TeeJay Publishers

P.O. Box 1375
Barrhead
Glasgow
G78 1JJ

Tel: 0141 880 6839
Fax: 0870 124 9189
e-mail: teejaypublishers@btinternet.com
web: www.teejaypublishers.co.uk

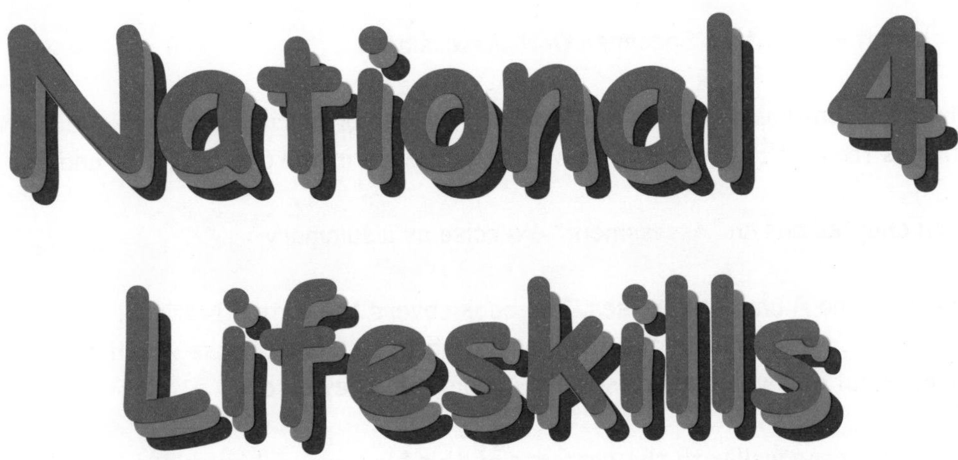

Produced by members of the TeeJay Writing Group

T Strang, J Geddes and J Cairns.

Thanks also to *Pamela Fraser*, Financial Education Training Officer for Dumfries & Galloway, for help with developing the material on pages 231-234 (Budgeting).

Front and Back Cover designed by *Fraser McKie*.
(http://www.frasermckie.com)

First Edition published by TeeJay Publishers - January 2015

National 4 Lifeskills Textbook

The book forms the basis of a one or two year course following the outcomes for National 4 Lifeskills as outlined by Education Scotland and the SQA.

- The book is based around our very successful N4-1 and N4-2 books.
- The assumption is that pupils embarking on this course will have been successful at CfE Level 2 and may have completed the National 3 Lifeskills course.
- The book covers the three Units, Numeracy, Geometry/Measure and Finance/Statistics in that order.
- Each Unit ends with a Specimen Unit Assessment.
- The book contains a short "Chapter Zero", which primarily revises all the relevant strands from CfE Level 2 that have been covered in our CfE Books 2a and 2b.
- Each chapter has an "Assessment" exercise as a summary.
- There are no A and B exercises. The book covers the entire National 4 Lifeskills Course without the teacher having to pick and choose which questions to leave out and which exercises are important. They all are !
- Pupils who cope well with the contents of this National 4 Lifeskills book should be able to be assessed at various stages throughout the course and be ready to sit an end-of-unit or end-of-course assessment or examination.
- Homework is available as a photocopiable pack.
- There is an End-of-Course Added Value Assessment Paper 1 and Paper 2.

T Strang, J Geddes, J Cairns

(January 2015)

Note :- Use of calculators throughout book - We have left this as discretionary, but certain exercises are specifically designated as "calculator free", particularly for those pupils being presented for the Added Value Assessment.

Index

FINANCE & STATISTICS

1. Round to the nearest 1000 :- a 12 498 b 35 501.

2. Copy and complete :- The answer to 4728 + 1876 is about 4700 + ... which equals .... .

3. Write the number that comes :- a 300 after 9900 b 500 before 17 200.

4. Write in words :- a 20 806 b 3 207 080.

5. Find the following :-

a $\begin{array}{r} 2680 \\ +\ 530 \\ \hline \end{array}$ b 22 708 + 9550 c $\begin{array}{r} 12\,000 \\ -\ 1836 \\ \hline \end{array}$ d 16 300 – 8762.

6. Find the following :-

a $\begin{array}{r} 2617 \\ \times\ 6 \\ \hline \end{array}$ b 12 070 x 9 c $5\overline{)7165}$ d 90 336 ÷ 8.

7. a Eight identical wooden blocks weigh 3576 grams. What is the weight of 1 block ?

b A bottle holds 750 ml of wine. How much wine is there in half a dozen bottles ?

8. To what numbers do these arrows point ?

a 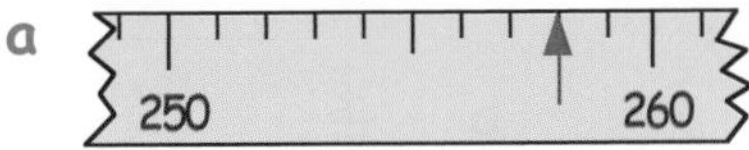

b 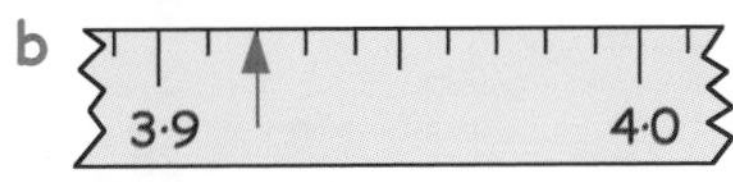

c 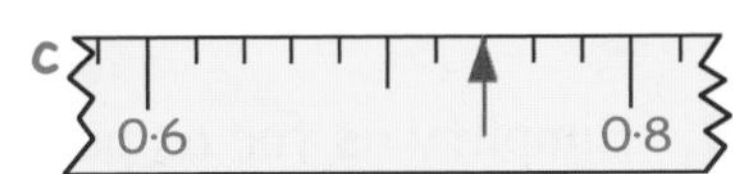

9. Write down the answers to the following :-

a 5017 x 1000 b 330 800 ÷ 100 c 321 x 300 d 6 400 000 ÷ 4000.

10. Round :-

a 29·663 to the nearest whole number b 12·149 to 1 decimal place

c 5·097 to 2 decimal places d 199·96 to 1 decimal place.

11. Do the following :-

a 19·8 + 2·77 b 121·83 – 35·9 c 8·07 x 6 d 31·26 ÷ 2

e 55 + 6·7 + 0·69 f 31 – 8·76 g 19·75 ÷ 5 h 13·16 x 8.

12. Find :-

a 6·0301 x 10 b 236 ÷ 1000 c 0·034 x 1000 d 6·8 ÷ 100.

13. Find :-

a 10 – 2 x 3 b 3 + 7 x 5 c 20 ÷ (4 + 6) d 28 + 12 ÷ 4 – 7.

14. What is the temperature on this thermometer ?

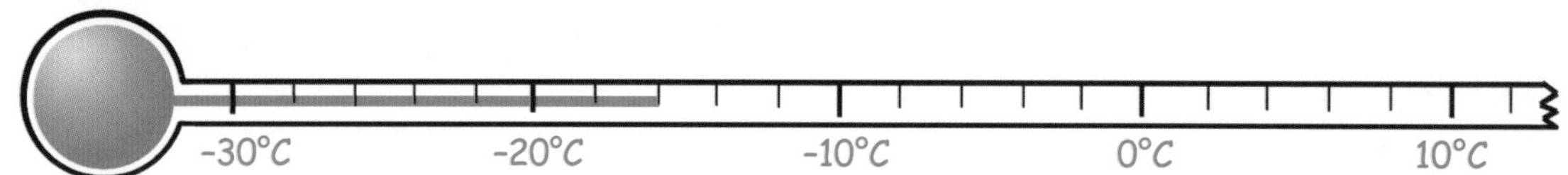

15. Find :-

a $5 - 11$ b $-2 + 8$ c $6 + (-10)$ d $(-21) - 9$.

16. What **fraction** of this triangle is coloured **red** ?

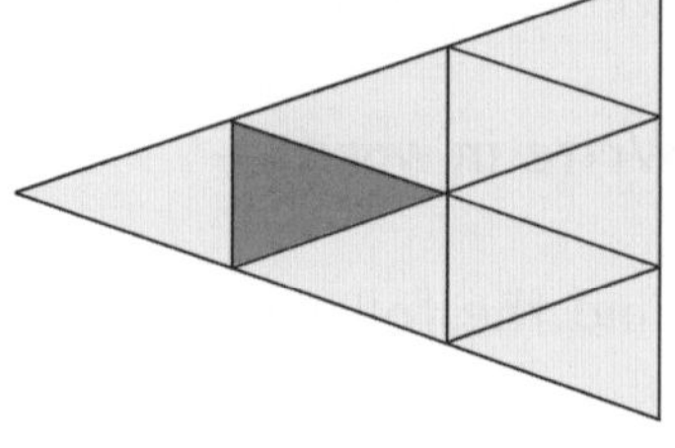

17. What **percentage** of this circular lattice has been coloured yellow ?

(*Do NOT count the white bits*).

18. At a birthday party, 25% present were men, 35% were women, 30% were girls and the rest were boys.

What **percentage** were boys ?

19. Write down any **fraction** equivalent to a $\frac{3}{5}$ b $\frac{7}{11}$.

20. Simplify as far as possible :- a $\frac{21}{28}$ b $\frac{12}{18}$.

21. What is :- a $\frac{2}{3}$ of £2·40 b $\frac{3}{7}$ of 350 metres ?

22. Find :- a 10% of £80·00 b 25% of £1·60 c 50% of £6·50.

23. 16 out of 20 people said their dog ate "*Cham*" dog food. What **percentage** is this ?

24. I picked up 2 shirts at £9·50 each, a top at £17·50 and a tie costing £6·75.

I checked my wallet and discovered a £20 note, two £10 notes and one £5 note.

Will I then have enough left over for my £1·50 train fare home ? (*Explain your answer*).

25. Which of these chocolate bars gives the better deal ? (*Explain your answer with working*).

£1 · 10

26. Write in 12 hour form, using am or pm :- a 1550 b 0010.

27. Change :- a 125 seconds to mins and secs. b 5 hours 25 mins to mins.

28. Find :- a 2 mins 35 secs + 5 mins 45 secs b 5 mins 20 secs - 1 min 55 secs.

29. The stopwatches show the times for the winner and the runner up in an 800 metre race.

Who won and by how much ?

30. On the 11th December 2014, the sun rose at 8.30 am and set at 3.45 pm.

How long was it between sunrise and sunset ?

31. a A car travelled the 560 kilometres from Glasgow to London. It took exactly 8 hours.

Calculate the car's average speed.

b I walked in the countryside for 4 hours. My average walking speed was 6 km/hr.

How far did I manage to walk ?

c I cycled the 60 kilometres from my house to the coast.

My average speed was 20 km/hr. How long did it take me ?

32. Measure the lengths of these lines and express your answer to each in 3 ways.

a b

33. Change to centimetres :- a 5 metres 36 cm b 10 m 4 cm.

34. Change to grams :- a 2 kg 345 g b 5 kg 50 g.

35. How many millilitres are in :- a 3 litres 200 ml b $4\frac{3}{4}$ litres ?

36. Write down three ways in which a rectangle and a parallelogram are different.

37. How many edges has a square based pyramid ?

38. Which solid 3-D shapes are made up from these nets ?

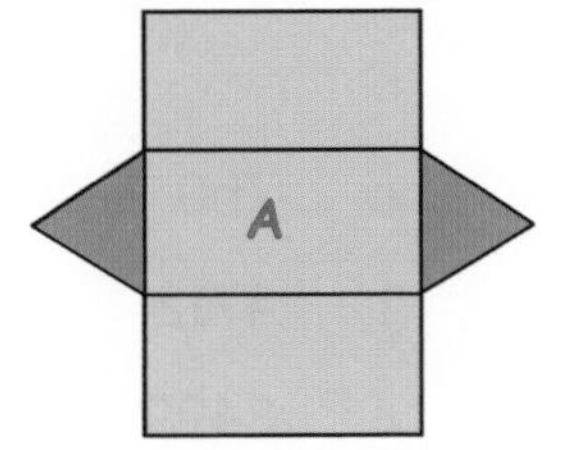

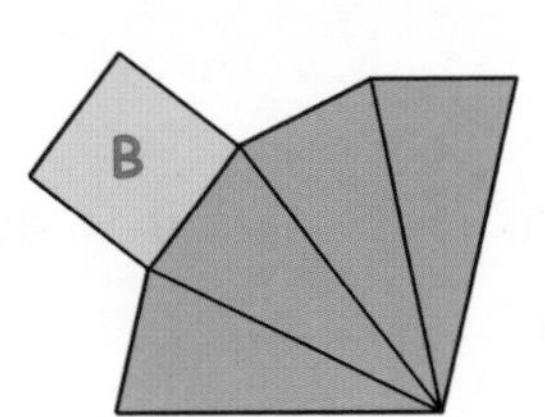

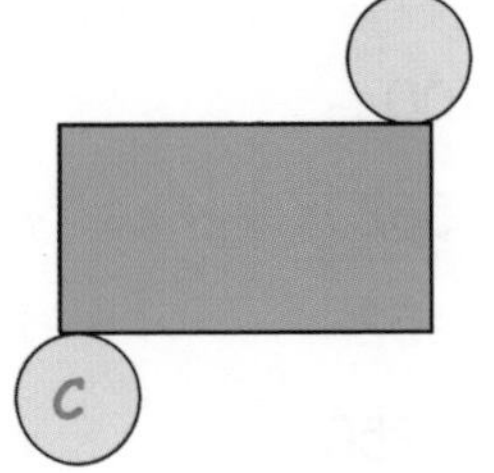

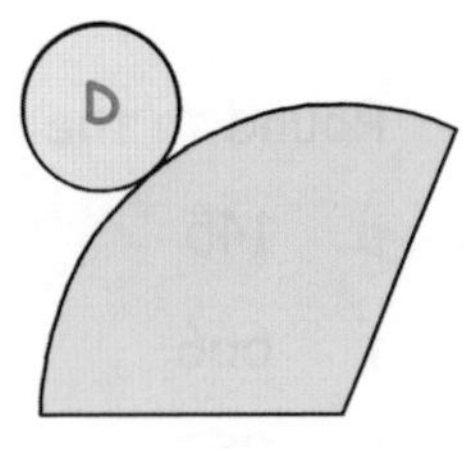

Whole Numbers

Rounding to the Nearest Whole Number

Exercise 1

1. Rounding to the nearest whole number. 12·7 13

   Copy these and round to the nearest whole number :-

a	1·9	b	5·6	c	8·3	d	19·9	e	47·4
f	81·1	g	22·5	h	2·18	i	32·71	j	96·53.

2. Round to the nearest second :-

a	12·2 sec	b	31·7 sec	c	16·1 sec	d	78·5 sec
e	83·8 sec	f	46·6 sec	g	7·47 sec	h	52·71 sec.

3. Using a calculator. 

   77 ÷ 8 = 9·625 (*check*)
   = 10 to the nearest whole number.

   Do these on a calculator, then round your answer to the nearest whole number :-

a	85 ÷ 6	b	80 ÷ 9	c	148 ÷ 5	d	513 ÷ 8
e	987 ÷ 25	f	1025 ÷ 64	g	2176 ÷ 72	h	6234 ÷ 98.

Rounding to the Nearest 10, 100 or 1000

Exercise 2

1. Round to the nearest 10 :-

a	47	b	33	c	18	d	49	e	65
f	84	g	91	h	58	i	6	j	105
k	314	l	417	m	645	n	704	o	5006.

2. Round to the nearest 10 cm :-

a	56 cm	b	72 cm	c	85 cm	d	91 cm	e	101 cm
f	176 cm	g	545 cm	h	804 cm	i	925 cm	j	1012 cm.

3. Round to the nearest 100 :-

a	145	b	562	c	826	d	491	e	750
f	666	g	452	h	58	i	6180	j	4712
k	2571	l	9250	m	8080	n	3555	o	8499.

4. Round to the nearest 1000 :-

a	1900	b	12 200	c	31 720	d	19 870	e	34 398
f	71 508	g	850	h	66 497	i	78 940	j	92 129
k	56 500	l	234 800	m	624 127	n	361 502	o	799 499.

Significant Figures and Estimating

If you round to 1 (or 2) figures of accuracy, no matter how many figures a number has, this is called rounding to 1 (or 2) significant figures, (*sig figs*)

Example :- 369 rounded to *2 sig figs* is 370 — 369 rounded to *1 sig fig* is 400

27 895 rounded to *2 sig figs* is 28 000 — 27 895 rounded to *1 sig fig* is 30 000

6078 rounded to *3 sig figs* is 6080 — 9865 rounded to *1 sig fig* is 10 000

It is possible to estimate mentally the answer to a question by rounding the numbers to "1 significant figure".

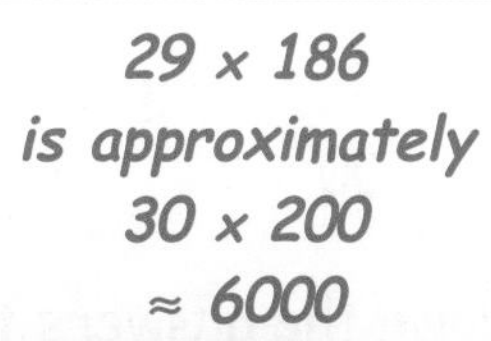
29 x 186
is approximately
30 x 200
≈ 6000

Example :- 578 ÷ 29

is approximately 600 ÷ 30

≈ 60 ÷ 3 ≈ **20.**

Knowing your tables will help here !

Exercise 3

1. Find approximate answers to these by rounding each number to 1 significant figure : -

a	29 x 29	b	17 x 52	c	68 x 58	d	189 x 31
e	204 x 79	f	185 x 304	g	389 ÷ 23 (note !)	h	791 ÷ 39
i	1927 ÷ 205	j	7856 ÷ 11	k	8019 ÷ 42	l	5962 ÷ 27.

2. The answer to 58 x 31 is either {178, 1798 or 17 908}. (*no calculator !*)

   By rounding 58 x 31 to 60 x ..... = ... , decide which of the 3 answers is likely to be the correct one.

3. By rounding your numbers to 1 significant figure before multiplying, decide which of the 3 given answers is most likely to be the correct one :-

a	28 x 32	Choice of {89·6, 896 or 1896}
b	72 x 19	Choice of {1368, 13 680 or 136 800}
c	298 x 61	Choice of {1878, 11 178 or 18 178}
d	499 x 21	Choice of {1479, 10 479 or 100 479}.

Multiplication by 10, 100, 1000

Learn these rules .....

Example :-

165 x 10 = 165**0**

Simple Rule for Whole Numbers :-

If you multiply by 10, simply put a 0 at the end.

If you multiply by 100, simply put two 0's at the end.

If you multiply by 1000, simply put three 0's at the end.

Exercise 4

1. Write down the answers to these :-

a	16 × 10	b	9 × 10	c	35 × 10	d	10 × 68
e	10 × 84	f	126 × 10	g	10 × 344	h	10 × 620
i	910 × 10	j	801 × 10	k	10 × 2309	l	6804 × 10.

2. Write down the answers to these :-

a	12 × 100	b	45 × 100	c	100 × 87	d	100 × 50
e	209 × 100	f	100 × 437	g	100 × 780	h	901 × 100.

3. Write down the answers to these :-

a	4 × 1000	b	26 × 1000	c	58 × 1000	d	1000 × 79
e	1000 × 90	f	435 × 1000	g	1000 × 760	h	1000 × 700.

Division by 10, 100, 1000

Learn these rules .....

Example :-

370~~0~~ ÷ 1~~0~~ = 370

Simple Rule for Whole Numbers :-

If you divide by 10, simply remove the last 0.

If you divide by 100, simply remove the last two 0's.

If you divide by 1000, simply remove the last three 0's.

Exercise 5

1. Write down the answers to these :-

a	40 ÷ 10	b	90 ÷ 10	c	220 ÷ 10	d	380 ÷ 10
e	910 ÷ 10	f	1600 ÷ 10	g	7200 ÷ 10	h	4630 ÷ 10
i	5000 ÷ 10	j	47 000 ÷ 10	k	87 700 ÷ 10	l	13 950 ÷ 10.

2. Write down the answers to these :-

a	7~~00~~ ÷ 1~~00~~ = ...	b	900 ÷ 100	c	1900 ÷ 100	d	5300 ÷ 100
e	8000 ÷ 100	f	21 000 ÷ 100	g	42 000 ÷ 100	h	86 100 ÷ 100.

3. Write down the answers to these :-

a	5000 ÷ 1000	b	18 000 ÷ 1000	c	24 000 ÷ 1000	d	60 000 ÷ 1000
e	225 000 ÷ 1000	f	390 000 ÷ 1000	g	510 000 ÷ 1000	h	800 000 ÷ 1000.

Multiplication by Multiples of 10, 100, 1000

To multiply 76×20

Step 1 Find $76 \times 10 = 760$

Step 2 Now find $760 \times 2 = 1520$

To multiply 118×400

Step 1 Find $118 \times 100 = 11\,800$

Step 2 Now find $11\,800 \times 4 = 47\,200$

Exercise 6

1. Calculate each of these, using the same method shown above :-

   a 42 x 20 (*Find 10 x 42 first = 420 and then find 420 x 2*).

   b 19 x 30 c 23 x 50 d 32 x 60

   e 45 x 80 f 124 x 50 g 325 x 40.

2. Work out each of these, using the 2 steps shown :-

   a 18 x 200 (*Find 18 x 100 first = 1800 and then find 1800 x 2*).

   b 41 x 300 c 17 x 500 d 22 x 700

   e 33 x 400 f 45 x 600 g 78 x 200

   h 500 x 14 i 3000 x 321 j 5000 x 25.

Division by 20, 30, 500, etc.,

To divide $19\,500 \div 30$

Step 1 Divide by 10 first $\frac{1950\not{0}}{1\not{0}} = 1950$

Step 2 Now divide by 3 $\quad 3\overline{)1950} = 650$

Exercise 7

1. Do the following divisions, using the same method as shown above :-

   a 390 ÷ 30 (*Find 390 ÷ 10 = 39 and then find* $3\overline{)39}$).

   b 180 ÷ 20 c 2250 ÷ 50 d 3200 ÷ 80

   e 13 200 ÷ 40 f 40 800 ÷ 60 g 46 000 ÷ 50.

2. Divide the following :-

   a 18 200 ÷ 200 (Find *18 200 ÷ 100 = 182 and then find* $2\overline{)182}$).

   b 21 900 ÷ 300 c 16 400 ÷ 400 d 32 500 ÷ 500

   e 17 600 ÷ 200 f 24 800 ÷ 800 g 819 000 ÷ 900.

Whole Numbers

Numeracy Assessment 1

1. Round to the nearest whole number :-

   a 23·7 b 12·51 c 197·498.

2. Round to the nearest 10 :-

   a 75 b 363 c 9458.

3. Round to the nearest 100 :-

   a 482 b 7149 c 54 750.

4. Round to the nearest 1000 :-

   a 2710 b 77 612 c 399 504.

5. Round to 1 significant figure :-

   a 539 b 8706 c 357 430.

6. By rounding each number to 1 significant figure, find an **estimate** to :-

   a 298 x 31 b 8245 ÷ 19 c 49 x 49.

7. Write down the answer to :-

   a 70 x 10 b 10 x 3103 c 45 x 100

   d 100 x 701 e 1000 x 20 f 114 x 1000.

8. Use the "two-step" method to find :-

   a 19 x 30 b 205 x 50 c 89 x 20

   d 300 x 60 e 500 x 75 f 207 x 4000.

9. Use the "two-step" method to find :-

   a 480 ÷ 20 b 5950 ÷ 50 c 30 420 ÷ 60

   d 1800 ÷ 300 e 33 400 ÷ 200 f 558 000 ÷ 900.

10. Joe bought cup-tie tickets for himself and his nineteen pals.

    If the tickets were priced £29 how much did Joe have to pay ?

11. Over a period of 30 months, a car travelled 26 100 miles.

    What does that work out at per month ?

Decimals

What are Decimals ?

Tenths and Hundredths

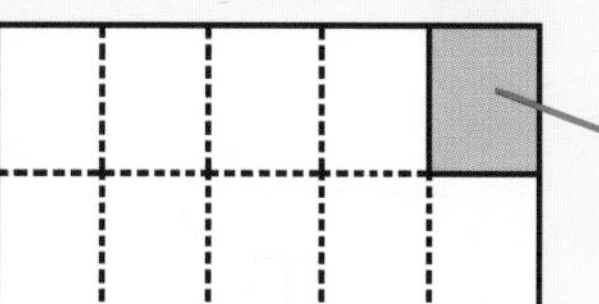

= $\frac{1}{10}$ (of 1 bar) or 0·1

= $\frac{1}{10}$ of $\frac{1}{10}$ of 1 bar

= $\frac{1}{100}$ of 1 bar = 0·01

1 (large) bar of chocolate

Exercise 1

1. [chocolate bar] represents 1 bar of chocolate. What numbers are represented here ?

a 

b 

c 

d 

e 

f 

2. These diagrams show pizzas (divided into 10 sections).
   What decimal number does each picture represent ?

a 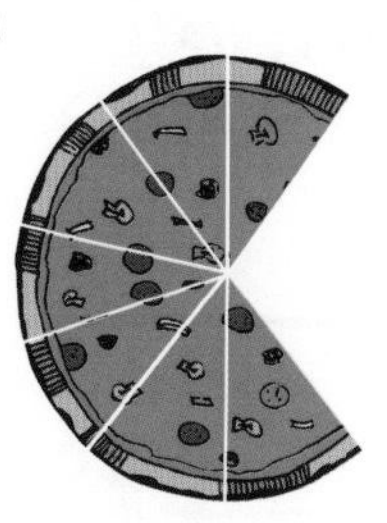

b 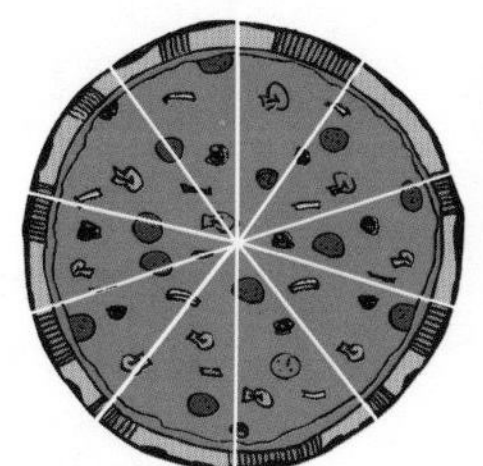  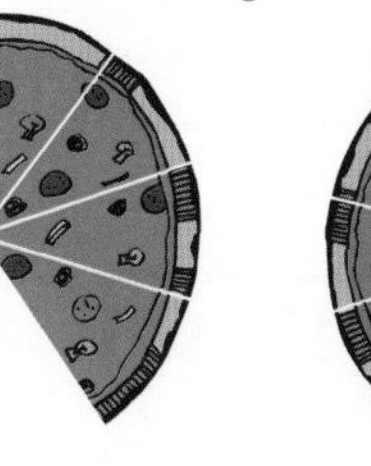

c 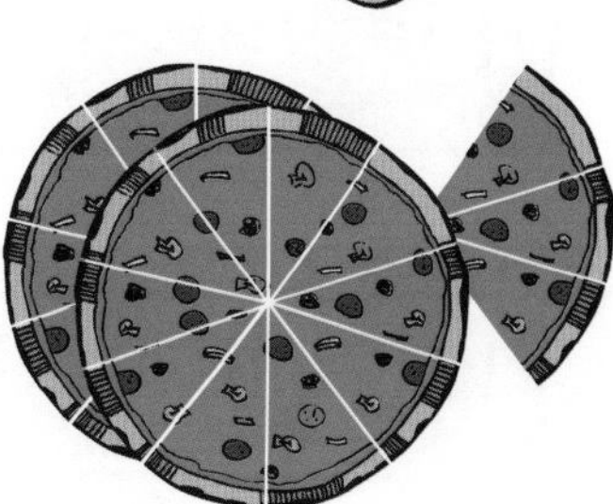

3. Given 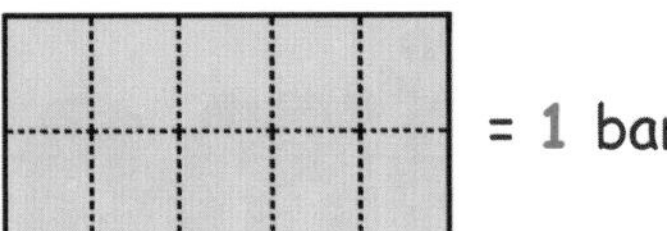 = 1 bar  = 0·1 bar and ▭ = 0·01 bar,

what numbers are represented by these pictures ?

a 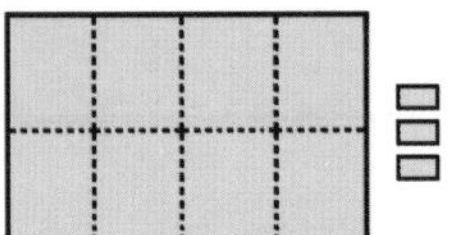

b 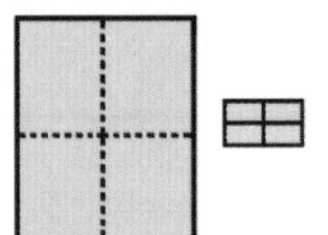

c 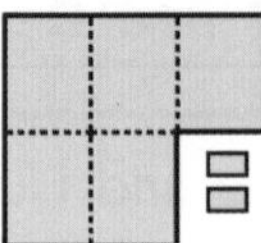

d 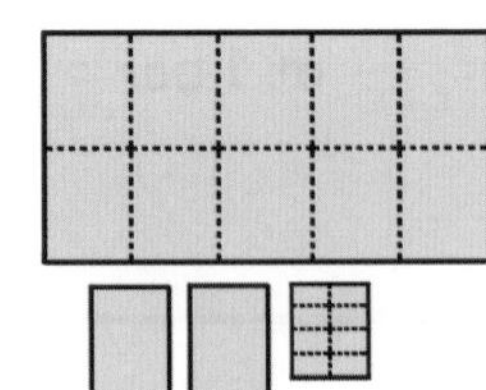

e 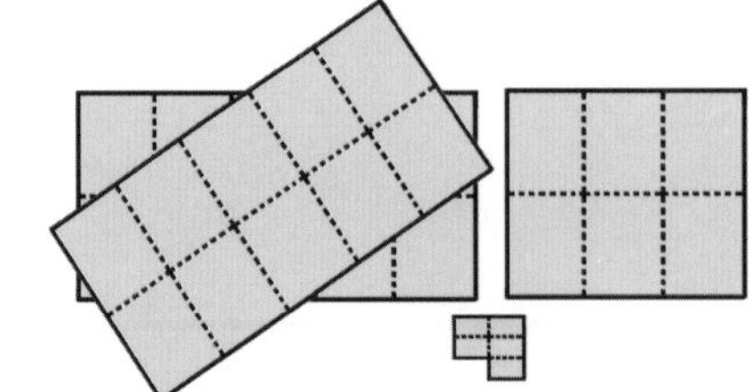

f 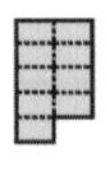

4. Use a ruler to draw neat pictures, similar to those above, to show the numbers :-

a 0·33 b 2·54 c 0·02.

Reading Decimal Scales

One Decimal Place

To decide where an arrow points to, decide first of all which 2 whole numbers it lies between.

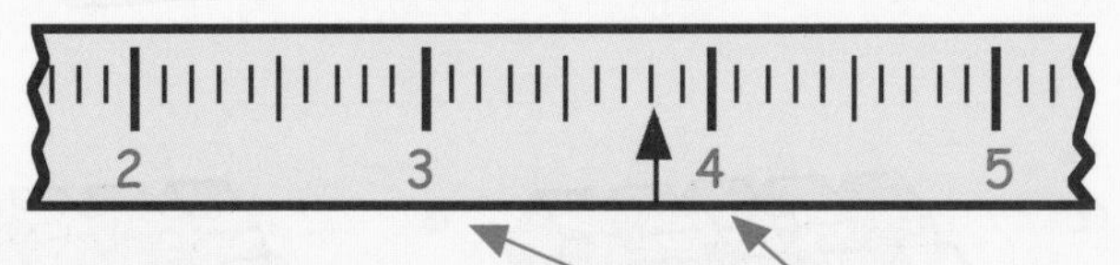

This arrow lies between 3 and 4.

It must be 3· (something).

It is in fact 3·8. (*Can you see this ?*)

Exercise 2

1. What numbers are these arrows pointing to ? State the units being measured :-

a 

b 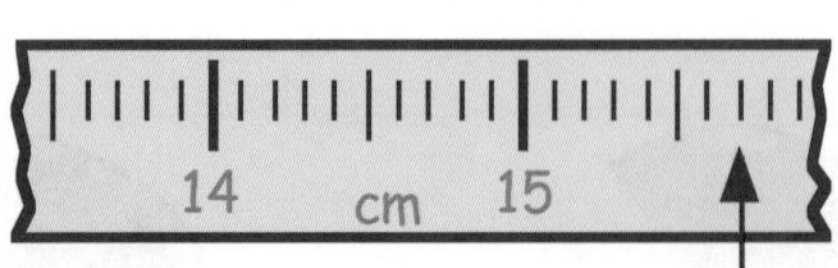

c 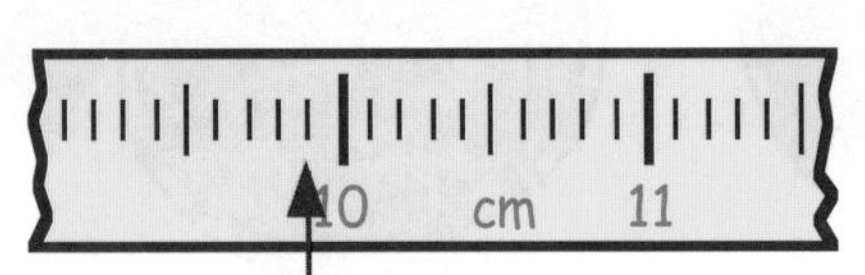

d 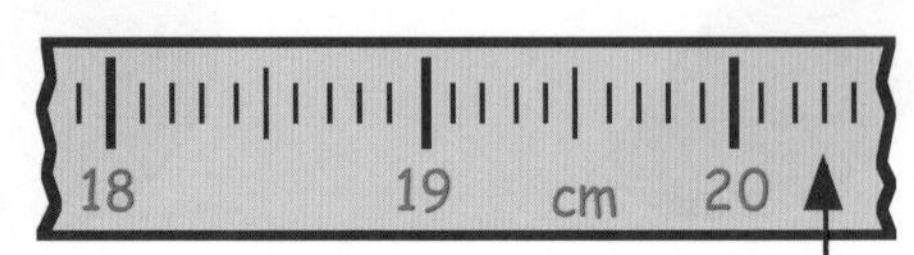

1. e

f

2. **Be careful here.** Write what number each of these arrows is pointing to :-

a

b

c

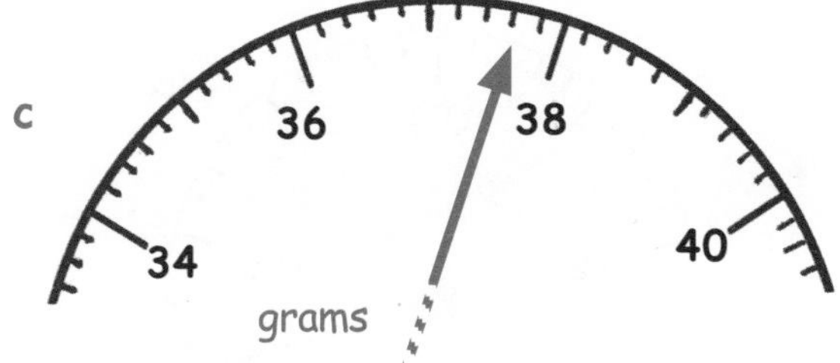

d

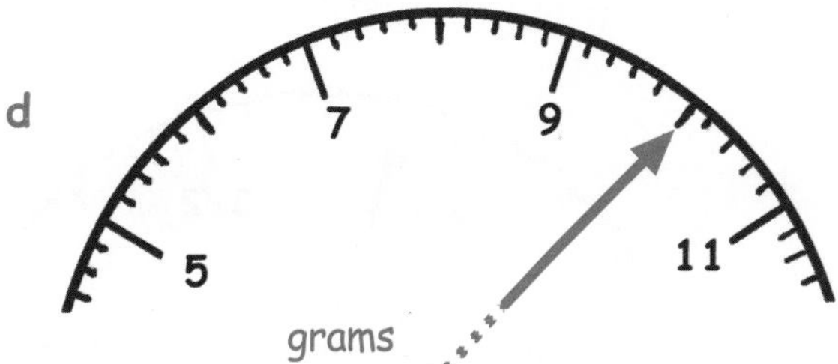

2 Decimal Places *(Harder)*

Always look at the 2 readings either side of the arrow. (*The 4·5 and 4·6*).

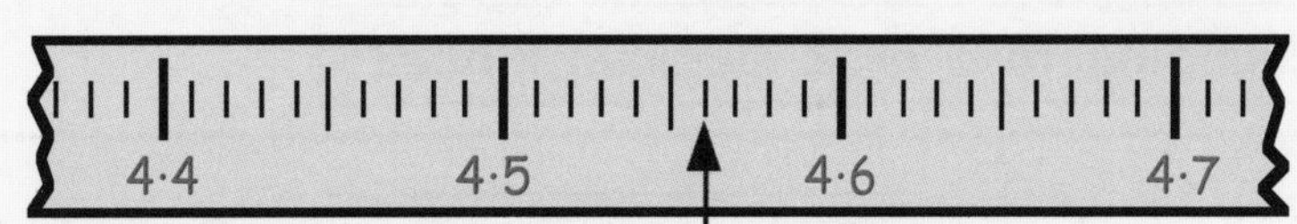

This arrow points to between **4 · 5** and **4 · 6**

It must be **4 · 5....** (4·5 something)

It points to **4 · 56**. (*Can you see this ?*)

3. Write what number each of these arrows is pointing to :-

a

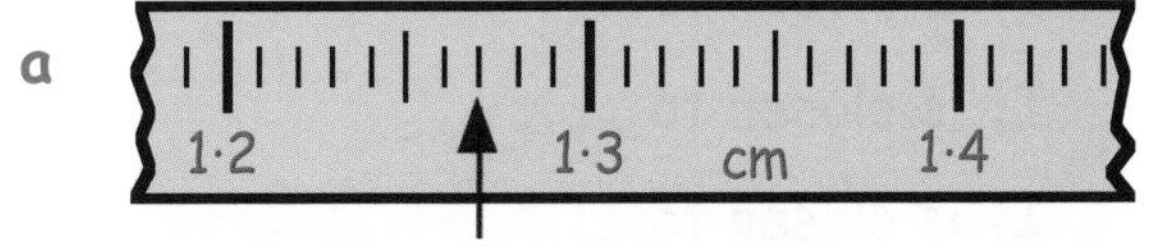

b

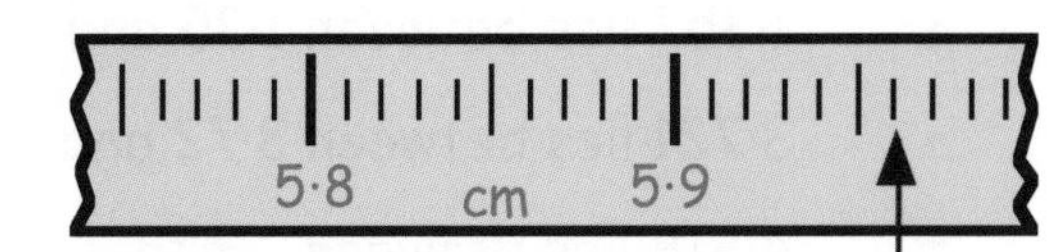

c

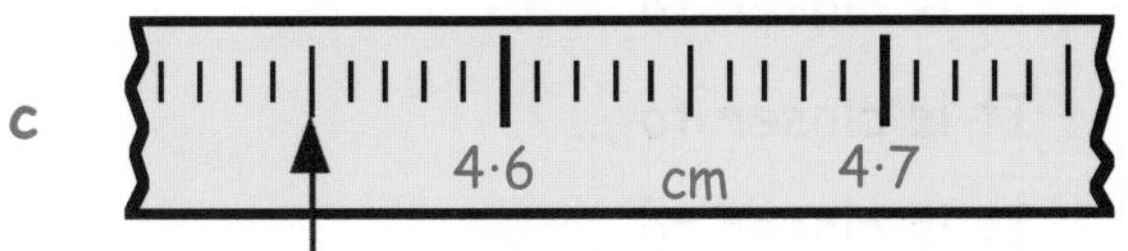

d

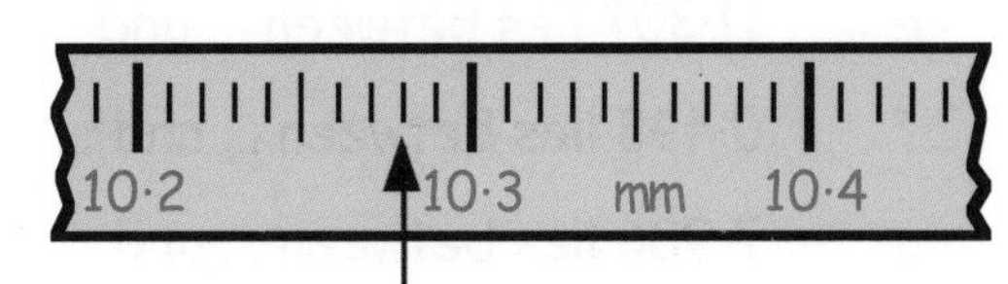

3. e 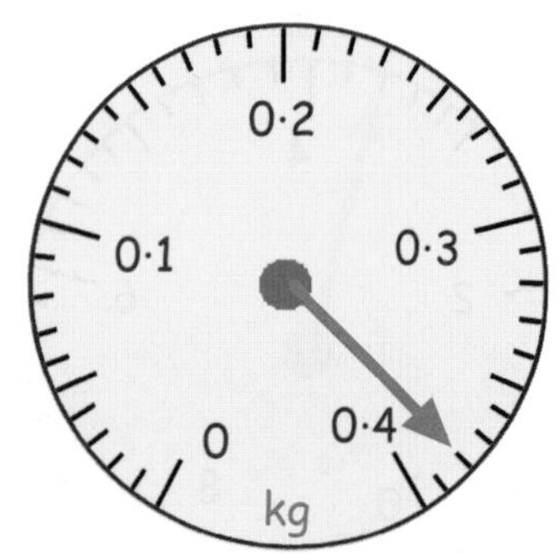

f 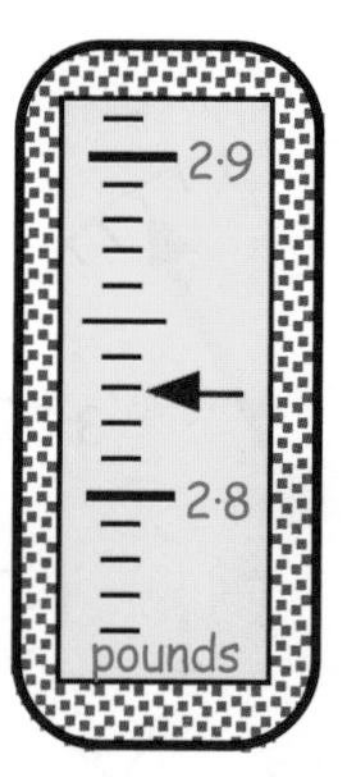

4. **Be careful here.** Write what number each of these arrows is pointing to :-

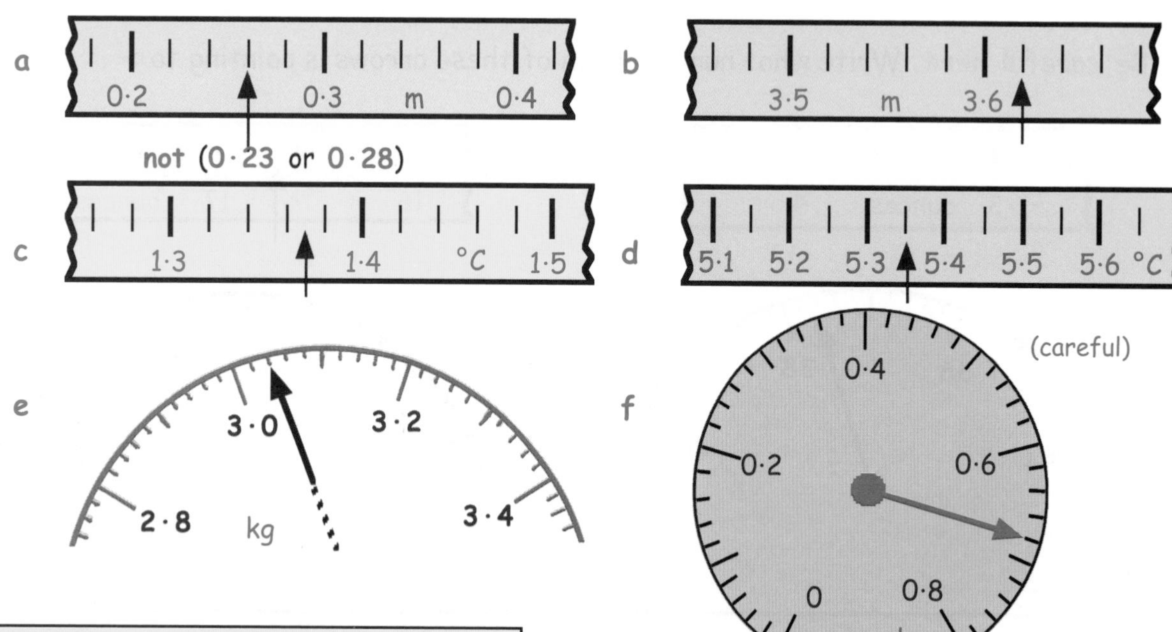

Rounding to 1 or 2 Decimal Places

Example 1 :- 2·273 lies between 2·27 and 2·28
It is closer to 2·27,
(*to 2 decimal places*).

Example 2 :- 14·819 lies between 14·81 and 14·82
It is closer to 14·82,
(*to 2 decimal places*).

Exercise 3

1. Copy and complete these statements :-

a 1·357 lies between 1·35 and 1·3... . It is closer to ...

b 3·721 lies between 3·72 and ... It is closer to ...

c 4·618 lies between ... and ... It is closer to ...

d 2·764 lies between ... and ... It is closer to ...

e 11·307 lies between ... and ... It is closer to ...

f 0·493 lies between ... and ... It is closer to ...

g 7·986 lies between ... and ... It is closer to ...

2. Which of the two numbers in the brackets is the correct answer when the number is rounded to 2 decimal places :-

a 1·437 (1·43 or 1·44)
b 6·053 (6·05 or 6·06)
c 2·848 (2·84 or 2·85)
d 0·781 (0·78 or 0·79)
e 15·388 (15·38 or 15·39)
f 9·009 (9·00 or 9·01)
g 12·585 (12·58 or 12·59)
h 0·032 (0·03 or 0·04) ?

To round "**longer**" numbers like <u>5·83724</u> to 2 decimal places :-

Step 1 - note that it lies between 5·83 and 5·84

Step 2 - say which number it is closer to –> 5·84.

3. Round these numbers to 2 decimal places, using this method :-

a 1·28512 –> 1·2...
b 2·97254 –>
c 5·32865 –>
d 6·18633 –>
e 9·92166 –>
f 8·04034 –>
g 4·97888 –>
h 6·05246 –>
i 10·86611 –>
j 0·27581 –>
k 12·1062 –>
l 0·09499 –>

4. Use your calculator to do these divisions and write down the answers.
Round each answer to 2 decimal places :-

a 60 ÷ 14
b 100 ÷ 23
c 67·1 ÷ 19·6
d 12·7 ÷ 0·66
e 500 ÷ 87·2
f 20·9 ÷ 28
g 0·98 ÷ 0·33
h 612 ÷ 114
i 2000 ÷ 400·5.

To change a fraction to a decimal :-

$\frac{7}{19}$ means 7 ÷ 19 = <u>0·36</u>8421..... = 0·37 (to 2 decimal places)

5. Change these fractions to decimals and round the answers to 2 decimal places :-

a $\frac{3}{7}$ = (3 ÷ 7) = <u>0·42</u>85714... = 0· . . . . . (to 2 decimal places)
b $\frac{7}{12}$ = (7 ÷ 12) = 0·
c $\frac{4}{9}$ = (4 ÷ ...) =
d $\frac{6}{7}$ =
e $\frac{10}{13}$ =
f $\frac{6}{11}$ =
g $\frac{2}{21}$ =

6\. 

a 3 workmen buy some sandwiches for lunch.

The total cost is £11·54.

They share the cost equally.

How much should each man pay ?
(*to the nearest 1 pence*).

b 6 bags of sugar weigh a total of 12·5 kilograms.

If each weighs the same, what is the weight of 1 bag of sugar ?
(*to 2 decimal places*).

c 

On Sunday, Paula was called in to work in the hotel.

She worked from noon until 8 pm and earned £60·40.

How much was she paid for each hour ?

d Which of these fractions is the biggest and which is the smallest :-

$$\{\tfrac{5}{7}, \tfrac{2}{3}, \tfrac{7}{9}\}?$$

Hint :- find $\frac{5}{7}$ = 5 ÷ 7 = ... find $\frac{2}{3}$ = 2 ÷ 3 ...... find $\frac{7}{9}$ = ...

Now compare your answers.

Add and Subtract Decimal Numbers

Example 1 **:-** 17·65 + 6·97

```
=>  17·65
   + 6·97
  = 24·62
     ↑
   line up
```

Example 2 **:-** 34·16 – 16·53

```
=>  34·16
  - 16·53
  = 17·63
     ↑
   line up
```

Make sure the decimal points are always beneath each other.

Exercise 4

1\. Set these down and find the answers :-

a
```
  16·72
 + 5·97
 ______
```

b
```
  28·68
+ 18·27
 ______
```

c
```
  53·19
 + 9·77
 ______
```

d 21·65 + 7·99

e 56·57 + 29·37

f 67·64 + 17·37

1. g 17·62 − 5·48   h 42·57 − 15·92   i 74·83 − 37·46

j 19·27 − 6·58   k 73·01 − 48·02   l 92·52 − 62·3.

To find 45·8 − 24·73 rewrite it as

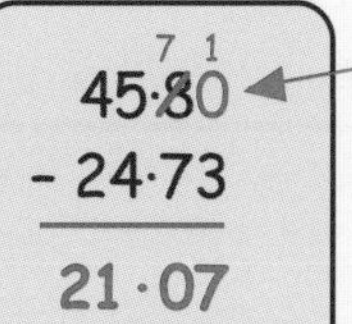

note (Adding 0's often helps).

2. Find the following :-

a 17·7 − 9·18   b 53·7 − 12·25   c 24·2 − 8·79

d 35·1 − 6·27   e 62·4 − 32·93   f 100·5 − 87·78.

To find 47 − 13·45 rewrite it as

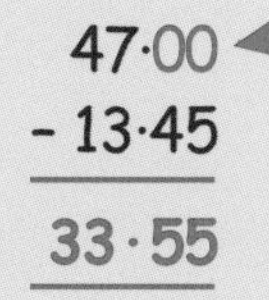

note (Adding 0's often helps).

3. Find the following :-

a 18 − 8·43   b 9 − 5·97   c 12 − 1·01

d 25 − 16·25   e 72 − 38·48   f 80 − 0·92.

4. a I got £7·51 change when I bought talcum powder with a £10 note.
How much did the talcum powder cost ?

b 2 bowls contain apples. One weighs 6·79 kg and the other weighs 5·25 kg.

(i) What is the total weight of the 2 bowls ?

(ii) By how much is the bigger bowl heavier than the smaller one ?

Multiplying Decimals

To find $7 \cdot 38 \times 9$

$$\begin{array}{r} 7{\cdot}38 \\ \times\ 9 \\ \hline 66{\cdot}42 \\ \hline \end{array}$$

remember the point

It helps to copy the decimal point straight down from where it is.

Exercise 5

1. Copy these and find the answers :-

a $\begin{array}{r} 4{\cdot}48 \\ \times\ 5 \\ \hline \\ \hline \end{array}$ b $\begin{array}{r} 3{\cdot}76 \\ \times\ 6 \\ \hline \\ \hline \end{array}$ c $\begin{array}{r} 6{\cdot}07 \\ \times\ 8 \\ \hline \\ \hline \end{array}$

d $\begin{array}{r} 9{\cdot}89 \\ \times\ 3 \\ \hline \\ \hline \end{array}$ e $\begin{array}{r} 13{\cdot}14 \\ \times\ 7 \\ \hline \\ \hline \end{array}$ f $\begin{array}{r} 0{\cdot}97 \\ \times\ 9 \\ \hline \\ \hline \end{array}$

g $\begin{array}{r} 47{\cdot}88 \\ \times\ 2 \\ \hline \\ \hline \end{array}$ h $\begin{array}{r} 24{\cdot}36 \\ \times\ 8 \\ \hline \\ \hline \end{array}$ i $\begin{array}{r} 7{\cdot}45 \\ \times\ 9 \\ \hline \\ \hline \end{array}$

j 19·74 x 5 k 12·57 x 6 l 8 x 11·25.

2. a 

A packet of Rolchies weighs 32·74 grams.

What is the weight of 5 packets ?

b The driver of this taxi charges £2·49 per mile.

My house is 7 miles from my office.

How much will I be charged for a taxi journey home from work ?

c Joe bought 8 metres of fencing at £7·85 per metre.

How much did it cost him ?

d I bought 9 two pint cartons of milk.

2 pints is the same as 1·14 litres.

How many litres of milk have I got ?

2. e A jug holds 2·75 litres of water when full.
8 full jugs of hot water are poured into an empty bath.
How much water is in the bath ?

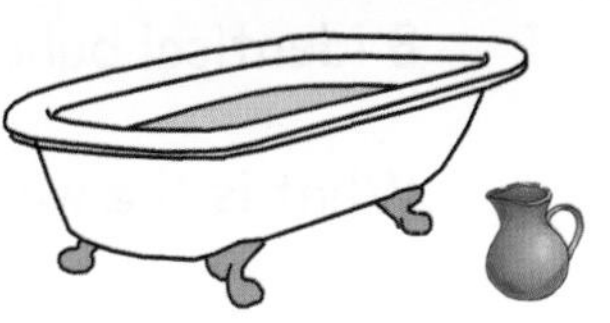

f 

These one year old twins each weigh 9·69 kg.
What is the combined weight of the 2 girls ?

g The average weight of a medium egg is 65·3 grams.
The empty carton weighs 52·5 grams.
What is the weight of the carton holding 6 eggs ?

Division by Decimals

Remember to copy the decimal point up to the line above.

To find :- 25·76 ÷ 7

=>

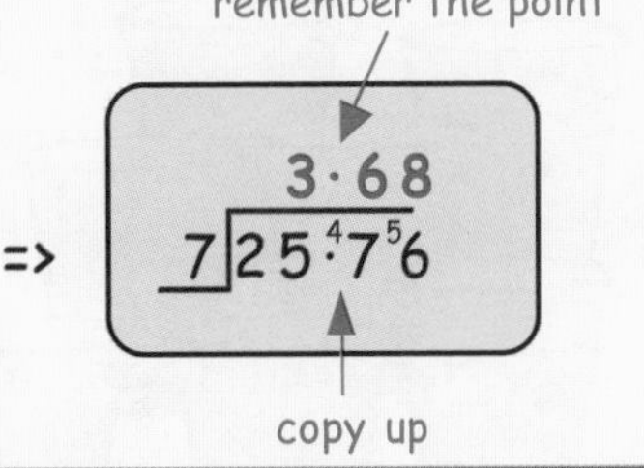

Exercise 6 *Again – Knowing your tables **really** helps here.*

1. Copy and do the following :-

a $2\overline{)14{\cdot}86}$ b $3\overline{)17{\cdot}01}$ c $4\overline{)27{\cdot}56}$

d $5\overline{)27{\cdot}75}$ e $6\overline{)46{\cdot}08}$ f $7\overline{)39{\cdot}34}$

g $8\overline{)53{\cdot}76}$ h $9\overline{)31{\cdot}77}$ i $6\overline{)2{\cdot}52}$

j 42·15 ÷ 5 k 20·32 ÷ 8 l 12·18 ÷ 7.

2. a Share £62·16 equally amongst 4 men.
How much will each receive ?

b 

Cut a piece of tape 43·62 centimetres long into 6 equal pieces.
What length is each piece ?

c Five farmers equally split 78·55 acres of land among themselves.
How much land will each farmer get ?

2\. d 8 identical bunches of pineapples weigh 12·48 kg in total.

What is the weight of 1 bunch ?

e 6·21 litres of juice is poured equally into 9 glasses.

How much juice will there be in each glass ?

f Thomas ran 4 laps round a running track near his home in a time of 182·96 seconds.

What was his average time for each lap ?

g (i) 7 new waste bins are delivered to the Glenboig Hotel.

The total weight of the bins is 20·23 kilograms.

What is the weight of 1 bin ?

(ii) The Armitage Arms orders 5 of the bins.

What is the total weight of these ?

Multiplication by 10, 100, 1000 - (Rules, Rules, Rules !!)

Can you remember when you multiplied a whole number by 10 you simply added a 0 on to the end ?

64 x 10 = 640

This rule does **not** work for decimals.

To find 2·79 x 10

=>

```
  2·79
   x10
 27·9
```

move all the figures 1 place left

To find 4·365 x 100

=>

```
  4·365
   x100
 436·5
```

move all the figures 2 places left

Exercise 7

1. Copy these down and find the following :-

a $\begin{array}{r} 5 \cdot 46 \\ \times 10 \\ \hline \\ \hline \end{array}$ b $\begin{array}{r} 3 \cdot 19 \\ \times 10 \\ \hline \\ \hline \end{array}$ c $\begin{array}{r} 0 \cdot 85 \\ \times 10 \\ \hline \\ \hline \end{array}$

d $\begin{array}{r} 14 \cdot 72 \\ \times 10 \\ \hline \\ \hline \end{array}$ e $\begin{array}{r} 8 \cdot 7 \\ \times 10 \\ \hline \\ \hline \end{array}$ f $\begin{array}{r} 0 \cdot 9 \\ \times 10 \\ \hline \\ \hline \end{array}$

g $\begin{array}{r} 2 \cdot 134 \\ \times 100 \\ \hline \\ \hline \end{array}$ h $\begin{array}{r} 0 \cdot 676 \\ \times 100 \\ \hline \\ \hline \end{array}$ i $\begin{array}{r} 8 \cdot 27 \\ \times 100 \\ \hline \\ \hline \end{array}$

Simple Rules :-

To multiply by 10	=>	move the figures 1 place to the left.
	=>	(*or move the point 1 place to the right.*)
To multiply by 100	=>	move the figures 2 places to the left.
	=>	(*or move the point 2 places to the right.*)

2. Write down the answers to the following by using the 1st rule above :-

a 10 x 7·61 b 10 x 1·82 c 10 x 0·69 d 10 x 6·32
e 16·18 x 10 f 47·5 x 10 g 0·03 x 10 h 10 x 1·08.

3. Write down the answers to the following by using the 2nd rule above :-

a 9·32 x 100 b 100 x 3·57 c 1·264 x 100 d 0·873 x 100
e 100 x 12·18 f 1·049 x 100 g 0·001 x 100 h 100 x 7·5.

4. A carpet tack weighs 0·19 grams.

Calculate the weight of :-

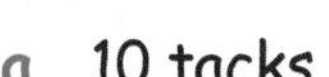

a 10 tacks b 100 tacks.

5. A bottle holds 1·15 litres of champagne.
How many litres are there in :- a 10 bottles b 100 bottles ?

6. Extend the above rules to help find the answers to the following :-

a 1·225 x 1000 b 0·467 x 1000 c 13·18 x 1000
d 0·00426 x 1000 e 1000 x 0·003 f 0·0505 x 1000.

Division by 10, 100, 1000 - (Yet More Rules !!)

We have just given a rule that said :-

To Multiply by 10		To Divide by 10
Move all the figures 1 place to the left	=> Now =>	Move all the figures 1 place to the right

25·9 ÷ 10 =>

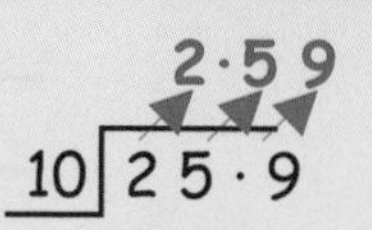

Exercise 8

1. Copy and find the following :-

a $10\overline{)5{\cdot}8}$ b $10\overline{)17{\cdot}2}$ c $10\overline{)2{\cdot}65}$

d $10\overline{)0{\cdot}76}$ e $10\overline{)59}$ f $10\overline{)0{\cdot}06}$

g 18·3 ÷ 10 h 33·72 ÷ 10 i 6 ÷ 10

The new rule for dividing by 100 is similar :-

To Multiply by 100		To Divide by 100
Move all the figures 2 places to the left	=> Now =>	Move all the figures 2 places to the right

j $100\overline{)42{\cdot}1}$ k $100\overline{)357}$ l $100\overline{)2421}$

m 85·6 ÷ 100 n 73·21 ÷ 100 o 9·8 ÷ 100

p $\frac{4{\cdot}5}{10}$ q $\frac{53}{10}$ r $\frac{0{\cdot}48}{10}$

s $\frac{77{\cdot}4}{100}$ t $\frac{239}{100}$ u $\frac{2{\cdot}6}{100}$.

Is it the point or the figures I move ? And is it left or right ? Hmmm !

The rules for dividing by 10 and 100 were simple.

To divide a number by 10, simply move all the figures 1 place to the right.

To divide a number by 100, simply move all the figures 2 places to the right.

2. Write down a similar rule for dividing by 1000.

3. Find the following :-

a $1000\overline{)247{\cdot}1}$ b $1000\overline{)1649}$ c $1000\overline{)23{\cdot}5}$

d $365{\cdot}2 \div 1000$ e $69 \div 1000$ f $6750 \div 1000$

g $\frac{650}{1000}$ h $\frac{3275}{1000}$ i $\frac{25{\cdot}8}{1000}$.

4. a If 10 packets of chews cost £5·40, what will one packet cost ?

b If a box of 100 doughnuts costs £4, what will one doughnut cost ?

c 1000 screws weigh 6·14 kg. What will one screw weigh ?

d 10 metal strips together measure 87 cm. What is the width of one strip ?

e 100 tins of beans weigh 15 000 grams. What will one tin weigh ?

To change from millimetres to centimetres, you "divide by 10".

5. Change each of the following to centimetres :-

a 12 mm b 42 mm c 5·8 mm d 3·0 mm e 0·7 mm.

To change from centimetres to metres, you "divide by 100".

Change each of the following to metres :-

6. a 422 cm b 805 cm c 99 cm d 46·7 cm e 5·8 cm.

To change from metres to kilometres, you "divide by 1000".

7. Change each of the following to kilometres :-

a 43 250 m b 437 m c 69 m d 32·6 m e 5·1 m.

Decimals

Numeracy Assessment 2

1. This stands for 1

   What number does this stand for ?

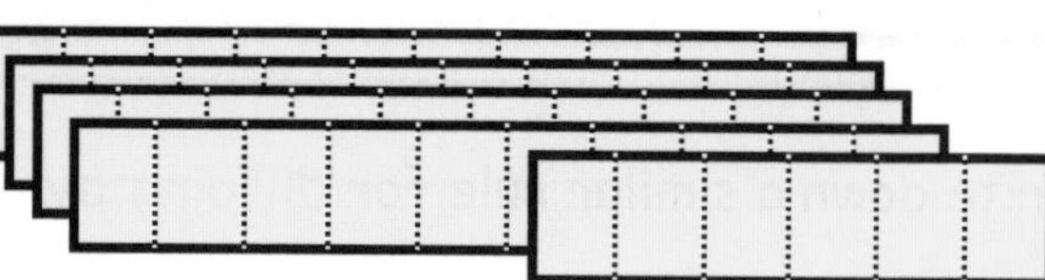

2. Round these numbers to 1 decimal place :-

   a 1·27 b 19·94 c 28·65 d 0·83 e 108·97.

3. Round these numbers to 2 decimal places :-

   a 5·293 b 12·496 c 0·955 d 7·174 e 0·0689.

4. Copy and work out the following :-

   a $\begin{array}{r} 3{\cdot}94 \\ +\ 4{\cdot}67 \\ \hline \end{array}$ b $\begin{array}{r} 19{\cdot}84 \\ -\ 7{\cdot}75 \\ \hline \end{array}$ c 0·88 + 9·2 d 25 – 5·05.

5. Copy and find the answers to the following :-

   a $\begin{array}{r} 7{\cdot}8 \\ \times\ 8 \\ \hline \end{array}$ b $6\overline{)23{\cdot}4}$ c $\begin{array}{r} 0{\cdot}89 \\ \times\ 9 \\ \hline \end{array}$ d $7\overline{)9{\cdot}52}$.

6. Write down the answers to the following :-

   a 7·9 × 10 b 100 × 0·374 c 0·0542 × 1000

   d 51·1 ÷ 10 e $100\overline{)6{\cdot}28}$ f $\frac{592}{1000}$.

7. What numbers are the arrows pointing to ?

   a

   b

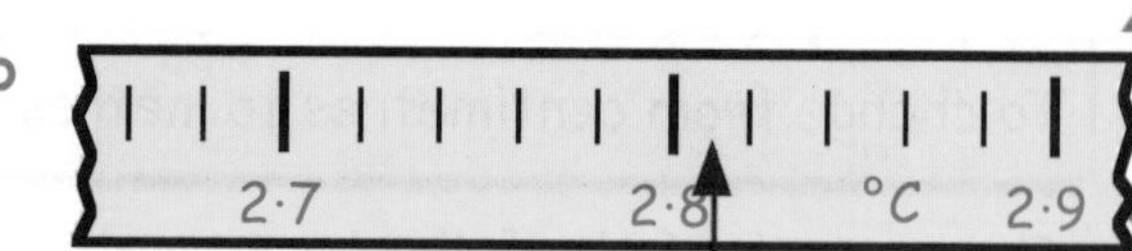

8. Change :-

   a 63 mm to cm b 75 cm to metres c 75 750 metres to km.

9. A photographer needs to mail 465 photographs to newspapers throughout the country.

   If he can get 5 photographs in each envelope, how many envelopes will he need ?

CHAPTER 3

Percentages

Percentages, Decimals & Fractions

Remember :-

15% means $\frac{15}{100}$ = 0·15 also 4% means $\frac{4}{100}$ = 0·04 (note)

Exercise 1

1. Write each of the following as a fraction AND as a decimal :-

a	17%	b	26%	c	48%	d	12%	e	75%
f	6%	g	2%	h	8%	i	10·5%	j	1·2%.

2. (*Knowing your multiplication tables will help here*).

Write these percentages as fractions and simplify where possible :-

a 45% = $\frac{45 \div 5}{100 \div 5}$ = $\frac{\square}{\square}$ b 30% = $\frac{30 \div 10}{100 \div 10}$ = $\frac{\square}{\square}$

c	35%	d	60%	e	50%	f	25%	g	75%
h	10%	i	5%	j	12%	k	36%	l	72%
m	4%	n	80%	o	65%	p	28%	q	90%.

To change a fraction (like $\frac{3}{5}$) to a percentage :-

$\frac{3}{5}$ means 3 ÷ 5 = 0·6 (calculator) => (0·6 x 100%) = 60%

$\frac{6}{8}$ means 6 ÷ 8 = 0·75 (calculator) => (0·75 x 100%) = 75%

3. Copy the following and use your calculator to change each fraction to a percentage :-

a $\frac{9}{50}$ = 9 ÷ 50 = 0·....... => (0·...... x 100%) = ☐ %

b $\frac{1}{4}$ = 1 ÷ 4 = 0·....... => (0·...... x 100%) = ☐ %

c	$\frac{3}{25}$	d	$\frac{2}{5}$	e	$\frac{3}{10}$	f	$\frac{11}{20}$	g	$\frac{1}{2}$	h	$\frac{1}{20}$
i	$\frac{7}{20}$	j	$\frac{7}{25}$	k	$\frac{1}{8}$	l	$\frac{5}{8}$	m	$\frac{7}{10}$	n	$\frac{3}{100}$.

4. Mary scored $\frac{19}{25}$ in a science test. To write this as a percentage :-

Score = $\frac{19}{25}$ = 19 ÷ 25 = 0·76 => (0·76 x 100%) = **76%**

Change each of these test scores to percentages in the same way :-

a Percy scored 21 out of 30 (= $\frac{21}{30}$ = 21 ÷ 30 = 0· .... => ..... %)

b Roddy scored 35 out of 50

c Pat scored 28 out of 40

d Charlie scored 3 out of 10

e Val scored 24 out of 25

f Cindy scored 54 out of 60

g Kath scored 70 out of 80

h Trevor scored 28 out of 56.

5. Rick sat 4 separate tests. Listed below are his marks.

French -	12 out of 60	Art -	18 out of 20
Geography -	9 out of 30	Music -	13 out of 25

By changing each score to a percentage, write his subjects in order, starting with his best subject.

Percentages using a Calculator

To find 13% of £500 =>

13% of £500 = $\frac{13}{100}$ x 500
= (13 ÷ 100) x 500 = £65

To find 8% of £70 =

8% of £70 = $\frac{8}{100}$ x 70
= (8 ÷ 100) x 70 = £5·6<u>0</u> note*

Exercise 2

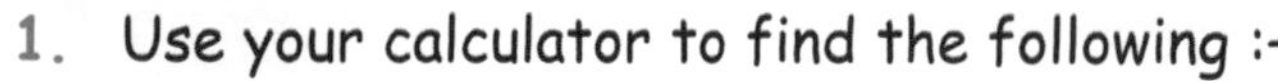

1. Use your calculator to find the following :-

a 12% of £50 = (12 ÷ 100) x 50 = £......

b 8% of £90

c 22% of £10

d 45% of £320

1. e 55% of £200 f 12% of £60 g 72% of £5400
h 75% of £7·80 i 2% of £5 j 1% of £110
k 32% of £9·50 l 25% of 44p m 22% of £2·50
n 4% of £12 o $17\frac{1}{2}$% of £50 (17·5)% p $2\frac{1}{2}$% of £200. (2·5)%

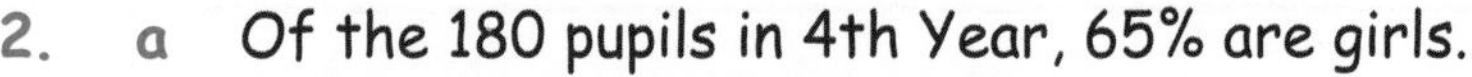

2. a Of the 180 pupils in 4th Year, 65% are girls.

(i) How many girls are there ?

(ii) How many boys are there ?

b 

The petrol tank in my car holds 80 litres.

When 95% of a full tank is used up, a warning light shines on the dashboard.

How many litres from a full tank will I have to use for the light to just come on ?

c A packet of cereal weighs 650 grams.

24% of it is sugar
48% of it is starch
16% of it is protein
7% of it is fibre
5% of it is fat

Calculate how many grams of sugar, starch, protein, fibre and fat are in the packet.

d 90% of the human body is made up of water.

If Joe weighs 60 kilograms, how much of him is water ?

e 

The value of my games console dropped by 45% in 1 year.

I paid £280 for it a year ago.

What's it worth now ?

f Cats are said to sleep on average 66·666% of the day.

Of the 24 hours in a day, how much of the time do cats spend sleeping ?

Percentage Rise

My new fridge should have cost me £400 but the price **rose** by 3%. =>

Old Price	£400	
Rise (3% of 400) =	£ 12	<- (3 ÷ 100) x 400)
New Price =	£412	

Exercise 3

(*For each question in this exercise, show the 3 lines of working neatly*).

1. A weekend in Paris was priced at £400. It has risen by 10%.

   What is the new cost for the break ?

2. Last year, a freezer cost £320.

   This year it has risen by 25%.

   What is the new price ?

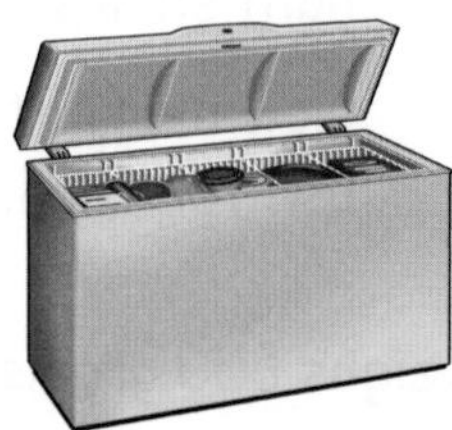

3. The pressure in a boiler was 70 poundals.

   The pressure rose by 5%.

   What was the new pressure ?

4. A military jet rose from a height of 3500 feet by 40%.

   What was its new height ?

5. The depth of water in a harbour at low tide was 2·5 metres.

   At high tide, the depth of the water rose by 50%.

   What was the depth of the water at high tide ?

6. Jessie weighed 50 kg, but because of her love for fry-up breakfasts, her weight has risen by 6%.

   Calculate Jessie's new weight.

7. In Spain, the average winter temperature is 16°C.

By spring, the temperature has increased by 75%.

What is the average spring temperature in Spain ?

8. 

The temperature in a furnace was 800°C.

The temperature rose by 12%.

What was the new temperature ?

9. With his old racing bike, Mark cycled at an average speed of 20 miles per hour.

On his new bike, he has upped his average speed by 38%.

What is his new average speed ?

10. 

A hill walker walked a total distance of 50 miles one weekend.

The next weekend, he was determined to walk at least 6% further.

How far had he to walk to do this ?

11. Bobby earned £40 000 last year doing gigs around the country.

This year, his earnings have increased by 2%.

How much is Bobby earning this year ?

12. 

Omar put £25 000 in a one year fixed rate bond in his bank at an interest rate of 3% per year.

If he closes the bond after one year, how much will he get out altogether ?

13. On average, employees at a particular company historically missed 40 days of work per year.

Then there was a management change.

Now the average is 7·5% more !

Now what is the average number of missed days per year ?

14. A **SURCHARGE** is simply an **increase** in the amount you pay for your holiday.

Ryanjet had to put a surcharge of **5%** on all their holidays due to increasing fuel prices.

	Ryanjet Holidays			Original holiday cost
Majorca	12th July	14 days	h/b	£620
Ibiza	17th July	11 days	h/b	£500
Lanzarote	19th July	10 days	room	£480
Minorca	1st August	7 days	h/b	£430
Tenerife	6th August	14 days	AI	£860

a With the surcharge, what will it **now** cost to go to Majorca for 14 days ?

b How much will it **now** cost to fly to Lanzarote for 10 days ?

c Mr Bentley and his wife booked for 2 weeks, all inclusive, to Tenerife.

(i) What **should** their bill have come to ?
(*For the two of them*).

(ii) How much "surcharge" did they have to pay ?

(iii) What did their new **final** bill come to ?

Percentage Fall

Sometimes prices fall.

For example, in a **SALE**.

This camera should cost £65, but it is REDUCED by 20% in the Autumn sale.

PHOTO STORE

SALE

20% OFF
ALL PRICES

£65

3 lines each time =>

Old Price = £65·00

=> Fall = $\frac{20}{100} \times 65 =$ (20 ÷ 100 x 65) £ 13·00 (calculator)

=> New Price = (£65 - £13) = £52·00

Exercise 4

(*For each question in this exercise, show the 3 lines of working neatly*).

1. The normal price for this tyre is £80.

   It has now been reduced by 40% in a sale.

   What is its new price ?

2. 

   This pair of trainers usually costs £65.

   The price dropped by 15% in a sale.

   What was their new price ?

3. The cost of a week's holiday to Portugal is advertised in a travel agent's window at £450.

   If you book online you can save 8%.

   What is the online price of the holiday ?

4. 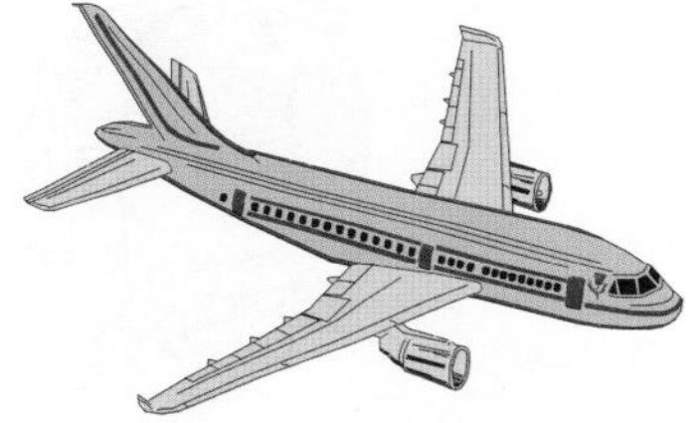

   A plane was flying at 25 000 feet.

   Due to turbulence, the plane's height dropped by 35%.

   What was the new height of the plane ?

5. Last December, the Green family used 725 units of electricity.

   This December, due to the milder weather, they have cut this by 12%.

   How many units will they pay for now ?

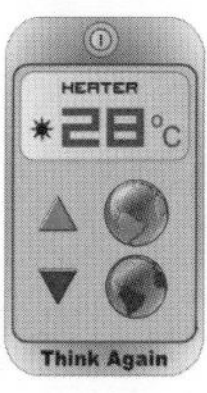

6. 

   A racing car was doing 210 mph along the straight during a practice lap.

   The driver slowed by 30% at a tight bend.

   What was the car's speed around the bend ?

7. In February, 120 millimetres of rain fell in Aberdeen.

   In March, there was a drop in rainfall of 15%.

   How much rain fell in March in Aberdeen ?

8. 

   The temperature in Barcelona in July was 36°C.

   By the 1st of October, it had dropped by 60%.

   What was the temperature in Barcelona on the 1st of October ?

9. 

Mr Roberts weighed in at 80 kilograms.

After dieting and exercising for 6 months, he found he had lost 9% of his original weight.

What was his new weight ?

10. The junior section in Gartland Golf Club used to have 150 members.

Now, only 14% of that number are still members.

How many members have left the club ?

11. 

11·6 centimetres of snow fell one night.

By tea time the following day, 25% had melted.

What was the depth of the remaining snow ?

12. A gent's leather jacket cost £350 when new.

When sold in a charity shop, the price dropped by 85%.

What was the price of the jacket in the charity shop ?

13. "SPORTS PALACE" had a winter sale.

They offered "45% off all goods".

In the sale, Jason bought each of the items below.

What was his total bill ?

SPORTS PALACE
dartboard £20
football boots £52
45% off these prices
football £18
weights £240
baseball bat £12·20
trainers £75

Percentages

Numeracy Assessment 3

1. Write 31% as :- a a fraction b a decimal.

2. Write each of the following as a fraction and simplify as much as possible :-

   a 60% b 85% c 22%.

3. Use your calculator to change each of the following fractions to a :-

   (i) decimal (ii) percentage :-

   a $\frac{9}{20}$ b $\frac{17}{25}$ c $\frac{25}{40}$.

4. Kendra scored 76 out of 80 in a Science Test. Write her score as a percentage.

5. Work out the following :-

   a 21% of £320 b 7% of £45

   c 68% of £20 d $12\frac{1}{2}$% of £5600.

6. Games consoles normally cost £425 at "*EasyGame*".

   a How much could be saved in the spring sale ?

   b How much will a console cost in the sale ?

EasyGame
SPRING SALE
40% off all items in stock.

7. A watering can had 4·8 litres of water in it.

   When a tap was opened, the volume of water in the can increased by 15%.

   a By how many litres did the volume rise ?

   b How much water was then in the can ?

8. Last winter, the caterers in a golf club took in a total of £2500.

   This winter, their takings have fallen by 8%.

   How much have they made this winter ?

9. Scotia Bank is offering interest at $\frac{1}{2}$% per year. Anglo Bank's rate is 0·75%.

   Tom puts £500 in the Scotia Bank and Jerry puts £500 in the Anglo Bank.

   How much more than Tom will Jerry have made when they close their accounts at the end of the year ?

Fractions

Simplifying Fractions

A fraction consists of 2 parts :-

$\frac{5}{8}$ ← this is the NUMERATOR (5) ← this is the DENOMINATOR (8)

The **denominator** is the name (or type) of fraction you are dealing with (*eighths here*).

The **numerator** tells you the number or "how many" of the eighths (*in this case five*).

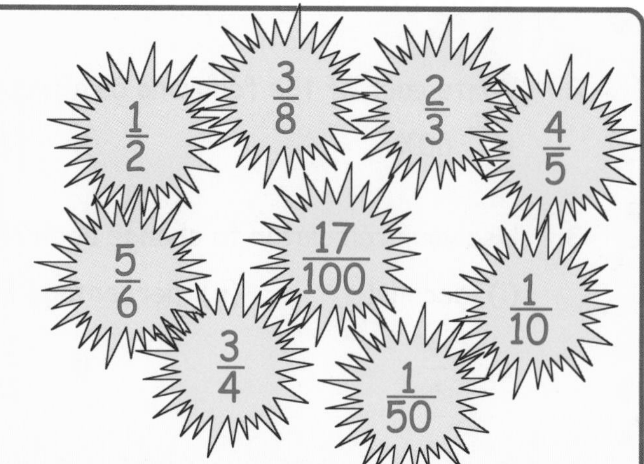

Exercise 1

1. For each of the following, say what fraction is YELLOW :-

a

b 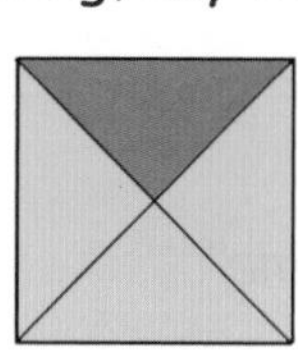

c 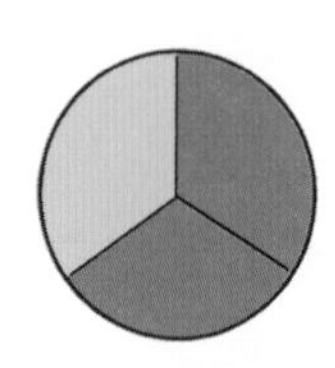

d 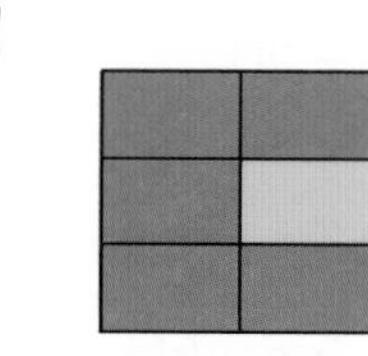

e 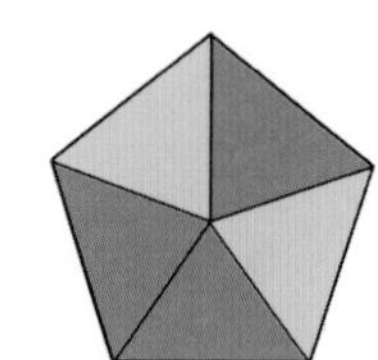

f 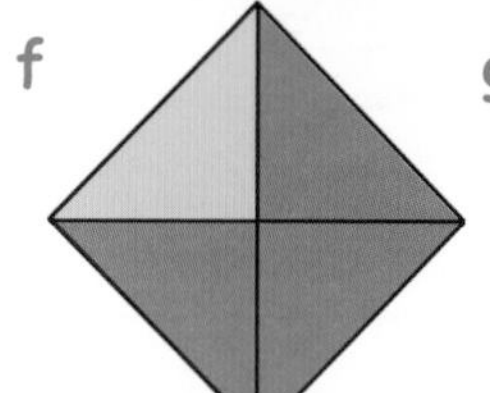

g 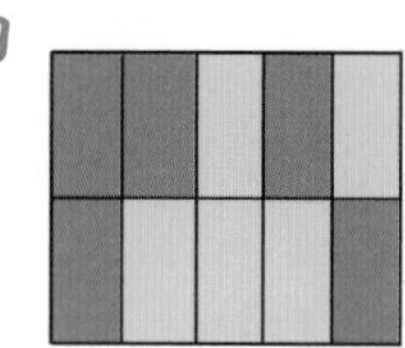

h 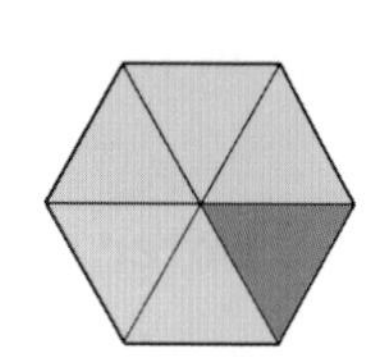

i 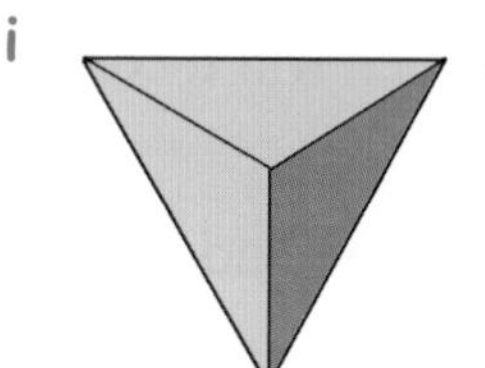

j 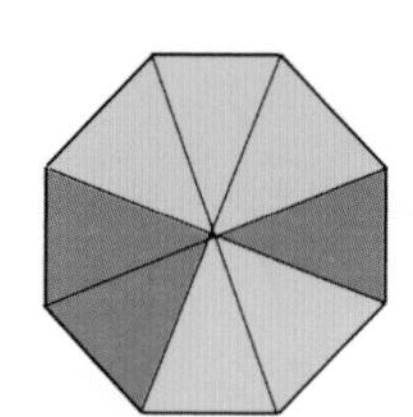

2. a Use a ruler to draw this rectangle measuring 6 boxes by 2 boxes. Shade in $\frac{1}{2}$ of it.

   b Draw the same box again. This time shade or colour in $\frac{1}{4}$ of the shape.

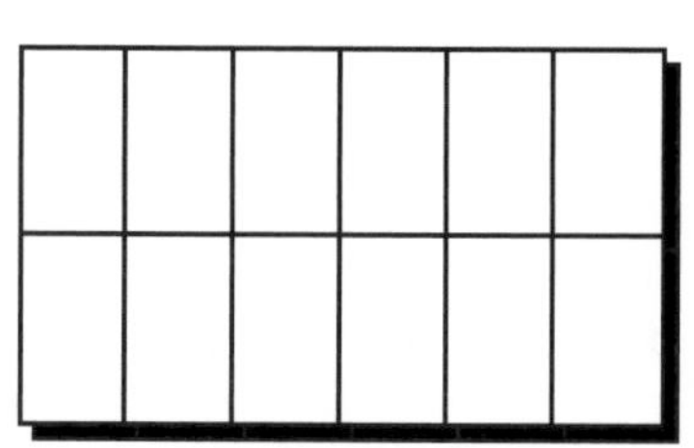

   c Draw the same box again. This time shade or colour in $\frac{1}{3}$ of the shape.

   d Draw the same box again. This time shade or colour in $\frac{3}{4}$ of the shape.

   e Draw the same box again. This time shade or colour in $\frac{5}{6}$ of the shape.

   f Draw the same box again. This time shade or colour in $\frac{7}{12}$ of the shape.

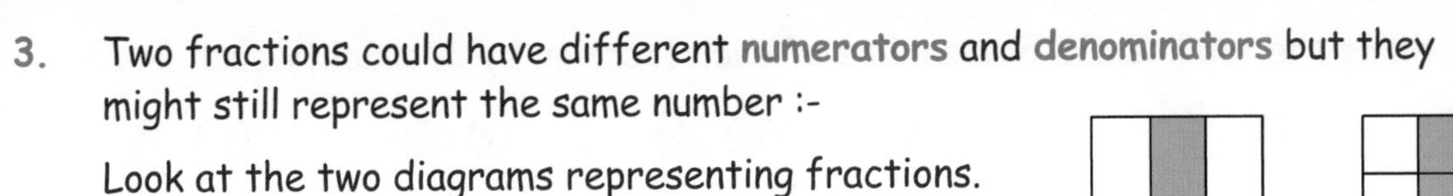

3. Two fractions could have different **numerators** and **denominators** but they might still represent the same number :-

Look at the two diagrams representing fractions.

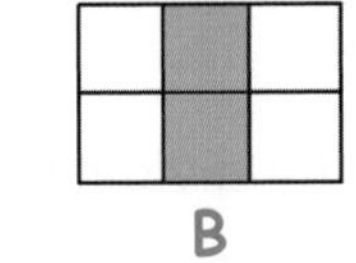

a What fraction is shaded in figure A ?

Can you see that the fraction shaded in B is $\frac{2}{6}$?

b What do the two diagrams tell you about the fractions $\frac{2}{6}$ and $\frac{1}{3}$?

4. Make neat sketches of the following and write down underneath each one the fraction represented by the colouring :-

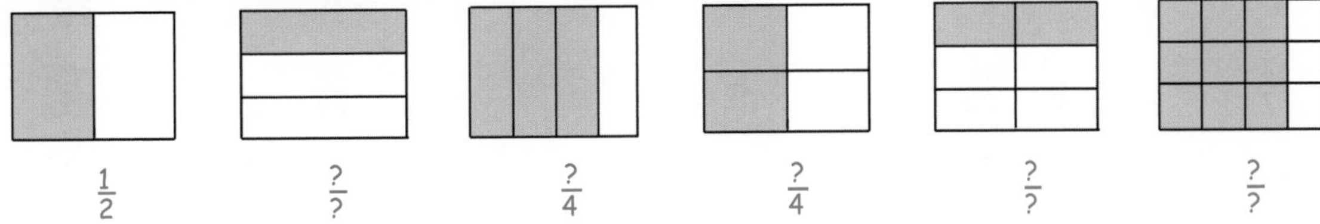

$\frac{1}{2}$ $\frac{?}{?}$ $\frac{?}{4}$ $\frac{?}{4}$ $\frac{?}{?}$ $\frac{?}{?}$

a From the six pictures you can see another fraction equal to $\frac{1}{2}$. $(\frac{1}{2} = \frac{?}{?})$.

b The second and fifth diagrams show that $\frac{1}{3}$ is the same as $\frac{?}{?}$

c The third and the last diagram shows that $\frac{?}{4}$ is the same as $\frac{?}{?}$

5. It is possible to find a fraction **equivalent** to $\frac{3}{4}$ by simply "multiplying the numerator and the denominator by any number" :-

=> $\frac{3}{4}$ becomes $\frac{3 \times 3}{4 \times 3} = \frac{9}{12}$ numerator × 3 / denominator × 3

a Multiply the top and the bottom of $\frac{3}{4}$ by 2 to create a new fraction. What is it ?

b Multiply the top and the bottom of $\frac{3}{4}$ by 4 to create a new fraction. What is it ?

c Find at least 5 more fractions equivalent to $\frac{3}{4}$.

6. By choosing any number (*not 0 or 1*) as a multiplier, find another fraction equivalent to :-

a $\frac{1}{2}$ b $\frac{2}{3}$ c $\frac{3}{5}$ d $\frac{5}{6}$ e $\frac{1}{3}$ f $\frac{7}{10}$.

7. It is possible to **simplify** fractions (like $\frac{10}{15}$) by "*dividing*" top and bottom by a number.

=> $\frac{10}{15}$ becomes $\frac{10 \div 5}{15 \div 5} = \frac{2}{3}$ (*This is the fraction in its **simplest form***).

a By dividing the top line and bottom line of each fraction by 2, simplify each one :-

(i) $\frac{2}{12}$ (ii) $\frac{6}{10}$ (iii) $\frac{14}{20}$ (iv) $\frac{10}{22}$ (v) $\frac{22}{30}$ (vi) $\frac{18}{28}$.

7. b By dividing the top line and bottom line of each fraction by 3, simplify each one :-

(i) $\frac{3}{12}$ (ii) $\frac{9}{15}$ (iii) $\frac{3}{21}$ (iv) $\frac{21}{27}$ (v) $\frac{30}{39}$ (vi) $\frac{6}{27}$.

c By dividing the top line and bottom line of each fraction by 5, simplify each one :-

(i) $\frac{5}{15}$ (ii) $\frac{15}{25}$ (iii) $\frac{65}{100}$ (iv) $\frac{35}{50}$ (v) $\frac{35}{55}$ (vi) $\frac{150}{205}$.

8. This is where it really pays to know your tables well !!

For each of the following fractions, find a number that will divide into both the numerator and the denominator to simplify the fraction fully :-

a $\frac{12 \div 4}{16 \div 4}$ b $\frac{3}{9}$ c $\frac{6}{12}$ d $\frac{14}{21}$ e $\frac{21}{28}$

f $\frac{18 \div 9}{27 \div 9}$ g $\frac{16}{20}$ h $\frac{9}{36}$ i $\frac{48}{60}$ j $\frac{70}{100}$

k $\frac{5}{15}$ l $\frac{33}{44}$ m $\frac{50}{55}$ n $\frac{15}{35}$ o $\frac{75}{100}$

p $\frac{4}{28}$ q $\frac{21}{49}$ r $\frac{27}{45}$ s $\frac{55}{66}$ t $\frac{40}{90}$.

Fractions of a Quantity

To find $\frac{1}{2}$ of 20, you simply divide 20 by 2 => $\frac{1}{2}$ of 20 = (20 ÷ 2) = 10

To find $\frac{1}{3}$ of 21, you simply divide 21 by 3 => $\frac{1}{3}$ of 21 = (21 ÷ 3) = 7

To find $\frac{1}{10}$ of 50, you simply divide 50 by 10 => $\frac{1}{10}$ of 50 = (50 ÷ 10) = 5

Exercise 2

1. Find the following :- (*no calculator*)

a $\frac{1}{2}$ of 16 b $\frac{1}{4}$ of 24 c $\frac{1}{3}$ of 27

d $\frac{1}{5}$ of 50 e $\frac{1}{10}$ of 90 f $\frac{1}{6}$ of 18

g $\frac{1}{8}$ of 40 h $\frac{1}{100}$ of 700 i $\frac{1}{20}$ of 60

j $\frac{1}{7}$ of 35 k $\frac{1}{5}$ of 75 l $\frac{1}{50}$ of 150.

2. You may use a calculator for this question :-

a $\frac{1}{4}$ of 368 b $\frac{1}{5}$ of 475 c $\frac{1}{3}$ of 345

d $\frac{1}{8}$ of 2096 e $\frac{1}{7}$ of 2261 f $\frac{1}{11}$ of 6006

g $\frac{1}{15}$ of 7500 h $\frac{1}{12}$ of 1476 i $\frac{1}{30}$ of 9300.

(Harder) To find $\frac{2}{3}$ of a number (like 15), you do it in 2 steps.

Step 1 :- Find $\frac{1}{3}$ of 15 (÷ 3) first => $\frac{1}{3}$ of 15 = 15 ÷ 3 = **5**

Step 2 :- Now find $\frac{2}{3}$ of 15 by (x 2). => $\frac{2}{3}$ of 15 = **5** x 2 = 10.

Here's how you should set down the working :-

$\frac{2}{3}$ of 15 => (15 ÷ 3) then 5 x 2 = 10

$\frac{3}{4}$ of 24 => (24 ÷ 4) then 6 x 3 = 18

$\frac{5}{6}$ of 18 => (18 ÷ 6) then 3 x 5 = 15

Rule :-
To multiply by a fraction like $\frac{5}{6}$
=> "divide by the denominator" (6)
=> then "multiply by the numerator" (5)

3. Do the following **without a calculator** :-

a $\frac{2}{3}$ of 21 => (21 ÷ 3) then 7 x 2 = ...

b $\frac{3}{4}$ of 16 => (16 ÷ ...) then ... x 3 = ...

c $\frac{2}{5}$ of 10 d $\frac{4}{5}$ of 20 e $\frac{5}{6}$ of 12

f $\frac{3}{8}$ of 24 g $\frac{3}{10}$ of 50 h $\frac{2}{9}$ of 27

i $\frac{3}{7}$ of 21 j $\frac{7}{8}$ of 80 k $\frac{7}{10}$ of 30

l $\frac{3}{100}$ of 500 m $\frac{9}{10}$ of 20 n $\frac{3}{4}$ of 120.

4. Do the following :- (*You may use a calculator*).

a $\frac{3}{5}$ of 180 => (180 ÷ 5) then 36 x 3 = ...

b $\frac{7}{8}$ of 120 => (120 ÷ ...) then ... x 7 = ...

c $\frac{2}{3}$ of 150 d $\frac{3}{4}$ of 680 e $\frac{7}{10}$ of 1400

f $\frac{3}{5}$ of 95 g $\frac{5}{9}$ of 360 h $\frac{3}{7}$ of 371

i $\frac{7}{8}$ of 656 j $\frac{5}{6}$ of 198 k $\frac{4}{5}$ of 925.

5. a A school has 1050 pupils. $\frac{3}{5}$ of them are boys.

(i) How many boys are there ? (ii) How many girls ?

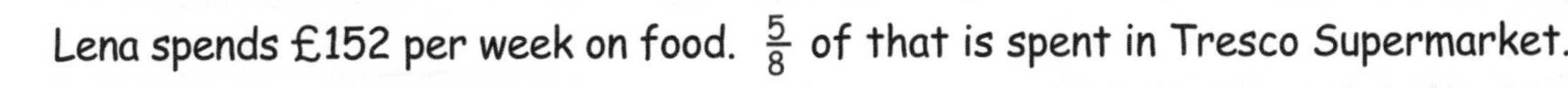

b Lena spends £152 per week on food. $\frac{5}{8}$ of that is spent in Tresco Supermarket.

(i) How much does she spend in Tresco ? (ii) How much is spent elsewhere ?

c Of the 84 words Aaron was asked to spell, he got $\frac{6}{7}$ of them correct.

(i) How many words did he spell correctly ? (ii) How many did he get wrong ?

Back to Percentages

In Chapter 3 on percentages, you discovered how to find 19% of £70 using a calculator.

$$19\% \text{ of } £70 = \frac{19}{100} \times £70 = (19 \div 100) \times £70 = 13{\cdot}3 = £13{\cdot}30.$$

note the 0

There are some very basic percentages which can be thought of as simple fractions.

Example :- $50\% = \frac{50}{100}\,{}^{\div 10}_{\div 10} = \frac{5}{10}\,{}^{\div 5}_{\div 5} = \frac{1}{2} \Rightarrow 50\% = \frac{1}{2}$

Exercise 3

1. Discuss with your teacher which of these percentages match up with which fractions.

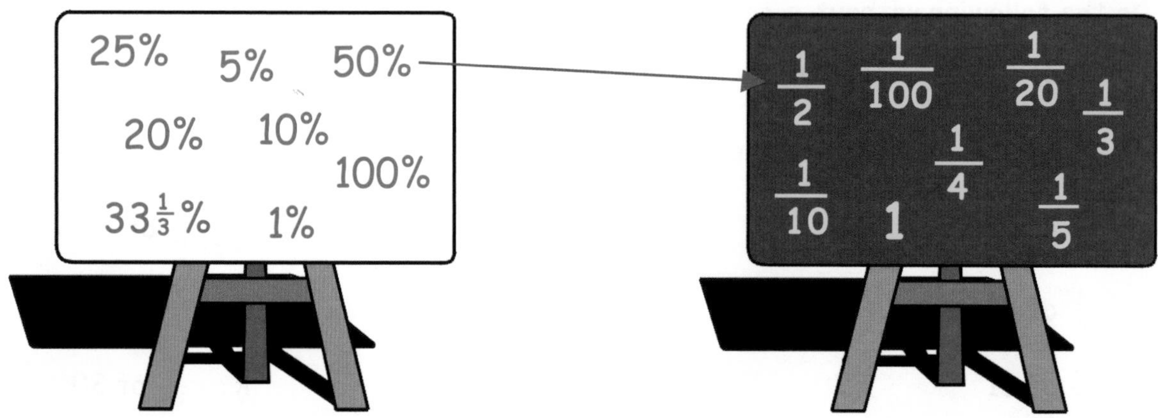

2. Copy and complete this table using your answers obtained from question 1.

percentage	100%	50%	$33\frac{1}{3}$%	25%	20%	10%	5%	1%
fraction	....	$\frac{1}{2}$	....	....	....	....	....	....

You **must** learn and know how to use these to answer basic percentage questions.

You can now do simple percentage work using the equivalent fraction instead :-

Example :- 50% of £60 means $\frac{1}{2}$ of £60 (= 60 ÷ 2) = £30

3. Do the following **mentally** :-

a 50% of £20 b 50% of £62 c 50% of £1400.

4. Find without a calculator :-

(Remember :- 25% means $\frac{1}{4}$).

a 25% of £12 (= $\frac{1}{4}$ of 12 = 12 ÷ 4 = £....)

b 25% of £200 c 25% of £28 d 25% of £360.

5. Find the following without a calculator :- (Remember :- 20% means $\frac{1}{5}$).

a 20% of £25 b 20% of £45 c 20% of £3500.

6. Find the following without a calculator :- (*Use fractions instead*).

a 50% of £170 b 25% of £44 c 20% of £60

d 10% of £110 e 100% of £3 f $33\frac{1}{3}$% of £66

g 25% of £48 h 1% of £4500 i 20% of £650

j 50% of £2600 k $33\frac{1}{3}$% of £180 l 5% of £80.

7. 20% of the 350 people who are learning to drive with *Able Motoring School* are female.

How many ladies is that ?

8. I earn £444 per week as a librarian and spend 25% of it on my mortgage.

a How much of the £444 is spent on my mortgage ?

b How much does that leave me with per week ?

9.

A coffee making machine is usually priced at £54.

This week, there is $33\frac{1}{3}$% off the price at *Satellite*.

a Calculate how much you could save.

b What's the sale price of the coffee machine ?

A few more Percentages

By now, you should have **memorised** the percentage <=> fraction equivalences.

Can you also see that :- 75% = 3 x 25% = 3 x $\frac{1}{4}$ = $\frac{3}{4}$

and 40% = 2 x 20% = 2 x $\frac{1}{5}$ = $\frac{2}{5}$?

Exercise 4

1. Copy the following and complete :-

a 75% = 3 x 25% = 3 x $\frac{1}{4}$ = ... b 40% = 2 x 20% = 2 x $\frac{1}{5}$ = ...

c 60% = 3 x 20% = 3 x $\frac{1}{5}$ = ... d 80% = 4 x ...% = 4 x $\frac{1}{5}$ = ...

e $66\frac{2}{3}$% = ... x $33\frac{1}{3}$% = ... x $\frac{1}{3}$ = ... f 30% = 3 x 10% = ... x $\frac{1}{10}$ = ...

g 70% = ... x 10% = ... x ... = ... h 90% = ... x ... % = ... x ... = ...

2. You now have an **extended** list to learn :-

percentage	50%	25%	75%	$33\frac{1}{3}$ %	$66\frac{2}{3}$ %	20%	40%	60%	80%	10%	30%	70%	90%
fraction	$\frac{1}{2}$	$\frac{1}{4}$	$\frac{3}{4}$	$\frac{1}{3}$	$\frac{2}{3}$	$\frac{1}{5}$	$\frac{2}{5}$	$\frac{3}{5}$	$\frac{4}{5}$	$\frac{1}{10}$	$\frac{3}{10}$	$\frac{7}{10}$	$\frac{9}{10}$

Copy this list into your jotter and **memorise** the above connections.

You will need them to do mental percentage work.

3. Copy and complete the following :- (*no calculator*)

a 40% of £30 = $\frac{2}{5}$ of £30 => (30 ÷ 5) => 6 x 2 = £....

b 80% of £40 = $\frac{4}{5}$ of £40 => (... ÷ 5) => ... x 4 = £....

c 75% of £16 = $\frac{3}{4}$ of £.... => (... ÷ ...) => ... x 3 = £....

d $66\frac{2}{3}$% of £21 = ... of £21 => (... ÷ ...) => ... x ? = £....

4. Do the following **MENTALLY** by using the fractions instead of the percentages :-

a (i) 25% of £60 (ii) 75% of £60

b (i) 20% of £25 (ii) 40% of £25

c (i) 20% of £90 (ii) 80% of £90

d (i) $33\frac{1}{3}$% of £24 (ii) $66\frac{2}{3}$% of £24

e (i) 10% of £70 (ii) 70% of £70

f (i) 10% of £140 (ii) 30% of £140

g (i) 20% of £180 (ii) 40% of £180

h (i) 10% of £500 (ii) 90% of £500

i (i) 10% of £160 (ii) 5% of £160 (half of 10%).

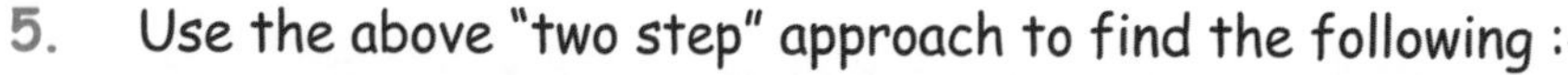

5. Use the above "two step" approach to find the following :-

a 75% of £28 (think of 25% = $\frac{1}{4}$ of £28 first, then ....)

b 40% of £15 c 60% of £25 d $66\frac{2}{3}$% of £48

e 30% of £110 f 70% of £60 g 60% of £55

h 6% of £400 i 75% of £88 j 80% of £130.

6. Betty saw a vacuum cleaner normally priced £112.

The label on it said "**75% OFF**".

a Calculate 75% of £112.

b How much did Betty end up paying for the hoover ?

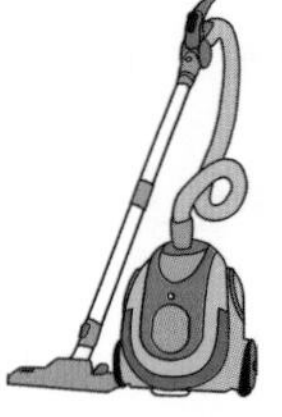

Fractions

Numeracy Assessment 4

1. What fraction of each of these shapes is coloured ?

a 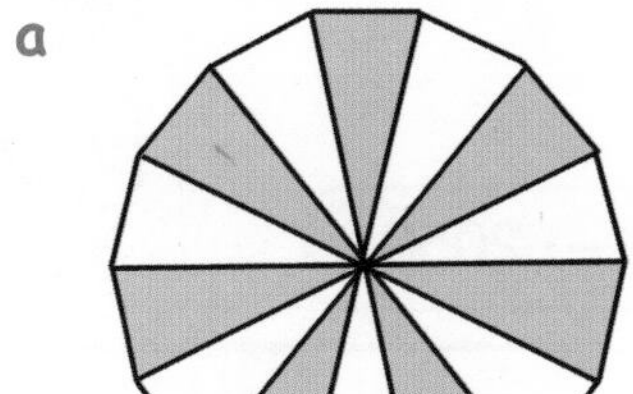

b 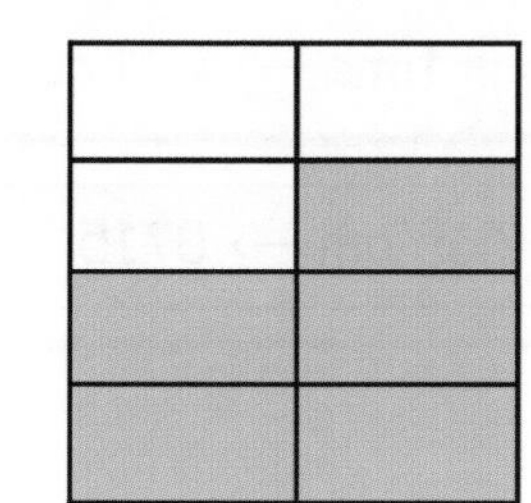

c 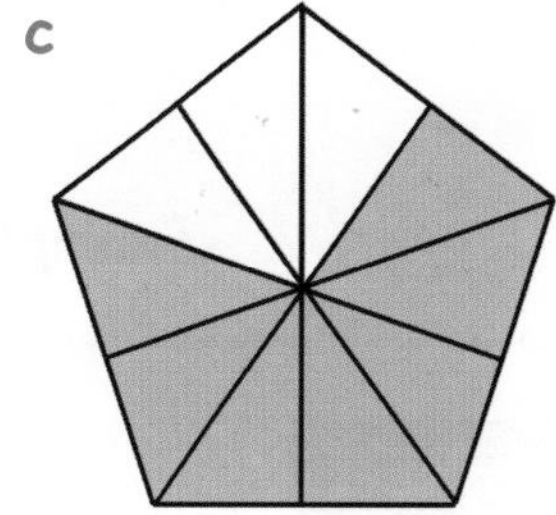

2. a Write down one other fraction equivalent to the fraction $\frac{7}{8}$.

   b Write down any two fractions equivalent to $\frac{4}{9}$.

3. Simplify the following fractions :-

   a $\frac{6}{10}$ b $\frac{36}{48}$ c $\frac{21}{35}$.

4. Find :- a $\frac{1}{2}$ of 38 b $\frac{1}{4}$ of 72.

5. Find :- a $\frac{3}{5}$ of 155 b $\frac{5}{6}$ of 144.

6. 90 people are sunbathing on a beach.

   $\frac{3}{5}$ of them are wearing sun glasses.

   How many of them are not ?

7. What **fraction** is equivalent to :-

   a 75% b 40% c 5% ?

8. Attempt the following without using a calculator :-

   a 50% of £74 b 10% of £14 c 25% of 64p

   d $33\frac{1}{3}$% of 45p e 20% of £85 f 1% of £30

   g 5% of £120 h 75% of £3·60 i 2% of £500

   j $33\frac{1}{3}$% of £1·08 k $66\frac{2}{3}$% of £1·08 l 200% of £500.

Time-Distance-Speed

12 & 24 hour Time

Remember :-

12 hour time —> 24 hour time

24 hour time —> 12 hour time

Example :- 7·15 am —> 0715 8·50 pm —> 2050

Exercise 1

1. Change the following 12 hour clock times to 24 hour clock times :-

a	1·30 am	b	4·45 am	c	6 am
d	7·30 pm	e	2·15 pm	f	3 pm
g	6·15 am	h	8·20 am	i	2·10 am
j	7·50 am	k	midday		
l	12·45 am	m	12·45 pm		
n	9·15 pm	o	3·25 am		
p	8·20 pm	q	11·55 pm		
r	9·55 am	s	10·20 pm		
t	11·34 am	u	8·47 pm.		

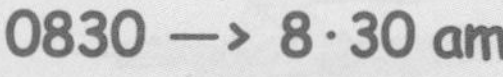

0830 —> 8·30 am 2040 —> 8·40 pm

2. Change the following 24 hour clock times to 12 hour clock times :-

a	0140	b	1110	c	0925
d	1430	e	1740	f	2315
g	0245	h	1915	i	1310
j	1903	k	1200		
l	0630	m	0525		
n	1520	o	2355		
p	1935	q	0020		
r	0758	s	1147		
t	2030	u	2155.		

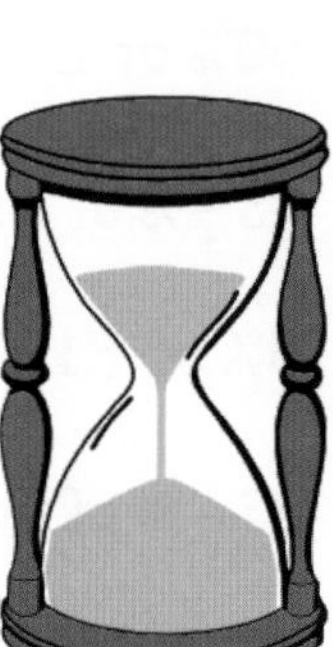

Time Intervals, Timetables, Programme Guides

Exercise 2

1. How long is it from :-

   a 2·15 pm to 6·15 pm b 6 am to 11·30 am

   c noon to 7·30 pm d 4·30 pm to 8·15 pm

   e 5·45 am to 8·20 am f 2·25 am to 5·10 am

   g 0820 to 1125 h 1845 to 2010

   i 1615 to 1905 j 2310 to 0200 (*next day*) ?

2. The clocks indicate the start and finish of a concert one evening.

   For how long did the concert last ?

Begins

Ends

3. Shown is part of the train timetable from Norton to Portville.

	Norton	*Douglas*	*Abbots*	*Weir*	*Portville*
Early Train	6·10 am	7·15 am	9·25 am	11·05 am	1·00 pm
Late Train	10·25 am	11·30 am			5·15 pm

   a How long does the early train take to travel from :-

      (i) Norton to Douglas ?

      (ii) Abbots to Weir ?

      (iii) Norton to Portville ?

   b Assuming that the late train travels at the same speed as the early train, when would it be expected to arrive at :-

      (i) Abbots ? (*Hint ! Notice how long the early train takes from Douglas to Abbots*).

      (ii) Weir ?

Time, Distance, Speed - Calculating Distance

Example :- A car travels at an average speed of 35 km/hr for 3 hours.

How far will the car travel ?

D = S x T

D = 35 x 3 = 105 km

Distance = **S**peed x **T**ime

Exercise 3

1. How far, in kilometres, can you travel :-
   - a walking at 5 km/hr for 2 hours
   - b jogging at 4 km/hr for 3 hours
   - c cycling at 12 km/hr for 3 hours
   - d driving at 42 km/hr for 5 hours ?

2. Calculate the distance travelled by :-
   - a a car, travelling at 46 mph for 2 hours
   - b a train, travelling at 90 mph for 6 hours
   - c a plane, flying at 320 mph for 4 hours
   - d a yacht, sailing at 13 mph for 3 hours.

3. What distances are covered by the following :-
   - a a lorry, travelling for 30 minutes at an average speed of 40 mph ?
   - b a $1\frac{1}{2}$ hour jog, at an average speed of 6 mph ?
   - c a car journey lasting $2\frac{1}{2}$ hours, at an average speed of 50 mph ?
   - d a speed boat ride for 4 hours 30 minutes, at an average speed of 30 km/hr ?
   - e a plane journey of 6 hours 30 minutes, at an average speed of 400 mph ?

4. What distances are covered by the following :-
   - a a canoe, moving at an average speed of 4 mph for $\frac{1}{4}$ of an hour ?
   - b a lion, running at an average speed of 28 mph for quarter of an hour ?
   - c a boat trip, sailing at an average speed of 12 mph for 1 hour 15 minutes ?
   - d a lorry, travelling at an average speed of 60 km/hr for 45 minutes ($\frac{3}{4}$ hour) ?
   - e an athlete, running at an average speed of 8 km/hr for 1 hour 45 minutes ?

5. a A plane left Amsterdam at 9·15 am and arrived at Glasgow at 11·15 am.

The plane flew at an average speed of 355 mph.

How long did the flight take and how many miles did it cover ?

b 

A sailing ship left the harbour at 3·35 pm and sailed at a steady speed of 15 mph.

How far is the ship from the harbour at 6·35 pm ?

c A jogger left George Square at 0930 and headed for the Erskine Bridge.

Jogging at an average speed of 10 mph, he arrived at the bridge at 1100.

How far had he travelled ?

Time, Distance, Speed - Calculating Speed

Example :- A train travels 280 miles in 4 hours. Find the **average speed** of the train.

S = D / T

S = 280 ÷ 4

S = 70 mph

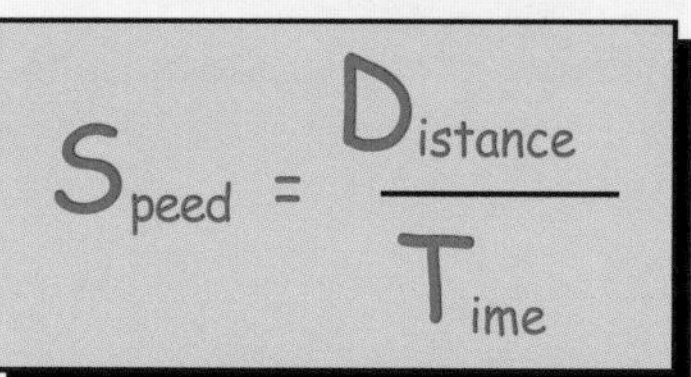

Exercise 4

1. Use the formula to find the average speed of these journeys :-

a 12 miles in 3 hours b 42 km in 6 hours

c 150 miles in 5 hours d 4200 km in 2 hours.

2. Calculate the average speed of these journeys (*watch the units*) :-

a 60 km in 2 hours b 400 miles in 5 hours

c 160 metres in 8 seconds d 26 km in 4 hours

e 45 000 miles in 9 hours f 280 000 km in 7 hours.

3. Calculate the average speed of these journeys (*in miles per hour*) :-

a A submarine sails 640 miles in only 8 hours.

b A plane flies 1550 miles in 5 hours.

c A train travels 249 miles in 3 hours.

d A marathon runner covers 22 miles in 2 hours.

e A coach travels 483 miles in 7 hours.

4. Find these average speeds :-

   a a van travelling 85 miles in 2 hours

   b a car travelling 17 miles in 30 minutes
      (*Hint - how far does it travel in 1 hour ?*)

   c a boat sailing 11 miles in $\frac{1}{2}$ hour

   d an athlete running 9 miles in 1 hour 30 minutes. ($1\frac{1}{2}$ *hours*).

   e a worm crawling $\frac{1}{2}$ metre in $\frac{1}{2}$ hour !

5. Find the average speed of :-

   a a runner who jogs 2 km in 15 minutes

   b a coach which travels 7 miles in $\frac{1}{4}$ hour

   c a ferry which sails 13 km in 30 minutes

   d a motor cyclist covers 90 km in 1 hour 30 minutes ($1\frac{1}{2}$ hrs)

   e a plane flying 1050 miles in 2 hours 30 minutes ($2\frac{1}{2}$ hrs).

6. A delivery van leaves Oban at 1015.
   By 1415, it has covered a distance of 280 kilometres.
   Calculate the average speed of the van.

7.

A plane left East Midlands Airport at 2·45 pm and flew 300 miles to Edinburgh, arriving at 4·15 pm.

   a How long did the journey take ?

   b What was the plane's average speed ?

8. Mike and Mandy hire a rowing boat and go out rowing on the loch.
   They row to an island, taking two hours to get there, but the return journey takes an hour longer.
   If the island is 7·5 miles from the hiring jetty, calculate the average speed for their round trip.
   (*Hint :- speed = total distance ÷ total time*).

Time, Distance, Speed - Calculating Time

Example :- A plane flies at an average speed of 300 km/hr.

How long will the plane take to travel 1200 kilometres ?

$T = D / S$

$T = 1200 \div 300$

$T = 4$ hours

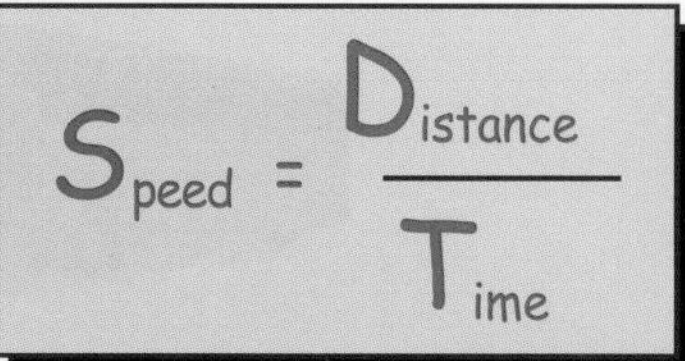

Exercise 5

1. Change these times to hours and minutes :-

a	$1\frac{1}{2}$ hours	b	$2\frac{1}{2}$ hours	c	$3\frac{1}{4}$ hours	d	$5\frac{3}{4}$ hours
e	$4\frac{1}{2}$ hours	f	$6\frac{1}{4}$ hours	g	7·5 hours	h	8·5 hours
i	2·25 hours	j	1·25 hours	k	4·75 hours	l	0·75 hours.

2. *3 hours 30 minutes is 3·5 hours, 2 hours 15 minutes is 2·25 hours* ($\frac{1}{4}$ of an hour)

What are these times in hours :-

a	2 hours 30 minutes	b	1 hour 15 minutes
c	3 hours 45 minutes	d	2 hours 15 minutes
e	5 hours 30 minutes	f	6 hours 30 minutes
g	4 hours 45 minutes	h	8 hours 45 minutes ?

3. Use the formula $T = \frac{D}{S}$ to calculate the time taken for each journey here :-

a	walking, 2 km at 2 km/hr	b	flying, 1600 miles at 400 mph
c	sprinting, 300 m at 10 m/sec	d	driving, 210 km at 30 km/hr
e	crawling, 8 cm at 2 cm/hr	f	jogging, 14 miles at 7 mph
g	running at 8 km/hr for 16 km	h	driving at 60 mph for 90 miles.

4. When will these trains arrive at their destinations :-

a **Steam Engine** –

departs 9 am – travels 140 miles at 70 mph

b **Electric Train** –

departs 2·30 pm – travels 135 km at 90 km/hr.

c **Diesel Train** –

departs 7·45 am – travels 280 miles at 80 mph ?

5. How long, in **hours** and **minutes**, or **minutes** and **seconds** did these journeys take :-

a a jet skier, travelling 30 km at an average speed of 20 km/hr ?

b a coach, travelling 125 miles at an average speed of 50 mph ?

c a caterpillar, covering 70 centimetres at an average speed of 0·7 cm/sec ? (*answers in minutes and seconds*)

d a van, travelling 70 km at an average speed of 20 km/hr ?

6. Use this **mileage chart** to find the distance between the towns and find how long each of the journeys would take :-

a Dunel —> Ropley at 30 mph

b Ropley —> Hartown at 70 mph

c Dunel —> Hartown at 60 mph.

Dunel		
60	Ropley	
90	70	Hartown

7.

A train left Fort William at 11·15 am.

It travelled the 100 miles to Glasgow at an average speed of 80 mph.

a How long did the journey take ?

b At what time did the train arrive in Glasgow ?

8. An aeroplane left Gatwick at 7·30 pm on Saturday.

Its holiday destination was an island 2200 miles away.

If it travelled at a steady 400 mph :-

a How long was the journey ?

b At what time did the plane land on the island ?

9. The speed of sound is about 345 metres per second.

Tina shouts to Tony who is standing 1380 metres away.

How many seconds does it take before Tony hears Tina's voice ?

Time, Distance, Speed - a Mixture

Use this triangle mnemonic* to help you use the correct formula to answer the questions in this exercise.

$D = S \times T$

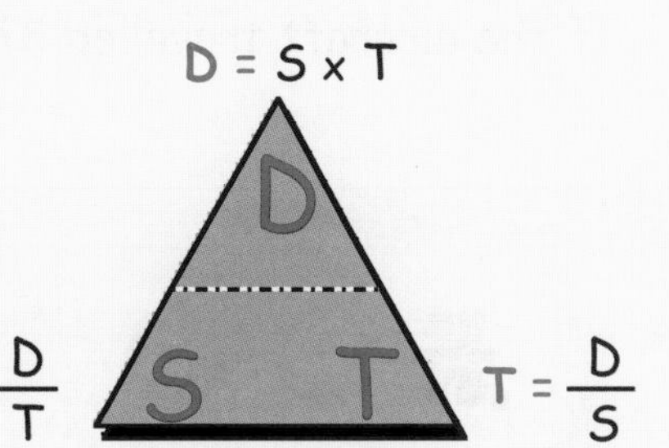

$S = \frac{D}{T}$ $T = \frac{D}{S}$

*A mnemonic is anything that helps you remember an important fact.

Exercise 6

1. a

Distance - 60 miles
Speed - 20 mph
Time ?

b

Distance - 150 km
Time - 6 hours
Speed ?

c

Speed - 25 mph
Time - 4 hours
Distance ?

d

Distance - 210 miles
Time - 3 hours
Speed ?

e

Distance - 450 miles
Speed - 100 mph
Time ?

f

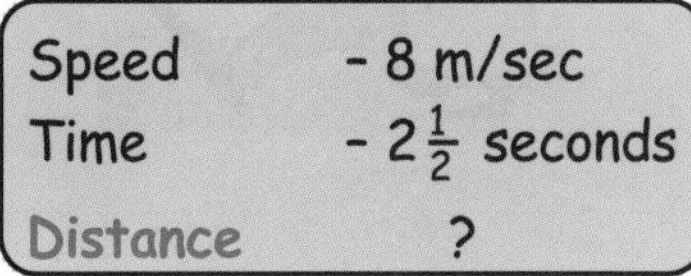

Speed - 8 m/sec
Time - $2\frac{1}{2}$ seconds
Distance ?

2. A fire engine sped to a fire 40 miles from the fire station.

The journey took 30 minutes.

What was the fire engine's average speed ?

3. 

A hot air balloon travelled 50 kilometres at an average speed of 20 kilometres per hour.

How long did it take to complete its journey ?

4. This bulldozer, going at a steady speed of 16 km/hr, took $2\frac{1}{2}$ hours to travel from its depot to the construction site.

What was the length of its journey ?

5. A pilot took off from an airfield at 0655 and flew north west to a meeting point, arriving there at 0855.

If the aircraft travelled 370 miles, what was its average speed ?

6. 

A tractor is travelling at 6 km/hr.

How long will it take to cover a field distance of 7·5 km ? (*Answer in hours and minutes*).

7. A communications satellite orbits a planet at an average speed of 12 400 mph.

It takes $1\frac{1}{2}$ hours to complete its orbit.

Calculate the length of the orbit.

8. 

Henry can walk to his office in 15 minutes.

The distance from his house to work is 1 mile.

a Calculate, in mph, Henry's average speed.

He can run twice as fast as he can walk.

b How long would it take him to run to work ?

9. A bird takes $12\frac{1}{2}$ days to migrate from the U.K. to U.S.A.

If it maintains an average speed of 200 miles per day, what distance will it fly to reach America ?

10. 

At full speed, a tortoise can travel at 50 centimetres per minute.

How long would it take a tortoise to cross a garden path measuring 1·5 metres wide ?

11. The police radar trap is set up in a "70 miles per hour" stretch of motorway.

Which of the following drivers cannot be charged with speeding ?

a Wilma, covering 17 miles in 15 minutes

b Freddie, covering 12 miles in 10 minutes

c Nina, covering 23 miles in 20 minutes.

Time-Distance-Speed

Numeracy Assessment 5

1. Here is part of a train timetable from Glasgow Central to Birmingham.

    a If I can get to Glasgow Central for about 2:20 pm what is the 1st train I can catch to Birmingham ?

    b How long would this train take to get me to Birmingham ?

    c Unfortunately, I don't arrive in Glasgow till 2:50 pm.

    How long must I wait for the next train ?

Glasgow Central [GLC] to Birmingham New Street [BHM]

Leaving	From	To	Arriving	Duration	Changes
14:00	Glasgow Central [GLC]	Birmingham New Street [BHM]	17:56	3h 56m	0
14:40	Glasgow Central [GLC]	Birmingham New Street [BHM]	18:55		1
16:00	Glasgow Central [GLC]	Birmingham New Street [BHM]	19:55	3h 55m	0
16:40	Glasgow Central [GLC]	Birmingham New Street [BHM]	20:55	4h 15m	1
17:40	Glasgow Central [GLC]	Birmingham New Street [BHM]		4h 10m	0

    d When does the 5:40 pm train from Glasgow Central arrive in Birmingham ?

    (Answer in 12 hour time notation)

2. A Redix petrol tanker leaves Grangemouth and travels for 5 hours at an average speed of 38 mph.

    How far will the vehicle have travelled ?

3. Mel and his girlfriend travelled the 150 miles from Dundee to Stranraer on his motorbike.

    They covered the journey in $2\frac{1}{2}$ hours.

    What was their **average speed**, in mph ?

4. Edna and Brian drove for 30 miles at an average speed of 40 mph.

    How long did they take, in minutes ?

5. Rick flew 150 km in his plane at an average speed of 120 km/hr.

    If he set off at 1745, **at what time** did he reach his destination ?

6. 

    A message in a bottle floats harmlessly on the surface of the ocean at a steady speed of 0·3 miles per hour.

    It floated for 200 hours before being picked up by a young girl on a beach.

    How far would it have travelled in that time ?

Area and Perimeter

Area

The AREA of a shape is defined as :-

The amount of space inside the boundary of a flat (2-dimensional) object such as a rectangle, square, triangle, circle ......

The square opposite measure 1 centimetre by 1 centimetre.

1 cm | 1 cm | $1\ cm^2$

We say it has an area of :-

1 square centimetre

or $1\ cm^2$ (for short).

(*note :- $1\ cm^2$ reads as "1 square centimetre"*).

Exercise 1

1. a How many boxes (*1 centimetre by 1 centimetre*) are shown here ?

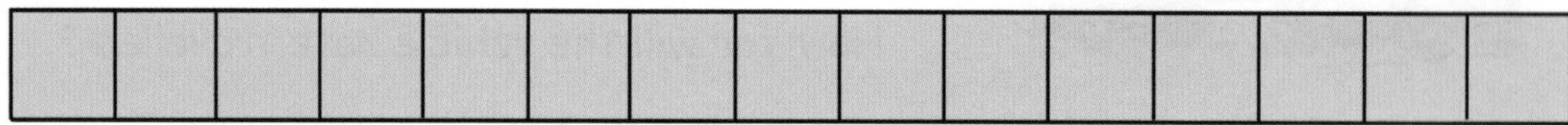

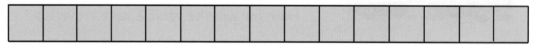

b Write down the area as :- Area = ... cm^2.

2. Write down the area (use cm^2) of each of the following shapes :-

a 

b 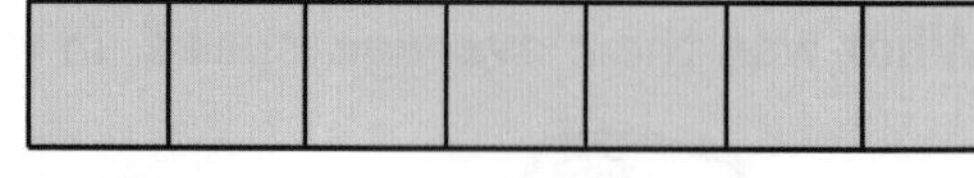

c 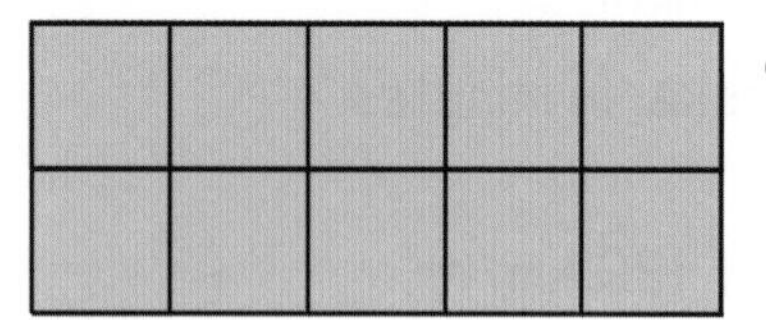

d 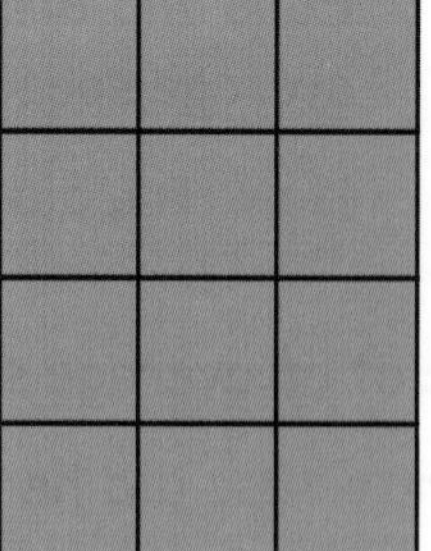

e 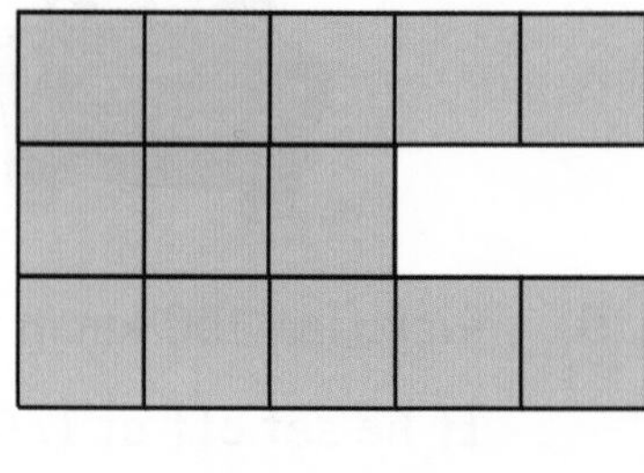

f 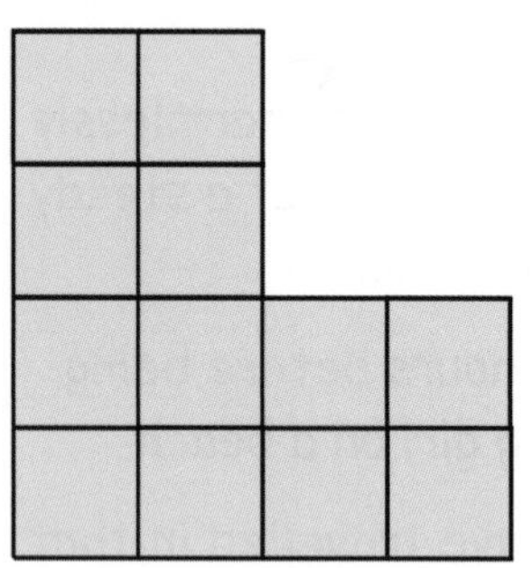

g 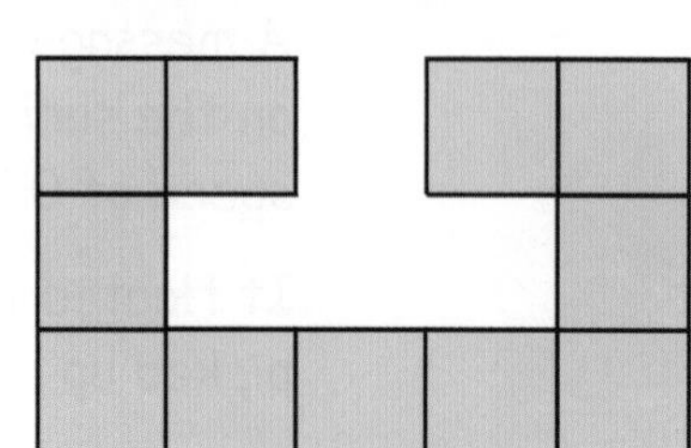

h 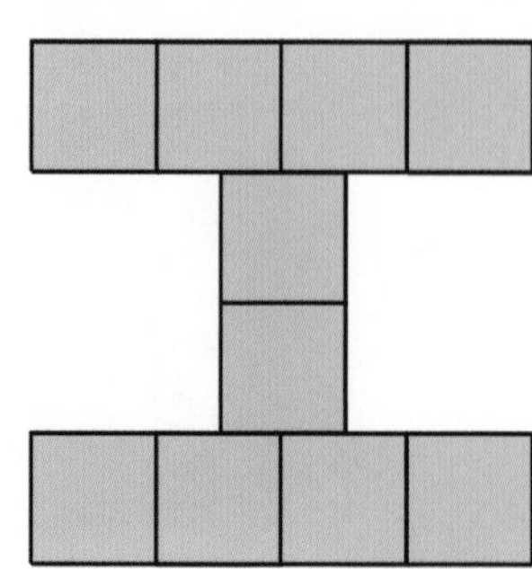

2. i

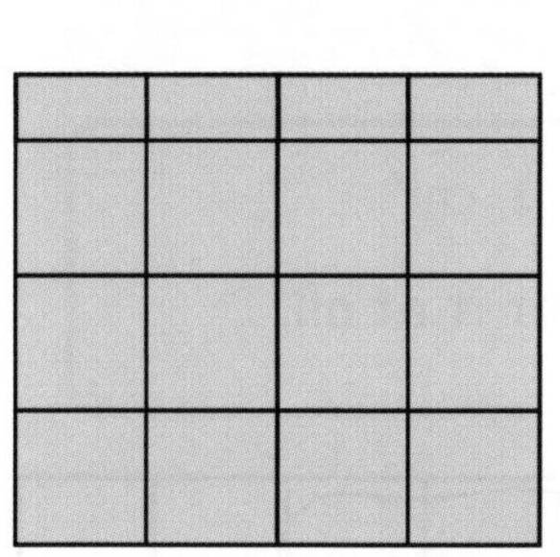

j

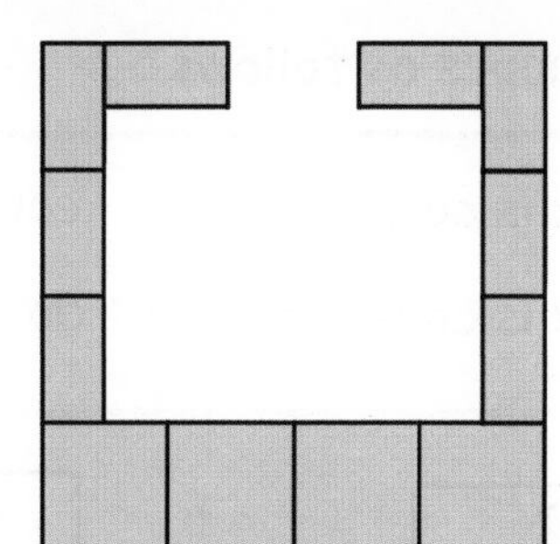

k

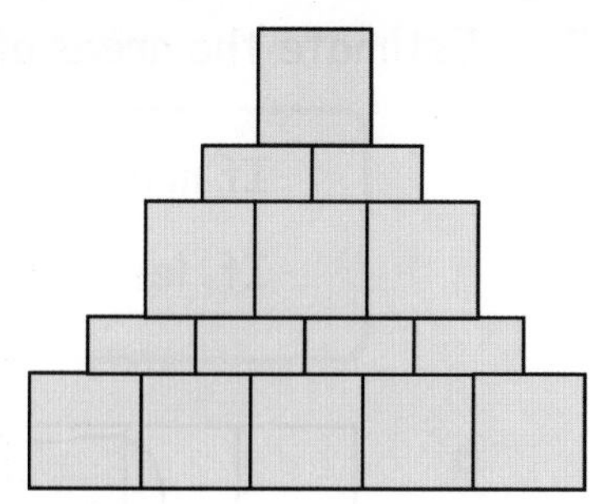

3. Find the shaded areas (don't include the holes) :-

a

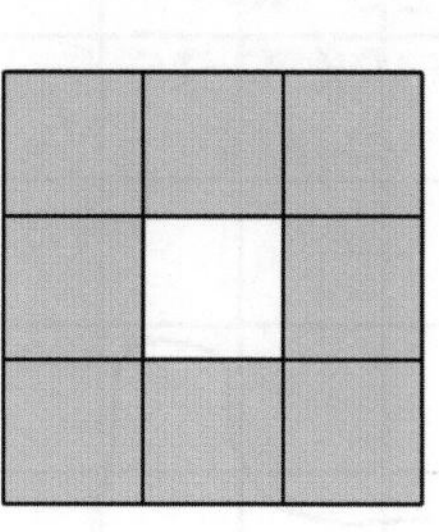

b

c

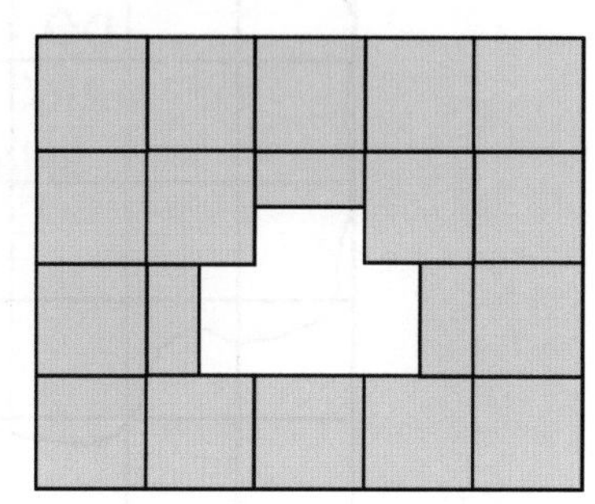

d

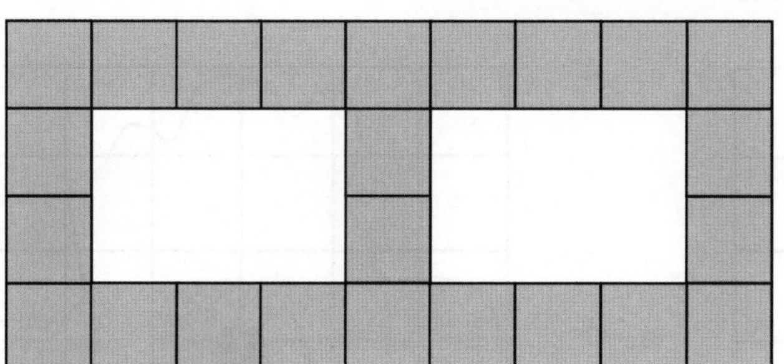

e

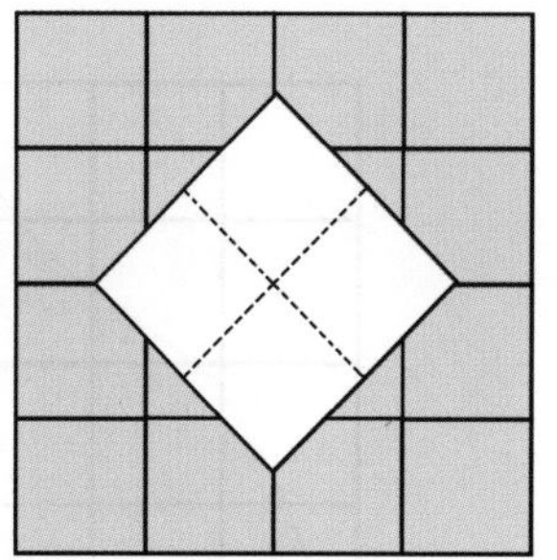

4. **Be careful here with $\frac{1}{2}$ squares !!** Find the areas of :-

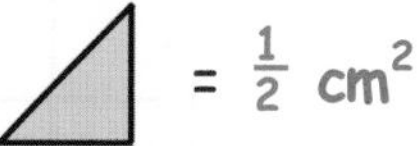

$= \frac{1}{2}$ cm^2

a

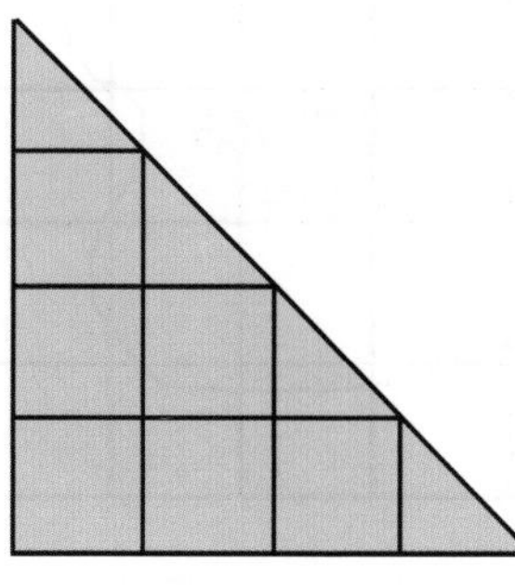

b

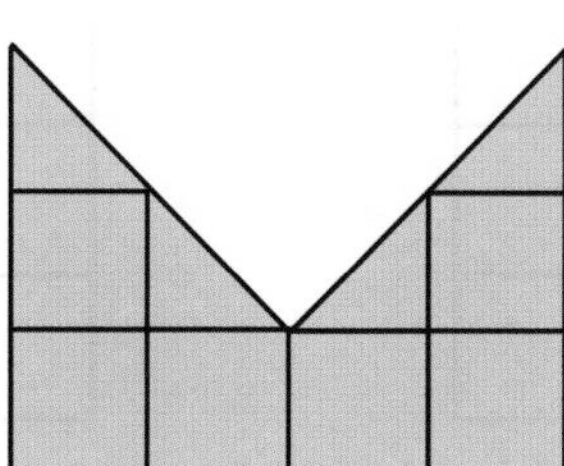

c

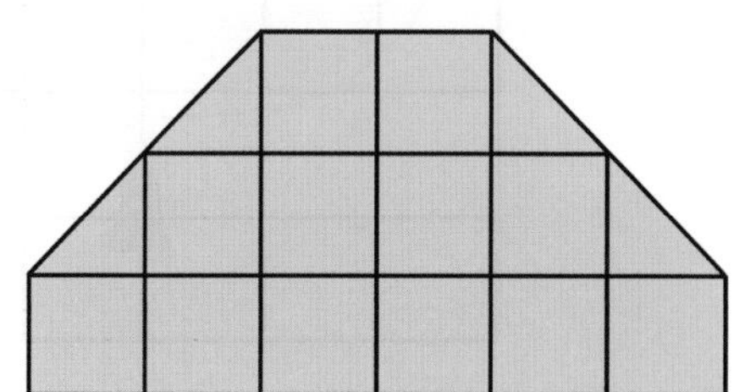

d

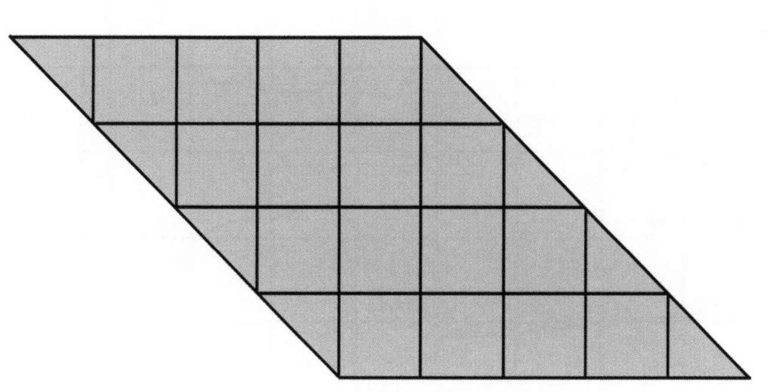

e

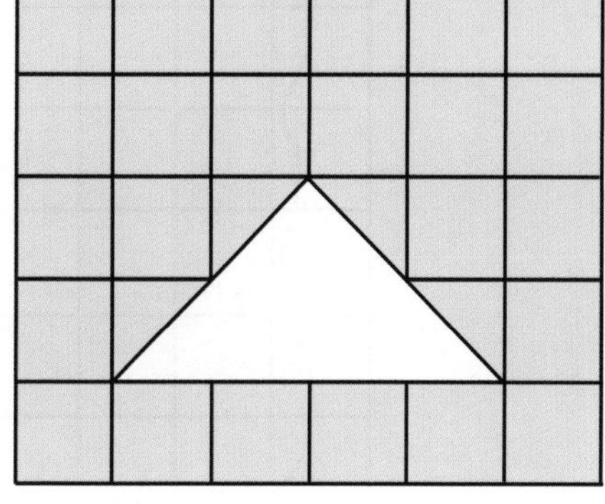

5. Estimate the areas of these shapes as follows :-

> If more than $\frac{1}{2}$ a box is covered —> count it as 1 cm^2
> If less than $\frac{1}{2}$ a box is covered —> do not count it at all.

a

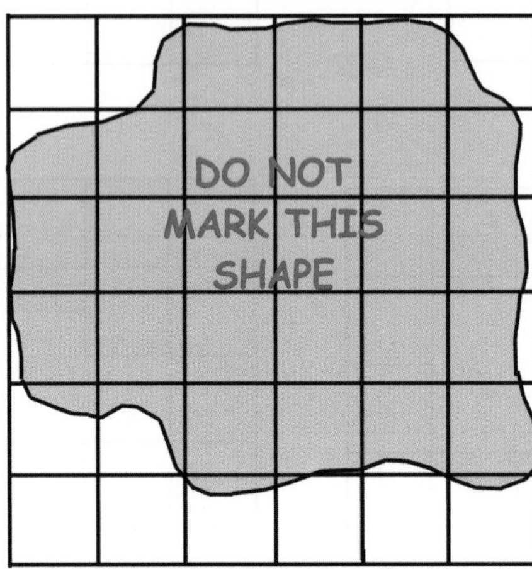

b

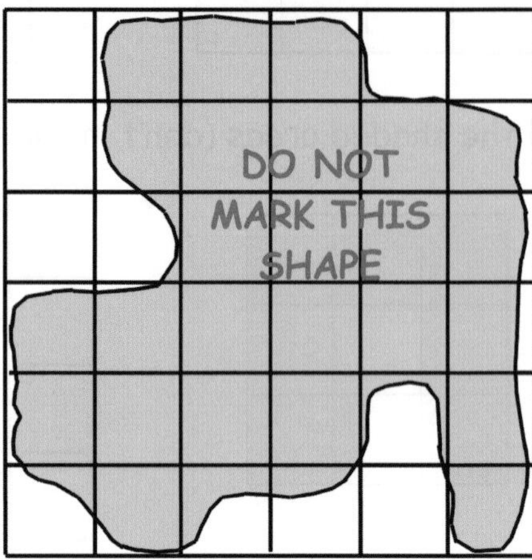

c

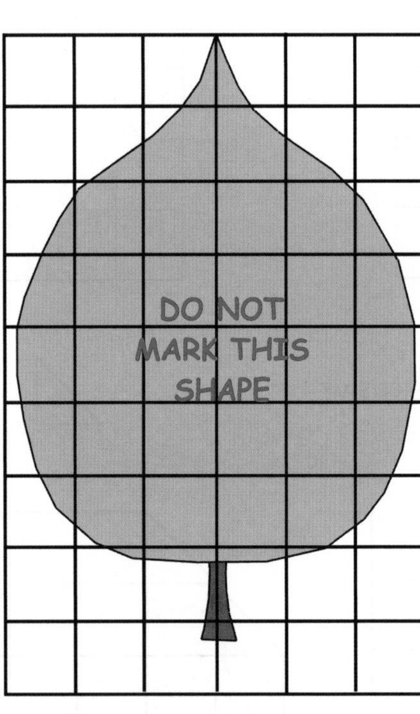

d

e

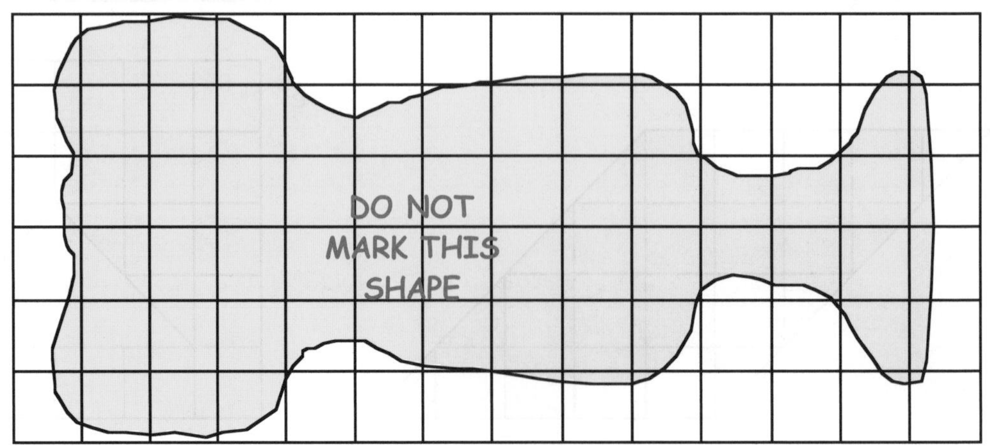

Area of a Rectangle (a Formula)

This rectangle measures 5 centimetres by 3 centimetres.

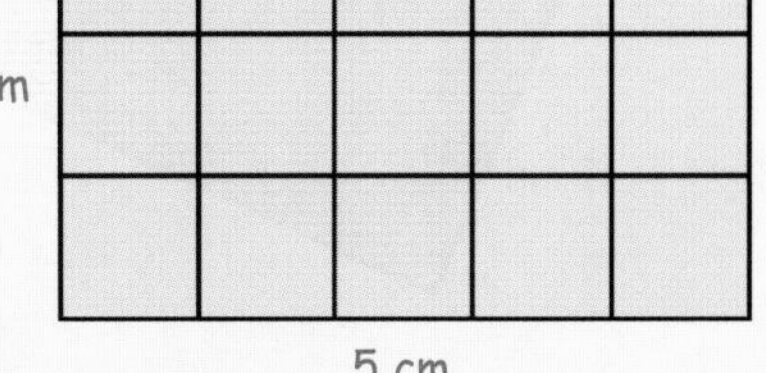

a Calculate its area (in cm^2) by counting all the boxes.

b Now write down the answer you get when you multiply its length by its breadth :-

=> 5 cm × 3 cm (do you get the same answer ?)

A really simple way of calculating the area of the rectangle is as follows :-

Area = length × breadth

or $A = L \times B$ for short.

=> $A = 5 \times 3$

=> $A = 15 \text{ cm}^2$

It is VERY important that you learn how to use the formula,

$A = L \times B$ when calculating the area of a rectangle.

Exercise 2

1. a Draw a rectangle 4 centimetres long by 3 centimetres wide.

   b Divide the rectangle neatly into 1 cm square boxes and count the boxes to find the area of the rectangle.

   c Use the formula $A = L \times B$ (with $L = 4$, $B = 3$) to calculate the area and check your answer is the same as that obtained in part b.

2. This is a sketch of a rectangle.

   Use the formula $A = L \times B$

   to calculate its area (in cm^2).

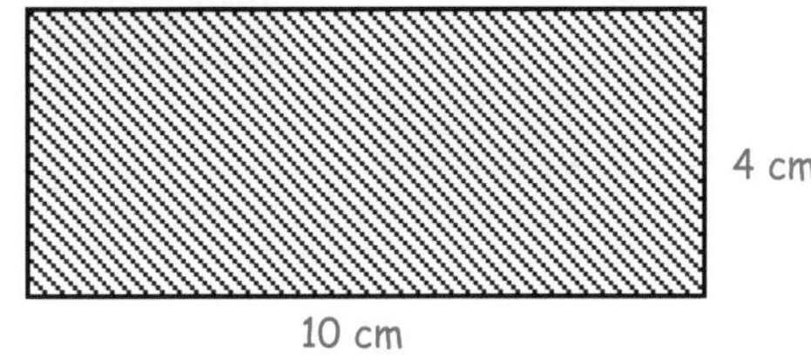

3. Calculate the area of each of the following rectangles.

   (In each case, write down the rule $A = L \times B$ and calculate the area in cm^2) :-

a

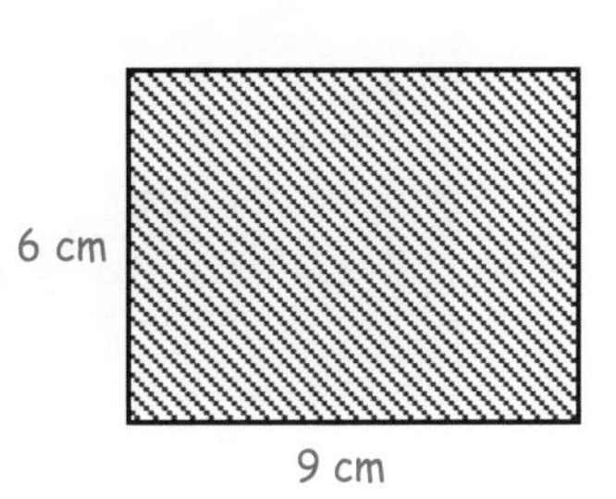

b

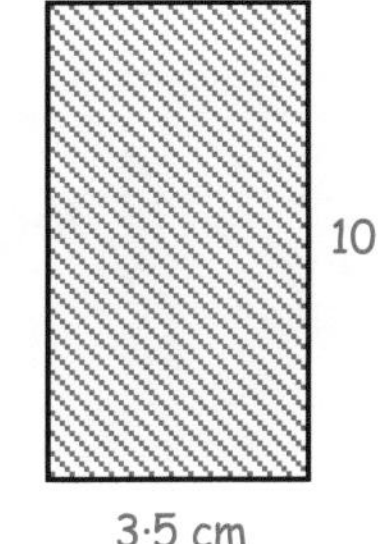

c

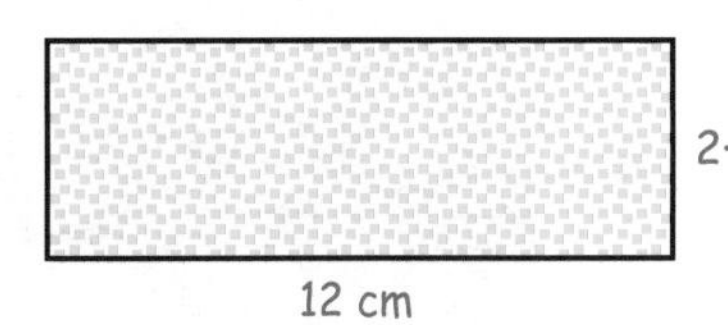

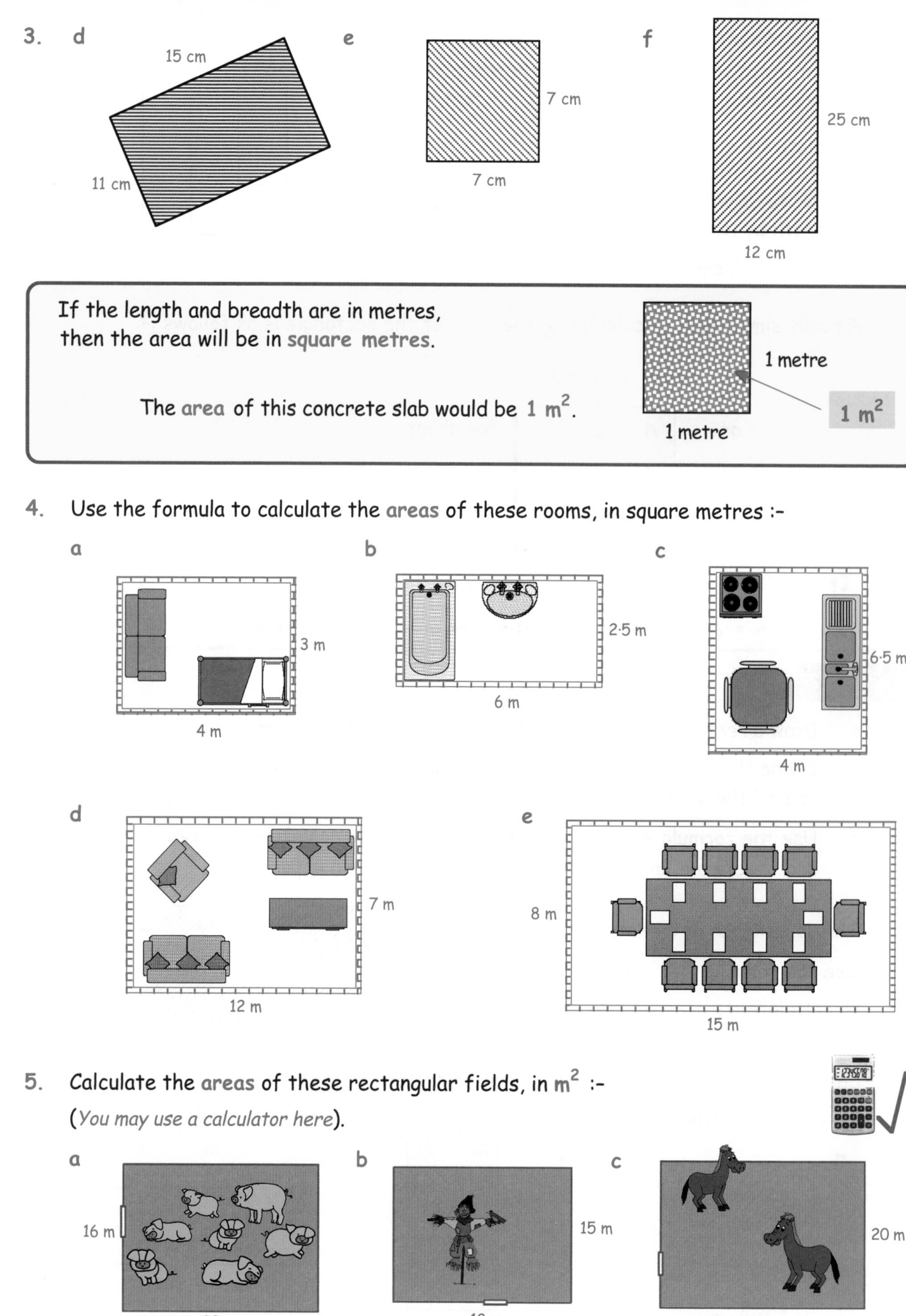

If the length and breadth are in metres, then the area will be in **square metres**.

The **area** of this concrete slab would be **1 m^2**.

4. Use the formula to calculate the **areas** of these rooms, in square metres :-

5. Calculate the **areas** of these rectangular fields, in m^2 :-
(*You may use a calculator here*).

Perimeter

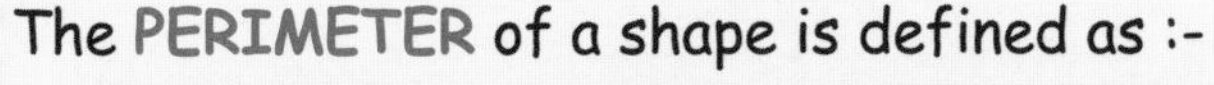

The **PERIMETER** of a shape is defined as :-

the total distance around its edges - (*its outside*).

The **perimeter** of this shape is

P = 15 cm + 16 cm + 11 cm = 42 cm

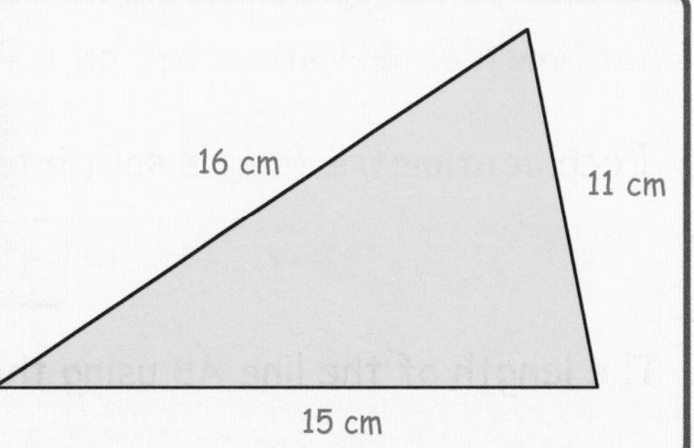

Exercise 3

1. Calculate the **perimeter** of these shapes :-

a

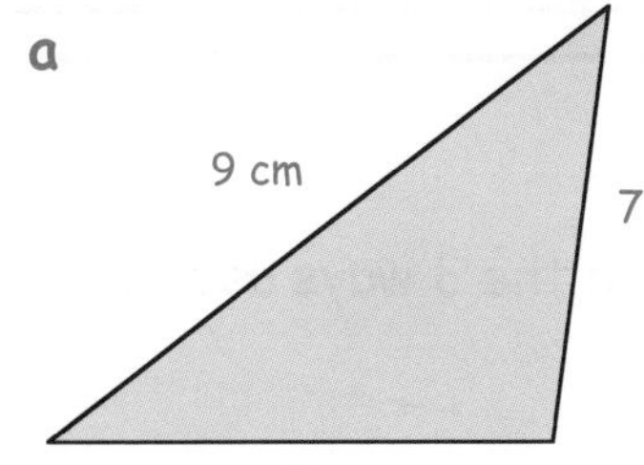

b

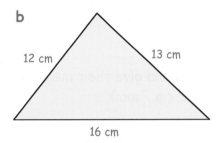

12 cm
13 cm
16 cm

c

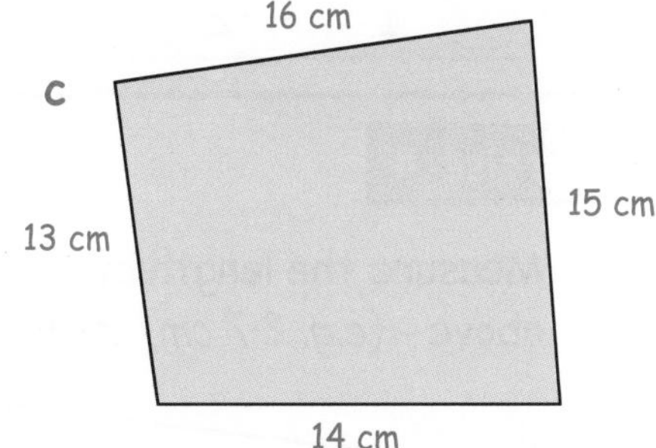

d

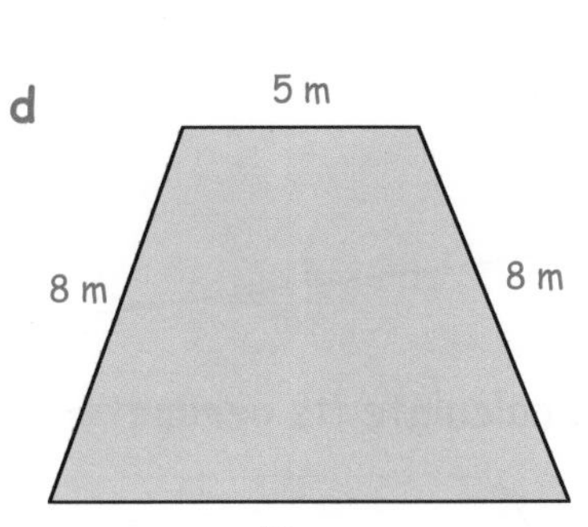

e

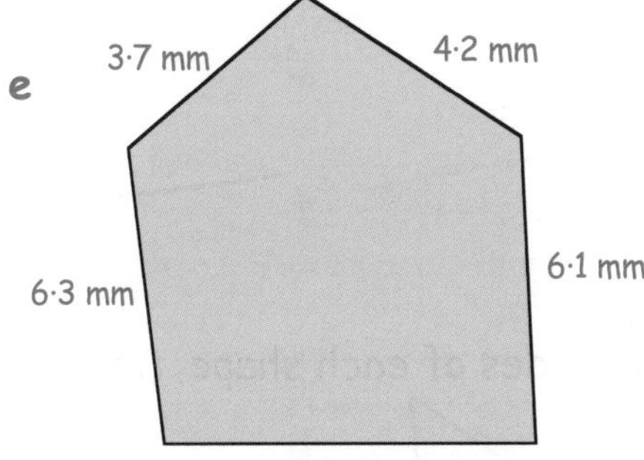

f

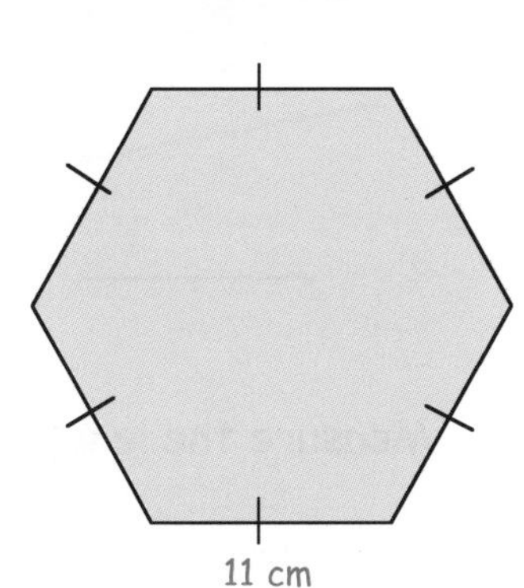

2. Calculate the **perimeter** of these rectangles :-

a

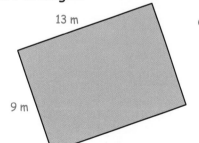

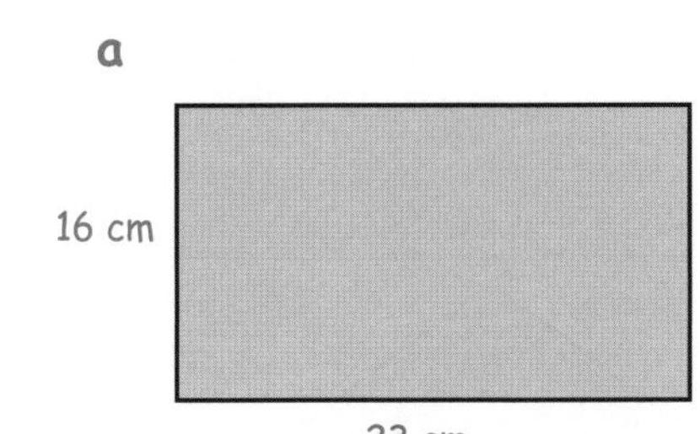

b

13 m
9 m

c

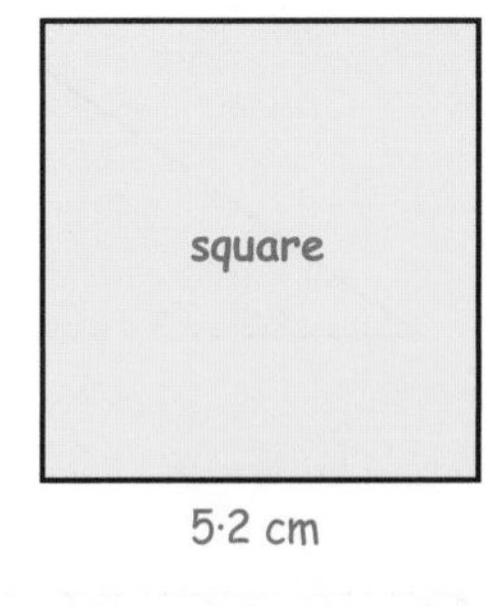

3. The **perimeter** of the floor of this rectangular room is 25·6 metres.

   It is 8·2 metres long.

   Calculate what the breadth (B) of the room must be.

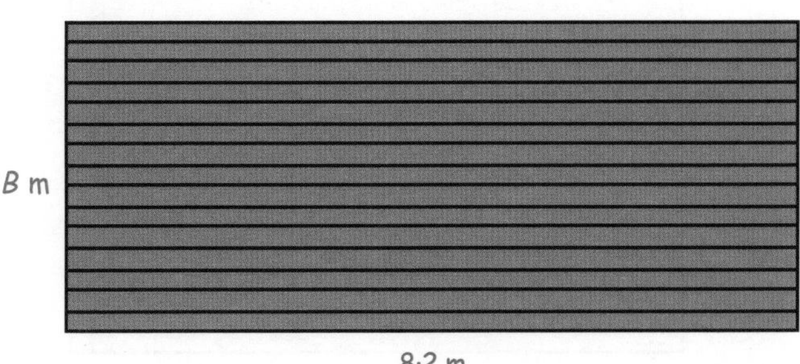

Measuring Lengths & Drawing Lines

Centimetres & Millimetres on a Ruler

Each centimetre (cm) is split into equal parts called millimetres (mm).

1 cm = 10 mm.

The length of the line AB using the ruler below is 7·8 cm or 78 mm or 7 cm 8 mm.

Exercise 4

1. Measure the length of these lines and give their measurement in the 3 ways as shown above - (*e.g. 2·7 cm, 27 mm or 2 cm 7 mm*).

a

b

c

d

e

f

2. Measure the lengths of the sides of each shape, (*in cm*) and calculate its perimeter.

a

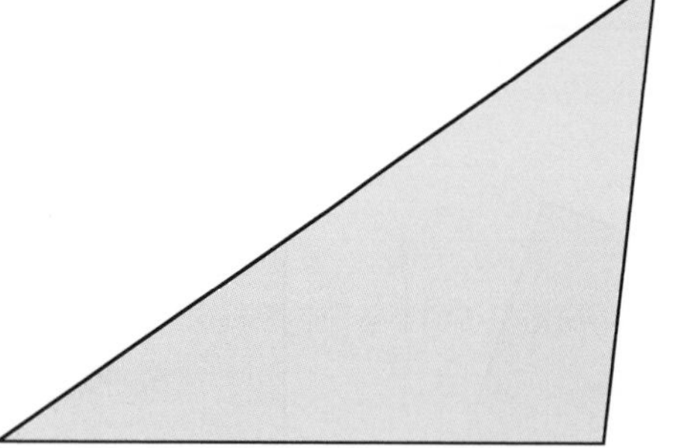

b

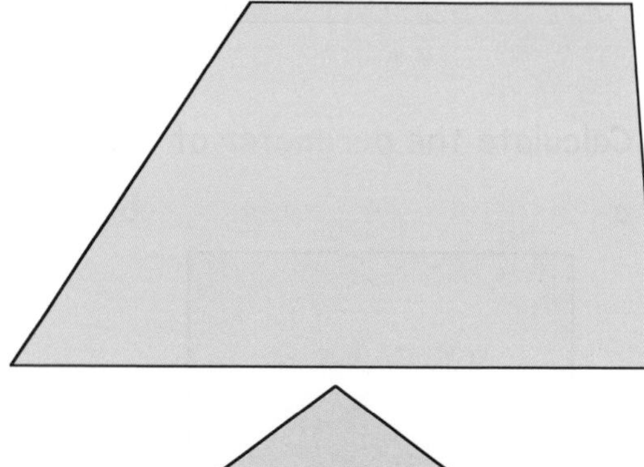

c

d

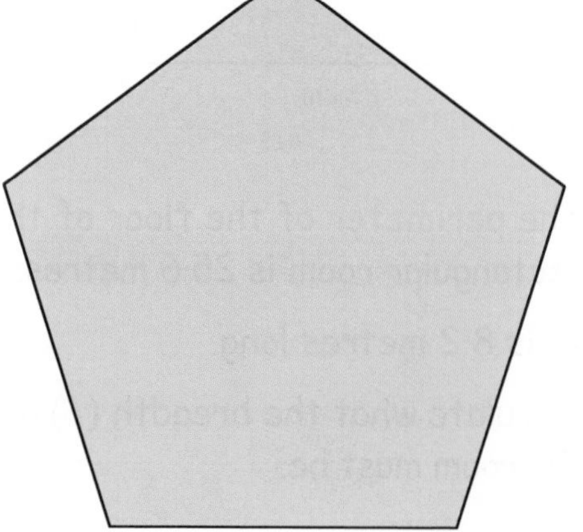

Measuring Angles

To measure an angle with a protractor :-

Step 1 : place the centre of the protractor on the vertex Q.

Step 2 : turn the protractor until the zero line lies along the arm PQ.

Step 3 : count from the zero (inside or out) and read the value where the arm RQ cuts the scale.

You should always estimate the size of angle (in degrees) before you measure it.

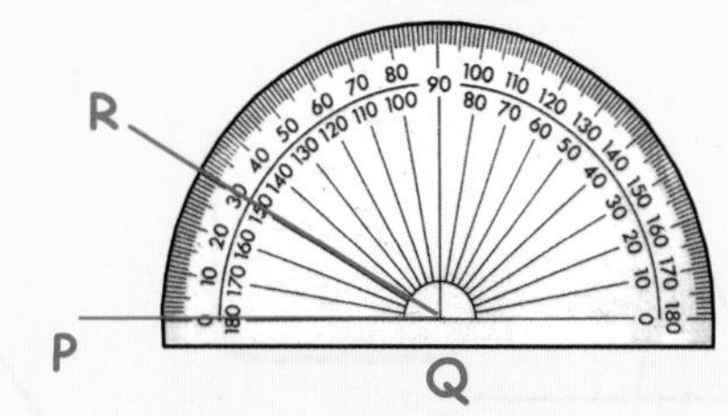

Use outside scale - angle PQR = 30°.

Example :-

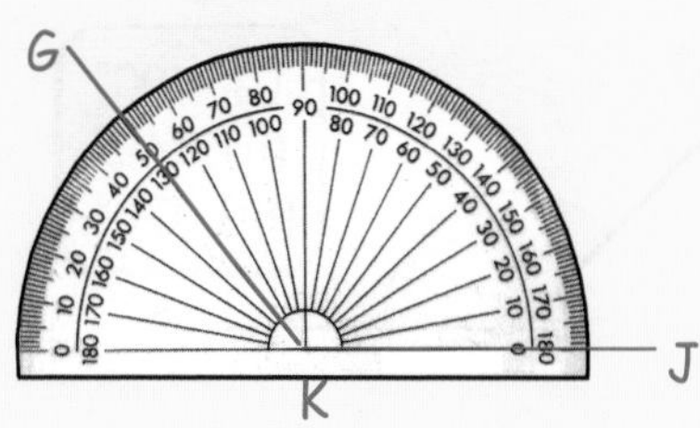

Use inside scale - angle GKJ = 130°.

Exercise 5

1. Write down the size of each angle below in degrees (°).

a
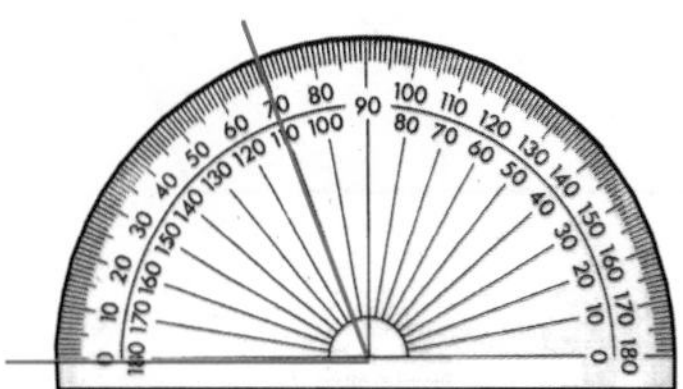

b
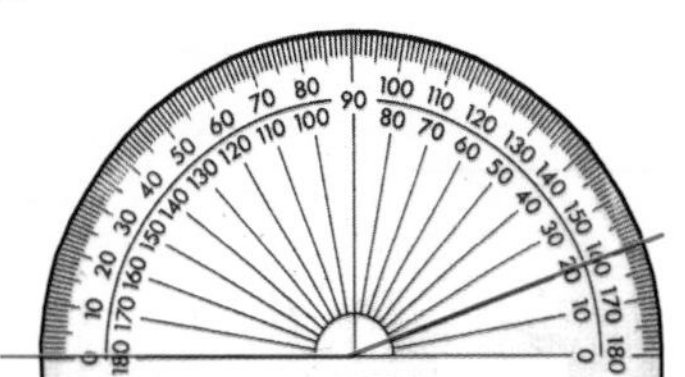

c
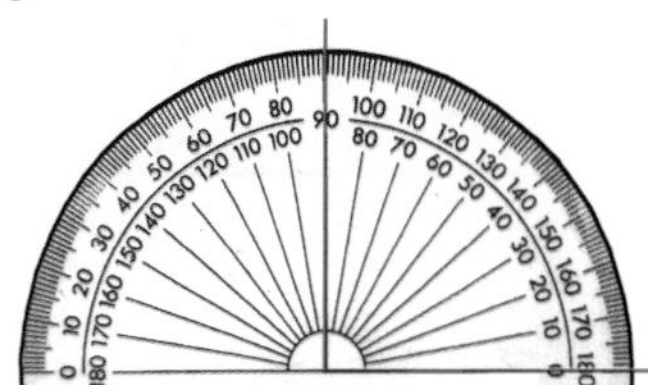

d
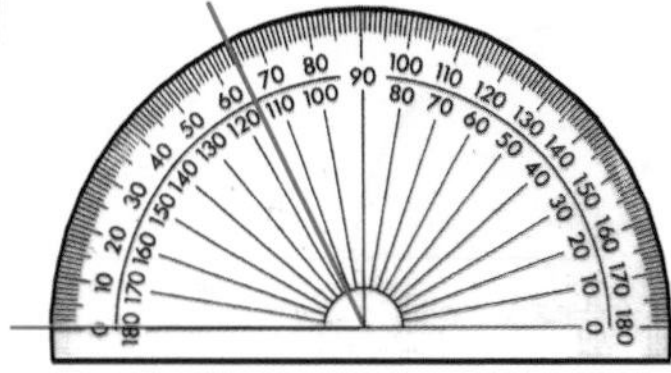

e
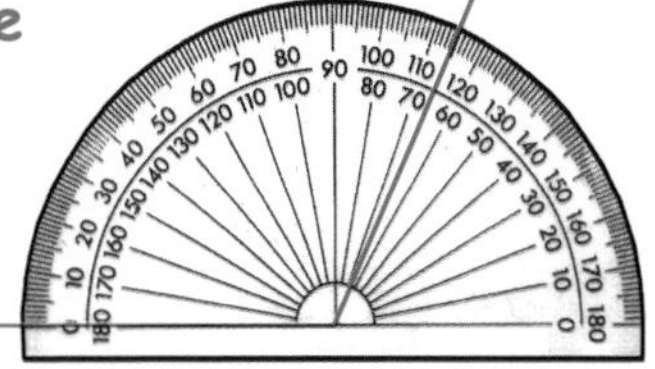

f

g
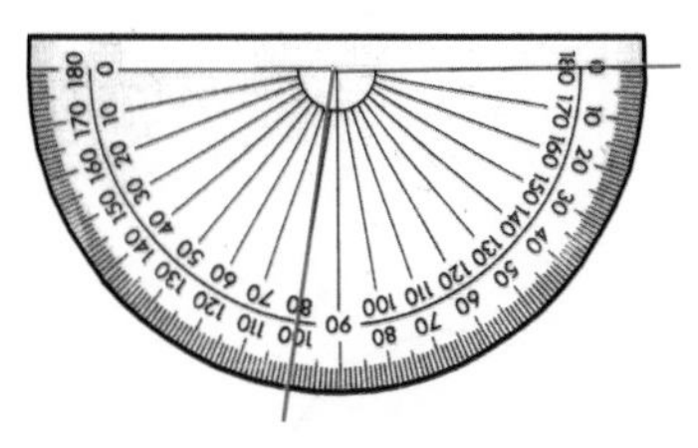

h
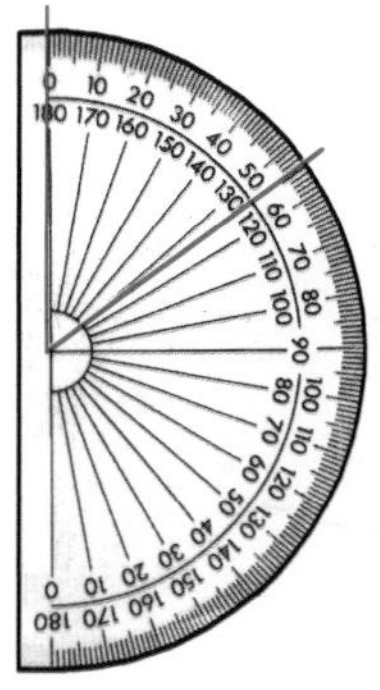

i
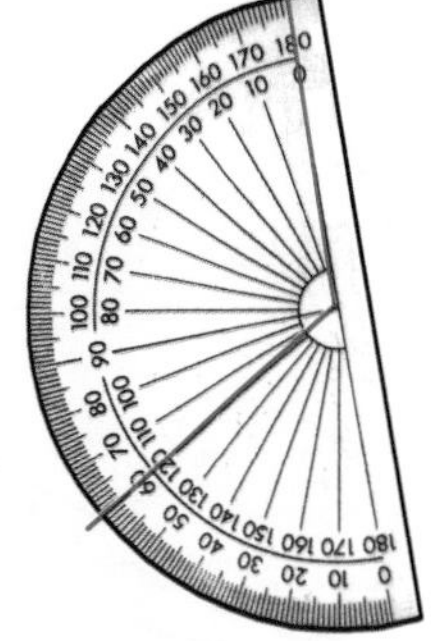

2. Do **not** use a protractor in this question.

Choose the estimate closest to what you think the angle is :-

3. For each **coloured** angle :- (i) **estimate** its size (then)

(ii) use a protractor to **measure** the size of each angle.

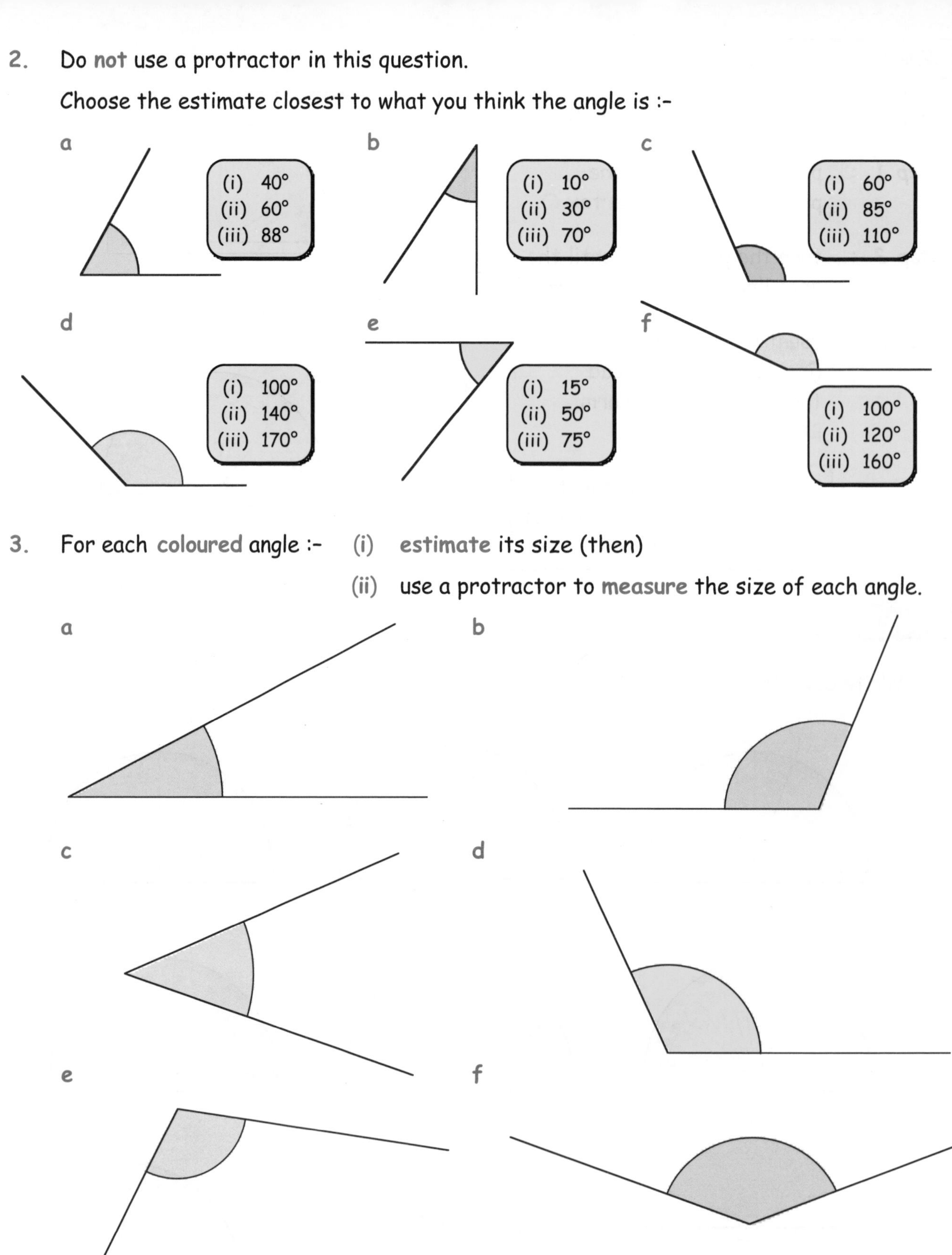

Area and Perimeter

Numeracy Assessment 6

1. Write down the area of shape A and the area of the yellow part of shape B.

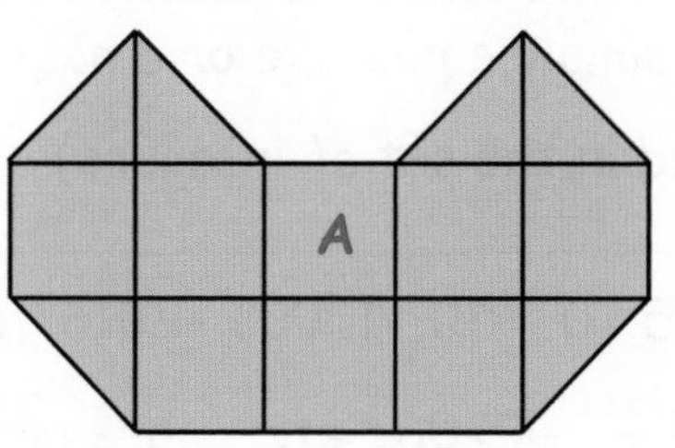

B

(*Each square is 1 cm by 1 cm*).

2. Calculate the areas of these rectangles :-
(*Use the formula and show your working*).

a

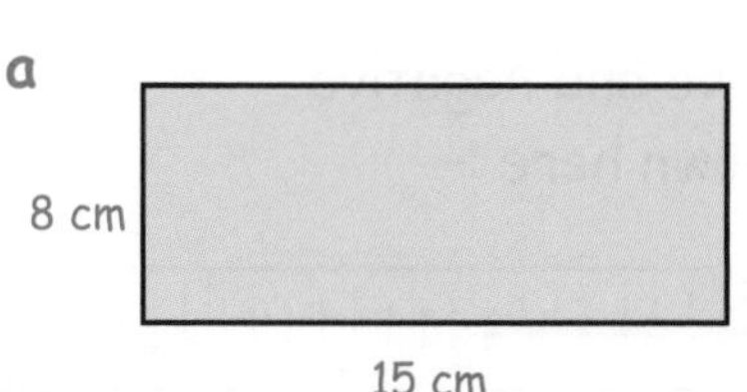

b

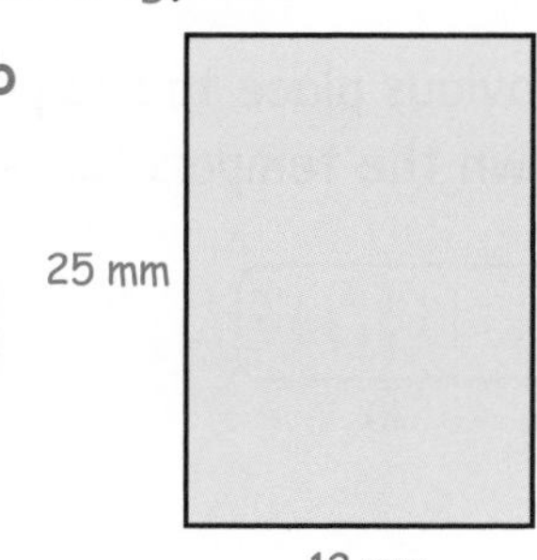

c

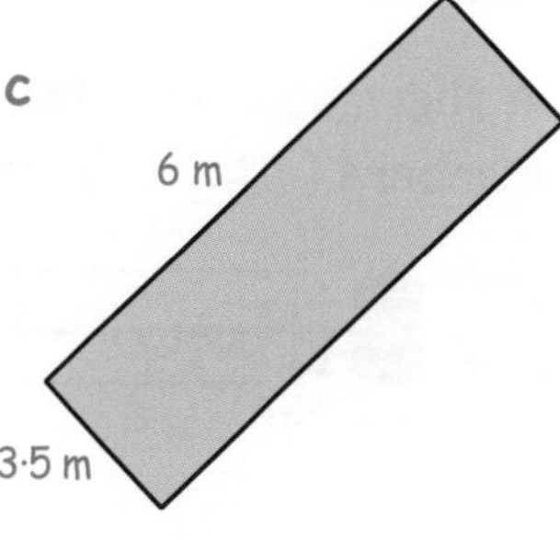

3. Calculate the perimeter of these three shapes :-

a

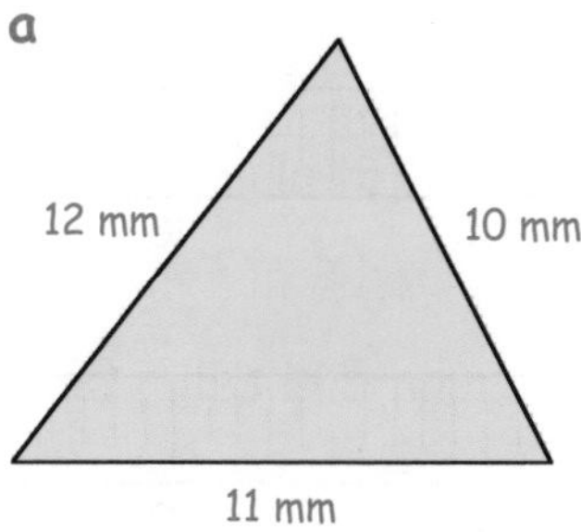

b

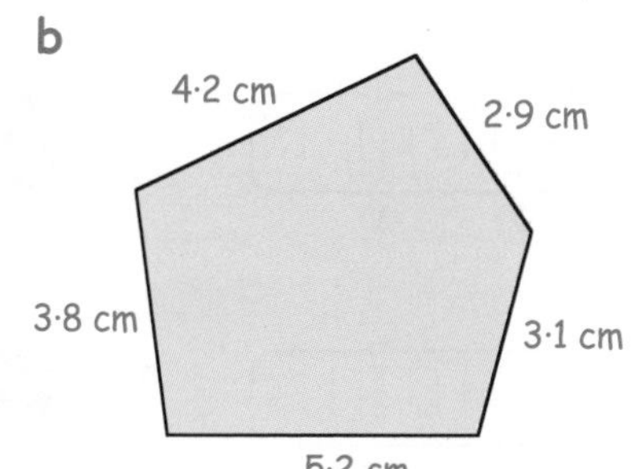

c

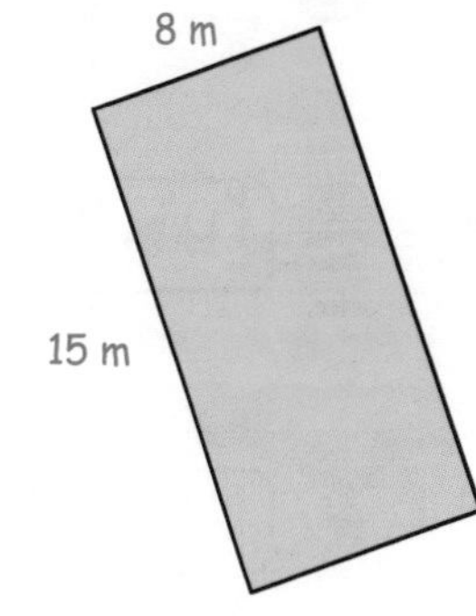

4. Measure the length of both lines. Answer in 3 ways (*2·9 cm, 29 mm or 2 cm 9 mm*).

a

b

5. Measure these two angles using a protractor :-

a

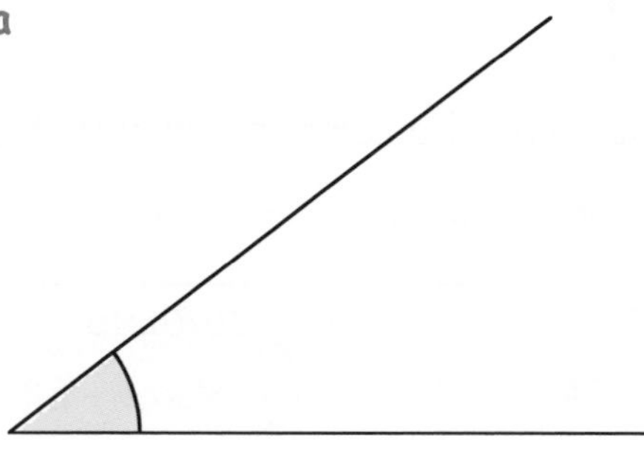

b

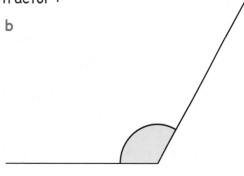

Negative Numbers

Integers in the Real World

Definition :- An INTEGER is simply a positive or a negative whole number.
(0 is also included in the set of integers).

Examples :- -2, -23, 7, 145, 0, -10, 1000, -2016, etc. are all **integers**.
6·2, $\frac{1}{2}$, -8·1, $1\frac{3}{4}$, -45·06, etc ... are **not** integers.

Exercise 1

1. A thermometer is the most obvious place to see positive and negative numbers (*integers*). Write down the temperatures shown here :-

a 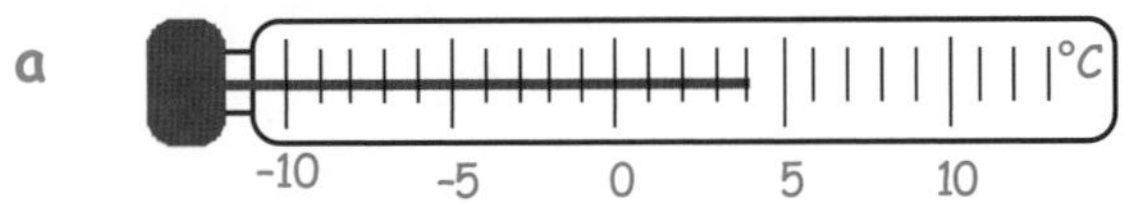

b 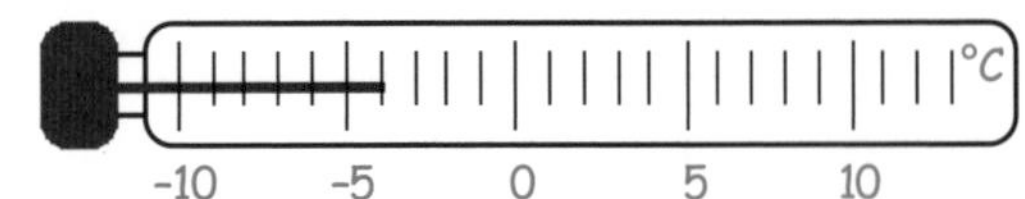

c 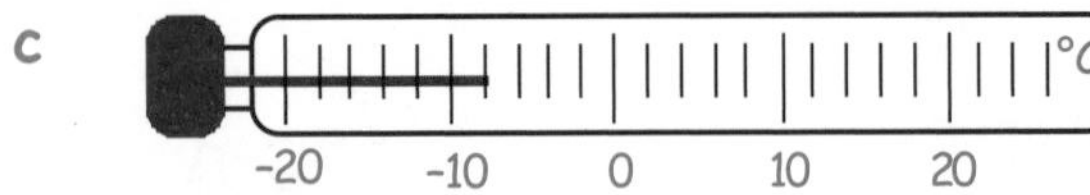

d 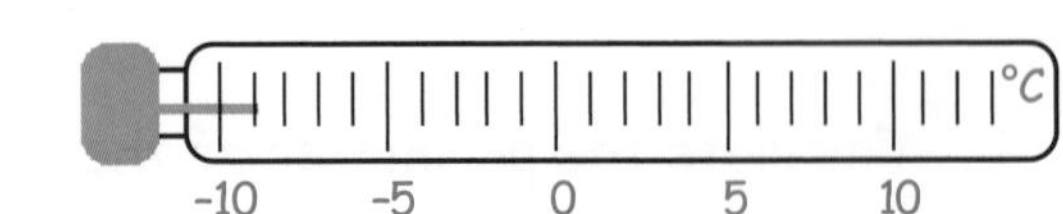

e 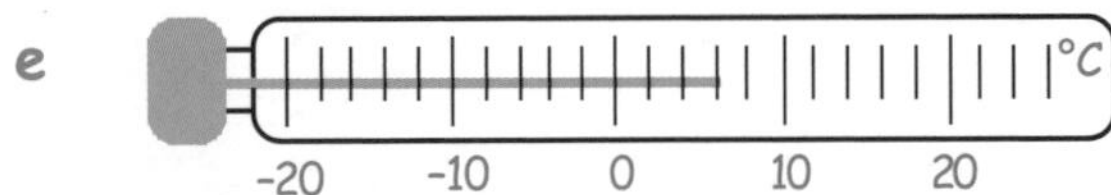

f 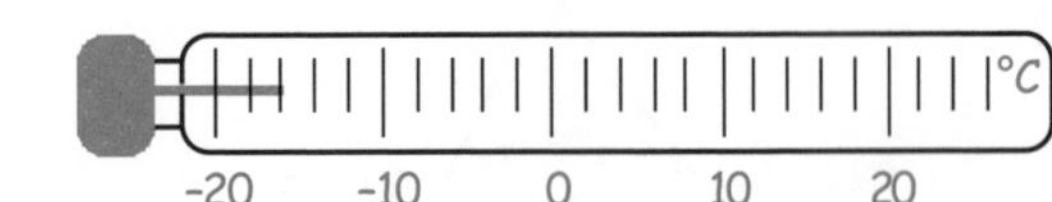

g 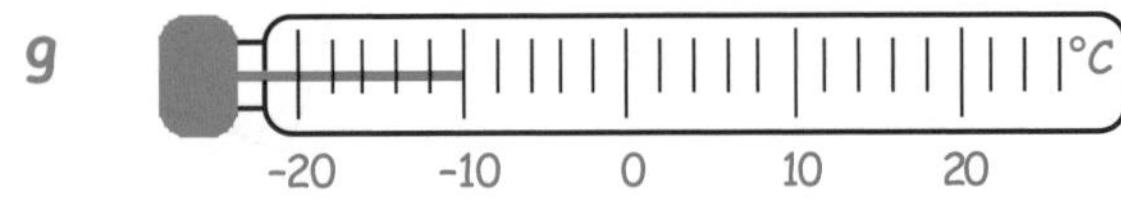

h 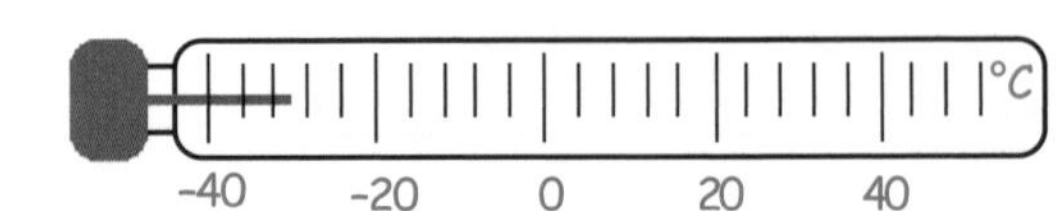

2. Negative numbers also occur when considering how much money you have (*or don't have !*) in a bank.

   If you have £50 in your bank account, the computer notes this as **+ £50·00**

   a If you are "*overdrawn*" by £50, what do you think the computer shows this as ?

   b State what each of the following "bank balances" mean, in real terms :-

(i) 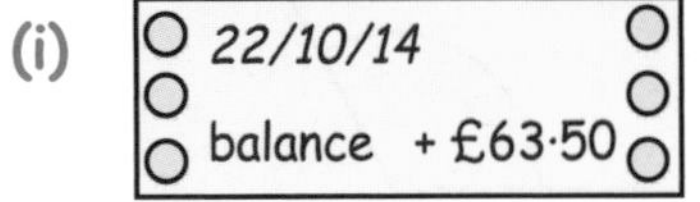

(ii) 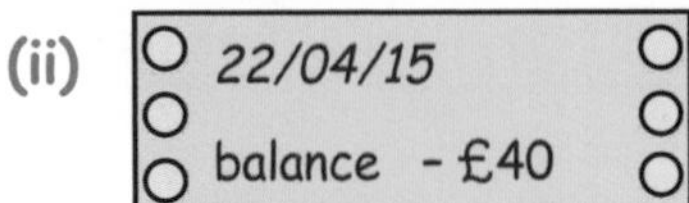

(iii) 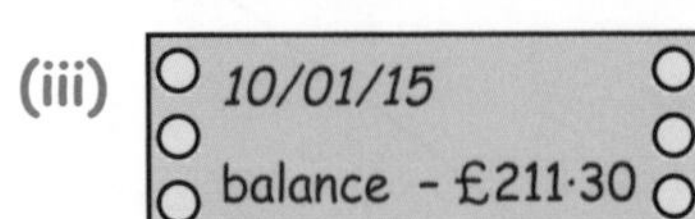

3. Write down the final balance for each statement below :-

a I had £15 in my bank account and withdrew £20.

b My bank balance shows £45. I pay £10 into my account.

c My bank balance was exactly £0·00. I withdrew £80.

d Last week, my bank balance stood at –£40·00. I withdrew a further £20.

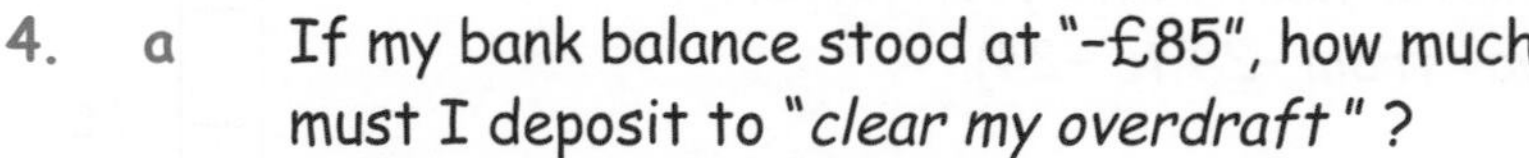

4. a If my bank balance stood at "–£85", how much must I deposit to "*clear my overdraft*" ?

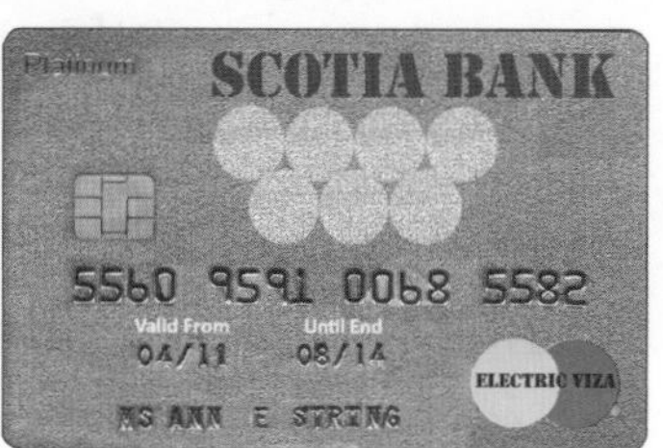

b My balance showed "+£15·50".

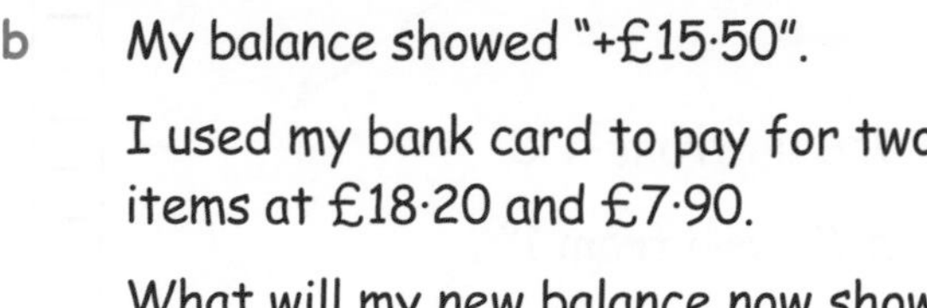

I used my bank card to pay for two items at £18·20 and £7·90.

What will my new balance now show ?

c Yesterday, my bank balance shows "–£345".

Today I deposited £400 and paid a £175 bill.

What is my balance now ?

5. When heights are measured as being above or below sea level, we can use negative numbers to describe them.

Heights **above** sea level are ***positive*** (+)

Heights **below** sea level are ***negative*** (–)

a Write down the heights or depths of the following :- (*use + or –*) (*all measurements are in metres*)

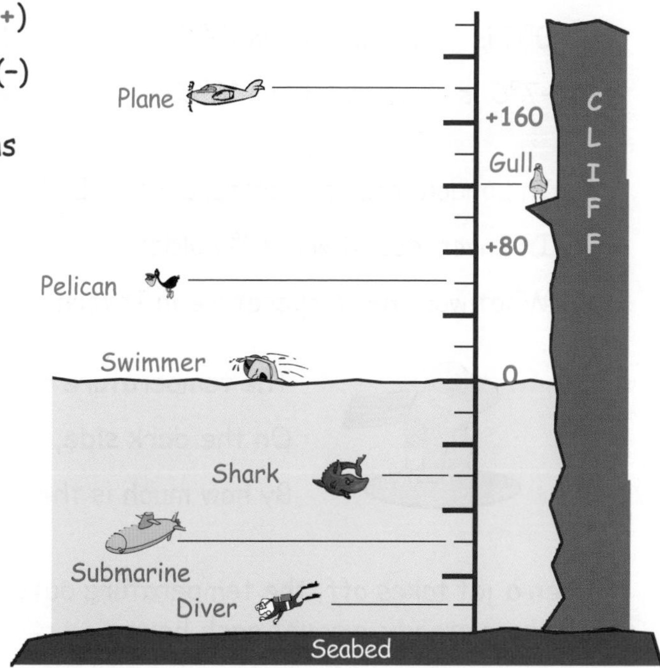

(i) the gull
(ii) the pelican
(iii) the shark
(iv) the cliff top
(v) the diver
(vi) the sea bed
(vii) the plane
(viii) the submarine.

b How high is the :- (i) pelican above the shark (ii) plane above the diver ?

6. **Investigate** negative numbers in time. (*Hint* - What year was it 2025 years ago ?)

Studying Integers

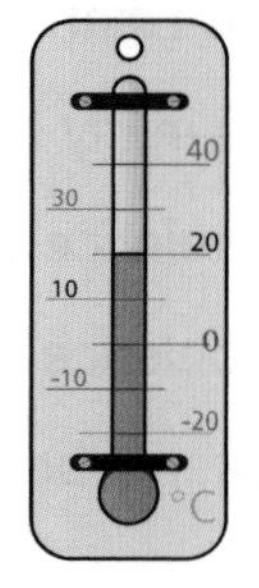

The easiest way to handle integers is to draw or imagine them as **temperatures** on a thermometer.

Exercise 2

1. Use a ruler to copy this thermometer neatly into your jotter.
   (*It does not have to go all the way from –24 to +24*).

2. Look at your thermometer.

   What is the temperature that is :-

   a 6°C **up** from 3°C
   b 7°C **up** from –1°C
   c 10°C **up** from –3°C
   d 5°C **down** from 1°C
   e 6°C **down** from 2°C
   f 5°C **up** from –8°C
   g 17°C **down** from 3°C
   h 10°C **up** from –16°C ?

3. Can you see that 4°C is "**6°C up from**" –2°C ?

   Copy and complete these in the same way :-

   (Say whether it's " .. up from" or " .. down from" each time.)

   a 10°C is .... from 2°C
   b 7°C is .... from 20°C
   c 0°C is .... from 15°C
   d 14°C is .... from –3°C
   e –7°C is .... from 10°C
   f 20°C is .... from –15°C.

4. a In London, the temperature was –15°C.

   In Inverness, it was 10° colder.

   What was the temperature in Inverness ?

   b 

   The temperature on the face of the moon was 120°C.

   On the dark side, it was –130°C.

   By how much is the drop in temperature ?

5. When a jet takes off, the temperature outside the jet falls by a **steady amount** each hour.

   At 1000 ft, the temperature is 6°C.

   At 2000 ft, the temperature is –1°C. At 3000 ft it is –8°C.

   What would be the temperature outside the jet at :-

   a 4000 ft
   b 6000 ft
   c 10 000 ft ?

Adding and Subtracting Integers

When adding and subtracting integers, the best way is to draw or imagine them as temperatures on a thermometer.

Example 1 :- To find 3 + 7,
imagine the 3 on a thermometer.
To do the "+ 7" bit you go **up** by 7. →

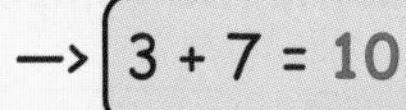

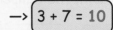

Example 2 :- To find 4 + (-6) ,
imagine the 4 on a thermometer.
To do the "+ (-6)" bit you go **down** by 6. → 4 + (-6) = -2

Example 3 :- To find 4 - 7,
imagine the 4 on a thermometer.
To do the "-7" bit you go **down** by 7. →

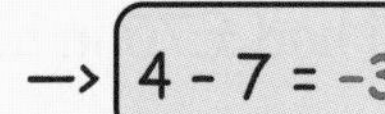

15
10
(+ 7)
5
(3)
0
-5
-10

Exercise 3

1. Use the thermometer which you drew from the last exercise, (or draw a new one), to help you here.

   Write down each question first, then the answer :-

a	8 + 5	b	9 - 2	c	4 - 5	d	8 - 11
e	2 + (-1)	f	2 + (-10)	g	5 + (-4)	h	8 + (-12)
i	0 + (-5)	j	(-5) + 7	k	(-8) + 8	l	(-3) + 7
m	(-20) + 10	n	(-25) + 15	o	20 + (-70)	p	(-200) + (-70).

2. Again use your thermometer to help here :-
   (*Remember :- 8 - 9 means "start at 8, then move down by 9"*).

a	11 - 8	b	9 - 10	c	7 - 10	d	11 - 15
e	8 - 20	f	2 - 10	g	0 - 47	h	(-1) - 2
i	(-5) - 2	j	(-10) - 4	k	(-3) - 20	l	0 - 137
m	23 - 43	n	(-25) - 35	o	150 - 450	p	(-56) - 137.

Remember :- If you **add** a **positive** number, move **up**.
If you **add** a **negative** number or take away a number, move **down**.

3.

a	3 - 4	b	1 + (-4)	c	11 - 17	d	(-5) + 7
e	-3 + (-3)	f	-9 - 2	g	(-6) - 6	h	(-10) + (-10)
i	-25 + 25	j	0 - 131	k	0 + (-33)	l	(-23) + (-13)
m	75 + (-70)	n	(-150) + 70	o	(-111) + 11	p	163 - 197.

Negative Numbers

Numeracy Assessment 7

1. Write down the temperature shown on each thermometer :-

a

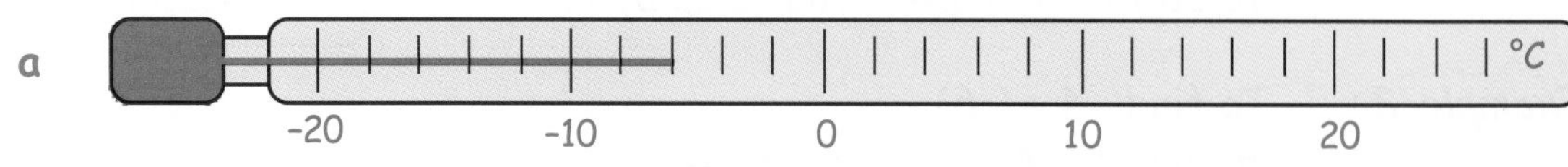

b

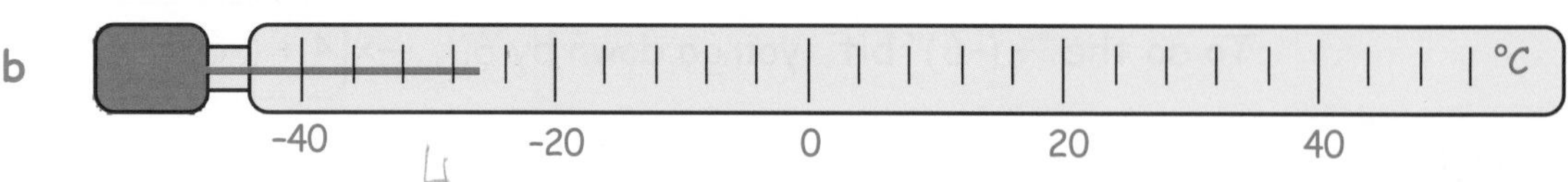

2. a Andi had £70 in her bank account and withdrew £90.

   What was her new balance ?

   b Risha's bank account read as –£140.

   She deposited £180 and then paid a £210 phone bill.

   What will her bank balance read now ?

3. What is the temperature that is :-

   a 8°C up from –3°C
   b 5°C down from –4°C
   c 28°C above –18°C
   d 27 °C below –3°C ?

4. a The temperature in an industrial freezer rose from –32°C to 48°C.

   By how much had it risen ?

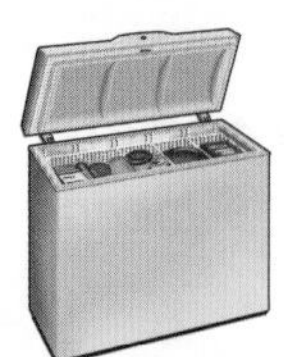

   b On holiday in Sweden, the temperature at noon was 14°C.

   By midnight, the temperature had dropped by 22°C.

   What was the temperature at midnight ?

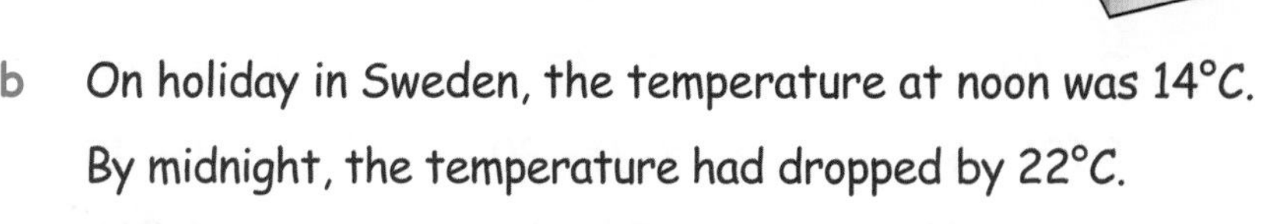

5. Find the following :-

a	3 – 5	b	(-1) + 3	c	(-8) + (-2)	d	12 – 15
e	(-4) – 3	f	(-8) – 12	g	(-5) + (-5)	h	6 + (-22)
i	(-8) - 34	j	0 + (-127)	k	(-112) + 67	l	(-85) + (-75).

6. Find :- a 5 + (-2) – 6 b (-45) + (-135) – 110.

Ratio & Proportion

Ratio

We can use ratios to compare two different quantities.

Example :-

This picture shows 3 hotdogs and 2 pizzas.

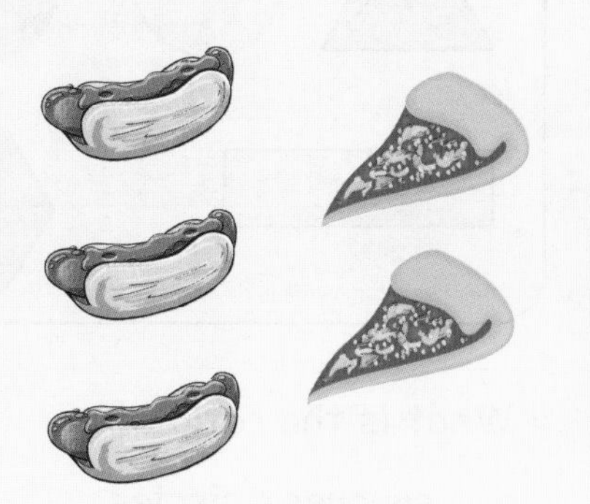

We say that "the ratio of hotdogs to pizzas" is 3 to 2, or for short :-

hotdogs : pizzas = **3 : 2.**

(: is the symbol for ratio)

Exercise 1

(RULER REQUIRED)

1. Look at this picture.

   Write down the ratio :-
   - a cars : buses.
   - b buses : cars.

2. 
   - a Write down the ratio, mice : cats.
   - b Write down the ratio, cats : mice.

3. In a pencil case, there are 7 HB pencils and 12 coloured pens.

   Write down the ratio of :-
   - a pencils to pens.
   - b pens to pencils.

4. At a depot, there are eighty seven vans and forty three trucks.

   What is the ratio of :-
   - a trucks to vans
   - b vans to trucks ?

5. A large hotel provides full breakfasts.

   The executive chef cooks 177 eggs, 211 sausages, 99 potato scones and 200 rashers of bacon every day.

   Write down the ratios of :-
   - a sausages : eggs
   - b eggs : scones.
   - c rashers : sausages
   - d meat items : non-meat items.

6. A boy has the following set of coloured tiles :-

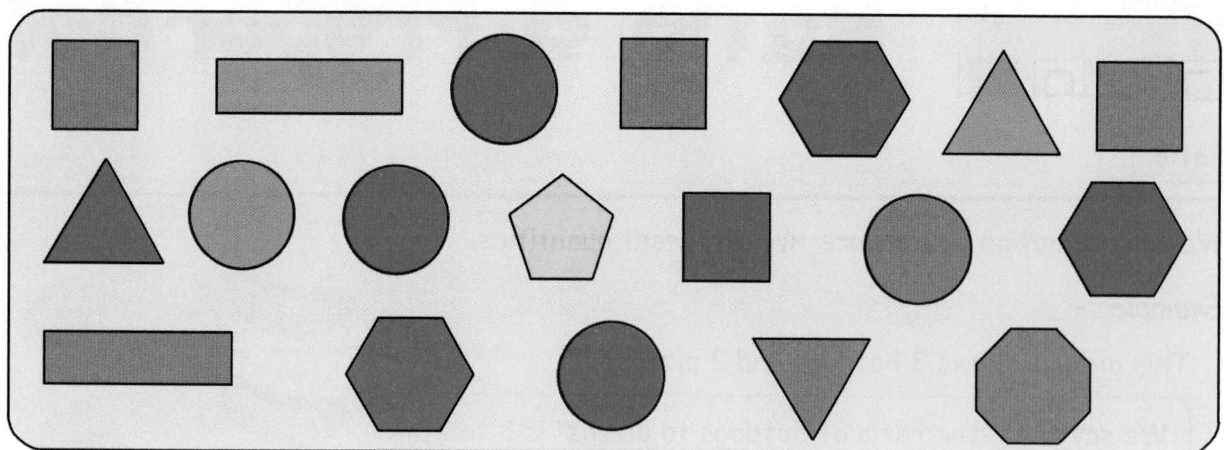

What is the ratio of :-

a squares : circles
b triangles : rectangles
c hexagons : circles
d red shapes : blue shapes
e octagons : red circles
f pentagons : circles
g brown squares : squares
h 3 sided shapes : quadrilaterals ?

7. Write down the ratio of female to male students in your classroom today.

8. a Measure and write down the length and breadth of the front cover of this book, in mm.

b Write down the ratio of :-

(i) length : breadth
(ii) breadth : length
(iii) length : perimeter
(iv) perimeter : area.

9.

It is 180 kilometres between Sanding and Kinister.

A bird flies 143 kilometres from Sanding heading for Kinister.

Write down the ratio of the :-

a distance travelled : distance to go.

b distance travelled : total distance.

10. A toolkit contains 140 items.

There are 45 screws, 57 nails and the rest are panel pins.

Write down the ratio of :-

a screws : nails
b items : nails
c screws : pins
d screws : nails : pins.

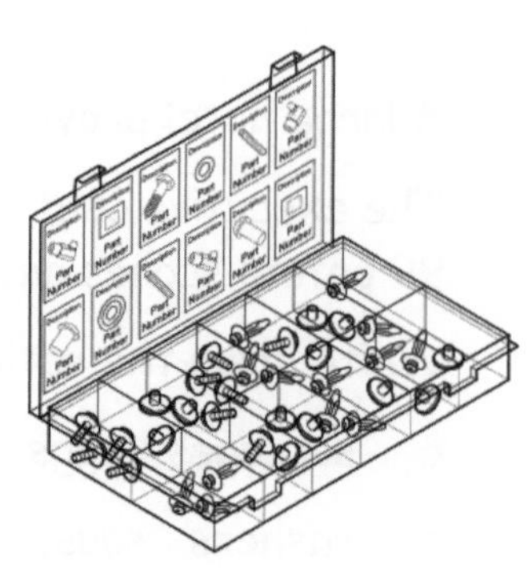

Simplifying Ratios

Earlier, you learned how to **simplify** fractions.

Example :- $\frac{4}{6}$ can be simplified, since 4 and 6 are part of the "2 times" table.

$$\frac{4}{6} \Rightarrow \frac{4}{6}\begin{matrix}(\div 2)\\(\div 2)\end{matrix} = \frac{2}{3}.$$

Similarly, the ratio **4 : 6** simplifies to **2 : 3** (*can you see this ?*)

Exercise 2

1. By dividing both numbers by 2, **simplify** the ratio 10 : 8.

2. By dividing both numbers by 6, **simplify** the ratio 36 : 42.

3. Copy each of the following ratios and **simplify** each as far as possible :-

a	4 : 6	b	6 : 20	c	7 : 28	d	2 : 28	e	9 : 3	f	18 : 9
g	15 : 12	h	48 : 10	i	36 : 9	j	21 : 49	k	30 : 48	l	90 : 80
m	180 : 150	n	55 : 25	o	72 : 9	p	11 : 88	q	3 : 3000	r	900 : 6
s	41 : 82	t	360 : 36	u	12 : 6000	v	8 : 16 000 000.				

4. What is the ratio of apples to bananas in each picture below ?
   Write each ratio in its **simplest** form.

a

b

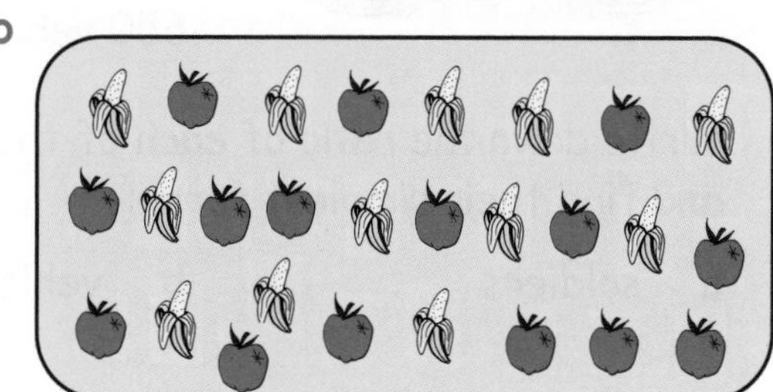

5. A concert arena uses 5 security people for every 1000 spectators.
   a What is the ratio of spectators to security people ?
   b Give this ratio in its **simplest** form.

6. The concert arena also has 10 VIP parking spaces for every 120 ordinary spaces.
   a What is the ratio of VIP spaces to ordinary spaces ?
   b Give this ratio in its **simplest** form.

7. For each of the following,

(i) write down the given ratio of the first to second quantity.

(ii) express the ratio in its simplest form :-

a There are 20 girls and 5 boys in a classroom.

b At a party, there are two adults and thirty children.

c There are 20 desks and 24 chairs in a room.

d There are 16 trolleys and 24 baskets in a supermarket.

e There are 4 parking bays and 34 spaces in each bay.

f There are 25 shop assistants and 150 shoppers.

g There are 36 000 tins and 8000 boxes in the shop.

h In an office, a manager earns £24 000 and a salesman earns £18 000 each year.

i A factory makes three million rivets and half a million bolts every week.

8. 

During a WW2 battle, two armies faced each other on a battlefield.

One army consisted of 30 000 soldiers, 1000 vehicles and 160 tanks.

The other had only 18 000 soldiers, 650 vehicles and 120 tanks.

Write down the ratio of each of the following (largest : smallest army) and find their simplest form :-

a soldiers b vehicles c tanks.

9. Sarah earns £30 000 per annum. Hilary earns £24 000. Alex earns £36 000.

Find each of these earning ratios in their simplest form :-

a Sarah : Hilary b Sarah : Alex c Alex : Sarah : Hilary.

10. Two photographs measure 5 cm by 8 cm and 7 cm by 4 cm.

Write down in simplest form, the ratio of :-

a their **perimeters**, big : small.

b their **areas**, big : small.

Ratio Calculations

This is the opposite of "simplifying" ratios.

Example :- To obtain a particular shade of **purple** paint, Q & B have to mix red and blue paint in the ratio, **red : blue = 3 : 4.**

For a large order, Q & B use 15 tins of red paint. How many blue tins are required ?

Set down like this :-

	red	blue	
×5	3	4	×5
	15	20	

Since 15 = **5** × 3

then blue = **5** × 4 = 20.

=> Needs 20 blue tins.

Exercise 3

1. A different shade of **purple** can be made by using red : blue = 2 : 3.

   a If Q & B used 8 tins of **red** paint, how many tins of **blue** are needed ?

   Start with this :-

	red	blue	
×?	2	3	×?
	8	...	

   b If Q & B used 12 tins of **red**, how many tins of **blue** are needed ?

   c If, this time, Q & B used 24 tins of **blue**, how much **red** is needed ?

2. | Cats | Dogs |
   |---|---|
   | 5 | 4 |
   | 40 | ... |

   In a Cat & Dog home, the ratio of cats : dogs is 5 : 4.

   a If there are 40 cats, how many dogs must there be ?

   b If in fact, there are 36 dogs, how many cats are there ?

3. Mr Rae buys rugby balls and footballs for a sports arena in a ratio of 2 : 7.

   a How many footballs should he order if he needs 10 rugby balls ?

   b How many rugby balls should he order if he needs 28 footballs ?

   c How many balls does he order **in total** if he orders 6 rugby balls ?

4. A florist stocks carnations and roses in the ratio 11 : 7.

   If there are :-

   a 33 carnations, how many roses are there

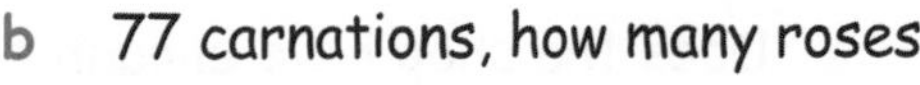

   b 77 carnations, how many roses

   c 35 roses, how many carnations are there

   d 98 roses, how many carnations ?

5. The ratio of "Hard" sums to "Easy" sums in a set of tests was 2 : 9.

a If a test consisted of 8 hard sums, how many easy ones were there ?

b If a second test consisted of 45 easy sums :-

(i) how many hard sums were there ?

(ii) how many sums were there altogether ?

c A third test had a total of 66 questions.

How many easy questions were in this test ?

6. 

Addy and James compare their weekly paper round money.

The ratio of their pay was :- Addy : James = 7 : 8.

a If Addy earned £70, how much must James have earned ?

b If James earned £88, how much must Addy have earned ?

c During Christmas week, they earned a total of £300.

How much did Addy earn that week ?

7. The ratio of words in the "*Chumbers*" dictionary to the "*Collings*" Dictionary is in the ratio of 6 : 7.

The "*Chumbers*" contains 480 000 words.

How many words are there in "*Collings*" ?

8. Look at this chart for making **purple** paint.

Which shade of **purple** will I get if I mix :-

	Mix in the Ratio		
Colour	***Red***	**:**	***Blue***
Very dark purple	5	:	1
Dark purple	7	:	2
Mid purple	2	:	1
Light purple	3	:	5
Very light purple	2	:	9

a 1000 ml of red with 200 ml of **blue**

b 120 ml of red with 200 ml of **blue**

c 6 tins of red with 3 tins of **blue**

d 350 ml of red with 100 ml of **blue**

e 4 litres of red with 18 litres of **blue** ?

9. To make a certain shade of tartan, a paint shop mixes blue and green paint in a 6 : 5 ratio.

The shop has 72 litres of blue in stock. Green paint must be ordered to make the tartan.

a How many litres of green should be ordered ?

b A customer needed 140 litres of tartan paint.

Does the shop have enough tins of paint for the order ?

(*Explain your answer*).

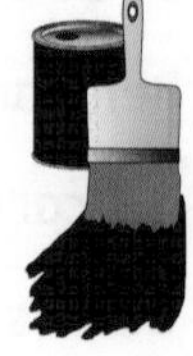

Proportion - Rates

If you know how many miles you drive and how many litres of petrol you use, you can calculate the number of miles per litre your car travels.

Example :- A van drives 48 miles on 8 litres of petrol, how many miles per litre ?

—> DIVIDE => 8 litres —> 48 miles
1 litre —> 48 ÷ 8 = 6 miles
Rate = **6 miles per litre**

Exercise 4 (*You may use a calculator here, but show your lines of working*).

1. A truck covered a distance of 120 miles on 6 gallons of petrol.
Calculate the rate in "*miles per gallon*".

Copy and **complete** :-

6 gallons —> 120 miles
1 gallon —> 120 ÷ 6 = ...
= .... miles/gallon.

2. A car covers 480 kilometres using 8 gallons of petrol.
Calculate the rate in "*kilometres per gallon*".

3. a A cheetah runs a distance of 120 metres in 10 seconds.
Calculate its speed in metres/second.

b  A tortoise covers 12 metres and takes 6 minutes.
Calculate its speed in m/min.

c A sheep eats 18·9 kilograms of grass in a week.
Calculate the weight of grass eaten per day.

d  Daisy the cow produces 56 litres of milk every week.
Calculate the rate per day.

e Daisy expels 1050 litres of methane every week.
Calculate her rate per day.

4. a A machine produces 84 000 paper clips every minute.
How much does the machine produce every second ?

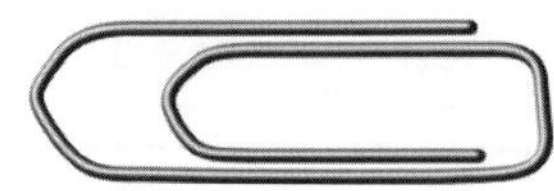

b 
Nine million pins are manufactured every hour.
How many are produced every :- (i) minute (ii) second ?

c Sandi can type 1188 words in nine minutes.
Calculate her rate in words per minute.

d 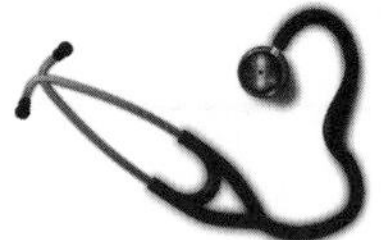
At rest, the average heart rate is 72 beats per minute.
How many beats is this per second ?

e A machine cog rotates three million times every day.
How many times does it rotate in :-
(i) an hour (ii) a second (*to the nearest whole number*) ?

5. 

David worked 8 hours as a labourer and earned £60.
Shona worked as a packer for 6 hours and earned £48.
Who has the higher rate of pay ?

6. In a factory, Ewan can pack 184 tins in 40 minutes.
Josh manages to pack 144 tins in 30 minutes.
Who is the faster worker ?
Justify your answer, showing your calculations.

7. 

a Sheri can get €84 for £70. How many €s to the £ ?
b Jamil can get $49 for £20. How many $s to the £ ?
c Farrah exchanges £6 for 3090 Baht. How many Baht/£ ?

8. Ali gets €47·60 for £40.
Dave gets €58·50 for £50.
Sal gets €53·10 for £45.
Who gets the best rate ? Explain.

9. **Investigate** different rates of currency exchange.

Direct Proportion

Two quantities, (for example, the **number** of *pens* and the **total** *cost*) are said to be in **direct proportion**, if :-

"*When you **double** the number of pens —> you **double** the cost*".

Example :- 9 Pens cost £33·75. What will 4 cost ?

Set down like this :-

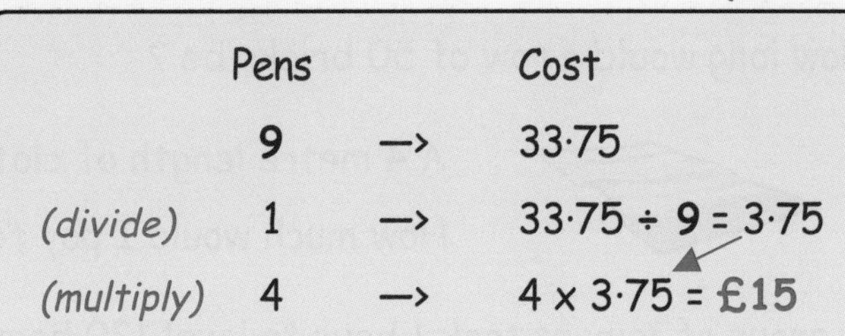

	Pens		Cost
	9	—>	33·75
(divide)	1	—>	33·75 ÷ **9** = 3·75
(multiply)	4	—>	4 x 3·75 = **£15**

Exercise 5 (*In each of these, show 3 lines of working, as well as two headings*).

1. Eight birthday cakes cost £72. Find the cost of 3 cakes.

Copy and **complete** :-

Textbooks		Cost
8	—>	£72
1	—>	£72 ÷ 8 = £......
3	—>	

2. 

Twenty teddy bears cost £350.

Find the cost of 11 teddy bears.
(*Hint - find the cost of 1 teddy first*).

3. When I exchanged £20 for euros, I received €22.

How many euros would I get for £9 ?
(*Hint - find how much I would get for £1 first*).

4. For each of the following, find the cost of one first :-

a A jet travels 880 km in 8 hours. How far would it travel in 7 hours ?

b A machine makes 6000 cogs in 6 minutes. How many would it make in 5 minutes ?

c It takes 4 minutes to file 32 folders. How long would it take to file 56 folders ?

d It takes a monkey 9 seconds to climb a 24 metre tree.
How long would it take the monkey to climb a 16 m tree ?

5. 

In 30 seconds, a turbine machine spins 18 000 times.

How many times will it spin in :-

a 1 second

b 7 seconds

c 12 seconds

d 2 minutes ?

6. a Eighty bricks, end to end, make a wall 24 metres long.

How long would a row of 50 bricks be ?

b 

A 4 metre length of cloth costs £8·32.

How much would I pay for 5 metres ?

c A group of joiners took 1 hour to level 120 beams on a roof.

How long would it have taken to level 80 beams ?

d On the planet Zeegard, five Splinkiis equals 120 Stoople.

How many Stoople will I get for six Splinkiis ?

7. 

When 30 000 millilitres of water are poured into an aquarium, it fills to a depth of 15 centimetres.

How many millilitres are needed to fill the aquarium to a depth of 8 centimetres ?

8. The pendulum of a clock swings backwards and forwards 180 times in 3 minutes.

How many times will it swing in 30 seconds ?

9. 

A book, which is 6 centimetres thick, contains 1260 pages.

How many pages would the book have had if it was only 5·5 centimetres thick ?

10. 10 square metres of turf cost £150.

My lawn has an area of 29 square metres.

What would I pay to re-turf my lawn ?

11. It takes a ten litre bottle of GrassGro to cover a 6 m by 10 m garden.

How many litres do I need to cover a garden 8 m by 12 m ?

Ratio & Proportion

Numeracy Assessment 8

1. In a classroom, there are 16 girls and 12 boys.

   a Write down the ratio of girls : boys.

   b Simplify this ratio as far as possible.

2. Simplify the following ratios as far as possible :-

a	12 : 16	b	25 : 45	c	16 : 48	d	36 : 18
e	120 : 200	f	88 : 99	g	360 : 240	h	$1\frac{1}{2}$: 6.

3. A gardener found the ratio of flowers : weeds was 5 : 2.

   He had 18 weeds. How many flowers did he have ?

4. 

   A bicycle shop sells mountain bikes and speed bikes.

   The ratio of mountain bikes : speed bikes is 4 : 3.

   If there were 28 mountain bikes :-

   a How many speed bikes were there ?

   b How many bikes were there altogether ?

5. Calculate the cost of one item for each of the following :-

   a Eight cakes costing £9·60

   b Seven books costing £84

   c Twenty Cd's for £180

   d 3 pizzas for £5·25.

6. Five T-shirts cost me £55·50.

   a What is the cost of 1 T-shirt ?

   b How much would it cost for 4 T-shirts ?

7. It took a satellite 130 hours to go round the earth 5 times.

   How long would the satellite take to go round 6 times ?

8. 

   Sara can run 24 kilometres in 3 hours.

   Sandi can run for 2 hours and cover 18 kilometres.

   Who is running faster ?

Converting Measures

Converting Lengths (mm cm m km)

Rules for changing

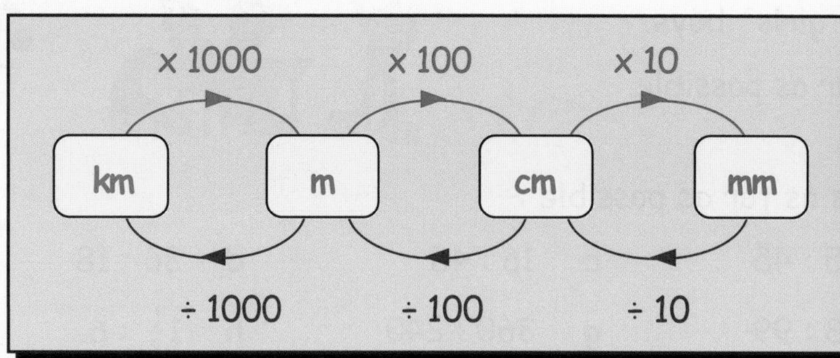

Examples :-

"To change **kilometres into metres - (x by 1000)"**

"To change **millimetres into centimetres (÷ by 10)"**

Exercise 1

1. Change from centimetres to millimetres :- **3 cm = (3 x 10) mm = 30 mm.**

   a 4 cm b 12 cm c 8·5 cm d 0·2 cm e 0·06 cm.

2. Change from millimetres to centimetres :- **800 mm = (800 ÷ 10) cm = 80 cm.**

   a 300 mm b 70 mm c 37 mm d 42 mm e 2 mm.

3. Change from metres to centimetres :- **7 m = (7 x 100) cm = 700 cm.**

   a 9 m b 20 m c 6·4 m d 0·75 m e 0·415 m.

4. Change from centimetres to metres :- **900 cm = (900 ÷ 100) m = 9 m.**

   a 400 cm b 150 cm c 50 cm d 1000 cm e 8 cm.

5. Change from kilometres to metres :- **4 km = (4 x 1000) m = 4000 m.**

   a 5 km b 200 km c 4·5 km d 0·25 km e 0·125 km.

6. Change from metres to kilometres :- **6000 m = (6000 ÷ 1000) km = 6 km.**

   a 3000 m b 6400 m c 500 m d 20 m e 1 m.

7. a One lap around a running track is 400 m.

Jason ran 20 laps.

How many kilometres did he run ?

b Sarah ran 30 laps of a 500 m track.

How many kilometres did she run ?

c Who ran further, and by how many kilometres ?

8. 

In an archery competition, the winner is the one whose arrow lands nearest to the centre of the Bulls-eye.

Zara is 27 cm away. Zak is 259 mm away. Zoe is 0·261 m away.

a Who won ?

b By how many mm did the winner beat third place ?

9. a Jerry throws his javelin 44·82 metres.

He is 44 cm short of the winning throw.

How far is the winning throw, in metres ?

b Three javelin throws are recorded using different units :-

Amy - 34·7 m, Jay - 3460 cm, Kia - 35 080 mm.

Put these throws in order *(longest* first).

10. Put each list in order, **smallest** first :-

a 184 cm, 2000 mm, 1·9 m, 0·003 km

b 1 000 000 mm, 10 000 cm, 1100 m, 0·112 km

11. Alice thinks she has put four lengths in order, smallest to largest :-

111 cm, 1110 mm, 1·11 m, 0·00111 km.

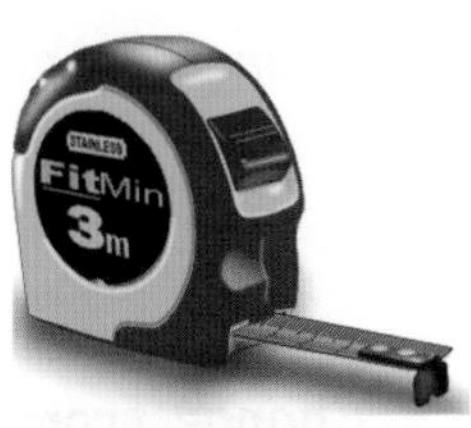

Is Alice correct ? Explain your answer.

12. 

Jack lives 860 metres from his office.

He walks there **and back** 6 days a week.

How many kilometres does he walk in total on his way to and from his office over these 6 days ?

Converting Volumes (litre, cl and ml)

Rules For Changing

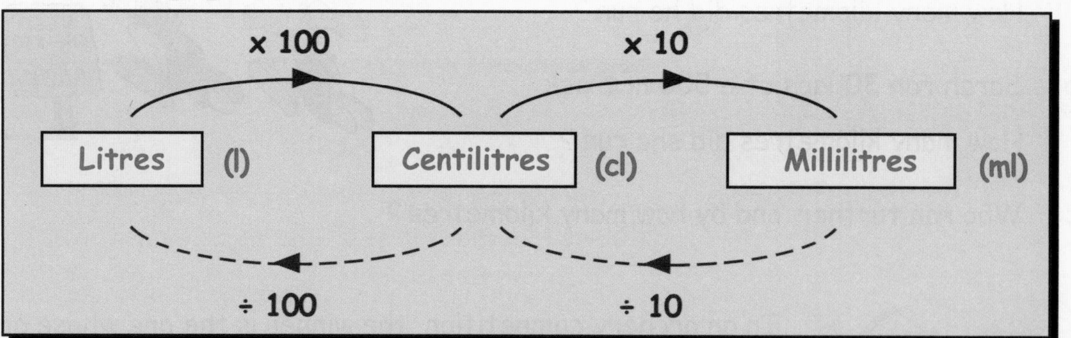

Volume conversions are carried out in a similar way to length conversions.

Examples :-

1. 4 litres = (4 × 100) centilitres = 400 cl
2. 70 millilitres = (70 ÷ 10) centilitres = 7 cl

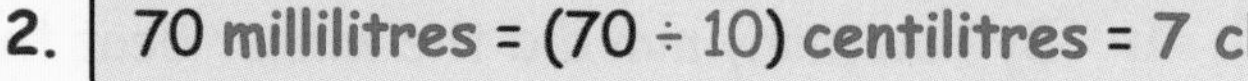

Exercise 2

1. Change from litres to centilitres :-

   a 8 litres b 40 litres c 0·2 litres d 0·03 litres.

2. Change from centilitres to litres :-

   a 700 cl b 2300 cl c 890 cl d 1 cl.

3. Change from centilitres to millilitres :-

   a 6 cl b 20 cl c 0·9 cl d 0·01 cl.

4. Change from millilitres to centilitres :-

   a 700 ml b 30 ml c 5000 ml d 10 ml.

5. Change from litres to millilitres :-

   REMEMBER :- 1 litre = 1000 ml.

   a 5 litres b 33 litres c 0·1 litres d 0·01 litres.

6. Change from millilitres to litres :-

   a 4000 ml b 50 000 ml c 350 ml d 10 ml.

7. Change :-

   a 40 000 ml to litres b 12·7 litres to ml
   c 50 ml to litres d 800 ml to litres.

REMEMBER :- 1000 cubic centimetres = 1000 ml = 1 litre (i.e. 1000 cm^3 = 1 litre)

8. Using the formula for the volume of a box :-

$$V = L \times B \times H,$$

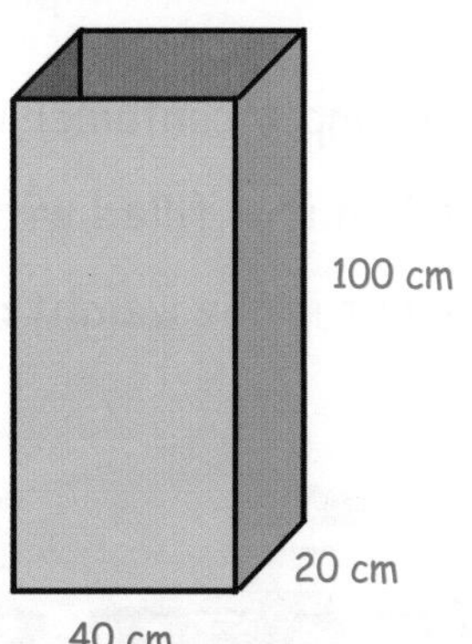

a Find the volume of this box, in cm^3.

b How many litres of water will it hold, when full ?

9. A hollow cube has all its sides of length 10 cm.

How many litres of liquid could it hold ?

Converting Weights (tonne, kg, g and mg)

Rules For Changing

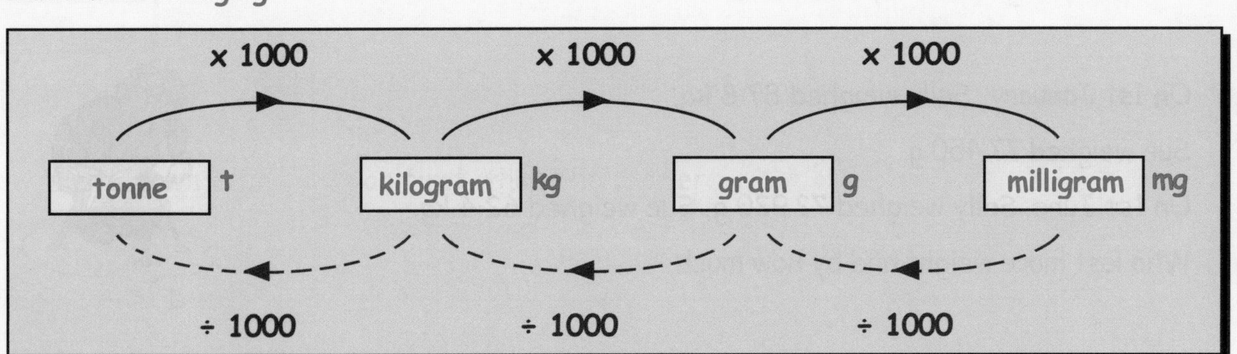

Weight conversions are similar to the others, but here, the x and ÷ are always by 1000.

Examples :-

1. 3 tonnes = (3 x 1000) kilograms = 3000 kg
2. 4000 milligrams = (4000 ÷ 1000) grams = 4 g

Exercise 3

1. Change from kilograms to grams :-

a 6 kg b 28 kg c 1·2 kg d 0·5 kg.

2. Change from milligrams to grams :-

a 7000 mg b 19 000 mg c 600 mg d 70 mg.

3. Change from tonnes to kilograms :-

a 8 tonnes b 40 tonnes c 9·5 tonnes d 0·24 tonnes.

4. Change from grams to kilograms :-

a 8000 g b 500 g c 57 000 g d 10 g.

5. An empty container weighs 1560 kg.

When it is filled with vending machines it weighs 3·8 tonnes.

What is the weight of the vending machines ?

6. A full truck weighs 14·6 tonnes.

The contents of the truck weigh 11 840 kg.

What is the weight of the empty truck ?

7. A chain of stores orders 0·85 tonnes of loose potatoes.

The stores sell them in 2 kg bags.

How many bags can they sell ?

8. On 1st January, Sally weighed 87·8 kg.

Sue weighed 77 450 g.

On 1st June, Sally weighed 72 920 g, Sue weighed 62·4 kg.

Who lost more weight and by how much ?

9. 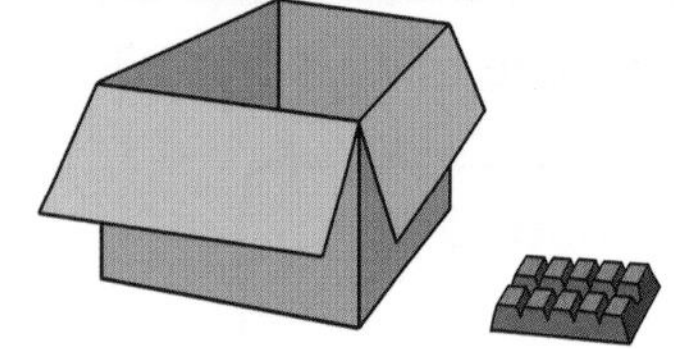

An empty box weighs 0·35 kg.

It is filled with 25 chocochunk bars, each weighing 40 grams and 10 bags of sweets, each weighing 25 grams.

Find the weight of the full box in :-

a grams b kilograms.

10. Gordon the "super" gardener bought the following :-

- 5 large slabs, each weighing 25 000 grams
- 10 medium slabs, each weighing 18 000 grams
- 20 small slabs, each weighing 8 kg
- 40 large rocks, each weighing 75 kg.

a Find the **total weight** of his purchases, in kilograms.

b Gordon's van can only carry at most 1 tonne on a single trip.

How many trips will he have to make ?

Converting Measures

Numeracy Assessment 9

1. Change :-

   a 8·1 cm to mm b 700 mm to cm c 0·3 metres to cm

   d 20 cm to metres e 7·2 km to metres f 6700 metres to km

   g 3000 cm to metres h 4 000 000 mm to m i 0·001 km to mm.

2. Eric lives 1·4 km from his school.

   He walks there and back 5 days a week.

   How many **metres** does he walk each week to school and back ?

3. Change :-

   a 9 litres to cl b 80 cl to litres c 3 litres to ml

   d 10 litres to ml e 40 ml to litres f 3100 ml to litres

   g 3 ml to litres h two million ml to litres.

4. a Calculate the volume of this box, in cm^3.

   b How many litres of water can the box hold when full ?

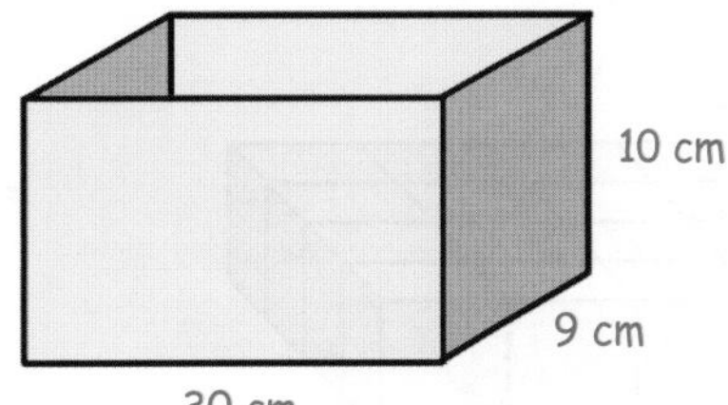

5. Change :-

   a 8·4 kg to grams b 2000 mg to grams c 4500 kg to tonnes

   d 3 tonnes to kg e 0·5 tonne to g f 4 000 000 mg to kg.

6. Sharon buys 7·5 litres of juice for her party.

   She has twenty guests and estimates they will **each** drink 350 ml.

   a If she is correct, how much juice will she have left ?

   b They actually drank 30 cl each.

   How many litres did she have left ?

Volume

Volumes by Counting

The volume of a shape is simply the amount of space it takes up.

One unit of volume is the cubic centimetre.

Each of these small cubes measures 1 cm by 1 cm by 1 cm.

Each has a volume of 1 cubic centimetre.

or for short :- 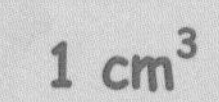 1 cm^3

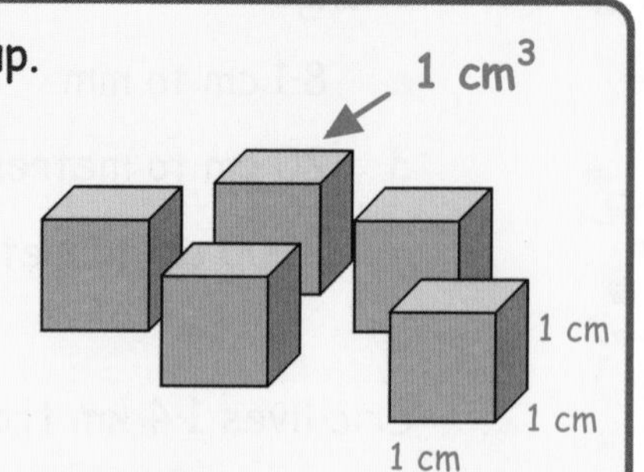

Exercise 1

1. A boy creates shapes using 1 centimetre cubes.
Write down the volume of each of the following shapes he made, in cubic centimetres (cm^3) :-
(*i.e. how many cubic centimetres are used to make each one ?*)

a 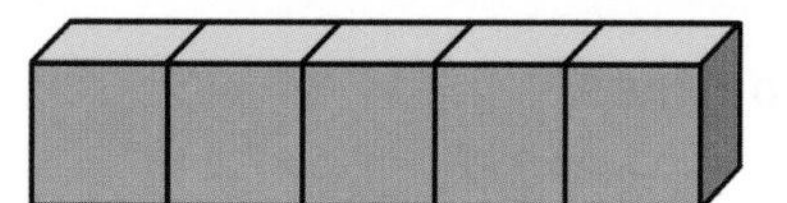

b 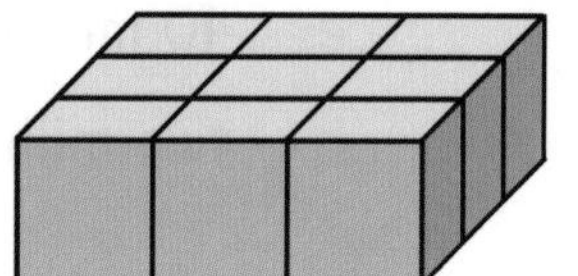

c 

d 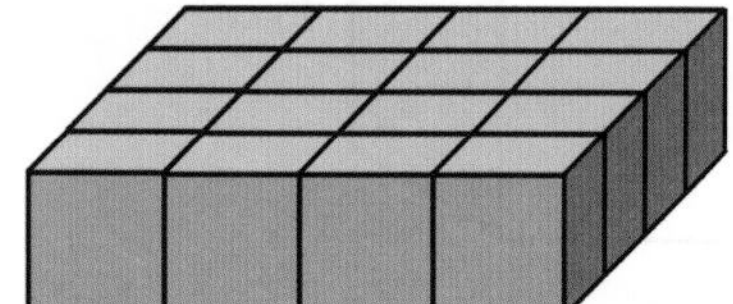

e 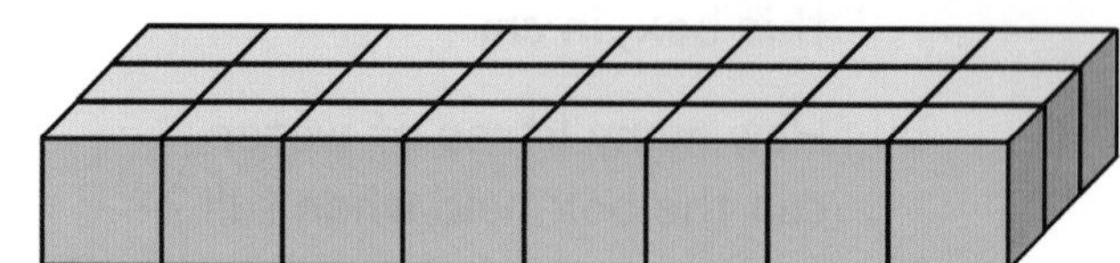

2. The boy began stacking them into cuboid shapes.
   a How many cubes are on the top layer of this shape ?
   b How many layers does it have ?
   c What is its total volume ?

3. 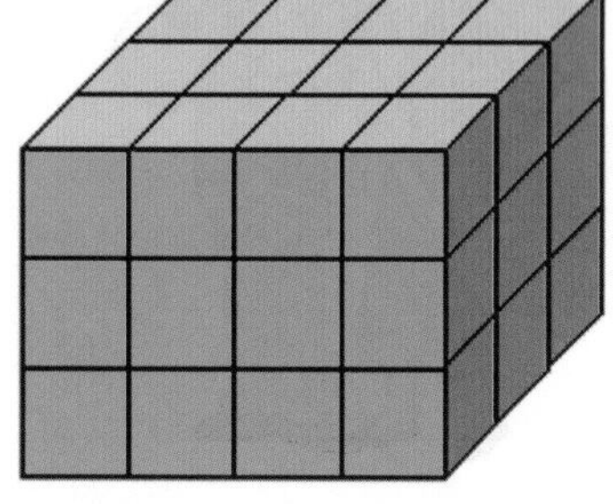
   a How many cubes are on the top layer this time ?
   b How many layers does it have ?
   c What is its total volume ?

4. By working out the volume of the top layer first, calculate the total volume (in cm^3) of each of the following shapes :-

a

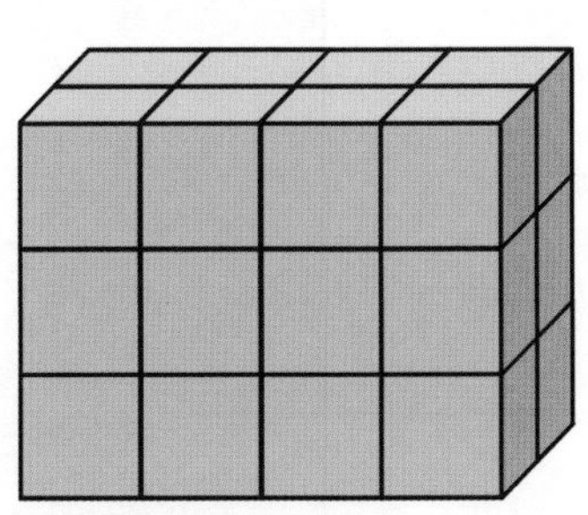

b

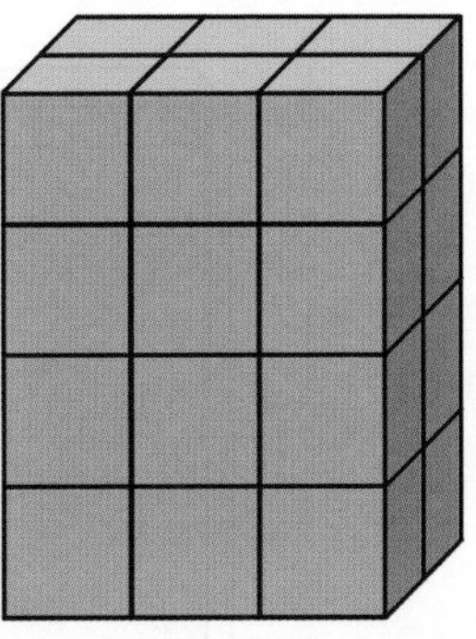

c

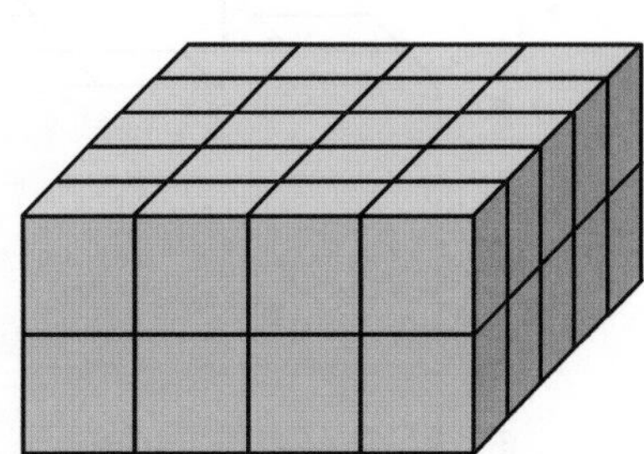

d

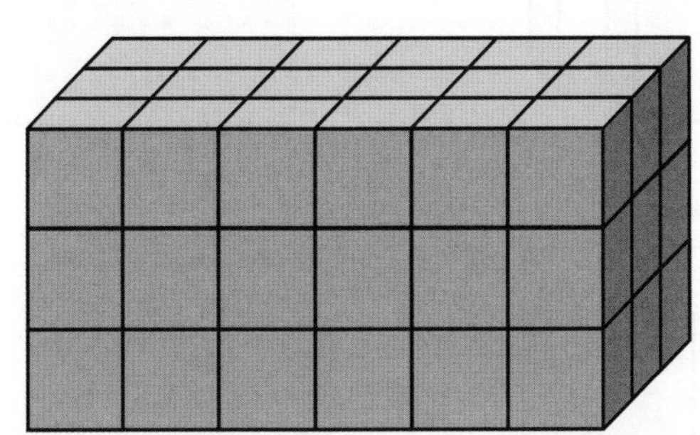

e

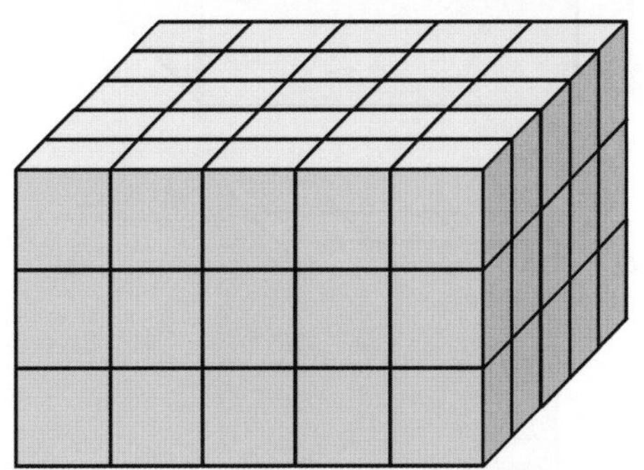

5. Calculate the volume of each cuboid :-
(*Show how you obtained your answers*).

a

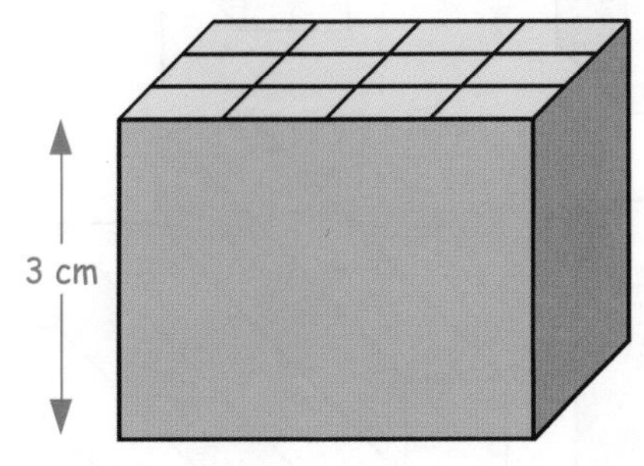

b

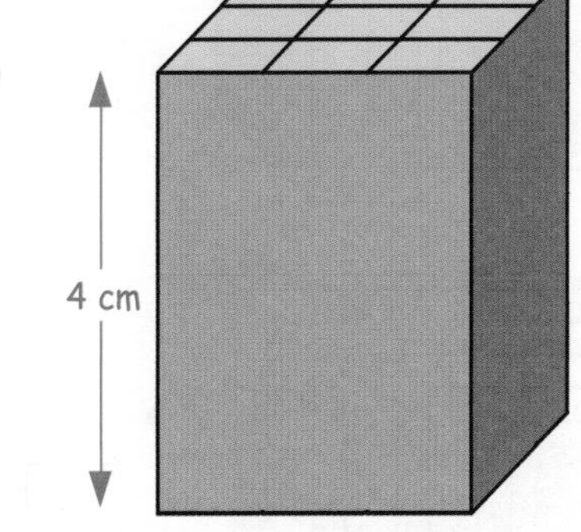

c

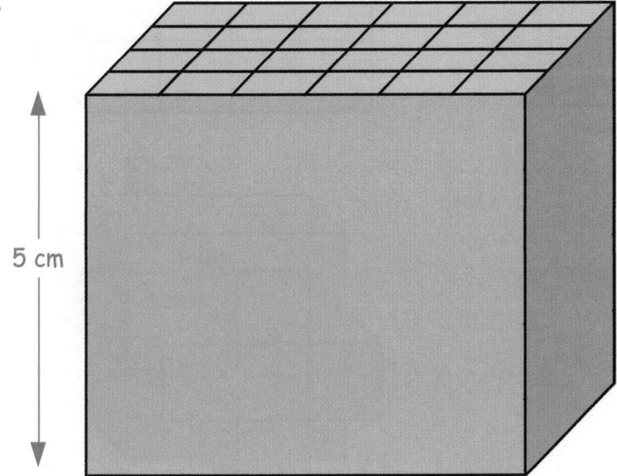

d

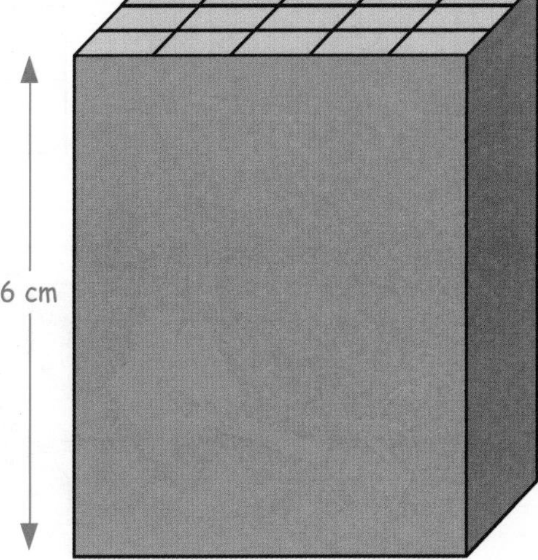

6. Calculate the volume of each shape :-
(*Show how you obtained your answers*).

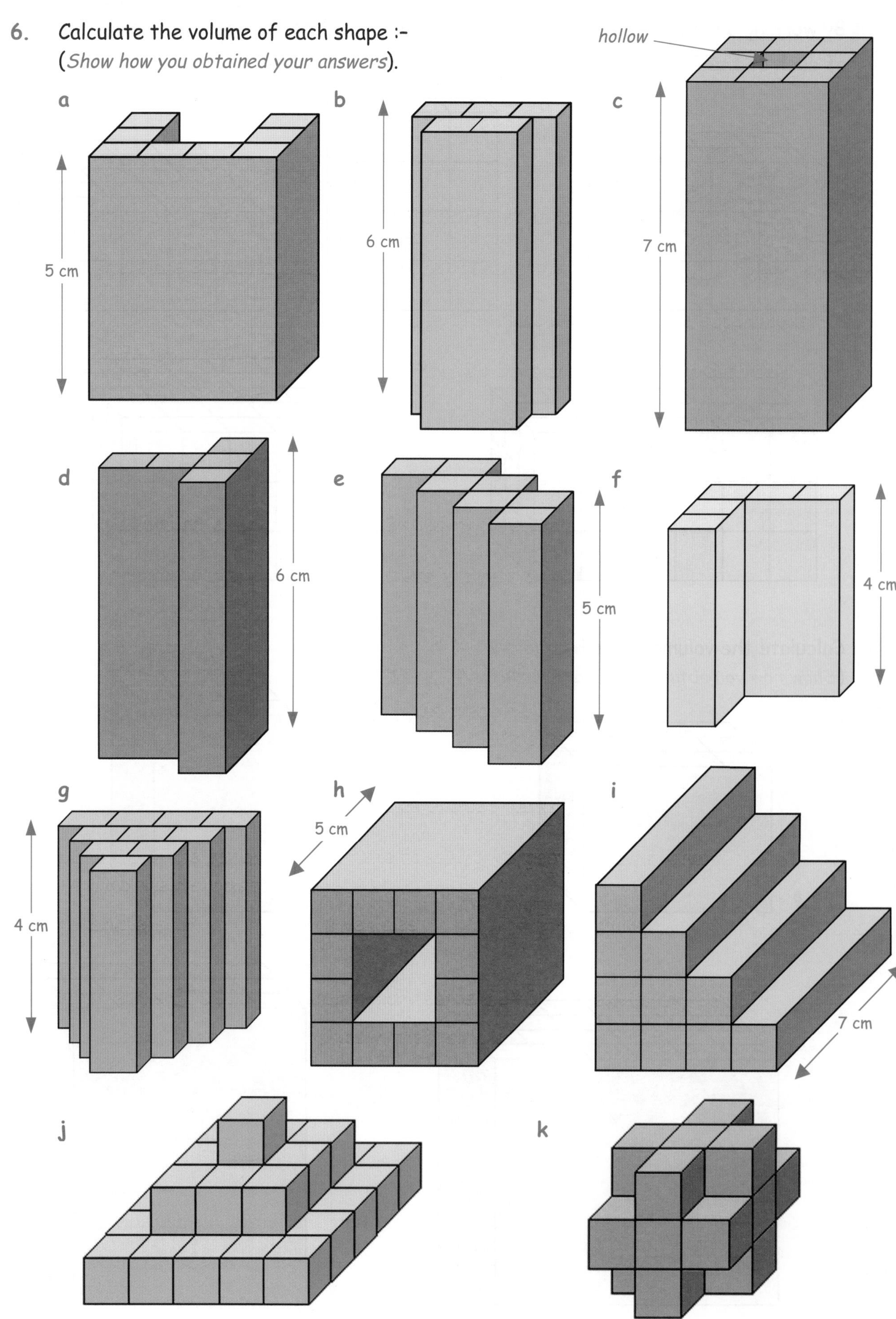

The Volume of a Cuboid - A FORMULA

(i) Can you see that the top layer of this cuboid is made up of

$(3 \times 6) = 18 \text{ cm}^3$?

(ii) Can you also see that there are 3 layers ? This means

Volume = $(3 \times 6) \times 3 = 54 \text{ cm}^3$?

To find the volume of a cuboid,
you can do so by simply multiplying

length × breadth × height

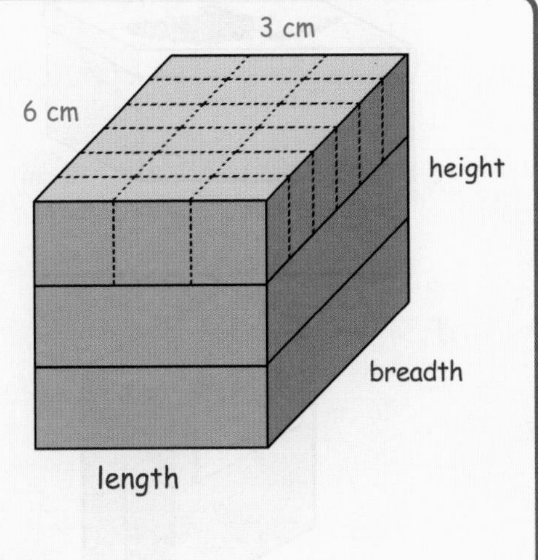

Formula :- **Volume = $l \times b \times h$**

Exercise 2

1. Copy and complete for this cuboid :-

$V = l \times b \times h$
$V = 10 \times 8 \times 6$
$V = \text{..........} \text{ cm}^3$

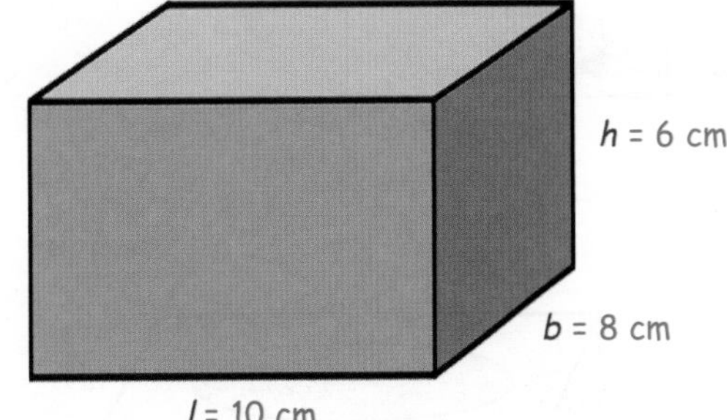

2. Use the formula $V = l \times b \times h$ to calculate the volume of this cuboid. (*Show your working*).

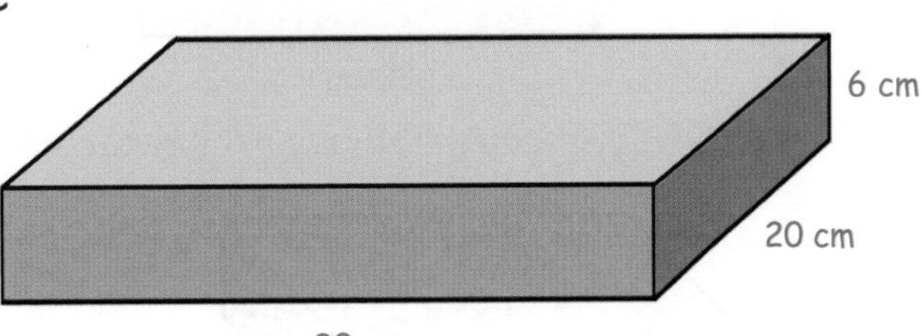

3. Use the formula again to calculate the volume of this cuboid.

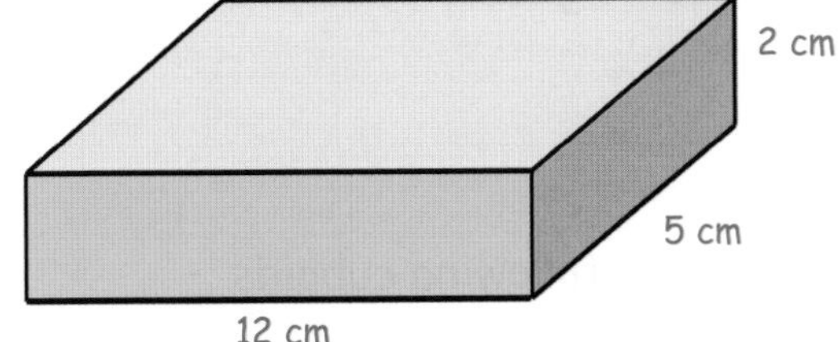

4. Find the volume of this ink cartridge box :-

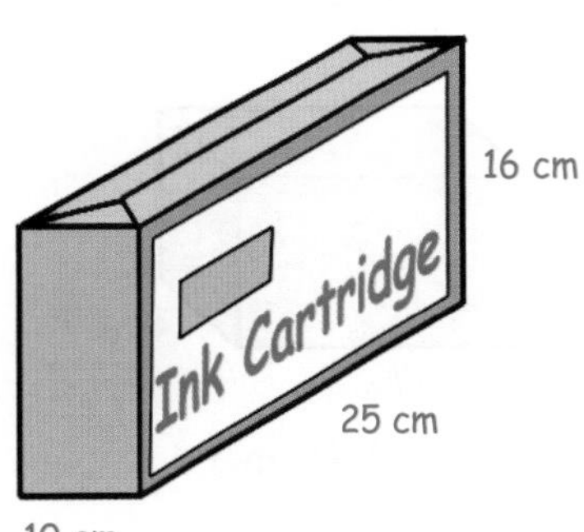

5. Calculate the volume of each of the following shapes :-

a

15 cm
18 cm
30 cm

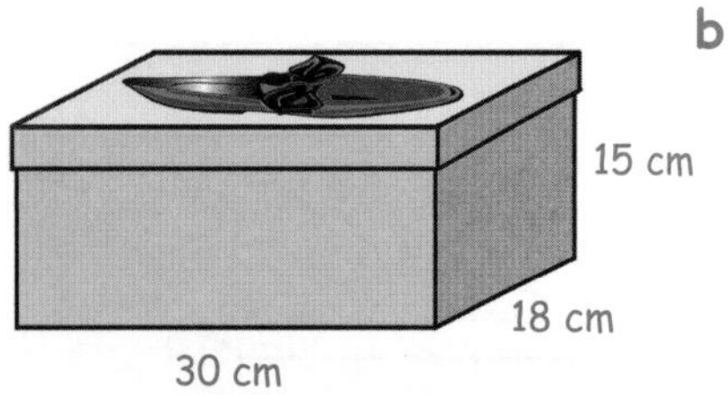

b

Marbles
contents - 30
9 cm
3 cm
5 cm

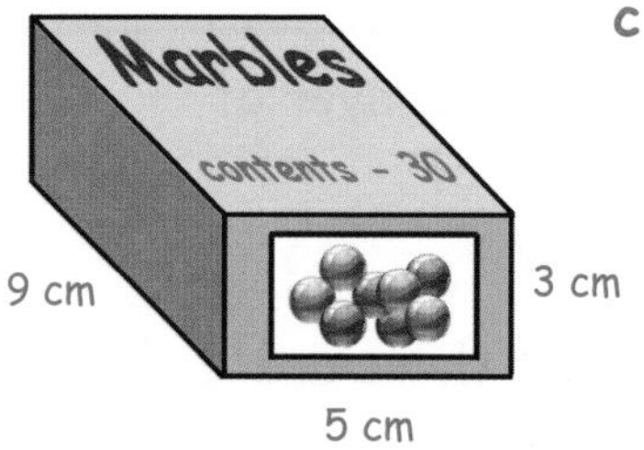

c

25 cm
20 cm
20 cm

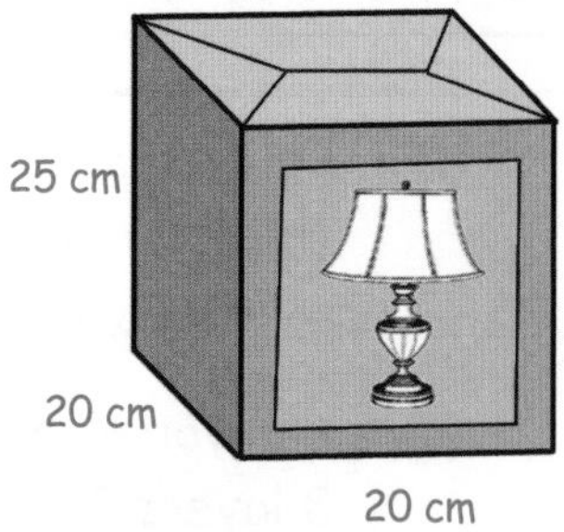

d

Apple Juice
16 cm
12 cm
8 cm

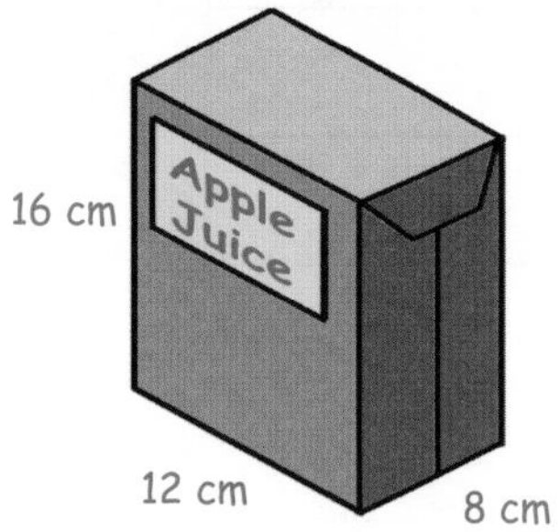

e

SCOTTS
BUTTER
7 cm
9 cm
15 cm

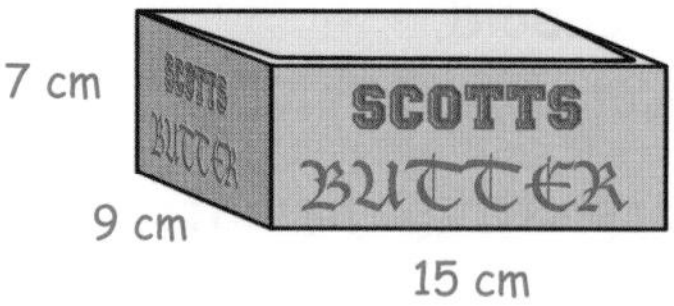

f

24 cm
16 cm
6 cm

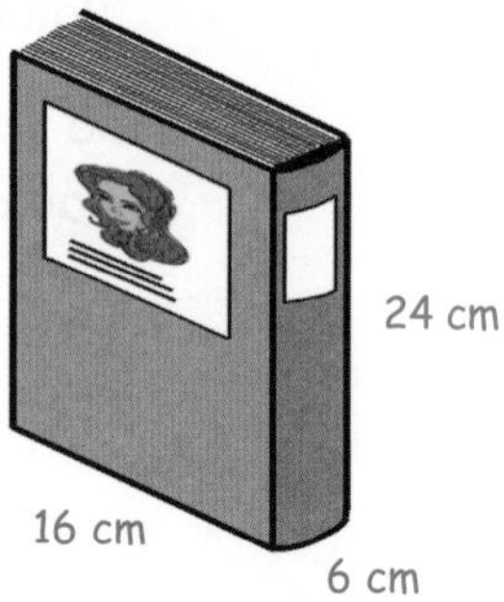

g

12 Dinner Plates
12 Plates
13 cm
30 cm
30 cm

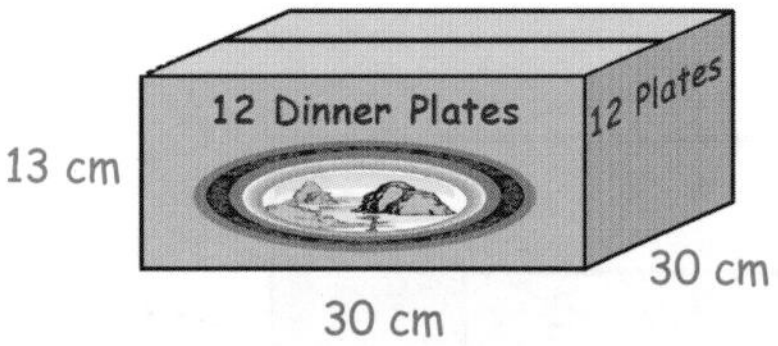

h

10 cm
5 cm
5 cm
Pro Flight Golf Ball

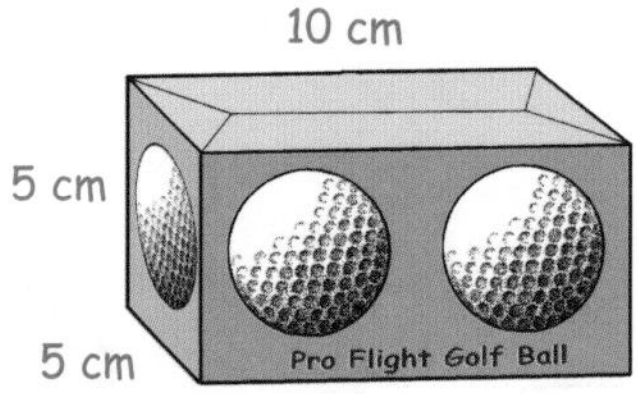

i

4 cm
26 cm
16 cm

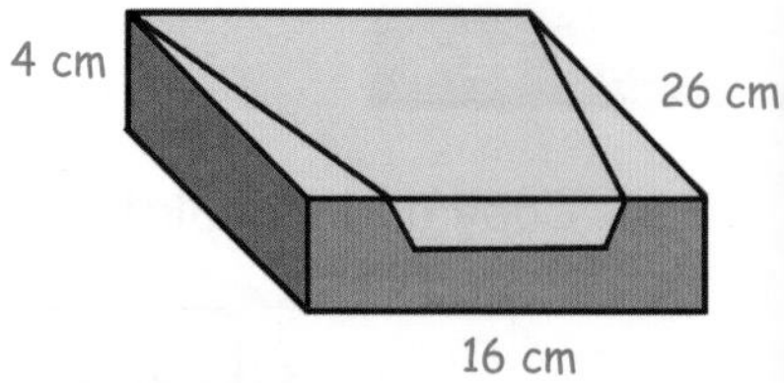

j

15 cm
4·5 cm
20 cm

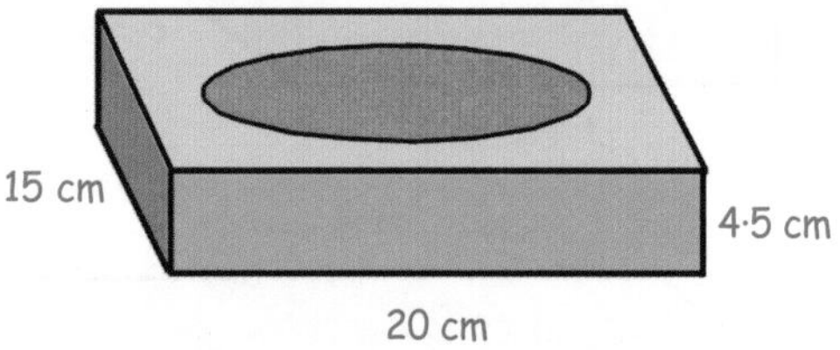

k

OIL
90 cm
50 cm
40 cm

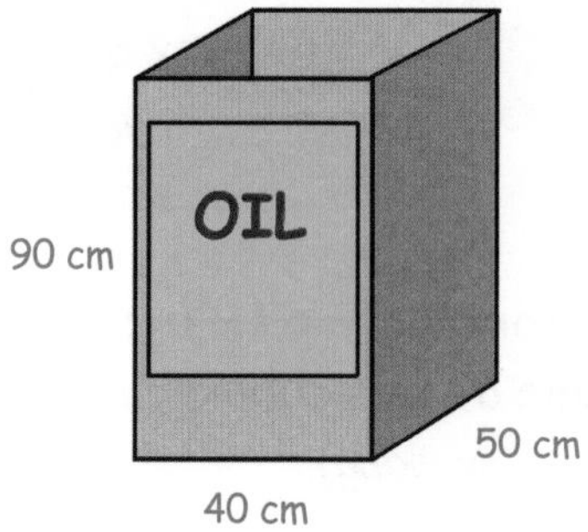

6.

h = ?
8 cm
10 cm

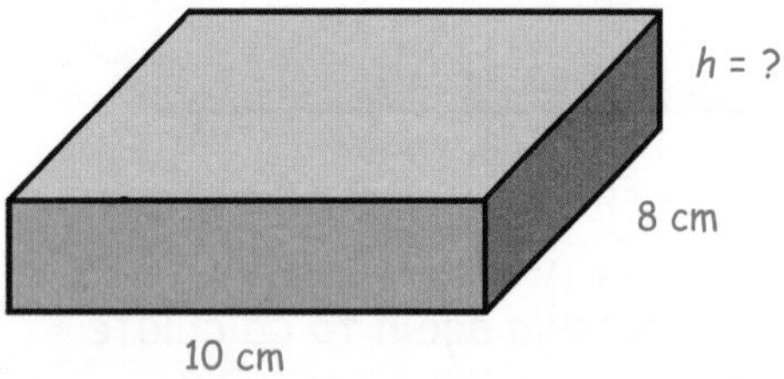

The volume of this cuboid is 120 cm^3.

Calculate its height.

7. Calculate the length of the missing edge in each of the following cuboids :-

a

5 cm
4 cm
L

(Vol = 120 cm^3)

b

4 cm
B
7 cm

(Vol = 140 cm^3)

c

Vol =
63 cm3
H
3 cm
3 cm

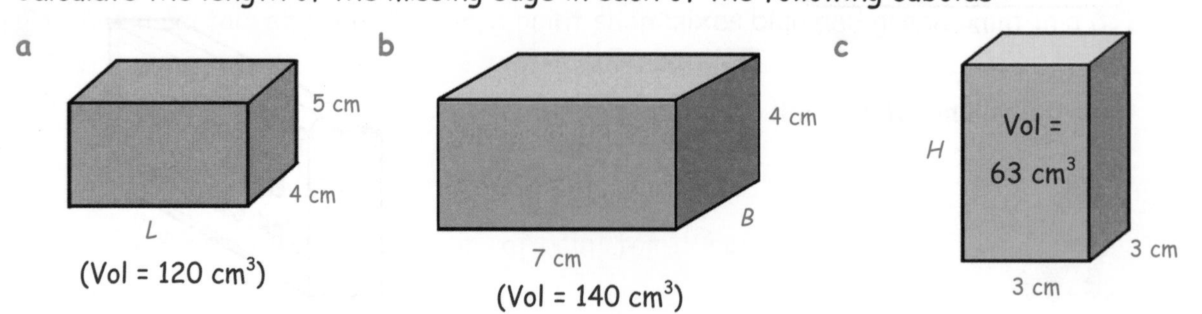

Liquid Volumes Capacity

If you take a hollow cube whose sides are all 1 centimetre, and fill it with water, we say it holds 1 millilitre of liquid.

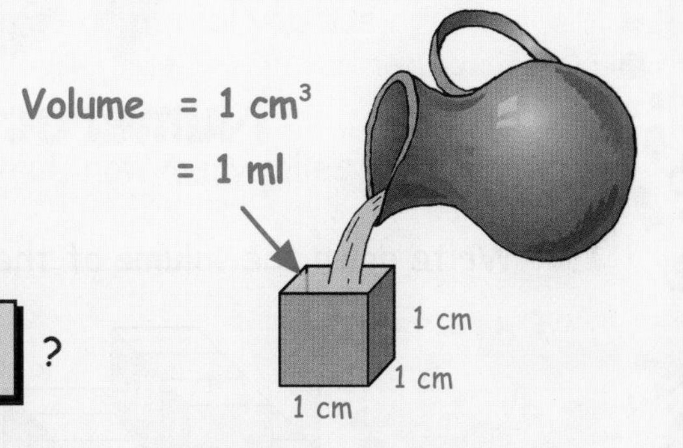

$1\ cm^3 = 1\ ml$

Can you see that $1000\ cm^3 = 1000\ ml = 1$ litre ?

Liquid volume is referred to as Capacity.

Exercise 3

1. a Calculate the volume of this rectangular tray, in cm^3.
   b How many millilitres of water will it hold ?

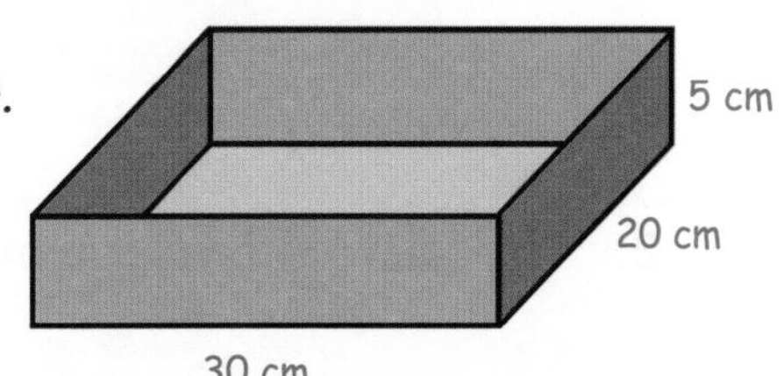

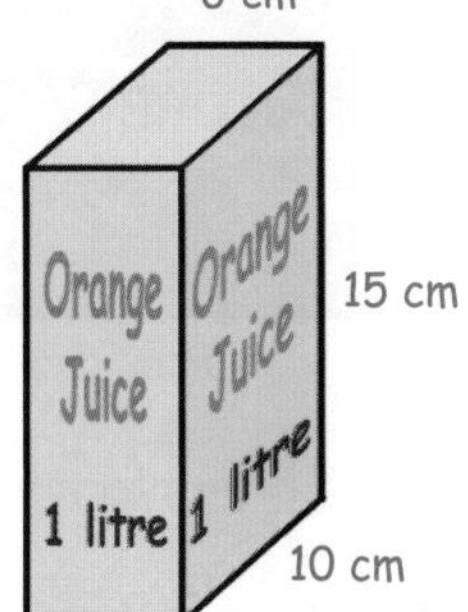

2. The label on this carton says it holds 1 litre (1000 ml) of orange juice.
   Why is the label misleading ?

3. A new milk carton is designed.
   It is a cuboid measuring :- 10 cm by 10 cm by 20 cm.
   a Calculate its volume, in cm^3.
   b Write down its volume, in millilitres.
   c How many litres will it hold ? (*Its capacity*).

Remember :- To change from millilitres —> litres, you simply ÷ 1000.

4. Change each of the following to litres :-

a	4000 ml	b	7000 ml	c	13 000 ml
d	1500 ml	e	2300 ml	f	10 250 ml
g	600 ml	h	400 ml	i	250 ml.

Volume

Numeracy Assessment 10

1. Write down the **volume** of these 2 shapes, in cm^3.

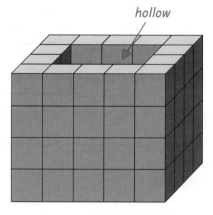

a

b

hollow

2. Calculate the **volume** of each cuboid :-

a

3·5 cm

10 cm

12 cm

b

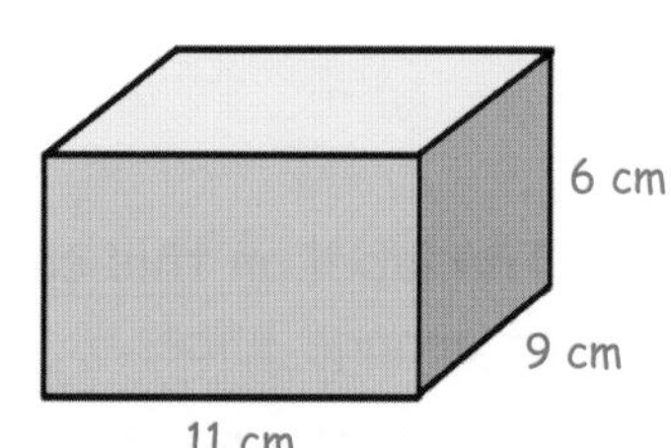

c

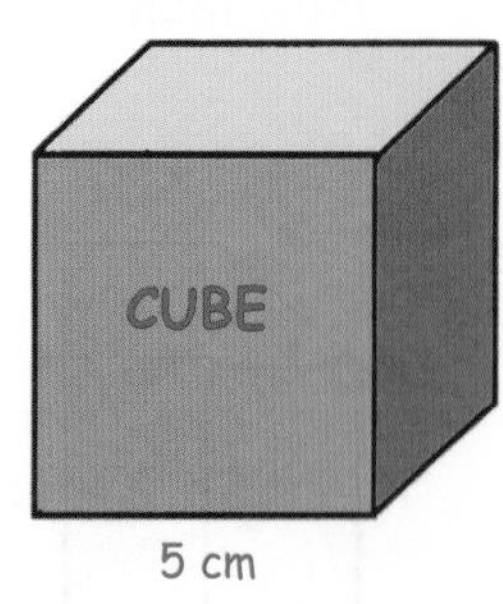

3.

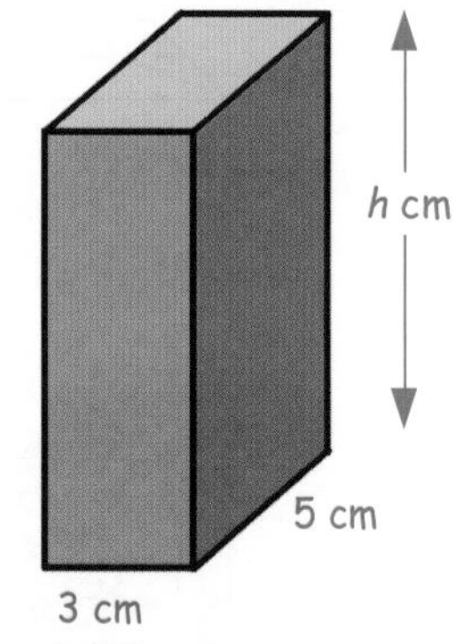

The volume of this cuboid is 150 cm^3.
Calculate its **height**.

4. Change to litres :- a 8000 ml b 7200 ml c 750 ml.

5. a Calculate the **volume** of water in this tank, in cm^3.

b How many millilitres of water can it hold ?

c Change your answer to litres.

d When the tap is opened fully, water flows out of the tank at a rate of 2 litres per minute.

How long will it take for the tank to empty ?

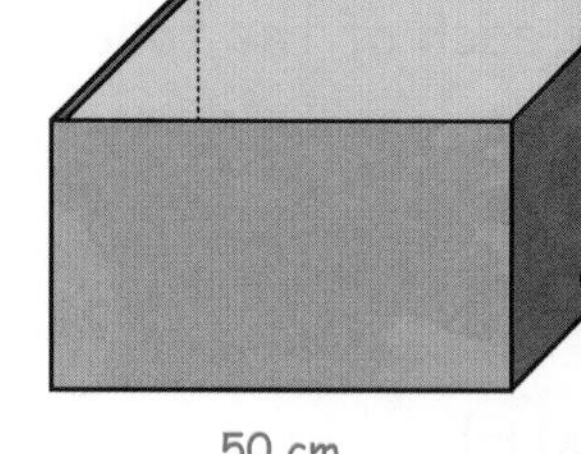

Graphs, Charts & Tables 1

Interpreting Graphs - Pictographs, Bar Graphs, Line Graphs & Pie Charts

Exercise 1

1. This pictograph shows the number of hours of sunshine recorded at Edinburgh Airport during the final five months of last year.

   = 50 hours

Aug	
Sept	
Oct	
Nov	
Dec	

   a How many hours of sunshine in August ?

   b How many hours of sunshine in December ?

   c How many **more** hours of sunshine were there in **September** than in **November** ?

2. This bar graph shows the number of animals presently residing at Denton Zoo.

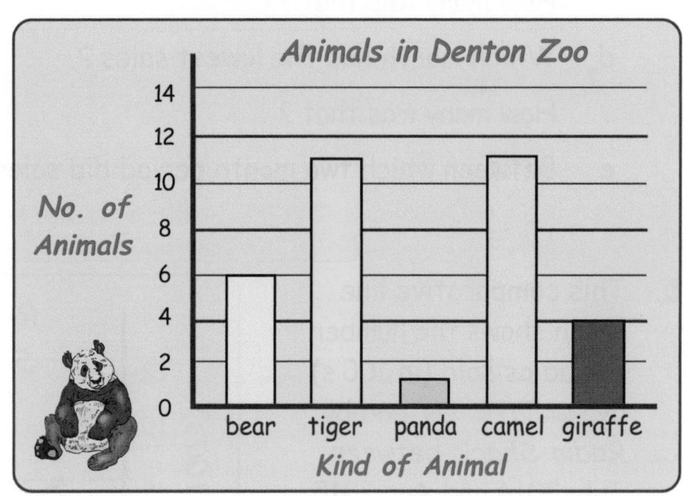

   a How many pandas live there ?

   b How many bears are there ?

   c How many **more** camels are there than giraffes ?

   d How many animals altogether reside in the zoo ?

   e Why are there so few pandas ? Investigate !

3. This bar chart shows the results of a large survey taken last year.

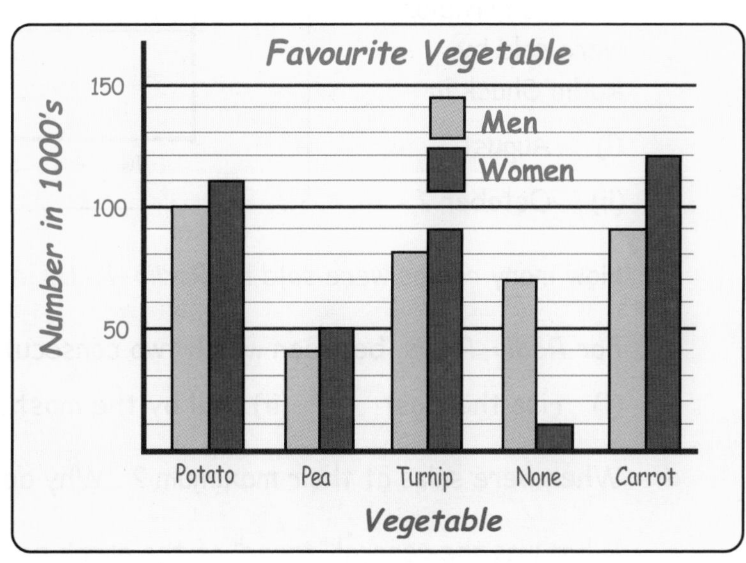

   a How many **men** chose :-

      (i) Potato (not 100)

      (ii) Turnip ?

   b How many **women** chose :-

      (i) Carrot

      (ii) Pea ?

   c How many people don't like vegetables ?

3. d What was the favourite vegetable of the :- (i) men (ii) women ?

e How many more women preferred Carrots to Turnips ?

f In the survey, what was the total number of :- (i) men (ii) women asked ?

g From this survey, who would you say was the healthier eaters, men or women ? Explain why you think this is so.

4. The line graph opposite shows the number of cars sold at *H V Kershaw's* garage during the first 7 months of 2014.

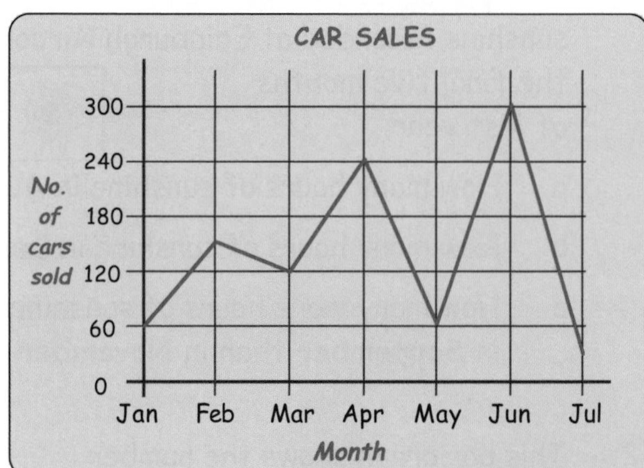

a How many cars were sold in :-

(i) February (ii) April ?

b How many times did sales **rise** ?

c Which month had the **highest** sales ?

How many was that ?

d Which month had the **lowest** sales ?

How many was that ?

e Between which two month period did sales **drop** the most ?

5. This comparative line graph shows the number of radios sold (in 100's) by ***Radio-R-Us*** and by ***Radio Shack*** between July 2014 and Apr 2015.

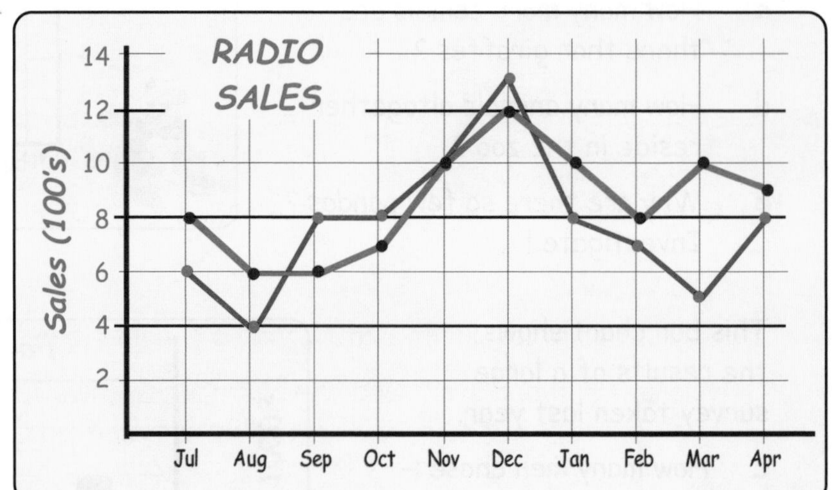

a How many radios were sold by Radio Shack in :-

(i) August

(ii) October ?

b How many radios were sold by ***Radio-R-Us*** in total ?

c For ***Radio-R-Us,*** between which two consecutive months did sales :-

(i) rise the most (ii) fall by the most ?

d When were sales at their maximum ? Why do you think this was the best month ?

e What was the general "*trend*" of the graph between September and December ?

6. The pie chart shows the results of a survey into favourite breeds of dog.

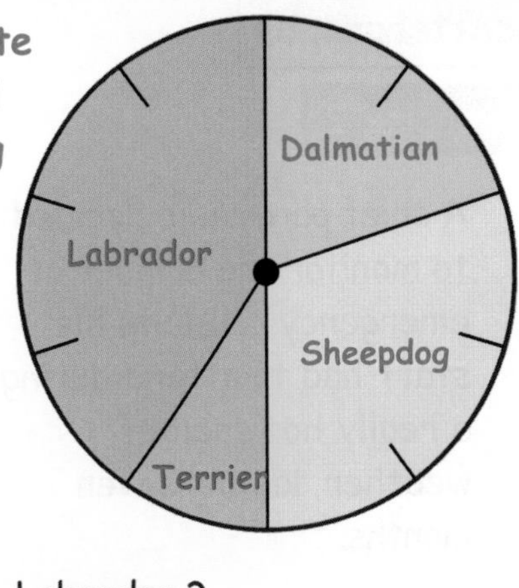

a What was the most and least popular dog ?

b Write down the fraction that chose :-

(i) Labrador (ii) Sheepdog

(iii) Dalmatian (iv) Terrier.

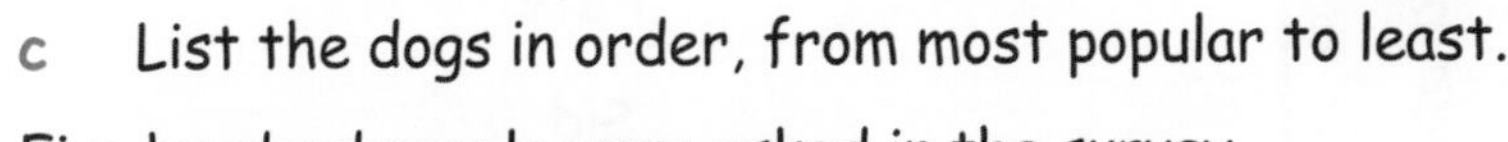

c List the dogs in order, from most popular to least.

Five hundred people were asked in the survey.

d How many people chose :- (i) Terrier (ii) Labrador ?

7. The pie chart shows the results of a survey into favourite types of cat.

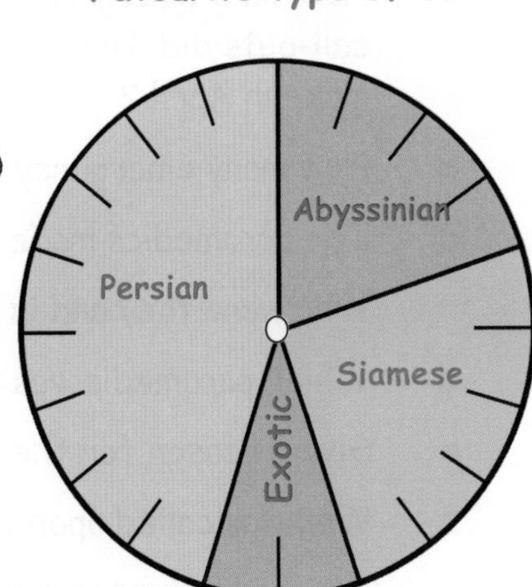

a What was the most and least popular cat ?

b Write down the fraction that chose :-

(i) Exotic (ii) Abyssinian.

c List the cats in order from most popular to least.

600 people took part in the survey.

d How many people chose :-

(i) Persian (ii) Siamese ?

8.

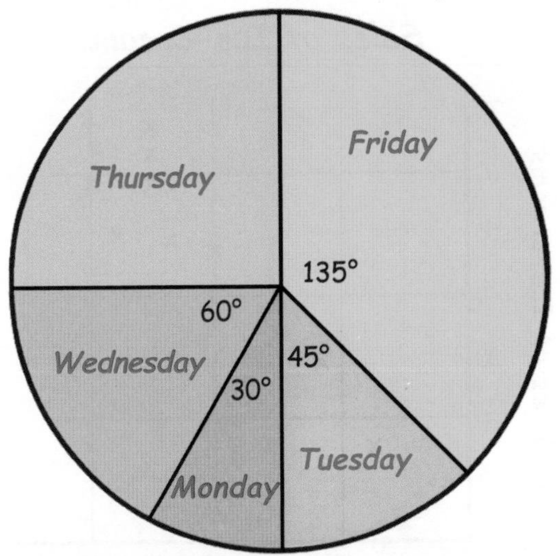

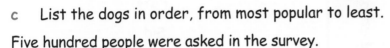

One hundred and twenty S4 students were surveyed to find their favourite school day.

This pie chart shows the result.

a Which day was the most popular ?

b Which day was the least popular ?

c What fraction of students voted :-

(i) Thursday (ii) Wednesday ($\frac{60}{360}$ *simplified*)

(iii) Monday (iv) Friday ?

d Calculate how many of the 120 students liked :-

(i) Thursday ($\frac{1}{4}$ of 120) (ii) Monday

(iii) Tuesday (iv) Friday ?

Scattergraphs

Exercise 2

1. A chief paramedic decided to monitor the number of emergency call-outs his staff had to attend during a really hot spell of weather, lasting seven months.

   The results are shown in this scattergraph.

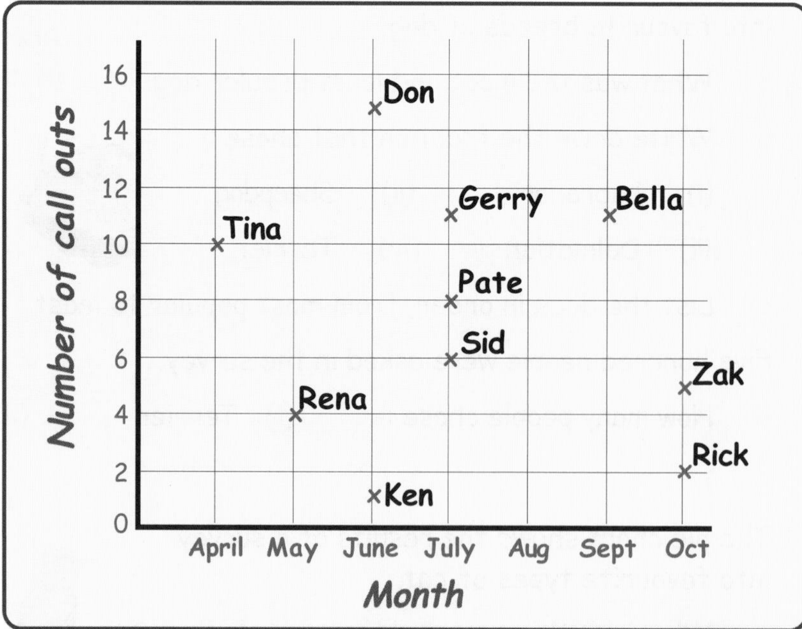

   a How many emergency call-outs did Tina make in April ?

   b How many emergency call-outs did Zak make in October ?

   c Two paramedics made the same number of call-outs.

   Who were they and in which months ?

   d Which paramedic was called out the most and in which month ?

   e Give a reason for the high number of call-outs in July.

   f Who was called upon the least and how many times was that ?

   g What was the total number of call-outs from April to June inclusive ?

2. This scattergraph shows a connection between the temperature during the day and the sales of ice-creams from Dave's Cafe.

   a Suggest in words a connection between the temperature and the sales of ice-creams.

   b Use the graph to estimate how many ice-creams were sold when the temperature was 18°C.

   c When the temperature was 10°C, how many ice-creams were sold ?

   d Estimate what the temperature might have been when 55 ice-creams were sold.

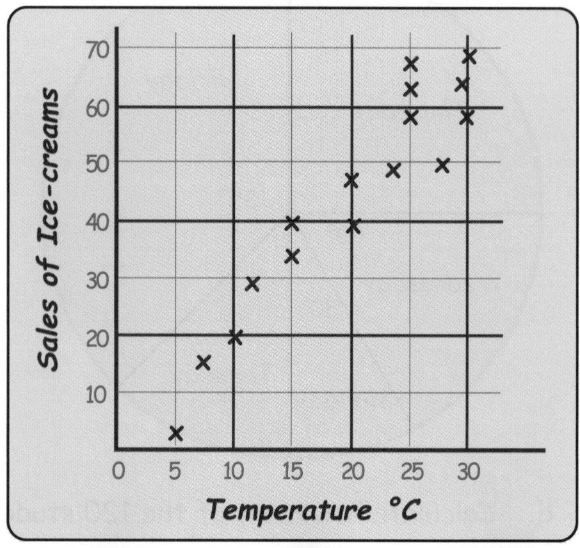

Stem & Leaf Diagrams

Exercise 3

1. A group of people were asked their ages while standing in a bank queue.

   The data is shown in this stem-and-leaf diagram.

   a The first level refers to these ages :-

   - **1**1 years, **1**4 years, **1**7 years, **1**9 years.

   Write out the ages in **level 2** in the same way.

   b What age was the youngest person surveyed ?

   c What age was the **oldest** person ?

   d How many people were in the survey ?

Age in years

1	1 4 7 9
2	1 2 4 4 8 9
3	0 7

Key :- 2 | 4 = 24 years

2.

Money taken

1	1 9
2	0 1 2 3 5 7 8
3	1 1 3 4 9
4	0
5	5 7 8 9

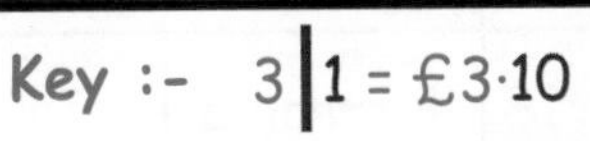
Key :- 3 | 1 = £3·10

Sales in a sweet shop were recorded over a 1 hour period.

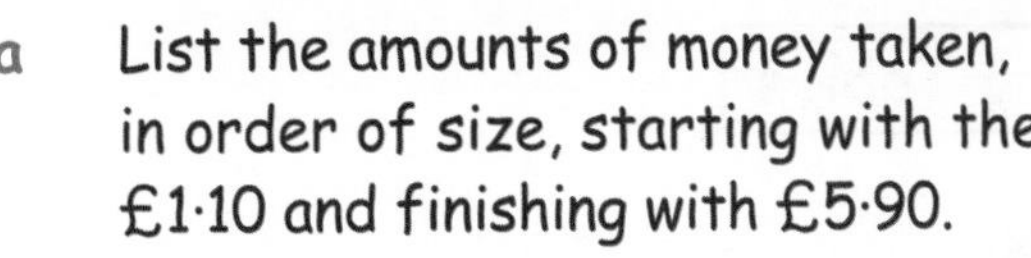

a List the amounts of money taken, in order of size, starting with the £1·10 and finishing with £5·90.

b Which level has the most data ?

c Which amount of money appears most often (the mode) ?

d How many takings are there **below** £2·30 ?

e How many customers bought items from the shop in the hour ?

3. A post office recorded the weight of parcels, in kilograms.

   a How many parcels were weighed ?

   b Write down the weights of all parcels over 3·5 kg.

   c How many parcels weighed less than one kilogram ?

   d Write down the weights of all the parcels under 1·5 kg.

   e What was the total weight of all the parcels ?

Weight (kg)

0	3 4 8 9
1	2 5 7
2	0 1 3 6 8
3	0 4 4 8
4	7 7 7 8 8 9
5	0

Key :- 1 | 2 = 1·2 kg

4. The ages of people receiving the flu vaccination in a surgery are recorded as shown.

Ages of people being vaccinated

Men		Women
1	**2**	2
5 4 0	**3**	3 5
	4	1 2 4
8 7 1	**5**	0 1
9 4	**6**	3 5 6
8 4 3 1	**7**	1 2 9

Key :- 4 | **3** means a 34 year old man, (note)

and **4** | 1 means a 41 year old woman.

a How many men in their 30's got vaccinated ?

b How many women in their 50's got vaccinated ?

c More men than women got vaccinated at this surgery. True or false ?

Interpreting Tables

Exercise 4

1. The local cinema shows 3 movies.

	5 pm	7 pm	9 pm
Studio 1	Batman 18	Horror 3	Jaws 9
Studio 2	Batman 18	Jaws 9	Horror 3
Studio 3	Horror 3	Batman 18	Horror 3

a What is showing in :-

(i) Studio 2 at 7 pm

(ii) Studio 3 at 9 pm ?

b Write down when and where you can watch Batman 18.

2. *SunShine Holidays* show the prices for three holidays for 1, 2, 3 and 4 weeks.

	1 week	2 weeks	3 weeks	4 weeks
Majorca	£200	£250	£275	£300
Tenerife	£225	£325	£350	£400
Zante	£240	£290	£390	£450

a How much would it cost for Ann to take a holiday to :-

(i) Majorca for 2 weeks

(ii) Zante for 3 weeks

(iii) Tenerife for 4 weeks ?

b Mr and Mrs Ross take a one week holiday to Zante.

How much will the holiday cost in total ?

3. This table shows the hire charges of sunbeds at the *Beach Hotel.*

The fee depends on what time you start the hire, until the end of the day.

Sunbed Hire Charges

Time (between)		Fee
6 am to 9 am	....	£4·00
9 am to noon	....	£3·50
noon to 3 pm	....	£2·50
after 3 pm	....	£2·00

a How much would it cost to hire a bed at :-

(i) 7 am (ii) 0930 hrs

(iii) 1330 hrs (iv) 1615 hrs ?

b Alan and Joy arrive at the beach at 1455.

They wait 6 minutes, then pay for their 2 sunbeds.

How much did they save by waiting ?

4. The table shows three different banks' Annual Percentage Interest Rate, which customers will receive in their savings accounts, depending on how much savings they have.

a Which bank should each person put their savings in :-

(i) Jay has £2750

(ii) Joy has £870

(iii) Jamie has £12 000 ?

	RSB	STB	ABS
less than £1000	1·3%	1·4%	1·2%
between £1000 & £10 000	2·1%	2·0%	2·2%
more than £10 000	3·0%	3·2%	3·1%

b Explain why you have chosen the banks for these people.

5. The charges for a delivery service are shown in the table.

What would be the charge for delivering a package weighing :-

a 4 kg for a distance of 8 km

b 12 kg for a distance of 14 km

c 7 kg for a distance of 4 km ?

Weight \ Distance	under 5 km	between 5-10 km	above 10 km
1 - 5 kg	£5·50	£6·00	£8·50
6 - 10 kg	£7·50	£8·50	£10·50
11 - 20 kg	£8·50	£9·00	£12·50
above 20 kg	£10·50	£11·00	£15·00

6. Dylan sends an 8 kg parcel 9 km, a 19 kg package 23 km and a 30 kg crate 3 km.

How much did he get charged in total ?

Graphs, Charts & Tables 1

Numeracy Assessment 11

1. A dentist recorded the number of fillings he had to perform on children between November and March.

   The results are shown in the comparative bar graph.

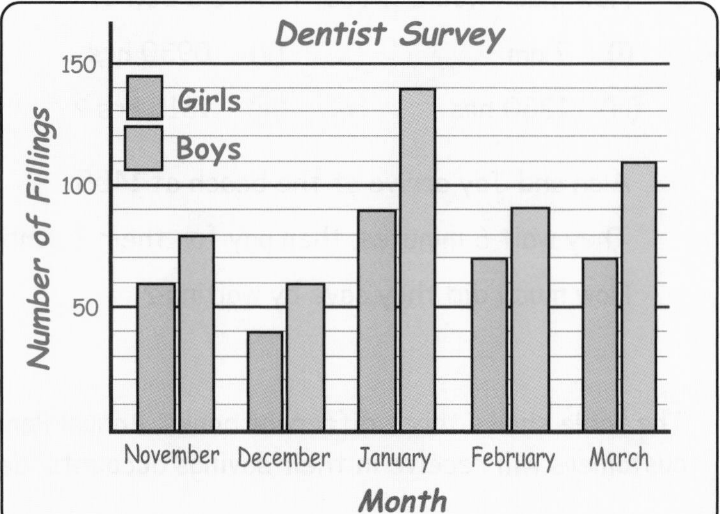

   a How many fillings did he give to :-

      (i) boys in December

      (ii) girls in March ?

   b How many fillings did he perform on :- (i) boys in total (ii) girls in total ?

   c From this survey, who looked after their teeth better, boys or girls ?

   d Why do you think the fillings rose dramatically in January ?

2. The comparative line graph shows two offices' heating bills over several months.

   - *Paper Co.* in red
   - *Cog Wheel Co.* **in black.**

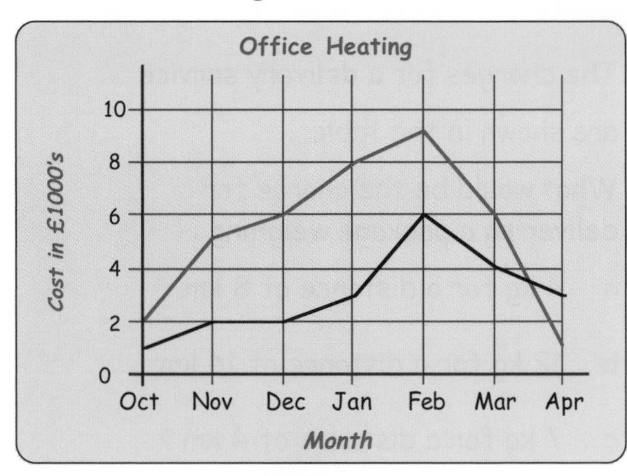

   a How much did Paper Co. pay in :-

      (i) November

      (ii) February ?

   b How much more did the *Paper Co.* pay in February than *Cog Wheel Co.* ?

   c If both offices operated at roughly the same temperature throughout this period, which company would you say had the better heating system ?

3. Some pupils were asked what their favourite school holiday was.

The results are shown in the pie chart.

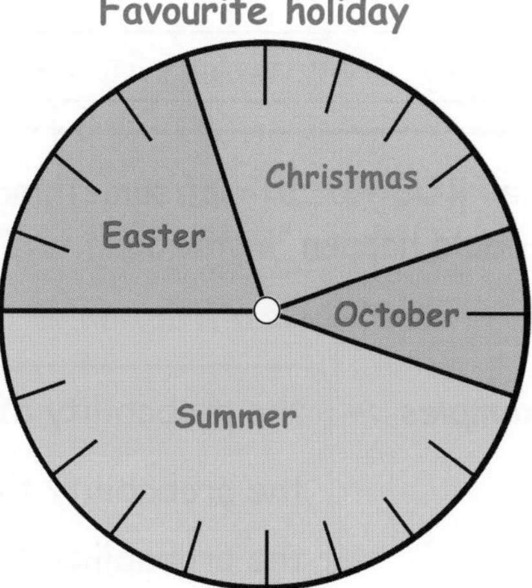

a List the holidays in order, starting with the favourite.

b What fraction of the pupils chose Christmas ?

c There were 800 pupils in the school.
How many pupils chose :-

(i) October (ii) Summer ?

4. The stem and leaf diagram shows the weights of pumpkins for sale in a supermarket one Halloween.

Weight (kg)

Stem	Leaf
0	9
1	4 7
2	2 2 5 6 8
3	0 1 6 9
4	0 1 2 3 5 6
5	1

Key :- 1 | 4 = 1·4 kg

a How many pumpkins weighed :-

(i) 3·6 kg (ii) 2·2 kg (iii) 4·4 kg ?

b List the pumpkins that weighed between 2·7 kg and 3·3 kg.

c How many pumpkins were on sale ?

5. A scattergraph is to be constructed using the sales of hot soup at football matches and the temperature in each stadium.

Write a short sentence explaining what connection you would expect to see in the scattergraph.

6. Three banks show their yearly interest rates charged for loans.

a Write down which bank each person should look to for a loan :-

(i) Rab needs £350

(ii) Beth needs £500

(iii) Ed needs £8000.

	ABB	RSB	CRB
less than £500	10·1%	10·3%	10·2%
between £500 & £5000	9·7%	9·5%	9·8%
more than £5000	7·0%	7·6%	7·5%

b Explain why you have chosen these banks.

Probability

Probability - what does it mean ?

The **PROBABILITY** of something happening simply means the **FRACTION** of times it would happen "**in the long run**".

Probability is a fraction or decimal and can only take values from 0 to 1.

Examples :-

- the probability of scoring a 1, 2, 3, 4, 5 or 6 on a dice is 1 (*certain*)
- the probability the next person you meet will be a female is $\frac{1}{2}$, (0·5)
- the probability the sun **won't** rise tomorrow is 0. (*impossible*)

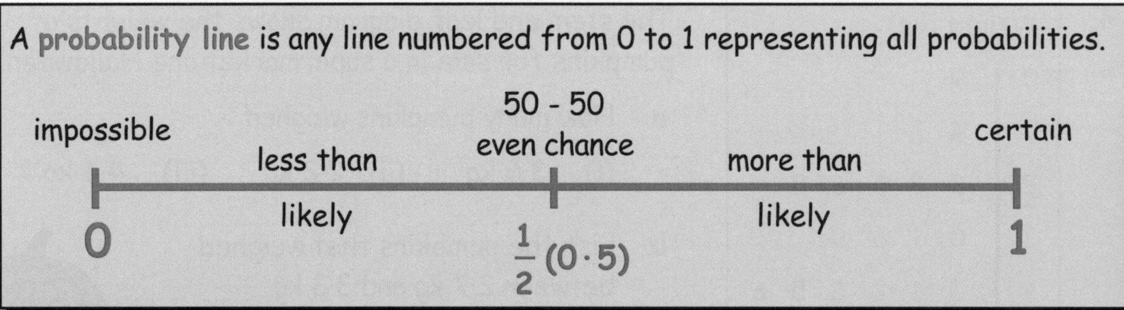

Introductory Exercise (*To be done orally*).

1. For each of these statements, say whether the probability of it happening is :-

impossible - less than likely - evens - more than likely - certain.

a Toss a coin and it lands showing a tail.

b Fall out of a two storey window and **not** hurt yourself.

c Switch the kettle on and the water will boil in under 10 minutes.

d It will rain **every** day in March.

e If I put my bare hand in a fire, I will burn myself.

f If I choose a card from a pack, it will be a spade.

g If I choose a month at random it will be one containing 3 or more letters.

h The first person I meet when leaving a shop will be over 10 years old.

i After baking a cake, my mum will unbake it.

j If I throw a tennis ball straight up in the air, it will come back down to earth.

k If I choose a number from 1 to 10 at random, it will be an odd number.

Probability - Some Calculations

The **PROBABILITY** of something happening can be thought of as a simple fraction.

$$\text{Probability of event happening} = \frac{\text{number of favourable ways}}{\text{number of possible ways}}$$

***Example* :-** This bag contains six £1 coins and four 1p coins.

If a coin is chosen at random, what is the probability that it will be a £1 coin ?

***Solution* :-** Look at this simple notation :-

$$\text{P(£1 coin)*} = \frac{6\ \text{(£1 coins)}}{10\ \text{(total coins)}} = \frac{6\ \div 2}{10\ \div 2} = \frac{3}{5} = 0{\cdot}6$$

**note :-* P(£1 coin) is shorthand for "the probability of choosing a £1 coin".

Exercise 1

1. The arrow of a 7 sided spinner is spun and the colour noted.

   Calculate, as a fraction, the probability it will point to :-

   a a yellow segment, P(yellow).

   b a red segment, P(red).

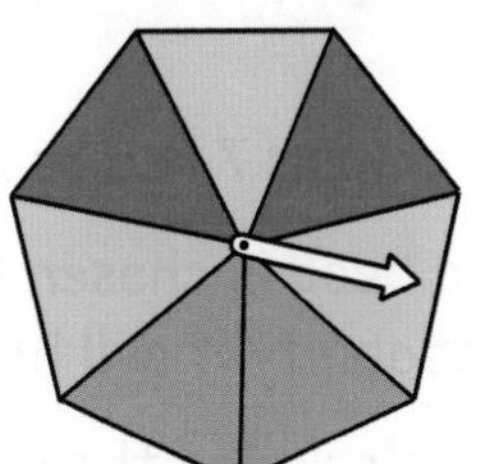

2. An octagonal dice is rolled and the number on top is noted.

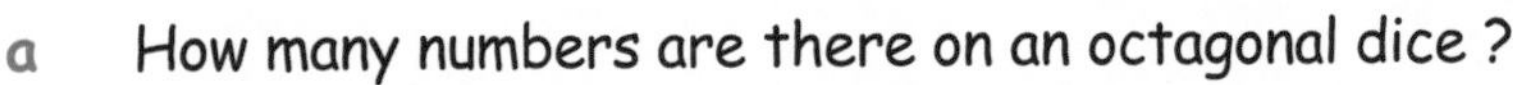

   a How many numbers are there on an octagonal dice ?

   b What is the probability it will show a two ? P(2) = ...

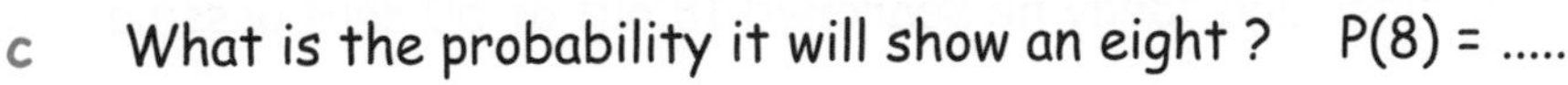

   c What is the probability it will show an eight ? P(8) = ...

   d What is the probability it will show an odd number ? P(odd) = ...

   e What is the probability it will show a number bigger than 3 ? P(> 3) = ...

3. The Ace (*low*) to the King of Hearts are shuffled and a card chosen at random.

   a How many Hearts are there in a pack of cards ?

   b What is the probability the card is red ? P(Red).

   c What is the probability the card is the 9 of Hearts ? P(9).

   d What is the probability the card is a face card ? P(Face).

   e What is the probability the card is a number from 3 to 7 ? P(3 to 7).

   f What is the probability the card is the 5 of Clubs ? P(Club 5).

4. A driver notes the times a set of traffic lights is at red, green, etc., and in a full "cycle" the times are as follows :-

red - 15 seconds	red/amber - 10 seconds
green - 20 seconds	amber - 5 seconds

A motorist drives up to the set of lights. What is the probability the lights will show :-

a red b green c amber or red/amber ?

(*Try to simplify your fractions as far as possible*).

5. At the fairground, one of the stalls contains the 4 by 4 grid shown opposite. People pay 20p and throw a counter onto the grid to try to win a prize.

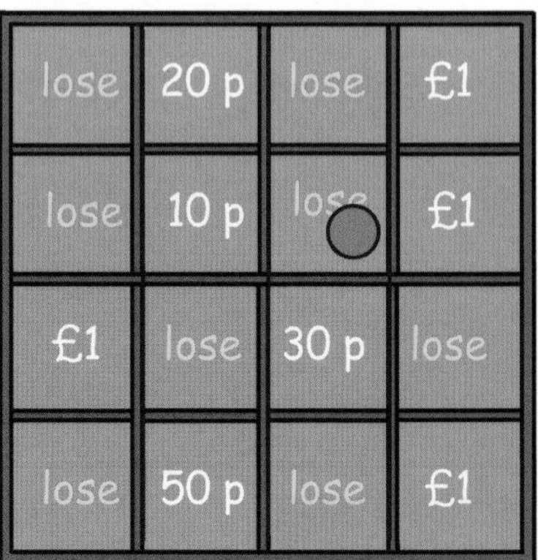

Assuming your counter actually lands on a square on the board, what is the probability :-

a you lose b you win a prize

c you win a 50p d you win £1

e you end up with less than your initial stake ?

6. Bag A contains 7 red beads and 3 blue beads and a bag B holds 6 red beads and 2 blue ones.

a If a bead is chosen from bag A without looking, what is the probability it will be red ? (*Give your answer as a decimal*).

b By calculating the probability of choosing a red bead from bag B, and expressing it also as a decimal, say which of the two bags gives a better chance of choosing red.

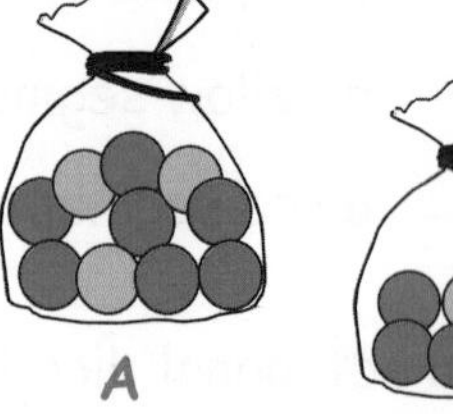

7. Mr White is a customs officer and today he searched 15 out of 40 cars passing him.

Mr Hay is also a customs officer and today he searched 18 out of 50 cars passing him.

By calculating the probability Mr White searches a car and the probability Mr Hay searches a car, decide which officer is less likely to check your car.

8. Which of these dartboards gives you the best chance of winning if you land on the board ?

Show all your working.

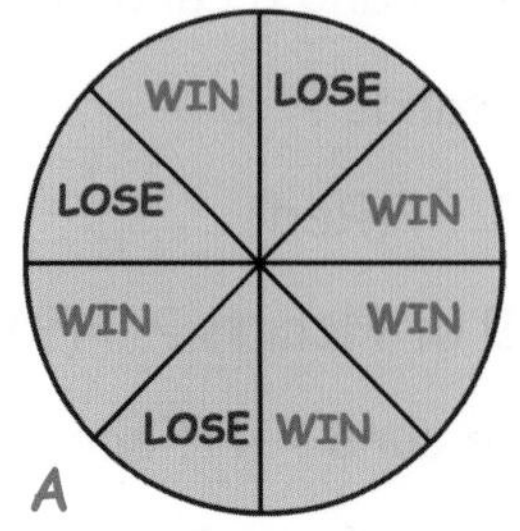

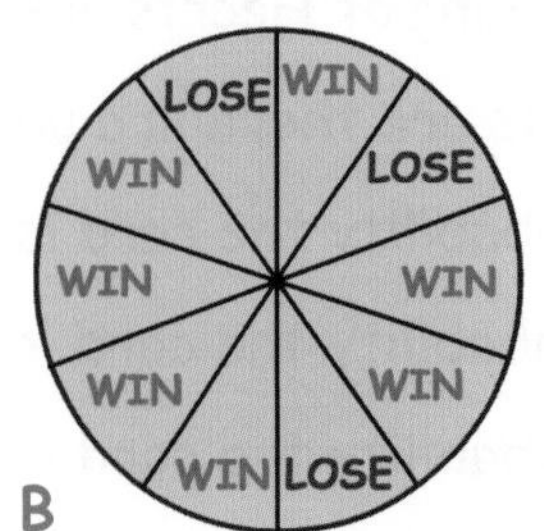

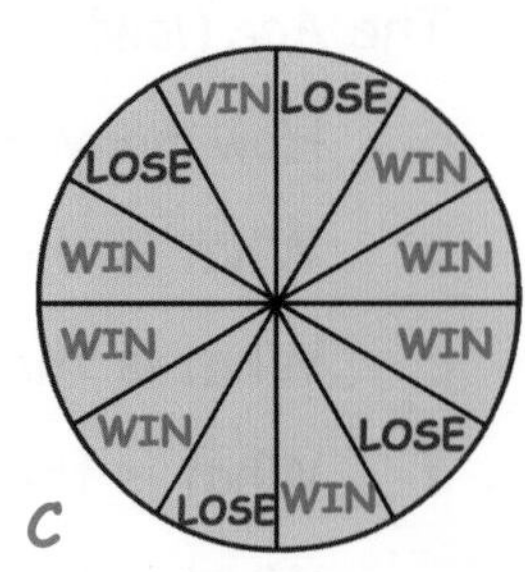

9. The probability of something happening is 0·6. What is the probability it will **not** happen ?

Probability

Numeracy Assessment 12

1. Shown is a "Probability Line".

impossible | highly unlikely | poorer than evens | 50–50 evens | better than evens | extremely likely | certain

For each of the following, decide what the best choice of probability is :-

A - If I flip a coin, it will land showing a "head".

B - If I enter a lift on the 18th floor heading for the ground floor, someone else will enter the lift before we reach the bottom.

C - I will meet someone today over 3 metres tall (*9 ft 10 inches*).

D - I will win the lottery this week.

E - In a swimming pool containing 23 boys and 18 girls, the next child to climb out of the pool will be a girl.

2. Identical cards, numbered 1 to 15, are turned upside down and shuffled.

If I pick one at random, what is the probability it will :-

a be the 10 b be an odd number

c not be the 12 d be a number bigger than 9

e be the number 0 f be a number smaller than 20 ?

3. A group of people were asked what their favourite meal was.

4 chose breakfast	6 chose lunch
12 chose dinner	2 chose supper.

If I pick one person at random, what is the probability the person :-

a chose breakfast b chose lunch or dinner c did not choose supper ?

4. A box contains 9 silver coins and 6 copper ones.

A jar contains 10 silver coins and 8 copper ones

A tin contains 9 copper coins and 12 silver ones.

If I can choose to pick a coin from any one of the above, which gives me the best chance of choosing a silver coin ? (*Explain why you made your decision*).

Unit Assessment
Numeracy

Assessment Tasks

1. I bought a guitar in 2010 for £320.

   I sold it in 2014 for 25% less than this.

   How much did I sell the guitar for ? (2)

2. 

   Mr Jenkins owns a tyre store.

   The tyres cost him £48·75 each.

   How many tyres can he buy if he has £1000 ? (2)

3. Copy and complete the bus timetable shown. (2)

Bus	Depart	Arrive	Journey Time
Ayr to Dundee	1800	....	2 hrs 20 mins
Skye to Aberdeen	....	1130	4 hrs 50 mins

4. Max drives from London to Glasgow, a distance of 420 miles.

   If his average speed is 60 miles per hour, how long will his journey take if he makes no stops ? (2)

5. 

   A chemical freezer unit was switched on at noon.

   The temperature in the unit was 8°C.

   By midnight the unit measured –47°C.

   By how many degrees had the temperature fallen ? (1)

6. a A factory makes a *Sunrise Cocktail* and uses orange and pineapple juice in a ratio of 5 : 3.

   If the factory has 850 litres of orange, how many litres of pineapple will it need ? (2)

   b The factory has orders for 1500 litres of *Sunrise Cocktail*.

   Does the factory have enough cocktail to fulfil this order ?

   Give a reason for your answer. (2)

7. A trapezium shaped piece of stainless steel is shown.

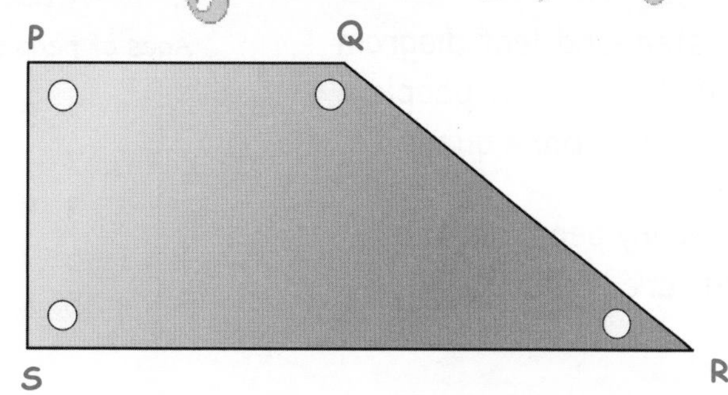

   a Measure the length of the sloping edge QR. (1)

   b Measure the size of the angle at R. (1)

8. A space between two walls measures 5·5 metres.

   Alice would like to fill this space with **eight** bookcases, each 70 cm wide, side by side.

   Can she do this ? *Give a reason for your answer.* (2)

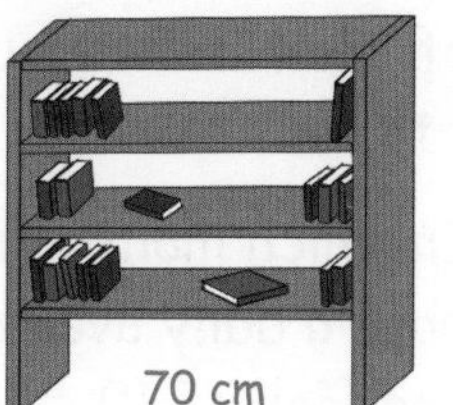

9. Ed pours some water into a marked beaker.

   He needs to have 2·5 litres altogether.

   How much more water must he add to the beaker ? (2)

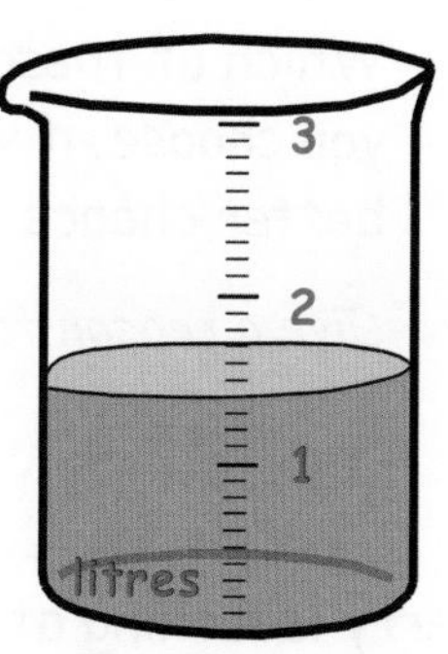

10. Miss Honey takes the train to work and back, Monday to Friday.

    A single fare costs £4·70.

    She can buy a 4-week SuperSaver ticket for £160.

    Would Miss Honey save money if she bought the SuperSaver instead of a single ticket ? *Give a reason for your answer.* (2)

11. 

    Over the next 75 days, Sally promises herself that she will try to walk her dog on at least 40 of those days.

    Sally manages to walk her dog on $\frac{3}{5}$ of the 75 days.

    Did Sally keep her promise ?

    Give a reason for your answer. (2)

12. There are 20 black balls, 12 white balls, 11 red balls and 6 blue balls in a bag.

    Andi says that the probability of picking, at random, a blue ball is $\frac{3}{25}$.

    Is Andi correct ? *Give a reason for your answer.* (2)

13. The stem-and-leaf diagram shows the ages of people waiting in a bank queue.

How many people in the queue are under 35 ?

Ages of people in a queue

1	1 3 5
2	0 7
3	3 3 9 9
4	1 6 7 8
5	4 5 8 8 8 9

Key :- 3 | 1 represent 31 years old

n = 19

(1)

14. A bar chart shows the average fall of snow in two winter resorts.

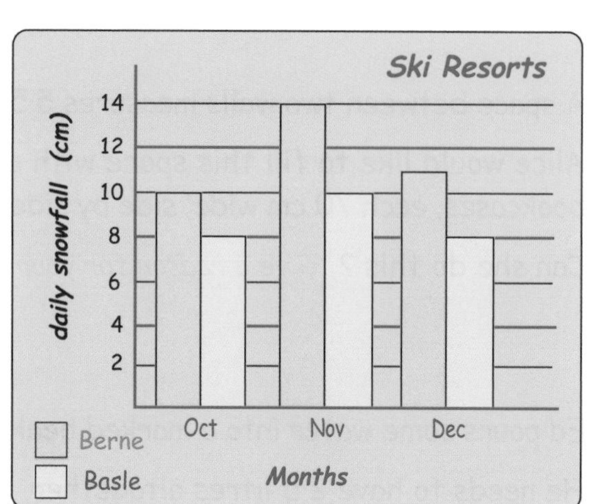

a In which month did Basle have a daily average snowfall of 10 cm ? (1)

b Which of these resorts would you choose, if you wanted a better chance of getting snow ?

Give a reason for your decision. (1)

15. Jerry is looking at three broadband packages.

Package	A	B	C
Connection (Mb)	20	15	25
Usage (Gb)	unlimited	9	12
Monthly cost	£15	£8	£10

a Which package has the cheapest offer ? (1)

b Jerry needs at least 10 Gb usage, and can't afford to pay any more than £12.

He chooses package B.

Did he choose correctly ?

Give a reason for your answer. (1)

16.

Ali buys 7 raffle tickets from a church raffle of 100 tickets.

Fizz buys 13 raffle tickets from a school raffle of 150 tickets.

Who has the better chance of winning ?

Give a reason for your answer. (2)

Gradients

Gradients

We can measure how steep a hill or road is, or how steeply a ladder is resting against a wall.

This is called the **slope** or the **GRADIENT** of the hill or ladder.

A gradient is usually written as a fraction.
(*It can be given as a decimal or as a percentage*).

Uphill Road has a **gradient** of 1 in 5.

This is written as :- **gradient** $= \frac{1}{5}$

This means that for every 5 metres moved across (horizontally), the road rises by 1 metre up the way (vertically).

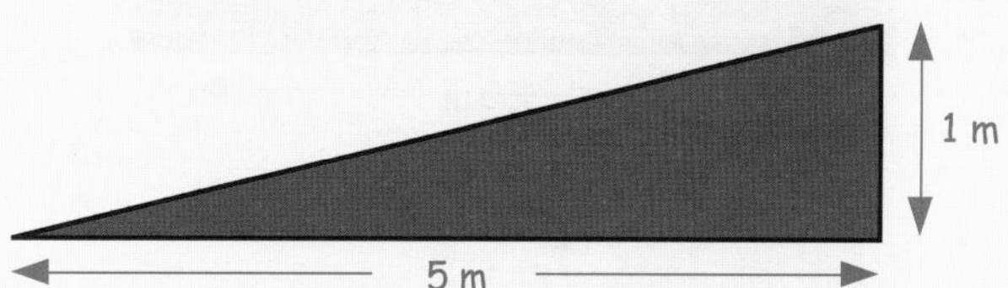

How to Calculate the Gradient of a Hill.

Example :- Ross Avenue rises by 3 metres.
It is 60 metres (horizontally) from the top end to the bottom.

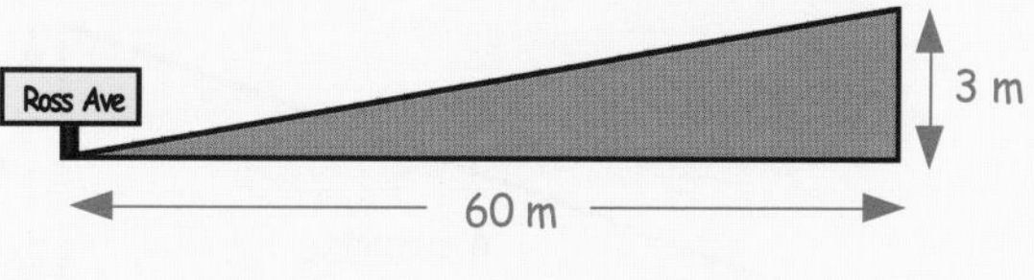

Gradient = 3 metres in 60 metres

$= \frac{3}{60}\begin{smallmatrix}\div 3\\ \div 3\end{smallmatrix} = \frac{1}{20}.$

[Can you see that $\frac{1}{20}$ is **smaller** than $\frac{1}{5}$?]

—> this means that Ross Avenue is **less** steep than Uphill Road.

Definition :- **Gradient** $= \dfrac{\text{vertical distance}}{\text{horizontal distance}}$

Exercise 1

1. Look at this picture of Moss Street.

   a Calculate the **gradient** like this :-

   Copy :-

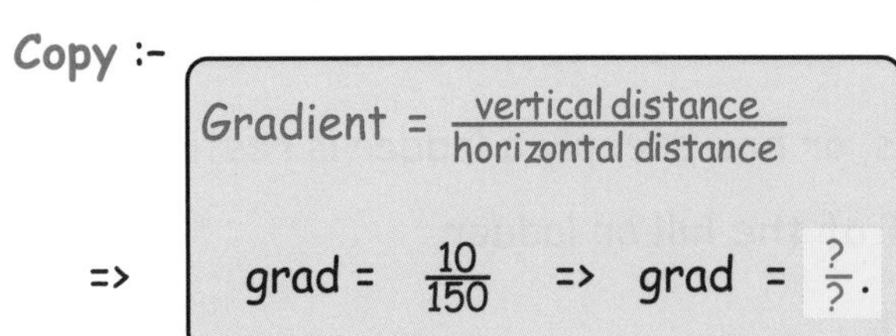

$$\text{Gradient} = \frac{\text{vertical distance}}{\text{horizontal distance}}$$

=> $\text{grad} = \frac{10}{150}$ => $\text{grad} = \frac{?}{?}$. (*simplify the fraction* $\frac{10}{150}$)

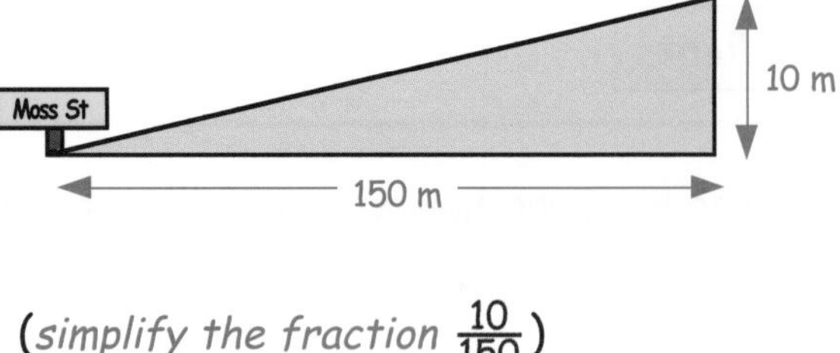

   b Compare the gradient of Moss Street with that of Uphill Road and Ross Avenue (*from the previous page*).

   Which stretch of road is :- (i) steepest (ii) the least steep ?

2. 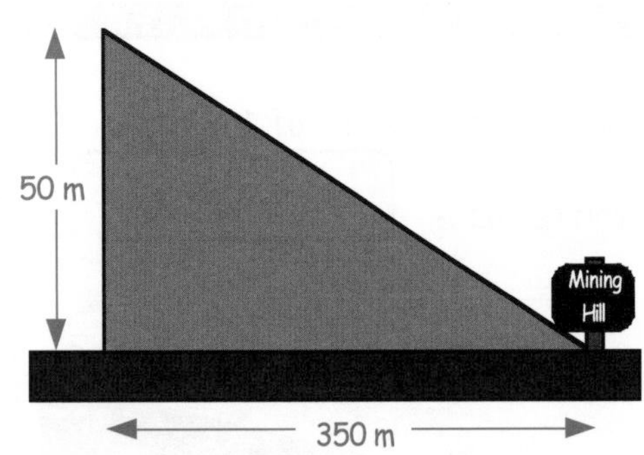

   Look at the sketch of Mining Hill.

   Calculate the **gradient** of the hill.

   Copy :-

$$\text{Gradient} = \frac{\text{vertical distance}}{\text{horizontal distance}}$$

=> $\text{grad} = \frac{50}{....} = \frac{?}{?}$.

(*Simplify the fraction*).

3. Shown below are two small hills.

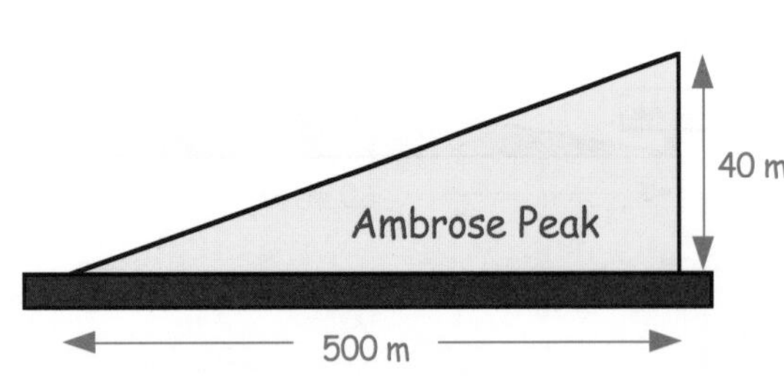

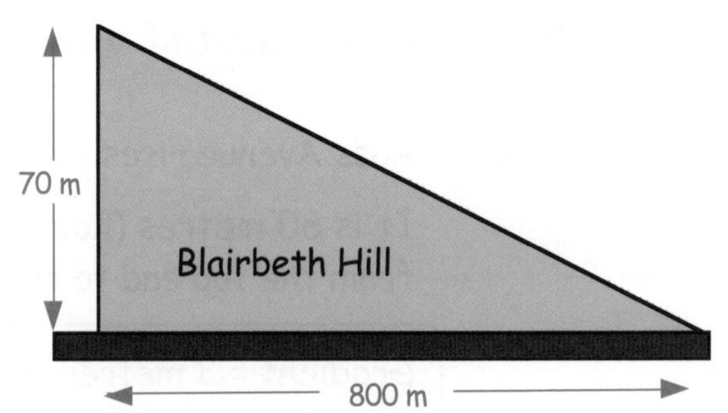

   Here is how we can find which one is steeper :-

   Copy and **complete** :-

   a Ambrose Peak – $\text{Gradient} = \frac{\text{vert}}{\text{horiz}} = \frac{40}{500} = \frac{?}{?}$.

   b The gradient of Blairbeth Hill can be found in the same way.

$$\text{Gradient} = \frac{\text{vert}}{\text{horiz}} = \frac{70}{800} = \frac{?}{?}.$$

3\. c It is **not** very easy to look at the two fractions and say which one is bigger.

To do this you :- **CHANGE THE FRACTIONS —> DECIMALS**

(i) Ambrose – Gradient = $\frac{40}{500}$ = 40 ÷ 500 = 0·08

(ii) Blairbeth – Gradient = $\frac{70}{800}$ = 70 ÷ .... = 0· . . .

(iii) Which is the bigger ? (*i.e. which hill is steeper ?*)

4\. Shown below are the side views of 4 hilly roads.

(i) Write down the gradient of each hill (*as a fraction*).

(ii) Change each fraction to a decimal (*see question 3c*).

(iii) Write the 4 hills in order, steepest first.

Copy and complete :- Love Street —> Grad = $\frac{\text{vert}}{\text{horiz}}$ = $\frac{5}{100}$ = (5 ÷ 100) = 0· . . .

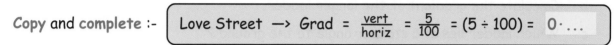

a

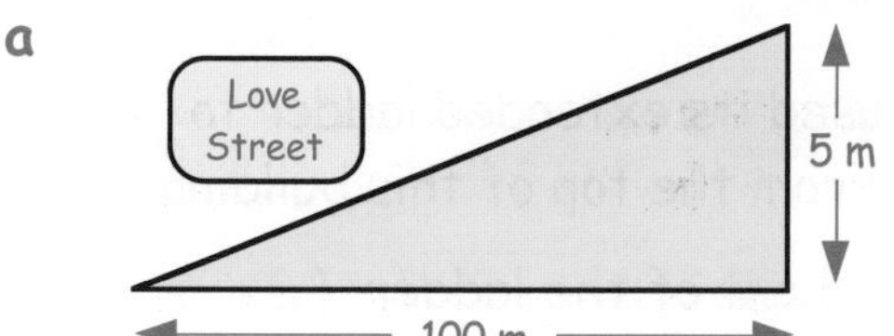

b

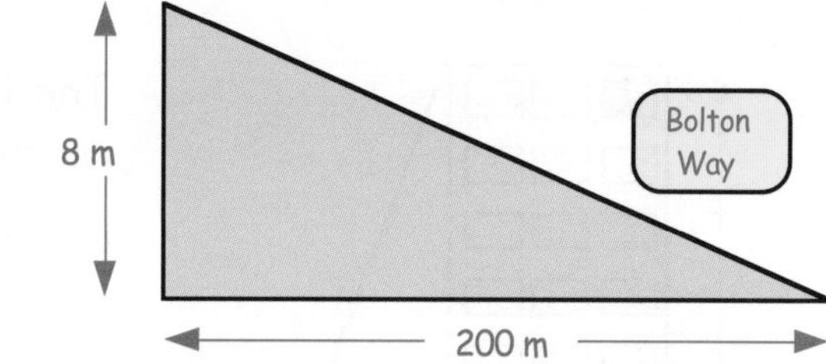

c

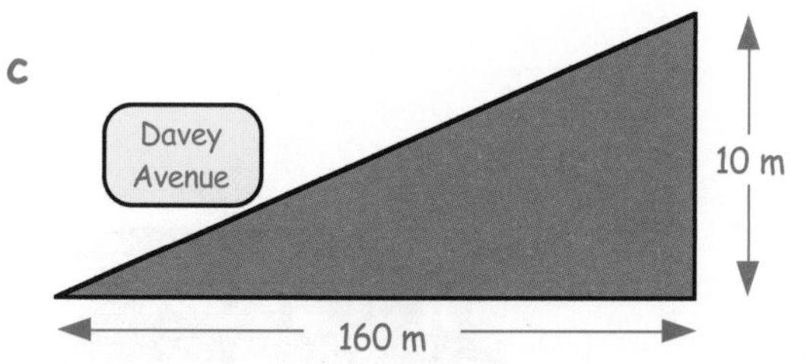

d

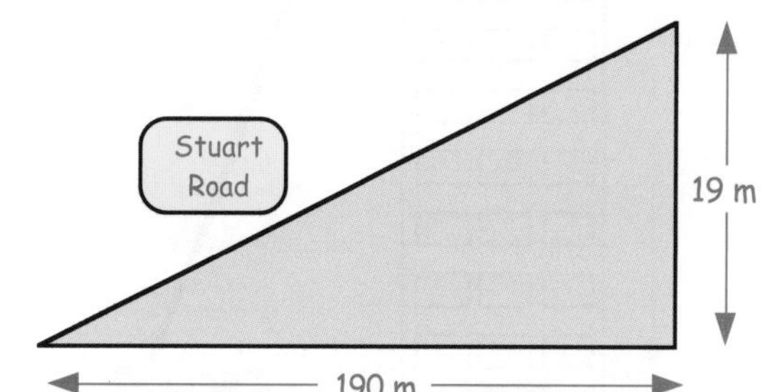

5\. This picture shows a ladder placed against a wall.

You can measure how steep the ladder is (the gradient) in the same way you worked out the gradient of the hills and roads.

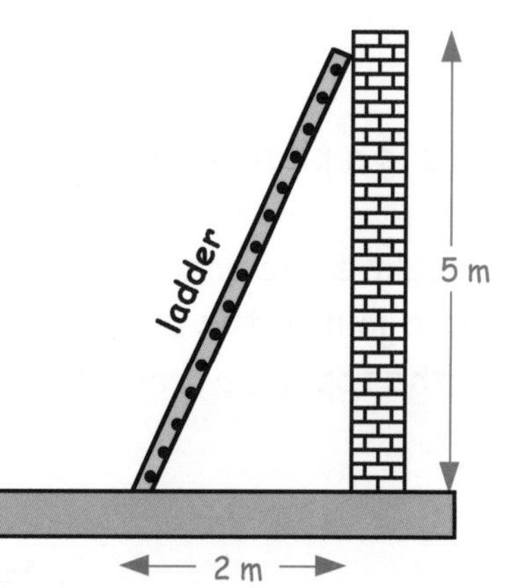

Copy :- Gradient = $\frac{\text{vert}}{\text{horiz}}$

=> Grad = $\frac{5}{2}$ = (5 ÷ 2) = 2· . . . .

This is a much bigger gradient (2 · . . .) than any of the roads measured in Question 4.

This means the ladder is resting **quite steeply** against the wall.

6. A window cleaner uses two ladders in his job.

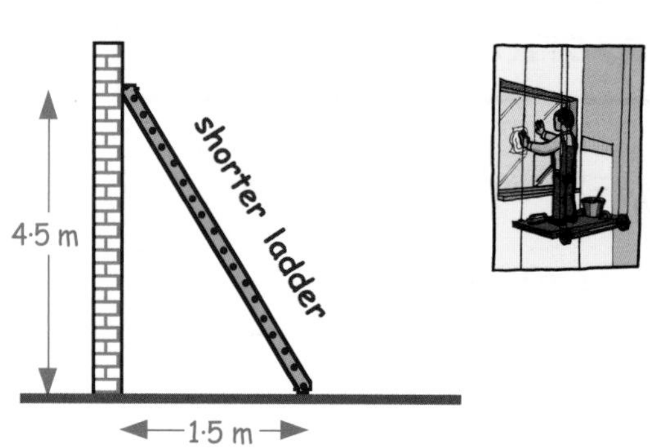

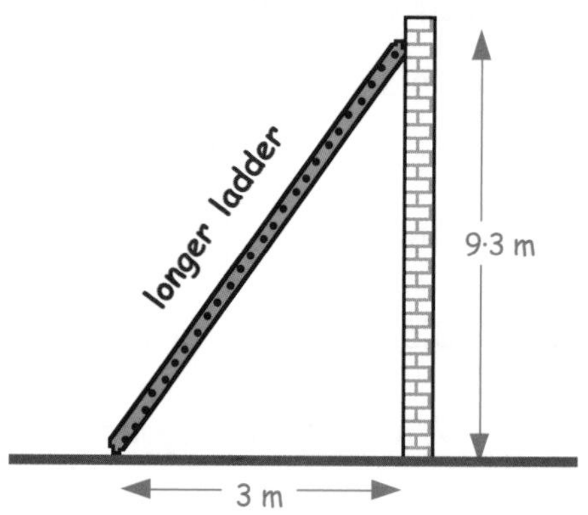

a Calculate the **gradient** of the shorter ladder.

$$\text{Grad} = \frac{\text{vert}}{\text{horiz}} = \frac{4 \cdot 5}{\dots} = \frac{?}{?}.$$

b Calculate the **gradient** of the longer ladder.

c Which ladder lies at a steeper angle to the ground ?

7. The fire engine used its extended ladder to rescue someone from the top of this building.

Calculate the **gradient** of the ladder, (*as a decimal*).

22 m

5 m

Fire Dept.

8. This is a picture of a cable car on Ben Mural Mountain.

Calculate the **gradient** of the cable joining the base point to the top, (*as a decimal*).

Top

cable car

cable

495 ft

Base Point

1650 ft

9. Calculate the gradient of this ski jump.

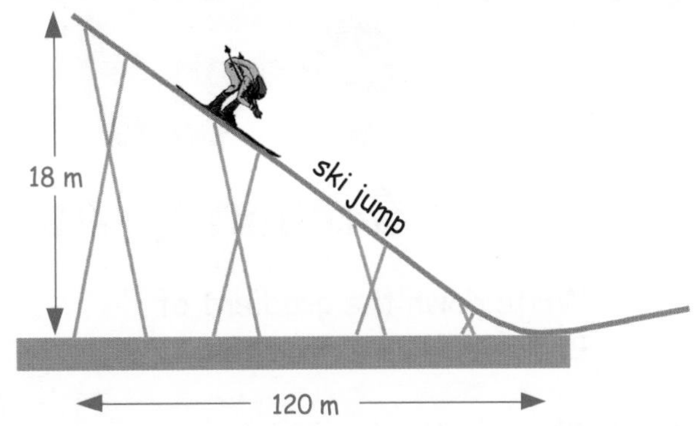

10. The steeper the slope – the faster a marble will run down it.

Calculate the gradient of each of the following slopes and say which is steepest and which is shallowest. (*Justify your answer showing your calculations*).

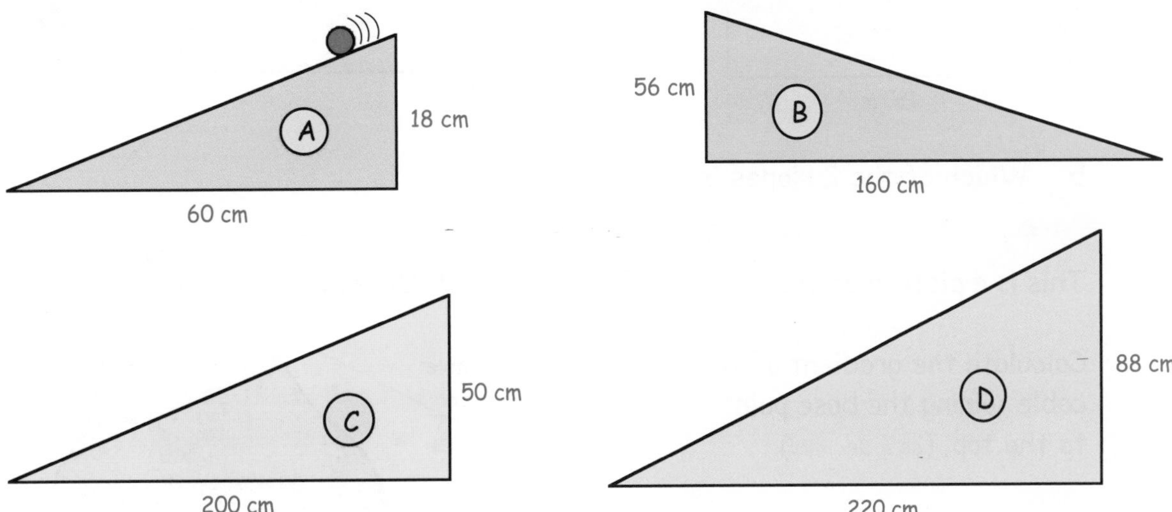

11. A hill runs up from a main road to the house at the top.

Use the information given in the picture to calculate the gradient of the hill.

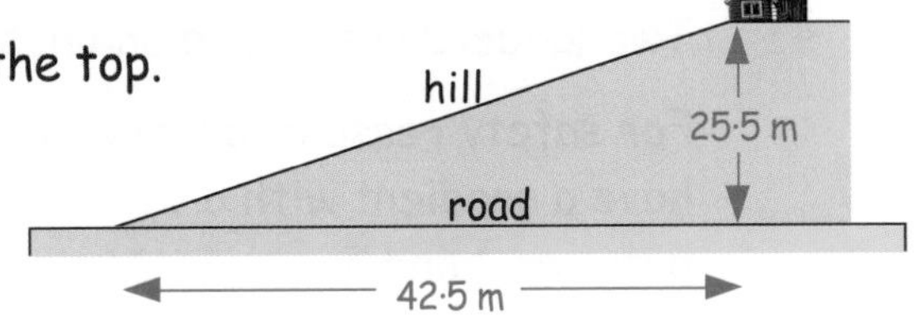

12.

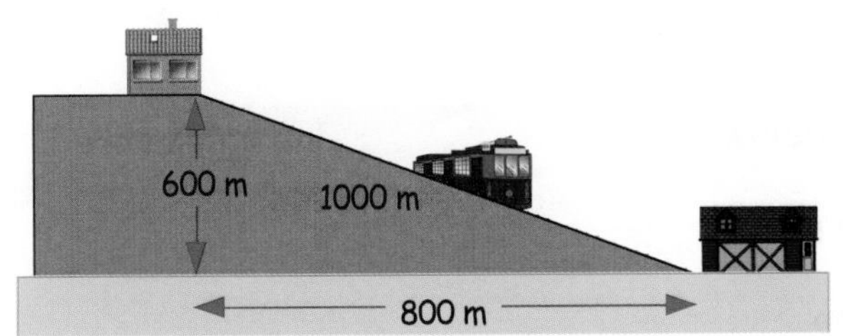

A funicular railway is 1000 metres long and the difference between the height from the top to the bottom is 600 metres.

The horizontal distance shown is 800 metres.

Find the gradient of the railway line.

Gradients

Geometry Assessment 1

1. a Write down the gradient of Brown Hill as a fraction.

   b Simplify the fraction.

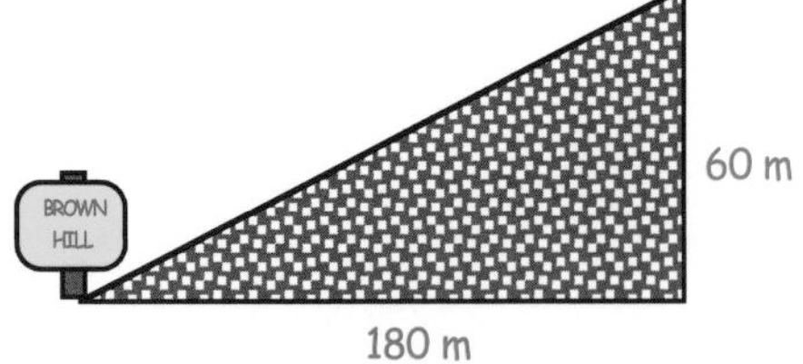

2. a Calculate the fractional gradients of Plum Brae and Mount View.

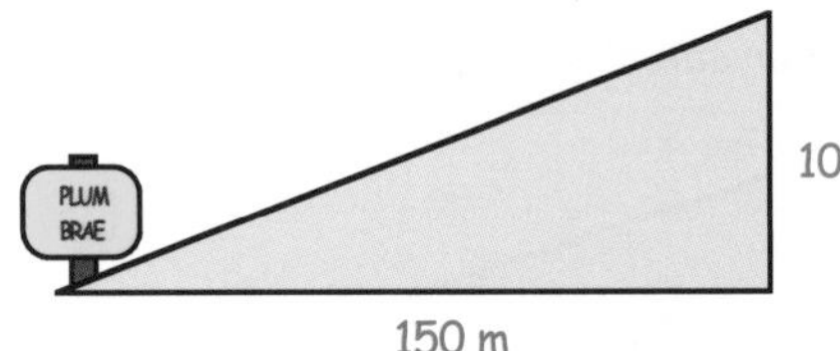

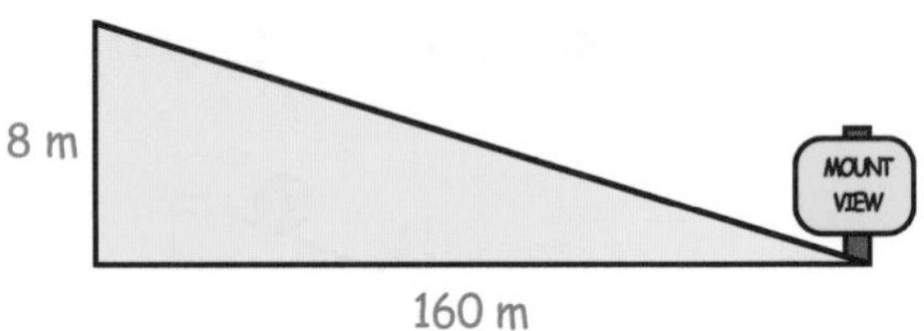

   b Which of the 2 slopes is **steeper** ?

3. This is a picture of the cable car on Ben Carrick Mountain.

   Calculate the gradient of the cable joining the base point to the top, (*as a decimal*).

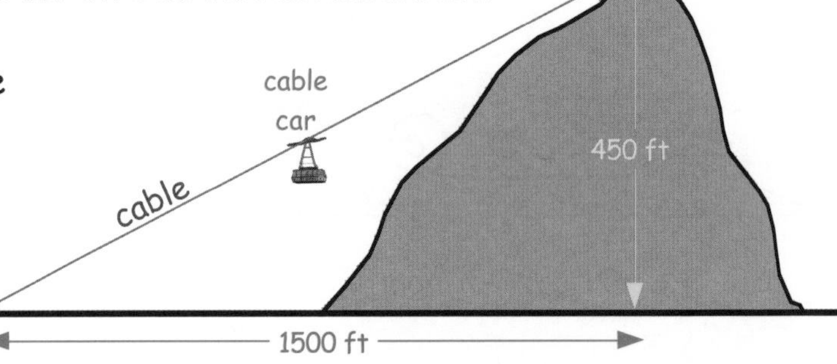

4. Two ladders are placed against a wall as shown.

   For safety reasons, a ladder must have a gradient with a value between **4** and **5**.

   Which of the ladders shown is/are safe ?

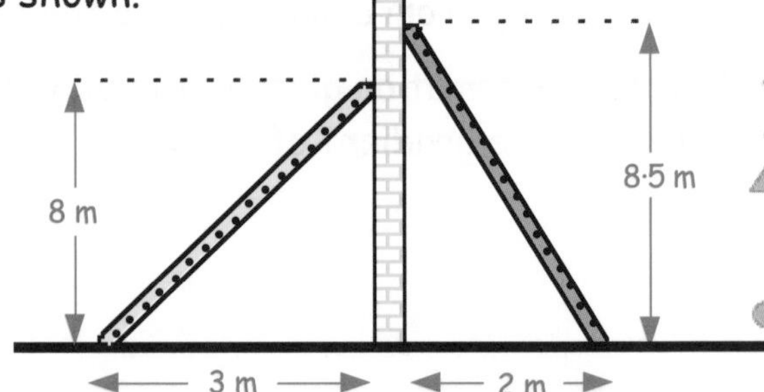

5. The gradients of four ramps are given below :-

car ramp	20%,	ski jump ramp	$\frac{3}{20}$,
skateboard ramp	0·175,	bike ramp	$\frac{1}{8}$.

   List the ramps in order, **steepest** first.

Perimeters

Perimeter of Rectilinear Shapes

The perimeter of a shape is simply :-

"the total distance around its outside".

This simply means you add all the outside lengths together.

Perimeter = (2·4 + 12·5 + 8·3 + 6·2) cm
= 29 · 4 cm

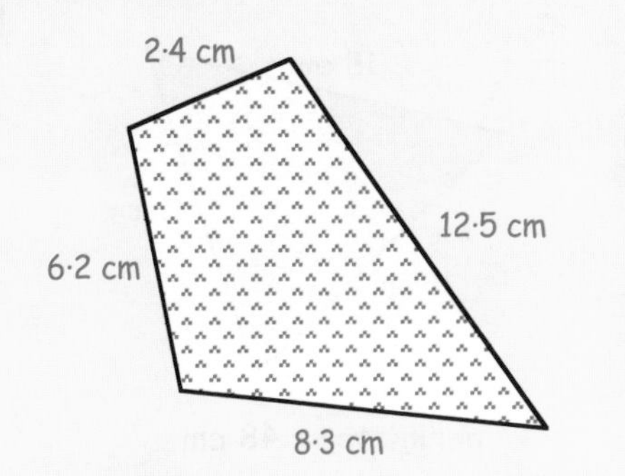

Exercise 1

1. Calculate the perimeter of this triangle.
(*Show your working*).

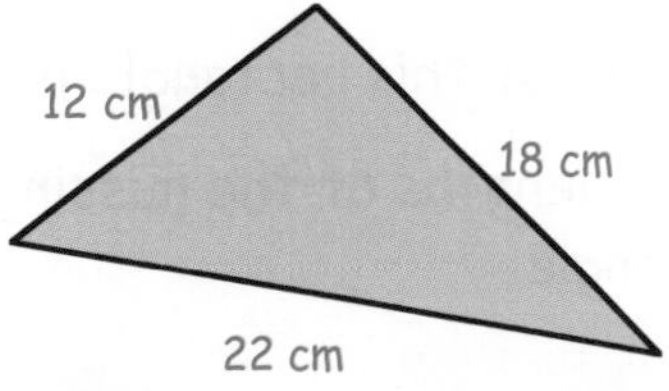

2. Calculate the perimeter of each of the following shapes :-

a
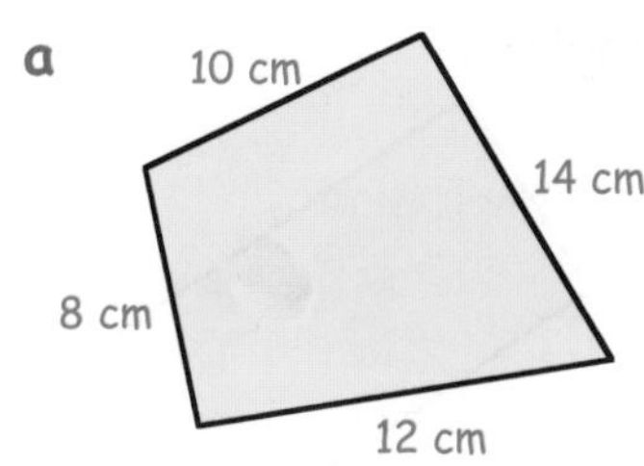

b
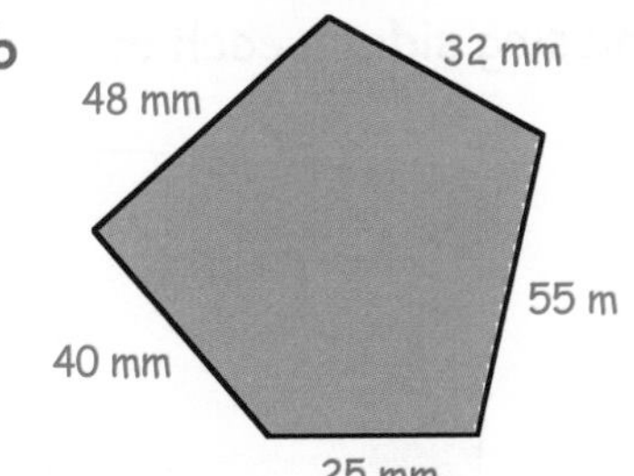

c
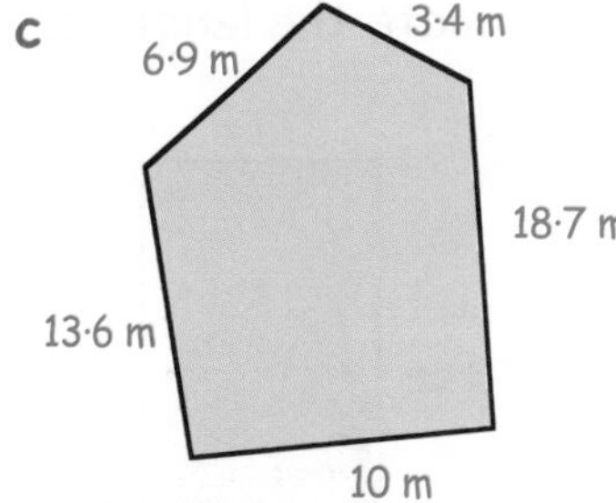

3. Calculate the perimeter of this rectangle.
(*it is not 10·6 cm + 4·4 cm !*)

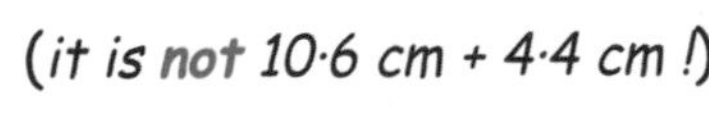

4. Calculate the perimeter of each of these rectangles :-

a
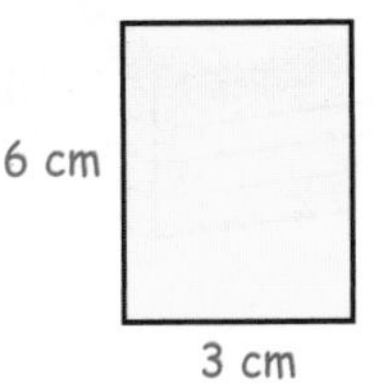

b

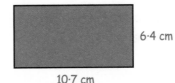

c
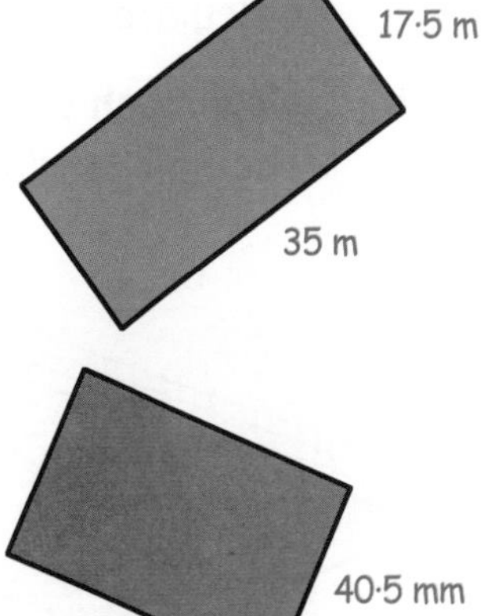

d
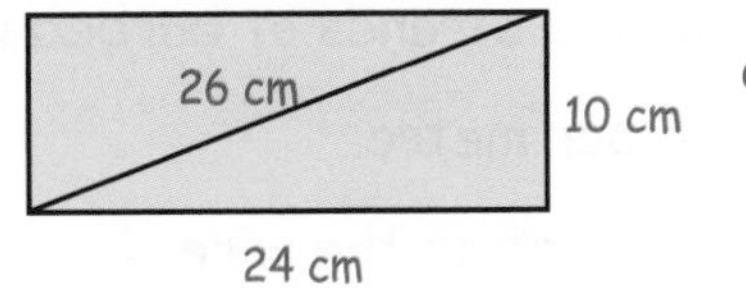

e
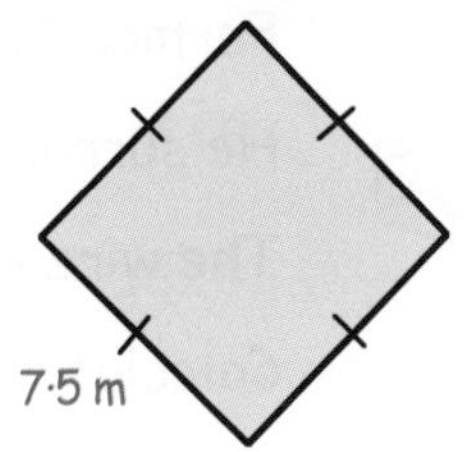

f

5. This triangle has a **perimeter** of 220 millimetres.

Calculate the length of the third side.

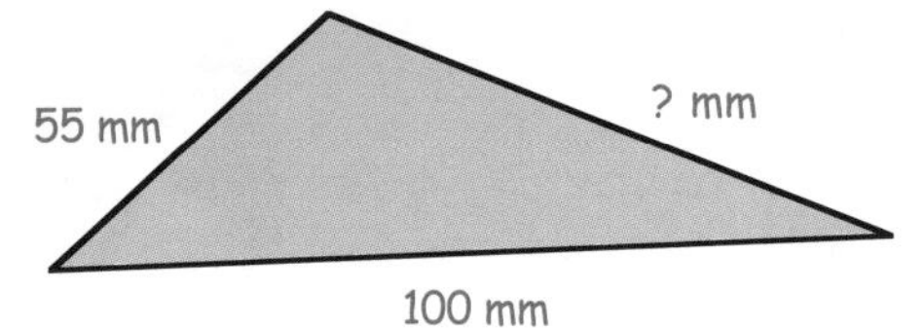

6. Calculate the lengths of the missing sides in the following figures :-

a

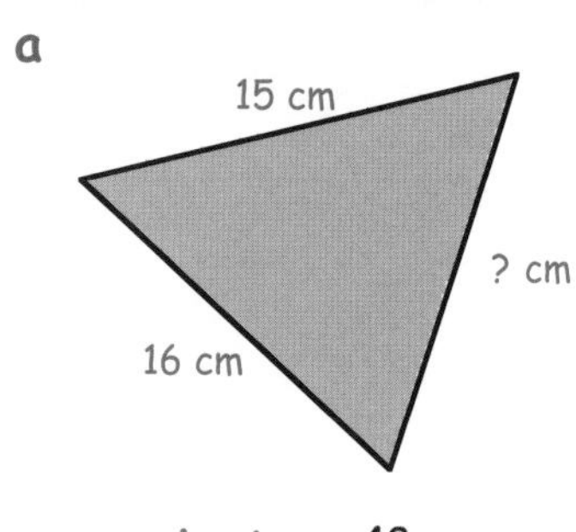

perimeter = 48 cm

b

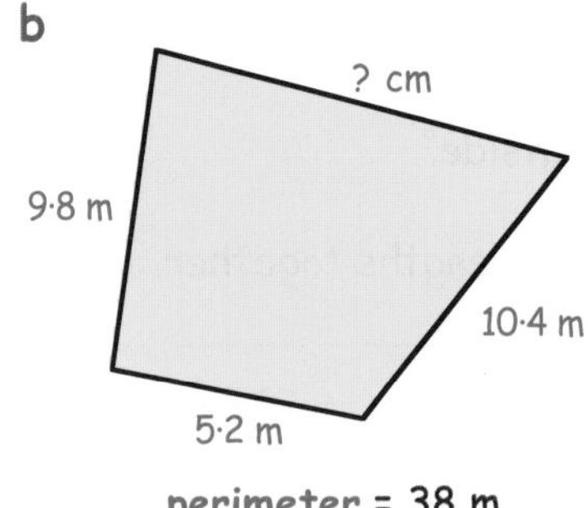

perimeter = 38 m

c

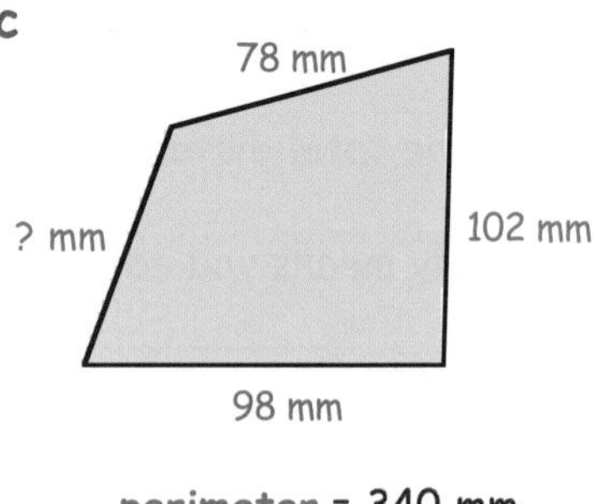

perimeter = 340 mm

7. The **perimeter** of this rectangle is 78 cm.

Calculate the lengths of the missing side of the rectangle.

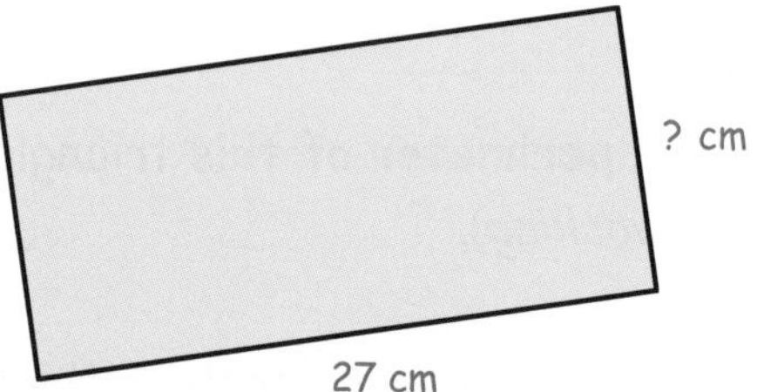

8. Calculate the length of the missing side in each of these rectangles :-

a

? cm

30 cm

perimeter = 88 cm

b

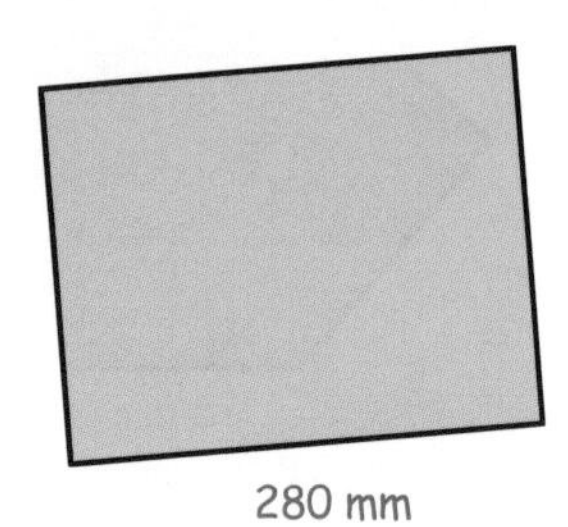

perimeter = 1000 mm

c

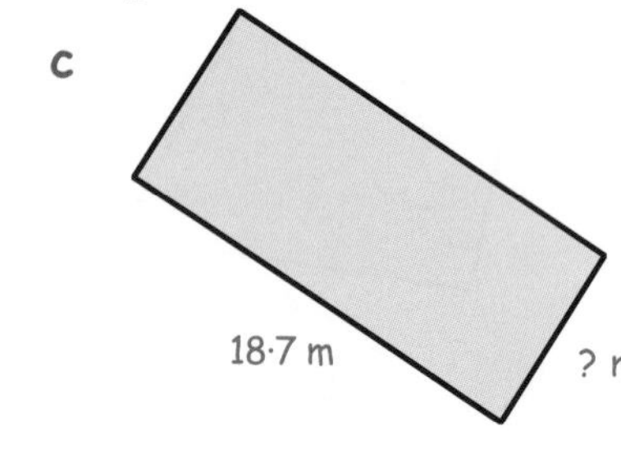

perimeter = 48 m

9. As a Christmas decoration, Mr Perry put strips of holly around his shed roof.

   a Calculate the **perimeter** of the roof.

   b How much will it cost to do this, if the holly strip costs 75p per metre.

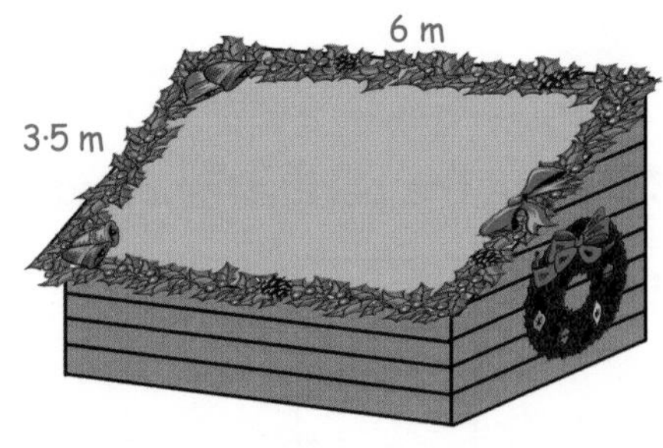

10. Farmer Jones owns a rectangular field.

He surrounds it with 3 strands of barbed wire.

The wire costs £6 per metre.

Calculate the total cost of the wire.

45 m

60 m

The Parts of a Circle

The curved distance around the edge of a circle is called the circumference (C) of the circle.

The line joining two points on the circumference passing through the centre is the diameter.

The shorter line joining the centre of the circle to the circumference is the radius.

The **diameter** is always twice the **radius**.

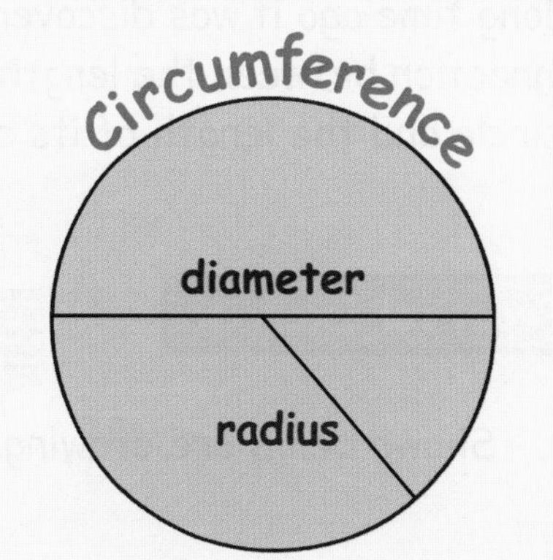

Exercise 2

(*You will need a **ruler** and a pair of **compasses** here*).

1. a Use a pair of compasses to draw a circle with a radius of 5 centimetres.
   b Draw in a diameter and label it diameter.
   c Draw in any radius and label it radius.
   d Label the circumference of your circle.

2. For each of these circles, say whether the dotted line is a radius or a diameter :-

   a 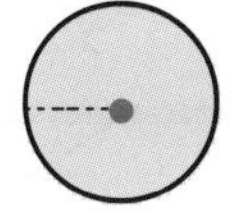 b 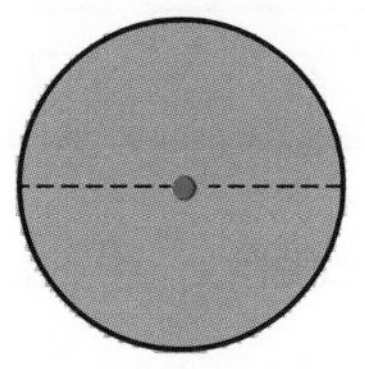 c 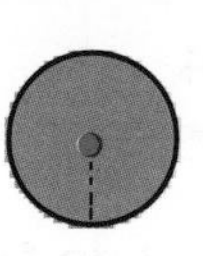 d 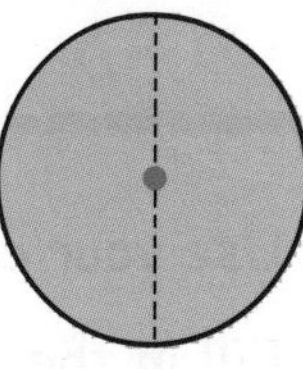

3. a Use two letters to name the line which is a diameter in this circle.
   b Name 3 radii (*plural of radius*) in the figure.

4. a Draw a circle with a radius of 6 centimetres. Put a point (O) at its centre.
   b Draw a radius OP on your circle and label the point P.
   c Draw any diameter QR on your circle and label the points Q and R.
   d Measure the length of QR and compare it with the length of radius OP.

5. a If the radius of a circle is 8 centimetres, what is the length of its diameter ?
   b If the diameter of a circle is 14 centimetres, what is the length of its radius ?
   c If the diameter of a circle is 47 centimetres, what is its radius ?
   d If the radius of a circle is 5·1 centimetres, what length is its diameter ?

The Perimeter of a Circle (Circumference (*C*))

A long time ago it was discovered that there was a connection between the length of the **diameter** of a circle and the length of its **circumference**.

Circumference

diameter

Practical Exercise

1. Shown below are drawings of circles with their **diameters** and **circumferences** given.

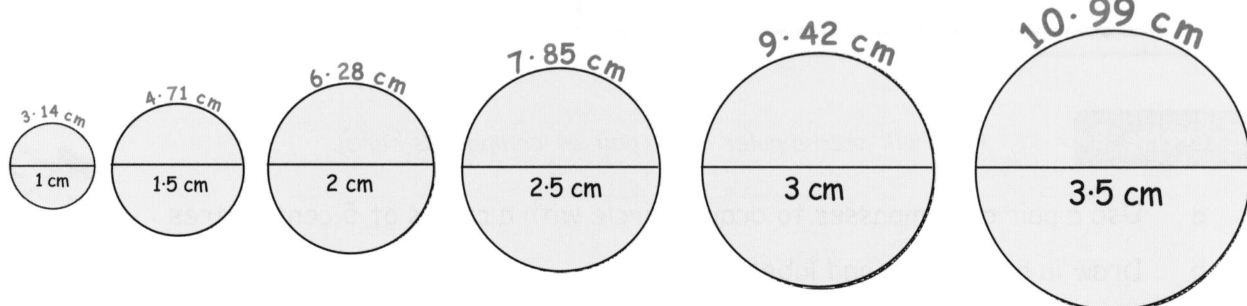

   a Copy this table and fill in the **first two rows** :-

diameter (***D***)	1	1·5	2	2·5	3	3·5
circumference (*C*)	3·14	4·71	6·28	?	?	?
C* ÷ *D	3·14	?	?	?	?	?

   b Use your calculator to **divide** the circumference of each circle by its diameter.

   Fill in the **third row** of your table.

   c What answer did you obtain each time ?

2. You may like to measure the diameters of a half dozen circular objects like tin lids.

   You could also measure their circumferences using a measuring tape or a piece of string. (*Check with your teacher*).

   If you have made your measurements accurately, you should check to see that when you divide the circumference of each circle by its diameter, you obtain the same answer as that discovered in Question 1.

3. (**Difficult**) If the pattern in question 1 continues, can you guess what the **circumference** of this circle with diameter 4 centimetres might be ?

4 cm

C = ?

The Circumference (C) of a Circle - A Formula

It has been known for a long time that when you divide the **circumference** of a circle by its **diameter** you always get the answer 3·14...

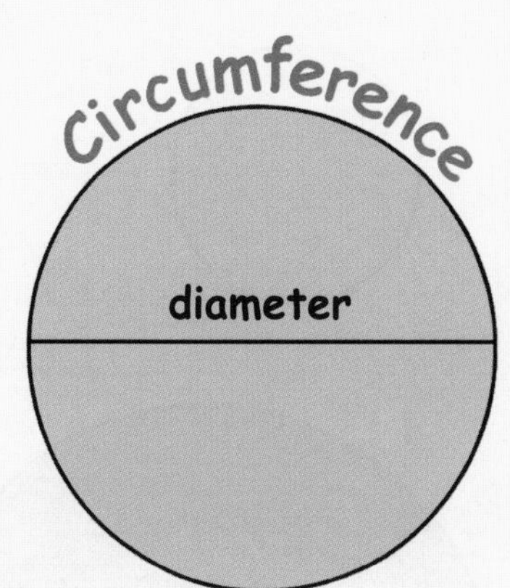

=> $\frac{C}{D} = 3 \cdot 14...$

This number (3·14...) is so famous in mathematics, it is given a name. It is called π (*pi* - pronounced "**pie**")

=> $\frac{C}{D} = \pi$ (where $\pi = 3 \cdot 14..$)

We can use the rearrangement of this to help us calculate the circumference of a circle as long as we know what its diameter is.

=> $C = \pi \times D$ (or $C = \pi D$ for short).

Example :- Calculate the **circumference** of this circle which has a diameter of 9 centimetres :-

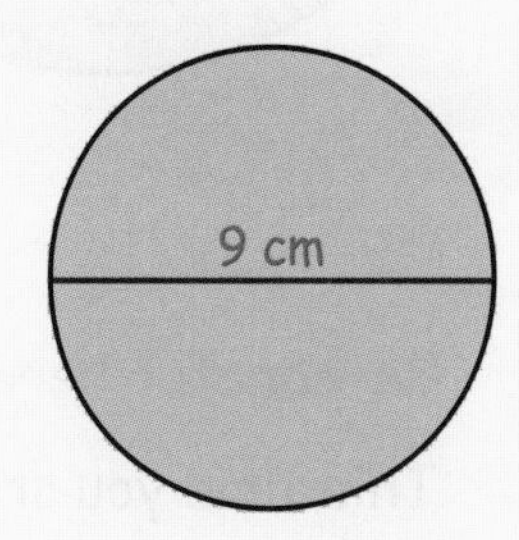

=> $C = \pi D$

=> $C = 3 \cdot 14 \times 9$ cm

=> $C = 28 \cdot 26$ cm

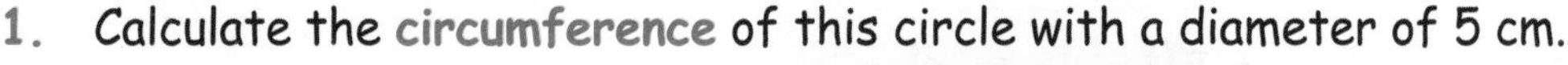

Exercise 3 (*In this exercise, use 3·14 as an estimate for π*).

1. Calculate the **circumference** of this circle with a diameter of 5 cm.

(*Copy this working*).

$C = \pi D$

=> $C = 3 \cdot 14 \times 5$ cm

=> $C = ...$ cm

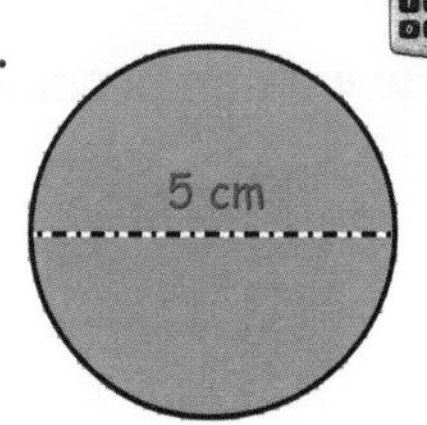

2. 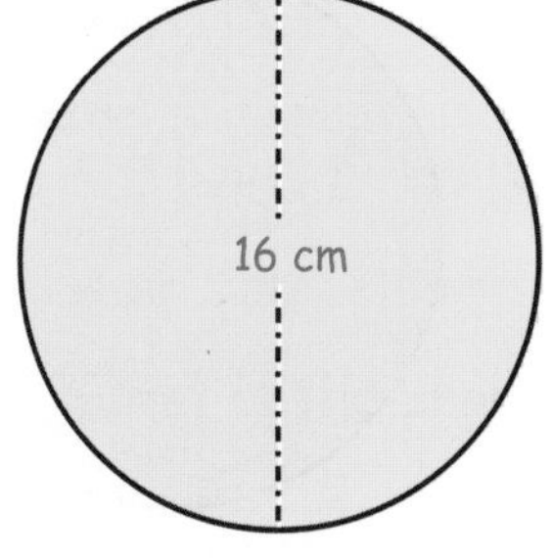

Calculate the **circumference** of the circle with diameter 16 centimetres. (*Show 3 lines of working*).

3. Calculate the **circumference** of this circle :-

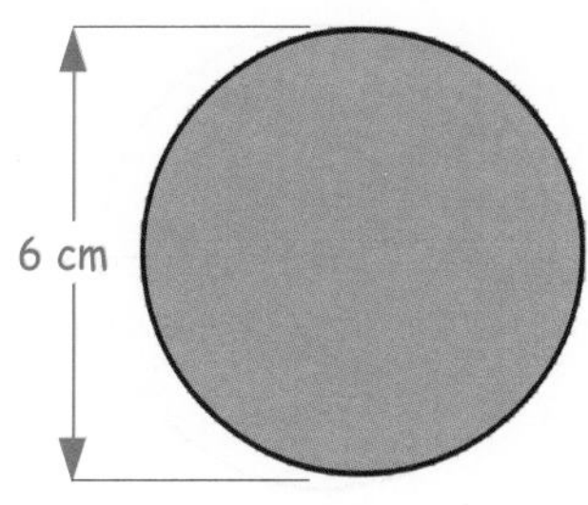

4. For each of these circles, set down the three lines of working and calculate the lengths of their circumferences :-

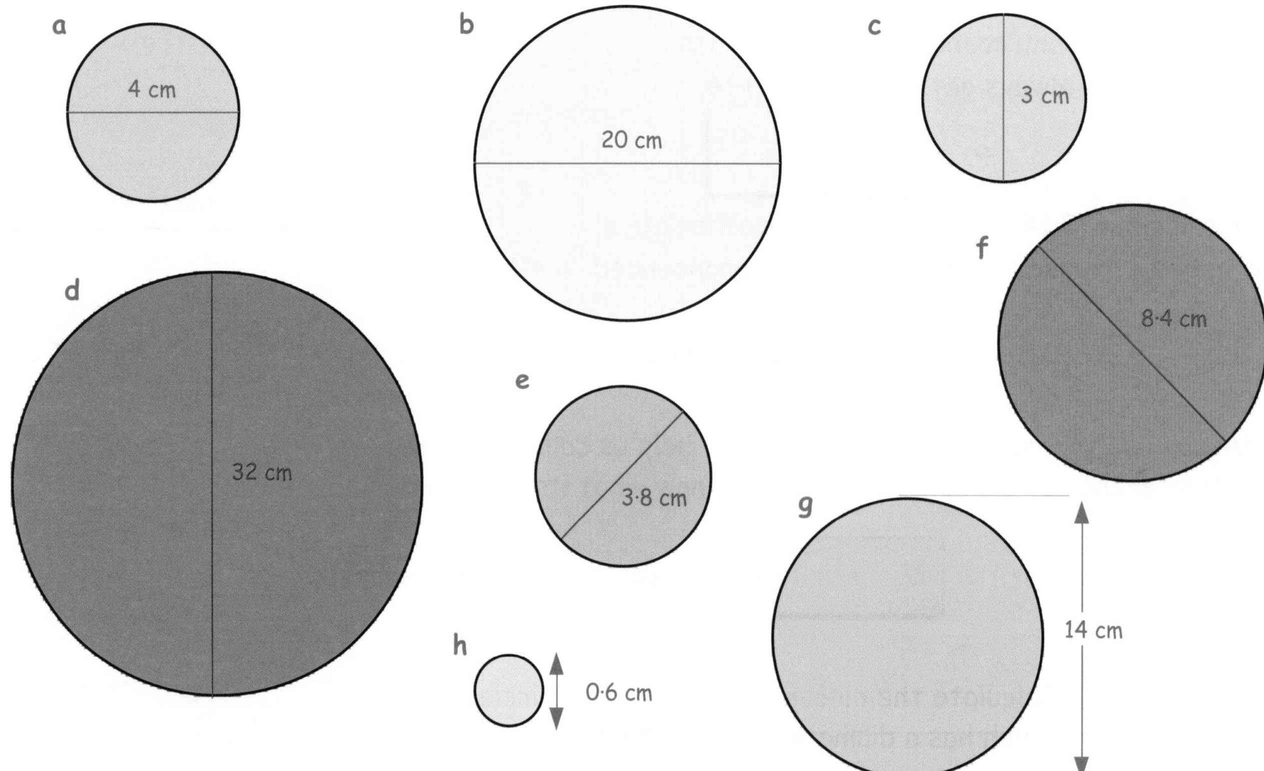

5. **Be careful here !!**

This time you are told that the radius is 6 centimetres.

To calculate the circumference, you have to find the length of the diameter first.

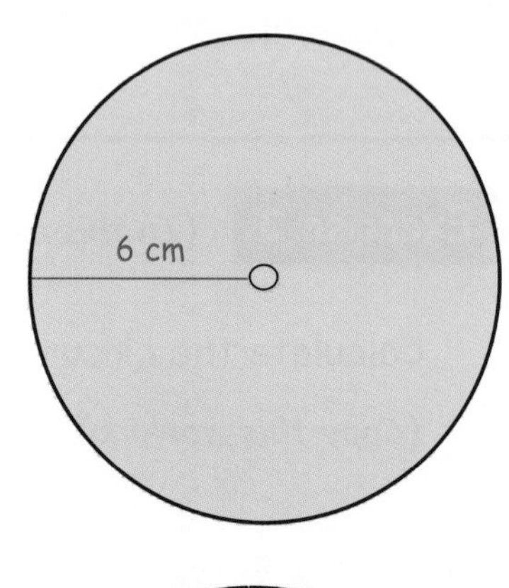

radius = 6 cm => **diameter = 2 x 6 = 12 cm**

Now we can proceed

$C = \pi D$

=> $C = 3{\cdot}14 \times 12$ cm (note)

=> $C = \ldots.$ cm

6. For this circle :-

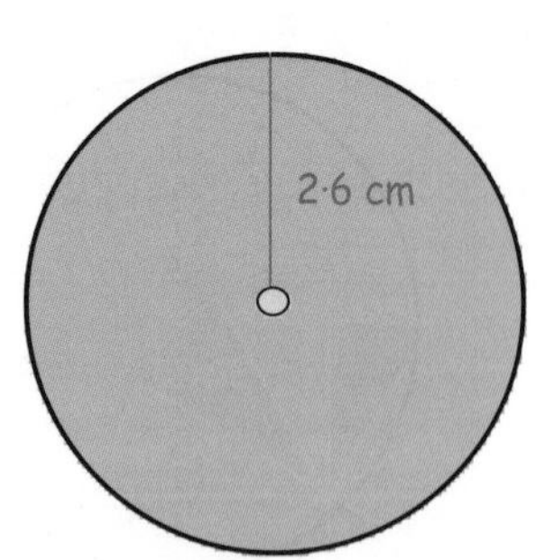

a Double the radius to get the diameter.

b Use the diameter to calculate the circumference.

7. (1·8 cm) Calculate the circumference of this circle.

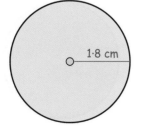

8. Calculate the diameter, then the circumference of each of these circles :-

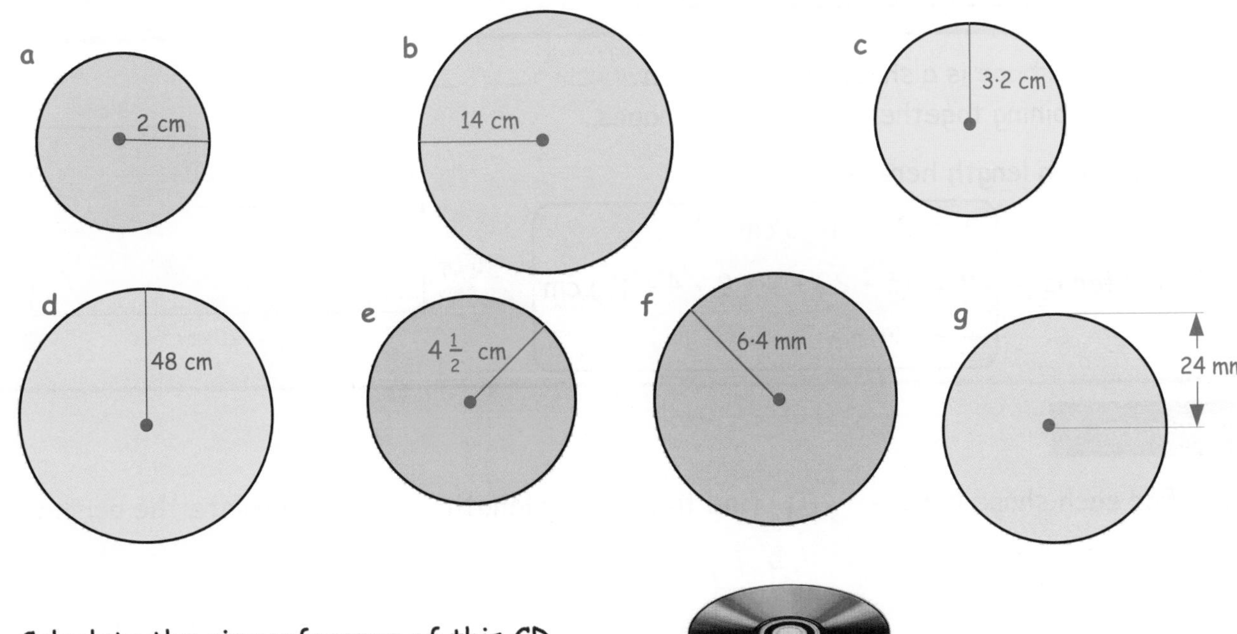

9. Calculate the circumference of this CD.

10. Calculate the circumference of a wheel on this bicycle.

11. The **radius** of this Mr Tearful face is 15 centimetres.

Calculate the circumference of the face.

12. The radius of the circular lid of this large soup pot is 22 centimetres.

Calculate its circumference.

13. The rim of this small frying pan has a diameter of 12·5 centimetres.

Calculate its circumference.

14. A circular helicopter landing pad has a radius of 5·25 metres.

Work out the circumference of the pad.

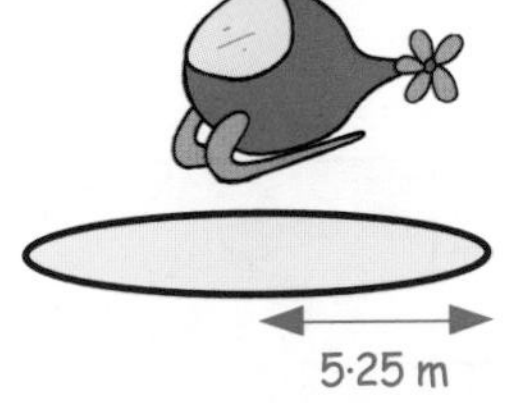

15. This road sign has a diameter of 40 centimetres.

Calculate the circumference.

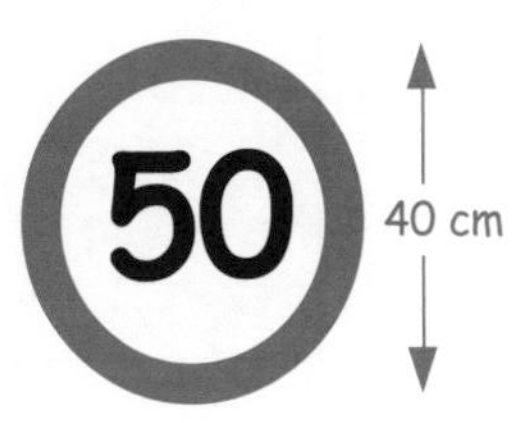

The Perimeter of a Compound Shape

A **compound shape** is a shape that has been formed by joining together two or more shapes.

The unknown length here is :-

$? = 20 \text{ cm} - 8 \text{ cm} = 12 \text{ cm}.$

Perimeter is :- $P = (5 + 20 + 9 + 8 + 4 + 12) \text{ cm}$

$P = 58 \text{ cm}$

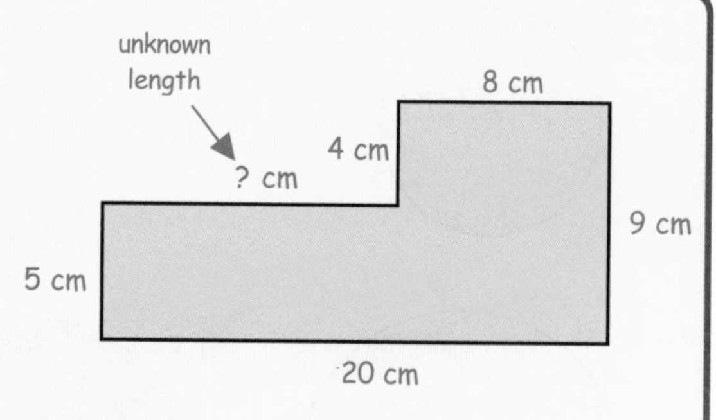

Exercise 4

1. For each shape here :- (i) find the missing length (ii) calculate the **perimeter**.

a

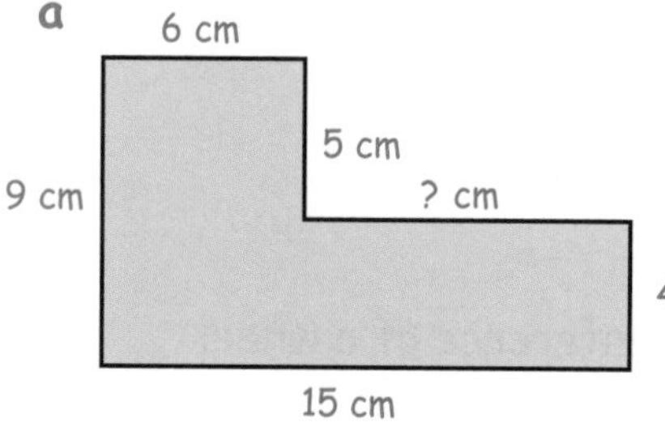

b

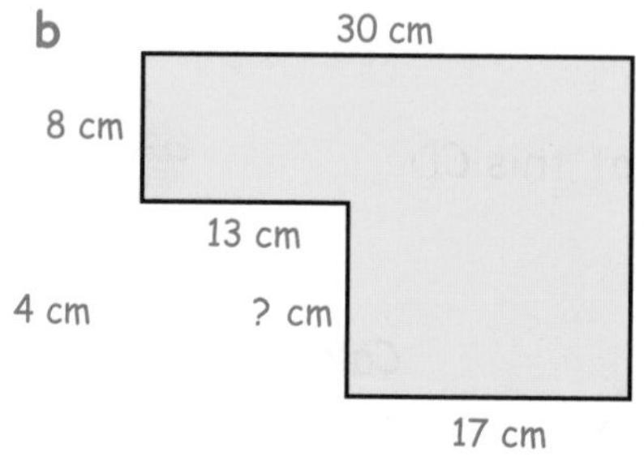

c

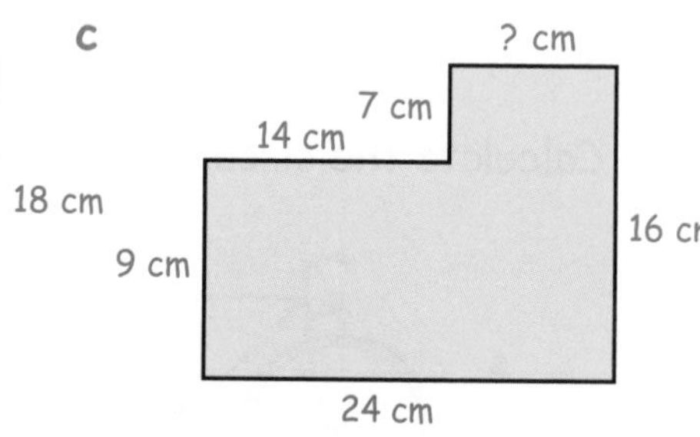

2. This time, there are several missing sides to find before calculating the **perimeter**.

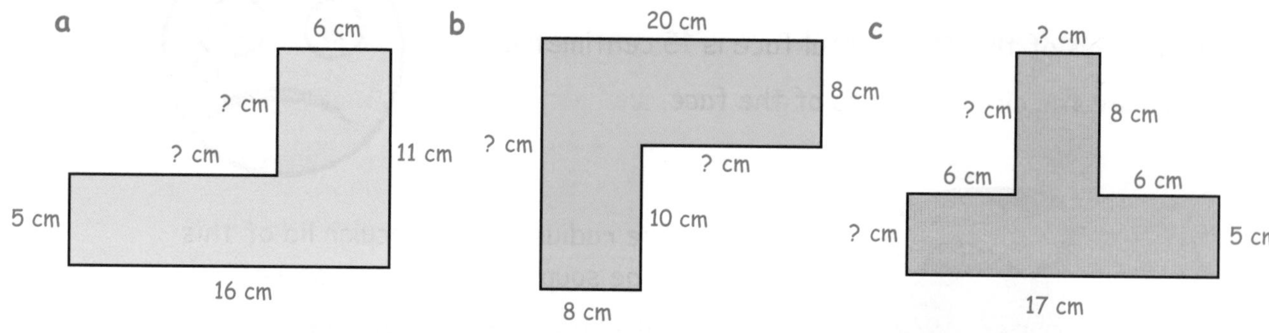

3. a Use a ruler to make an **accurate** drawing of this shape

   b Measure the length of the sloping side in your drawing.

   c Calculate the **perimeter** of the shape.

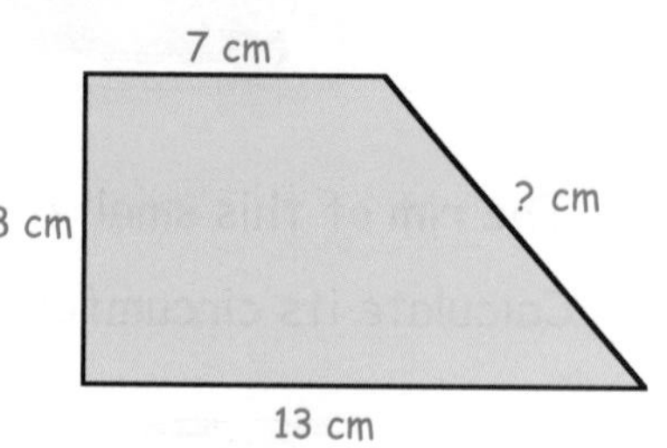

4. Calculate the **perimeter** of each shape :-

a

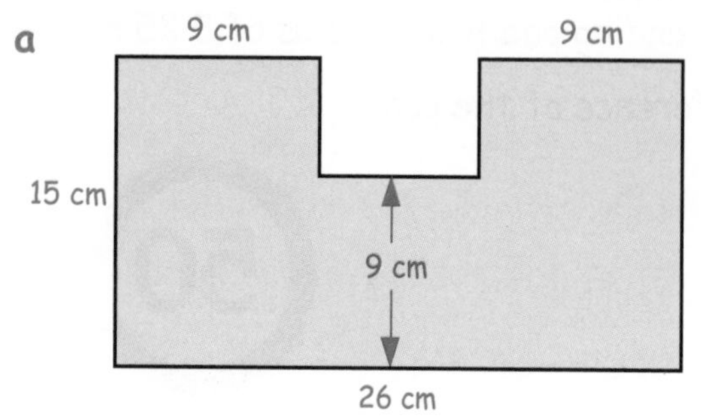

b

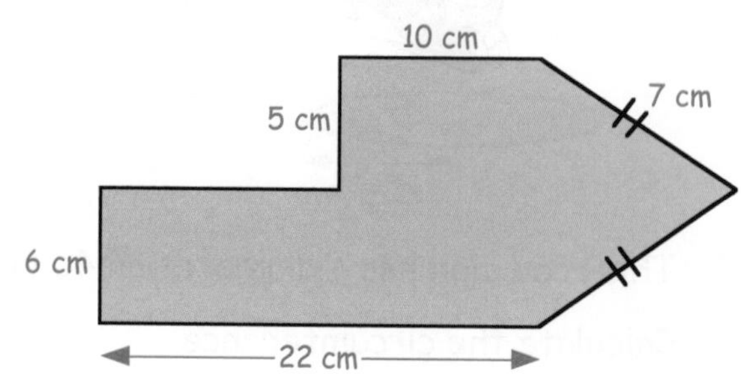

Perimeters

Geometry Assessment 2

1. Calculate the perimeter of each of these shapes :-

a

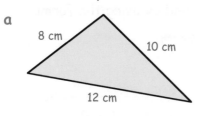

8 cm

10 cm

12 cm

b

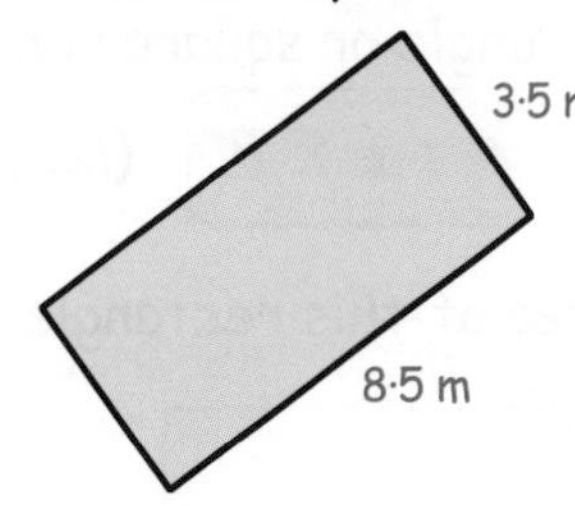

c

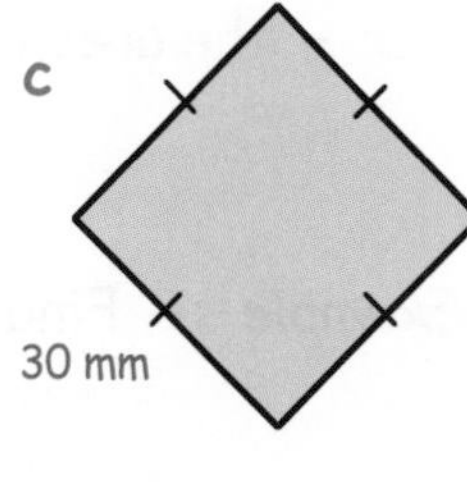

2. The perimeter of this rectangle is 62 cm.
Calculate the missing side of the rectangle.

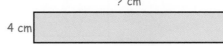

? cm

4 cm

3. The diameter of the lid of this wooden barrel is 31 cm.
What is its radius ?

4. Calculate the circumference of each of these :-

a

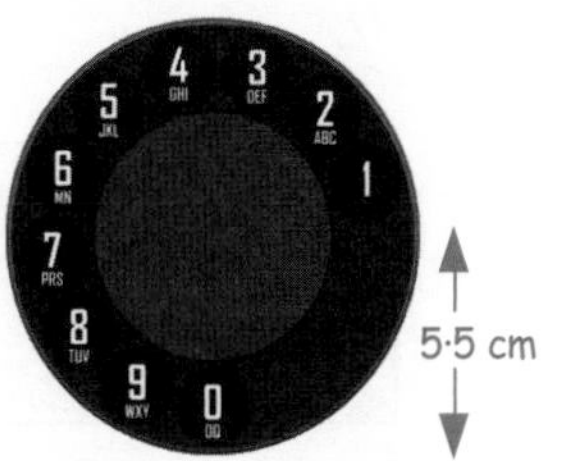

b

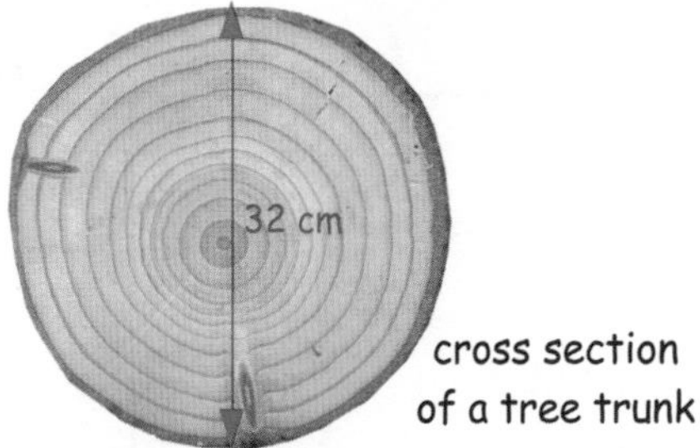

cross section of a tree trunk

5. a Calculate the circumference of this bicycle wheel.

b How far will the bike travel if the wheel rotates 50 times ? (*Answer in metres*).

6. a Calculate the length of the side marked x.

b Now calculate the perimeter of the whole shape.

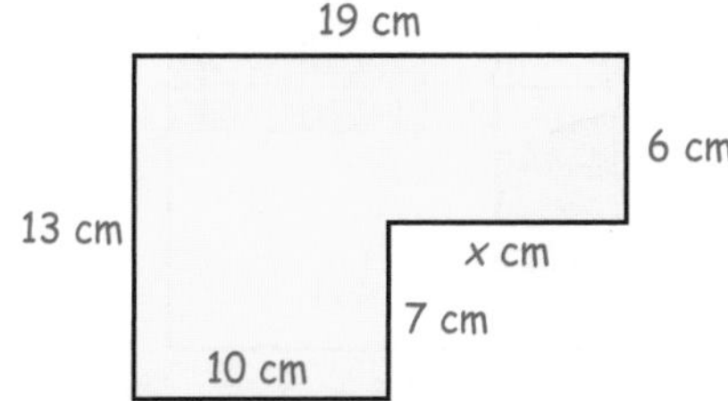

7. Calculate the perimeter of this shape.

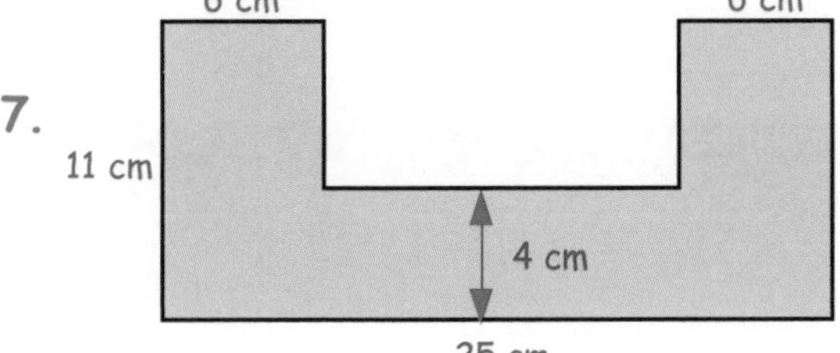

Area of a Rectangle   Revision

Remember - the area of a rectangle or square can be found by using the formula :-

$$A = L \times B$$ (*Length x Breath*)

Example :- Find the area of this rectangle :-

4 cm

12 cm

$A = L \times B$
$= 12 \times 4$
$= 48 \text{ cm}^2$

Exercise 1

1. Calculate the area of each of the following rectangles.
   (Write down the rule $A = L \times B$ and calculate the area in cm^2) :-

a

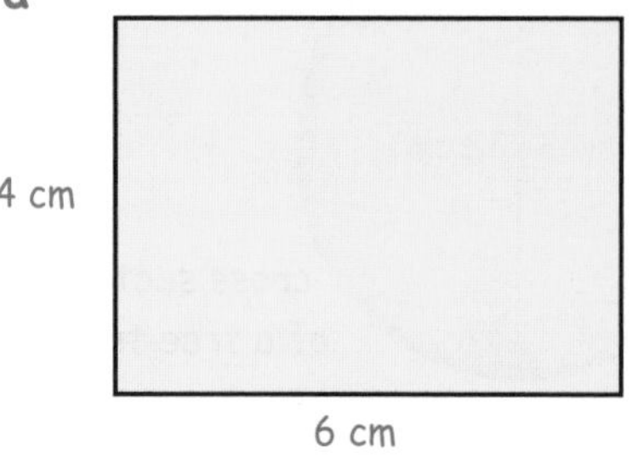

b

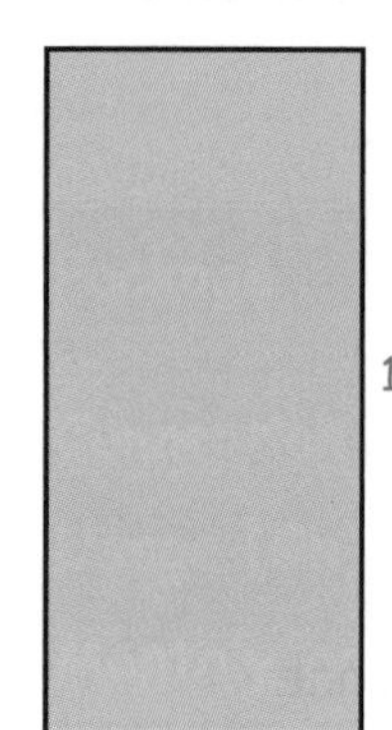

c

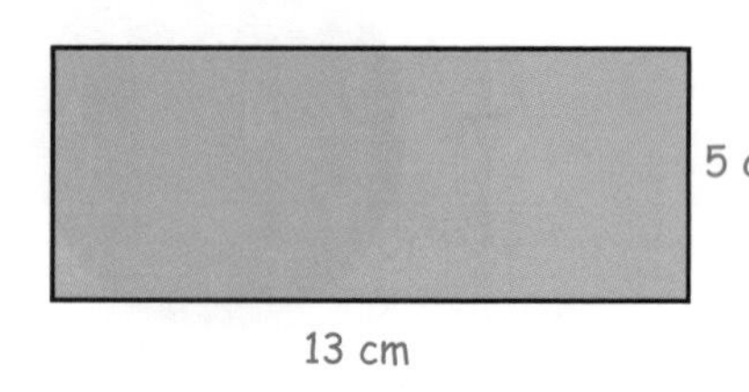

2. Calculate the areas (remember area can be measured in mm^2 and m^2) :-

a

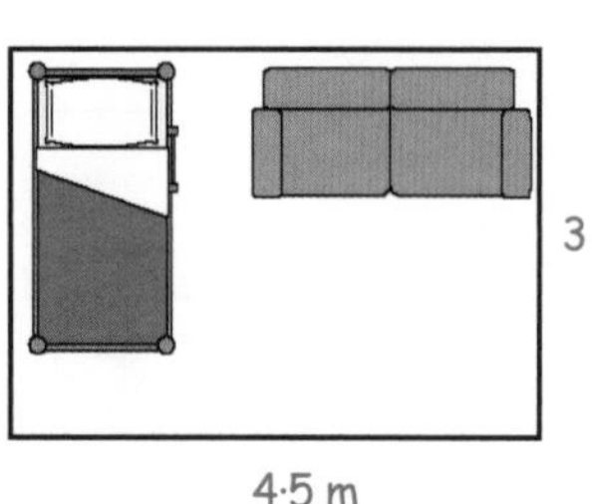

b

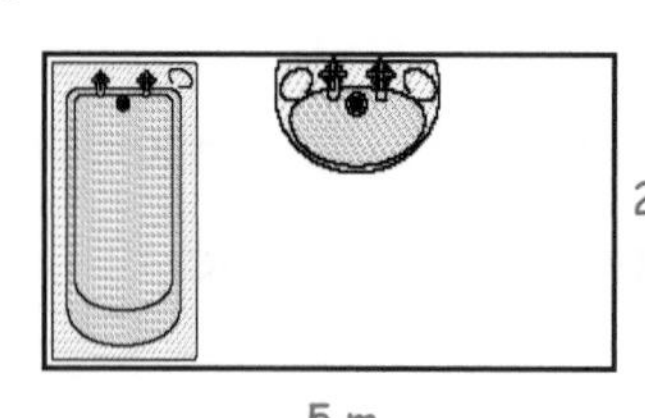

c

d

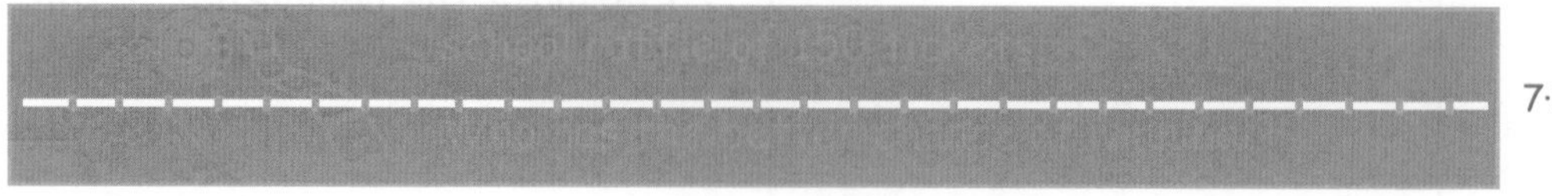

Area of a Right Angled Triangle

To calculate the area of a Right Angled Triangle :-

Step 1 - Look at the surrounding rectangle

=> Area = $6 \times 3 = 18$ cm^2.

Step 2 - Halve your answer =>

=> Area = $\frac{1}{2}$ of $18 = 9$ cm^2.

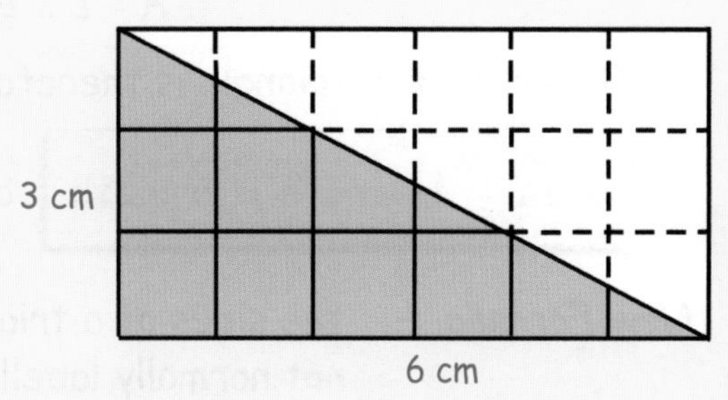

Exercise 2

1. a Make an accurate drawing of this right angled triangle.

   b Complete the figure by drawing the surrounding rectangle.

   c Calculate the area of the rectangle.

   d Now write down the area of the triangle.

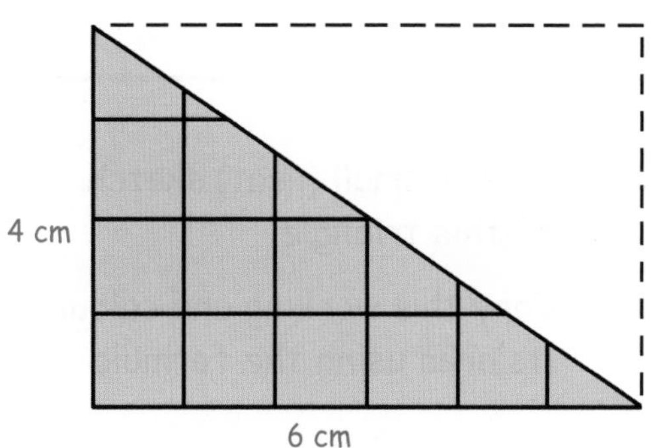

2. For the following right angled triangles :-

   (i) make a small neat sketch

   (ii) draw the surrounding rectangle

   (iii) find the area of the rectangle

   (iv) calculate the area of the triangle.

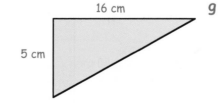

a

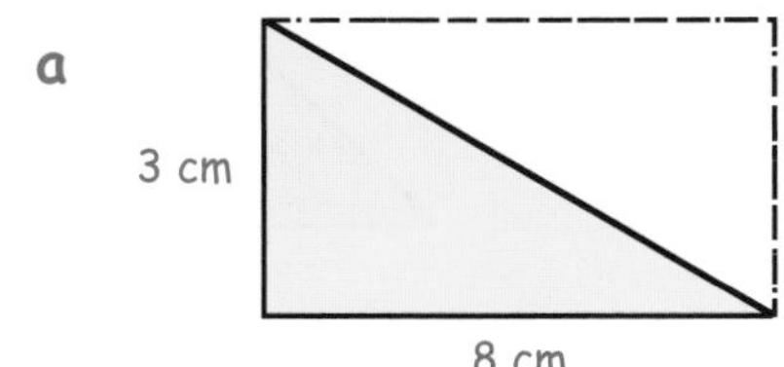

Area $_{(rectangle)} = L \times B = 8 \times 3$

$= 24$ cm^2

Area $_{(triangle)} = \frac{1}{2}$ of $24 = ...$ cm^2

b

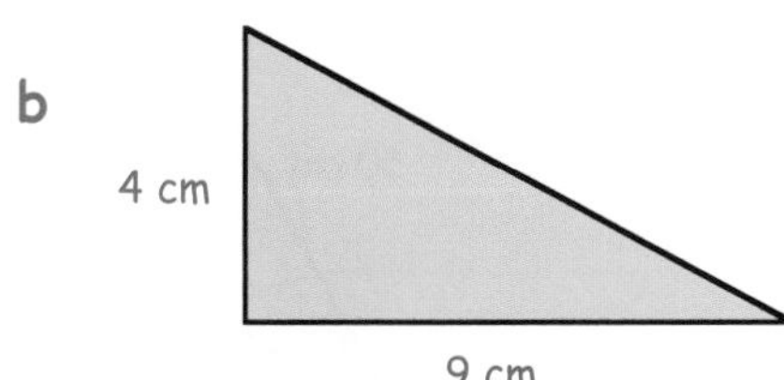

c

3 cm

14 cm

d

e

7 cm

8 cm

f

16 cm

5 cm

g

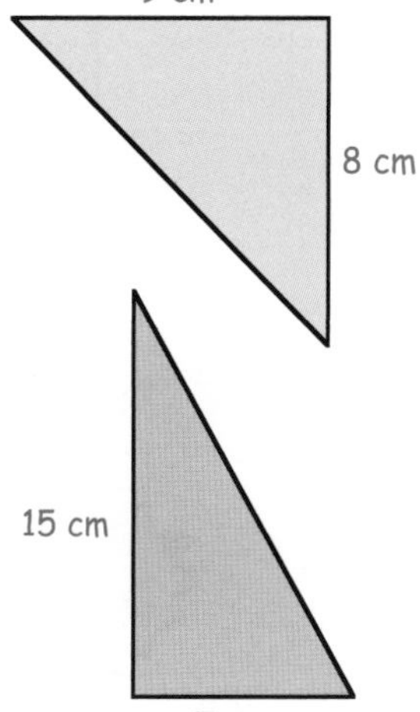

A Formula (rule) for the Area of a Right Angled Triangle

Remember :- the area of a rectangle is given by :-

$$A = L \times B$$

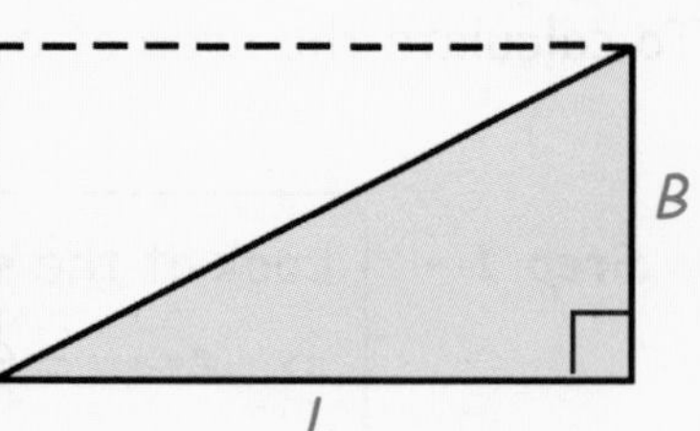

The area of a triangle is therefore given by :-

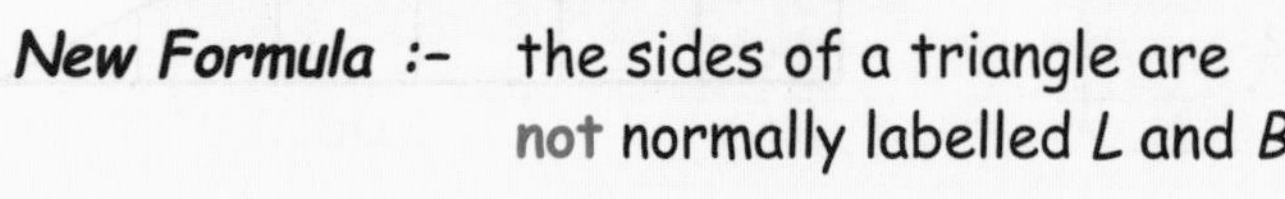

or $A = \frac{1}{2}(L \times B)$

New Formula :- the sides of a triangle are not normally labelled L and B.

Base (B) and Height (H) are used.

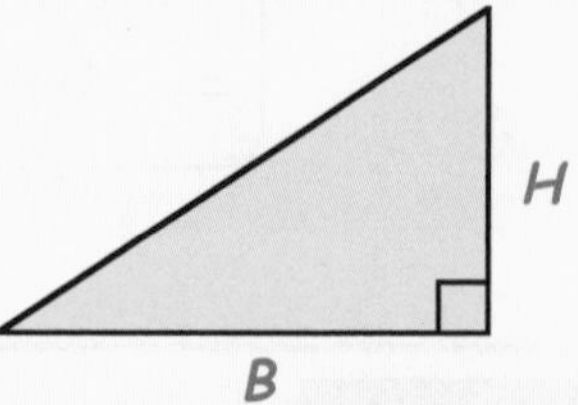

The area of a triangle is now given by :-

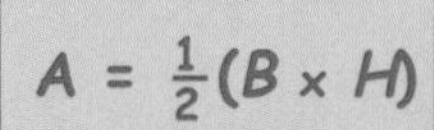

To be learned !!!

3. a Make a small (neat) sketch of this triangle.

   b Copy this working and calculate its area using the formula :-

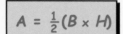

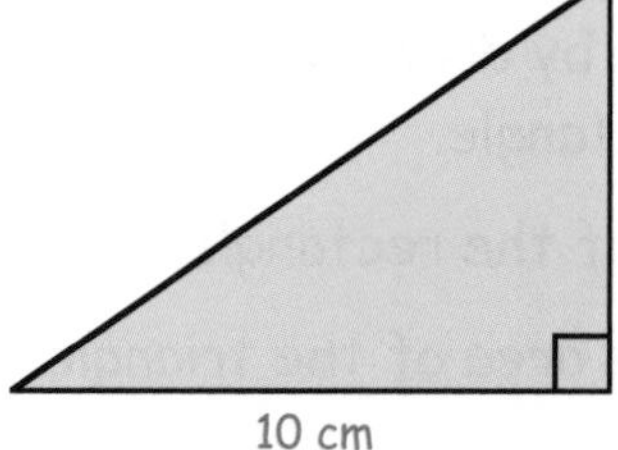

$A = \frac{1}{2}(B \times H)$

$A = \frac{1}{2}$ of (10×7)

$A = \ldots\ cm^2$

4. Use the formula to calculate the area of each of these right angled triangles :-

a 12 cm, 8 cm

b 15 cm, 10 cm

c 16 cm, 20 cm

d 32 cm, 10 cm

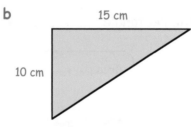

e 20 cm, 20 cm

f 50 cm, 23 cm

g 37 cm, 100 cm

h 155 cm, 80 cm

i 70 cm, 110 cm

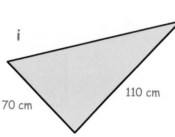

5. Calculate the **area** of these **right angled triangles** (*in* mm^2, cm^2 *or* m^2) :-

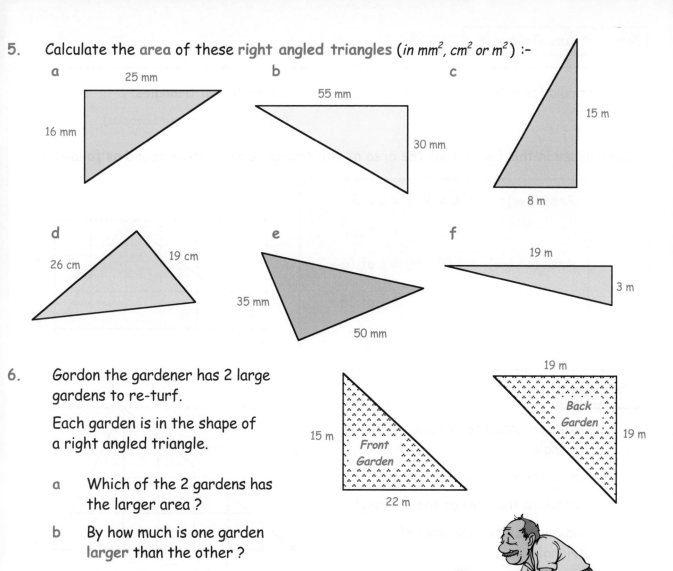

a 25 mm, 16 mm

b 55 mm, 30 mm

c 15 m, 8 m

d 26 cm, 19 cm

e 35 mm, 50 mm

f 19 m, 3 m

6. Gordon the gardener has 2 large gardens to re-turf.

Each garden is in the shape of a right angled triangle.

Front Garden: 15 m, 22 m

Back Garden: 19 m, 19 m

a Which of the 2 gardens has the larger area ?

b By how much is one garden **larger** than the other ?

c The turf costs £2·50 per square metre.

How much will it cost to re-turf both gardens ?

7. Three identical aluminium brackets are used to support a shelf.

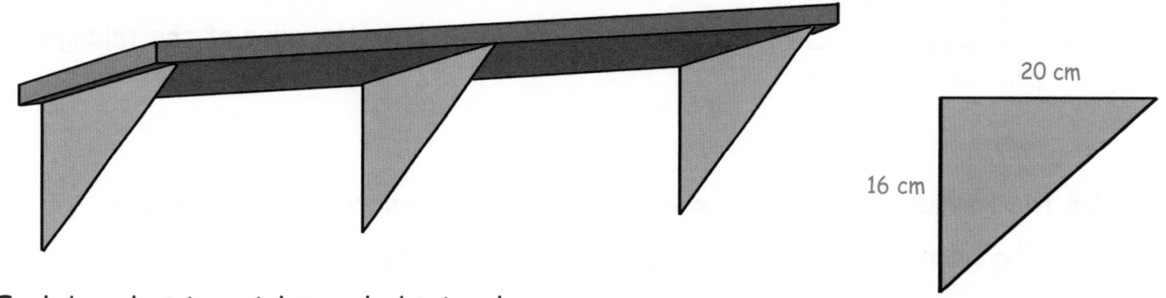

20 cm, 16 cm

Each bracket is a right angled triangle.

a Calculate the **total area** of aluminium needed to make all 3 brackets.

b The aluminium weighs 13·5 grams for every **ten** square centimetres.

The wooden shelf itself weighs 1·35 kilograms.

Calculate the total weight of the shelf and the three brackets.

Area of any Triangle

The formula (or rule) :- *Area* = $\frac{1}{2}(B \times H)$ works for **all** triangles.

(*Not just right angled triangles*).

Can you see in this figure that the area of the triangle below can be found as follows ?

Area (*rect*) = $L \times B$ = 6×3

= 18 cm^2

Area (*triangle*) = $\frac{1}{2}(B \times H)$ = $\frac{1}{2}$ of (6×3)

= $\frac{1}{2}$ of 18

= 9 cm^2

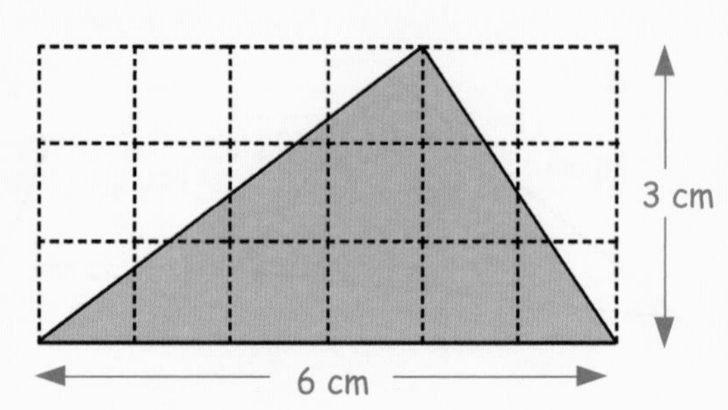

Exercise 3

1. a Make an accurate drawing of this triangle.
   b Draw the surrounding rectangle.
   c Calculate the area of the rectangle.
   d Now write down the area of the triangle.

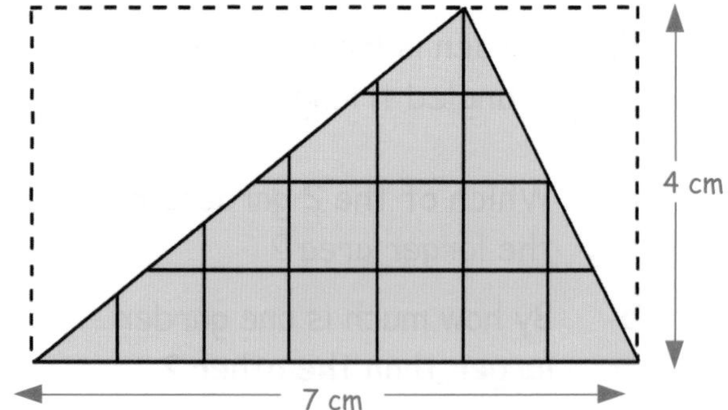

2.

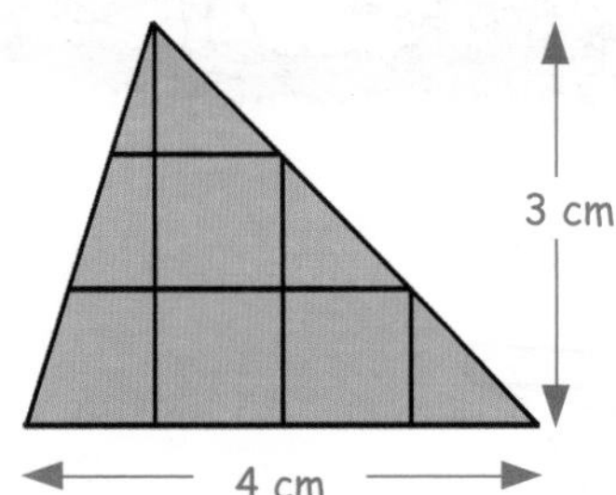

   a Make an accurate drawing of this triangle.
   b Draw the surrounding rectangle.
   c Calculate the area of the rectangle.
   d Now write down the area of the triangle.

3. Use the formula *Area* = $\frac{1}{2}(B \times H)$ each time to calculate the areas of the following triangles (*make a neat sketch of each triangle*) :-

a

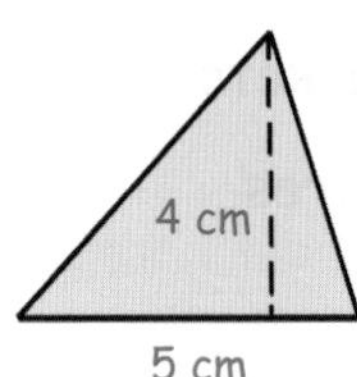

$A = \frac{1}{2}(B \times H)$

=> $A = \frac{1}{2}$ of (5×4)

=> $A =$ ..... cm^2

b

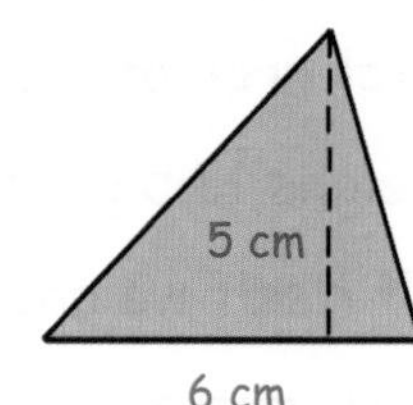

$A = \frac{1}{2}(B \times H)$

=> $A = \frac{1}{2}$ of $(6 \times ...)$

=> $A =$ ..... cm^2

3. c

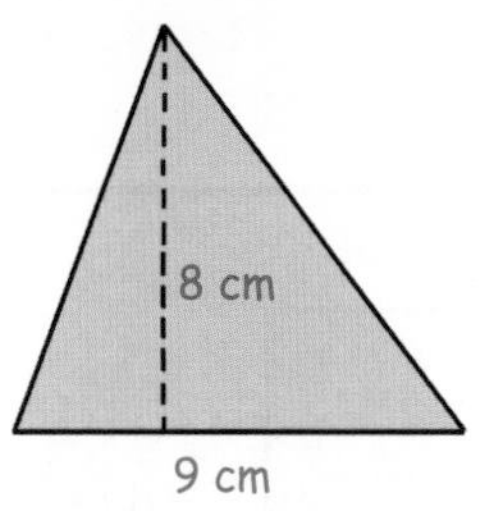

d

8 cm
15 cm

e

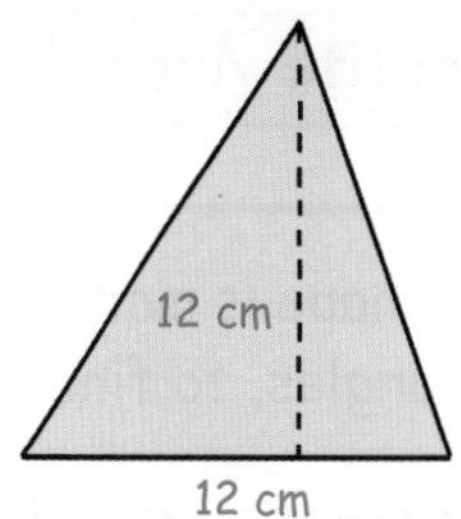

f

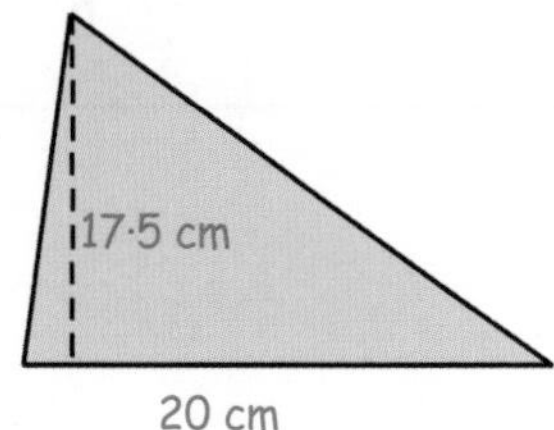

g

50 cm
23 cm

h

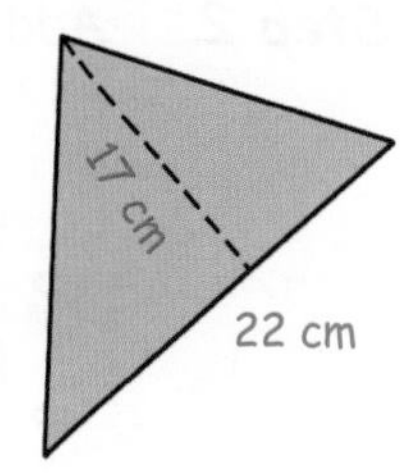

4. Which of these triangles has the **bigger** area ?

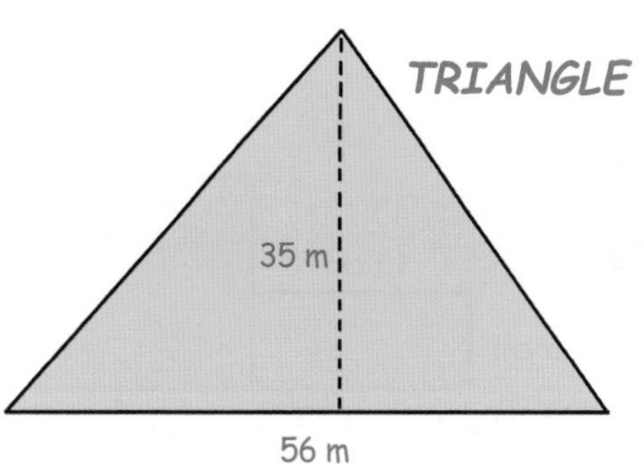

TRIANGLE B
42 m
47 m

5. Triangular wooden fencing is used to edge a lawn.

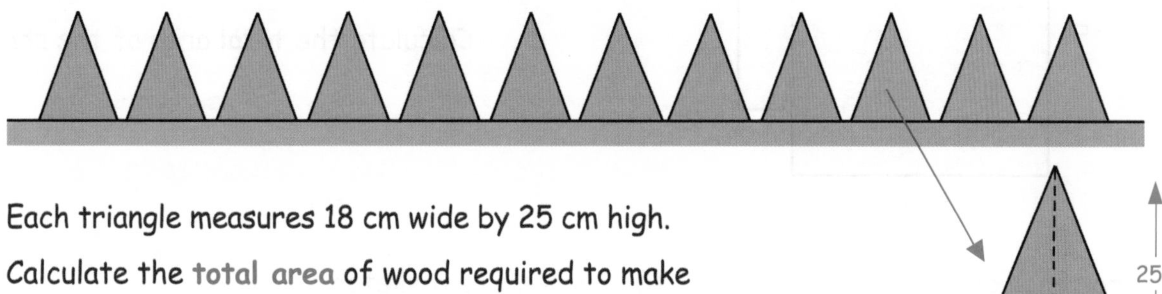

Each triangle measures 18 cm wide by 25 cm high.

Calculate the **total area** of wood required to make all 12 triangular edging pieces.

25 cm
18 cm

6.

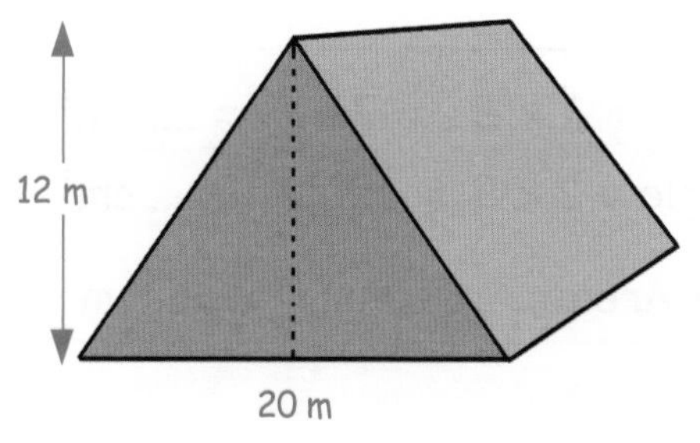

The end face of a large wooden storage building is in the shape of a triangle, as shown.

This face is to be painted with a special paint.

Each tin costs £45·75 and covers 15 m^2 per tin.

What is the total cost to paint both the **inside** and the **outside** of this triangular side with one coat of the special paint ?

Composite Areas

If a shape is made up of 2 (or more) rectangles, to find its area, simply :-

Step 1 Calculate the area of each rectangle.

Step 2 Add the areas together.

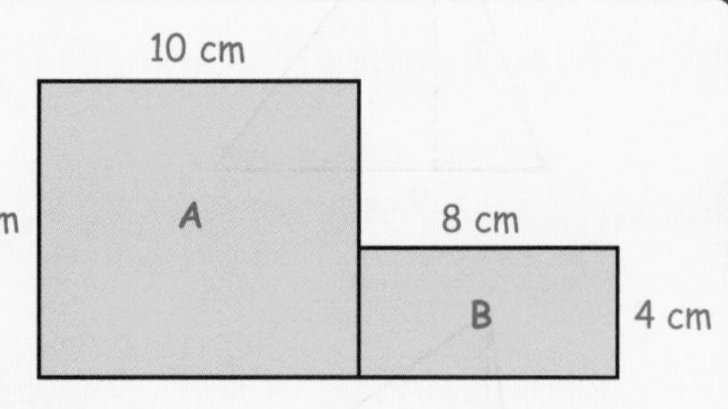

=> Area (of A) = $L \times B = 10 \times 9 = 90\ \text{cm}^2$

=> Area (of B) = $L \times B = 8 \times 4 = 32\ \text{cm}^2$

=> **Total Area = 90 + 32 = 122 cm^2**

Exercise 4

1. a Calculate the area of the big rectangle.
   b Calculate the area of the small rectangle.
   c Calculate the **total** area of the shape.

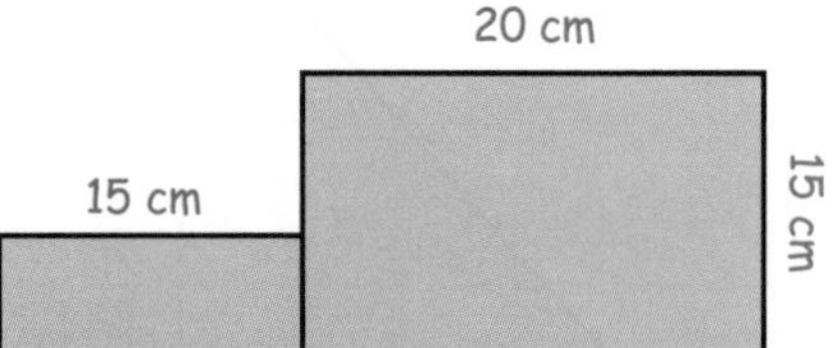

2.

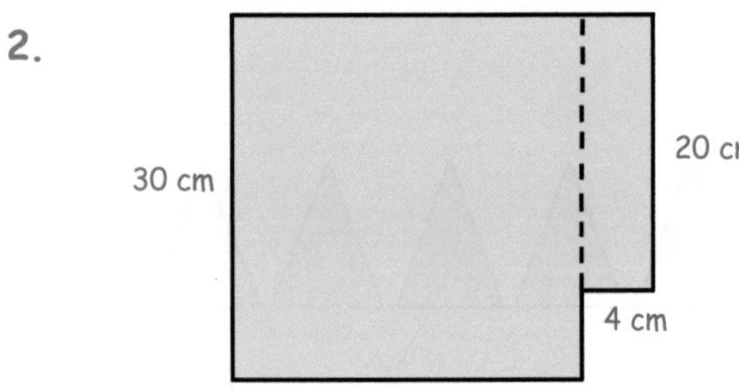

   a Calculate the area of the square.
   b Calculate the area of the rectangle.
   c Calculate the **total** area of the shape.

3. For each of these shapes :- (i) make a neat sketch
   (ii) calculate the area of each part (*show working*)
   (iii) calculate the area of the whole shape.

   a

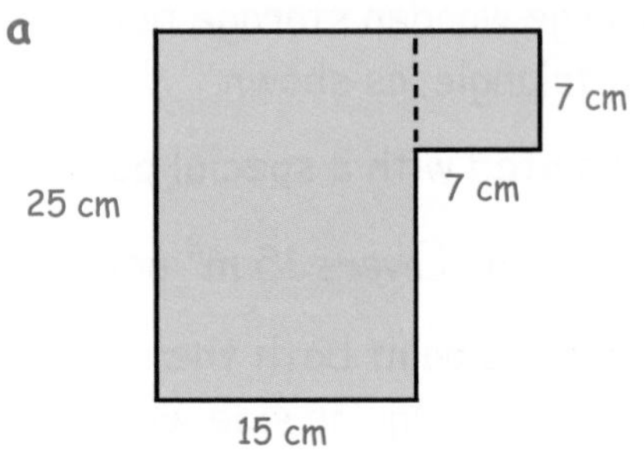

Area of square = $L \times B$ = 7×7 = ... cm^2

Area of rectangle = $L \times B$ = $15 \times ?$ = ... cm^2

=> **Total Area** = ... + ... = ... cm^2

3.

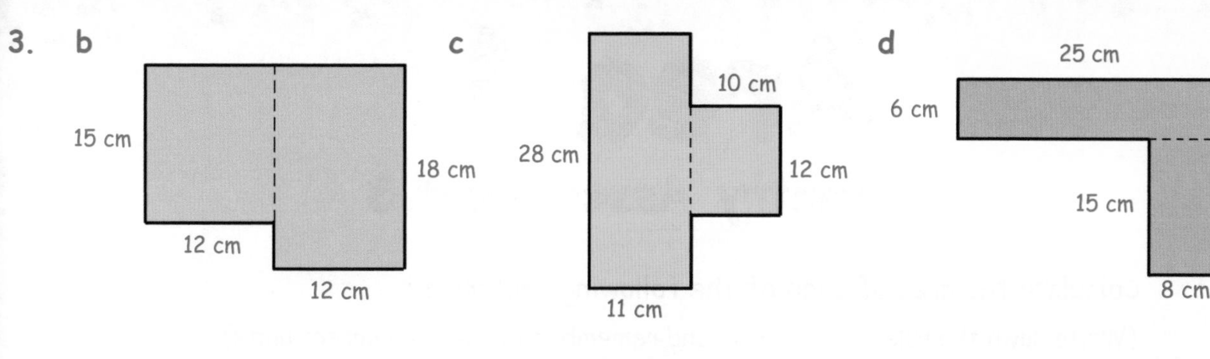

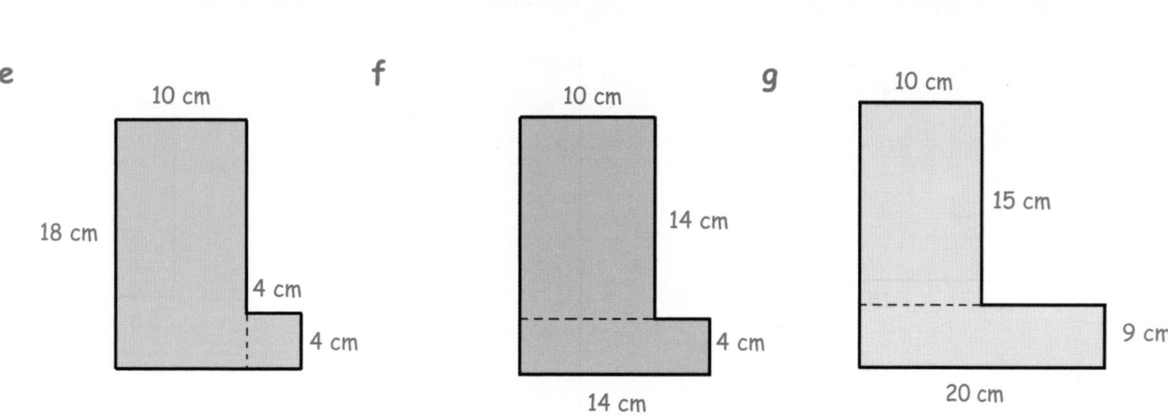

4. This shape consists of a rectangle and a right angled triangle.

Copy the working and complete it :-

Area of rectangle $A = L \times B = 10 \times 5 = ... \text{ cm}^2$

Area of triangle $B = \frac{1}{2}(B \times H) = \frac{1}{2}$ of $10 \times 4 = ... \text{ cm}^2$

=> **Total Area** = ... + ... = ... cm^2

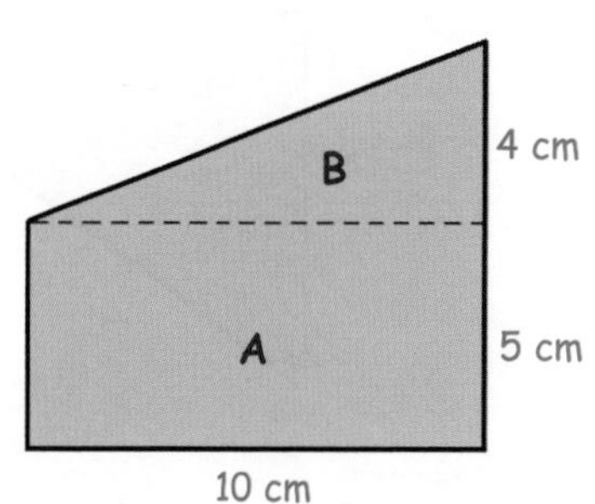

5. For each shape here, calculate the area of the rectangle, the area of the right angled triangle and the **total area** of the shape :-

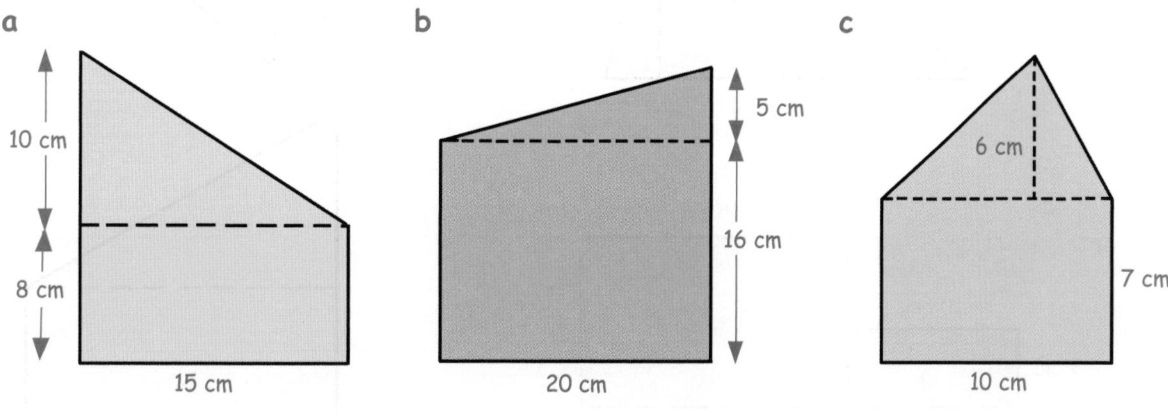

Area 1

Geometry Assessment 3

1. Calculate the area of each of the following rectangles.
(Write down the rule $A = L \times B$ and remember to use the correct units) :-

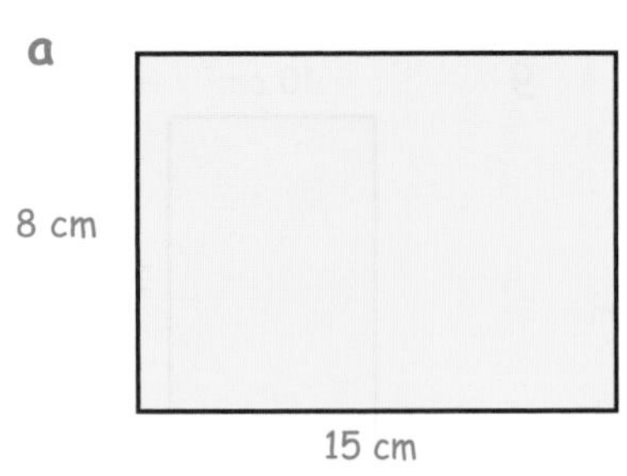

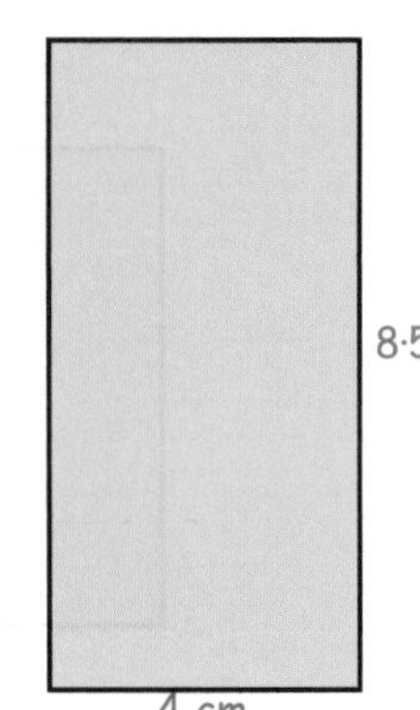

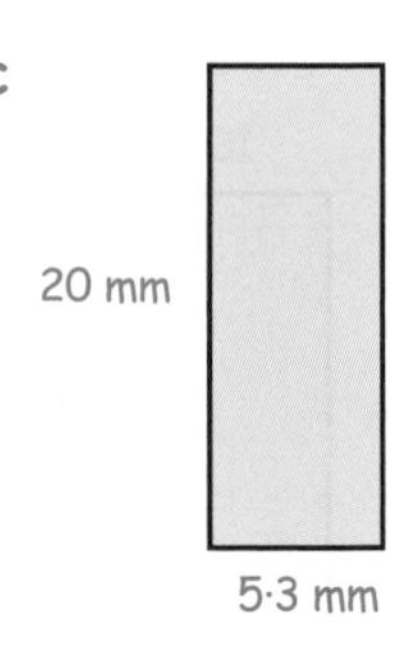

2. Calculate the areas of these right angled triangles (*in* mm^2, cm^2 *or* m^2) :-

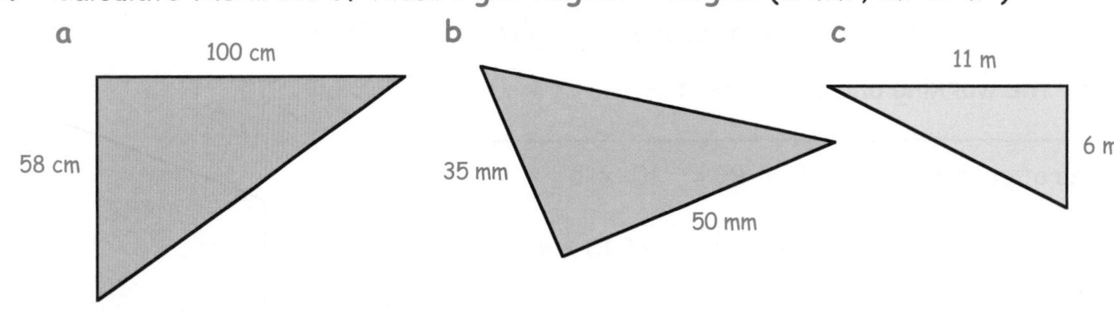

3. Calculate the area of each of the following shapes :-

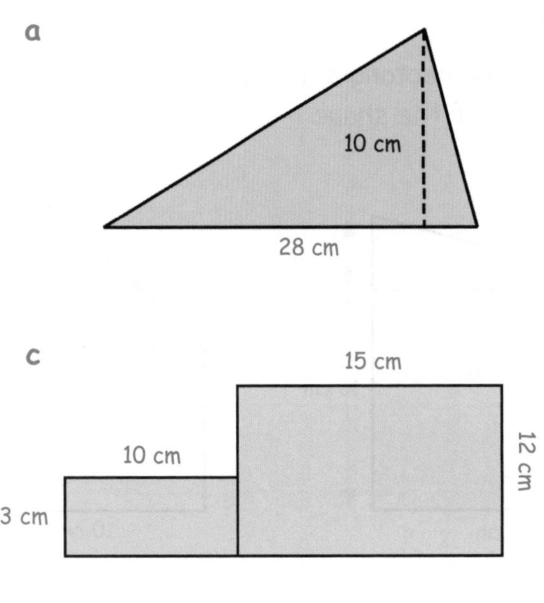

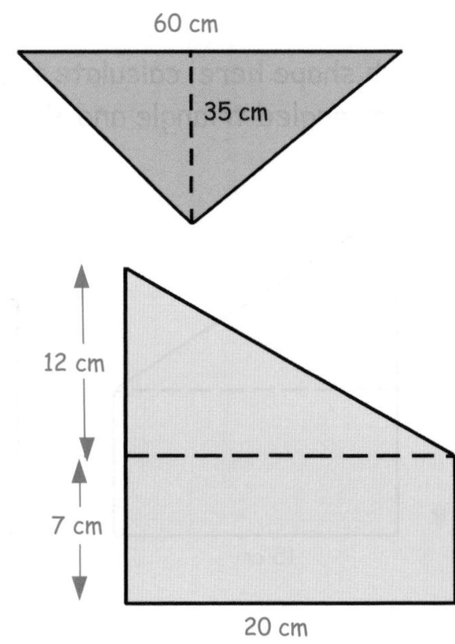

Scale Drawings 1

Enlargements

Exercise 1

1. Make a neat "**two-times**" enlargement of each of these shapes :- (*Each box = 1 cm*).

a

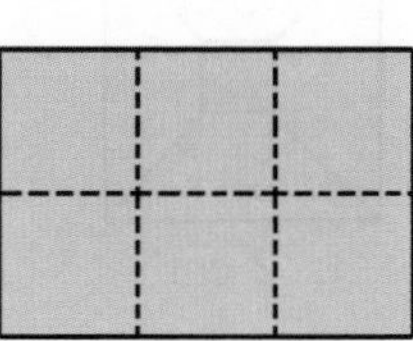

b

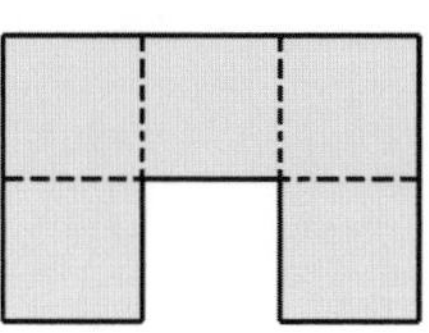

c

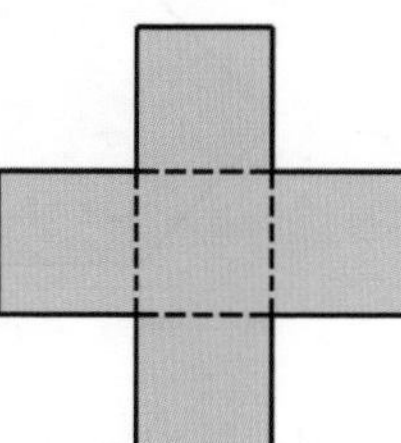

d

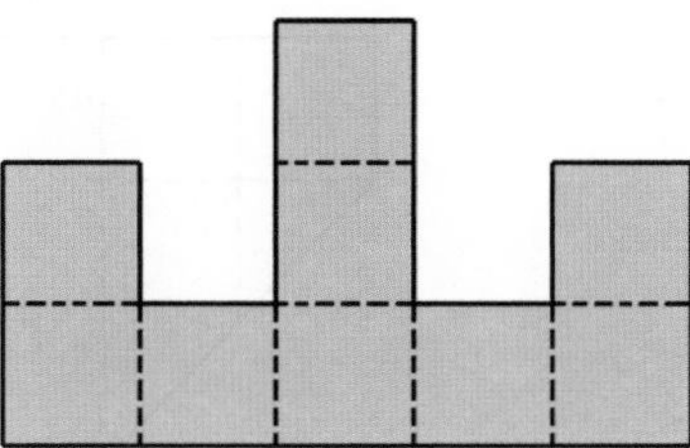

e

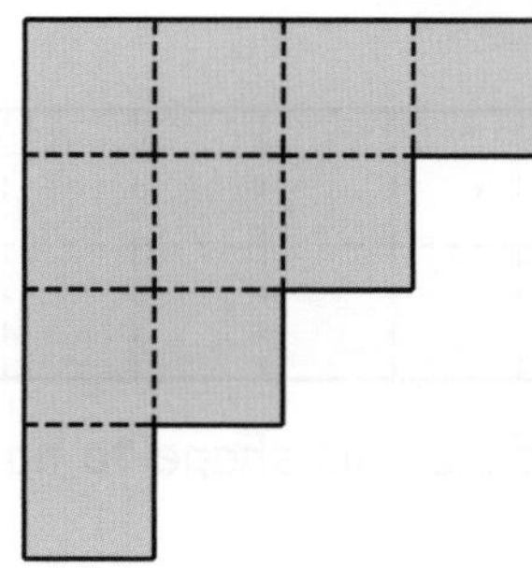

f

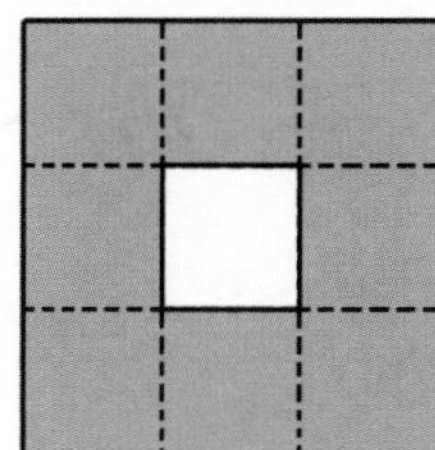

g

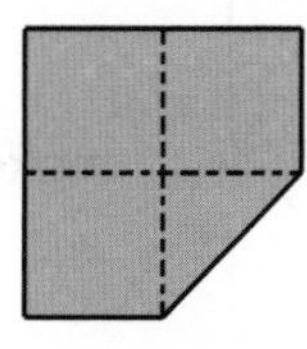

h

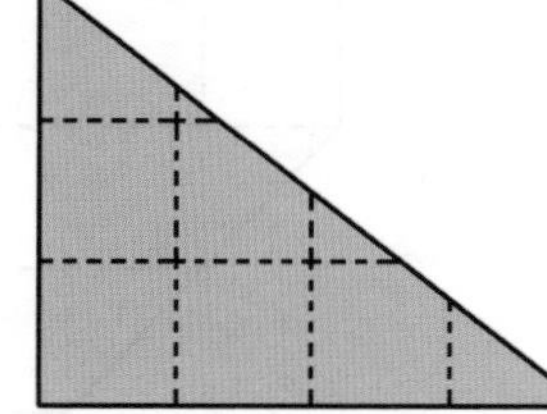

i

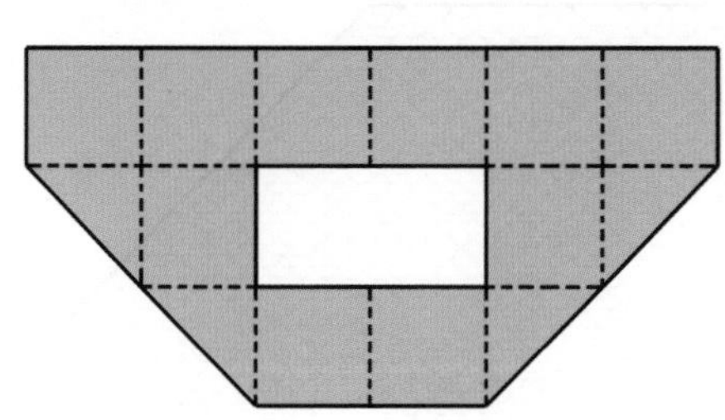

j

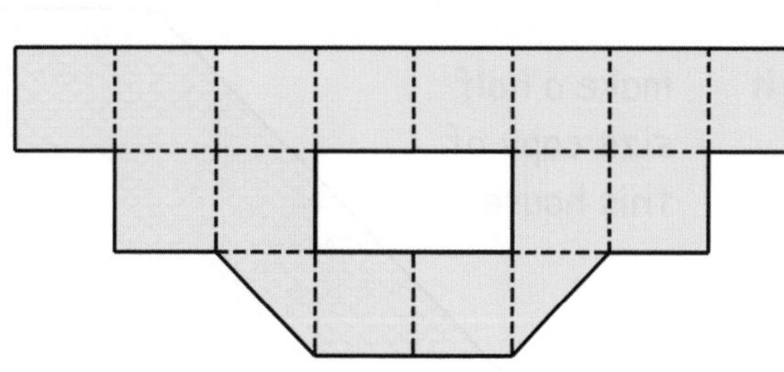

k

10 cm

3 cm

1·5 cm

3 cm

2 cm

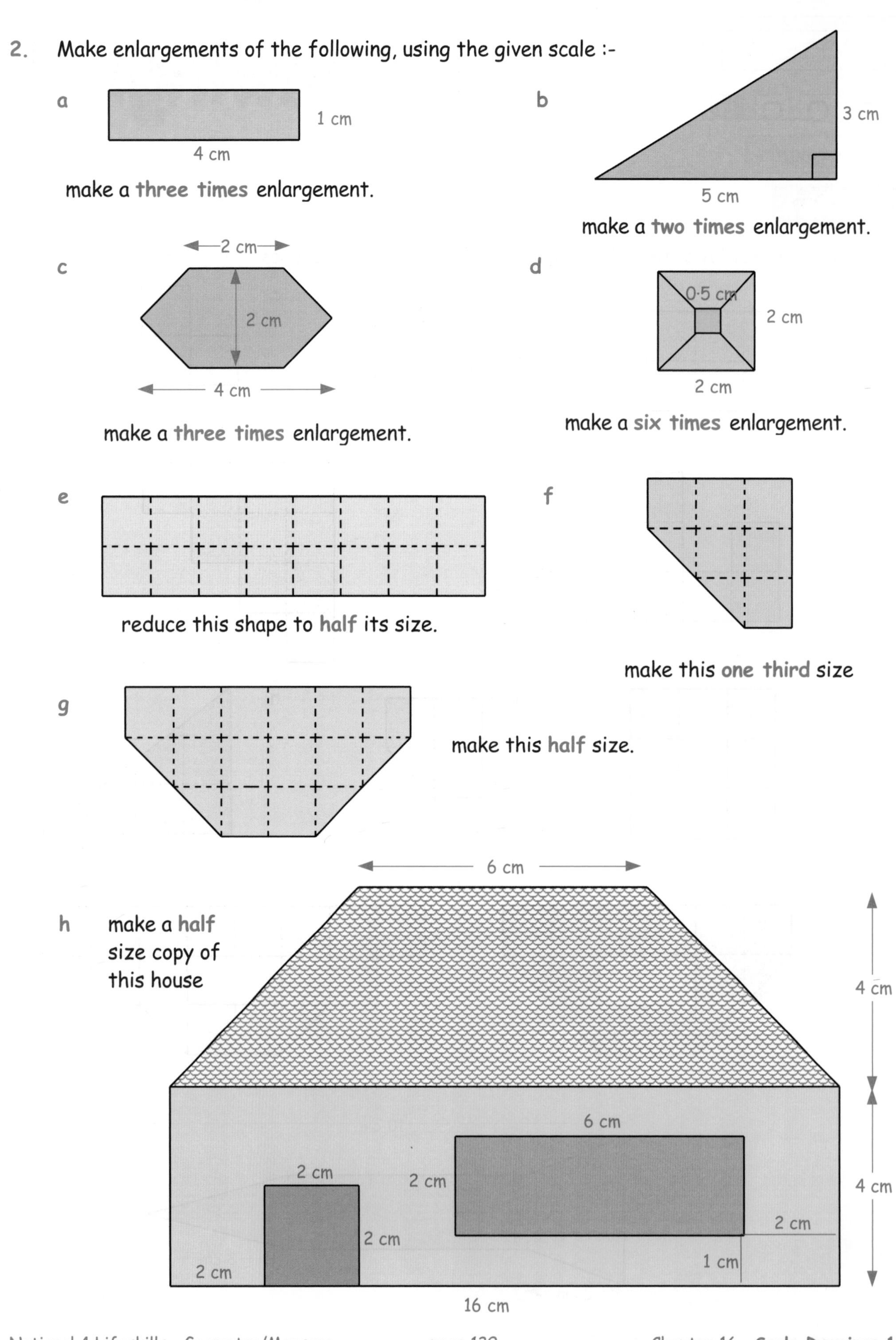
2. Make enlargements of the following, using the given scale :-
a
1 cm
4 cm
make a three times enlargement.
b
3 cm
5 cm
make a two times enlargement.
c
2 cm
2 cm
4 cm
make a three times enlargement.
d
0·5 cm
2 cm
2 cm
make a six times enlargement.
e
reduce this shape to half its size.
f
make this one third size
g
make this half size.
h
make a half size copy of this house
6 cm
4 cm
4 cm
6 cm
2 cm
2 cm
2 cm
2 cm
2 cm
1 cm
16 cm

Scale Drawings (basic)

If you know the scale used in a drawing,

e.g. *1 cm = 4 m*

then you simply multiply any length (in centimetres) by 4 to determine the real length of the object (in metres).

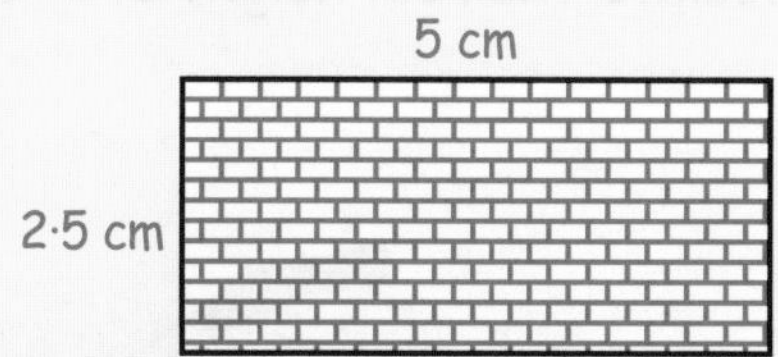

=> real length = 5 x 4 = 20 m

=> real width = 2·5 x 4 = 10 m

Exercise 2

1. This scale drawing of a garage forecourt is drawn to a scale of :-

   1 cm = 6 m.

   a Calculate the real width of the forecourt.

   b Now calculate the real length of the forecourt.

2. This drawing of a car was done using a scale :-

   1 cm = 20 cm.

   a Calculate the real length of the car (... x 20).

   b Calculate the real width of the car.

   c Write the real length and breadth in metres.

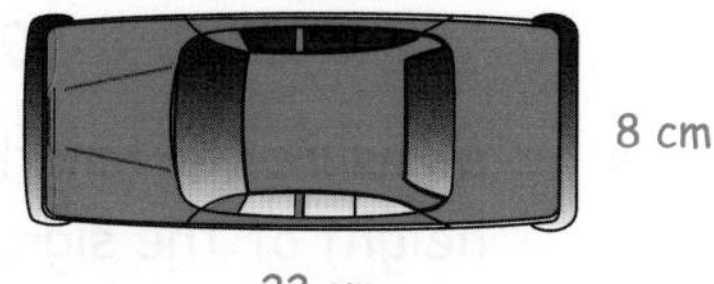

3. 

   This door has been drawn to a scale of :-

   1 cm = 25 cm.

   a Calculate the real height of the door.

   b Calculate the real width of the door.

4. Farmer Stokes' field is in the shape of a rectangle.

   The scale is :- *1 cm = 15 metres.*

   a Calculate the real length and the real breadth of the field.

   b Calculate the perimeter of the field.

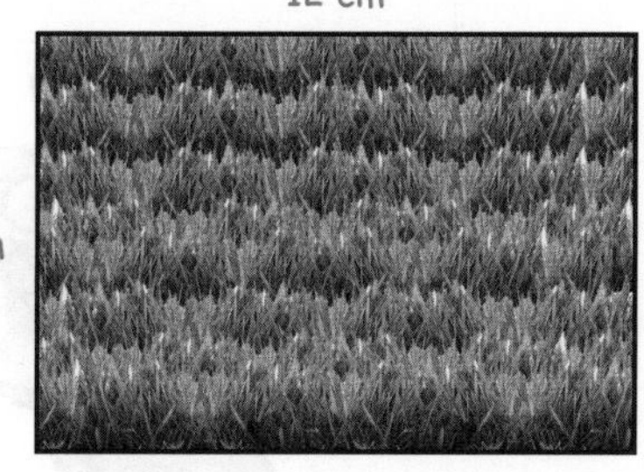

5. This picture of a photocopier is shown to a scale :-

1 cm = 40 cm.

Calculate the real height of the copier.

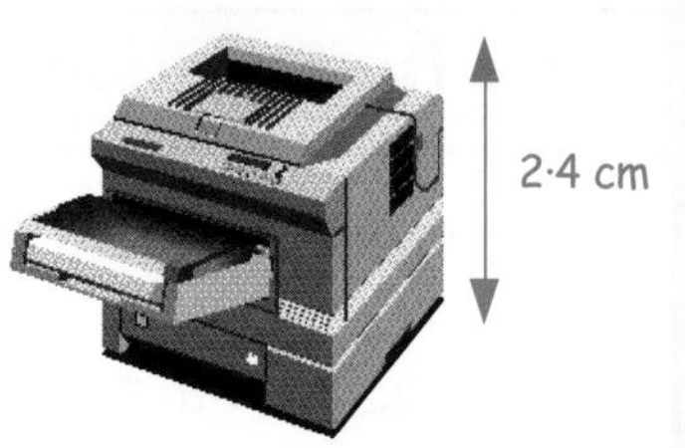

6. 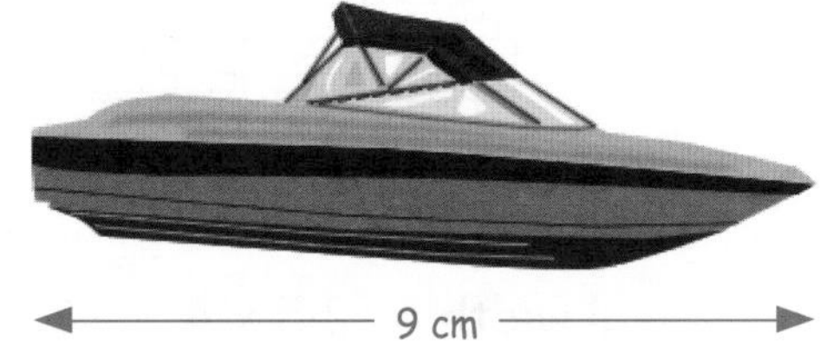

This speed boat has been drawn to a scale of :-

1 cm = 0·5 metres.

Calculate the length of the real boat.

7. This garden shed has been drawn to a scale of :-

1 cm = 1·5 metres.

a Calculate the real height of the shed.

b Calculate the real length of the shed.

*You will need a **ruler** for the remainder of this exercise.*

8. This road sign has been drawn to a scale of :-

1 cm = 50 cm.

a Measure the length and measure the height of the sign, in centimetres.

b Calculate the real length and height of the road sign.

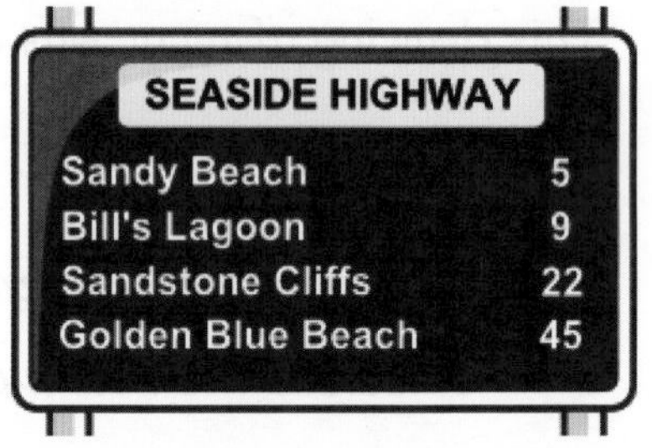

SEASIDE HIGHWAY
Sandy Beach 5
Bill's Lagoon 9
Sandstone Cliffs 22
Golden Blue Beach 45

9. a Measure the height of this lorry, in centimetres.

b If the scale of the drawing is :-

1 cm = 1·2 metres,

calculate the real height of the lorry.

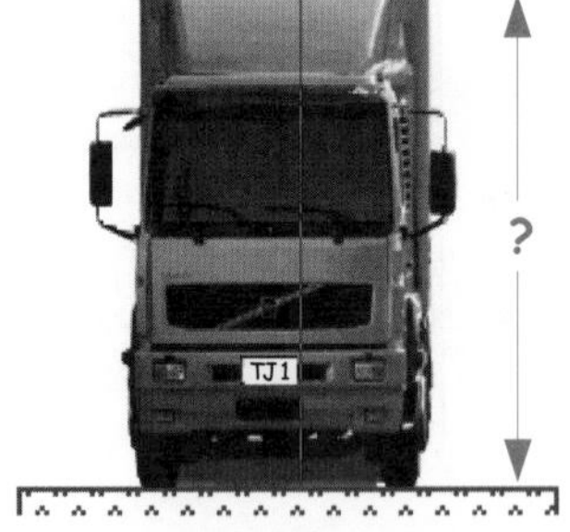

10. 

This picture has been drawn to a scale :-

1 cm = 40 cm.

Measure the length of the log in the picture and calculate its real length.

11. a Use your ruler to measure the height of this lighthouse, in centimetres.

The scale is :- *1 cm = 5 m.*

b Calculate the real height of the lighthouse.

12.

Wick
Inverness
Aberdeen
Glasgow
Edinburgh
Carlisle
York
Liverpool
Norwich
Birmingham
Cardiff
LONDON
Plymouth

This map of Britain has been drawn to a scale :-

1 cm = 50 miles.

a Check that the line from Glasgow to Aberdeen is 2·8 centimetres long.

Calculate the **real** distance from Glasgow to Aberdeen, in miles.

b For each of the following, measure the **shortest** distances between the towns in centimetres, then calculate the **real** distances between the towns in miles :-

(i) Inverness to Wick

(ii) Edinburgh to Liverpool

(iii) Plymouth to London

(iv) York to Glasgow

(v) London to Wick.

c Ryanjet flight RJ3456 flew from London City Airport to Birmingham, then on to Edinburgh. From there it returned to London City.

(i) Measure each of the three parts of the flight, in centimetres.

(ii) Calculate each of the distances, in miles.

(iii) Calculate the total distance flown by flight RJ3456.

Scale Drawings

Geometry Assessment 4

1. Make a two-times enlargement of these shapes, each large box being 1 cm by 1 cm.

a

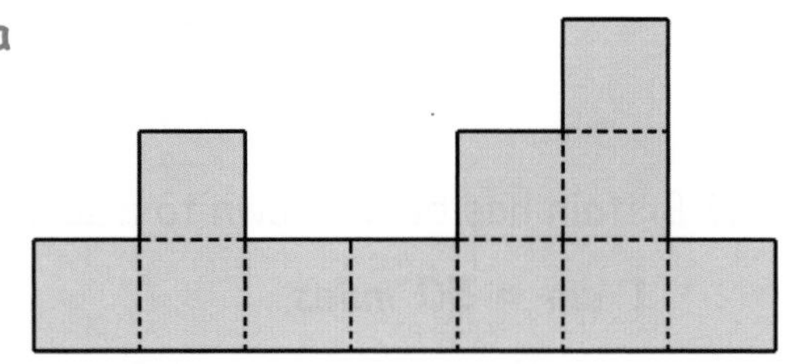

b

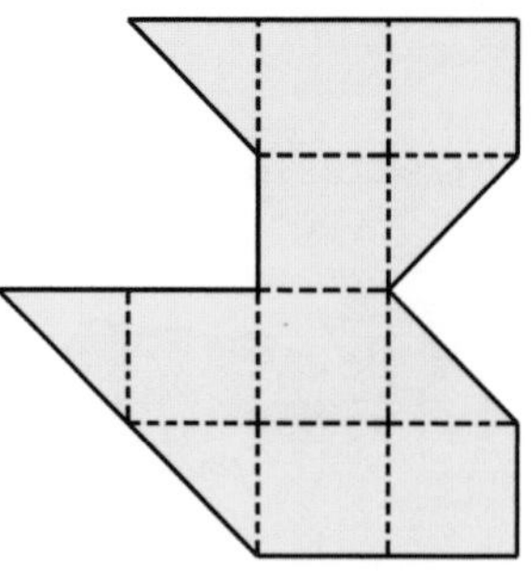

2. Make a copy of this shape but half its size.

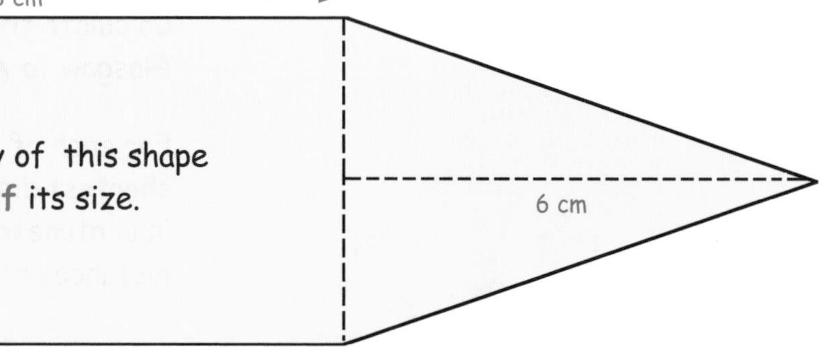

3. This picture frame is drawn to a scale of :-

1 cm represents 7·5 cm.

a Calculate the real width of the frame.

b Calculate the real height of the frame.

c The real length of a diagonal is 37·5 cm.

Calculate the length of the diagonal in the picture.

4. Shown is a drawing of one of the modern buildings in the new harbour area in the town of Dunston.

It has been drawn using a scale :- **1 cm = 5·5 m.**

Work out the real height of the building.

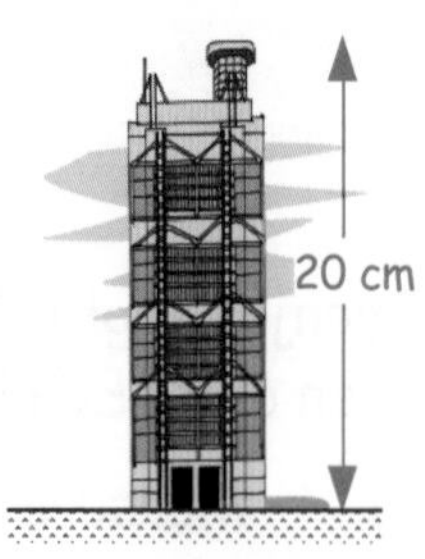

5.

Port Allen

1 cm = 50 km

Brodich

The map opposite shows 2 islands in a stretch of water between two countries.

a Use your ruler to measure the distance from Port Allen to Brodich.

b Use the scale of the map to work out the real distance between them.

Area 2

Area of a Parallelogram

This parallelogram has base length 6 centimetres and height 3 centimetres.

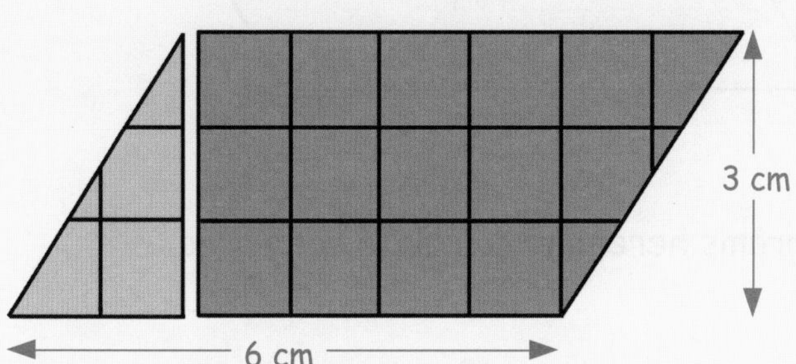

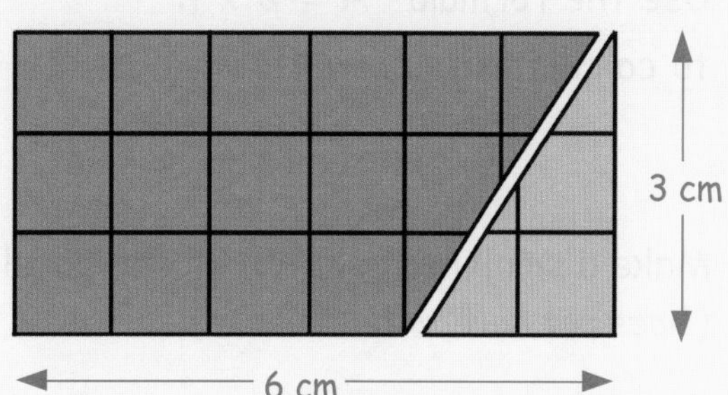

By cutting off the right angled triangle on the left and moving it round to the right, we can change the parallelogram into a rectangle measuring 6 cm long and 3 cm high.

Since the area of a rectangle is :- $A = 6 \times 3 = 18 \text{ cm}^2$,

=> The area of the **parallelogram** is also given by

Area = base × height = 6 × 3 = **18 cm^2**.

Rule for finding **area** of **parallelogram** is :- Area = base × height

Exercise 1

1. a Trace this parallelogram **neatly** using a ruler.

   b On your tracing paper, cut along the dotted line.

   c Lie the larger piece flat in your jotter and place the small triangle onto the right to create a rectangle.

   d What is the length and breadth of the rectangle ?

   e Calculate the **area** of the rectangle. (*A = length x breadth*).

   f Now calculate the **area** of the original parallelogram.

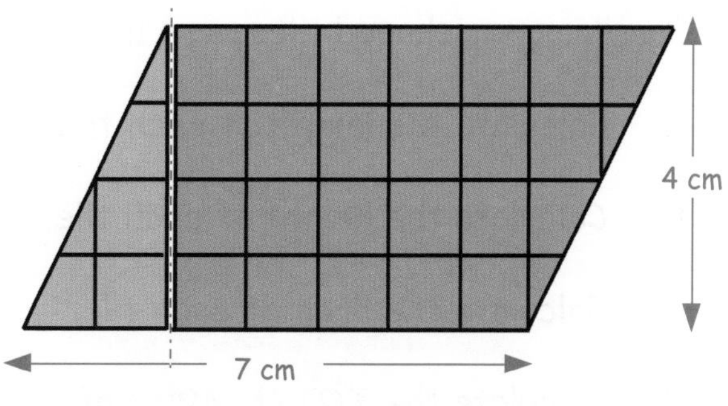

2. Use the formula :-

Area = b x h

to calculate the area of this parallelogram measuring 8 cm long and 2 cm high.

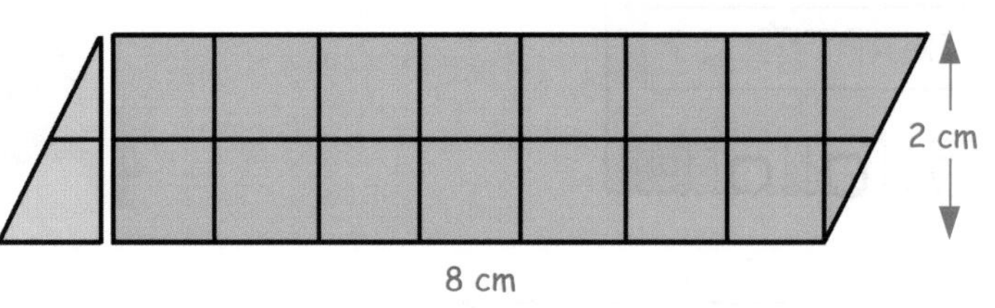

3. This is a sketch of a parallelogram.

Use the formula *A = b x h*

to calculate its area. (*in cm²*).

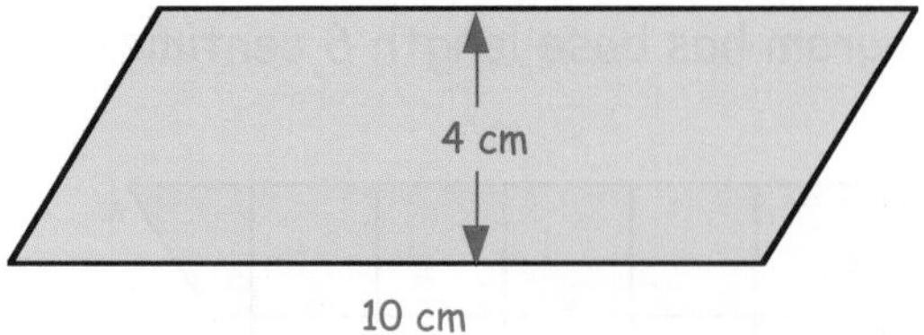

4. Make a small neat sketch of the parallelograms here, and calculate each area :-
(*Does **not** have to be full size*).

a

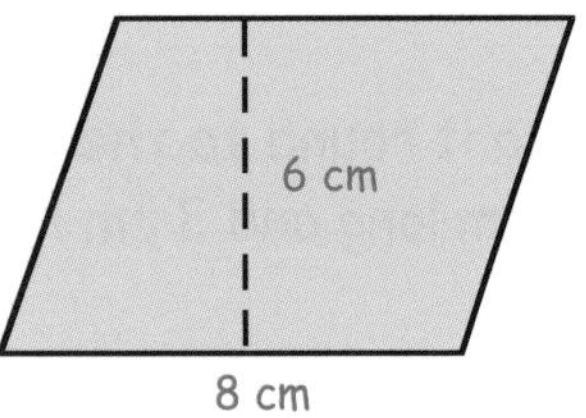

b

7 cm

15 cm

c

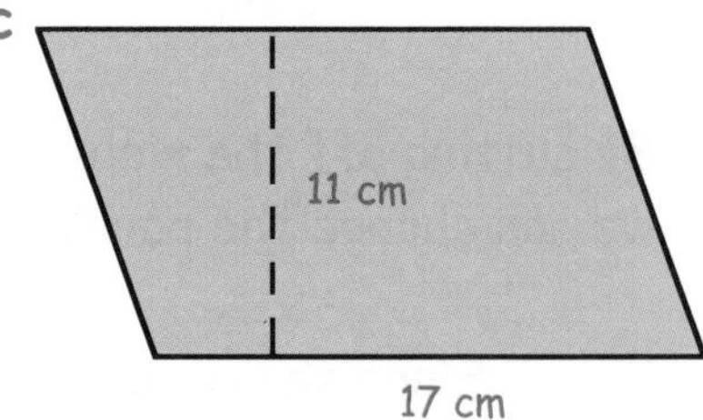

d

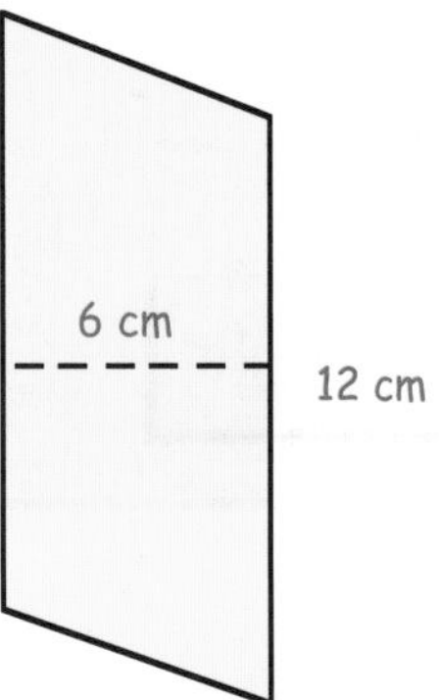

e

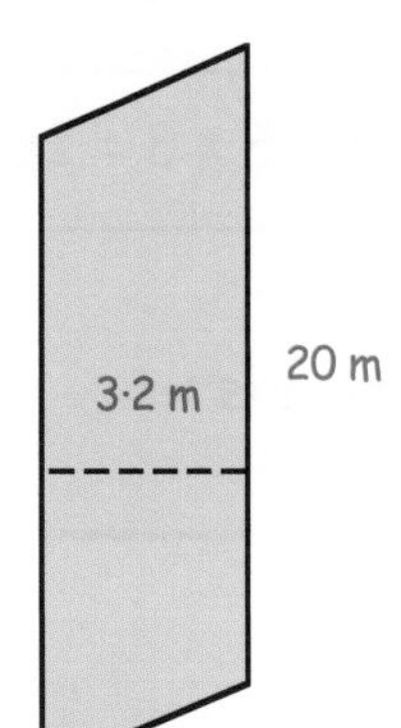

f

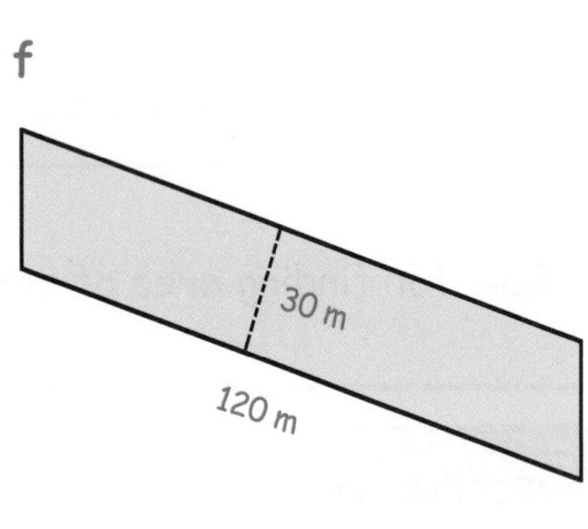

5. Shown is a section of tiling on a bathroom wall.

Parallelogram shaped tiles were used.

a Calculate the **length** of each tile.

b Calculate the **height** of each tile.

c Calculate the **area** of each tile.

d Calculate the TOTAL AREA of the tiling shown.

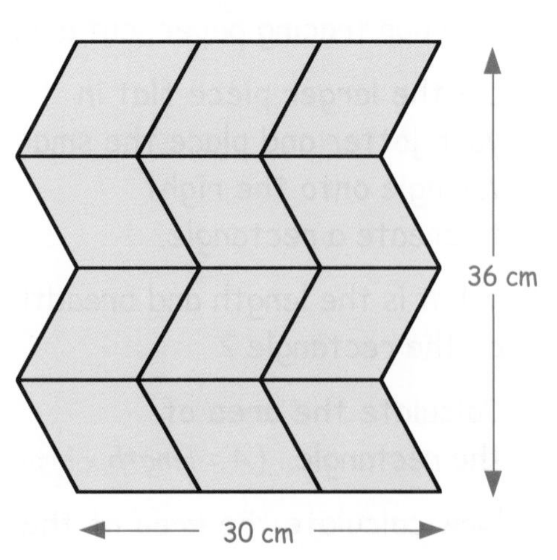

Area of a Kite and a Rhombus

Remember what a **Kite** and what a **Rhombus** looks like ?

Kite   rhombus (diamond)

It is fairly simple to find the **area** of a rhombus (or kite) by drawing (or imagining) the rectangle surrounding it.

This rhombus measures 8 centimetres long by 4 centimetres high.

We have drawn a (dotted) rectangle around it.

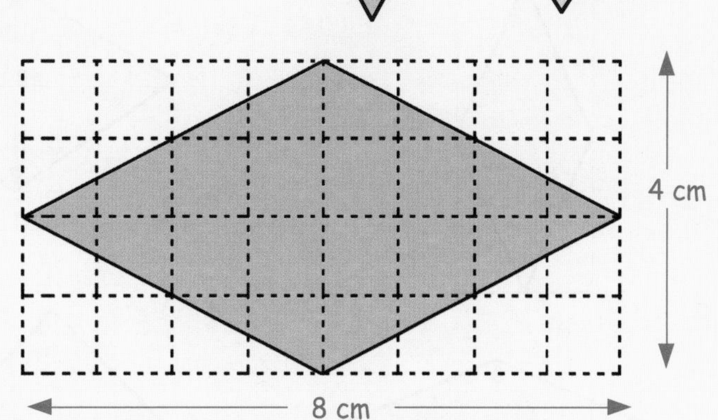

Can you see => Area of (surrounding) rectangle = $l \times b = 8 \times 4 = 32\text{ cm}^2$?

Can you also see => Area of rhombus = $\frac{1}{2}$ of this area = $\frac{1}{2}$ of 32 = 16 cm^2 ?

=> To find the **area** of a **rhombus** :-

find the area of the surrounding rectangle then find HALF of this answer.

Exercise 2

1. a Make an accurate drawing of this rhombus, 6 cm by 4 cm.

   (*You are probably better drawing the two diagonals 6 cm by 4 cm meeting at right angles in the middle first*).

   b On your diagram, draw a rectangle round the rhombus.

   c Calculate the **area** of the rectangle.

   d Now calculate the area of the **rhombus** (÷ 2).

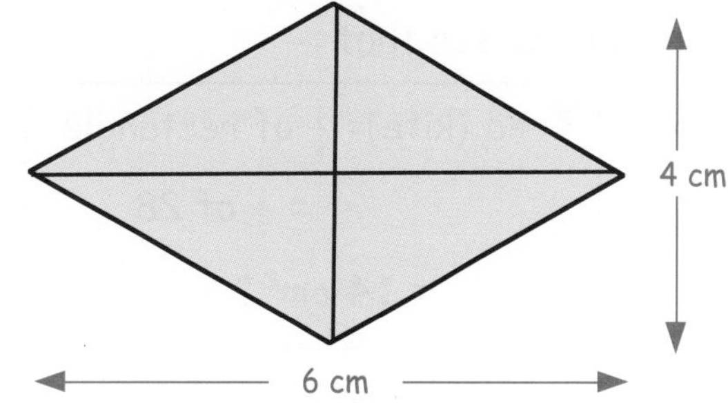

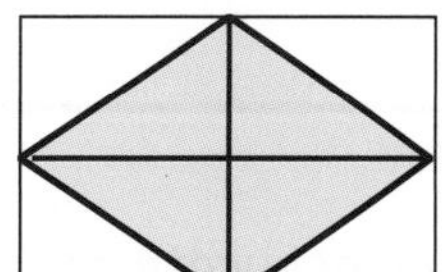

2. a Make a small neat *sketch* of this rhombus.

   b Draw in the (dotted) surrounding rectangle.

   c Calculate the area of the rectangle.

   d Now calculate the area of the rhombus.

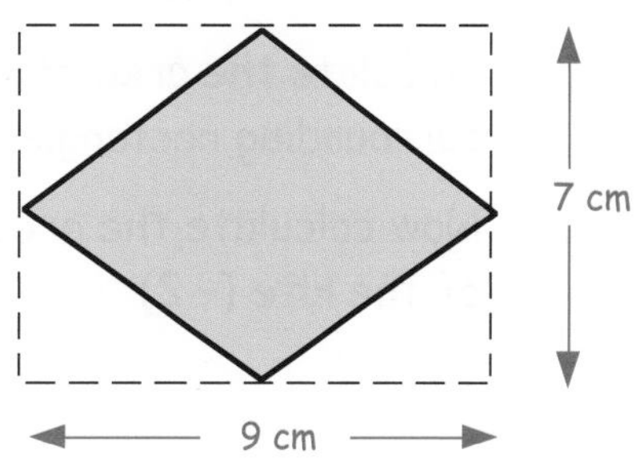

3. For each rhombus below :-

(i) **Sketch** the rhombus. (ii) Surround it with a rectangle.

(iii) Calculate the area of the rectangle. (iv) Calculate the area of the rhombus.

a

4 cm

9 cm

b

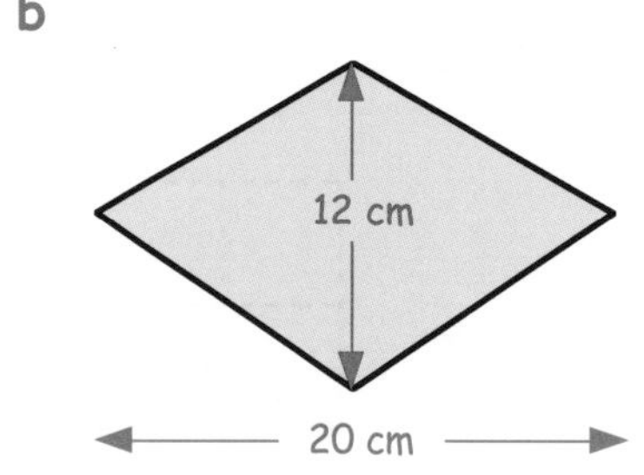

c

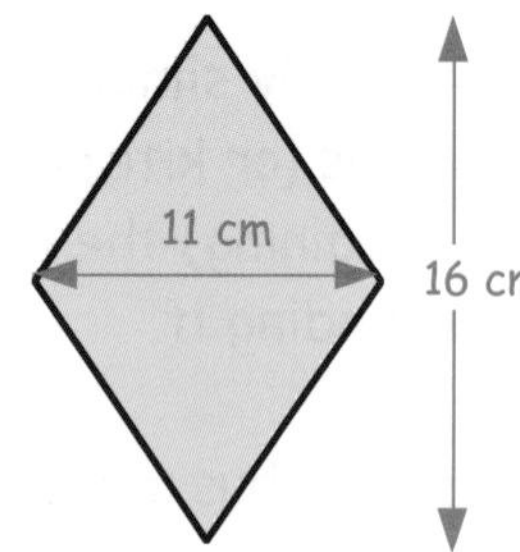

d

7 cm

18 cm

e

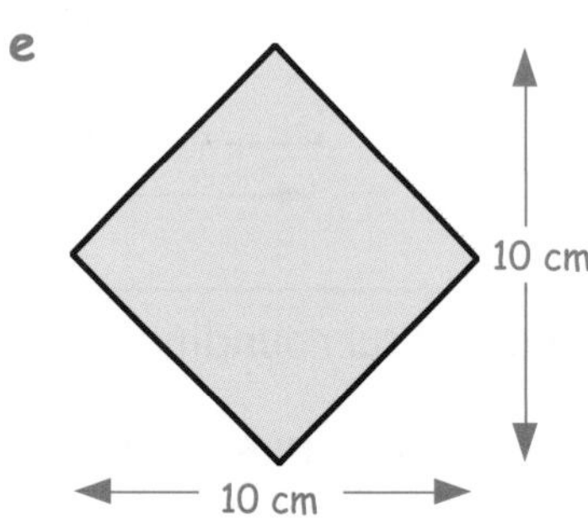

f

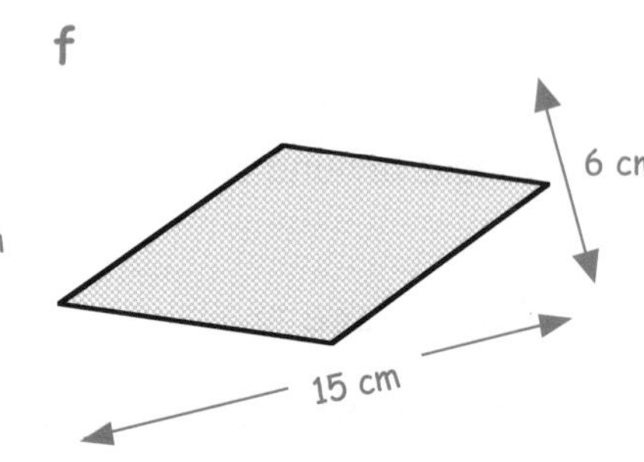

The **area of a kite** is found in the same way.

Can you see that :-

Area (rectangle) = $l \times b$ = 7×4 = 28 cm^2 ?

Can you also see that :-

=> **Area** (kite)= $\frac{1}{2}$ of rectangle

= $\frac{1}{2}$ of 28

= **14 cm^2** ?

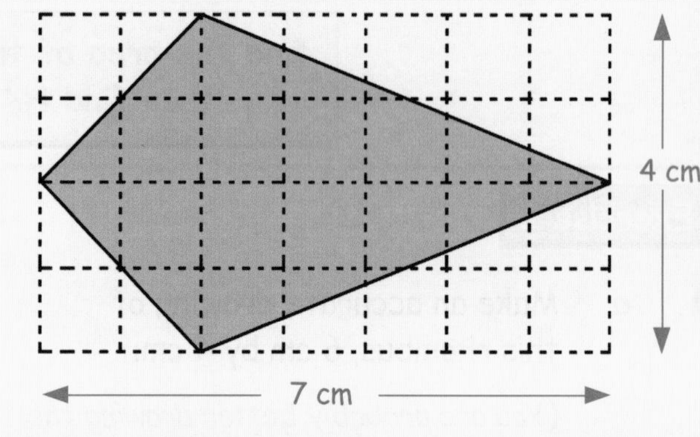

=> To find the **area of a kite** :-

find the area of the surrounding rectangle then find HALF of this answer.

4. a Make an accurate drawing of this kite, using a ruler.

b Calculate the area of the surrounding rectangle.

c Now calculate the area of the **kite** (÷ 2).

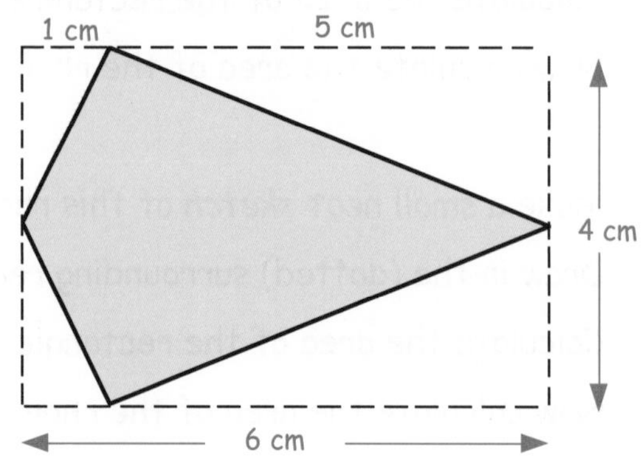

5.

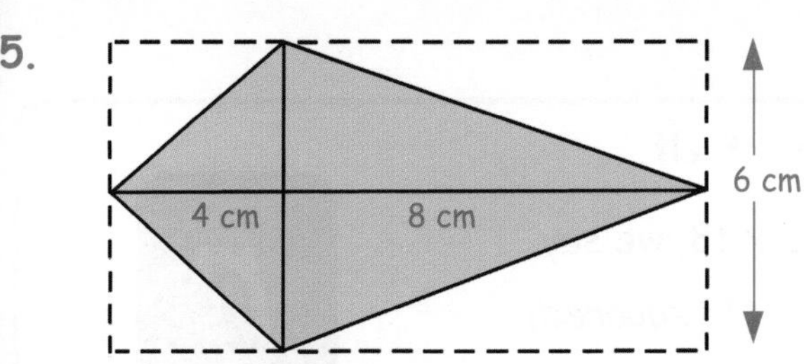

a Make a small neat sketch of this kite.

b Calculate the area of the surrounding rectangle.

c Now calculate the area of the kite.

6. For each kite :-

(i) **Sketch** the kite.

(ii) Surround the kite with a rectangle.

(iii) Calculate the area of the rectangle.

(iv) Now, calculate the area of the kite.

a

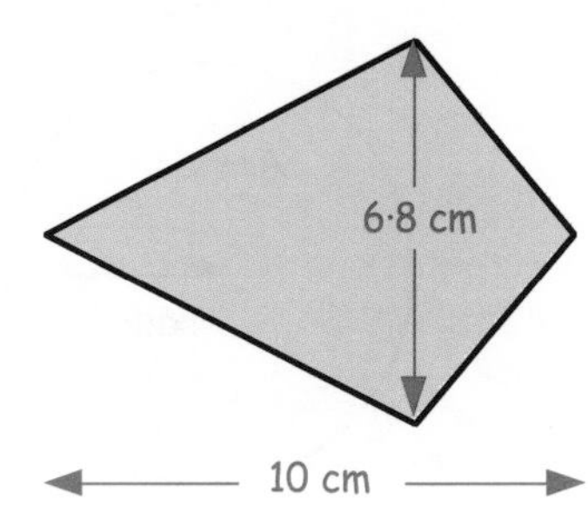

b

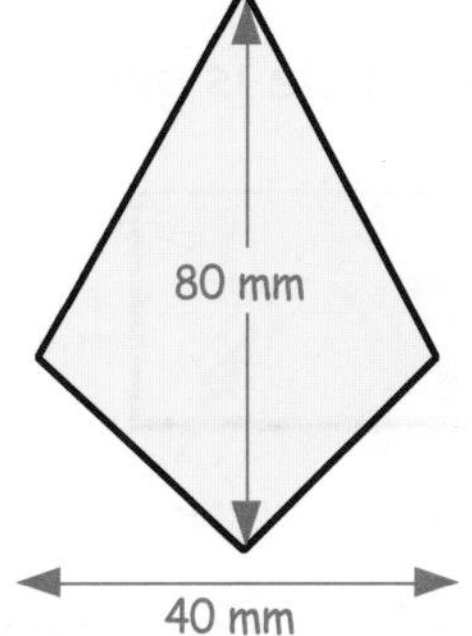

c

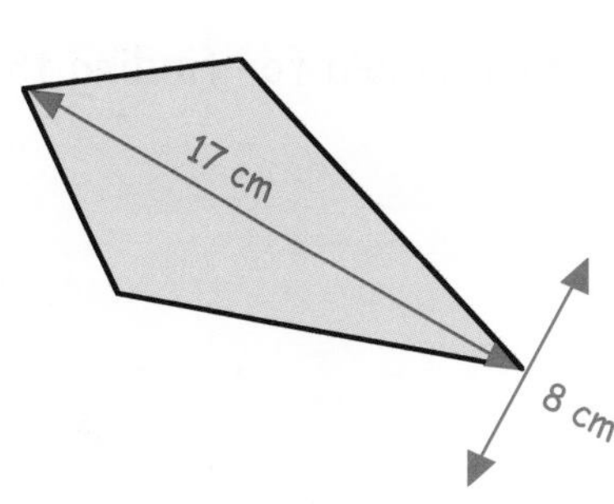

d

6·8 cm

10 cm

e

80 mm

40 mm

f

17 cm

8 cm

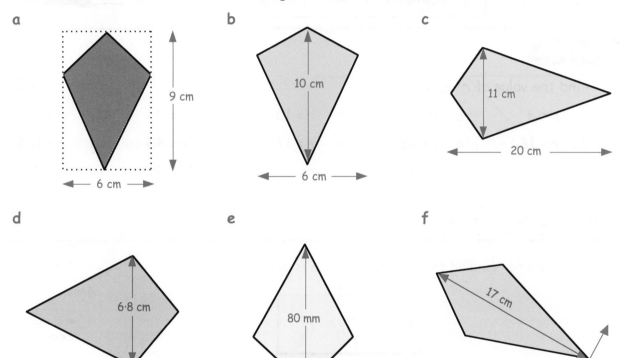

7. Which has the bigger area :- the rhombus or the kite, and by how much ?

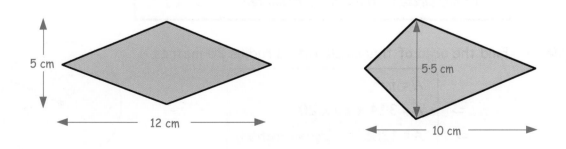

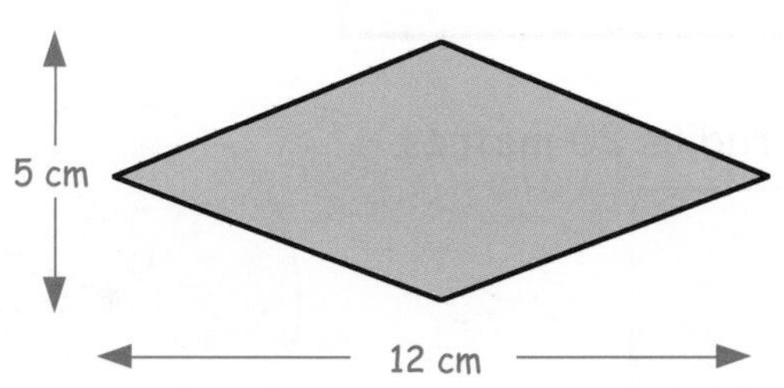

5·5 cm

10 cm

"Squaring" a Number

To square a number means to multiply the number by itself.

If we wish to multiply a number by itself, e.g. 13 x 13, we say we have squared the number, and write it as 13^2. (*13 squared*)

Examples :- $3^2 = 3 \times 3 = 9$ $7^2 = 7 \times 7 = 49$

Example :- If the radius of a circle is 4 cm, find the value of the "radius squared" (r^2).

$r = 4$ (cm) $= r^2 = 4 \times 4 = 16$ (cm^2)

Exercise 3

1. Find the value of r^2 given that :-

a	$r = 3$	b	$r = 2$	c	$r = 10$	d	$r = 9$	e	$r = 5$
f	$r = 12$	g	$r = 25$	h	$r = 17$	i	$r = 40$	j	$r = 120$
k	$r = 1·2$	l	$l = 3·5$	m	$r = 101$	n	$r = 9·5$	o	$r = 0·5$

The Area of a Circle

The formula for finding the area of a circle is given as :-

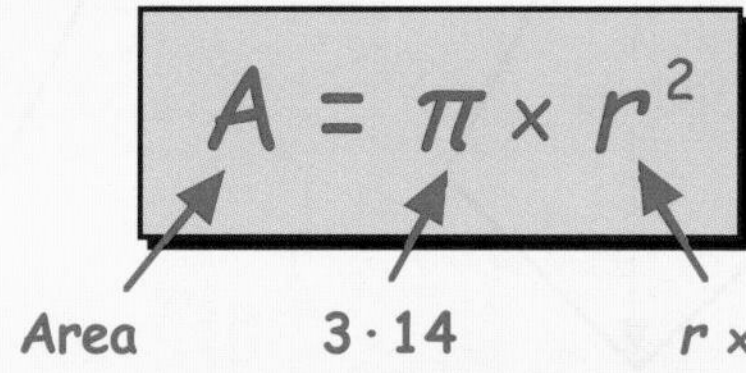

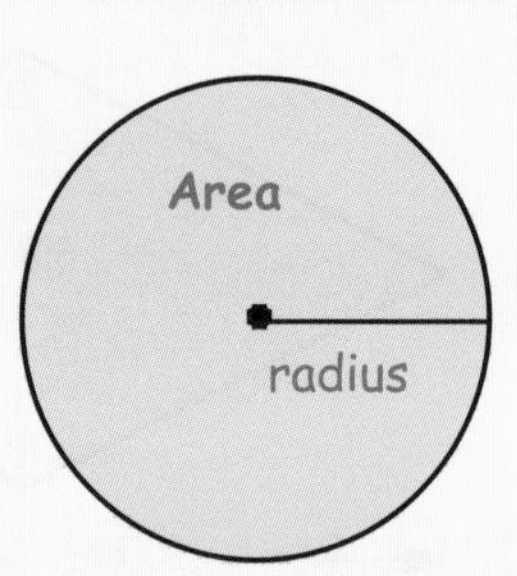

where A is the area, π is Pi (= 3·14), and r is the radius.

> *You met π in the previous chapter.*
> *It's the value you get when you divide the Circumference of any circle by the circle's Diameter. ($\pi = C \div D$)*

Example :- Find the area of this circle with a radius 20 metres.

$A = \pi r^2$

=> $A = 3·14 \times 20 \times 20$

=> $A = 1256$ m^2 (*square metres*)

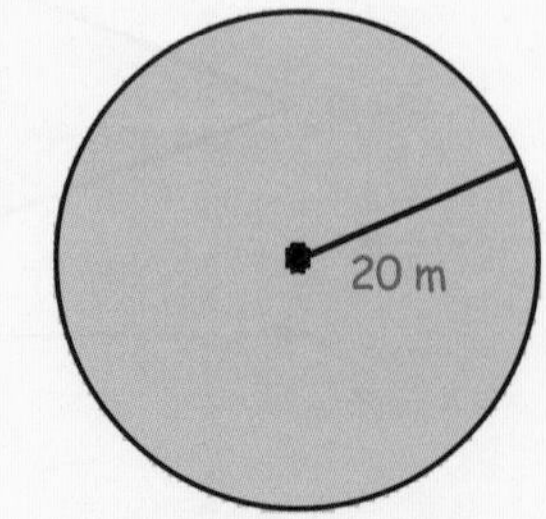

Exercise 4

Give your answers to 2 decimal places where necessary.

1. Calculate the area of each of these circles :-

a

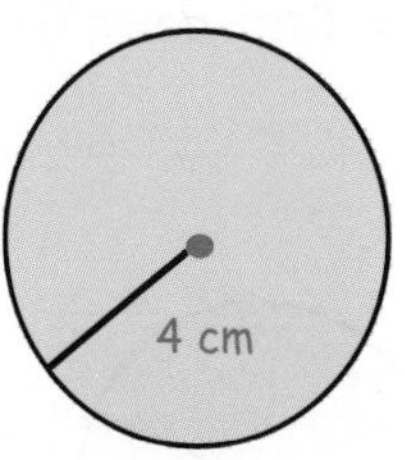

b

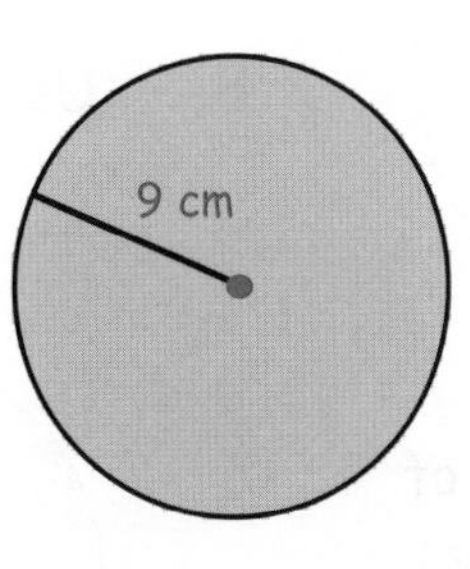

2. Calculate the area of this circle.

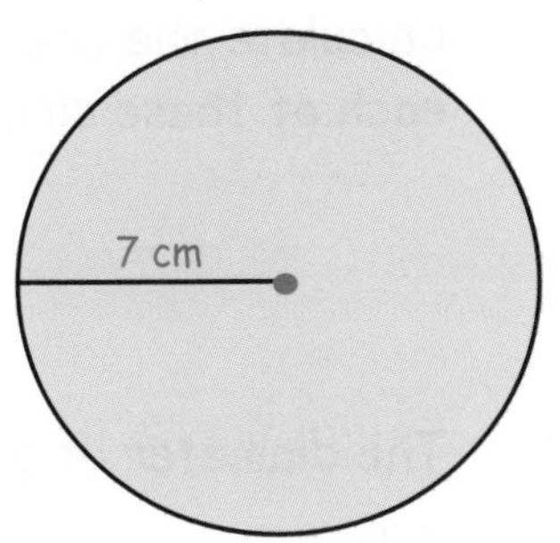

3. For each of the following circles, set down the three lines of working and calculate its area :-

a

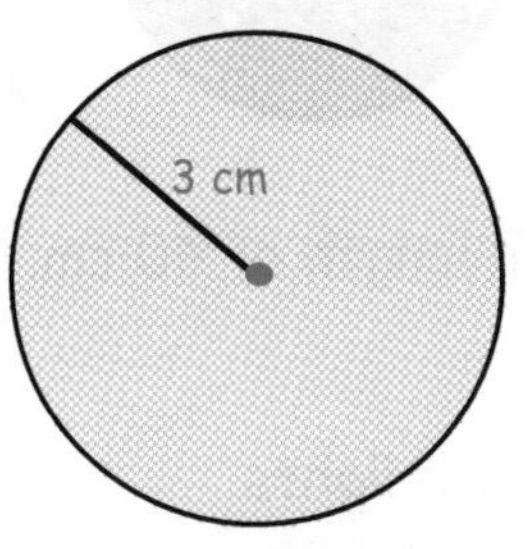

b

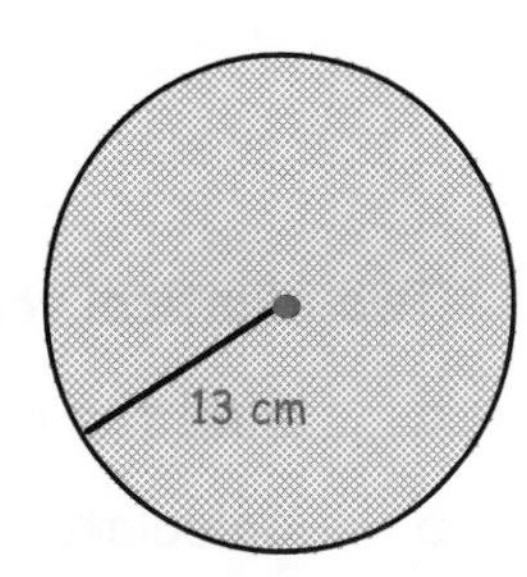

c

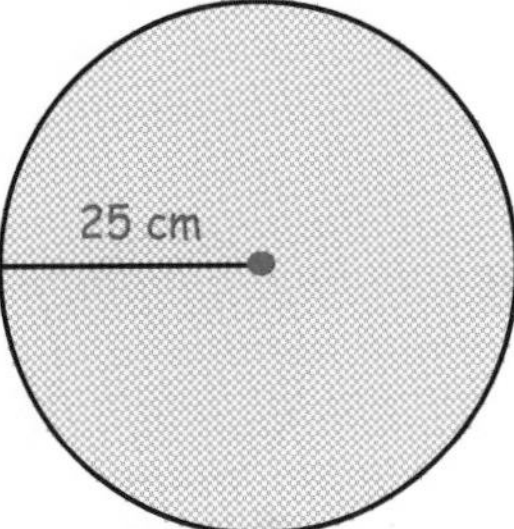

d

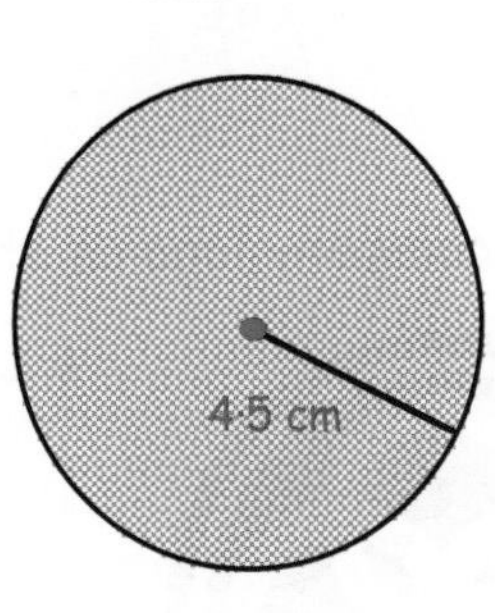

e

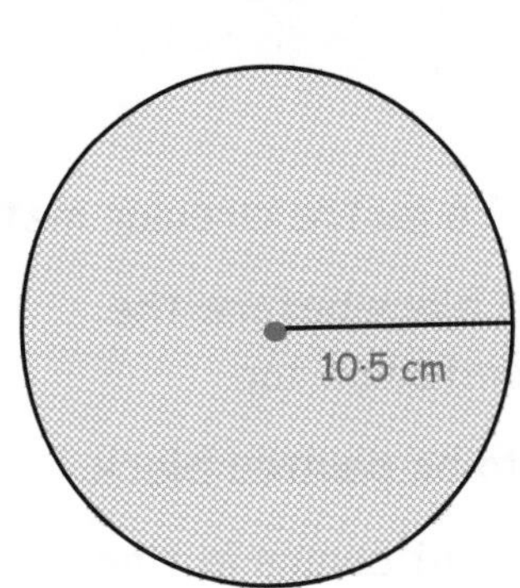

f

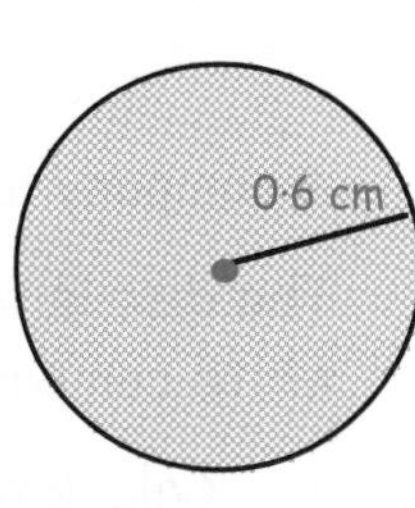

4. **Careful !!**

In this question, you are given the **diameter** (not the radius).

Copy and complete to calculate the **area** :-

Step 1 :-

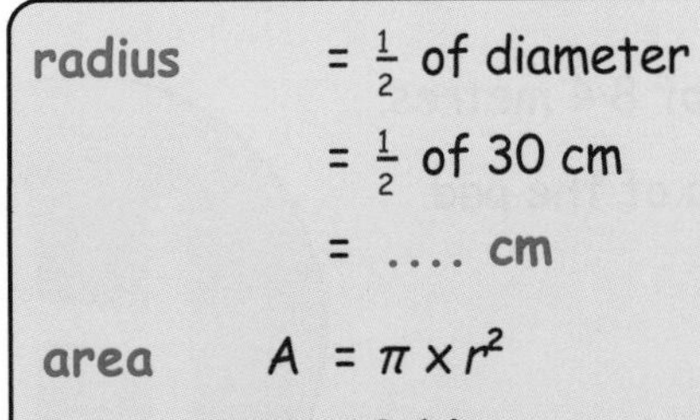

radius $= \frac{1}{2}$ of diameter

$= \frac{1}{2}$ of 30 cm

$=$ .... cm

Step 2 :-

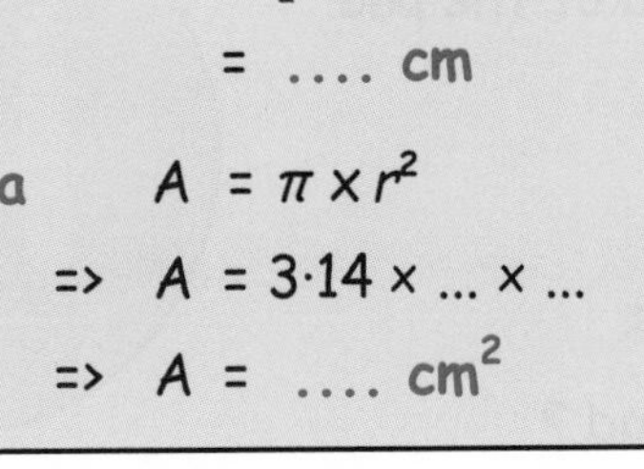

area $A = \pi \times r^2$

=> $A = 3{\cdot}14 \times ... \times ...$

=> $A =$ .... cm^2

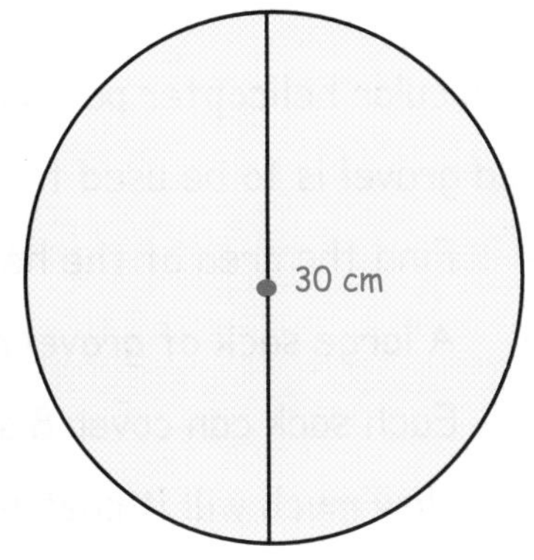

5. For this circle :-

18 cm

a Halve the diameter to get the radius.

b Use this to calculate its **area** (*set down !*)

6. Calculate the **area** of each of these circles :-

a 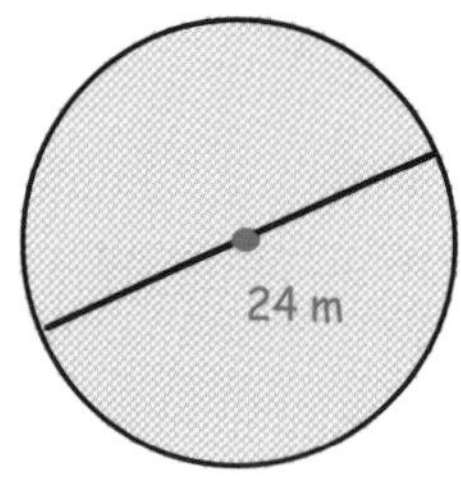

b 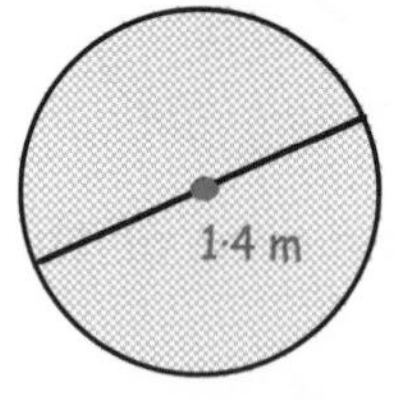

7. The diameter of an old Vinyl L. P. record is 30 centimetres.

Calculate its **area**.

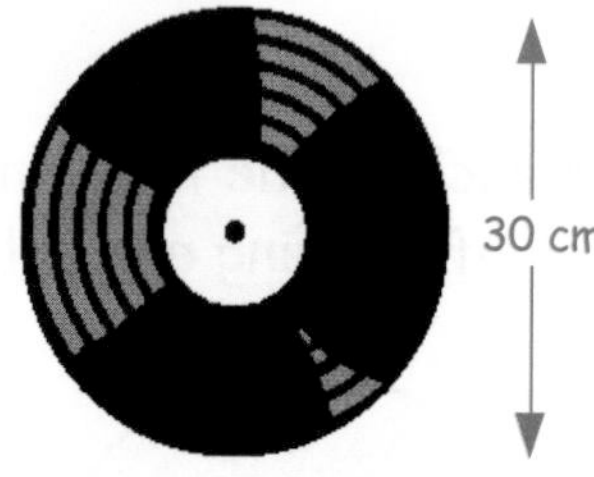

8. 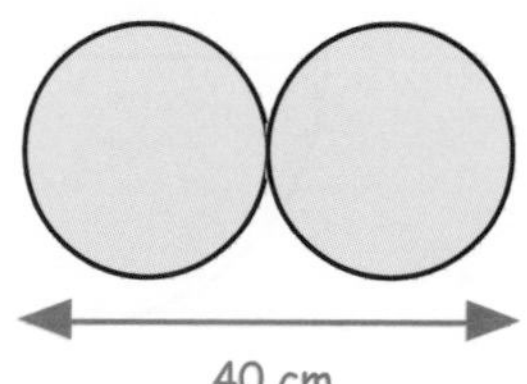

Two identical touching lights have a **length** of 40 cm.

a Find the radius of each light.

b Calculate the **total area** of both lights.

9. A company uses a large 4·6 metre circular metal disc for its company logo as shown.

The disc is to be painted black before the white company logo is painted on top.

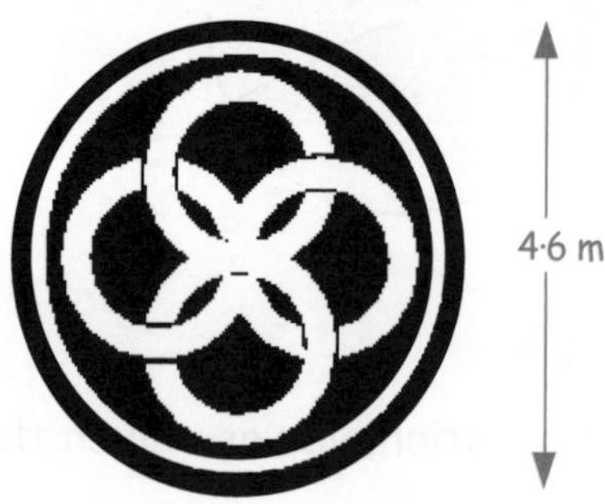

a Calculate the area to be painted black.

b The black metallic paint comes in tins.

Each tin covers 2·5 square metres.

How many tins of paint are needed ?

10. A circular helicopter pad has a diameter of 8·4 metres.

Red gravel is to be used to cover the area of the pad.

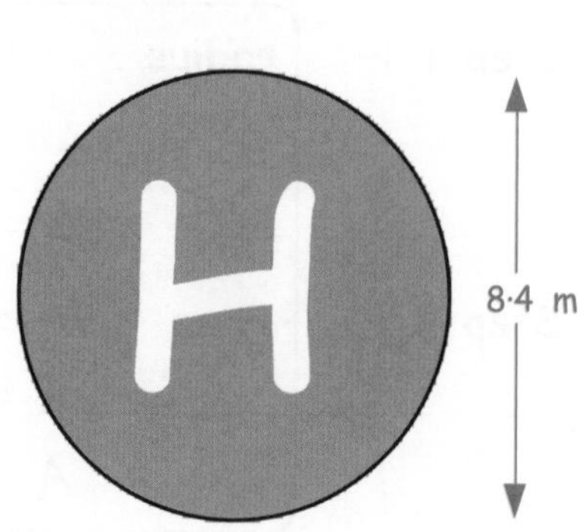

a Find the area of the helicopter pad.

b A large sack of gravel costs £4·80.

Each sack can cover 8 square metres.

How much will it cost to cover the pad ?

Area 2

Geometry Assessment 5

1. Calculate the area of each of these shapes :-

a parallelogram

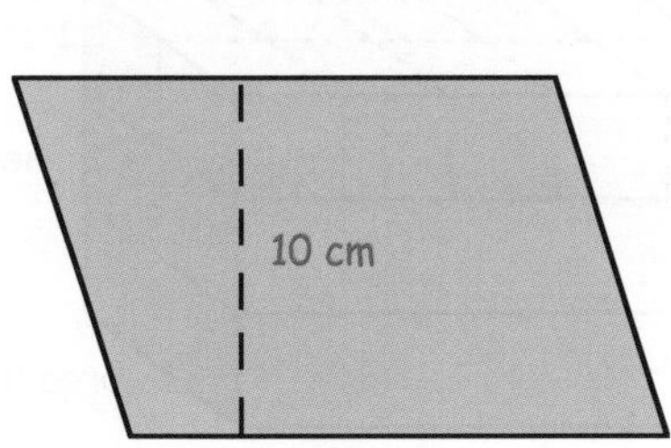

b rhombus

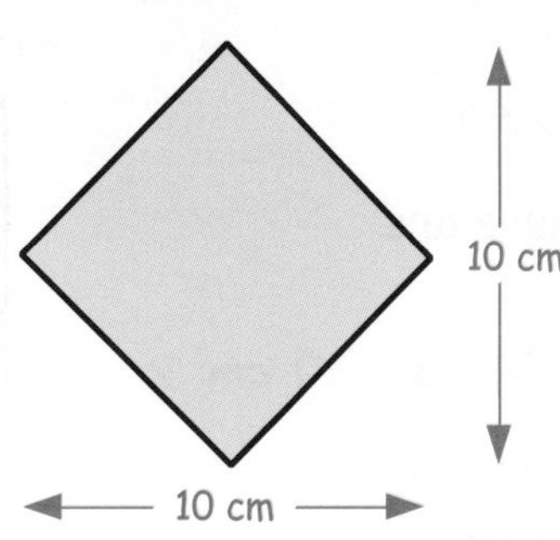

c kite

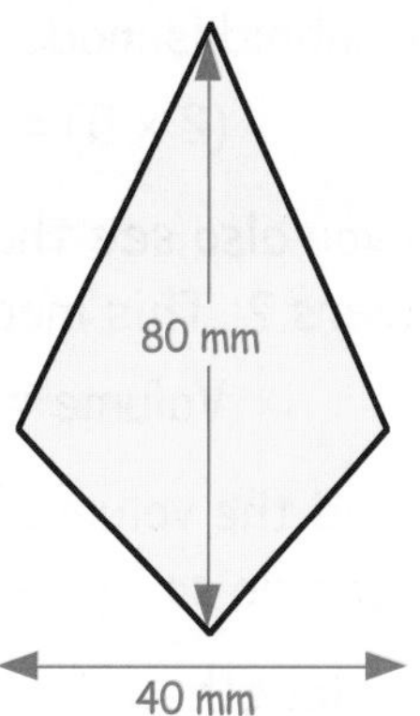

2. Calculate the area of each circle below :-

a

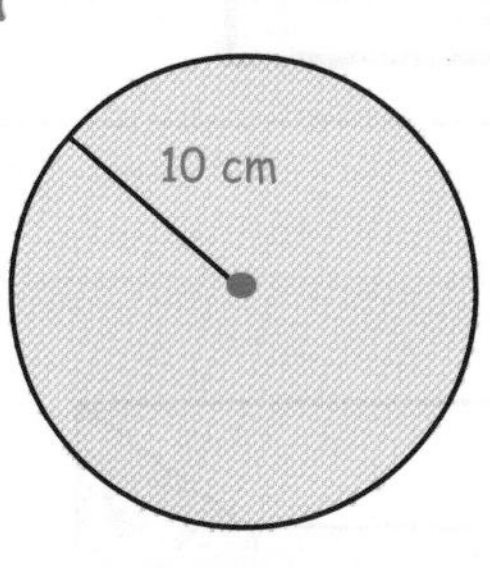

b

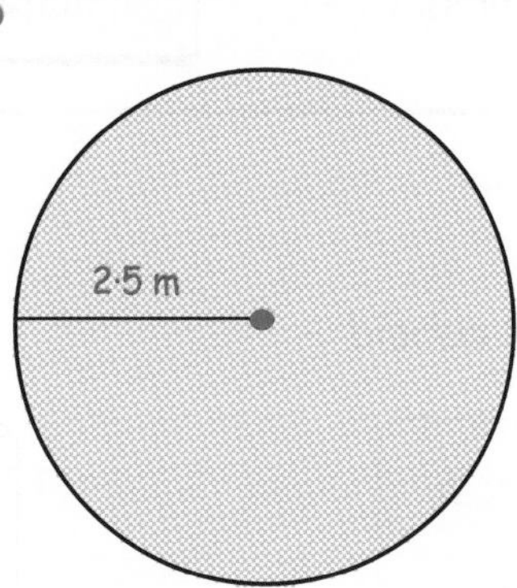

c

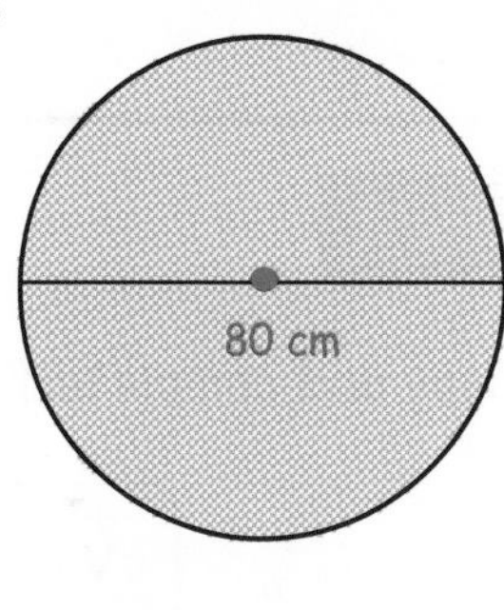

3. Grass is to be grown on the large circular garden plot shown.

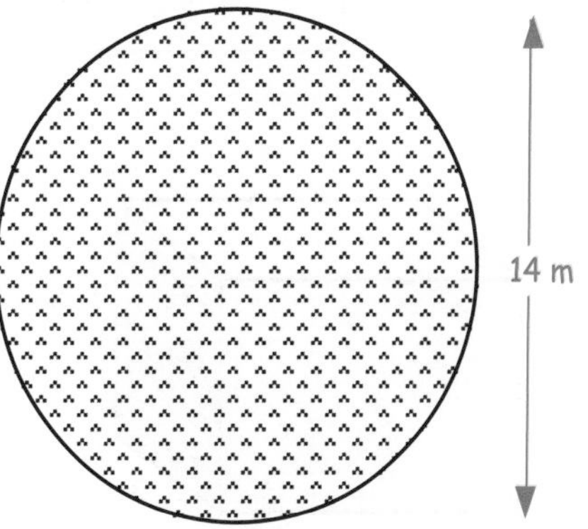

a Find the area of the plot of land.

The grass seed used is sold in bags costing £5·75 each.

Each bag of seed covers **ten** square metres.

b Find the cost of the grass seed needed to cover the entire garden.

Volume

The Volume of a Cuboid Revision

(i) Can you see that the top layer of this cuboid is made up of

$(2 \times 5) = 10 \text{ cm}^3$?

(ii) Can you also see that there are 3 layers ? This means

Volume = $(2 \times 5) \times 3 = 30 \text{ cm}^3$?

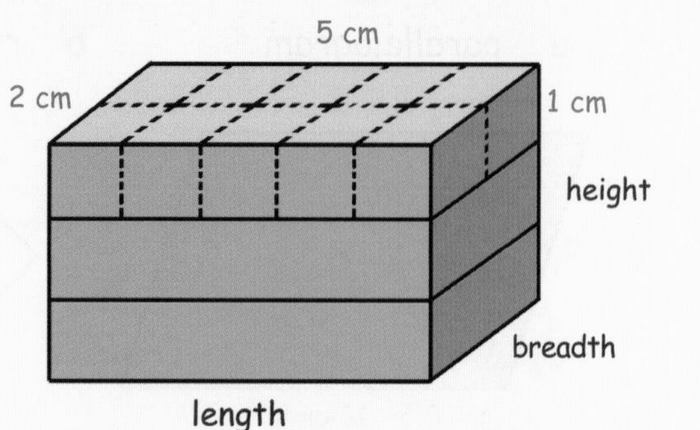

To find the volume of a cuboid, you can do so by multiplying :-

length × breadth × height

Formula :- **Volume = $l \times b \times h$**

Exercise 1

1. Copy and complete for this cuboid :-

$V = l \times b \times h$
$V = 9 \times 4 \times 6$
$V = \text{..........} \text{ cm}^3$

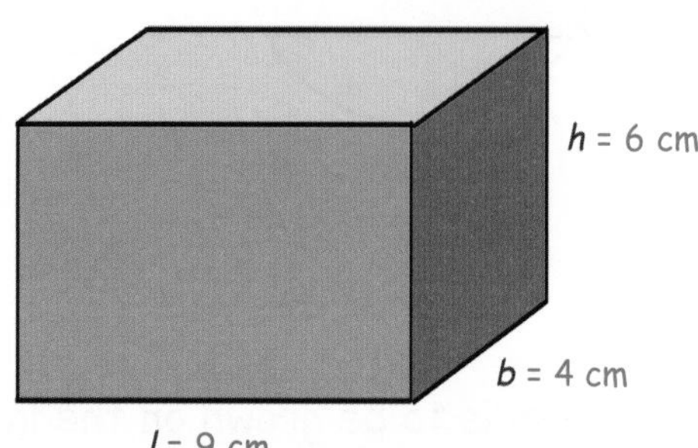

2. 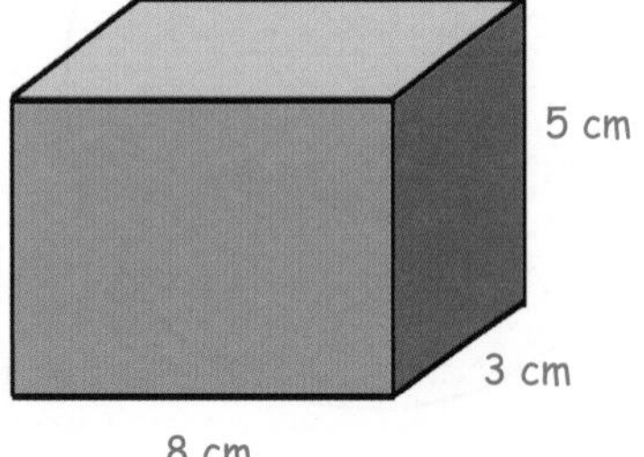

Use the formula $V = l \times b \times h$ to calculate the volume of this cuboid.
(*Show your working*).

3. Use the formula again to calculate the volume of this cuboid.

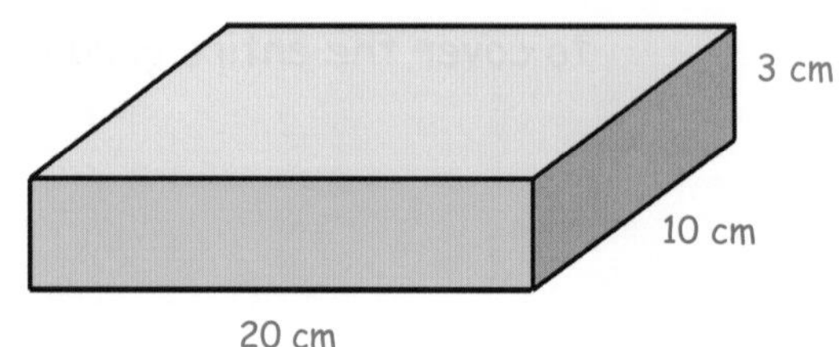

4. Calculate the **volume** of each of the following cuboids, in cm^3 (*Show your working*) :-

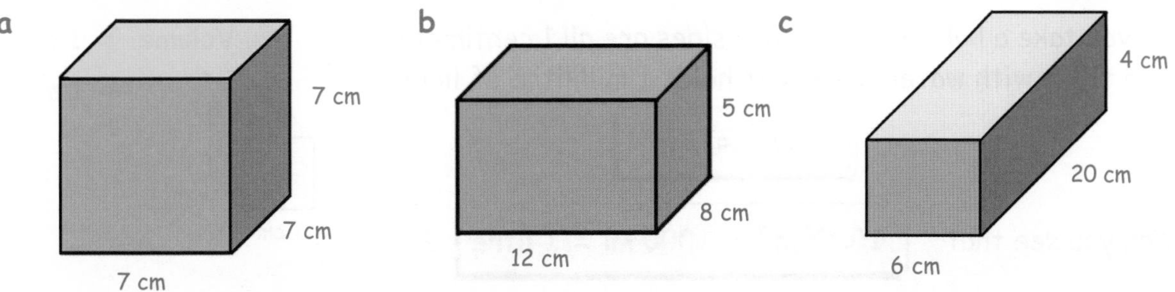

5. Calculate the **volume** of each of the following cuboids, in m^3 (*Show your working*) :-

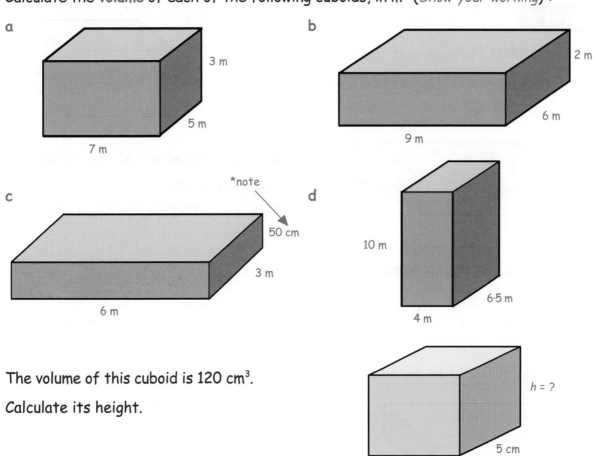

a
3 m
5 m
7 m

b
2 m
6 m
9 m

c
*note
50 cm
3 m
6 m

d
10 m
6·5 m
4 m

6. The volume of this cuboid is 120 cm^3.

Calculate its height.

h = ?
5 cm
6 cm

7. Calculate the length of the missing edge in each of the following cuboids :-

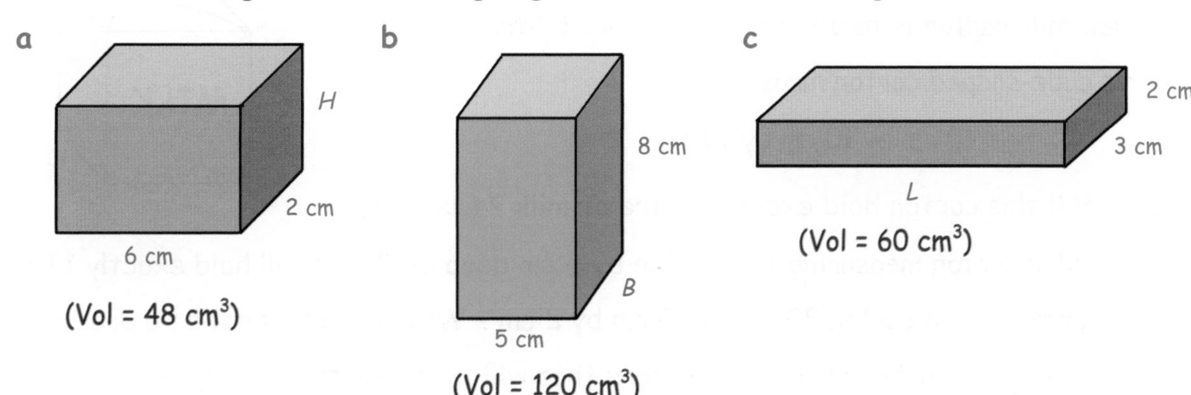

Liquid Volumes - Capacity Revision

If you take a **hollow cube** whose sides are all 1 centimetre, and fill it with water, we say it holds 1 millilitre of liquid.

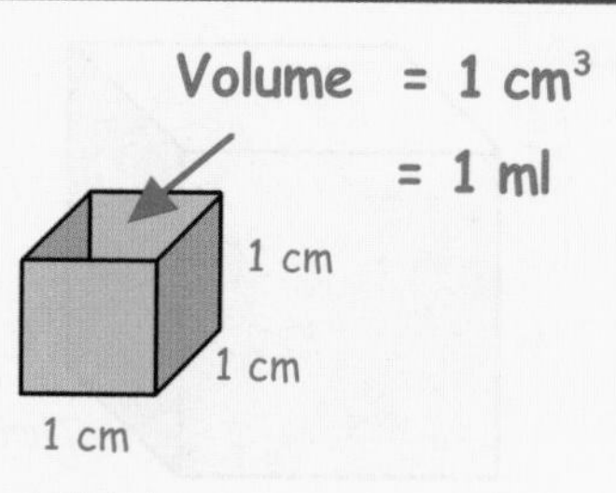

$1 \text{ cm}^3 = 1 \text{ ml}$

Can you see that $1000 \text{ cm}^3 = 1000 \text{ ml} = 1 \text{ litre}$?

Liquid volume is referred to as **Capacity**.

Exercise 2

1. a Calculate the **volume** of this container, in cm^3.

   b How many millilitres of liquid will it hold ?

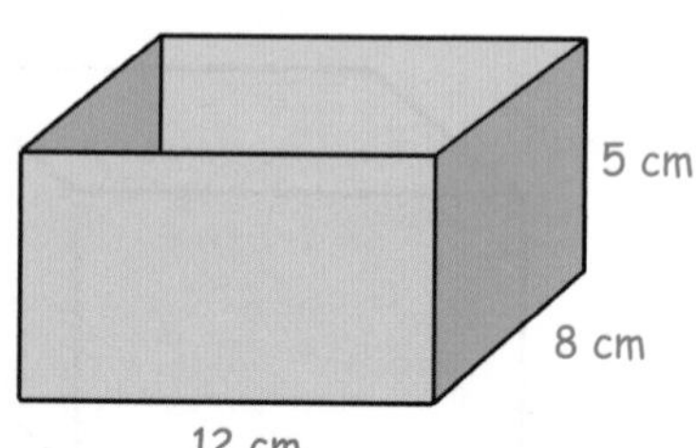

2. 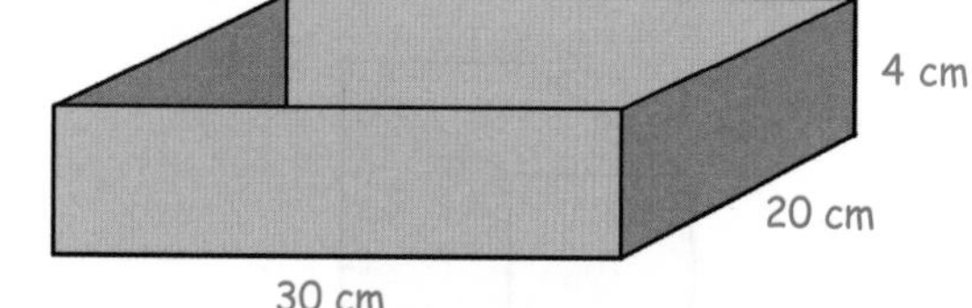

   a Calculate the **volume** of this rectangular container, in cm^3.

   b How many millilitres of liquid will it hold ?

3. Change each of the following to litres :-

a 4000 ml	b 8000 ml	c 15 000 ml
d 1500 ml	e 2300 ml	f 750 ml.

4. This tray collects rain water from a roof.

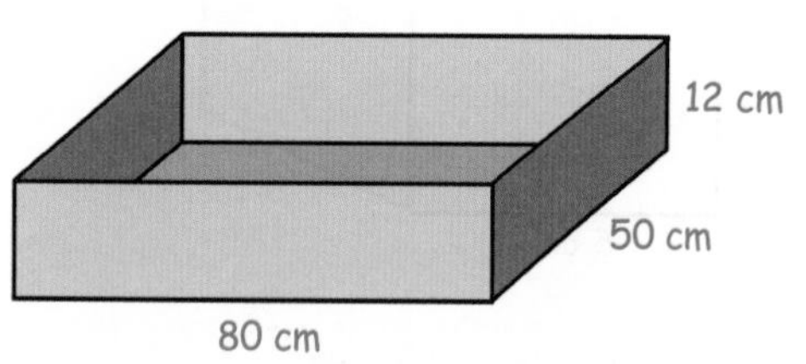

   a Calculate its volume, in cm^3.

   b How many millilitres will it hold when full ?

   c Write its **capacity**, in litres.

5. A new milk carton is to be designed to hold **1 litre**.

   This cube-shaped carton measures :-

   10 cm by 10 cm by 10 cm.

   a Will this carton hold exactly a litre of milk ? (*explain*)

   b Will a carton measuring 10 cm wide by 5 cm deep by 20 cm tall hold exactly 1 litre ?

   c What about a carton 20 cm by 25 cm by 2 cm ? Why would this not be a good design ?

   d **Investigate** other shapes of cartons that will hold exactly 1 (or 2) litres of milk.

The Volume of a Prism

A **prism** is simply a solid geometric figure whose two ends are identical and parallel, and whose corresponding pairs of corners are joined with straight lines.

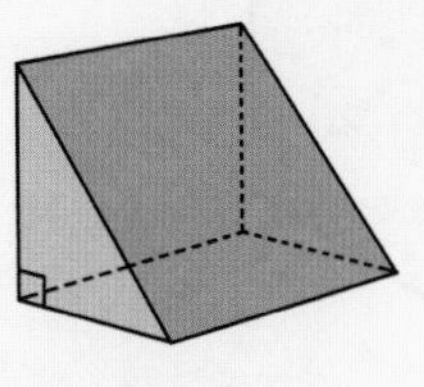
right angled triangular prism

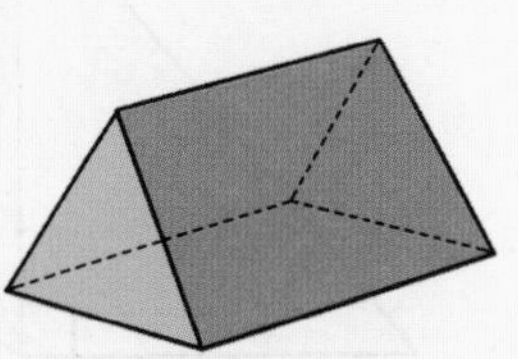
triangular prism

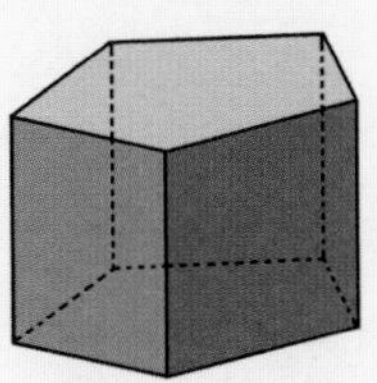
pentagonal prism

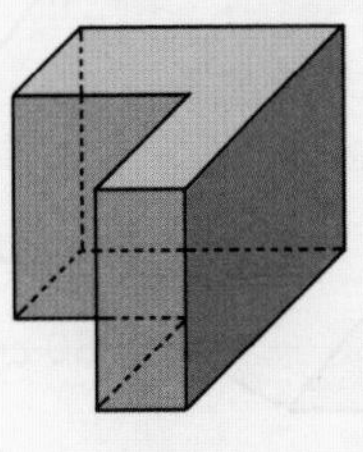
L-shaped prism

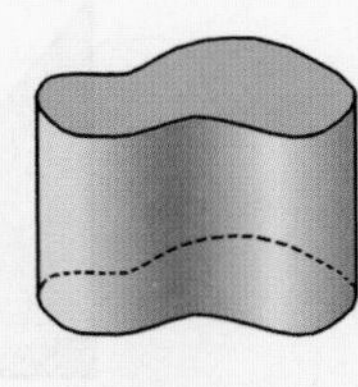
irregular prism

The **Volume** of a **Prism** is found by multiplying the **area** (*A*) of the common face by the **distance** (*d* or *h*) between the two faces.

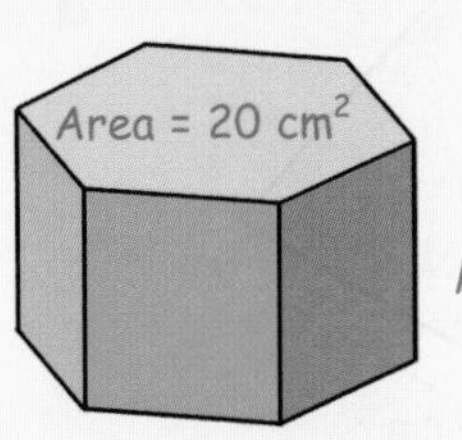

$V = \text{Area}_{(base)} \times \text{height}$

$\Rightarrow V = 20 \text{ cm}^2 \times 7 \text{ cm}$

$\Rightarrow V = 140 \text{ cm}^3$

Exercise 3

1. Use the formula $V = \text{Area}_{(base)} \times \text{height}$ to calculate the volumes of these prisms :-

a

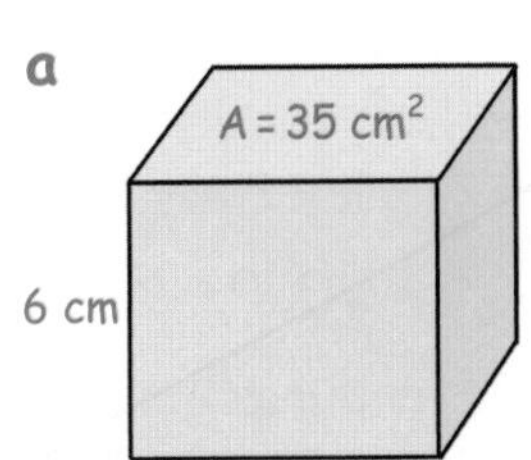

b

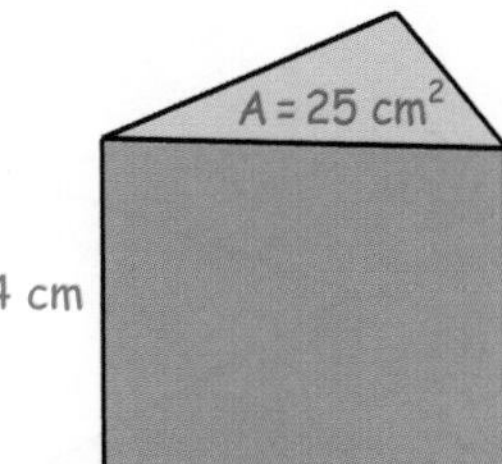

c

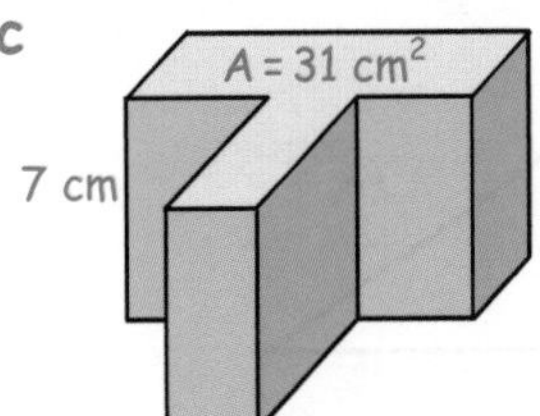

d

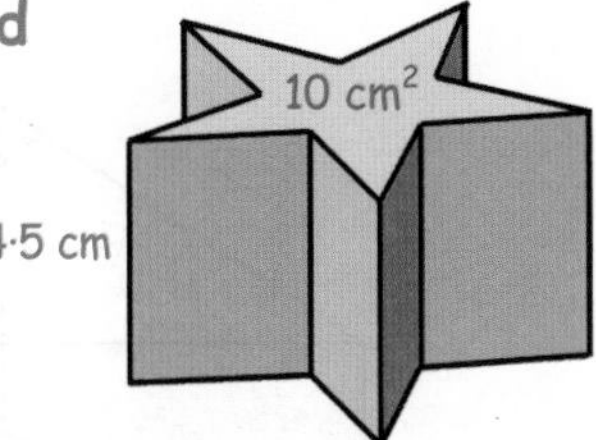

2. Shown is a rectangular based prism (*a cuboid*).
   - a Calculate the **area** of the top face.
   - b Now calculate the **volume** of the prism.

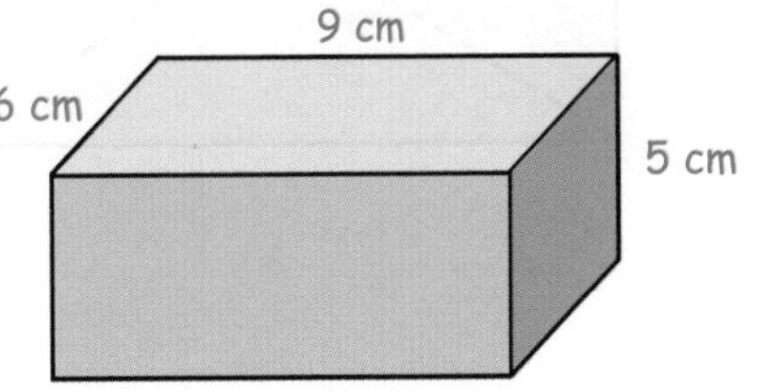

3.

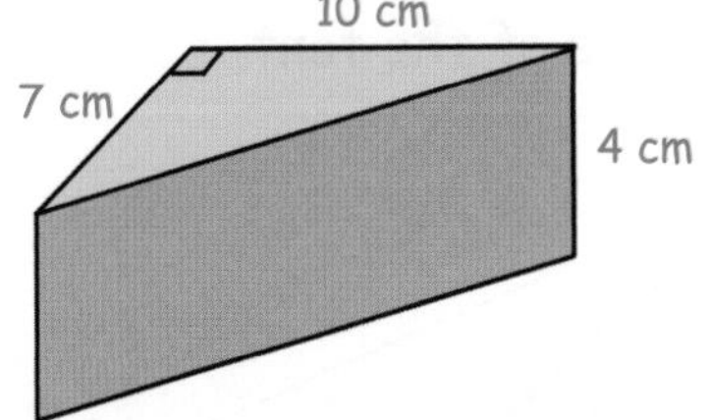

Shown is a right-angled triangular prism.
   - a Calculate the **area** of the triangular top.
   - b Now calculate the **volume** of the prism.

4. Shown is an isosceles triangular prism.
   - a Calculate the **area** of the front triangular face.
   - b Now calculate the **volume** of the prism.

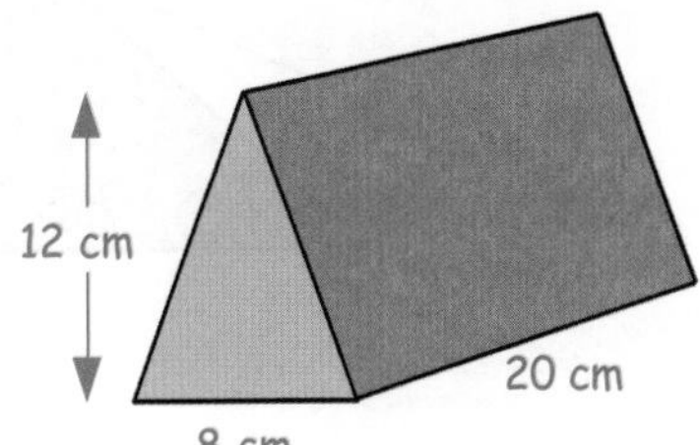

5. Calculate the volume of each of the following triangular prisms :-

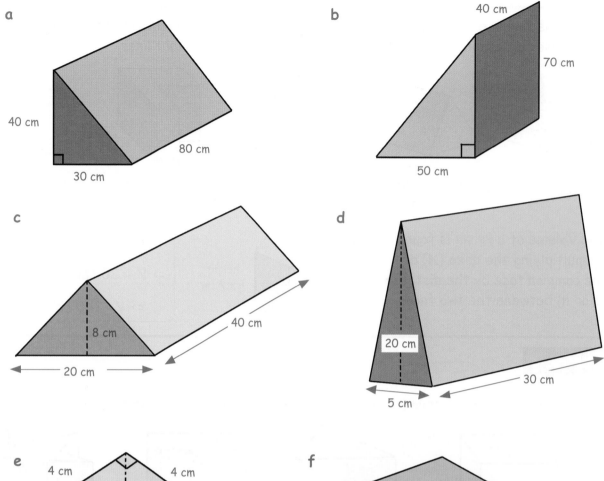

a

40 cm

80 cm

30 cm

b

40 cm

70 cm

50 cm

c

8 cm

40 cm

20 cm

d

20 cm

30 cm

5 cm

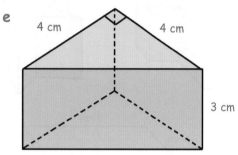

e

4 cm

4 cm

3 cm

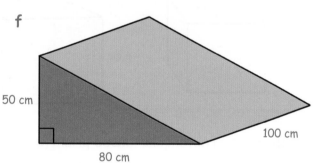

f

50 cm

100 cm

80 cm

6. For the tent shown below, calculate :-

a the area of the triangular front.

b the volume of the tent.

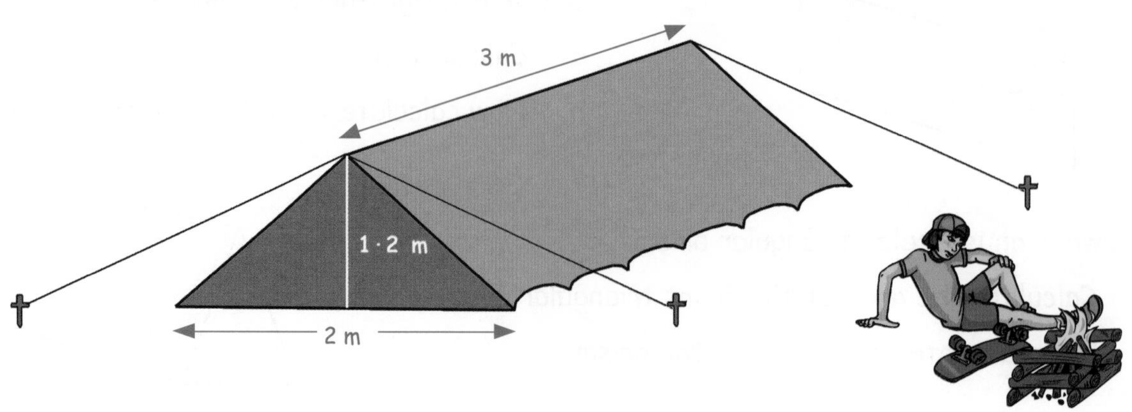

The Volume of a Cylinder

A circular based prism is better known as a cylinder.

To find the Volume of a Cylinder :-

> find the Area of the Base (*a circle*),
> then
> multiply the answer by the Height of the Cylinder
> $V = A_{(base)} \times h$

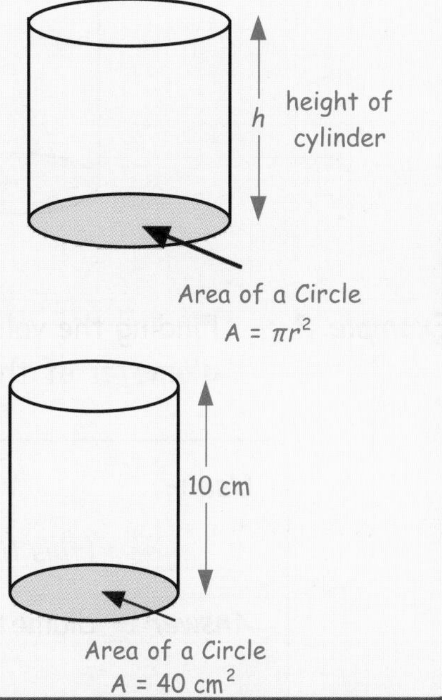

Example **:-** Finding the volume of a cylinder when the area of the base is already given.

V = Area of base × height
= 40 cm² × 10 cm
= 400 cm³

Exercise 4

1. Find the volume of each of the following cylinders :-
   (*The areas of the circular bases are given*).

a

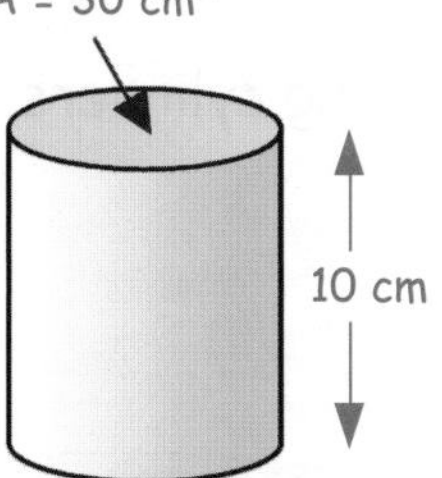

b

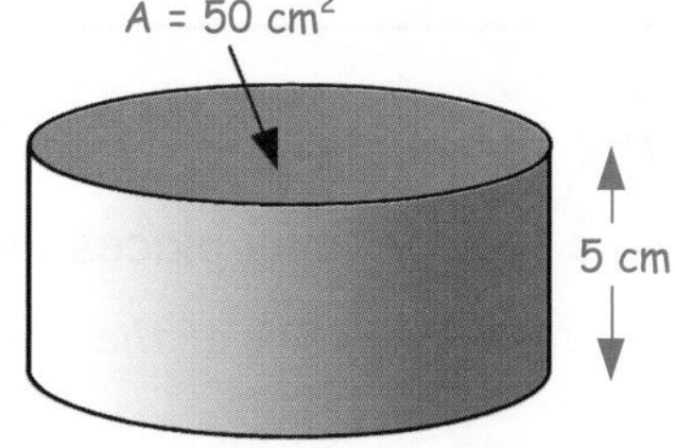

c

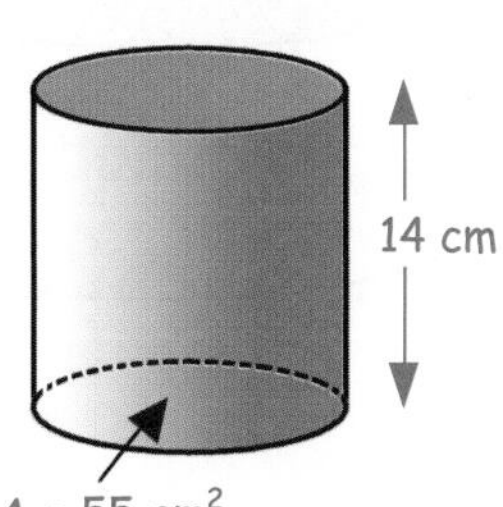

d

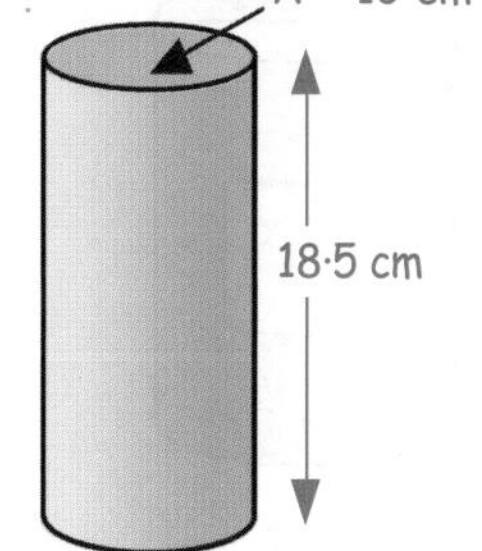

e

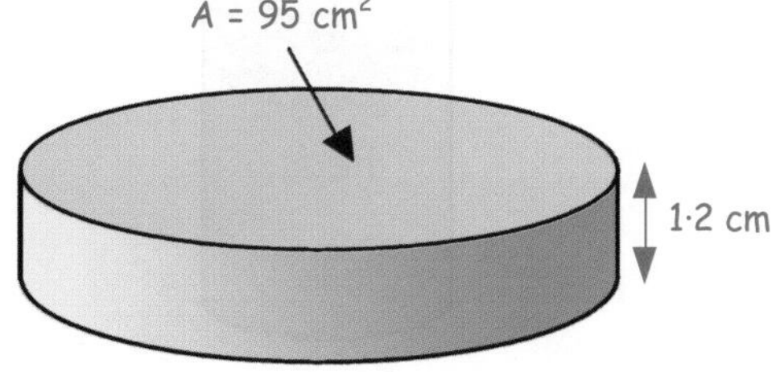

f

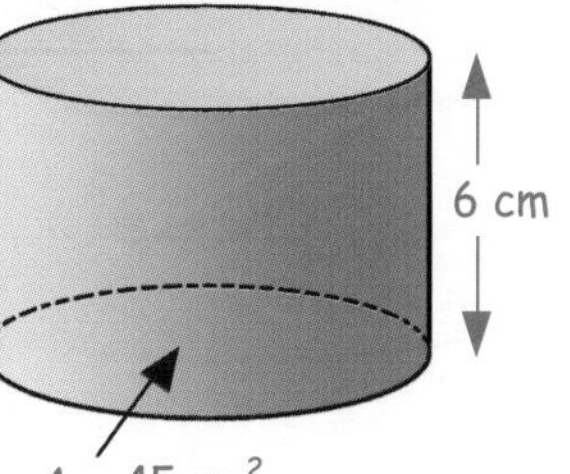

Example 1 :- Finding the volume of a cylinder given the **radius** of the circular base.

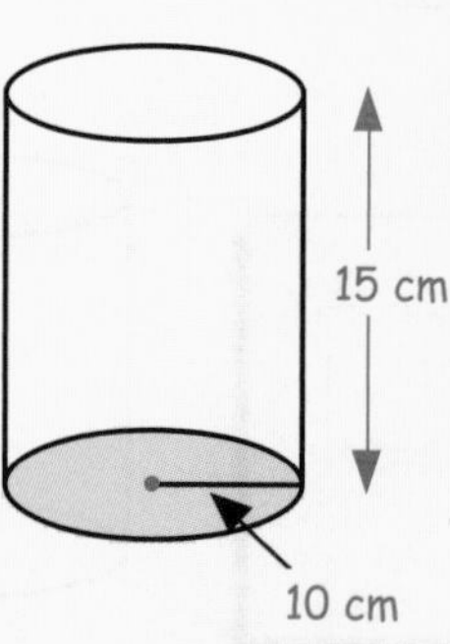

Remember :- $Area_{circle} = \pi r^2$

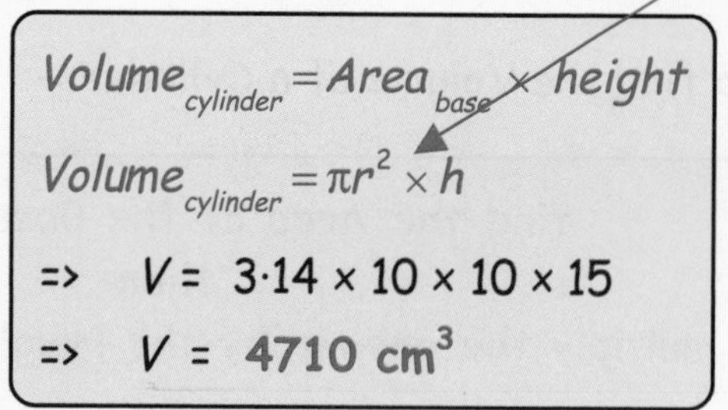

$Volume_{cylinder} = Area_{base} \times height$

$Volume_{cylinder} = \pi r^2 \times h$

=> $V = 3{\cdot}14 \times 10 \times 10 \times 15$

=> $V = \mathbf{4710\ cm^3}$

Example 2 :- Finding the volume of a cylinder given the **diameter** of the circular base.

Use :- $V = \pi r^2 h$

(*this time, the radius has to be found first*)

Answer :- diameter is 12 cm, so radius is 6 cm.

$V = \pi r^2 h$

$= 3{\cdot}14 \times 6 \times 6 \times 15$

$= \mathbf{1695{\cdot}6\ cm^3}$

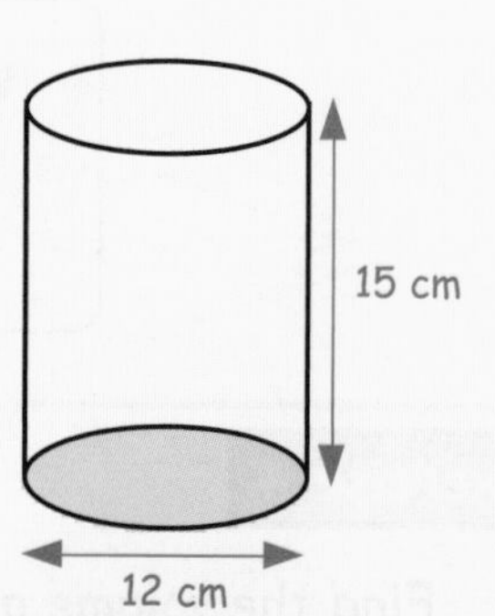

2. Use the formula $V = \pi r^2 h$ to find the volumes of the following cylinders, giving your answers to 2 decimal places :-

(*In each case, the* **radius** *of the circular base is given*).

a

b

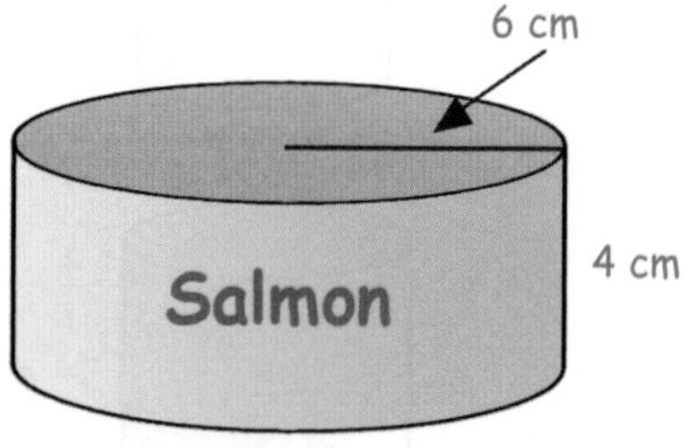

c

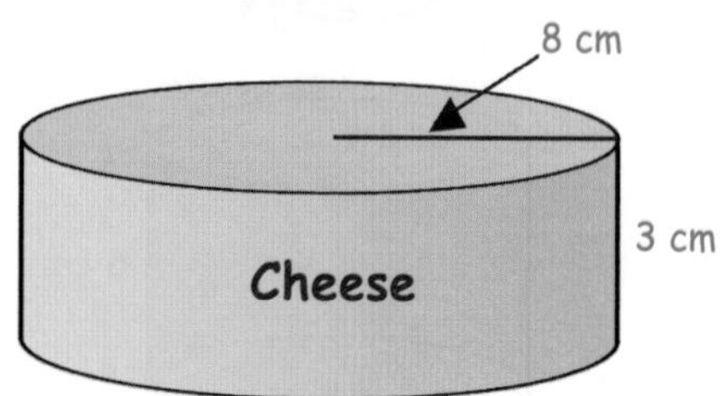

d

3. Write down the radius of each circular base.

Use the formula $V = \pi r^2 h$ to find the volume of each of the following cylinders :-

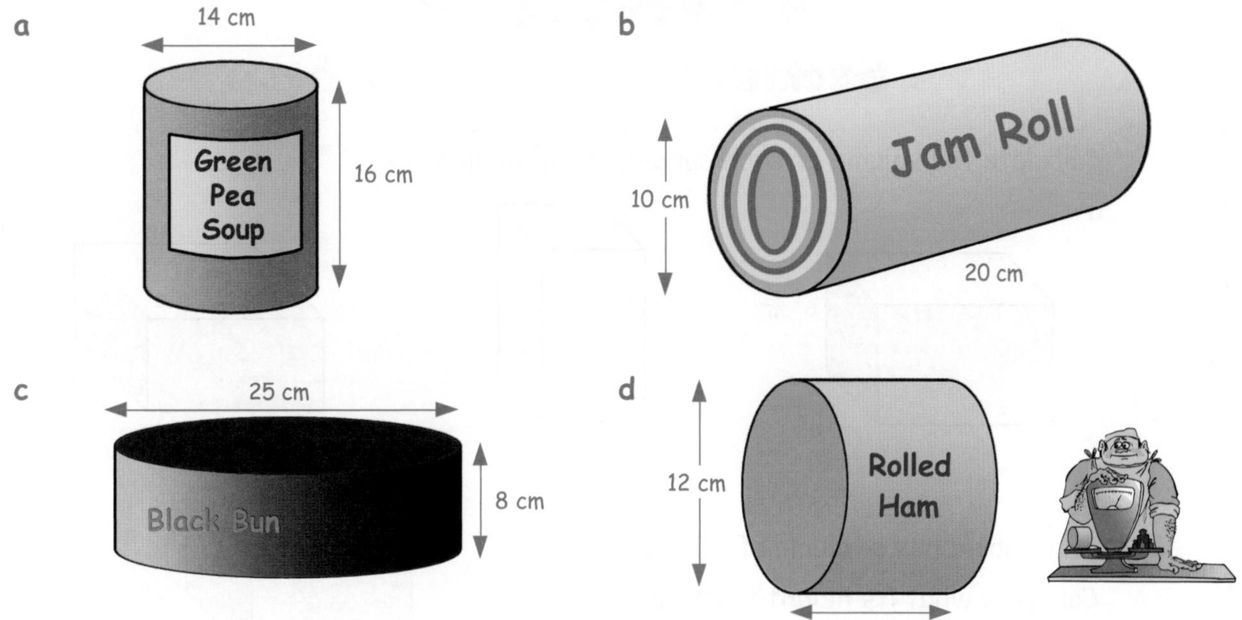

4. Calculate the volumes of the following cylinders :-
(*Give your answers to the nearest whole number each time*).

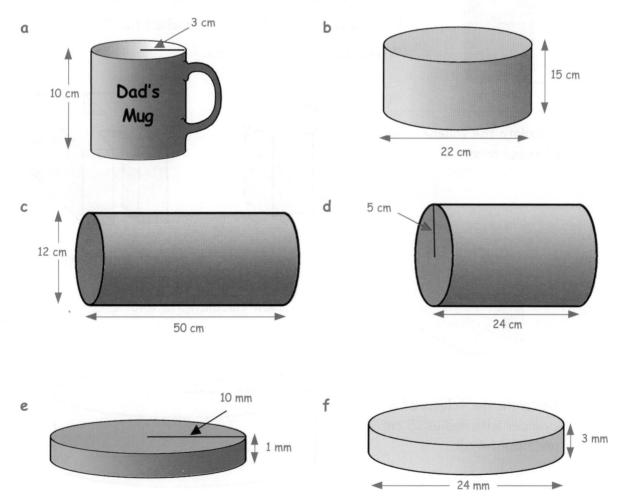

a

3 cm
10 cm
Dad's
Mug

b

15 cm
22 cm

c

12 cm
50 cm

d

5 cm
24 cm

e

10 mm
1 mm

f

3 mm
24 mm

Volume

Geometry Assessment 6

1. Calculate the volume of each cuboid, in cm^3 or in m^3 :-

a

6 cm
7 cm
10 cm

b

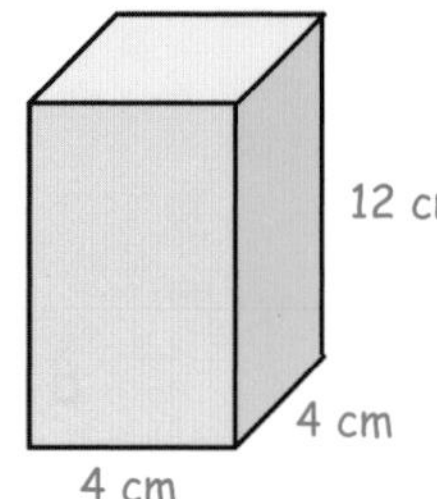

c

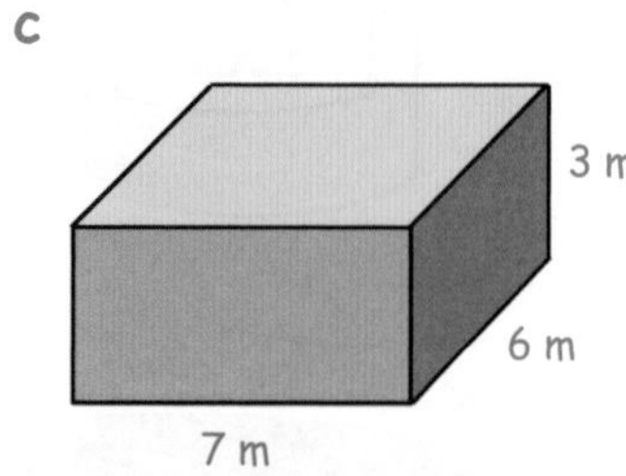

2. This cuboid has a volume of 90 cm^3.
Calculate what its height must be.

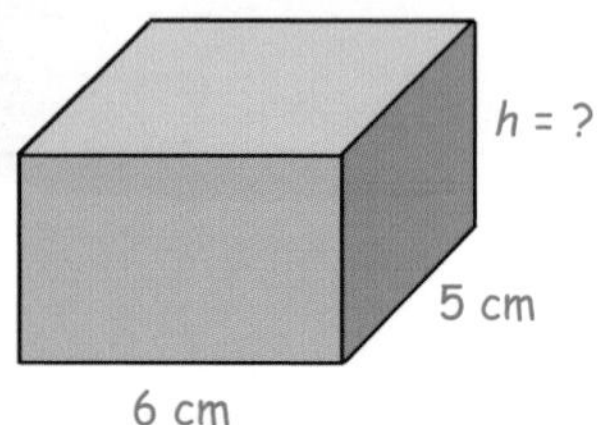

3.

30 cm
8 cm
25 cm

a Calculate the volume of this olive oil tin, in cm^3.

b How many millilitres will it hold when full ?

c Write its capacity, in litres.

4. Calculate the volume of these prisms :-

a

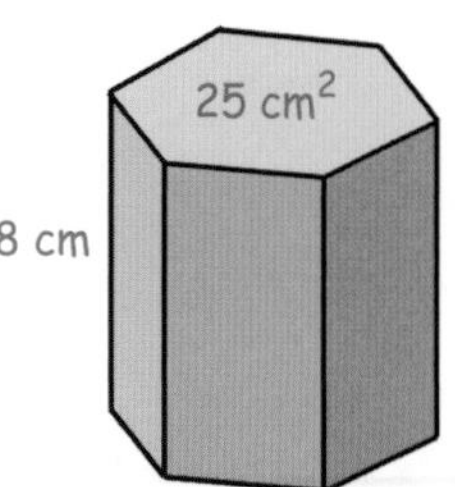

b

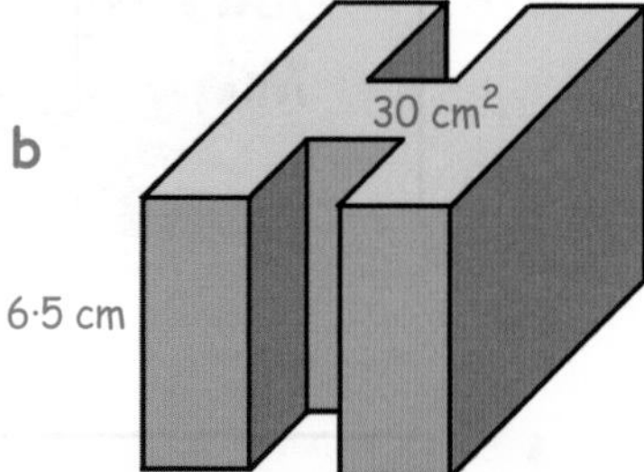

5.

8 cm
15 cm
5 cm

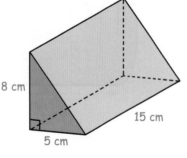

a Calculate the area of the triangular end face of this prism.

b Now calculate its volume.

6. Calculate the volume of a cylinder with radius 10 cm and height 4 cm.

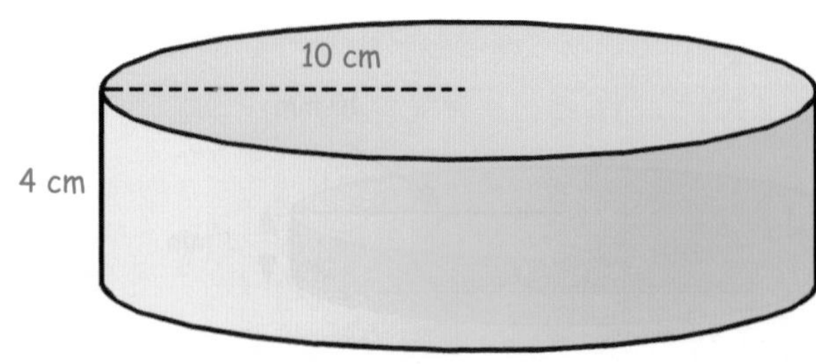

CHAPTER 19

Pythagoras

Squares and Square Roots

You now know how to find $4^2 = 4 \times 4 = 16$.

In reverse, we sometimes want to know "which number - times itself - gives 16"?

The answer, as can be seen from above, is obviously 4.

We say "the SQUARE ROOT of 16 is 4",

which shortens to $\sqrt{16} = 4$ (this reads as "the square root of 16 is 4")

Exercise 1

1. No calculator in this question. Copy each line and complete :-

   a since $2^2 = 4 \Rightarrow \sqrt{4} = 2$ b since $5^2 = 25 \Rightarrow \sqrt{25} = ...$

   c since $6^2 = 36 \Rightarrow \sqrt{36} = ...$ d since $7^2 = 49 \Rightarrow \sqrt{49} = ...$

2. Find the following :-

   a $\sqrt{81}$ b $\sqrt{1}$ c $\sqrt{100}$ d $\sqrt{64}$.

3. In this question, you should use the "$\sqrt{\ }$" button on your calculator to find :-

   a $\sqrt{0}$ b $\sqrt{121}$ c $\sqrt{144}$ d $\sqrt{169}$ e $\sqrt{256}$

   f $\sqrt{196}$ g $\sqrt{400}$ h $\sqrt{900}$ i $\sqrt{2500}$ j $\sqrt{2{\cdot}56}$.

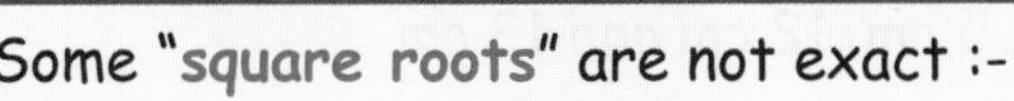

Some "square roots" are not exact :-

$\sqrt{29} = 5{\cdot}385164..... = 5{\cdot}39$ (to 2 decimal places) - check this !

4. Use your calculator to find the following to two decimal places :-

   a $\sqrt{13}$ b $\sqrt{22}$ c $\sqrt{35}$ d $\sqrt{69}$ e $\sqrt{89}$

   f $\sqrt{110}$ g $\sqrt{200}$ h $\sqrt{300}$ i $\sqrt{550}$ j $\sqrt{750}$.

5. 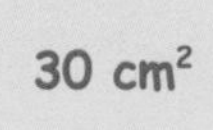

   The square shown has an area of 30 cm^2.
   Calculate the length of one of its sides. ($\sqrt{30}$).

Pythagoras' Theorem

Pythagoras was a famous Greek Mathematician who discovered an amazing connection between the three sides of a right angled triangle. This connection means it is possible to calculate the length of one side of a right angle triangle as long as you know the length of the other two.

Look at this right angled triangle with sides 6 cm, 8 cm and 10 cm.

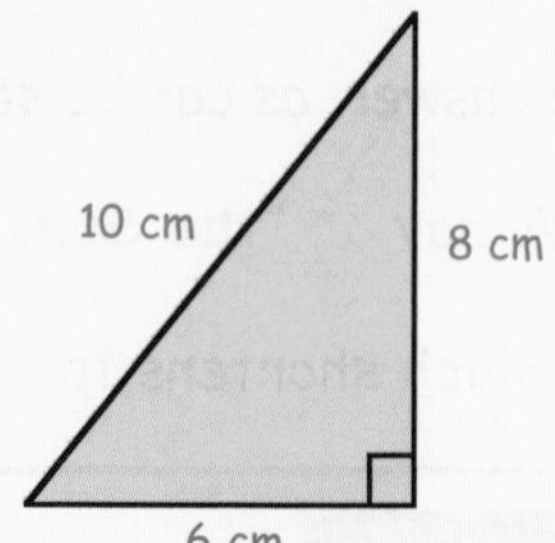

If you add the two smaller sides (6 cm and 8 cm) together do you get the longer side (10 cm) ? - No !

Can you see that $6^2 = 36$, $8^2 = 64$ and $10^2 = 100$?

Can you also see that:- $6^2 + 8^2$
$= 36 + 64$
$= 100 = 10^2$?

Pythagoras found that this connection between the three sides of a right angled triangle was true for every right angled triangle.

Exercise 2

1. The three sides of this right angled triangle are 3 cm, 4 cm and 5 cm.

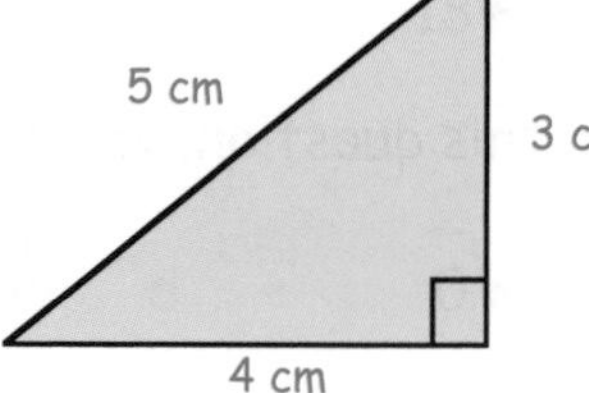

   a Write down the values of 3^2, 4^2 and 5^2.

   b Find the value of $3^2 + 4^2$.

   c Check that $3^2 + 4^2 = 5^2$.

2. The three sides of this right angled triangle are 5 cm, 12 cm and 13 cm.

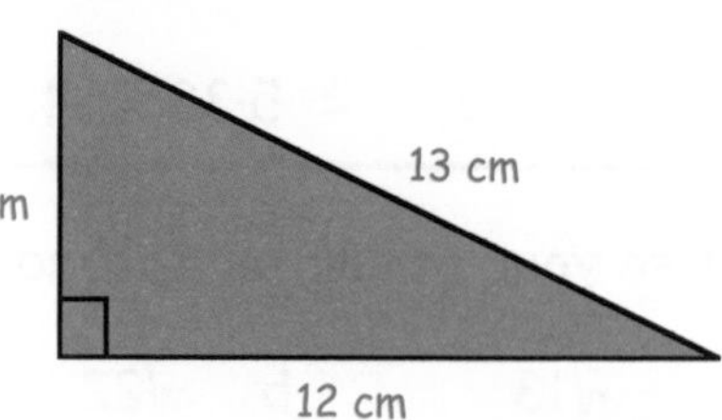

   a Write down the values of 5^2, 12^2 and 13^2.

   b Find the value of $5^2 + 12^2$.

   c Check that $5^2 + 12^2 = 13^2$.

3. The three sides of this right angled triangle are 9 cm, 12 cm and 15 cm.

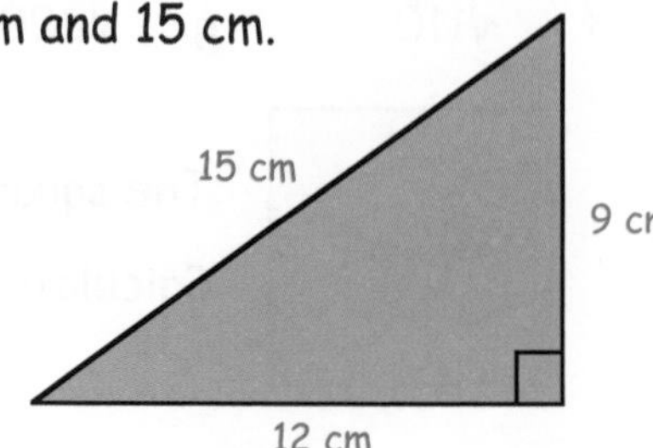

   a Write down the values of 9^2, 12^2 and 15^2.

   b Find the value of $9^2 + 12^2$.

   c Check that $9^2 + 12^2 = 15^2$.

4. The three sides of this right angled triangle are 8 cm, 15 cm and 17 cm.

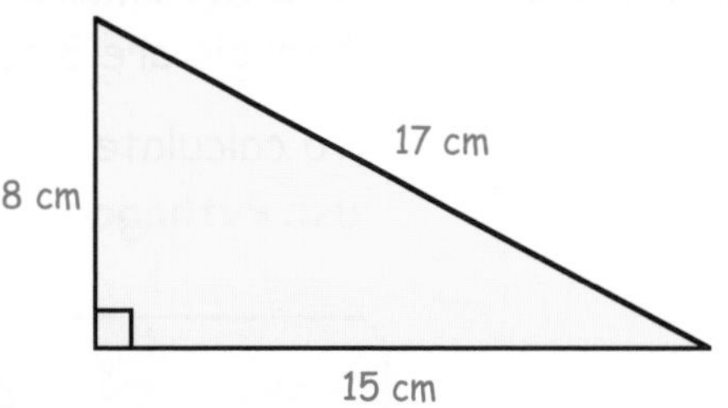

a Write down the values of 8^2, 15^2 and 17^2.

b Find the value of $8^2 + 15^2$.

c Check that $8^2 + 15^2 = 17^2$.

5.

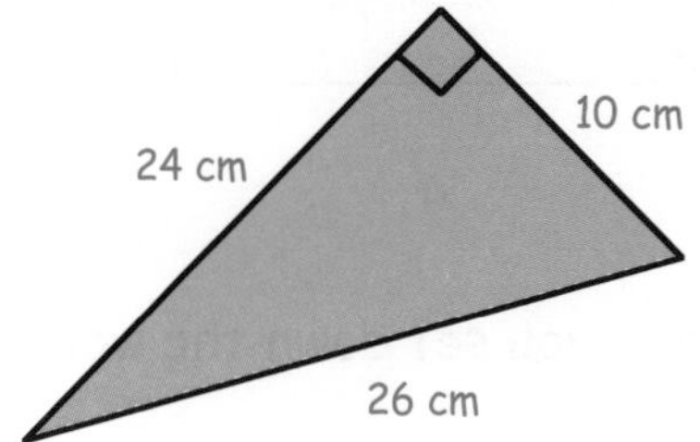

The three sides of this right angled triangle are 10 cm, 24 cm and 26 cm.

a Write down the values of 10^2, 24^2 and 26^2.

b Find the value of $10^2 + 24^2$.

c Check that $10^2 + 24^2 = 26^2$.

6. The three sides of this right angled triangle are 15 cm, 20 cm and 25 cm.

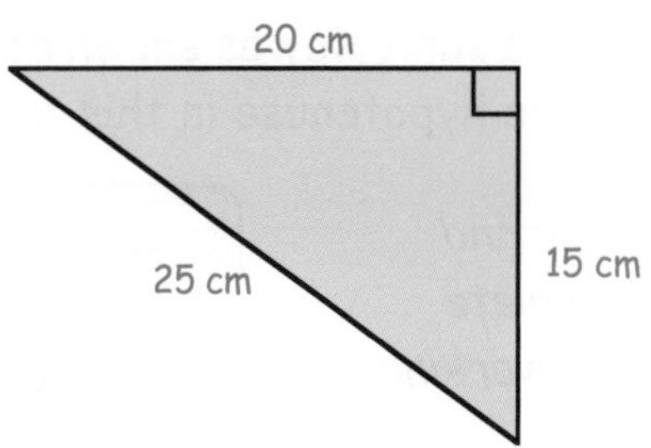

a Write down the values of 15^2, 20^2 and 25^2.

b Find the value of $15^2 + 20^2$.

c Check that $15^2 + 20^2 = 25^2$.

Pythagoras Theorem (a formula)

Pythagoras made up a small rule which shows the connection between the three sides of any right angled triangle.

The **longest** side of a right angled triangle is called the **hypotenuse**.

If the three sides are *a* cm, *b* cm and *c* cm (the hypotenuse), then Pythagoras' rule states :-

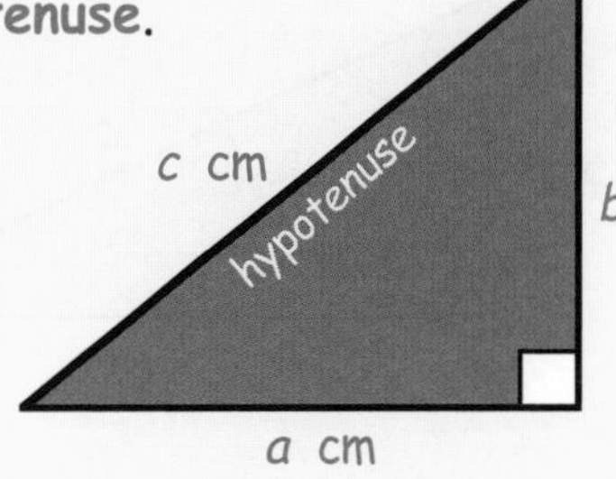

=> $c^2 = a^2 + b^2$

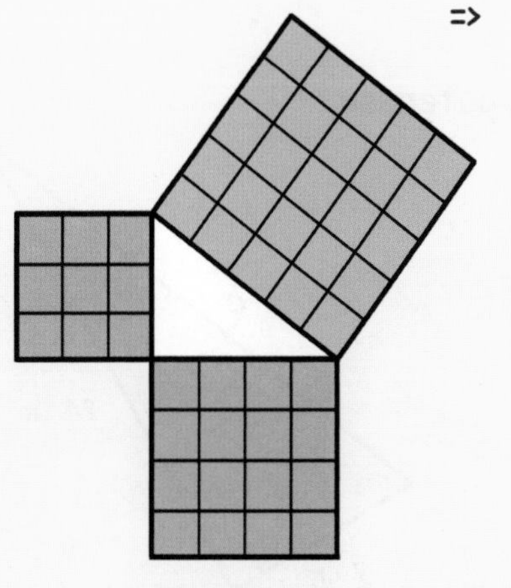

We can use this rule to calculate the length of the **hypotenuse** of a right angled triangle if we know the lengths of the **two smaller** sides.

Example 1 :- The two smaller sides of this right angled triangle are 3 centimetres and 4 centimetres.

To calculate the length of the hypotenuse, use Pythagoras' Rule, (or Pythagoras' Theorem).

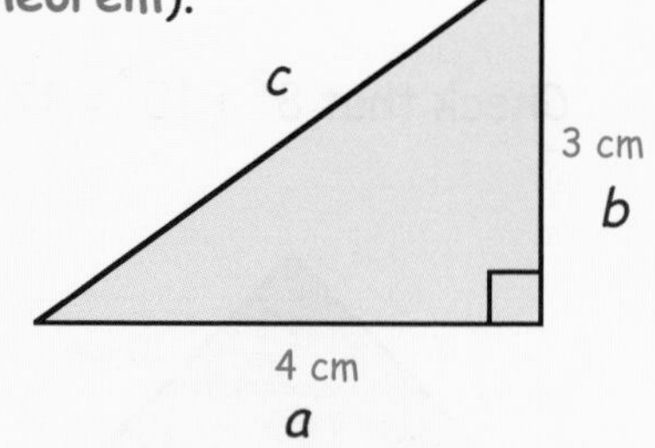

=> $c^2 = a^2 + b^2$

=> $c^2 = 3^2 + 4^2$

=> $c^2 = 9 + 16 = 25$

=> $c = \sqrt{25} = 5$ cm

This is how you set down the working.

Exercise 3

1. In the same way as shown above, use Pythagoras' Theorem to calculate the length of the hypotenuse in this triangle :-

Copy and complete the working.

=> $c^2 = a^2 + b^2$

=> $c^2 = 8^2 + ...^2$

=> $c^2 = 64 + ... = ...$

=> $c = \sqrt{...} = ...$ cm

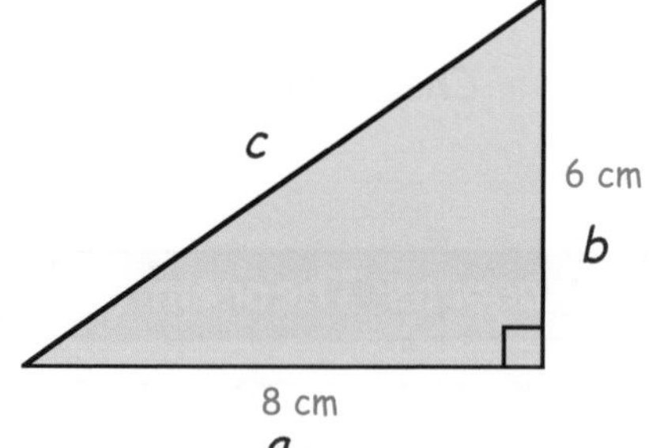

2. 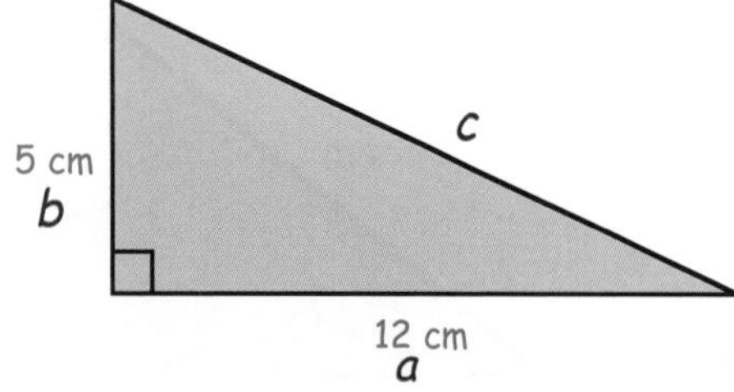

Use Pythagoras' Theorem to calculate the length of the hypotenuse in the right angled triangle shown on the left.

(*Set down your 4 lines of working as shown*).

3. Use Pythagoras' Theorem to calculate the length of the hypotenuse in each of these triangles :-

a 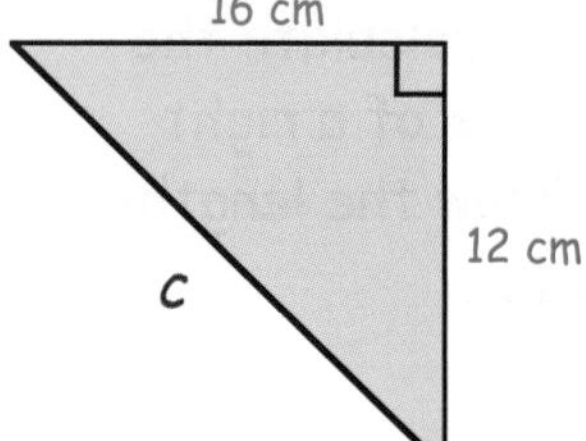

b 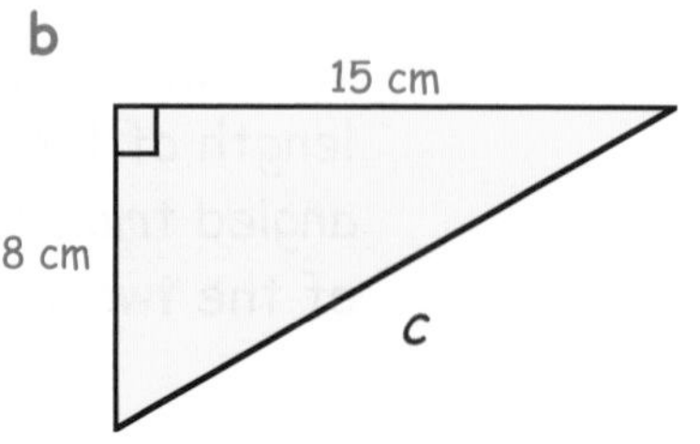

c 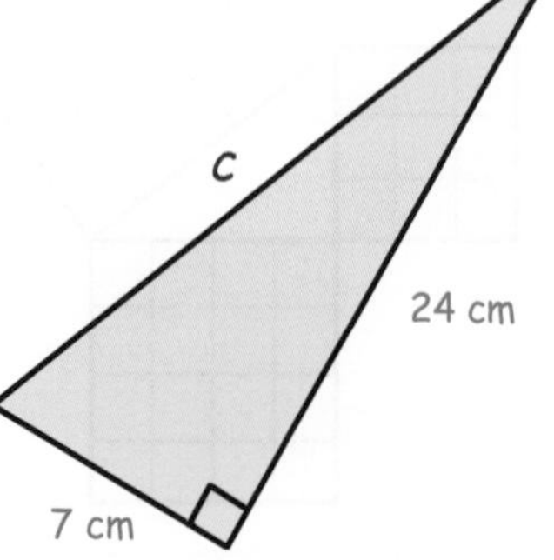

Example 2 :- You do not always get whole number answers.

$$\Rightarrow \quad c^2 = a^2 + b^2$$

$$\Rightarrow \quad c^2 = 12^2 + 6^2$$

$$\Rightarrow \quad c^2 = 144 + 36 = 180$$

$$\Rightarrow \quad c = \sqrt{180} = 13 \cdot 4164\ldots \text{ cm}$$

$$= 13 \cdot 42 \text{ cm}$$

(to 2 decimal places.)

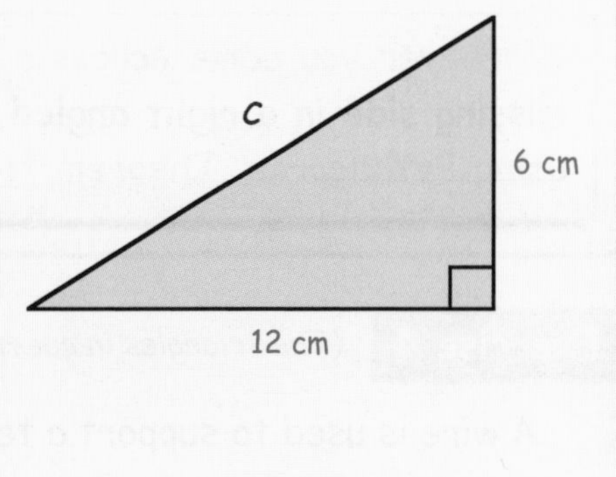

4. In the same way as shown above, use **Pythagoras' Theorem** to calculate the length of the hypotenuse in this triangle, to 2 decimal places.

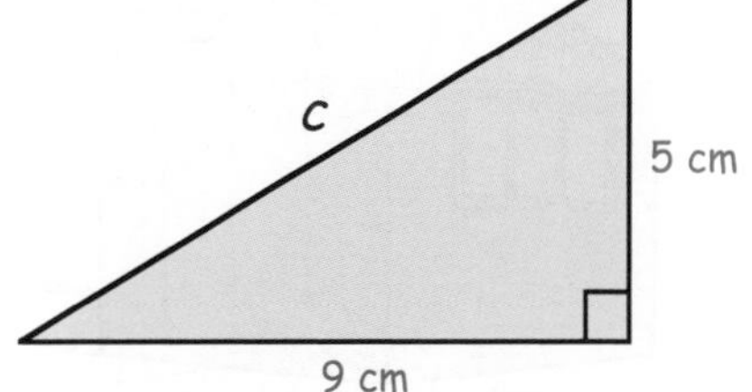

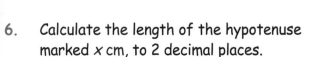

5. Use **Pythagoras' Theorem** to calculate the length of the hypotenuse in the right angled triangle shown, to 2 decimal places.

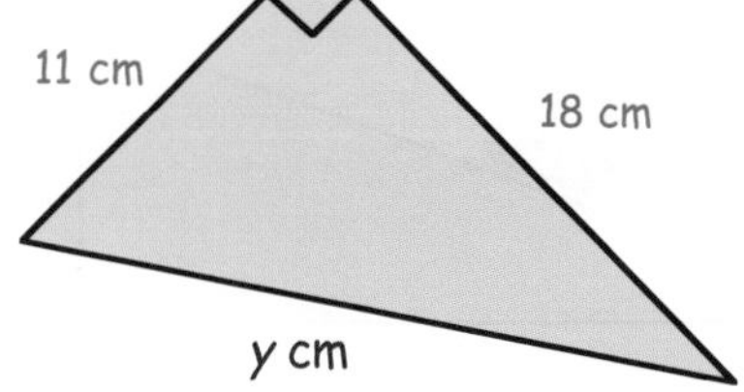

6. Calculate the length of the hypotenuse marked x cm, to 2 decimal places.

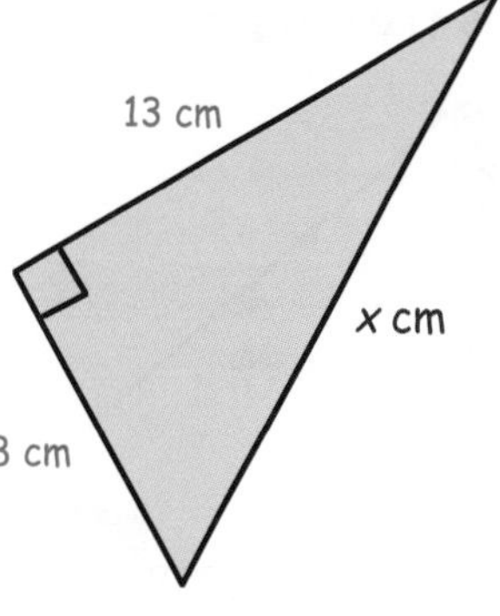

7. Calculate the length of the line marked y cm, to 1 decimal place.

8. Calculate the length of the hypotenuse in this right angled triangle, to 1 decimal place.

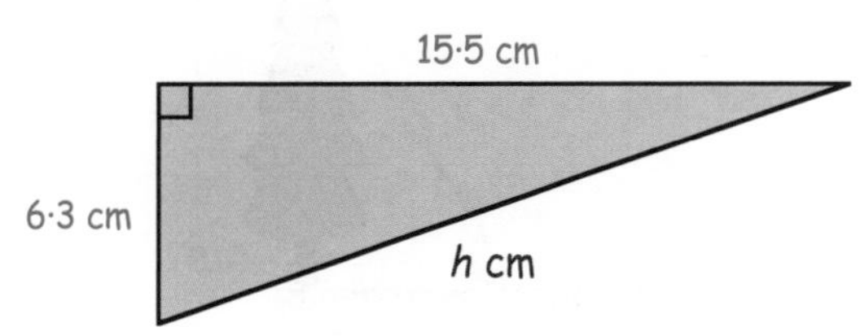

Problems involving Pythagoras' Theorem

> Whenever you come across a problem involving **finding a missing side in a right angled triangle**, you should consider using Pythagoras' Theorem to calculate its length.

Exercise 4

(*The triangles in questions 1 to 7 are right-angled*).

1. A wire is used to support a telephone pole.

   Calculate the length of the wire.

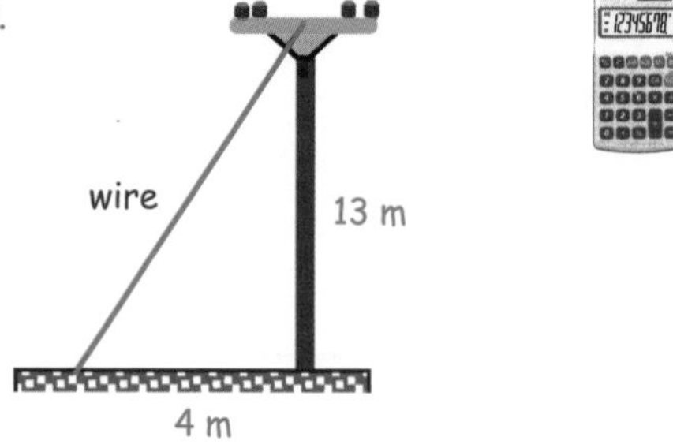

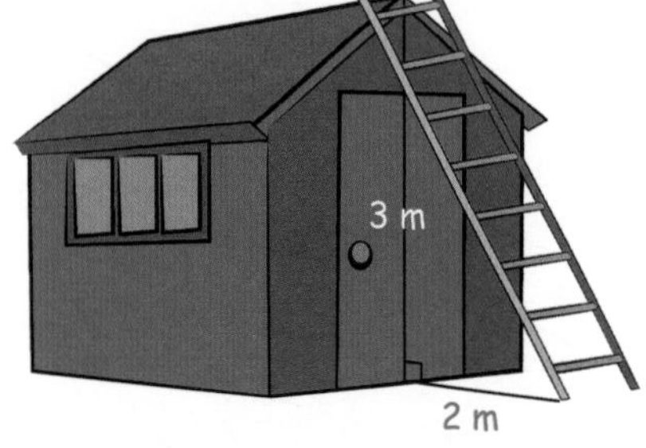

2. A ladder rests against the roof of a shed.

   The bottom of the ladder is 2 metres from the base of the 3 metre high shed.

   Calculate the length of the ladder.

3. A helicopter left Aberdeen Airport.
   The pilot flew 90 kilometres West.

   He then flew 60 kilometres due North.

   Calculate how far away the helicopter then was from the airport.

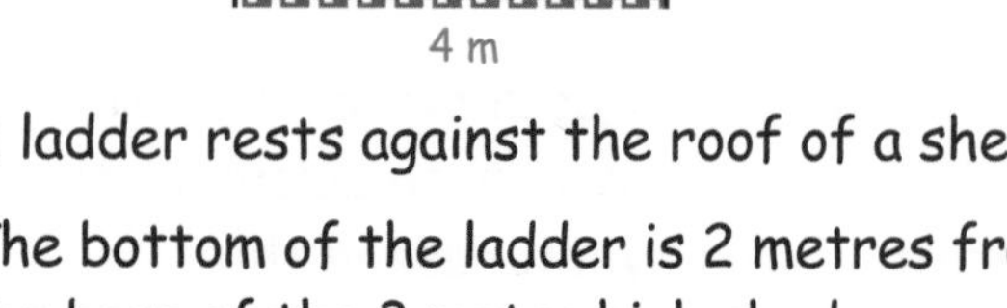

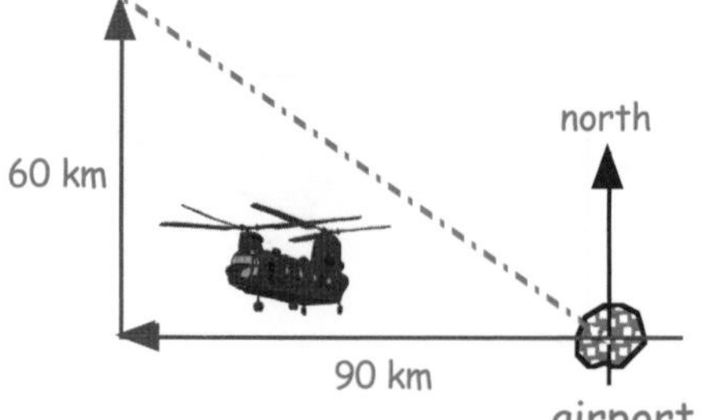

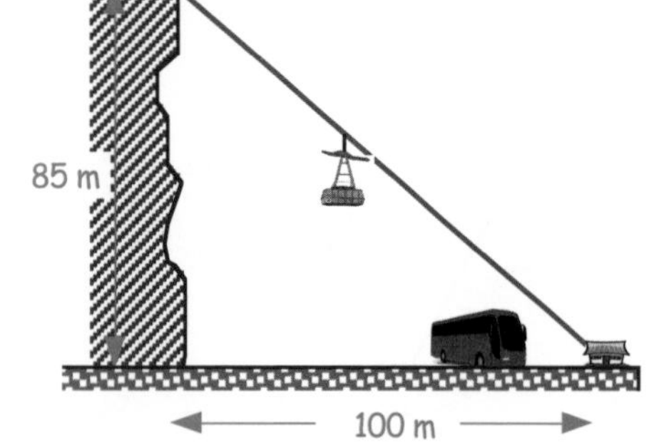

4. A cable-car, attached to a strong wire cable, takes tourists to the top of the mountain.

   Calculate the length of the cable.

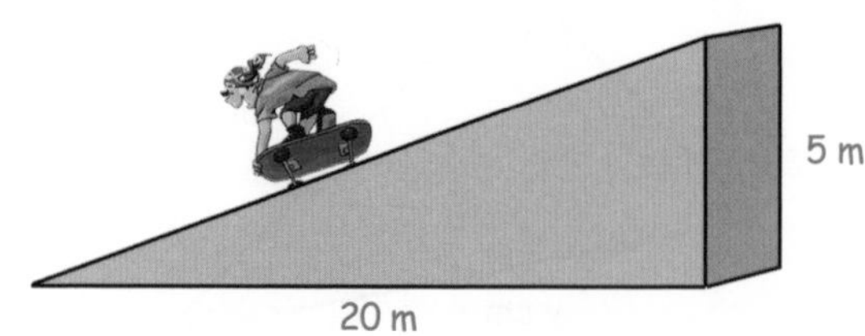

5. Shown is a concrete skateboard ramp.

   Calculate the length of the ramp.

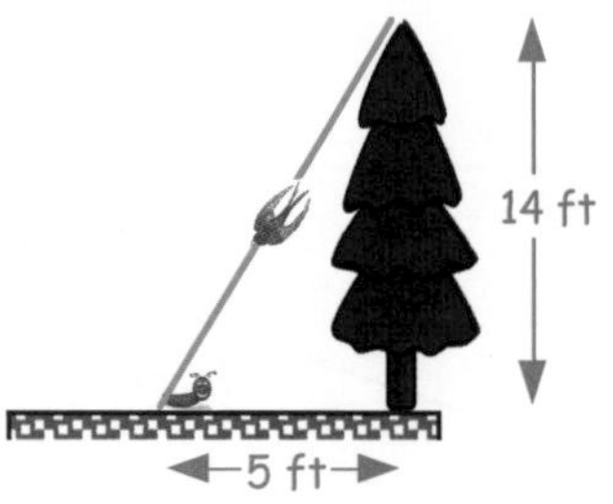

6. A bird lives in a nest at the top of a 14 feet high tree.

   How far will the bird have to glide in a straight line to reach a worm that is 5 feet from the base of the tree ?

7. A triangular bracket is fixed to a wall to support a shelf 16 centimetres wide.

Calculate the length of the sloping side of the bracket.

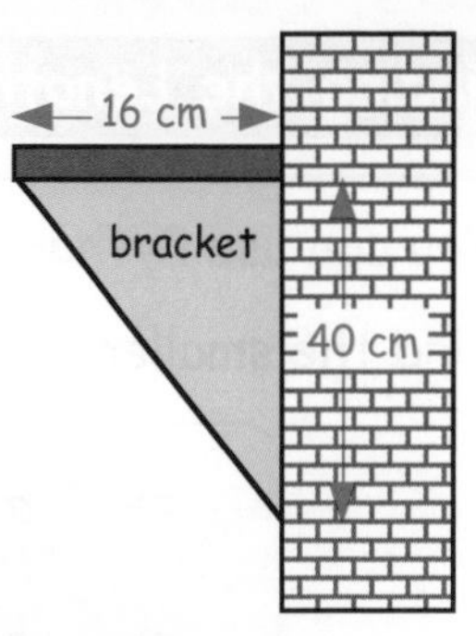

8. 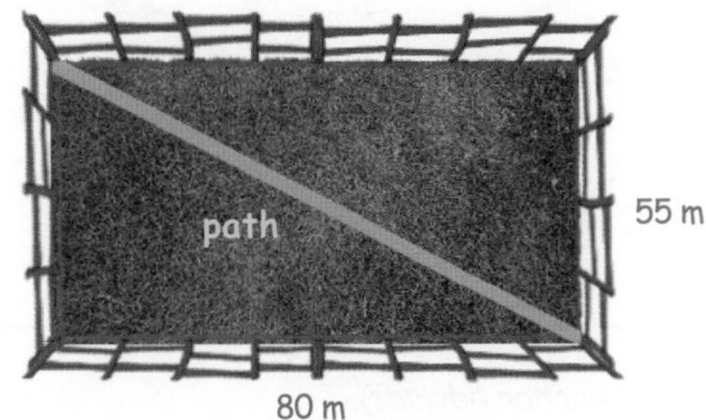

Farmer Jones has a field in the shape of a rectangle 80 metres long by 55 metres wide.

A diagonal pathway runs across the field.

Calculate the length of the pathway.

9. The picture shows the side view of a "lean-to" shed.

Calculate the length of the sloping roof.

(*Hint :- just consider the right angled triangle at the top*)

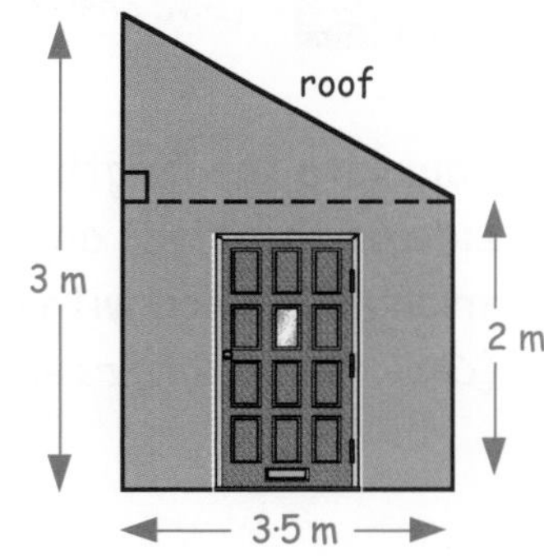

10. 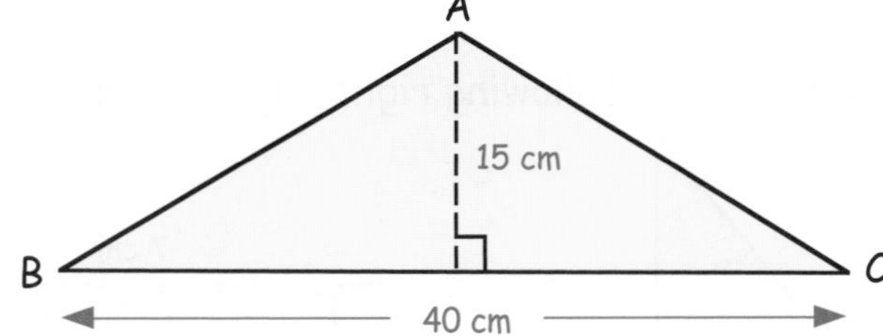

Triangle ABC is not right angled !

It is **isosceles**.

Calculate the length of the side AC.

(* **not** $AC^2 = 40^2 + 15^2$)

11. 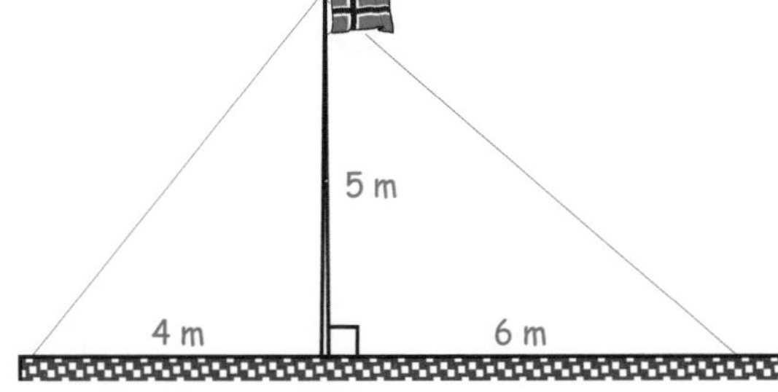

Two wires are used to support a flag pole, as shown in the diagram.

Calculate the **total** length of wire required.

12. The diagram shows a 3 bar gate with a diagonal plank fitted to strengthen it.

Calculate the length of the sloping strengthening plank.

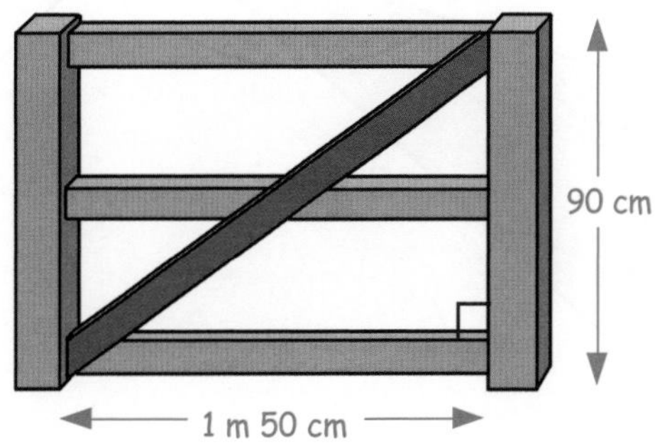

Finding the Length of a Smaller Side

You can use Pythagoras' Theorem to calculate one of the smaller sides as follows :-

Find the smaller side (a) :- *Can you see why the "-" sign ?*

$\Rightarrow \quad a^2 = c^2 - b^2$

$\Rightarrow \quad a^2 = 13^2 - 5^2$

$\Rightarrow \quad a^2 = 169 - 25 = 144$

$\Rightarrow \quad a = \sqrt{144} = \mathbf{12\ cm}$

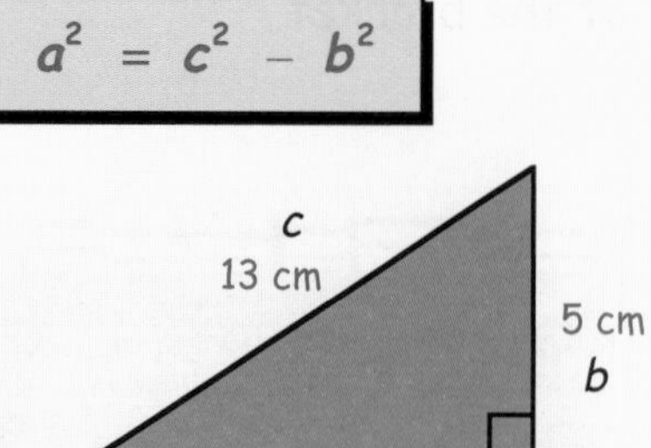

Exercise 5

(*Give answers to 3 figure accuracy or to whatever teacher advises*).

1. Calculate the length of the side of this right angled triangle marked with an x. (*Copy the working as shown*).

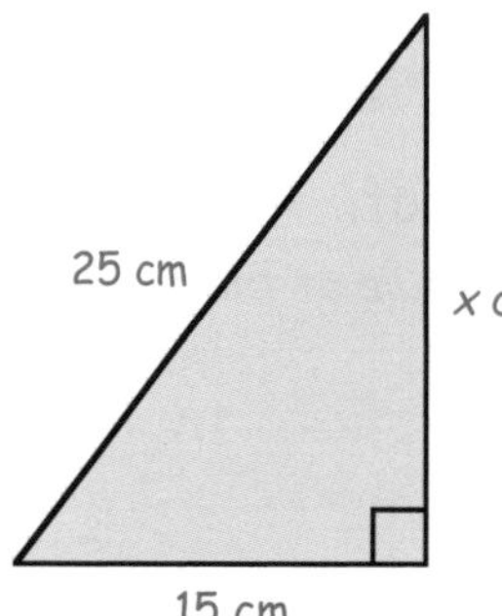

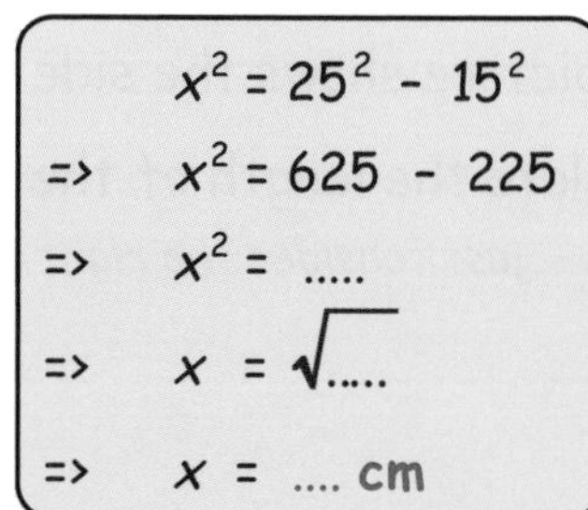

2. Calculate the size of each of the smaller sides in the following right angled triangles.

a

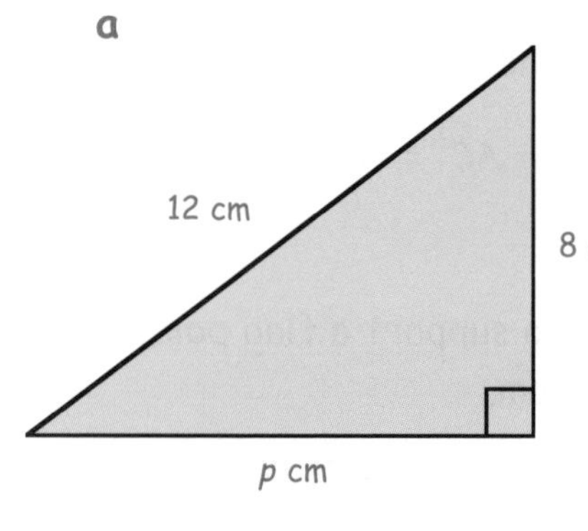

b

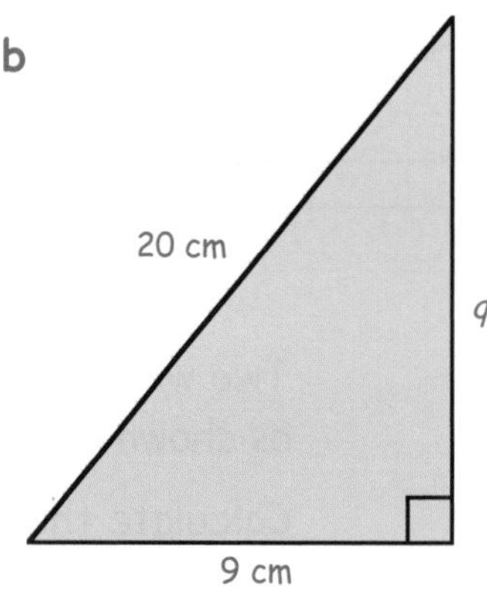

c

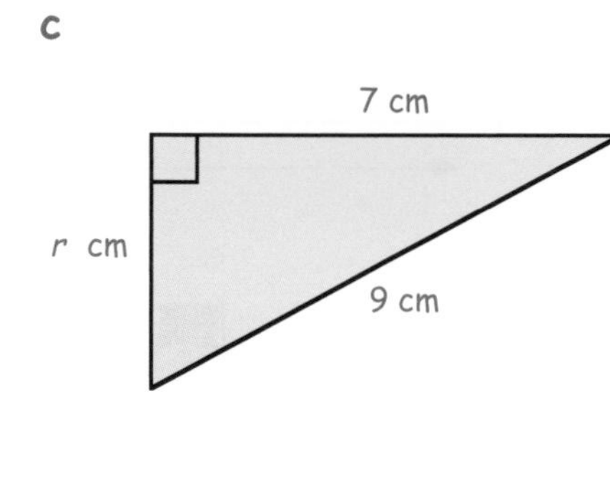

d

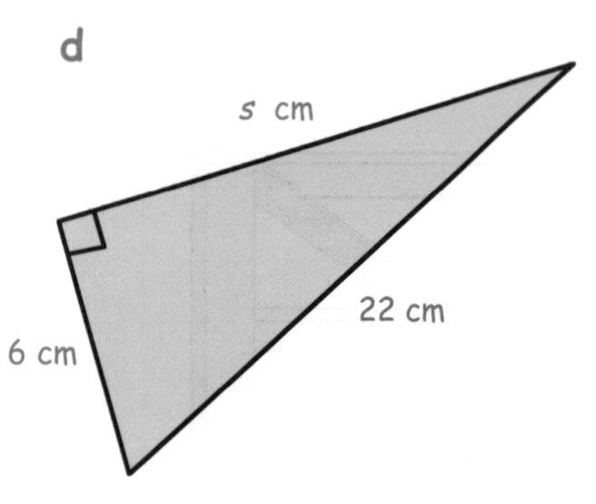

e

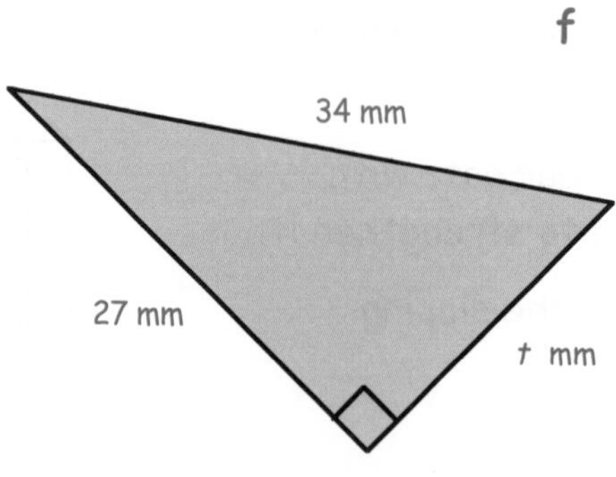

f

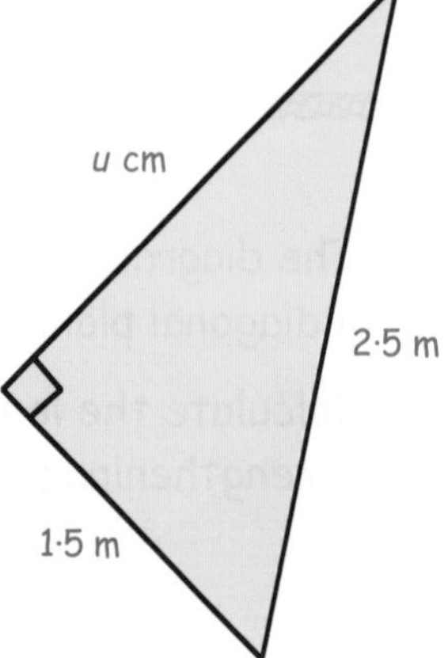

3. A 5 metre wire and three bricks are being used to support a crossroads sign.

The wire is fixed to a point 2 metres from the base of the pole.

Calculate the **height** of the sign.

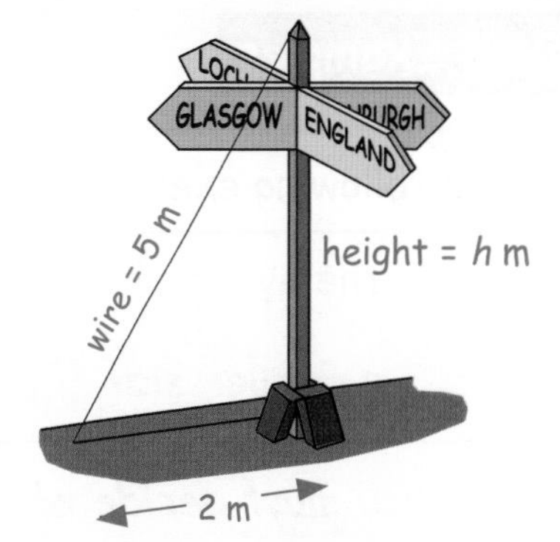

4.

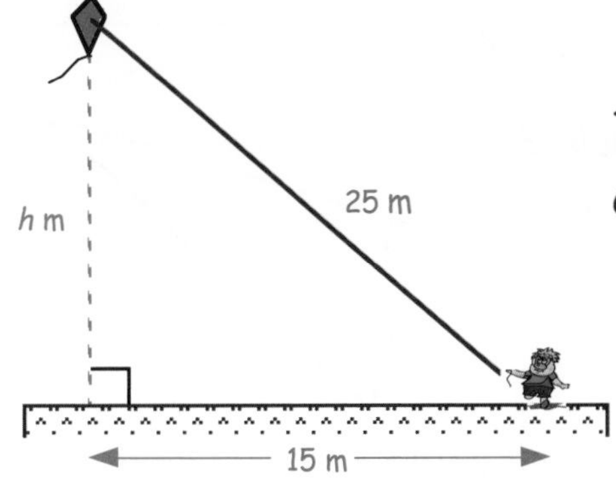

Toby is flying his kite at the end of a 25 metre rope.

Calculate the height of the kite above the ground.

5. The diagonal of a rectangle is 23 metres long.

The small side is 10 metres.

Calculate the length of the longer side.

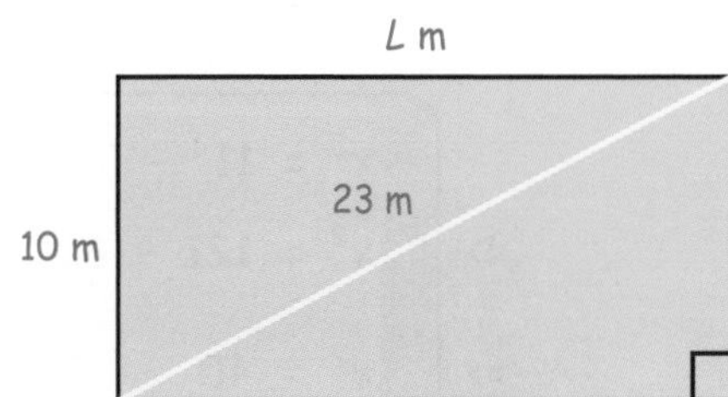

6.

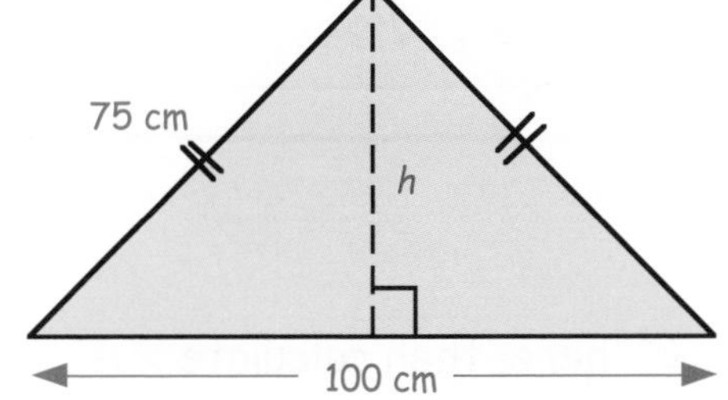

The base of an **isosceles** triangle is 100 cm long.

The length of each of its sloping sides is 75 centimetres.

Calculate the **height** of the triangle.

7. This is the side view of a pine bread box.

The base is 50 cm wide and the top is 30 cm wide.

The sloping edge is 40 cm long.

a Write down the length from A to B.

b Calculate the height of the bread box.

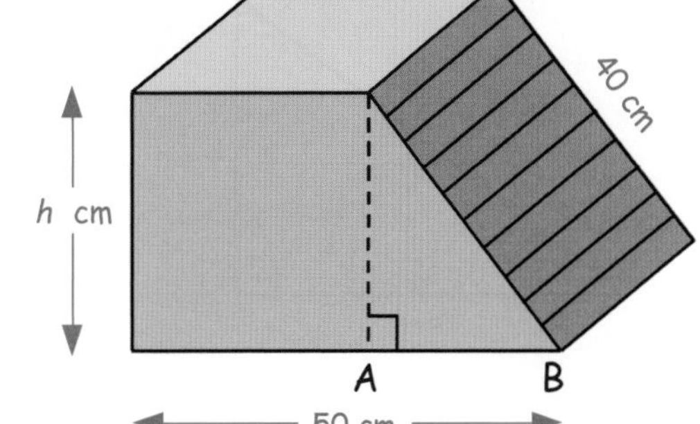

8.

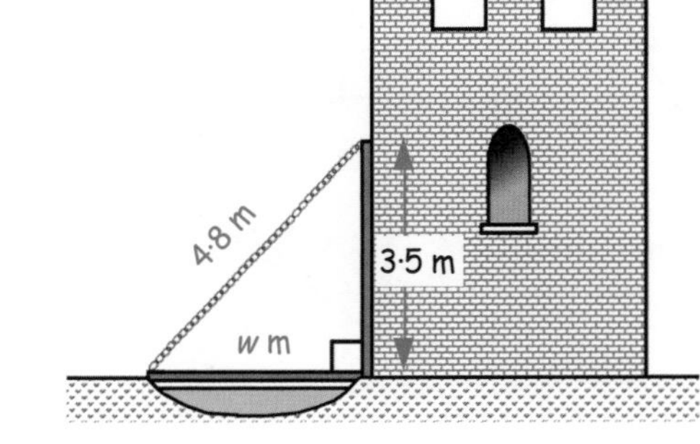

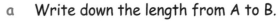

The entrance to the castle is 3·5 metres high.

The chain which operates the drawbridge is 4·8 metres long.

Calculate the width of the moat which the drawbridge goes over.

Mixed Examples

In the following exercise you will be asked to find :-

- the **hypotenuse** (use $c^2 = a^2 + b^2$)
- a **smaller side** (use $a^2 = c^2 - b^2$)

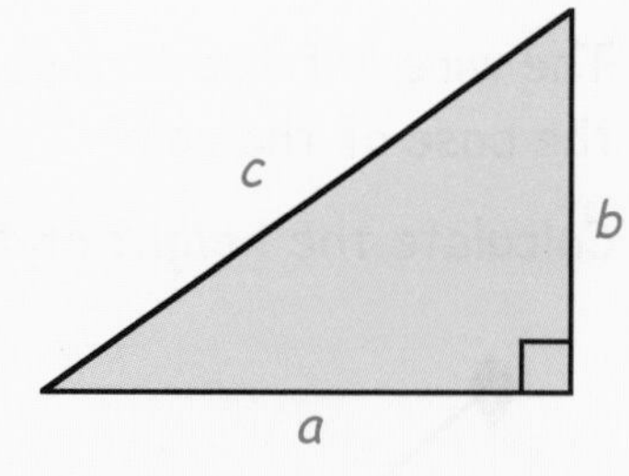

* *You must decide which formula you have to use.*

Example 1 :-

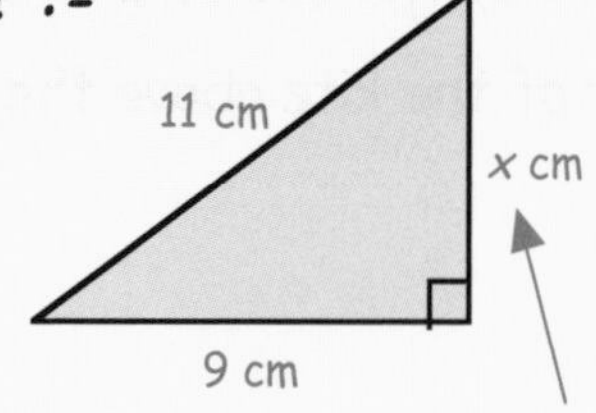

(Here you are looking for a **short side**).

$$x^2 = 11^2 - 9^2$$
=> $x^2 = 121 - 81$
=> $x^2 = 40$
=> $x = \sqrt{40} = \mathbf{6 \cdot 32\ cm}$

Example 2 :-

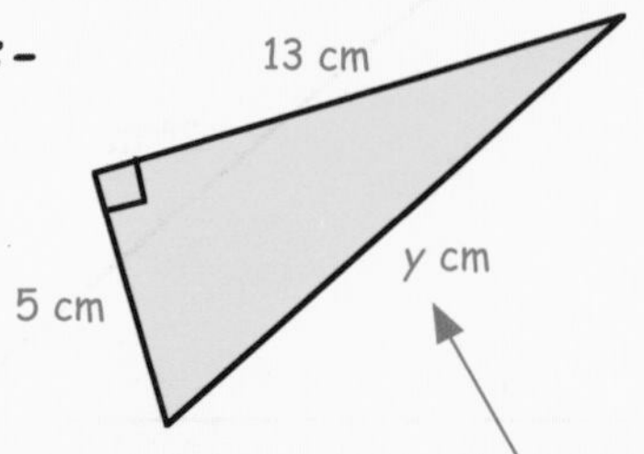

(Here you are looking for the **hypotenuse**).

$$y^2 = 13^2 + 5^2$$
=> $y^2 = 169 + 25$
=> $y^2 = 194$
=> $y = \sqrt{194} = \mathbf{13 \cdot 9\ cm}$

Exercise 6

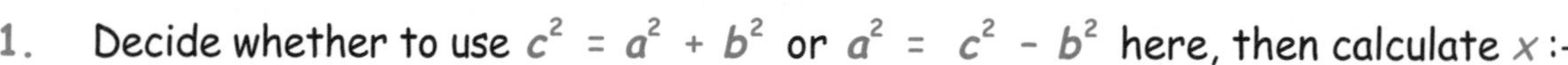

1. Decide whether to use $c^2 = a^2 + b^2$ or $a^2 = c^2 - b^2$ here, then calculate x :-

a

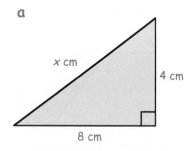

x cm
4 cm
8 cm

b

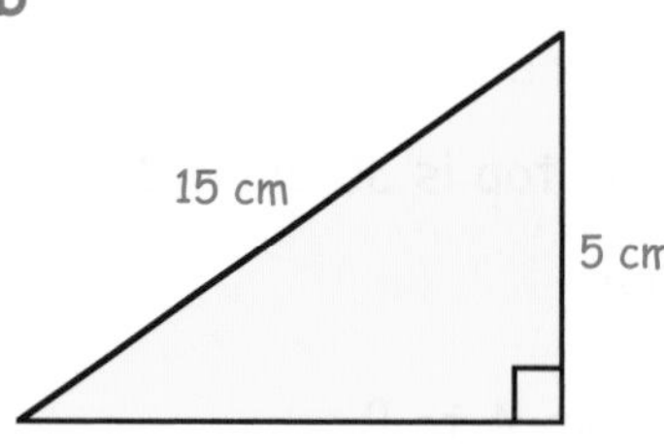

c

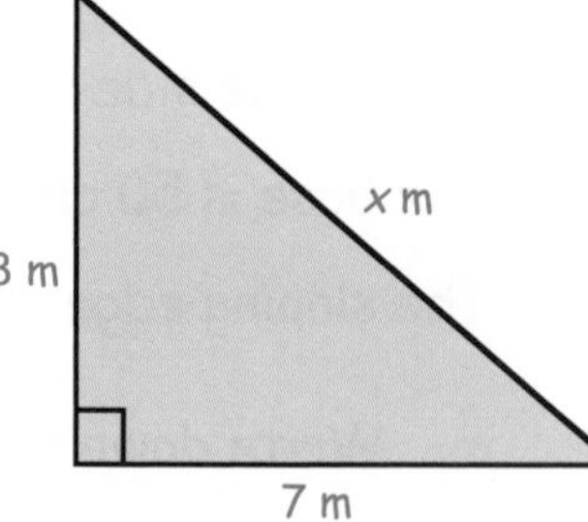

d

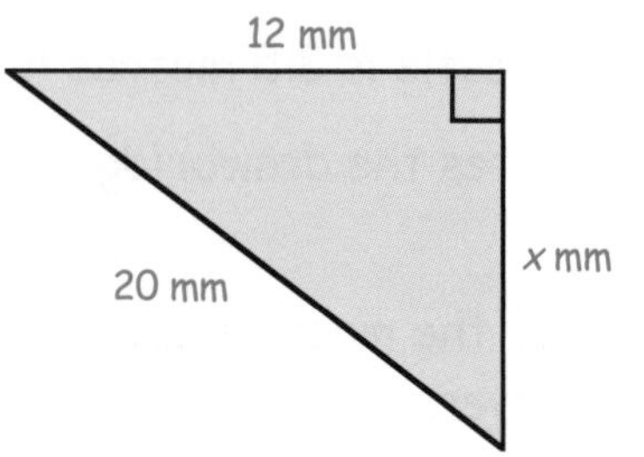

e

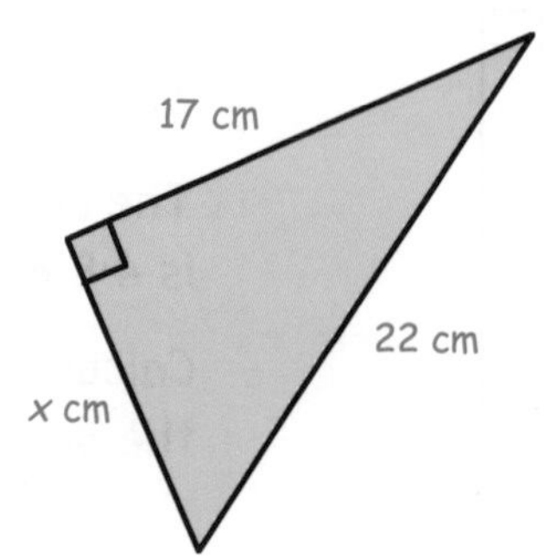

f

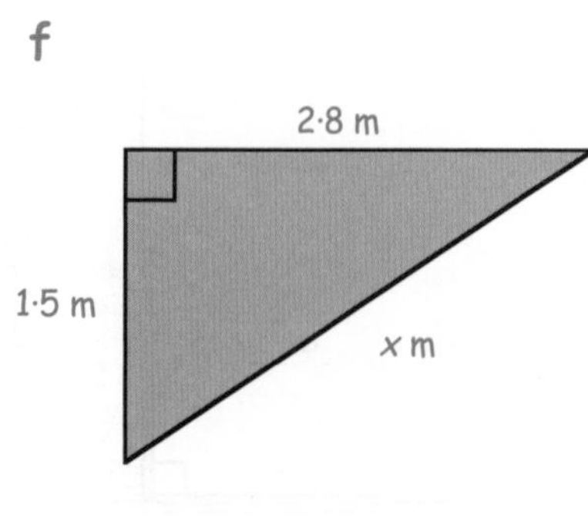

2. When Donnie was asked to calculate the value of x, he proceeded as follows :-

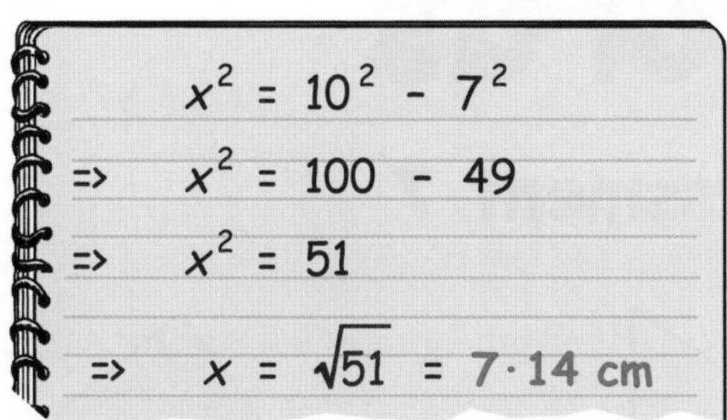

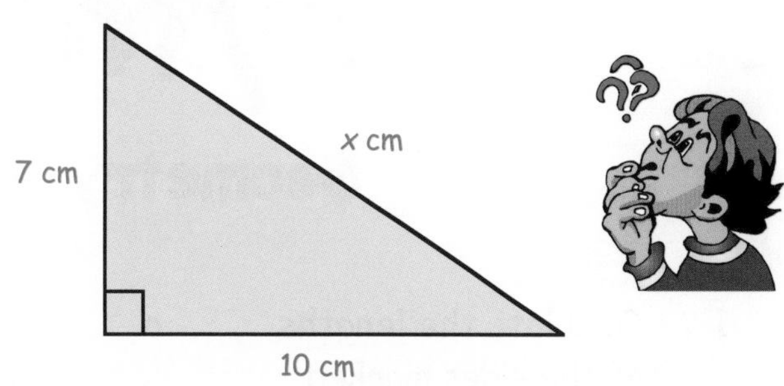

Explain in words, when Donnie looked at his answer and at the triangle, why he should have known immediately that his answer **had** to be **wrong**.

3. One of the following two answers is known to be the **correct** value for p.

$p = 16{\cdot}1$ cm or $p = 19{\cdot}1$ cm

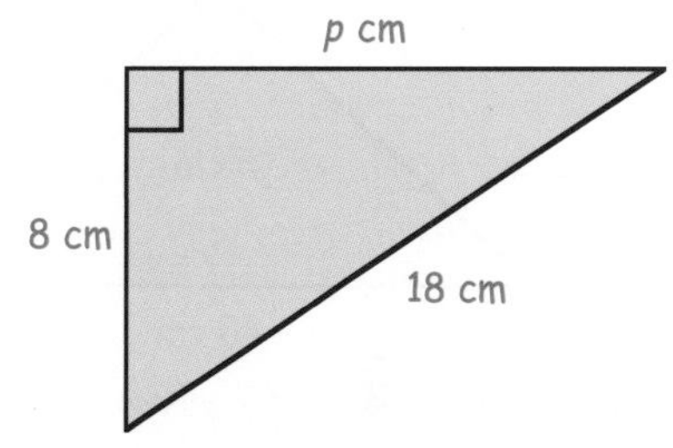

Without actually doing the calculation, say which answer must be correct and why the other is obviously wrong.

4. 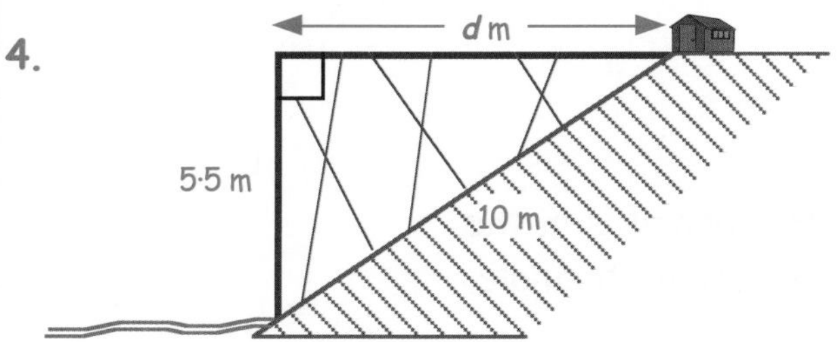

A wooden pier 5·5 metres high is shown.

It is in the shape of a right angled triangle.

Calculate the distance ***d*** from the fishermen's hut to the end of the pier.

5. To make two triangular shelf bracket supports, Colin saws "diagonally" across a rectangular piece of wood.

Calculate the length of the sawn edge.

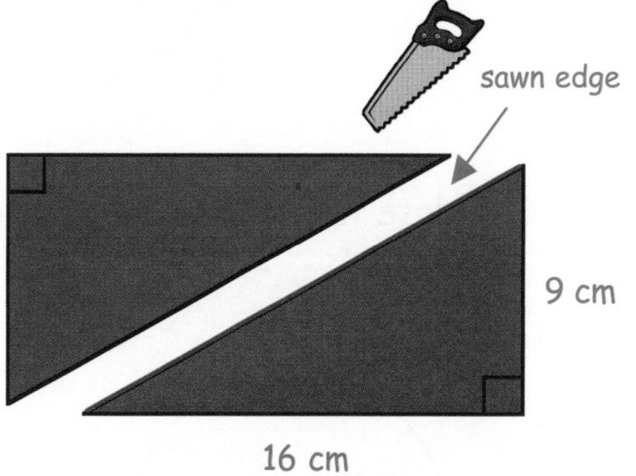

6. 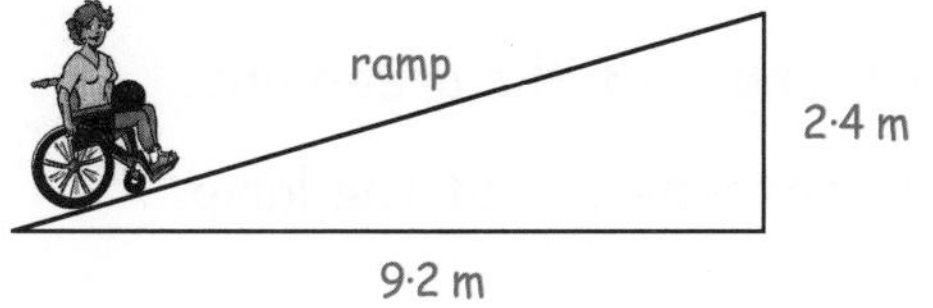

Shown is a design for a wooden wheelchair ramp.

Calculate the length of the ramp.

Pythagoras

Geometry Assessment 7

1. Calculate the lengths of the sides marked x and y here.

a

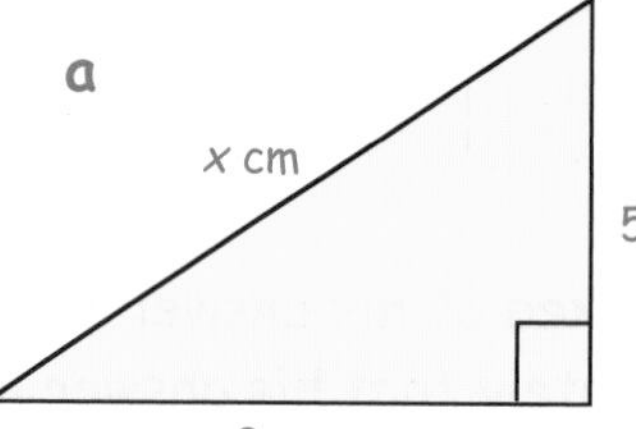

b

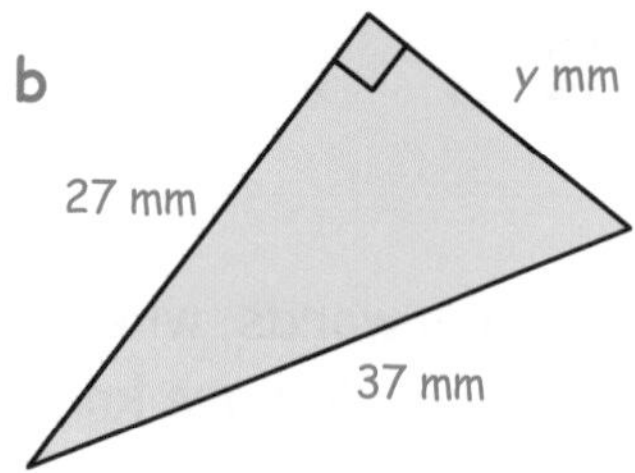

2. A

25 cm

h cm

B C

40 cm

Triangle ABC is isosceles with AB = AC.

   a Calculate the height of triangle ABC.

   b Now calculate its area.

3. A triangular corner unit (shown in yellow), is built to house a television.

   Calculate the length of the long edge of the unit (x).

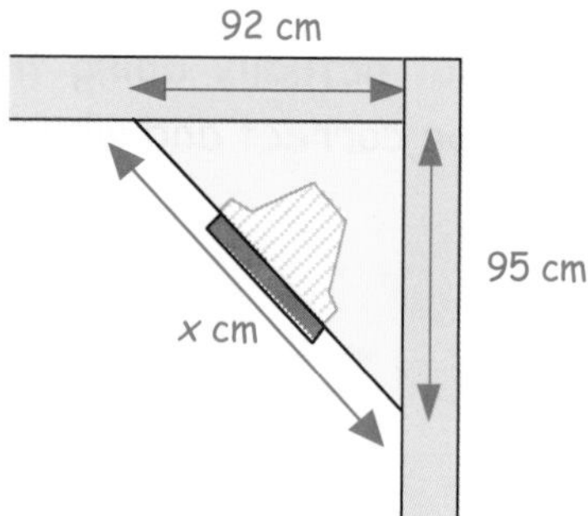

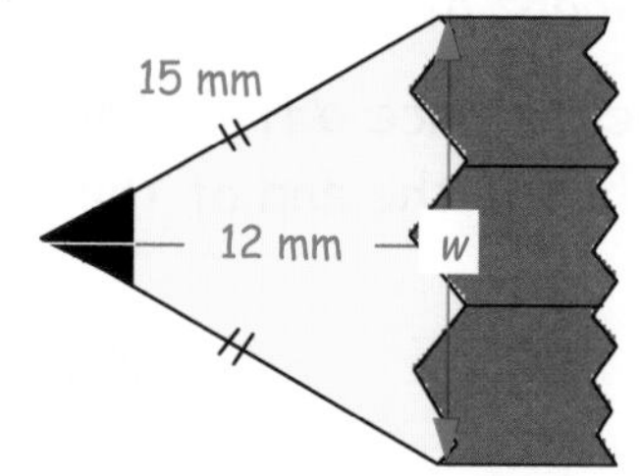

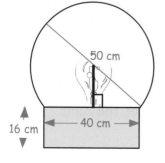

4. The tip of this pencil is in the shape of an isosceles triangle.

   Calculate the width of the pencil (w).

5. Calculate the **perimeter** of this shape.

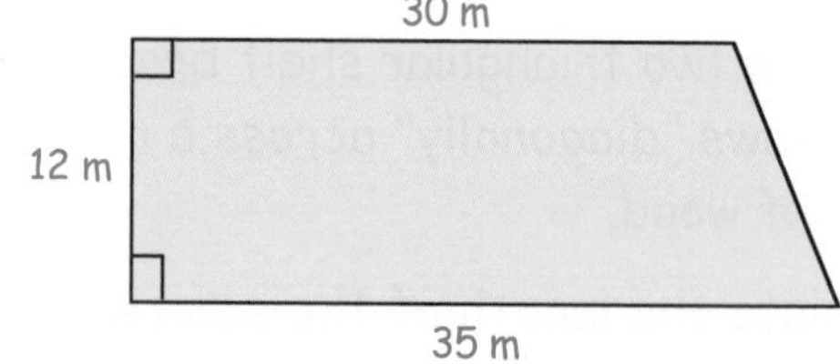

6. 50 cm

16 cm

40 cm

The picture shows a glass lamp, consisting of part of a spherical globe on top of a rectangular base.

   a Calculate the length of the green line.

   b Calculate the total height of the lamp.

Time & Timetables

12 & 24 hour Time

Revision

Remember :-

12 hour time —> 24 hour time
24 hour time —> 12 hour time

Example :- 6·55 am —> 0655 9·25 pm —> 2125

Exercise 1

1. Change the following 12 hour clock times to 24 hour clock times :-

a	2·30 am	b	5·35 am	c	9 am	d	8·30 pm	e	3·45 pm
f	4 pm	g	8·25 am	h	8·25 pm	i	1·50 am	j	6·25 am
k	midday	l	12·10 am	m	12·10 pm	n	11·15 pm	o	4·25 am.

Remember :- 0830 —> 8 · 30 am 2040 —> 8 · 40 pm

2. Change the following 24 hour clock times to 12 hour clock times :-

a	0250	b	1010	c	0725	d	1530	e	1650
f	2345	g	0135	h	2020	i	1405	j	2107
k	1200	l	0430	m	1725	n	1620	o	2259.

3. How long is it from :-

a	4·25 pm to 7·25 pm	b	5 am to 9·30 am	c	noon to 6·45 pm
d	5·20 pm to 8 pm	e	7·45 am to 9·15 am	f	3·40 am to 6·20 am
g	0950 to 1125	h	1515 to 1705	i	2245 to 0245 (*next day*) ?

4. The alarm clock indicates when Billy went to sleep at night and awoke in the morning.
   For how long was Billy asleep ?

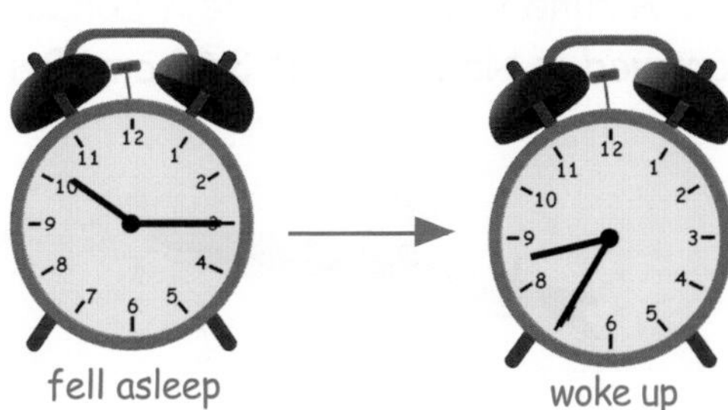

Interpreting Timetables

Exercise 2

1. Here are the coach timetables for "Falkirk <—> John O'Groats".

Falkirk <—> John O'Groats			
Falkirk	leave	0850	2155
Perth	arrive	0945	2250
	leave	0950	2255
Dunkeld	arrive	1015	2320
Pitlochry	arrive	1055	midnight
	leave	1205	0015
Newtonmore		1325	0135
Carrbridge		1403	0205
Inverness	arrive	1453	0300
	leave	1535	0300
John O'Groats	arrive	1755	0525

John O'Groats <—> Falkirk			
John O'Groats	leave	0755	1955
Inverness		1035	2235
Carrbridge		1127	1127
Newtonmore	arrive	1155	midnight
	leave	1240	0005
Pitlochry		1320	0045
Dunkeld	arrive	1350	0115
	leave	1400	0115
Perth	arrive	1427	0146
	leave	1427	0210
Falkirk	arrive	1505	0335

a How long does it take from Inverness to John O'Groats on each of the 0850 and the 2155 services from Falkirk ?

b At what times do the coaches leave Newtonmore for Pitlochry ? (*Use a.m. or p.m.*).

c Where will you have time for an early lunch on **each** of the **day time services** ? How long in each case ?

d On the **night time services** – where will you have time for a comfort stop and for how long in each case ?

e Which of the two evening services takes longer and by how much ?

f If you dislike travelling by coach, but had to undertake a journey from John O'Groats down to Falkirk, which coach would you choose to take and why ?

2. A plane left Prestwick Airport at 2335 on Thursday.

It touched down in Gran Canaria at 0415 (*British time*) on Friday.

How long did the flight take ?

3. PD Airline flight PD747 left London City Airport at 8·25 pm on Wednesday and arrived in New York at 3·10 am (British time) on Thursday morning.

a How long did the flight take ?

b New York is 5 hours **behind** UK.

What time (*New York time*) was it when the plane touched down ?

4. Shown is a TV programme listing for a Monday evening.

BBC one — BBC 1 Scotland	BBC TWO — BBC 2 Scotland	stv — STV South	4 — Channel 4
7:00 The ONE Show 7:30 Viva Variety	7:00 Tom Kerridge's Best Ever Dishes 7:30 Children's Hospital: The Chaplains	7:00 Emmerdale 7:30 Coronation Street	7:00 Channel 4 News 7:55 The Political Slot
8:00 East Enders 8:30 Room 101	8:00 University Challenge 8:30 Only Connect	8:00 On Weir's Way with David Hayman 8:30 Coronation Street	8:00 How the Rich get Richer Channel 4 Dispatches 8:30 Sarah Beeny's How to Sell Your Home
9:00 Holby City	9:00 Intruders 9:45 Some Irish People with Jokes	9:00 I'm a Celebrity ... Get Me Out of Here !	9:00 24 Hours in Police Custody
10:00 BBC News at Ten 10:25 Reporting Scotland 10:35 Scot Squad	10:00 Never Mind the Buzzcocks 10:30 Scotland 2014	10:00 ITV New at Ten & Weather 10:30 Scotland Tonight	10:00 8 out of 10 Cats 10:50 Toast of London

Use it to answer the following :-

a Which channel is showing a quiz involving **university** students ?

b You are in the process of trying to sell your house.

Which programme should you watch ?

On which channel and at what time ?

c How long does "**The Political Slot**" last for ?

d "**Reporting Scotland**" lasts for how long ?

e How long in total is "**Coronation Street**" on for ?

f On which channel and at what time is there an **Irish Comedy** programme showing ?

g If you watch all of "**Reporting Scotland**" then switch over to BBC2 for "**Scotland 2014**" how much of that programme will you have missed ?

h If you switch on to Channel 4 to watch "**The Political Slot**" and stay with that channel until the end of "**8 Out of 10 Cats**", for how long will you have been watching TV ?

i Imagine you had wanted to record "**Emmerdale**", "**Intruders**", "**BBC News at Ten**" and "**Reporting Scotland**" on a 2 hour DVD.

Would that have been possible ? *Explain* !!

5. Jocelyn's flight from Edinburgh to New York left Edinburgh Airport at 9.35 pm on Monday.

The flight time was 6 hours and 45 minutes.

a At what time did the plane land ? (*UK time*)

b If New York is 5 hours **behind** UK time, at what time (*local*) did she arrive in New York ?

6. 

Rod caught the 2130 overnight train from London to Rome on Friday night.

The total journey time is 19 hours and 20 minutes.

Rome is 1 hour ahead of Britain.

At what time (*local time*) should he arrive in Rome ?

7. I caught the overnight ship from Portsmouth to St Malo in France which left Portsmouth at 1955 on Friday night.

The crossing took 10 hours and 45 minutes and it took a further 35 minutes to get to my car and leave the ship.

France is 1 hour ahead of Britain.

When did I finally drive off the ship in St Malo ?

8. 

Jenny caught the overnight coach on Friday in Wick at 7.25 pm, heading for London.

The bus timetable said the journey time was 11 hours and 45 minutes.

Unfortunately, the coach had a puncture and the company had to send for a mechanic to repair it.

She got into London at 8.25 am on Saturday.

Calculate how long the mechanic took to repair the coach to allow it to continue.

9. Archie caught the 2340 train from London to Edinburgh on Monday night for an important meeting.

When he got to Edinburgh, he waited 15 minutes for a taxi and the taxi then took a further 35 minutes to drive him to his meeting in Dunfermline.

He got to his meeting at 0655 on Tuesday morning.

How long must his train journey have been ?

Time & Timetables

Measure Assessment 1

1. Write the times shown below as 24 hour times :-

   a 8:17 pm

   b twenty to five in the morning

   c 11:29 pm

   d seven minutes to seven at night.

2. Write these as 12 hour times :-

   a 0745 b 1635 c 2259 d 0015.

3. How long, in hours and minutes, is it from :-

   a 9:45 am till 2:10 pm

   b 2250 Monday till 0815 Tuesday ?

4. Shown is the bus timetable from Edinburgh to North Berwick.

Edinburgh		Musselburgh		Longniddry		North Berwick	
Arrive	Depart	Arrive	Depart	Arrive	Depart	Arrive	Depart
	0708	0742	0747	0803	0808	0851	0859
1005	1010	1044	1049	1105	1110	1153	1201
1317	1322	1356	1401	1417	1422	1505	1523
1629	1634	1708	----	----	----	----	----
----	----	----	1825	1841	1846	1929	----

   a When the bus leaves Edinburgh at 0708, at what time does it arrive at North Berwick ?

   b The bus arrives at North Berwick at 1929.

   Where did it set out from and when did it leave ?

   c I am at the bus stop in Musselburgh at 4:55 pm.

   How long do I have to wait for the next North Berwick bus to come along ?

   d How long does the journey take from :-

   (i) Edinburgh to Musselburgh (ii) Edinburgh to Longniddry

   (iii) Musselburgh to Longniddry (iv) Edinburgh to North Berwick ?

5. It takes 10 hours and 45 minutes to travel by train from London to Barcelona in Spain.

   If I catch the 2050 train from London, at what time will I arrive in Barcelona ?
   (*Remember - Spain is 1 hour ahead of us*).

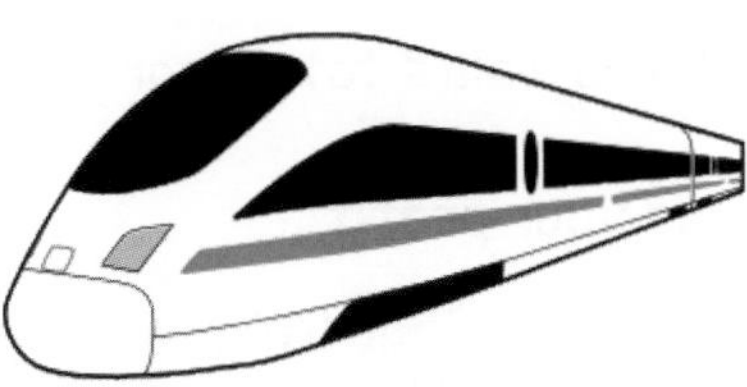

6. BBC1 showed the 3 Hobbit films, back to back, with 10 minutes between each.

   An Unexpected Journey lasted 2 hrs and 49 mins, The Desolation of Smaug lasted 3 hrs and 2 mins and The Battle of the 5 Armies lasted 2 hrs and 24 minutes.

   The first film started at 8.30 pm on Saturday. At what time did the last film end ?

Rules & Formulae

Formulae Expressed in Words

Example 1 :-

There are 10 chocolate Rolchies in a pack. How many Rolchies will there be in 8 packs ?

1 pack has 10 Rolchies

=> 8 packs must have 10 × 8 Rolchies = **80** Rolchies

Example 2 :-

To find the area of a parallelogram :- "Multiply the **base** by the **height**".

Find the area of a parallelogram with base 6 cm and height 9 cm.

Area = **base** × **height**

= 6 × 9

= **54 cm²**

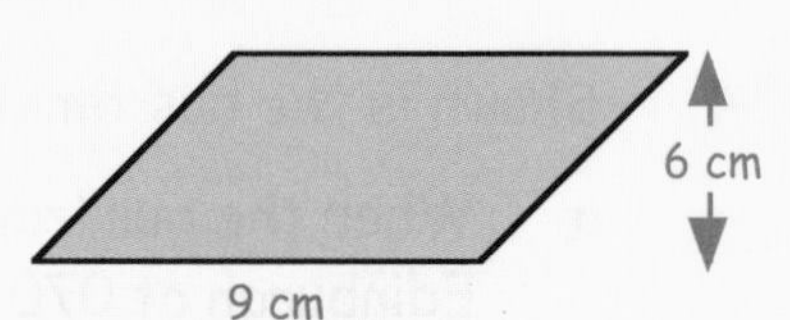

Exercise 1

1. A garden tub can hold twenty tulip bulbs.

   How many bulbs will there be in 5 tubs ?

2. 

   Chef has placed 12 cakes on each of his trays.

   a How many cakes can four trays hold ?

   b How many trays will be required for :-

   (i) 36 cakes (ii) 60 cakes ?

3. Tom had nine rolls with a bowling ball.

   He scored ten points with each of his first eight balls, but only four points with his last ball.

   What was Tom's total score ?

4. To find your **profit** :-

   "Subtract how much you paid for the goods in the first place from the amount you actually sold them for".

   a How much profit did a shopkeeper make when he sold a bicycle for £325, having previously bought it for £190 ?

   b He made a £35 profit by selling a bicycle helmet he bought for £38.

   How much did he sell the helmet for ?

5. To find how many legs a number of ants have, you simply multiply the number of ants by six.

How many legs do 450 ants have ?

6. To find the time, in hours, which a train takes to complete a journey :-

"Divide the distance travelled by the average speed of the train".

How long did it take a train to travel 360 miles going at 80 miles per hour ?

7. breadth AREA length

The breadth of a rectangle can be found by :-

"dividing the area of the rectangle by its length".

Find the breadth of a rectangle which has an area of 63 cm^2 and a length measuring 9 cm.

8. The cost of hiring a motor mower from the local garden centre is :-

"£30 basic, plus £5 per day".

How much will it cost to hire a mower for :-

a 2 days b 1 week c a fortnight ?

9. To work out the cost of ordering polo shirts online, use the following formula :-

"Multiply the number of shirts you want to buy by 20 and then add 2·99".

The answer is then given in pounds (£'s).

a How much will it cost to order 2 polo shirts ?

b What do you think the *2·99* in the formula represents ?

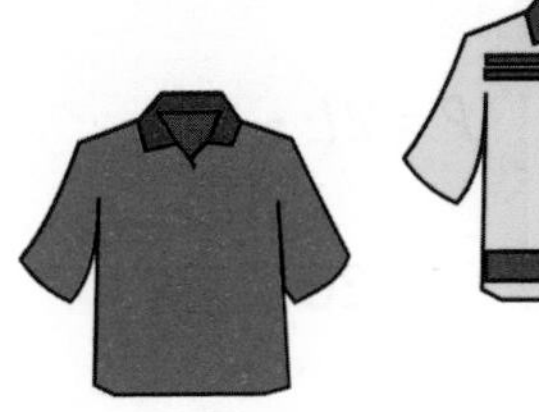

10.

To cook a ham joint in the oven :-

"Give it 30 minutes per kg and then add an extra 20 minutes".

For how long should you cook a eight kilogram ham ?

11. In an intelligence test, the rules were :-

2 marks for each correct answer, but 1 mark OFF for each wrong answer.

What score did James get :-

a if he had 15 correct and 5 wrong answers ?

b if he had 7 correct and 13 wrong answers ?

Formulae with Symbols

Example 1 :-

If $A = B \times C$

find A when $B = 6$ and $C = 8$.

$$A = B \times C$$
$$= 6 \times 8$$
$$= \mathbf{48}$$

Example 2 :-

If $P = \frac{mn}{10}$,

find P when $m = 4$ and $n = 6{\cdot}5$.

$$P = \frac{mn}{10}$$
$$= \frac{4 \times 6{\cdot}5}{10}$$
$$= \frac{26}{10}$$
$$= \mathbf{2{\cdot}6}$$

Exercise 2

1. The following formulae are often used in Mathematics and Science.

   For the formula :-

   a $P = s - b$ find P, when $s = 32$ and $b = 18$.

   b $D = S \times T$ find D, when $S = 20$ and $T = 14{\cdot}5$.

   c $V = I \times R$ find V, when $I = 14$ and $R = 8$.

   d $Q = m \times s \times t$ find Q, when $m = 200$, $s = 1{\cdot}5$ and $t = 3$.

   e $P = 2L + 2B$ find P, when $L = 9{\cdot}5$ and $B = 10$.

   f $T = 20 + 7W$ find T, when $W = 6$.

   g $V = u - 10t$ find V, when $u = 100$ and $t = 3$.

   h $D = \frac{m}{v}$ find D, when $m = 450$ and $v = 45$.

   i $P = \frac{mv}{10}$ find P, when $m = 80$ and $v = 5$.

   j $K = 8M \div 5$ find K, when $M = 10$.

   k $F = \frac{9C}{5} + 32$ find F, when $C = 15$.

   l $A = L^2$ find A, when $L = 30$.

2. The volume of a cuboid is found using :-

$$V = L \times B \times H$$

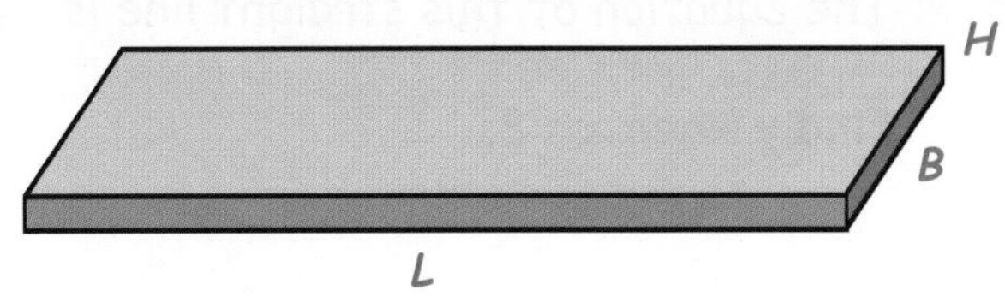

Calculate the volume of a cuboid when :-

$L = 20$, $B = 5$ and $H = 0{\cdot}5$.

3. 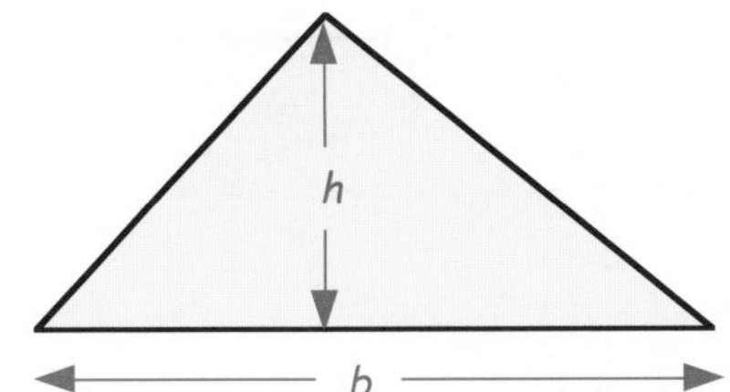

The area of a triangle is found by using $A = \frac{1}{2}(b \times h)$.

Find A when $b = 14$ and $h = 5$.

4. When a kettle is switched on, the temperature rises.

The formula for calculating the temperature is $T = 0{\cdot}9t + 16$ where t is the time (in seconds) and T is the temperature (in °C).

Calculate the temperature (the value of T) when :-

a $t = 0$ b $t = 10$

c $t = 20$ d $t = 50$.

5. 

When a window is opened, the temperature in the room falls.

A formula for working out the temperature in a room with an open window is $T = 24 - 0{\cdot}2m$, where m is the time in minutes and T is the temperature in degrees Celsius.

Calculate the temperature (T) when :-

a $m = 0$ b $m = 5$

c $m = 50$ d $m = 120$.

6. The perimeter of the shape shown can be worked out using the formula :- $P = 2a + b + c$.

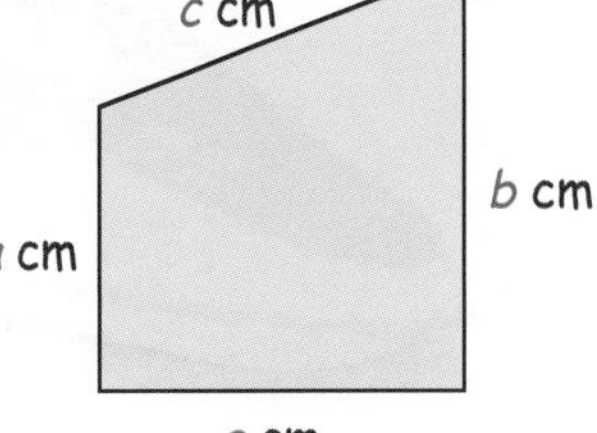

Find P when :- $a = 10$, $b = 14$ and $c = 10{\cdot}8$.

7. The cost of a ticket for a football league match for an adult is £A.

A child's ticket is £C.

The total cost for a group of adults and children is £T.

For a group of 5 adults and 4 children the cost is given by

$$T = 5A + 4C.$$

Find the value of T when :-

a $A = 20$ and $C = 10$ b $A = 25$ and $C = 12{\cdot}50$.

8. The equation of this straight line is $y = \frac{1}{2}x + 3$.

Find y when $x = 8$.

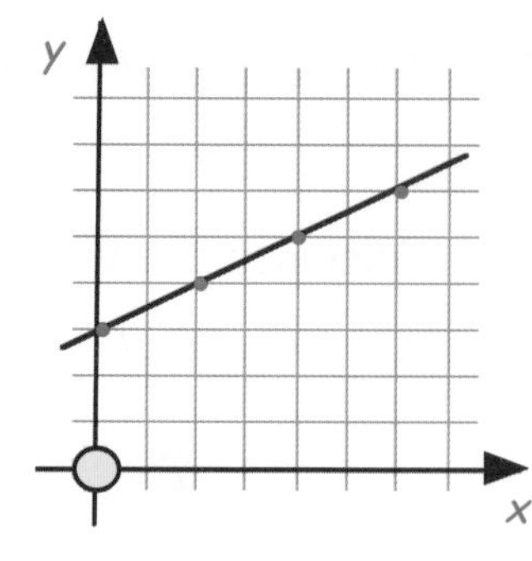

9. The length of an arc is found by using the formula

$$L = \frac{1}{3}(8h - c).$$

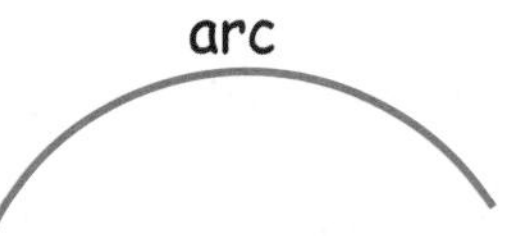

Find L when $h = 2$ and $c = 7$.

10. To find the **mean**, (*average*), of any three numbers v, w and x, use the formula :-

$$M = \frac{v + w + x}{3}$$

Calculate the value of M when $v = 20$, $w = 30$ and $x = 70$.

11. A plumber estimates the cost of a job by using the formula

$C = nr + t$, where

- C is the cost of the job in £'s
- n is the number of hours required to be worked
- r is the rate per hour and t is the travel charge to drive to the job.

Calculate the cost of a job which took 10 hours to complete, where the hourly rate was £40 and the travel charge was £25.

12.

The cost of hiring a jet ski is given by the formula

$C = f + 25h$

where
- C is the total cost (in £'s)
- f is a fixed value and
- h is the cost per hour.

Find the cost of hiring a jet ski for 2 hours with a fixed value of £20.

13. The volume of a cube is found by using the formula

$V = L^3$, ("$L \times L \times L$")

where L (cm) is the length of one side of the cube.

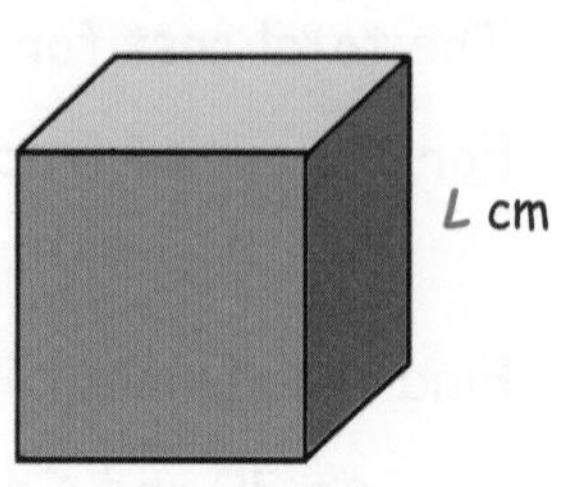

Calculate V when $L = 5$.

(*to cube a number :- multiply it by itself and itself again*)

Rules & Formulae

Measure Assessment 2

1. The average speed (in mph) at which a train travels is found by using the rule :-

   "Divide the distance travelled by the time taken for the journey".

   What is the average speed of a train covering 90 miles in $1\frac{1}{2}$ hours ?

2. The area of a kite, in cm^2, is found as follows :-

   "multiply the larger diagonal by the smaller diagonal and halve the answer".

   Find the area of a kite with diagonals 9 cm and 6 cm.

   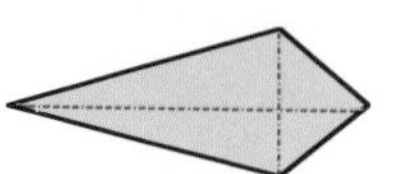

3. For each formula, find the value of the letter asked for :-

a	$T = r - s$	find T, when $r = 17{\cdot}5$ and $s = 9{\cdot}5$.
b	$D = S \times T$	find D, when $S = 20$ and $T = 2{\cdot}5$.
c	$U = v \times w \times z$	find U, when $v = 100$, $w = 5$ and $z = 0{\cdot}5$.
d	$M = n - 100p$	find M, when $n = 1000$ and $p = 9$.
e	$C = 9 \times A \div 27$	find C, when $A = 3$.

4. The advert shows the cost of hiring a car.

   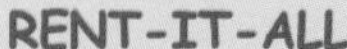

   RENT-IT-ALL

   25 pounds per day plus ten pence per mile

   What did it cost me to hire a car for 4 days and drive a total of 200 miles ?

5. The net profit made by a computer store is given by the formula :-

   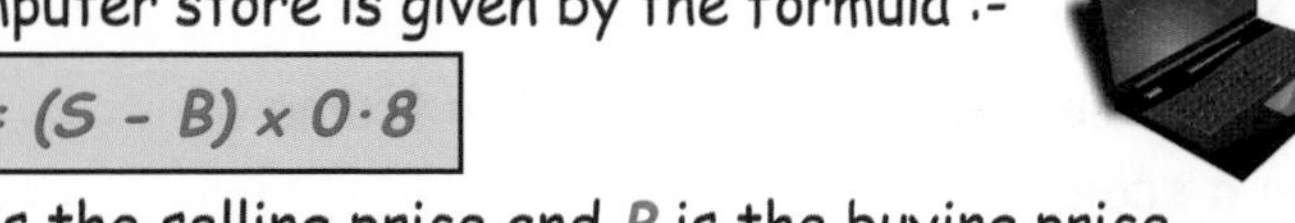

   $P = (S - B) \times 0{\cdot}8$

   where P is the net profit, S is the selling price and B is the buying price.

   Calculate the store's profit on a laptop bought for £220 and sold for £420.

6. A library charges a fine (£F) for any book returned late.

   To find F, use the formula shown :- $F = 0{\cdot}64 + 0{\cdot}6d$,

   (where d is the number of days late).

   How much will you be fined for taking a book back 6 days late ?

Scale Drawings 2

Making Simple Scale Drawings

*You will need a **ruler** to draw these figures.*

Exercise 1

1. This is a "rough" sketch of the floor of a conservatory.

   Make an accurate scale drawing of it using a simple scale of :-

   1 cm = 1 metre.

2. 

   This is a sketch of Mr Craig's allotment.

   Make an accurate scale drawing of the allotment using a scale of :-

   1 cm = 4 metres.

   a If 4 metres is represented by 1 centimetre in the scale drawing,

   => 24 metres (length) will be represented by (24 ÷ 4) = ... centimetres.

   Start your scale drawing by drawing a line ..... centimetres long.

   b Also => 16 metres (breadth) will be represented by (16 ÷ 4) = ... cm.

   Now finish your scale drawing by drawing the breadth .... centimetres long and completing the rectangle.

3. This window frame measures 140 centimetres by 70 centimetres.

   Make a scale drawing of the window frame using a scale :-

   1 cm represents 20 cm.

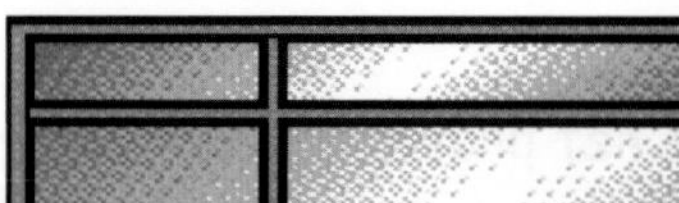

4. 

   This foot bath measures 40 inches by 30 inches.

   Make a scale drawing of the bath.

   Scale :- *1 cm = 4 inches.*

5. Here is a sketch of a kitchen.

Make an accurate scale drawing of it using a scale of :-

1 cm = 0·5 metres.

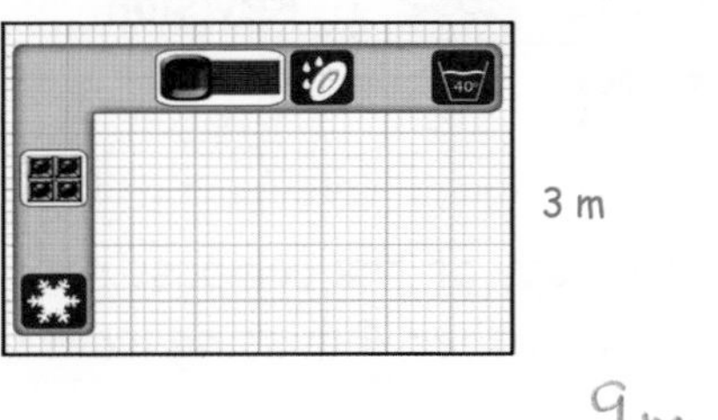

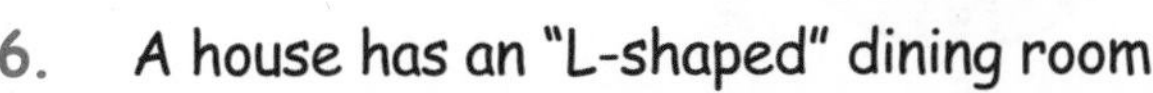

6. A house has an "L-shaped" dining room.

Not all of the actual sizes of the room are shown.

a Write down the two sizes which are missing.

b Make a scale drawing of the room, using the scale :-

1 cm represents 1·5 m.

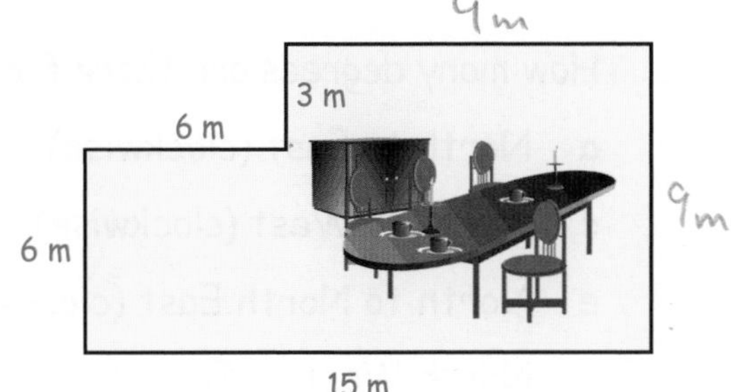

7. A rescue team set off from the airport in a helicopter and fly 160 kilometres East to Storm Island.

From Storm Island, they then fly North for 100 kilometres to the hospital, before returning to base.

a Make a scale drawing of the trip.

b Measure the length of the line on your drawing from the hospital to the airport.

c Calculate the **real** distance from the airport to the hospital, in km.

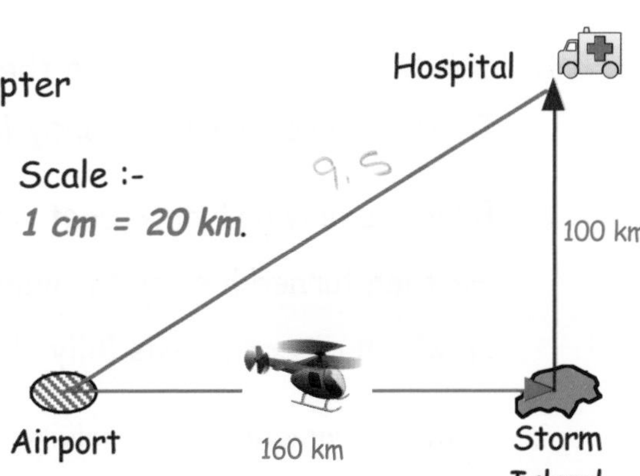

8.

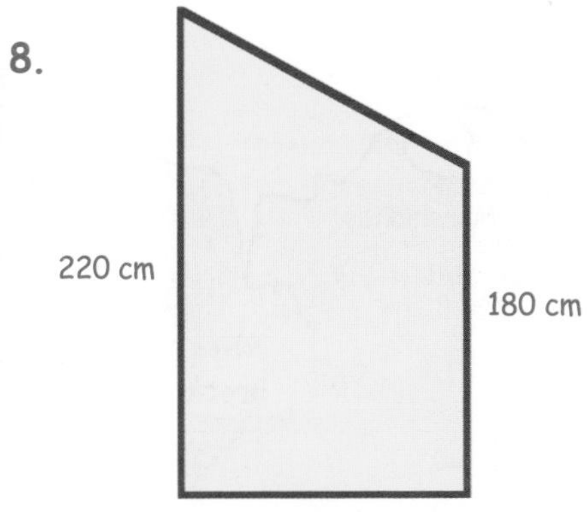

A side view of a shed is shown.

It is in the shape of a right angled triangle on top of a rectangle.

a Make a scale drawing of the side view,

Scale :- *1 cm represents 20 cm.*

b Measure the sloping line on your drawing and calculate the **real** length of the sloping roof, to the nearest centimetre.

9.

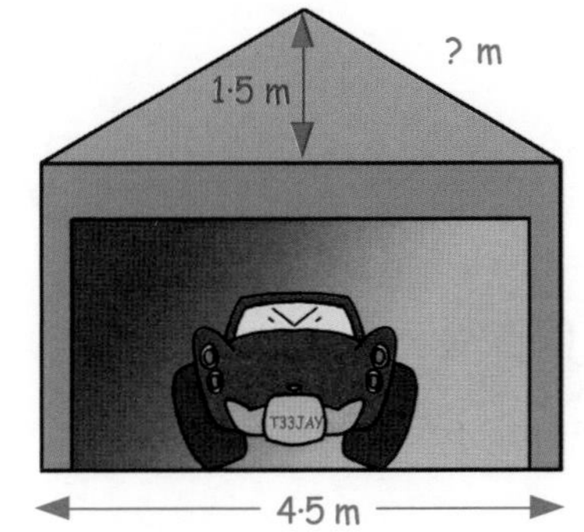

The garage roof is in the shape of an isosceles triangle.

a Make a scale drawing of the **roof** using a scale :-

1 cm represents 50 cm.

b Measure one of the sloping lines and calculate the **real** length of the sloping garage roof on one side.

The Compass Rose   Revision

Exercise 2

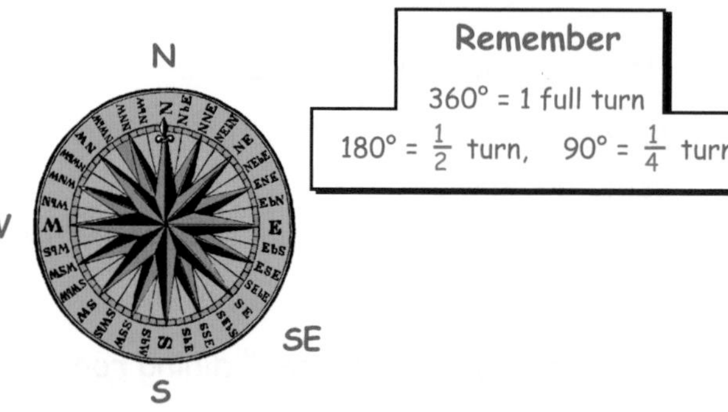

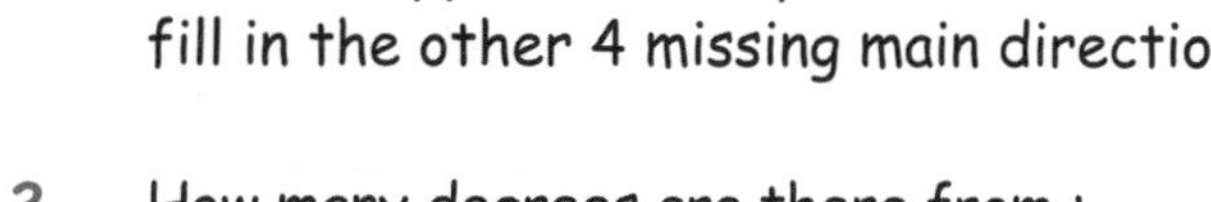

1. Make a copy of the compass rose and fill in the other 4 missing main directions.

2. How many degrees are there from :-

   a North to East (clockwise)
   b North to South (clockwise)
   c North to West (clockwise)
   d North to West (anti-clockwise)
   e North to North East (clockwise)
   f North to South East (clockwise)
   g North West to East (clockwise)
   h East to North West (anti-clockwise).

3. a Sandy was facing West. He then made a $\frac{1}{4}$ turn anti-clockwise.
   In which direction was Sandy facing ?

   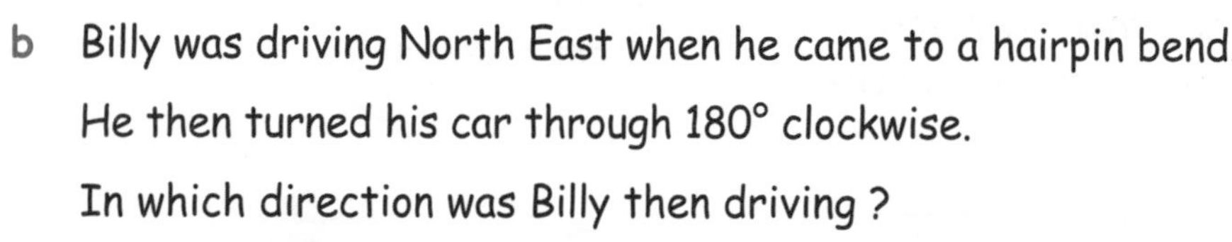

   b Billy was driving North East when he came to a hairpin bend.
   He then turned his car through 180° clockwise.
   In which direction was Billy then driving ?

   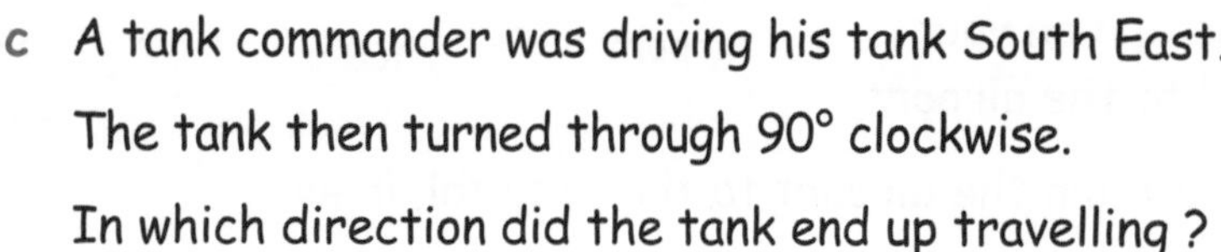

   c A tank commander was driving his tank South East.
   The tank then turned through 90° clockwise.
   In which direction did the tank end up travelling ?

4. The map shows Foggy Island.
   The town of Kirkton lies at a point around the middle.

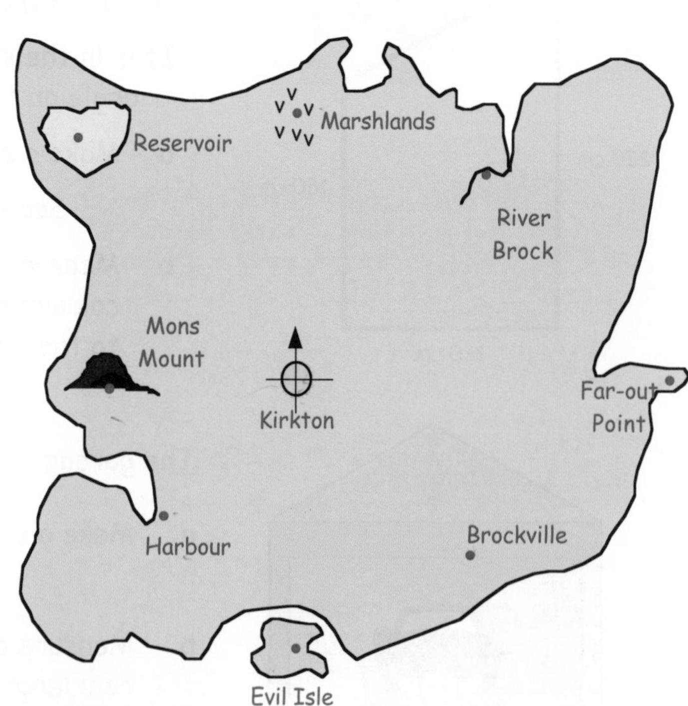

   a If I was in Kirkton, where would I be looking towards if I faced :-

   (i) South (ii) East
   (iii) N West (iv) S East ?

   b Where are the following in relation to Kirkton :-

   (i) the Marshland
   (ii) the River Brock
   (iii) Mons Mount
   (iv) the Harbour ?

   c Describe where Kirkton is in relation to Brockville.

Three Figure Bearings and Scale Drawings

A different way of describing directions is to give them as **3-figure bearings**.

The diagram shows Ayrton with the North direction through it.

Can you see that if you stand at Ayrton, **facing North** and turn through **60° clockwise**, then you will end up facing Prassie ?

=> We say that Prassie lies "**on a bearing 060°**" from Ayrton.
(*notice how we have used three figures to give the bearing*).

Can you see also that if you stand at Ayrton, **facing North** and turn through **135° clockwise**, then you will end up facing Tonga ?

=> We say that Tonga lies "**on a bearing of 135°**" from Ayrton.

Note:-
(i) Bearings are **always** measured **CLOCKWISE** from the North direction.
(ii) **Three figure bearings** are always used.
(iii) Use your protractor, turned **on its side** to measure bearings.

Exercise 3 You will need a **protractor** for this exercise.

1. Look at the diagram showing Brigton and Whirl.
   What is the 3-figure bearing of Whirl from Brigton ?

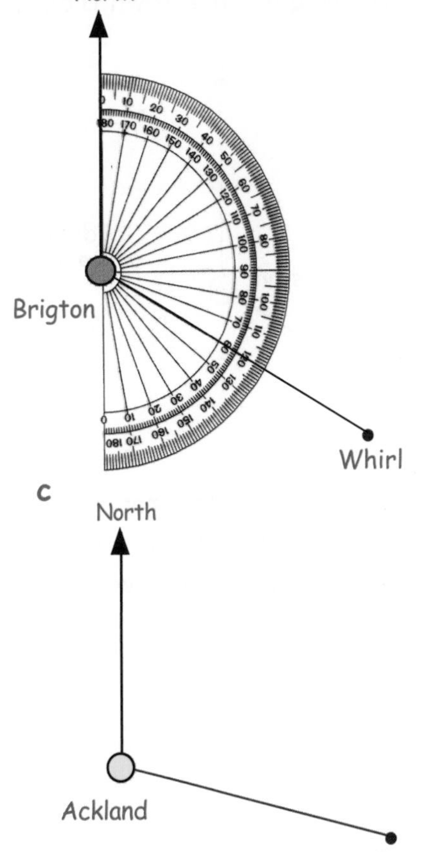

2. Use a protractor (turned round) to measure the bearing of each town from Ackland.

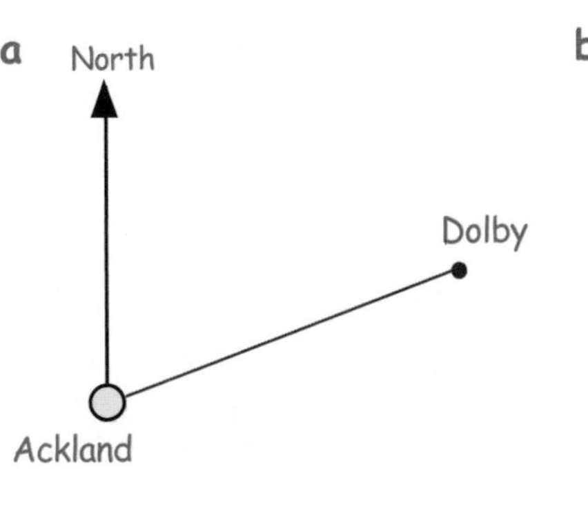

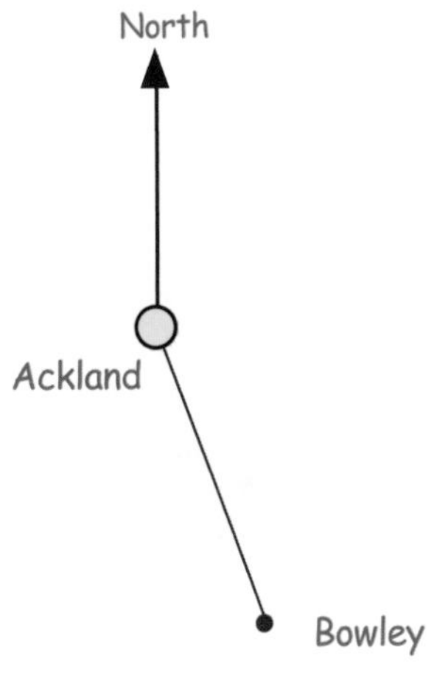

3. North, obviously, in 3-figure bearing terms is **000°**.

Write down the 3-figure bearing of the following :-

a South b East (3 figures !)

c South-East d North-East.

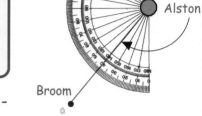

> Even if the direction you are dealing with is further round than **South**, you still measure it "**clockwise**" from the North.
>
> Can you see that Broom, in this figure, is 40° further round than South ?
>
> => it is (40° + 180°) = 220° round from North
>
> => the 3-figure bearing of Broom from Alston is **220°**.

4. Write down the 3-figure bearing of the following directions :-

a West b South West c North West.

5. The diagram shows 2 towns - Brent and Norley.

Write down the 3-figure bearing of Norley from Brent.

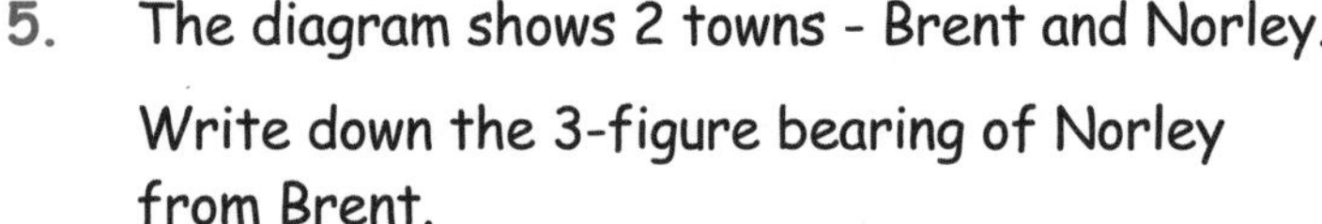

6. Use a protractor (turned round) to measure the bearing of each town from Dunstan.

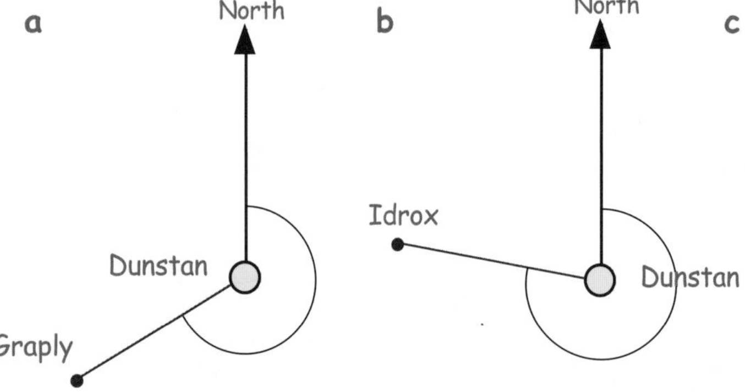

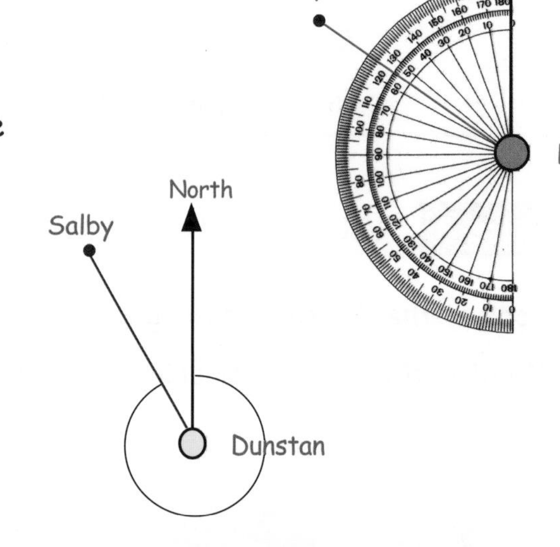

7. Use your protractor to write down the 3-figure bearing of each of these towns from Edinglow.

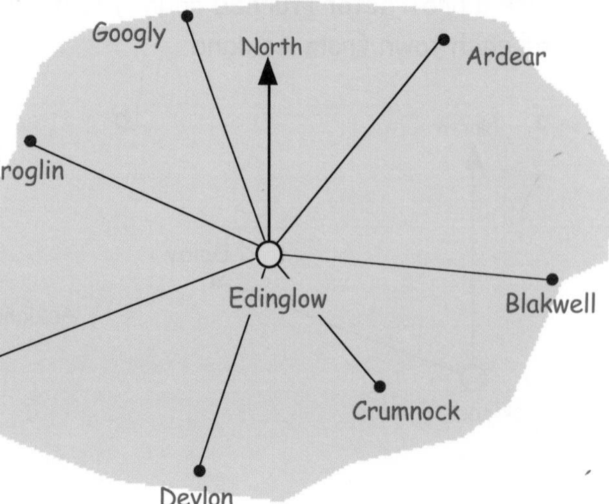

8. Mark a point on the page of your jotter and call it Arwick.

Draw a North line through your point.

Use your protractor to show Bouley, on a bearing 085° from Arwick.

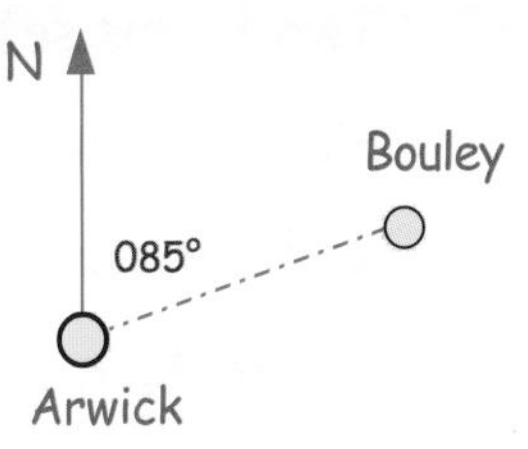

9. A plane leaves Norton airport and flies 80 km on a bearing 120° to Darvel.

To make a scale drawing of this journey :-

- Put a dot on your page and draw a North line.
- Use your protractor to show a bearing 120°.
- Use a scale *1 cm = 10 km* to show the journey of 80 kilometres.

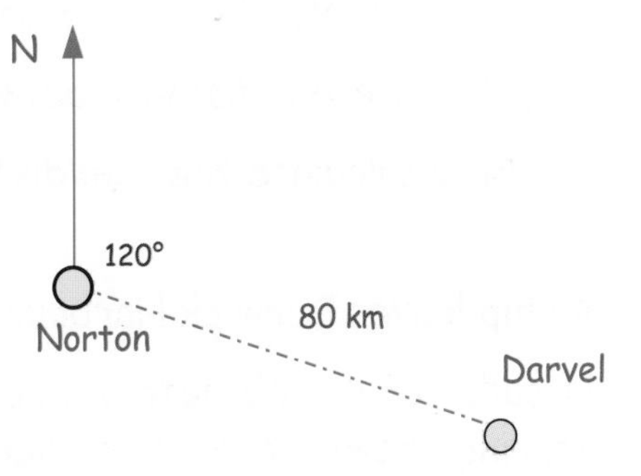

10. A boat leaves the harbour and sails 30 km on a bearing 040° to Tor Island.

It then leaves Tor, and sails on a bearing of 140° to Maine Marina, 40 km away from Tor.

a Make a scale drawing showing the combined journey using a scale *1 cm = 5 km*.

b Measure, in centimetres, how far the Marina is away from the harbour and calculate the **real** distance between them, in kilometres.

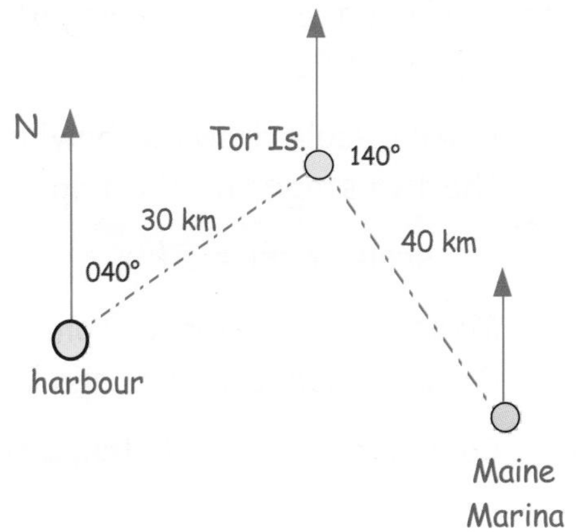

11. Two aircraft leave Edinburgh Airport at the same time.

The Cessna plane travels 95 kilometres on a bearing of 040°.

The helicopter flies 55 kilometres on a bearing of 145°.

a Make a scale drawing of the two journeys.

scale *1 cm = 10 km*.

> - start by marking a point on your page to show E.
> - draw in the north-south and east-west lines thru' E.
> - use your protractor to show the 40° from north.
> - use your ruler to show the Cessna's journey.
> - repeat for the helicopter's trip.

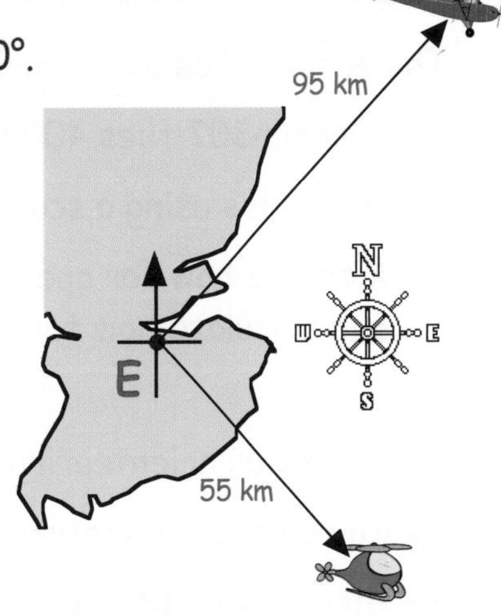

b Measure the distance between the two aircraft, in centimetres.

c Now calculate the **real** distance between them, in kilometres.

12. Two teams set off from a base camp as part of a military exercise.

Blue command travel for 13 kilometres on a bearing 250°.

Red command travel for 16 kilometres on a bearing 140°.

a Make a scale drawing of the two journeys.

scale *1 cm = 2 metre.*

b Measure the distance between the two teams, in centimetres.

c Now calculate the **real** distance between the two teams, in kilometres.

13. A ship leaves Dorwick Harbour.

It sails for 45 kilometres on a bearing of 060° to Parker Island.

It then sails from Parker Island for 30 kilometres on a bearing of 130° to Scapa Point.

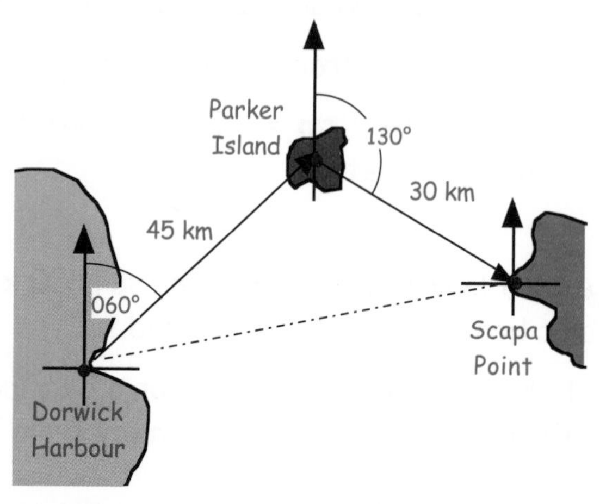

a Make a scale drawing showing the two stages of the trip.

scale *1 cm = 5 km.*

b Measure the distance from Dorwick Harbour to Scapa Point, in centimetres.

c Calculate the **real** distance from Dorwick Harbour to Scapa Point, in kilometres.

*For the following two questions, make a **rough** sketch first then an accurate drawing.*

14. Two planes leave Glasgow Airport at the same time.

The Airbus flies on a bearing of 075° and travels 350 miles.

The Boeing 307 flies 400 miles on a bearing of 165°.

a Show this using a scale *1 cm = 50 miles.*

b Measure how far apart the two planes are, in centimetres, and calculate how far apart they are, in miles.

15. As part of an orienteering competition, Mark sets off from base.

He walks for 1600 metres on a bearing of 165° to Marker 1.

He then travels 1200 metres on a bearing 070° to Marker 2,

Finally, he walks for 800 metres due North to the finish point.

a Draw Mark's route using a scale of *1 cm = 200 metres.*

b Calculate how far he is from the base, in metres.

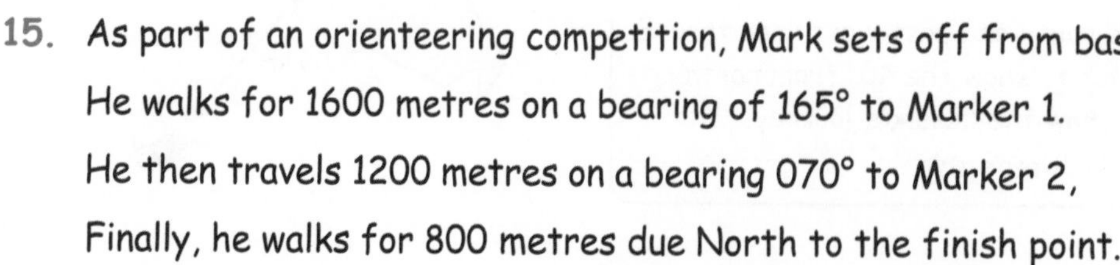

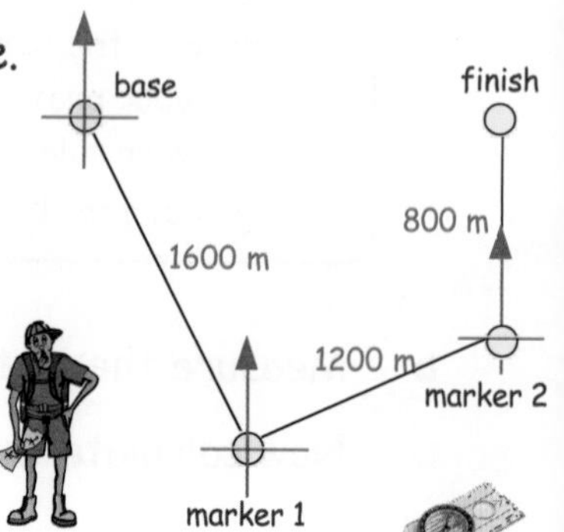

Scale Drawings 2

Measure Assessment 3

1. Farmer Smythe has a rectangular field with a plot of ground laid out as his wife's garden.

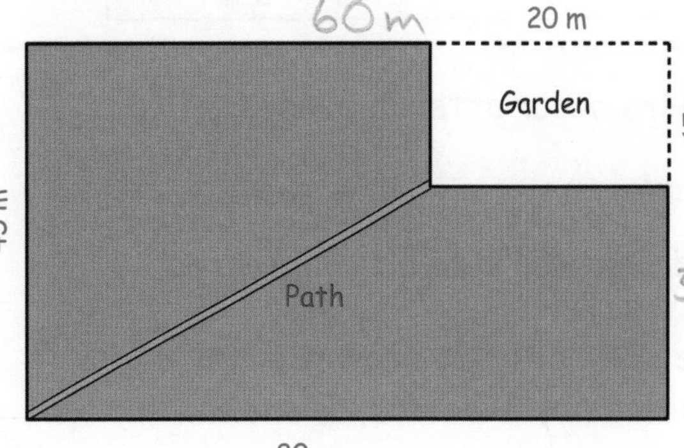

   a Make a scale drawing of this L-shaped field, using a scale :-

   1 cm = 10 m.

   b Measure the length of the path from the garden to the corner of the field, (*in cm*), on your drawing.

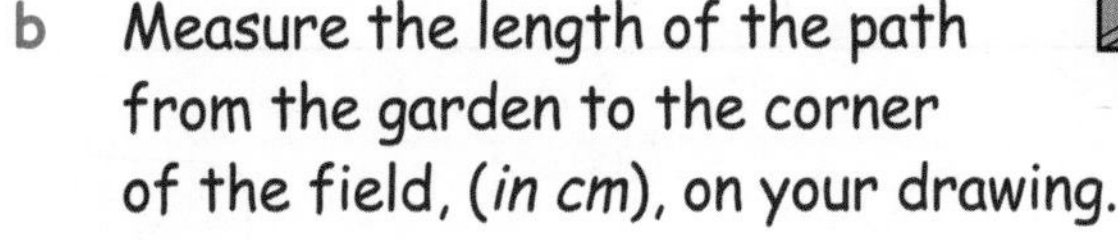

   c Calculate the real length of the path, in metres.

2. A pilot was flying North West, but on receiving a distress call, turned his plane clockwise till he was then flying due South.

   By how many degrees had the pilot rotated his plane ?

3. Use a protractor to measure the bearing of each island from Kryton airport.

a

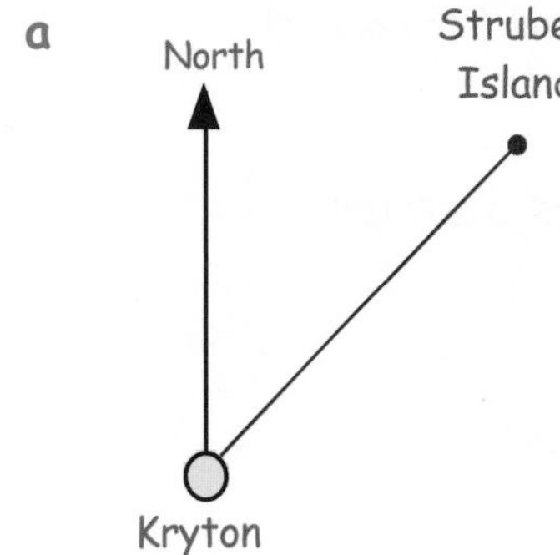

b

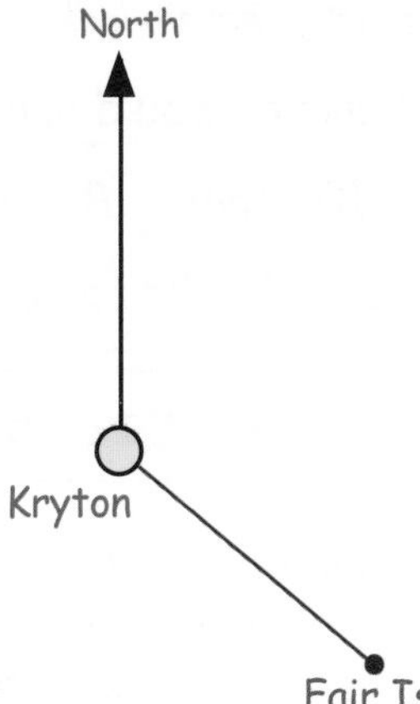

c

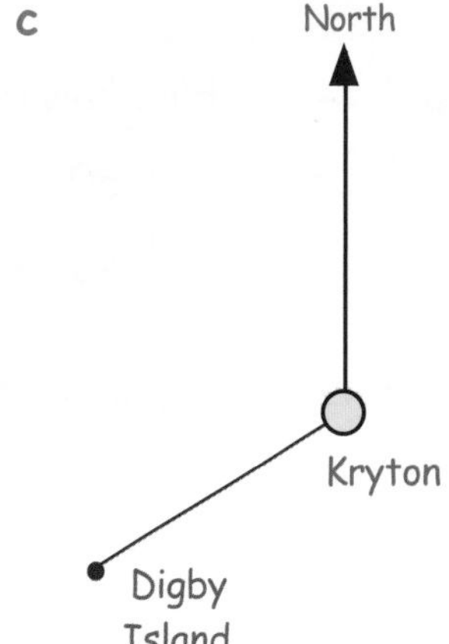

4. The *Lindhurst* sends out a distress call which is picked up by two naval vessels.

   The *Bitanic* is on a bearing of 025° from the *Lindhurst* and is 35 miles away.

   The *Hercules* is on a bearing of 130° from the Lindhurst and is 40 miles away.

   a Make a scale drawing showing all 3 ships using a scale *1 cm = 5 miles.*

   b Measure the distance between the *Bitanic* and the *Hercules,* in centimetres, and calculate how far apart the ships are, in miles.

Problem Solving

Real Life Problems involving Area

Problems occur often in everyday life.

Example :-

A bedroom wall is to be wallpapered.

The wall has been measured and is 6 metres by 3 metres, as shown.

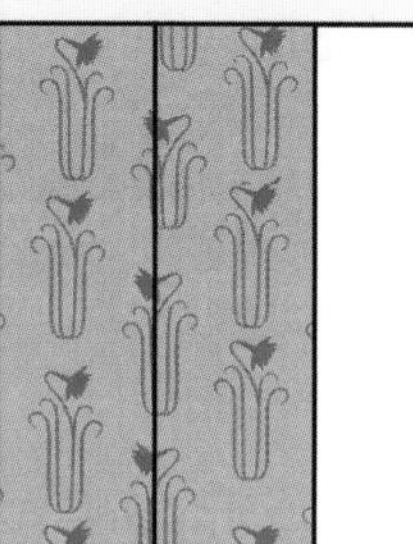

60 cm

6 m (600 cm)

3 m (300 cm)

The rolls of wallpaper to be used measure 60 cm wide and have a length of 11 metres when unrolled.

The wallpaper costs **£12·75** per roll.

Step 1 :- Find how many strips can be cut from 1 roll.

> one roll = **11 m** ÷ **3 m** = 3 full strips
> (*with a bit left over*).

Discuss why you might need extra paper ?
(Hint :- have a look at the pattern of the paper).

Step 2 :- Find how many rolls you would need.

> 600 ÷ 60 = 10 strips *But 1 roll gives 3 strips !*
> You would need 4 rolls to cover the wall.

Step 3 :- Calculate the cost. **4 × £12.75 = £51·00**

Discuss what other costs are involved in wallpapering a wall.
(Hint :- What keeps the paper on the wall ?
What tools/items do you need ?)

Exercise 1

1. Using the same rolls of wallpaper above, find how many strips, how many strips per roll, how many rolls are needed and the cost of wallpapering this wall.

3 m

15 m

2. Using the same wallpaper as question 1, find the cost of wallpapering a rectangular wall :-

   a 8 m long by 250 cm high   b 7 metres long by 2·4 metres high .

3. A rectangular kitchen floor, 5 m by 4 m, is to be tiled using square tiles of side 50 cm.

   a How many tiles will be needed to tile the floor ?

   b The tiles cost £22·50 for each pack of ten.

   How much will the tiles cost in total ?

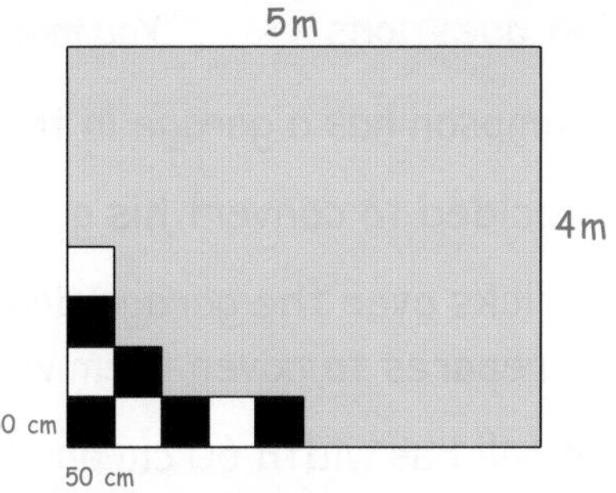

4. This floor is to be tiled using square tiles of side 30 cm.

   These tiles cost £24·50 per pack of eight tiles.

   How much will it cost to tile the floor ?

   (Remember - if you need part of a tile, count it as a full tile).

2·3 m (230 cm)

3·6 m (360 cm)

5. A bathroom wall is to be tiled.

   The wall has dimensions as shown.

   Each tile used is 40 cm by 40 cm.

   The tiles are sold in boxes of twenty at £56 per box.

   How much will it cost to buy the tiles for this wall ?

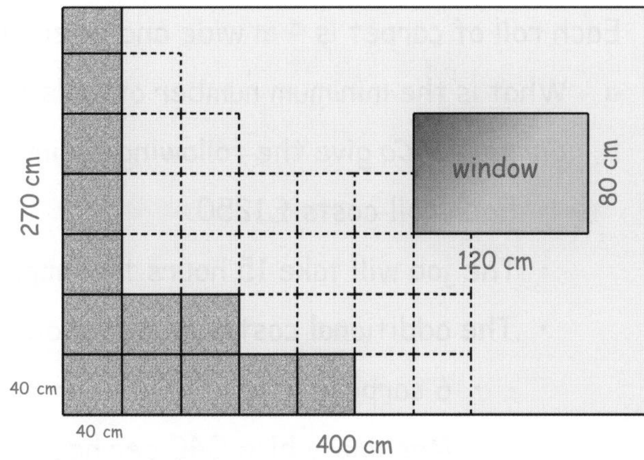

6. Tania has to paint the outside walls of her garden shed which is in the shape of a cuboid measuring 3 m by 2·5 m by 2 m.

   There is only one window (*shown*) which measures 1 m by 50 cm.

   A one litre tin of paint covers 6 m^2.

   The paint costs £6·95 per tin.

   What will be the total cost of the paint ?

50 cm

1 m

2 m

3 m

2·5 m

7. A playground is in the shape of a large **square** and a right angled **triangle** as shown.

   The playground is to have its surface covered in a special weather resistant rubberised material.

   This material costs £108 per square metre.

   How much will it cost to cover the playground with the special weather resistant material ?

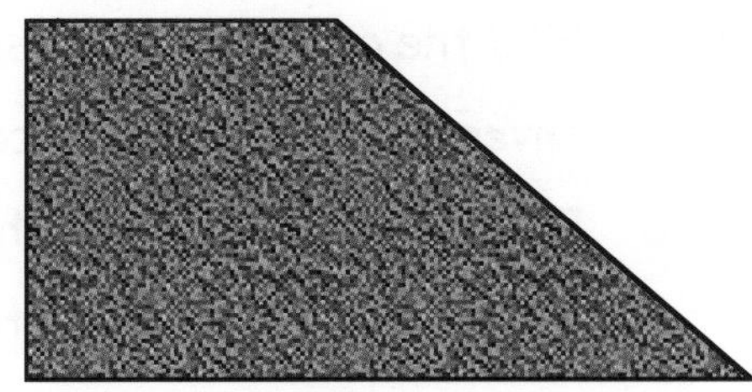

Extension questions :- *You may find questions 8 to 10 difficult - but try them.*

8. Mr Simpson has a garage in the shape of a cuboid.

   He decided to convert his garage into a play room.

   He bricks over the garage door, plasters all 4 walls and prepares to cover them with yellow wallpaper.

   Each roll has width 60 cm and has a length of 10 metres.

   The wallpaper costs £8·95 per roll.

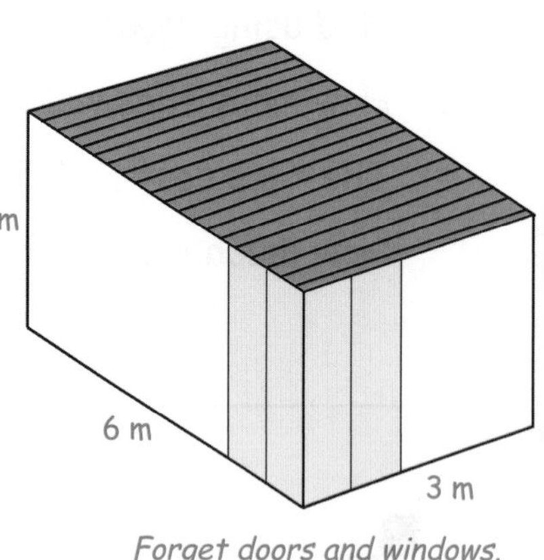

Forget doors and windows.

   a Find how many strips of wallpaper, and hence how many rolls he needs to wallpaper the 4 walls of the new room.

   b Calculate the total cost of the wallpaper.

9. The Grand Hotel has a rectangular ballroom 60 m by 40 m. The Ballroom is to be carpeted.

   Each roll of carpet is **4 m** wide and when unrolled is **24 m** long.

   a What is the minimum number of rolls required to carpet the ballroom ?

   b *Carpets & Co* give the following estimate :-

   - Each roll costs £1250.
   - The job will take 15 hours to complete.
   - The additional costs are as follows :-
     - 6 carpet fitters @ £24 per hour each
     - Machinery hire £40 per hour.

   60 m

   40 m

   How much will it cost the Hotel to carpet the ballroom ?

   c *Carpets-R-Us* can fit a one-piece carpet 60 m by 40 m.

   This will cost 5% more than *Carpets & Co's* total estimate for the actual cost of the carpet.

   They estimate it only will take 12 hours, using 4 men at £25 per hour using the same machinery.

   How much are *Carpets-R-Us* quoting ?

   d The Hotel use *Carpet-R-Us* to carpet their ballroom.

   Why do you think they chose this company ?

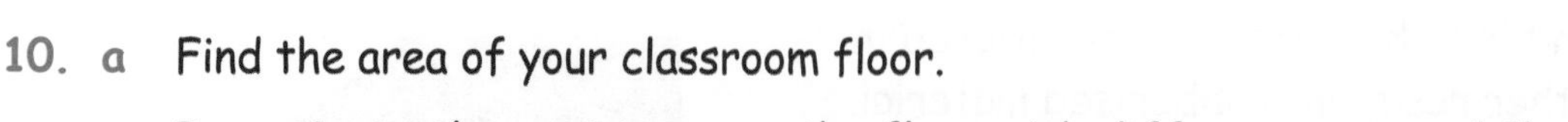

10. a Find the area of your classroom floor.

   Investigate the cost to cover the floor with different types of flooring.

   b Find the area of one of the walls in your classroom.

   Investigate the cost of tiling this area with different types of tiles.

   c Write a report or cost proposal on your findings for **a** and **b**.

Real Life Problems involving Volume

Problems, involving space and volume occur often in everyday life.

Example :-

A delivery van has a storage space which is in the shape of a cuboid, 4 m by 3 m by 3·5 m tall.

How many boxes 50 cm by 50 cm by 50 cm will fit into the van ?

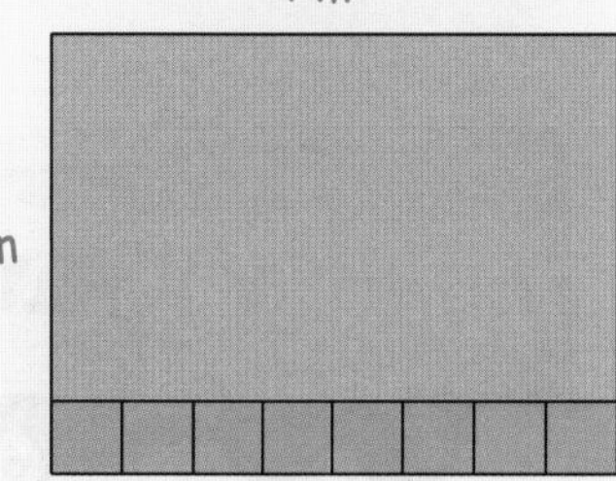

Step 1 :- Find how many boxes will fit along one side of the van.

(4 m) 400 cm ÷ 50 cm = 8 boxes.

Step 2 :- Find how many will sit on the floor in total.

(3 m) 300 cm ÷ 50 cm = 6

there can be 6 rows => 48 boxes.

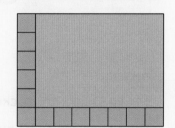

Step 3 :- Find how many layers stacked on top you can have.

(3·5 m) 350 cm ÷ 50 cm = 7 stacks high

Step 4 :- Find total number of boxes.

8 x 6 x 7 = 336. The van can hold 336 boxes.

N.B. The van is completely full - no spaces.

Exercise 2 *All boxes and containers are cuboidal unless otherwise stated.*

1. A smaller van has a storage space 2 m by 2 m by 1 m high.

   (*Boxes cannot be stored above the 1 metre height*).

   How many boxes can the van hold if the boxes measure :-

   a 25 cm by 25 cm by 25 cm b 50 cm by 25 cm by 20 cm ?

2. A storage depot in Aberdeen has to deliver three hundred boxes to its Dundee depot.

   The van from question 1 is used.

   The boxes this time are 40 cm by 30 cm by 30 cm.

   (This time there is some empty space on the van).

   How many trips will the van have to make to deliver all 300 boxes ?

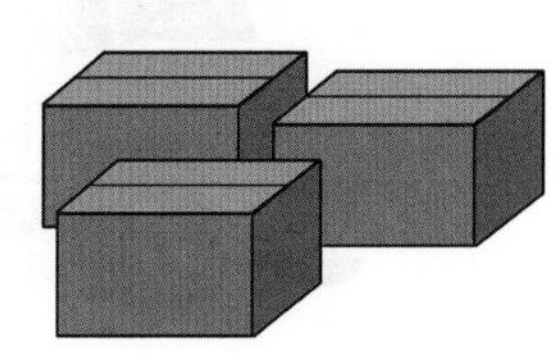

3. DVD cases 2 cm wide are stacked along a shelf.

a How many cases can be stacked along a shelf 2 metres long ?

b What is the minimum length of shelf needed to stack 120 DVDs ?

4. 

A van has a storage capacity of 450 cm by 300 cm by 200 cm.

a How many Plasma TV boxes 150 cm by 100 cm by 20 cm can be put into the van ?

b How many toy boxes 40 cm by 40 cm by 40 cm can be put into the van ?

5. Sirloin steaks are packed into boxes 20 cm by 20 cm by 10 cm.

The boxes are to be put into a sealed freezer unit 100 cm by 80 cm by 60 cm.

How many boxes can be packed into each freezer unit ?

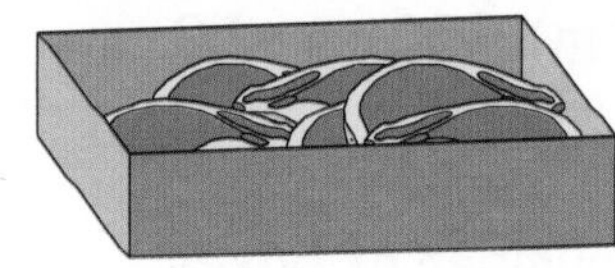

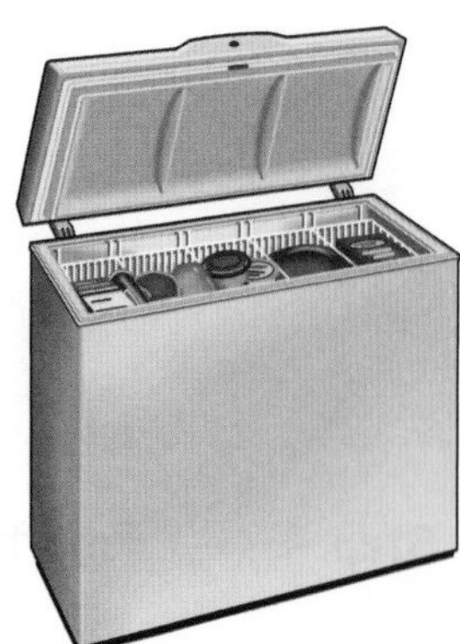

6. Wooden roof joists are stored in a barn measuring 30 m long by 9 m wide by 3 m high.

Each joist is 6 m long, 30 cm wide and has a depth of 10 cm.

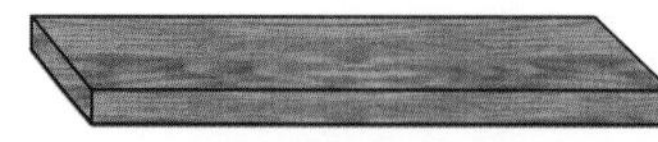

What is the maximum number of joists that can be stored in the barn ? (*Disregard the roof space*).

7. The container on the truck below measures 8 m by 4 m by 3 m wide.

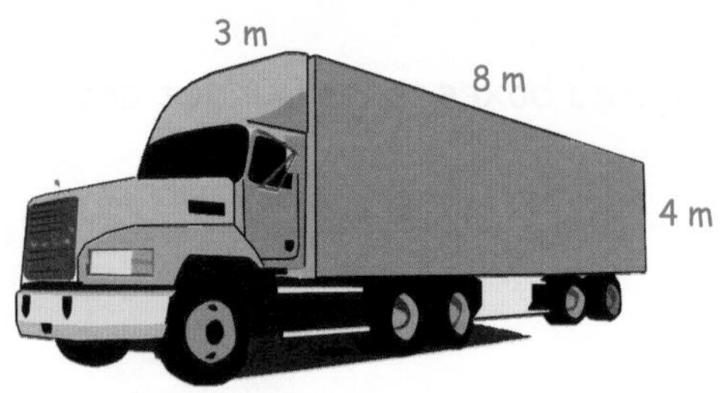

a How many boxes 40 cm by 40 cm by 40 cm can be put onto this truck ?

b How many boxes 75 cm by 80 cm by 65 cm can be put in this truck ?

Extension questions :- *You may find questions 8 to 11 difficult - but try them.*

8. A large cargo ship's hold carries 200 containers.

   - Each container is 8 m by 5 m by 4 m.
   - Each container is full of identical crates.
   - Each crate measures 1 m by 50 cm by 50 cm.
   - Each crate is full of identical boxes.
   - Each box, 25 cm by 25 cm by 25 cm, contains a Teddy Bear.

   How many Teddy Bears are on the ship ?

9. A large can of Cole Cola has dimensions as shown.

   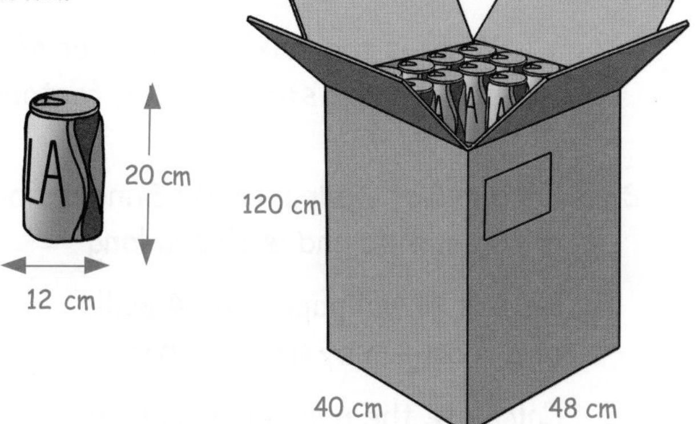

   a How many cans (*upright*) can be put into a box 48 cm by 40 cm by 120 cm tall ?

   b Explain why this size of box is better than a box measuring 60 cm by 35 cm by 135 cm tall.

   c The boxes in a are transported by trucks which have a storage capacity of 5 m by 4 m by 3·6 m tall.

   How many trips would the truck need to make to transport one million cans ?

10. A room measures 6 metres by 6 metres.

    Tony is going to tile it with pink and blue tiles.

    - The blue tiles measure 50 cm by 50 cm.
    - The pink tiles measure 25 cm by 25 cm.

    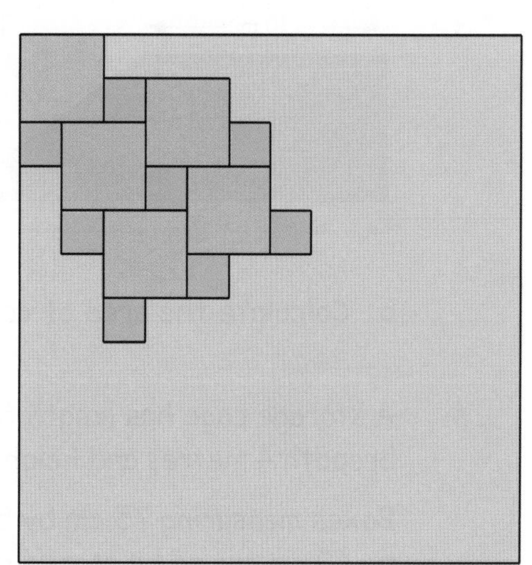

    He starts to draw out on paper the pattern shown.

    a Make a scale drawing on squared paper showing the blue and pink tiles, following this pattern.

    b How many pink tiles does he need ?

    Tony finds he has to halve some of the blue tiles, but can use both halves to fill in the gaps.

    c How many blue tiles is Tony going to need ?

    Both tiles are sold in packs of 6, the blue ones costing £18·50 per pack and the pink ones costing £5·95 per pack.

    d Calculate the total cost for all the tiles.

Problem Solving

Measure Assessment 4

1. A factory stores boxes 45 cm by 45 cm by 45 cm on a shelf **ten metres** long, **1 metre** deep and **50 cm** high.

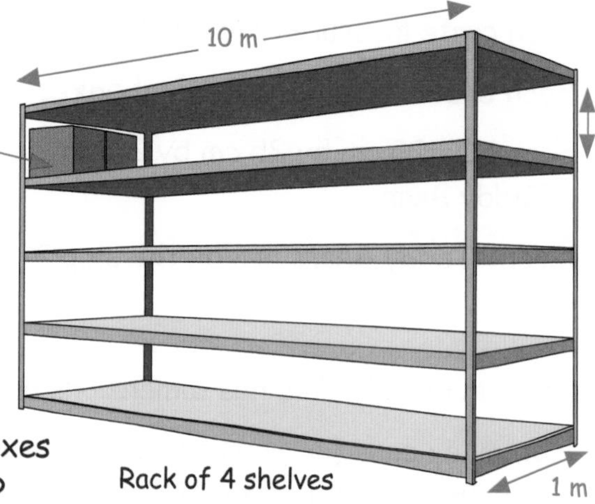

Rack of 4 shelves

   a How many boxes can be placed on one shelf ?

   b There are 4 shelves in each rack and 80 racks in the factory.

   What is the maximum number of boxes that can be stored in the factory ?

2. Each roll of wallpaper Mr Sanders buys is 70 cm wide and is 10·5 m long

He has to wallpaper the 4 walls of a room 4 m by 6 m by 2·5 m.

Calculate the number of rolls of wallpaper Mr Sanders should buy.

(*Forget the door and window, and there is no pattern to match*).

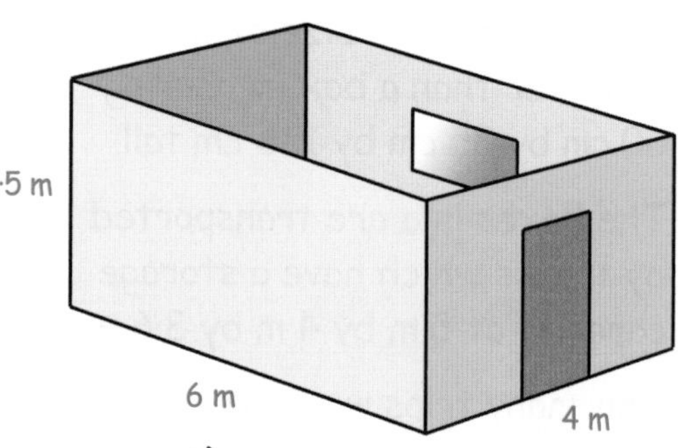

3. 10 m

3·5 m

16 m

The floor shown is to be fully carpeted with no joins.

The carpet is 4 metres wide, and can be bought to the nearest metre in length.

The carpet costs £28 per square metre.

   a Calculate the cost of carpeting this floor.

   b Calculate the area of carpet that is "wasted".

4. A storage cage has length 6 metres, breadth 4 metres and height 3 metres.

Boxes measuring 75 cm by 50 cm by 40 cm are to be stored in the cage.

The boxes must be stored using the instructions written on the boxes.

What is the maximum number of boxes that can be stored in the cage ?

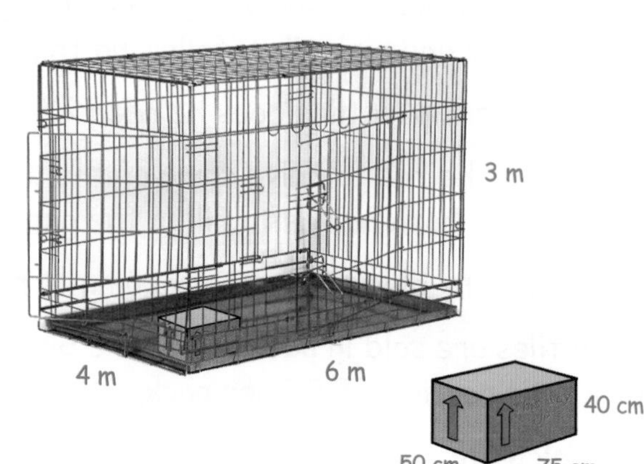

Tolerance

Tolerance

When a tractor manufacturer orders steel bolts to build his tractor engines, he would like them to be 30 millimetres long **exactly**.

As this is not always possible, the manufacturer allows a "little error" either side of this.

He might be willing to accept any bolt as long as it lies between 28 mm and 32 mm.

This means he will accept a bolt which is **within 2 mm** of the 30 mm he asked for.

This is referred to as the **tolerance** for the measurement.

This means add or subtract 2 mm to/from 30 mm

He will then specify the *acceptable limits* as => (30 ± 2) mm

This means :- **minimum** length is (30 – 2) mm = **28 mm**.
maximum length is (30 + 2) mm = **32 mm**.

Exercise 1

1. An onion grower ideally wants her onions to have a diameter of 80 millimetres.

   She states the tolerance as (80 ± 4) mm.

   a What is the **minimum** acceptable diameter (80 – ? = ... mm) ?

   b What is the **maximum** acceptable diameter ?

2. For each of the following tolerances, write down the **minimum** (min) and **maximum** (max) allowable sizes :-

a	(30 ± 1) mm	b	(25 ± 2) cm	c	(15 ± 3) kg
d	(20 ± 4) kg	e	(50 ± 5) ml	f	(45 ± 2) ft
g	(100 ± 1) g	h	(150 ± 10) mg	i	(200 ± 25) cm
j	(2·5 ± 0·1) km	k	(8·2 ± 0·2) m	l	(22·7 ± 0·3) m
m	(44·7 ± 0·1) miles	n	(20 ± 0·5) kg	o	(60 ± 0·2) mm
p	(95 ± 0·5)°C	q	(9·2 ± 0·3) litres	r	(18·5 ± 1·5) km.

3. Write down the **maximum** and **minimum** values given by these tolerances :-

a	(2·25 ± 0·01) mm	b	(4·75 ± 0·03) cm	c	(9·15 ± 0·05) g
d	(0·76 ± 0·06) kg	e	(3·21 ± 0·05) miles	f	(30·57 ± 0·03) ml
g	(1·98 ± 0·02) litres	h	(2·222 ± 0·002) ml	i	(4·054 ± 0·004) g.

4. In the manufacture of aeroplane seats, all bolts must have a length of (19 ± 3) millimetres.

   a Write down the minimum and maximum acceptable lengths.

   b State which of the following bolts should be rejected :-

   (i) 21 mm (ii) 16 mm (iii) 23 mm (iv) 14 mm

   (v) 20 mm (vi) 21·9 mm (vii) 15·8 mm (viii) 22·1 mm.

5. A hole has to be drilled in a metal plate so that it lines up with a bolt projecting from a wall.

   The hole is to be at a distance of (7·9 ± 0·2) cm from the left side of the plate.

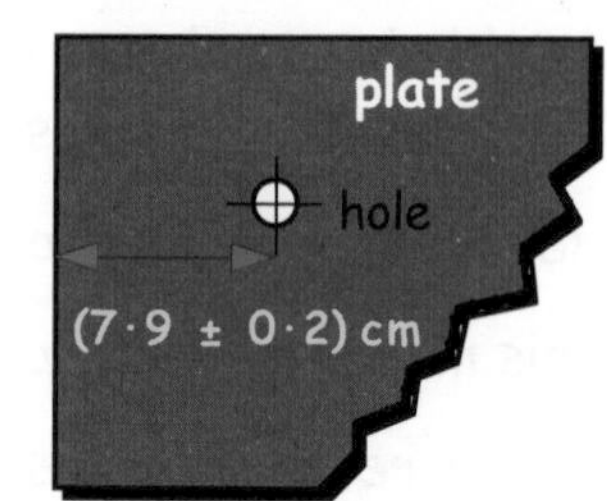

   a What is the minimum and maximum acceptable distance ?

   b It is discovered that the hole has been drilled 7·69 cm in from the left hand side of the plate. Is this acceptable ?

6. 

   Most stopwatches are only accurate to a certain degree.

   Formula One racing driver Lou Hambone's average pit stop time was reported as (8·98 ± 0·05) seconds.

   a What was Lou's fastest possible time, (*using the tolerance*) ?

   b What was his slowest time ?

7. In the baking of a farmhouse sultana cake, the weight of soft brown sugar used is important.

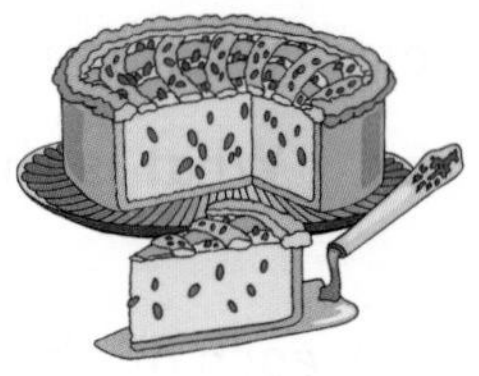

   The recommended weight is (8 ± 0·75) ounces.

   a What is the minimum weight of soft brown sugar required ?

   b What is the maximum weight of soft brown sugar required ?

8. 

   When "Talc Jars" mechanically fill their bottles of talcum powder, they expect the bottles to hold (250 ± 12) grams.

   a What is the minimum and maximum acceptable volume ?

   b 1 bottle is found to have 235 grams of powder. Is this o.k. ?

9. To cook the christmas turkey, a particular recipe recommends a temperature of (180 ± 5)°C for (3 ± 0·25) hours.

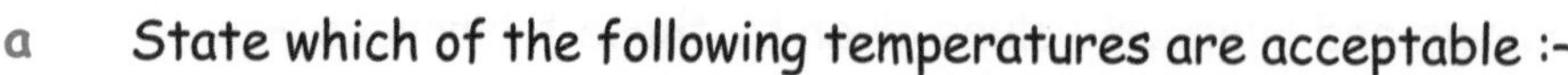

   a State which of the following temperatures are acceptable :-

   (i) 180°C (ii) 174°C (iii) 184°C (iv) 185·2°C.

   b State which of the following times are acceptable :-

   (i) 3 hours (ii) 2·85 hours (iii) 3 hrs 10 mins (iv) 2 hrs 40 mins.

Using Tolerance Notation

Example 1 :- When blowing up balloons for an office party, the boss decides that, for effect, their diameters should be between 35 and 45 centimetres.

This can be put into "**tolerance form**" as follows :-

Step 1 Find the "**middle**" of 35 and 45 => $\frac{(35 + 45)}{2}$ = 40.

Step 2 Write it as (40 ± 5) cm .

Example 2 :- The diameter of a button is to be between 2·1 and 2·5 centimetres.

=> Mid-point is $\frac{(2 \cdot 1 + 2 \cdot 5)}{2}$ = 2·3 => Tolerance is (2·3 ± 0·2) cm

Exercise 2

1. The length of a tennis court should be between 26 and 30 feet.

   Put this into tolerance notation (.... ± ....) feet.

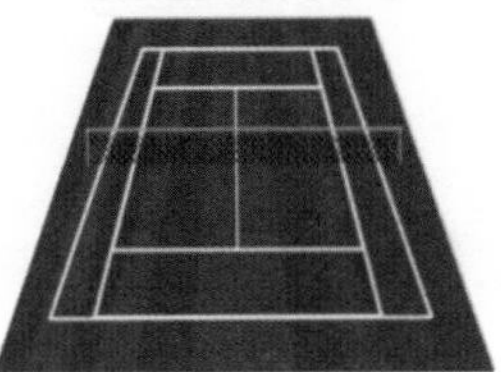

2. 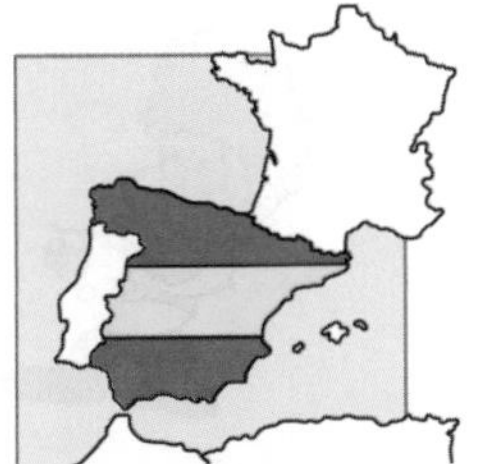

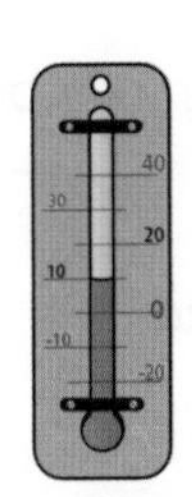

The afternoon temperature in Spain during January varies between 9°C and 15°C.

Write this in tolerance form.

3. Write each of the following in tolerance form :-

a	min = 15 cm max = 17 cm	b	min = 40 cm max = 50 cm	c	min = 5 cm max = 6 cm	d	min = 110 cm max = 130 cm
e	min = 9 kg max = 10 kg	f	min = 35 mm max = 41 mm	g	min = 4·4 m max = 4·8 m	h	min = 14·1 km max = 14·5 km
i	min = 0·7 cm max = 1·1 cm	j	min = 30·2 m max = 30·8 m	k	min = 12·4 g max = 13·4 g	l	min = 200 miles max = 800 miles.

4. Change the following to tolerance form :-

a	min = 8·12 g max = 8·14 g	b	min = 4·03 cm max = 4·07 cm	c	min = 0·74 m max = 0·78 m	d	min = 13·71 km max = 13·77 km
e	min = 7·28 ft max = 7·32 ft	f	min = 0·01 km max = 0·09 km	g	min = 3·95 g max = 4·05 g	h	min = 0·060 miles max = 0·064 miles.

5. In a recording studio, the sound engineer tries to keep the volume between 70·2 and 70·8 decibels.

   a Write this in tolerance notation.

   b Say whether the following are "too quiet", "too loud" or "just right" :-

   (i) 70·1 db (ii) 70·67 db (iii) 70·31 db (iv) 70·81 db.

6. 

Monty suggests that when hitting a golf ball into a high wind you want to keep it low, flying between 3 feet and 11 feet from the ground.

Write this in tolerance notation.

7. It is claimed that, on average, people write about 31 words per minute from memorised text and 23 words per minute while copying from a piece of writing.

Compare both using tolerance notation.

8. 

Whilst following a recipe for fruit scones, Debbie uses between 215 grams and 235 grams of self raising flour.

Express this in tolerance notation.

9. Tina knows she has between £10·70 and £11·30 in her piggy bank.

   a Write this in tolerance form.

   b Is it possible she has two £5 notes, a 50p coin and nine 10p coins in her bank ?

10. 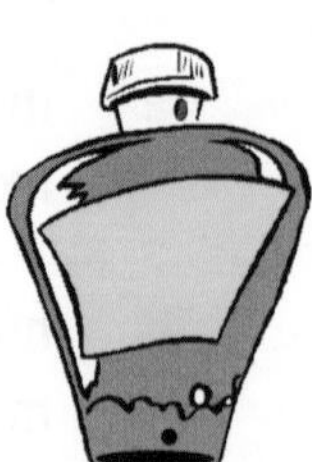

All 10 drivers in a go-kart race took between 30·5 and 31·3 seconds to complete the first lap.

Write this in tolerance notation.

11. In a chemist shop, when cough mixture is poured into a bottle, each bottle should contain between 230 ml and 244 ml.

   a Write this in tolerance form. b Is 229·5 ml acceptable ?

12. "Aldo Stores" won't put watermelons out on display unless they have a diameter between 16·0 cm and 24·8 cm.

   a Write this in tolerance form.

   b The store manager measured one at random and found its diameter to be 15·9 cm.

   Should that melon have been on display ?

Tolerance

Measure Assessment 5

1. For the 2 weeks before his big fight, a boxer finds that in training, his weight ranges from (81 ± 4) kg.

   a What is his lightest weight ? b What is his heaviest ?

2. Write down the minimum and maximum values for each of the following :-

   a (70 ± 5) cm b (125 ± 6) kg c (130 ± 20) volts

   d (2000 ± 150) tonnes e (9·1 ± 0·3) ml f (0·1 ± 0·01) litres.

3. All four competitors in the 100 metre final finished in a bunch.

   Their times were (9·84 ± 0·05) seconds.

   a What was the winning time ? b What was the last runner's time ?

4. The number of calories in a forty gram fruit scone should be (126 ± 10).

   Which of the following calorie numbers are acceptable :-

   a 106 b 135·9 c 117 d 137 ?

5. During training, a rowing team tries to maintain a "stroke rate" of between 28 and 34 strokes per minute.

   Write this in tolerance form as (.... ± ....) strokes/min.

6. Put the following into tolerance form :-

   a min = 20 cm, max = 30 cm b min = 147 kg, max = 153 kg c min = 2400 g, max = 1600 g

   d min = 1·9 sec, max = 2·0 sec e min = 31·5 m, max = 32·1 m f min = 0·02 mm, max = 0·08 mm.

7. The idle speed of a car is between 775 revs/min and 875 revs/min.

   Write this in tolerance form.

8. *"Lido Stores"* only accept pears with weights lying within a certain tolerance.

   The tolerance is given by (.... ± 10) grams. The maximum value allowed is 170 g.

   What is the minimum acceptable weight ?

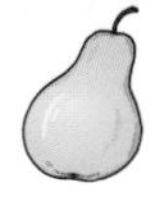

Unit Assessment
Geometry/Measure

Assessment Tasks

1. The cost, in £'s, of hiring a cement mixer is given by the formula :-

$$C = 12{\cdot}5d + 8{\cdot}5.$$

where d = number of days
and C = cost in £'s

a What is the cost of hiring the cement mixer for 5 days ? (2)

b A building manager was presented with a bill of £158·50 for hiring the cement mixer.

For how many days must he have hired it ? (2)

2. A cruise liner and a tall-ship leave port (P) at the same time.

The cruise liner travels 60 kilometres north east.

The tall-ship sails 30 kilometres south east.

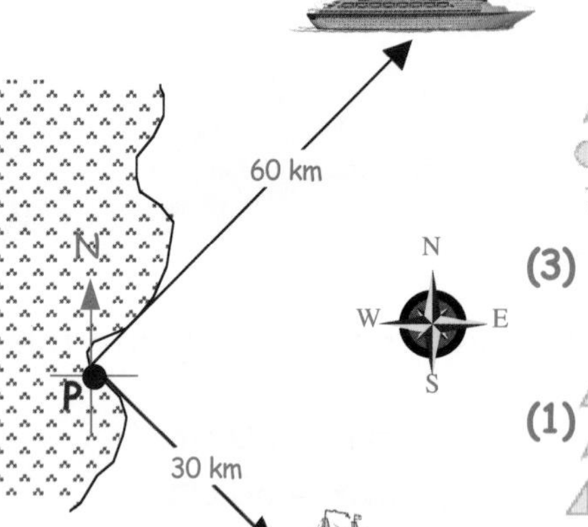

a Make a scale drawing of the two journeys.

Scale *1 cm = 10 km*. (3)

b Measure the distance between the two ships, in centimetres. (1)

c Now calculate the **real** distance between them, in kilometres. (1)

3. Small individual puddings produced at a factory must weigh between 119 grams and 125 grams.

Puddings that are not within the tolerated weights must be thrown out.

Write the allowable pudding weights in tolerance form, (.... ± ....) grams (2)

4. A ladder has slipped down the wall it was leaning against.

A small fence stopped it from falling onto the ground.

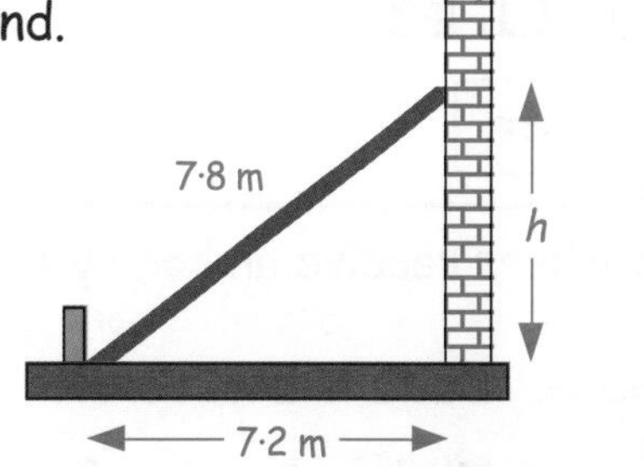

a How high is the ladder up the wall, to the nearest metre ? (4)

b This type of ladder is deemed to be unsafe if it has a gradient less than 0·4.

Is this ladder unsafe ? *Explain your answer.* (3)

5. A salesman, who sells boxes of matches, packs as many boxes as he can into his briefcase.

A match box measures 50 mm by 35 mm by 12 mm and his case is 300 mm by 420 mm by 90 mm.

What is the greatest number of match boxes he can pack into his case ? (4)

6. a Calculate the volume of this tank, in cm^3. (3)

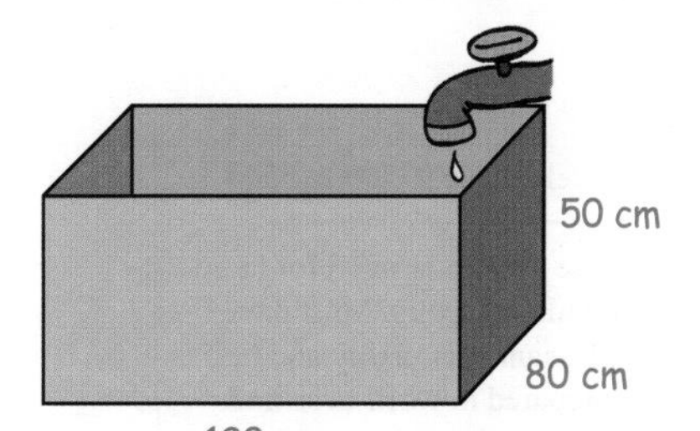

b How many litres is this ? (1)

($1000 \text{ cm}^3 = 1$ litre)

c When the tap is opened fully, water flows in at the rate of 6 litres per minute.

How long before the tank overflows ? (2)

7. Roddy wants to paint the outside of his garage - walls and door.

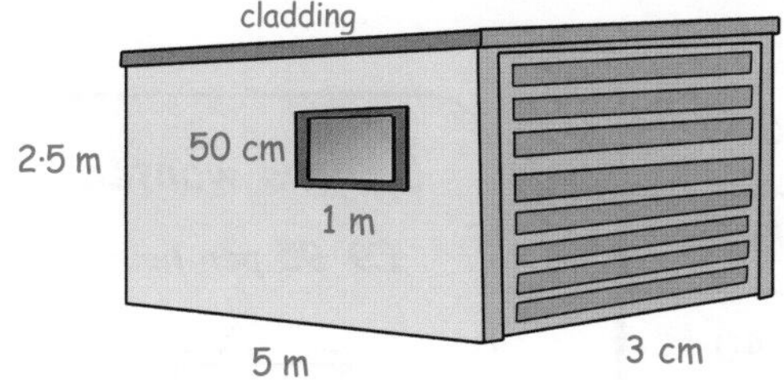

It is in the shape of a cuboid measuring 5 m by 3 m by 2·5 m.

It has two windows - the one (*shown*) which measures 1 m by 50 cm and another one, the same size, on the wall opposite.

a What is the total area of the four walls and door needing painted ? (3)

b How many litres of paint will Roddy need to buy if a one litre tin covers an area of 8 m^2 ? (1)

c If the paint is £19·50 per litre, how much will it cost him ? (1)

d For appearance, Roddy puts grey PVC cladding around the garage roof.

If the cladding is £4·50 per metre how much will this job cost him ? (2)

Income

Hourly Rate

Many workers receive an **hourly rate** of pay.

Example :- David is a labourer.
His hourly rate of pay is £8·50.
Last week he worked 38 hours.
What was his **basic** pay ?

Pay = 38 × £8·50 = £323·00

Exercise 1

1. Tam is an electrician's assistant, with a basic rate of pay of £8·25 per hour.
   If he worked 40 hours last week, how much was he paid ?

2. ....telephone 07799 665544

   Office Worker wanted for large textile company. Must have pleasant personality and be prepared to work overtime if required.
   Hourly rate £8·40
   phone 012345 678 901

   Joiner's assistant required .....

   a Ted applied for and got the job shown.
   In his first week, he worked 30 hours.
   Calculate his basic pay for this week's work.

   b In his 2nd week, he worked 36 hours.
   Calculate his pay for this week's work.

   c How much **more** did he earn in the 2nd week ?

3. James was calculating the pay for each of his 5 drivers.

Name	*Bob*	*Bill*	*Ted*	*Sue*	*Fred*
Hours	30	44	56	35	40

   a Calculate the pay due to each of the 5 drivers.

   b How much **more** did Ted earn than Fred ?

   c Calculate James' **total** wage bill for the week.

4. Sally works in an office.
   She earns £11·55 per hour.
   How much did she earn in February if she worked :-

Week 1	(1st - 5th February)	-	36 hours
Week 2	(8th - 12th February)	-	39 hours
Week 3	(15th - 19th February)	-	43 hours
Week 4	(22nd - 26th February)	-	32 hours

Calculating the Hourly Rate

If you know the total weekly wage for someone, and you know the number of hours worked, you can calculate their hourly rate of pay, by **dividing**.

Example :- Sara is a fitness instructor and worked 38 hours last week.

Her total basic pay for the week was £482·60.

What was her hourly rate of pay ?

Hourly Rate = £482·60 ÷ 38 = 12·7 = **£12·70.**

Exercise 2

1. Jack's payslip last week showed he earned £392.

   He knew he had worked for 40 hours.

   Calculate Jack's hourly rate.

2. Shown in the table are the weekly wages and hours worked by four different workers in *Capital Computing Co.*

Ari Analyst	*Tina* Telephonist	***Clara* Cleaner**	***Edith* Engineer**
£582·00	*£310·40*	***£267·30***	***£471·60***
40 hours	*32 hours*	***33 hours***	***24 hours***

   Calculate the hourly rate for each of the 4 workers.

3. Vera is a vet. Her wage last week was £1282·50.

   She had worked for 54 hours.

   a Calculate her hourly rate of pay.

   b This week she worked for 40 hours.

   How much did she earn this week ?

4. Last week, Toni worked 40 hours and earned £1328·40.

   How much will she earn this week if she works 48 hours ?

5. During the month of October, Bill worked 36 hours the 1st week, 42 hours the 2nd week, 40 hours the 3rd week and 44 hours the 4th week.

   a How many hours did Bill work altogether in October ?

   b If his total wage for the month was £1782, calculate Bill's hourly rate of pay.

Weekly & Monthly Pay

If you know a person's :-

monthly pay —> (x 12) to calculate the annual pay.

weekly pay —> (x 52) to calculate the annual pay.

Remember

52 weeks = 1 year

12 months = 1 year

Exercise 3 (Annual means yearly).

1. a Alistair's monthly pay at *The Paper Mill* is £1490.

   Calculate his annual (*yearly*) pay.

   b Ella's payslip shows she earns £1742·25 every month.

   Calculate her annual pay.

   c By how much is Ella's annual pay greater than Alistair's ?

2. Stevie does a part-time milk round each morning.

   He is paid £51·50 per week.

   Calculate Stevie's annual pay.

3. Calculate each person's annual wage :-

   a Fran earns £275·85 per week b Julie earns £987·90 per month

   c Sally gets £2010·95 monthly d Guri gets £1109·85 weekly.

4.  

   Jean is paid monthly and earns £1860·50 per month.

   Gina is paid weekly and gets £440·25 per week.

   Who earns more annually and by how much ?

5. Viv and Trish, both secretaries for the same company, decide to check if both receive the same wage.

   Viv is paid monthly and receives £1907·80 per month.

   Trish is paid weekly and earns £470·80 per week.

   Is one of them paid more than the other ? *Explain* !!

If you know your ANNUAL pay you can easily calculate :- your weekly pay -> by dividing by 52.

your monthly pay -> by dividing by 12.

52 weeks = 1 year

12 months = 1 year

6. a Arianna earns £27 588 per year as a sales manager.

Calculate her monthly salary.

b  Cheri has an annual (yearly) salary of £16 584.

Calculate her monthly pay.

7. a Nadia works as a dental hygienist.

She is paid an annual salary of £12 753.

Calculate Nadia's weekly wage.

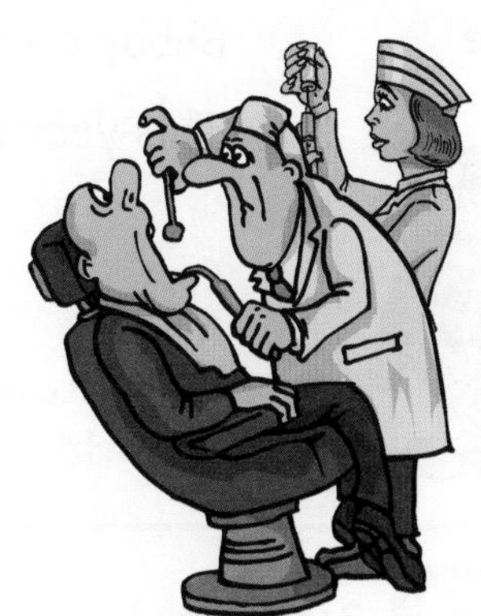

b Francesca is a laboratory assistant and is paid an annual salary of £22 022.

Calculate how much Francesca is paid each week.

8. Two models earn different annual wages.

Cathy is paid £27 378 per year. Ada receives £11 700.

Calculate each model's weekly wage.

9. 

Mo works for *Macro Robotics* and gets £44 426·20 per year.

a Calculate what he should be paid every week.

b *Macro* pay their employees every two weeks.

How much is Mo paid every 2 weeks ?

10. Leanne is offered a job as a Computer Analyst.

She can choose to be paid weekly or monthly.

a How much would her monthly salary be ?

b Now calculate how much she would earn weekly if this was the chosen method of payment.

11. 

Darren works a 40 hour week as a cattle auctioneer.

His annual salary is £27 040.

a Calculate his weekly pay.

b Now calculate Darren's hourly rate of pay.

c From this April, Darren will be paid £2133·33 monthly.

Is this an increase or decrease in his annual salary ?

Wage Increase & Decrease (Percentage Work)

Remember :- To find 5% of £700 using a calculator.

$$5\% \text{ of } £700 = \left(\tfrac{5}{100} \times 700\right) = (5 \div 100) \times 700 = £35.$$

Example :- Bobby earned £25 500 last year as a policeman.

This year he got a 4% pay increase. Calculate his new annual salary.

Last year's salary =	£25 500
Rise = $\left(\frac{4}{100} \times 25\,500\right)$ =	+ £1020
This year's salary =	£26 520

N.B. For a decrease in salary subtract instead of add.

Exercise 4 *Remember to set down the 3 lines of working as shown above.*

1. a Alan earned £19 400 last year as a telephonist.
   This year he was given a 6% pay rise (*increase*).
   Calculate his new annual salary.

   b 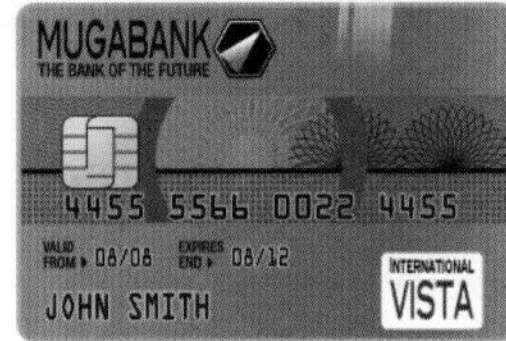

   Theresa is a clerk and earns £18 800 per year.
   The bank awarded her a pay increase of 2%.
   Calculate her new annual salary.

2. a Mr Johnson, an engineer, earns £48 700 per annum (*annually*).
   Unfortunately he has been asked to take a pay cut of 2%.
   How much will he earn per annum after the cut ?

   b George is to get a pay cut of 3% on his £22 600 annual salary.
   How much will he earn after the pay cut ?

3. Calculate each new salary after the increase or decrease :-
   a Kay £11 900 (*increase 8%*) b Jon £32 400 (*decrease 1%*)
   c Fern £40 800 (*pay rise of 4%*) d Harry £18 750 (*pay cut of 6%*).

4. Two Store Managers are paid different salaries.
   Jeff gets paid £30 700. Alec gets £32 450.
   Jeff is to get a pay increase of 3%.
   Alec is to get a pay cut of 4%.
   Who is then paid more, and by how much ?

Commission

Some people, particularly salespeople, do not get paid a weekly or monthly fixed wage.

They receive a percentage of the value of whatever they make by selling cars, carpets, etc.

This is called **COMMISSION**.

Example :- Ted sells cars. He is paid a **commission** of 5% on any car he sells. Last week, Ted sold £9000 worth of cars.

Commission = 5% of £9000 = $\frac{5}{100} \times 9000$ = **£450.**

Exercise 5

1. In a magazine, commission is paid at **3%** on all sales of advertising space.

   Calculate the **commission** due by selling the following amount of advertising :-

   a £22 600 (i.e. $\frac{3}{100} \times$ £22 600) b £8750 c £140 000.

2. Richard gets 7% commission on handmade curtain sales.

   Last month, he sold £20 400 worth of curtains.

   Calculate Richard's **commission**.

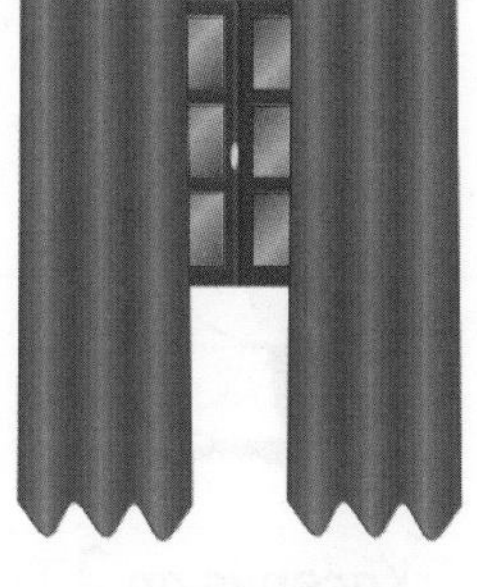

3. Find the commission (*given in brackets*) for each of the following sales :-

   a £8000 (7%) b £120 000 (9%) c £100 000 (8·5%).

4. Brad is an agent for "*PhoneU*". He has a monthly pay of £850.

   On top of this, he also gets 12% commission on all his sales.

   In January, he sold £8250 worth of goods.

   a Calculate his **commission** for January.

   b Calculate his total pay for January.

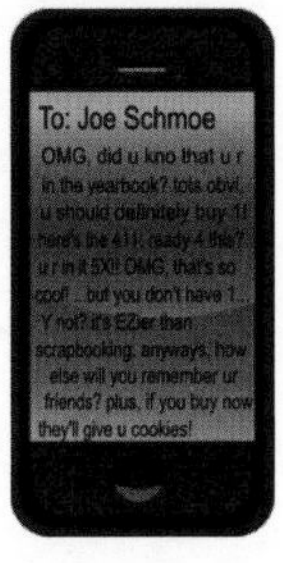

5. 

   Jackson and Kenny are both yacht salesmen.

   Jackson earns 4% commission on sales. Kenny earns 5%.

   Last month Jackson sold £87 000. Kenny sold £77 000.

   Who earned more commission **and** by how much ?

6. Write a sentence or two explaining why you think companies use commission to pay employees.

Overtime Pay & Bonuses

Overtime is when you work **extra hours** above your basic number of hours.

You usually get paid a HIGHER RATE of pay for overtime.

Double Time :- If your basic rate of pay is £8·50 per hour, you will get paid £17·00 per hour for every overtime hour you work (at **double time**).

Exercise 6

1. Richard works in a Hairdressing Salon and his basic rate is £11·00 per hour.

   Last Sunday, he worked 6 hours **overtime** at **double time**.

   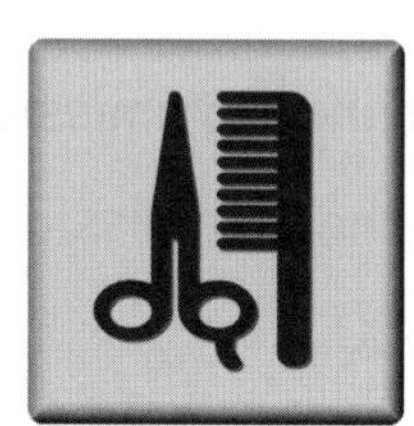

   a Calculate Richard's **overtime** hourly rate (*£11 doubled*).

   b Calculate Richard's total **overtime pay**.

2. 

   Cyril is a chemist who is paid a basic rate of £23·70 per hour.

   On Tuesday night, he worked 4 hours overtime at **double time**.

   How much did Cyril earn in **total** for his 4 overtime hours ?

3. a Karen is an ATM engineer and is paid £14·60 an hour. She worked 8 hours on Bank Holiday Monday as **overtime** at **double time**.

   How much was she paid for this overtime ?

   b Sergie worked 12 hours overtime on New Year's Day.

   His basic rate is £12·78 per hour.

   How much would he be paid for his New Year's Day overtime at double time ?

4. 

   a Daisy works for £9·80 per hour as a waitress in an American diner in Dundee.

   If she works on Xmas Day, she will be given **treble** time.

   How much will she earn on Xmas Day for 5 hours ?

   b How much will Wally the Waiter earn for 3 hours on Xmas Day, in the same diner, if his basic hourly rate is £14·90 ?

CANDOR & SONS
BUILDERS & FITTERS
Hourly Rate as shown
Plumber £19·40
Brickie £10·75
Electrician £17·80
Secretary £12·50
Joiner £13·60
Driver £9·80

5. For each of the jobs shown above in "*CANDOR & SONS*", calculate what someone would earn if they worked **overtime** for 4 hours when the rate was set at double time.

Example :- Tim's pay rate as a courier is £12·20 per hour.

He works 5 hours overtime at "**time and a half**".

How much does he earn ?

Basic rate per hour	=	£12·20
Overtime rate = (1·5 x £12·20) [* note]	=	£18·30
=> Overtime pay = (5 x £18·30)	=	£91·50

*** note**
"time and a half" means $1\frac{1}{2}$ or 1·5 times your basic rate

6. Jimmy works as a lift operator for Highland Council.

His basic hourly rate of pay is £13·20.

a Calculate his overtime rate of pay, (*at time and a half*).

b How much does he get paid if he works 4 hours overtime ?

7. Jane is a gardener at Cathray Country Park.

Her basic hourly rate of pay is £11·80.

Jane had to work 12 hours overtime, (*at time and a half*).

How much was she paid for this ?

8. Lionel is an office junior and is paid £8·85 per hour.

Last month, he worked a total of 22 hours overtime altogether at time and a half.

Calculate how much he earned for his 22 overtime hours.

9\. 

Mr Moss works for "*Dog Groomers & Co.*".

He is paid a rate of £13·40 per hour.

On Sunday, he worked 5 hours overtime at time and a half.

a Calculate his overtime rate of pay.

b Calculate how much he earned altogether for his 5 hours overtime.

10\. Bronte works as a party coordinator.

Her basic hourly pay rate is £23·40.

She works 6 hours overtime on Saturday.

a Bronte thought she was getting paid at **DOUBLE TIME** for these overtime hours.

What was she hoping to earn for her Saturday work ?

b The company only paid her an overtime rate of **time and a half**.

How much did Bronte actually earn for her Saturday work ?

c How much **less** did she earn than she originally thought ?

A **bonus** is money **added** on to your pay for a job well done or done within a set timescale.

11\. Aileen works for "*Ace Computers*" and has a monthly salary of £1475.

Last month she received a **bonus** of £380.

What was her total salary for the month ?

12\. 

Sandy is a joiner and works on a building site.

He gets a bonus of £4·50 for every window frame he builds.

This week he built 32 frames.

Calculate Sandy's total **bonus** for the week.

13\. Clara is a joiner for a housing group. She is paid £225·50 per week and gets a **bonus** of £1·90 for every door she hangs.

In a normal week she hangs 140 doors.

a Calculate Clara's bonus for one week.

b Calculate Clara's total pay for that week.

14\. Last year Ollie got £17 850 (which included his Xmas bonus).

How much was his bonus if he usually earns £16 900 ?

The following questions require you to calculate the basic pay, the overtime pay and the total pay.

15. Ali is an agent, and has a basic rate of pay of £9·20 per hour.

    Last week, he worked his "normal" basic 40 hours.

    He also worked 8 hours overtime at time and a half.

    COPY this payslip for Ali and **complete** it.

Ali Siniti	*Payroll Number 0761*		*Date w/e 02/02/15*
Basic Rate = £9·20	*Overtime Rate = (1·5 x ....)*	=	£ ......
Basic Pay	= 40 x £9·20	=	£
+ Overtime Pay	= 8 x £..........	=	£
	Total Pay	=	£

16. Yani works as a cleaner in an office block.

    Her basic hourly rate is £8·60.

    Last week, she worked her "normal" basic 36 hours.

    She also worked 12 hours overtime at time and a half.

    COPY this payslip for Yani and **complete** it.

Yani Estuti	*Payroll Number 0904*		*Date w/e 02/02/15*
Basic Rate = £8·60	*Overtime Rate = (1·5 x ....)*	=	£ ......
Basic Pay	= 36 x £8·60	=	£
+ Overtime Pay	= 12 x £..........	=	£
	Total Pay	=	£

17. Make up a similar payslip for George Young, a head chef.

    George's basic hourly rate of pay is £15·40.

    This week, he worked his "normal" basic 38 hours.

    He also worked 7 hours overtime at time and a half.

    His payroll number is 0183. It is week ending 9th February, 2015.

    Calculate his basic pay, overtime pay and total pay for the week.

18. Calculate Sean's total pay for the week. (*Do **not** write on the page*).

McGubbins					
Name : Sean O'Toole		Works Number - 0333			Week No. 17
Pay Rate	Basic Rate per hour			=	£13·20
	Overtime Rate (*double time*) = (2 x £13·20)			=	£ ......
	O'time Rate (*time and a half*) = (1·5 x £........)			=	£......
Wage	Basic Pay	=	40 x £13·20	=	£......
	Sunday Pay (*double time*)	=	(4 x £....)	=	£......
	Tuesday Pay (*time and a half*)	=	(3 x £....)	=	£......
	Total Pay for week			=	£......

Gross Pay, Deductions, Net Pay, and Payslips

GROSS PAY :- This is what you are paid by your employer.

DEDUCTIONS :- These are taken from your pay for various reasons. Find out about Income Tax, National Insurance, Superannuation, etc.

NET PAY :- This is your **take home** pay after DEDUCTIONS.

NET PAY = GROSS PAY - DEDUCTIONS

Exercise 7

1. Calculate the Net (*take home*) pay for each of the following :-

	Gross Pay	Deduction
a ***Tom***	£1750/month	£435
b ***Dick***	£1904/month	£705
c ***Harry***	£17 817/year	£4140
d ***Joe***	£1375·45/month	£418·15
e ***Andy***	£50 180/year	£19 009

	Gross Pay	Deduction
f ***Kay***	£505/week	£156
g ***Fay***	£21700/year	£5 980
h ***Anni***	£488·50/week	£87·35
i ***Una***	£662·80/week	£233·75
j ***Kori***	£878·60/f'night	£208·75

2. 

Toni works as a teacher and earns £2450·75 per month.

His deductions usually come to £363·40 per month.

Calculate Toni's net (take home) pay.

3. Emma starts work as a computer programmer at a salary of £22 500 per year.

She calculated that her total deductions come to £3960.

a Calculate Emma's **net** pay for the year.

b Calculate her net **monthly** pay. (*Do you divide or multiply by 12 ?*).

4. Jimmy's boss, on the building site, promised him a wage of £530·50 last week.

Jimmy found that his total deductions came to £123·75.

Calculate Jimmy's **net** pay last week.

5. Some payslips have a different layout from the previous slips.

They are usually still calculated (*horizontally*) for Gross Pay, and for Deductions.

Then the net pay is calculated (*vertically*). (Gross Pay - Deductions).

Calculate the net pay for each of these pay slips :-

a

Name	N.I. No.	Emp. No.	Week
Bob	QT42127	007651	14
Basic Pay	Overtime	Bonus	Gross P
£210	£37·40	£00·00	£..........
Nat. Ins	Inc.Tax	Pension	Deduct
£27·82	£41·18	£12·65	£..........
		Net Pay	**£ ......**

b

Name	N.I. No.	Emp. No.	Week
Tam	QP11252	006109	18
Basic Pay	Overtime	Bonus	Gross P
£340	£67·40	£20·00	£..........
Nat. Ins	Inc.Tax	Pension	Deduct
£40·80	£62·44	£20·40	£..........
		Net Pay	**£ ......**

c

Name	N.I. No.	Emp. No.	Week
Lia	QK37754	000897	41
Basic Pay	Overtime	Bonus	Gross P
£748	£137·40	£100·00	£..........
Nat. Ins	Inc.Tax	Pension	Deduct
£89·76	£142·12	£59·84	£..........
		Net Pay	**£ ......**

d

Name	N.I. No.	Emp. No.	Week
James	QT43915	007409	23
Basic Pay	Overtime	Bonus	Gross P
£1268	£00·00	£300·00	£..........
Nat. Ins	Inc.Tax	Pension	Deduct
£152·16	£240·92	£00·00	£..........
		Net Pay	**£ ......**

6. Calculate the Net (take home pay) for each of the following pay slips :-

a

McDOUGALLS MACHINES								
Name :- Andy Robins			Works No. :- 31307			Week No :- 16		
Income	Basic -	£703·65	O/Time -	£95·50	Bonus -	£70·00	Total -	£..........
Deducts	I. Tax -	£140·73	Superan -	£42·18	Nat Ins -	£84·44	Total -	£..........
					Net Pay			£........

b

McDOUGALLS MACHINES								
Name :- Pete Taunton			Works No. :- 31308			Week No :- 18		
Income	Basic -	£843·05	O/Time -	£84·20	Bonus -	£70·00	Total -	£..........
Deducts	I. Tax -	£168·61	Superan -	£50·58	Nat Ins -	£44·74	Total -	£..........
					Net Pay			£........

c

McDOUGALLS MACHINES								
Name :- Sarah Laburnum			Works No. :- 31310			Week No :- 18		
Income	Basic -	£1100·05	O/Time -	£195·50	Bonus -	£70·00	Total -	£..........
Deducts	I. Tax -	£230·73	Superan -	£110·30	Nat Ins -	£121·01	Total -	£..........
					Net Pay			£........

d

McDOUGALLS MACHINES								
Name :- Delia Ronnie			Works No. :- 30143			Week No :- 23		
Income	Basic -	£2108·00	O/Time -	£00·00	Bonus -	£70·00	Total -	£..........
Deducts	I. Tax -	£421·60	Superan -	£105·00	Nat Ins -	£94·11	Total -	£..........
					Net Pay			£........

e

McDOUGALLS MACHINES								
Name :- Andy McCoist			Works No. :- 30565			Week No :- 48		
Income	Basic -	£2703·65	O/Time -	£100·80	Bonus -	£70·00	Total -	£..........
Deducts	I. Tax -	£548·77	Superan -	£135·18	Nat Ins -	£108·15	Total -	£..........
					Net Pay			£........

Income

Finance Assessment 1

1. a Al gets £11·24 per hour. How much will he get for a 40 hour week ?

   b Ted gets paid £541·80 for 42 hours work. Find his hourly rate.

   c Pia earns £257·12 every week. What is her yearly earnings ?

   d Gina earns £21 460·40 a year. How much does she earn weekly ?

   e Sam gets £17 463 per annum. How much does he get paid monthly ?

2. Bill is paid an annual salary of £22 000.

   He is to get a 4% pay rise.

   a How much will Bill earn after his pay **rise** ?

   b Bill's wife Jill gets £25 400 per annum.

   She has to take a 3% pay **decrease**.

   Who now earns more and by how much ?

3. Jake earns 8% commission on all sales.

   How much will Jake get on £52 000 sales ?

4. Don gets paid £9·70 per hour as a labourer.

   a How much will he be paid for 12 hours at ***double time*** ?

   b How much will he get for 9 hours at ***time and a half*** ?

5. George has a gross pay of £764·80.

   His deductions total £118·75.

   Find his ***net*** (*take-home*) pay.

6. Copy and complete the pay slip below to find the net pay.

Sharkey & Sons

Name :- Jan Mullins   Works No. :- 30565   Week No :- 48

Income	*Basic* -	£2503·85	*O/Time* -	£108·80	*Bonus* -	£170·00	Total -	£.........
Deducts	*I.Tax* -	£538·17	*Superan* -	£133·78	*Nat Ins* -	£101·05	Total -	£.........
							Net Pay	£.......

Foreign Exchange

Exchanging GBP for Foreign Currency

Many countries use different currencies, although Britain still uses the GBP, the Great British Pound.

Euros (€) are widely used throughout Europe.

Initially we will look at how to change from our currency to the currencies of other countries.

You will have to do this if you ever holiday abroad.

Exchange Rates

£1 = €1·25 (All Europe)

£1 = \$1·53 (America)

£1 = 1·82 (Australian Dollars)

Example 1 :- To change £200 to Euros you simply MULTIPLY :-

£200 = 200 x €1·25 = **€250**

Example 2 :- To change £120 to American Dollars, again, you simply MULTIPLY :-

£120 = 120 x \$1·53 = **\$183·60**

Rule :- *When changing from British money to foreign money, always* ***MULTIPLY****.*

Exercise 1

1. Alan went to Santa Ponsa in Majorca. He changed £500 to Euros before leaving. How many Euros did he receive ?

2. Taylor went to Berlin at Easter and changed £280 to Euros. How many Euros did Taylor get ?

3. The Hendrys flew to Las Vegas (in America) and changed £1200 to dollars. How many dollars did they get ?

4. Winnie and Tom went to Australia for a month's holiday. They changed £2100 to Australian dollars. How many dollars did they receive ?

5. Change the following :-
   a £250 to Euros
   b £8 to Euros
   c £340 to American dollars
   d £750 to Australian dollars.

Not every country uses the Euro or the USA/Australian dollar.

Shown are some of the **world exchange rates** :-

British Pound (January 20...)	£1 =
American Dollar ($)	1·53
Australian Dollar	1·82
Chinese Yuan Renminbi	9·30
Danish Kroner	9·20
Euro	1·25
Hong Kong Dollar	11·85
Indian Rupee	90
Japanese Yen	185
Mexican Peso	21
New Zealand Dollar	1·95
Norwegian Kroner	10
South African Rand	17·2
Swiss Franc	1·50

6. a If I changed £200 to Hong Kong Dollars how many would I receive ?

   b Joe changed £500 to Yen before flying to Japan.

   How many did he get ?

   c The Frasers changed £750 to Rupees for a stopover in Mumbai.

   How many Rupees did they receive ?

   d During our two week stay in Norway, we spent £925 which we had changed to Kroner.

   How much was this in Kroner ?

7. 

Jenny went camping around Denmark for 3 months.

Before she went, she changed £1500 to Danish Kroner.

How many did Jenny receive ?

8. Sam bought a new Samsung Galaxy S11 for £250. How much would this be in :-

   a American Dollars   b Euros

   c Swiss Francs   d Pesos ?

9. Sam saw the same Galaxy S11 phone when he was in New Zealand, priced 500 dollars.

   Was this cheaper or dearer than he paid for it back home ? (*Show working*).

10. Decide which is the cheaper :-

   a Scotland - £950, Germany - 1100 Euros.

   b

   Britain - £1800.

   America - $2754.

   c Car price in Britain - £10 200.

   Same car in India - 920 000 Rupees.

Exchanging Foreign Currency for GBP

If you want to change foreign currency back to pounds => you simply **DIVIDE**.

When you bring Euros, dollars etc. home from your holiday you will have to divide by the present rate to get your £'s.

Exchange Rates

£1 = €1·25 (All Europe)

£1 = $1·53 (America)

£1 = 1·82 (Australian Dollars)

Example :- To change 800 Euros back to pounds you have to **DIVIDE** :-

€800 = 800 ÷ 1·25 = **£640**

Rule :- *When changing foreign money back into British money, always* ***DIVIDE****.*

Exercise 2

1. Hazel returned from Paris with 50 Euros.

   How much would she get by changing them back to £'s ?

2. 

   Walter spent a week in Italy, staying in Pisa.

   He brought €93·75 back and changed them back to £'s.

   How much did he receive ?

3. Troy returned from America with $229·50.

   How many £'s will he get when he exchanges his dollars ?

4. 

   I brought 236·60 Australian dollars back from holiday.

   How many £'s will I get for them ?

5. How much would be given when the following amounts were exchanged for £'s :-

   a 10 Euros b 18·75 Euros c $1530

   d $3·06 e 1911 Australian dollars f 2500 Euros ?

6. 

   I changed £500 to Euros before travelling to Rome.

   a How many Euros did I receive ?

   b I spent €600 when I was in Italy and changed the rest back to £s when I got home.

   How many £'s did I have when I returned home ?

7. a If I changed 711 Hong Kong Dollars to £'s how many would I receive ?

   b Chesney changed 3700 Yen to £'s before flying home from Japan.

   How many £'s did he get ?

   c The Johnsons spent 27 300 Pesos while on holiday in Mexico.

   What was that in £'s ?

   d When Sadie returned from Denmark she exchanged 414 Kroner for pounds.

   How many did she get ?

British Pound (January 2015)

	£1 =
American Dollar ($)	1·53
Australian Dollar	1·82
Chinese Yuan Renminbi	9·30
Danish Kroner	9·20
Euro	1·25
Hong Kong Dollar	11·85
Indian Rupee	90
Japanese Yen	185
Mexican Peso	21
New Zealand Dollar	1·95
Norwegian Kroner	10
South African Rand	17·2
Swiss Franc	1·50

8. Charlie returned from China with 465 Yuan.

   How much will he get when he changes his money back to £'s ?

9. Anne paid 1·75 Euros for a notepad at a market in Strasbourg.

   She wondered what that had cost her in British money.

   Work out the price for Anne.

10. Edwina bought her laptop in Hamburg, Germany for €425.

    Kendra bought the same laptop in New York, America for $459.

    Lotti had paid £320 in Dundee for an identical laptop.

    Who got the best deal ? *Explain.*

11. Mr and Mrs Gordon and their two children went on a skiing holiday to Switzerland.

    Weekly ski hire was 112·50 francs per adult and 60 francs per child.

    What was the total cost of ski hire for the Gordon family for the week, in GBP ?

12. When the Whitehouse family visited India they hired a car which travelled 14·5 kilometres on one litre of petrol.

    a How much petrol did they need for a journey of 609 kilometres ?

    Petrol cost 117 **Rupees** per litre.

    b How much did their petrol cost, in British money ?

Foreign Exchange

Finance Assessment 2

1. | £1 sterling can be exchanged for :- | |
|---|---|
| • 90 | Indian rupee |
| • 185 | Japanese yen |
| • 21 | Mexican peso |
| • 1·53 | American dollars ($) |

Change each of the following :-

a £30 to yen
b £85 to pesos
c 10800 rupees to £'s
d $428·40 to £'s.

2. Denise went on a weekend break to Paris.

She took £480, which she changed to euros at a rate of €1·25 to the £.

How many euros did Denise receive ?

3. 

The Wilson's took their son Andrew to visit Legoland in Denmark.

If they exchanged £1200 for kroner at a rate of 9·20 kroner to the £, how many did they get ?

4. The exchange rate from euros to £'s is varying between €1·20 to the pound and €1·25 to the pound.

a Going on holiday from the UK to Belgium, which gives the better rate ? *(Explain)*.

b Returning from Belgium, I change my euros back to £'s.

Which is the better rate now ? *(Explain)*.

Dollarate

£1 = $1·50

EuroChange

£1 buys you €1·20

5. On his way back from California USA, Eck stopped off and spent some time in Portugal.

When he got home, he had 76·50 dollars and 66 euros left.

If Eck changed them back to £'s, which of the two currencies would give him the greater amount, and by how much ?

6. 

Alana went on holiday to China.

She changed £2200 into Yuan at a rate of 9·30 Yuan to the pound and spent 19 488 Yuan while on holiday.

Alana changed the Yuan she had left back into pounds at a rate of 9·00 Yuan to the pound.

How many pounds did she get for that ?

Banking

Simple Interest

There are many different types of bank accounts.

Savings Account 6% gross

SuperSaver Account 7·1%

High Interest Account 3·7% net

Exercise 1

1. There are two main reasons why, if you were to come into a sum of money, you should put it in a bank (or building society). Write down the reasons.

2. Dave and Sally put their combined savings of £8000 into "*SCOTIA BANK*".

SCOTIA BANK
"come bank with us"
Annual Interest Rate
A.P.R. = 3%

How much **interest** would they receive after 1 year ?
(*3% of £8000*).

3. 

Kenny sells his flat for £35 000 and leaves the money in *SCOTIA BANK* for 1 year whilst he travels around Australia.

How much **interest** is Kenny due at the end of the year ?

4. Some friends compare the **interest** they are due from various banks and building societies for 1 year.

a	Tanya left £6500 for a year.	Rate = 4% p.a.
b	Alan deposited £9200 for a year.	Rate = 2·5% p.a.
c	Alison banked £11 400 for a year.	Rate = 3·5% p.a.
d	Richard invested £6850 for a year.	Rate = 4·1% p.a.

Calculate how much **interest** each person is due.

5. 

Tony won £18 000 on the *Rovers' Pools*. He was about to invest it in his savings account at *Edinburgh Regal Bank*.

a How much interest would he receive if he invests the money into his savings account ?

b Instead, he asks for the "Special" Saver's Rate.

How much interest will he actually get at the end of the year ?

6. Brian invested £5200 in a special savings account at his bank for 1 year.

   The annual interest rate was 3·7%.

   His friend Julie saved £4800 in her building society account for 1 year and received a rate of 4·0% per annum.

   Which of the two received more interest after 1 year ?
   (*You will have to calculate both Brian's and Julie's interest*).

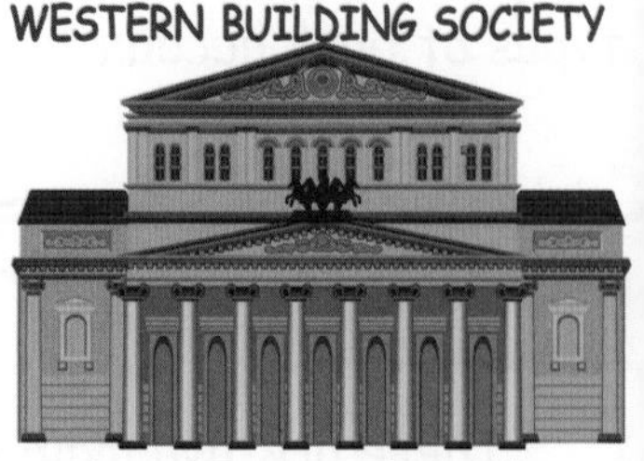

7. I decide to invest £6000 with the "*Western Building Society*".

   a How much interest should I expect after 1 year ?

   b How much would my total savings then be ?
   (*£6 000 + £......... =*)

8. I deposited £3400 in my bank account for 1 year. The annual interest rate was 3·5%.

   a Calculate my interest after 1 year.

   b How much did I then have in my bank account ?

9. For each of the following, calculate how much the savings would be worth **in total** at the end of 1 year :-

   a Sally invested £4000. Annual Interest Rate = 5% p.a.

   b Nadine invested £800. Annual Interest Rate = 3% p.a.

   c Stewart invested £2200. Annual Interest Rate = 2·5% p.a.

   d Ralph invested £17 400. Annual Interest Rate = 5·5% p.a.

10. Karen had £7000 and decided to invest it with "*Morden Building Society*".

   a What **rate** of interest should she expect (2·3%, 2·9% or 3·2%) ?

   b Calculate how much **interest** Karen would receive after 1 year.

MORDEN BUILDING SOCIETY

"The more you bank – The higher the rate"

up to £1000	-	2·3%
£1000 - £10 000	-	2·9%
over £10 000	-	3·2%

11. Decide what **rate** of interest each of the following is due with *Morden Building Society* and calculate the amount of interest due after 1 year :-

   a Nell has £700 to invest for 1 year.

   b Naomi has £11 000 to invest for 1 year.

   c Jennifer has £4500 to invest for 1 year.

   d Andrew has £24 000 to invest for 1 year.

Bank Cards - Debit Cards

Many banks now issue a Bank Card or **Debit Card** when you open a bank account.

BANK

Bank cards can be used in most places to pay for goods or services instead of money.

PLATINUM
SCOTIA BANK
2311 3234 5898 0041
Valid From 04/14
Until End 08/18
Mrs Anne E Strange
20 03 47
00176502
DEBIT CARD

16 digit Card Number.

Dates are given as month/year eg 08/18 is end of ....

Memory Chip for Security

Sortcode identifies which bank branch is being used.

Account Number is the actual bank account number being used.

When using a card you need a secret *Personal Identification Number* (PIN) which ONLY you know.

Exercise 2

1. Look at the bank card above.
   - a Which bank has issued this card ?
   - b What is the name of the person who uses this card ?
   - c Write down the expiry date (end date) in full.
   - d When was the card issued ?

2. Write down all the information shown on each of the following cards :-

a

PLATINUM
SCOTIA BANK
2311 3234 5898 0041
Valid From 02/13
Until End 01/15
Mrs Ruth Woolie
20 03 47
00176502
DEBIT CARD

b

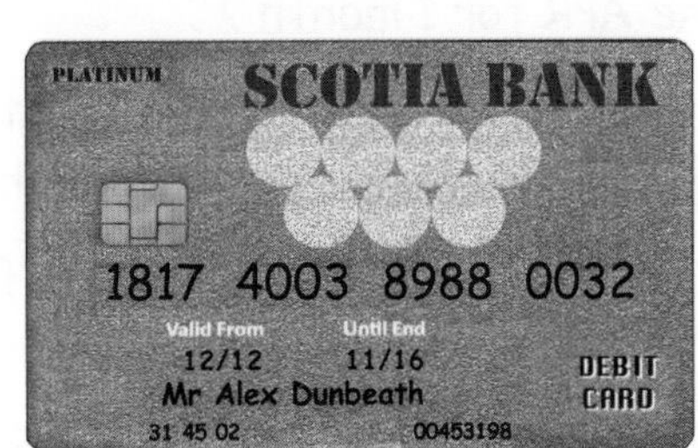

PLATINUM
SCOTIA BANK
1817 4003 8988 0032
Valid From
12/12
Until End
11/16
Mr Alex Dunbeath
31 45 02
00453198
DEBIT CARD

3. Discuss the following :-
   - a Why does each bank need a (sort) code ?
   - b Why does each person need an account number ?
   - c Why should the PIN be secret and known only to the card holder ?
   - d Do you think using a card is better than money ?

4. Write a few sentences about each point in question 3, or discuss as a class.

5. Find out more about banks and banking terms such as ATM, overdraft, direct debit etc.....

Credit Cards

Credit Cards are used in a very similar way to bank cards.

The main difference is that a credit card does **not** have money stored in an account.

When you use a credit card you are borrowing money (very much like a loan).

Scotia Bank's *Electrik Viza* card has an **APR** charge (**A**nnual **P**ercentage **R**ate) of 36%.

This means every **month** there will be a (36% ÷ 12) = 3% interest charge.

Example :- Ms String uses £200 from her credit card.

How much interest will she owe after one month ?

3% of £200 = 3 ÷ 100 x 200 = £6

Ms String will owe £206 after one month.

Exercise 3

1. Ms String uses her card (see above) and pays for a new bicycle costing £160.

   How much will she owe after one month ?
   (*Remember to use an APR of 36%*).

   Copy and complete :-

   36% APR means one month is ...%
   ...% of £160 = ... ÷ 100 x 160 = ...
   She owes £ ..... interest after 1 month.

2. How much would she owe after one month if she used £480 on her card ?

3. Mrs Wilson has a *Viza Card* which has an APR of 24%.

   a What is the APR for 1 month ?

   b How much would she owe after one month if she had used each of the following amounts on her card :-

   (i) £780 (ii) £1800 (iii) £345·50 ?

   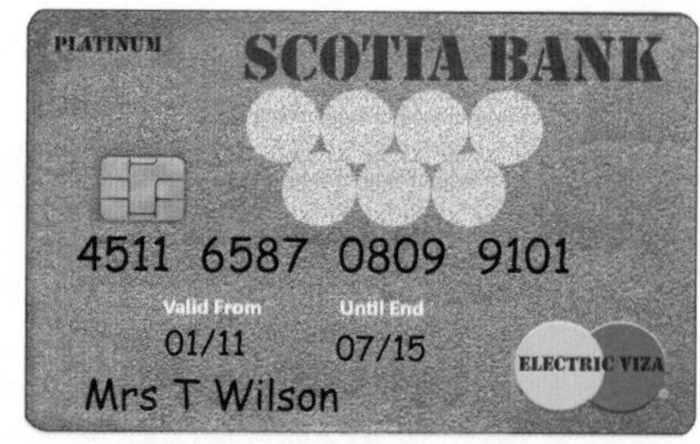

4. Erin uses a *SIMLA* card offering a 30% APR.

   How much would she owe after one month if she had used :-

   a £80 b £880 c £2140 ?

   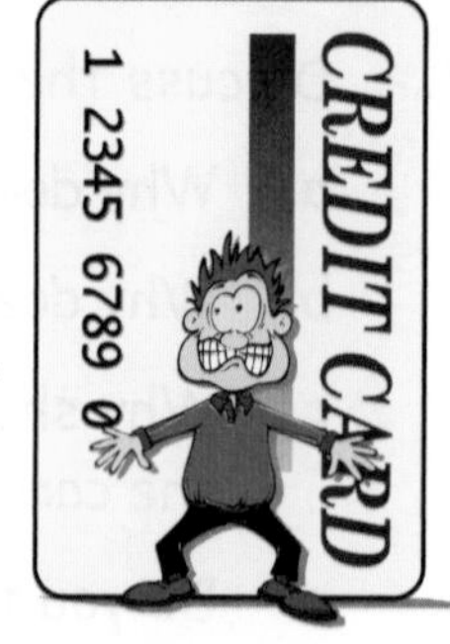

5. Paul considers various credit cards as shown.

Card	APR
Zamex	40%
Vira	33%
Banco	35%

   Which credit card should he choose ?
   (*Explain why*).

6. a Find the differences between a bank card, a credit card and a store card.

   b Many people fall into a lot of debt by using cards. Discuss.

Borrowing Money

Individuals and small to large companies sometimes need to borrow money.

Discuss :-

why people might need a loan.

why companies might need a loan.

places people can go to for loans - Banks, Private Loans, Pay Day Loans, Brighthouse, etc.

the benefits and disadvantages of these lenders.

what APR means

Example :- Mr Hay needs to borrow £2000 to pay for a 2nd hand car. He has two options :-

a *Scotia Bank* will charge him 14·9% if he repays it monthly over 1 year.

b *Sunshine Personal Loans* will charge him £571 per month over 6 months.

Which of the two will mean he pays less interest ?

Answer :-

a *Scotia* - 14·9% of £2000 = 14·9 ÷ 100 × 2000 = £298 total interest
Monthly payments = (£2000 + £298) ÷ 12 = £191·50.

b *Sunshine* - Total payment over 6 months = 6 × £571 = £3426.
Total interest due = £3426 - £2000 = £1426.

Discuss :-

- which is obviously the better deal.
- why someone might have to take out a *Sunshine Personal Loan.*

Exercise 4

Scotia Bank has different APRs. The more you borrow, the lower the interest rate becomes.

Loan	under £500	£500-£1000	£1000 - £2000	£2000-£5000	over £5000
APR (1 year)	11·6%	9·2%	8·4%	6·5%	4·9%

1. Jamie wants to borrow £400 for 1 year to buy a new bike.
   a What is the APR Jamie would expect to be charged ?
   b Calculate the added interest and the total amount payable.
   c If Jamie sets up a standing order to pay the loan, what will his monthly payments be ?

2. Caroline wishes to borrow £650 to pay for her holiday in Ibiza.
   a Calculate the added interest she must pay and the total amount payable.
   b How much will Caroline's monthly payments be ?

3. Lucy and her partner Billy need to borrow £1800 for a year for a new kitchen in their flat.
   a Calculate the total amount repayable.
   b How much will their monthly payments be ?

4. Stewart and Katie need to borrow £12 000 for a deposit on a new apartment.

They take out a loan over a 5 year period and Scotia charges them a total of 14·5% interest.

a Calculate the total amount repayable over 5 years.

b How much will their monthly payments be ?

5. 

Sophie needs a short term loan from Scotia of £2500.

She wishes to pay it back within 6 months.

a How much interest would this be for 1 year ?

b How much for 6 months and what would the amount payable be ?

c What would each of Sophie's six monthly payments work out at ?

6. The Hills want to borrow £3000 to pay for flights to Australia to see their family.

Scotia offers them 2 different loan options :-

	Annual Interest Rate	Loan term
Loan payment 1st option	9·5%	12 months
Loan payment 2nd option	8·6%	6 months

a Calculate the monthly repayments for both the 1st and the 2nd options.

b Which option do you think they might choose and explain your reasoning ?

7. Jenny borrows £800 to pay for her wedding dress from *Scotia Bank*.

Their annual rate is 9·2% and she hopes to pay it back over 1 year.

She reckons she can afford £75 per month at most from her pay.

a Calculate how much interest she is due in a year.

b Will she be able to stay within her budget with her monthly payments ?

8. A *Pay Weekly Company* offers this "amazing deal" on a 49" Ultra HD Flat Screen TV.

The actual cost of the TV in various electrical shops was £749.

TV with 5* service	£1520·50
Weekly Payment	£18·25
Number of weeks (3 years)	156
Representative APR	64·7%
Total payable	....

a Calculate what the "Total Payable" worked out at with the *Pay Weekly Company*.

b Do you think a "*Pay Weekly Company*" is a good idea ?

c Why might people still decide to use one of these companies ?

Banking

Finance Assessment 3

Forthdale Building Society		
"Variable Interest Rate"		
up to £500	-	1·8%
£500 - £5 000	-	2·2%
over £5 000	-	3·0%

1. Tess deposited £1500 her gran gave her in the *Forthdale Building Society*.

   How much interest will she be due if she removes her money 1 year later ?

2. Tommy deposited £3000 in one account and his wife paid in £3000 to her account, both with *Forthdale Building Society*.

   How much **more** interest would they have received if they had invested the £6000 in one single account ?

3. Mr Jones has a *Viza Card* which has an **APR** of 18%.

   a What is the APR for 1 month ?

   b How much would he owe after one month if he had used each of the following amounts on his card :-

   (i) £400 (ii) £1800 ?

4. Stewart needs to borrow £1200 to buy his girlfriend an engagement ring.

   Barcloyds Bank charges an annual interest rate of 8·75% on loans.

   a Calculate how much interest will be due if the loan is for 1 year.

   b How much will Stewart's monthly payments be ?

5. 

   Billy needs to borrow £6000 to start up his own TV repair business. Barcloyds rate this time is only 5·5% per year.

   a How much interest would build up over a 1 year period ?

   b How much for 6 months and what would the amount payable be ?

   c What will each of Billy's six monthly payments be ?

6. *Darkhouse Pay Weekly* offers this "special" deal.

   You can buy the iPad Deluxe in *Liddy's* for £425.

iPad Deluxe	£650·99
Weekly Payment	£16·25
Number of weeks (2 years)	104
Representative APR	87·5%
Total payable	....

   a Calculate how much you would end up paying for the iPad over the 2 year period.

   b How much less would it cost you to buy it from *Liddy's* ?

Comparing Prices

Managing Your Money - Buying Goods

When running a home, most people have to work to a budget.
(*A specific amount they can afford to spend*).

When shopping, lots of money can be saved by finding the **best buys** for individual items.

Example :-

Lorne Dog Food comes in two sizes.

- The small one costs £2·65.
- The large one costs £3·64.

By calculating the cost of **100 grams** of food for each size of tin, decide which is the **better deal**.

Cost of small tin per 100 g :-

£2·65 ÷ 5 = £0·53.

Cost of large tin per 100 g :-

£3·64 ÷ 7 = £0·52.

Better Deal is large tin.
A saving of 1p per 100 g.

Exercise 1

1. *"Zad Soap Powder"* is offered in two different sizes.
   - The small box costs £15 for 600 grams.
   - The large box costs £19·20 for 800 grams.

   Which one is the better deal ? Explain.

2. Two bottles of the same wine are priced £7·70 for the 700 ml bottle and £10 for the one litre bottle. Which is the better deal ? *Explain.*

3. *"Belgique Chocolates"* costs £4·16 for a 400 gram box or £5·25 for a 500 gram box.

   Which is the better deal ? *Explain.*

4. 

   "Puss Puss" cat treats come in two sizes of tin.
   - The small tin costs £3·50 for 350 grams.
   - The large tin costs £4·40 for 550 grams.

   Which is the better deal ? *Explain.*

   (*Hint :- find the cost per 50 g or the cost per gram*)

5. *"Ryanjet Holidays"* offers special deals at the Constantino Hotel in Torremolinos.

Which of the two deals is better value for money ? *Explain.*

6. Ken is comparing two holiday companies' offers.

Which of the two should he choose ? *Explain.*

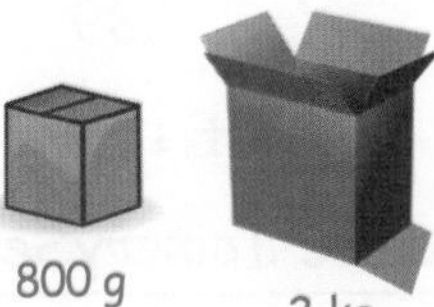

7. 

Fence paint can be bought in two tin sizes - 750 ml and 2·5 litres.

The larger tin costs £20. The smaller tin costs £7·50.

Which of the two tins offers the better value ?

8. Three cartons of rice are on offer.

- The small 800 gram carton costs £1·60.
- The 2 kilogram carton costs £3·60.
- The large 5 kilogram trade carton costs £7·50.

Which of the boxes offers :-

a the best value

b the poorest value ?

800 g

2 kg

9. Golf balls are sold in boxes of 3, 6 and 10.

- A box of three costs £5·40.
- A box of six costs £10·20.
- A box of ten costs £17·50.

Which would you choose ? *Explain.*

10. Benny paid £78·60 for 60 litres of diesel for his car at *"Erskine Filling Station"*.

Tanya put 48 litres of diesel in her car at *"Braehead Gas"*, costing £60·48.

Which petrol station offered the better deal ?

11. 

Jake has a rectangular lawn 6 metres by 10 metres.

Hannah's rectangular lawn measures 8 metres by 12 metres.

- Jake paid £924 to have his lawn re-turfed.
- Hannah paid £1344 to have her lawn re-turfed.

a Work out the area of Jake's lawn, in square metres.

b Work out the area of Hannah's lawn, in square metres.

c By calculating the cost of one square metre of turf, determine who got the better deal.

Managing Money - Paying for Services

Most people in real life will "shop around" to find the best deal for service providers like plumbers, joiners etc.

Many of the service industry workers will charge a **call-out charge**, then a **rate per hour** and finally any **parts** or items that need purchased.

Example :-

- *JoinerMan* has a call-out charge of £39 and charge a rate of £30 per hour.
- *JoineryServices* have a £60 call-out charge and a £25 per hour rate.

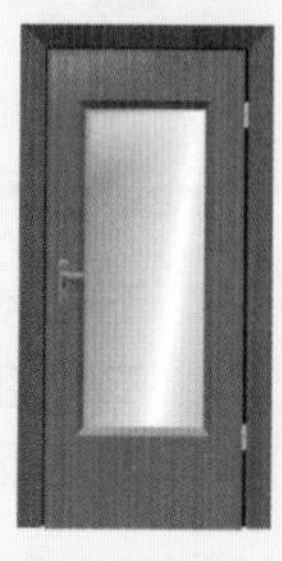

Mrs Craig wants new internal doors and is told it will be a 5 hour job.

Which company should she choose ?

JoinerMan		*JoineryServices*	
labour £30 x 5 =	£150	labour £25 x 5 =	£125
call-out	£39	call-out	£60
total	**£189**	**total**	**£185**

She should use JoineryServices, as it is **£4 cheaper**.

Exercise 2

1. a Both companies had miscalculated the time it would take for Mrs Craig's doors. (above)
   It actually only took 4 hours. Which company would have given the **better deal** ?

   b Mrs Craig decided to have all her window sills renewed.

   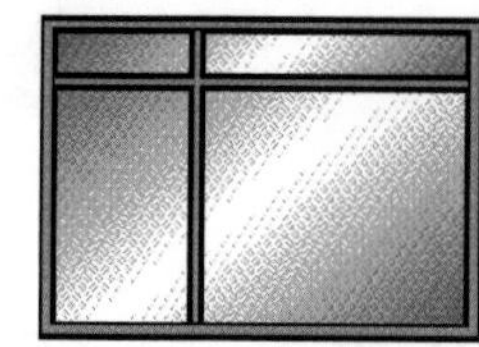

   "JoinerMan" gave her a quote for the job which would take 8 hours.
   "JoineryServices" quoted her for a 10 hour job.

   Which was the **cheaper** quote and by how much ?

2. 

   "PL Plumbing" charge a rate of £35 per hour and have a £25 call-out fee.
   "The Water Co." have a £20 call-out charge and a rate of £30 per hour.

   PL Plumbing has quoted Mr Sim for a four hour job to fit a new bath.
   The Water Co. have quoted five hours to do the same job.

   a Which company provided the **lower quote** and by how much ?

   b If the job only took 3 hours, calculate each company's bill.

3. *"Tele Media"* charge £80 call-out and £40 per hour.
   "Phone Wire" charge £48 per hour with a £70 call-out fee.

   Mrs Davis needs a new phone line installed (a two hour job).

   Which would be the **cheaper** option ?

4. Two freezer repair men have different charges.

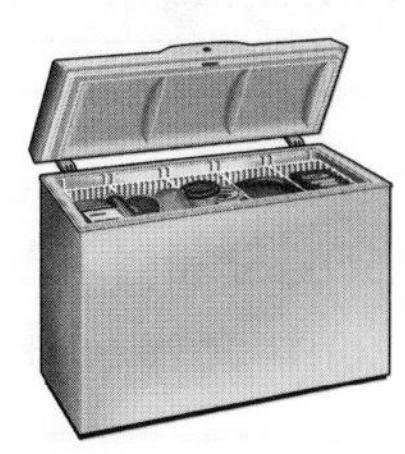

Chas - £75 for the 1st hour - £35 per hour thereafter
Dave - Call-out charge £50 - £30 per hour.

Mr Hove employed Chas who took 3 hours to repair his washing machine.

a How much was he charged in total ?

b Would he have been cheaper if he had called Dave ?

5. 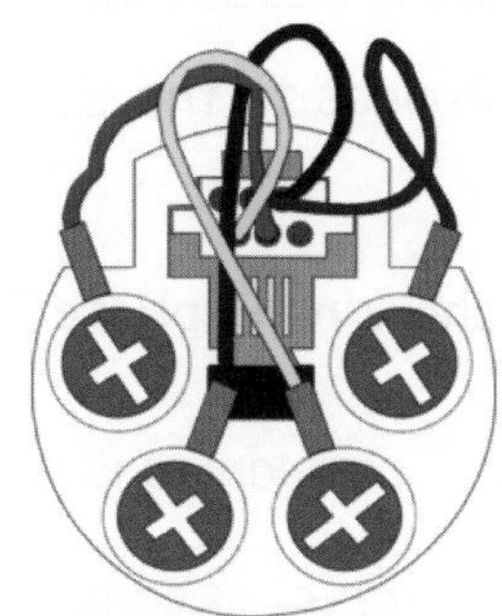

Colin called *ElectroFix* to rewire two rooms.

ElectroFix had a call-out fee of £40 and charged £45 per hour for the 4 hour job.

They also charged him for 14 metres of cable at £5 per metre.

SparkServices would have charged him a call-out of £50, a rate of £55 per hour, but the cable was included in the price.

Would *SparkServices* have been cheaper ? (*Explain*).

6. Aaron repairs dish washers.

He charges according to the graph shown.

a After 0 hours what will he charge ? (*Hint - his call-out fee*).

b What is his rate per hour ?

c What would he charge in total for :-

(i) $3\frac{1}{2}$ hours (ii) 10 hours ?

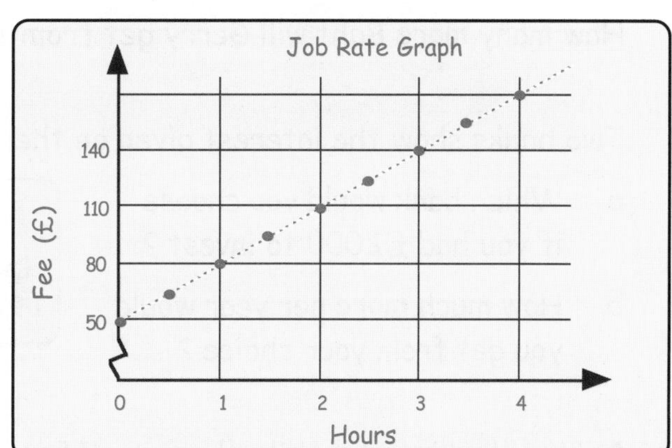

7. 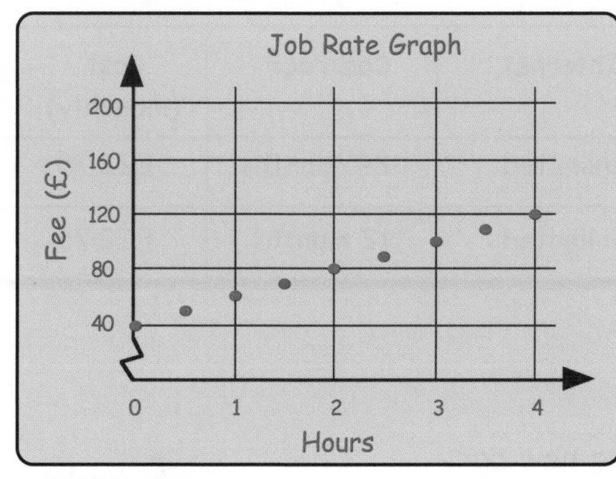

Alison repairs televisions and she uses this graph to show her charges.

a What is Alison's call-out fee ?

b What does she charge per hour ?

c What would she charge for a job lasting :-

(i) 5 hours (ii) $8\frac{1}{2}$ hours ?

8. Euan and Terry repair cars from their mobile garages.

Euan has a tow charge of £30 and charges £40 per hour.

Terry charges £60 for a tow and a rate of £35 per hour.

a Who charges more for a 3 hour job ?

b How many hours are needed for Terry to be cheaper than Euan ?

Managing Money - Rates or Contracts

Again, most people will wish to compare rates or contracts of telephone, broadband, TV, gas and electricity providers before taking out or renewing contracts with them, to make certain they are receiving the best value, and to save money.

Exercise 3

1. Mr Sahni is looking for the best currency exchange rate to change his Rupees into £'s.

   Xchange gives a rate of 80 Rupees to the £. RupRate offers 90 Rupees to the £.

   a What rate should he take ? *Explain.*

   b If Mr Sahni has 3600 Rupees, how much **less** would he get by choosing RupRate ?

2. Gerry has £5000 and is flying to Thailand. The exchange rate for 3 companies is :-

   X-rate : £1 to 49·1 Baht *X - Money* : £10 to 503 Baht *Xpound* : £100 to 4898 Baht

   How many **more** Baht will Gerry get from the **best** rather than the **poorest** deal ?

3. Two banks show the interest given on their deposit accounts.

   a Which bank would you choose if you had £2000 to invest ?

   b How much **more** per year would you get from your choice ?

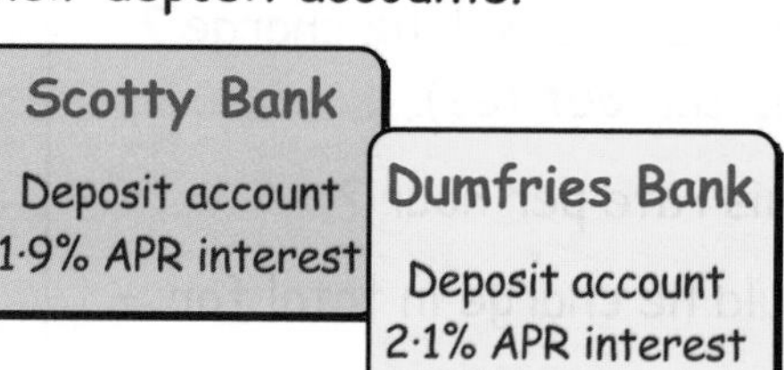

4. Daisy is looking at mobile phone tariffs.

Phone Company	Free mins	Free texts	Internet	Contract	Cost (monthly)
O3	100	1000	unlimited	24 months	£22·75
Oringe	100	1000	unlimited	12 months	£22·75

Explain why most people would choose Oringe.

5. Mrs Girvan is taking out a £15 000 loan to buy a new car.

   Three companies offer different interest rates as shown :-

   a Which company should she use ? (*Explain*).

   b Calculate the **least** amount of **interest** she will have to pay for her loan.

   c How much will she save by taking the middle rate rather than the poorest rate ?

CarLoan	-	11% interest
Loan Car	-	12% interest
Loans-R-us	-	15% interest

Comparing Prices

Finance Assessment 4

1. *Eazy Clean* floor polish comes in 2 sizes.

   The 500 ml bottle costs £3·10 and the
   2 litre plastic container costs £11·80.

   a How much does it cost per 100 ml for the bottle ?

   b How much does it cost per 100 ml for the container ?

   c Which is better value ?

2. Which pack of Cola is the best buy - the 6-pack, the 8-pack or the 9-pack ?

£1·98

£2·48

£2·88

3. I need to hire a heavy duty hoover to remove stains from my carpets.

   I estimate it will need to be hired for 4 hours.

   > *PowerVac* charge a basic hiring fee of £17 plus £9 per hour after that.
   >
   > ***CarpetClean*** don't charge any basic fee but their rental charges are £12 per hour.

   a Which company should I hire it from ? (*Explain*).

   b It actually took 6 hours to clean all the carpets in my house.

   Would I have been better hiring it from the other company ? (*Explain*).

4. Pete's electricity bill with *ScotElect* last year was £1200.

   GenGas charged Pete £1446 for his gas.

   This year he has been offered a combined deal with ***GasGlow*** whereby his total bill for gas and electricity is estimated to be £215 per month.

   Should Pete take up ***GasGlow's*** offer ? (*Explain*).

Budgeting

Budgeting

Most people have to budget their money so that they can decide whether or not they can afford to buy certain items.

Example :- Pete saves £35 a week so that he can buy a scooter costing £840.

a Can he afford the scooter after 18 weeks ?

b How many more weeks will he need to save ?

Answer :-

a 35 x 18 = £630.
No, he cannot afford it after 18 weeks.

b 840 ÷ 35 = 24 weeks. He needs to save 6 more

Exercise 1

1. Ross is saving £30 a week to buy a ring costing £595 for his girlfriend.

   a Can he afford to buy the ring after 19 weeks ?

   b For how many more weeks will he need to save ?

2. Josh saves £12·00 every week for 9 weeks to buy a pair of hiking boots costing £129.

   For how many more weeks will he need to save ?

3. Anne saves £25 a week, saving for an outfit costing £196.

   Tom saves £40 per week for a new £275 suit.

   Who will be able to buy their item first and by how many weeks ?

4. George saves £25 every week, saving up for a new computer costing £315.

   a How many weeks will he need to save to be able to afford the computer.

   b After 8 weeks, he notices a sale where the computer is only £225.

   For how many more weeks will he have to save ?

5. Barry works 5 days a week and has budgeted £60 per week from his pay.

   £40 is for his train fares to and from work and he wants to spend £5 a day on his lunch.

   a What is wrong with his calculations ?

   b What should he do to correct this ?

Managing a Budget Topic 1 - Saving for a Trip

Eve is a single mother with two young sons Alfie & Finn. Both boys want to go on a weekend school trip to York but the trip will cost £200 per pupil. Eve explains to her sons that the only way they can go is if they pay **half** of the cost themselves.

Exercise 2

1. The boys each receive pocket money of £7 per week, but they also like to spend their pocket money every week.

   Below are pages from their notebooks showing how they spent their money last week.

Alfie

Sweets	£1·00
Swimming	£1·35
Stickers	£0·45
Mum's Birthday Card	£1·95
New Pencil	£0·15

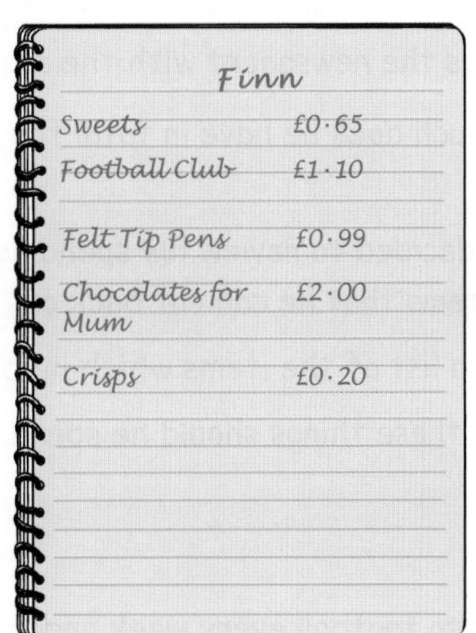

Finn

Sweets	£0·65
Football Club	£1·10
Felt Tip Pens	£0·99
Chocolates for Mum	£2·00
Crisps	£0·20

   a How much did Alfie spend last week ?

   b How much did Finn spend last week ?

2. The boys decide that they will have to do something to make sure that they have more money to save for their trip.

   What are the 2 different ways that they can do this ?

3. The trip is 30 weeks away, so how much will each boy have to save **each week** to achieve the £100 ?

4. Alfie plans to wash some cars. He borrows the equipment for washing from his mum then he charges £1·50 for a wash and £3·00 for a wash & polish.

   Alfie manages to get 12 customers - 4 cars wash only and 8 cars had a wash & polish.

   a How much money did Alfie make from the car washing ?

   b How much money does he still have to find to go on the trip ?

5. Alfie had forgotten that he hadn't bought a birthday present for his mum.

He needs to get her something.

What could Alfie do for his mum's birthday which wouldn't cost him any money ?

6. With 20 weeks left to go before the school trip, Alfie gets a job as a paperboy delivering a few local papers every Friday after school.

The newsagent pays him a wage of £2·50 per week.

a How much money will he make from the new job before his trip ?

b Alfie is offered £25 by the newsagent for helping him count stock one Sunday, but Alfie is taking part in a football match on that day.

What should he do ?

7. Alfie helps the newsagent with the stock count.

So how much does he have in total for the cost of the school trip ?

8. Finn has decided to review his spending to see if there are any items that he can cut back on.

Shown is a list of the items which he buys most often.

Which of these things should he spend less money on ?

Finn	
Crisps	£0·25
Chocolate	£0·75
Comics	£0·99
Football Club	£1·10
Cinema	£2·25

9. Finn goes to football every week and to the cinema every second week.

a How much would Finn save, over the 30 week period, if he only went to football every 2 weeks instead of every week ?

b Which item should Finn stop paying for to save the most money and how much money would he save over the 30 weeks ?

c How much money would Finn save after 30 weeks if he stopped all of the items on his list ?

10. Finn only decides to stop going to the cinema and buying comics until his trip.

He also gets £40 for his birthday but spends it all on a new pair of trainers.

What was the consequence of doing this ?

11. At the end of the 30 weeks, Eve reviews the boys' budget to check how much they have managed to save.

Who gets to go on the trip ?

Managing a Budget Topic 2 - Monthly Budgeting

Eve is concerned about managing her finances properly. She works part time in an office and receives benefits from the government to help her look after her children, but she has a lot of expenses each month. She decides to set up a monthly budget so that she knows how much money she is spending.

Exercise 3

1. Eve has listed her income and expenditures. Some of these are weekly - others are monthly.

Council Tax	£55 per month	Gas	£80 per month
Wages	£750 per month	Food	£80 per week
Electricity	£45 per month	Rent	£350 per month
Child benefit	£33·70 per week	Fuel	£70 per month
Child Tax Credit	£113·50 per week	Working Tax Credit	£68 per week
Car Loan	£108 per month	Car Ins	£51 per month
Credit card	£100 per month	TV Licence	£15 per month
Clothing & Shoes	£80 per month	Mobile Phone top-up	£60 per month

Can you calculate the following **monthly** amounts to assist Eve ? (*Use 1 month = 4 weeks*)

a Food per month -

b Child Benefit per month -

c Child Tax Credit per month -

d Working Tax Credit per month -

2. Draw up a planner, similar to that shown below, and transfer the information from the table above onto the appropriate side on the Income/Expenditure list.

3. By subtracting her expenditure from her income, Eve calculates how much money she has left each month. How much does she have ?

Monthly Budget Planner Sheet for Eve Jones	
INCOME	EXPENDITURE
	Copy
Over/Under Spend (Income - Expenditure)	£..................

Make up and fill in a Budget Planning sheet like this.

4. Eve has both fixed and variable amount expenses.

List her fixed amount expenses.

5. Eve takes her car to the garage for an MOT and she gets a bill for £220 for repairs needed to be carried out.

How much money will Eve have left this month once the bill is paid ?

6. Eve currently works 21 hours a week, but her manager asks if she could increase her hours to 28 hrs per week. This would mean her pay would go up to £1000 per month but her working tax credit would decrease to £150 per month.

What affect would this have on her budget ? Should she increase her hours ?

7. Look at Eve's income and expenditure, what other changes could effect her budget ?

Managing a Budget Topic 3 - Needs & Wants

Discuss the 5 Basic NEEDS necessary for survival.
Eve is trying hard to budget her money efficiently, but still finds it difficult at times, especially when she confuses things that she WANTS with things that she NEEDS. She is thinking of ordering her supermarket shop online. She plans to keep to a weekly budget of £75 for her food and for other household items.

Exercise 4

1. Eve starts by buying her regular basic foodstuffs first. She buys cheese, milk, bread, cereal, potatoes, chocolate spread, salad vegetables and crisps. The total amount spent on these items is £18·00.

   a Are these all NEEDS foodstuffs ?

   b Why do you think she believes that she needs these items ?

2. Once she has these items in her virtual shopping bag, she now plans the meals that she will make for the week, Monday to Friday. She buys chicken £6·20, minced beef £4·55, pasta £1·07, tomato sauce £0·65, onions £0·63 and mushrooms £0·70.

   a How much has she spent on the food for meals ?

   b Assuming that she has enough for 5 days' meals how much has she spent on each day's meal ?

3. The supermarket has recommended some extra items for Eve, based on what she has purchased previously. She has been offered a new brand of make-up at £9·99, a frozen pizza for £3·49 and a child's winter coat for a special price of £18·99.

   a Which of these items are NEEDS ?

   b Which of these items are WANTS ?

4. Eve does not buy the recommended items, but she does spend a further £25·30 on other essential items for the home. Now she starts to plan what to buy for Finn's birthday party.

   a What items are essential and NEEDED for a birthday party ?

   b Finn has asked for birthday bags for his friends, but Eve is not sure whether these are NEEDS or WANTS. What are they ?

5. Eve spends £15·75 on party food, £6·10 on cola & juice, and a further £7·25 on other items for the party. How much has the party cost her ?

6. Eve has received loyalty vouchers from the supermarket. One offers 40p off a bar of chocolate, one offers 100 points for buying a certain brand of washing powder and the last one is 25 points for buying a box of plasters.
   Are any of the vouchers for her 5 basic NEEDS ?

7. Total all the items that Eve has bought in her virtual shopping basket.
   Has Eve kept to her budget of £75 ?

8. If she were to order her shop online, Eve would have to pay a delivery charge of £6·00 to get the shopping delivered straight to her door.
   Are there any circumstances in which this WANT could in fact be a NEED ?

Budgeting

Finance Assessment 5

1. In January, George decides to set up a standing order which pays £25 per week into a special account to pay for his surfing holiday to Florida. He has to pay for it in 18 weeks time, (*10 weeks before the holiday date*).

   If the holiday costs £525, how much extra does George need to add to his savings to pay for the holiday fully ?

2. George's girlfriend, Jenna works in *Taras* ladies fashion shop. Her hourly rate of pay is £8·75 and in January she worked a total of 144 hours.

   Her payslip showed deductions of £225·50.

   As well as this, she works 8 hours on each of four Saturday evenings in a bar in Aberdeen, where the hourly rate is £7·20, with no tax.

   a Calculate Jenna's total **net** income for the month of January.

   Jenna rents a flat and estimates her outgoings for January.

Rent - £440	Car Loan - £135	Electricity - £95	Food - £220
Petrol - £70	Mobile - £32·90	Entertainment - £200	Savings - ?????

   Whatever she has left, Jenna puts into her savings account.

   b How much can Jenna save in January ?

   c What could she cut down on to help with her savings ?

3. Jenna's bill for her car being put through its MOT is £790.

   She needs to borrow £800 for 1 year and the bank charged her 5% for the loan.

   Calculate the overall amount payable and decide if Jenna has enough funds in January to meet the monthly payment.

4. She decides that from January to August, she will cut her spending each month on entertainment by a quarter.

   a Assuming her monthly income remains the same from January to August, and George pays the £525 for her trip to Florida with him, how much will she have in her savings, by August ?

   b She changes £400 of her savings to dollars at an exchange rate of £1 = $1·65. How many dollars will she have to spend ?

Comparing Data Sets

Averages

A Measure of Spread - The Range

The RANGE is a mathematical tool used to measure how widely spread a set of values is.

=> **Range = Highest score − Lowest score**

Example :- For the set of numbers :- 7, 3, 4, 6, 9, 7, 8, 11, 18, 13.

=> Range = 18 − 3 = 15

Averages - Mode, Median and Mean

There are three measures of average :- the mode, the median and the mean.

MODE - The number that occurs "most".

2, 6, 6, 5, 7, 7, 5, 8, 8, 5, 10, 10, 11, 4, 5.
mode = 5

MEDIAN - The "middle" number, (*as long as the numbers are in "order"*).

1, 5, 6, 6, 7, 7, 7, 8, 8, 8, 10, 10, 12, 15, 18.
median = 8

MEAN - "Add" all the data together and "divide" by the number of pieces of data.

mean of 4, 3, 1, 3, 9 is :-

$$\frac{4+3+1+3+9}{5} = 4$$

Exercise 1

1. Find the range of these numbers :-

a 2, 5, 8, 1, 3, 3
b 14, 12, 42, 51, 17, 47
c 8, 25, 14, 7, 31, 19, 52, 25
d 11, 107, 240, 98, 145
e 9, 6, 5, 4, 3, 12, 5, 4, 2, 17, 9
f 94, 36, 65, 32, 95, 29, 47, 22, 25
g 2·3, 5·1, 8·6, 1·9, 3·7, 6·8, 4·3, 7·5
h 5·22, 2·77, 3·44, 6·11, 4·66, 2·78.

2. Find the mode for each set of data :-

a 1, 1, 2, 2, 2, 2, 3, 3, 5, 6, 9
b 4, 4, 5, 5, 5, 3, 3, 7, 7, 8, 9, 9, 1
c 8, 7, 9, 8, 6, 7, 8, 9, 7, 6, 8
d 3, 4, 3, 5, 4, 3, 3, 4, 7, 4, 7, 4
e 29, 27, 26, 27, 28, 25, 27, 26, 25
f 4·2, 4·2, 4·3, 4·4, 4·5, 4·3, 4·5. 4·3.

3. Work out the **median**. (*Put the numbers in order first !*)

a 1, 1, 2, 2, 3, 3, 6, 7, 7

b 6, 9, 5, 3, 2, 7, 4

c 41, 44, 51, 16, 39, 57, 45, 38, 51

d 2·7, 3·3, 2·4, 3·5, 2·1

e 122, 133, 78, 184, 155, 129, 168

> If there is not a single middle number :-
> take the **mean of the middle two numbers.**
>
> **Example** :- 2, 2, 4, 5, 8, 9, 9, 10
>
> The **median** is (5 + 8) ÷ 2 = 6·5.

Continue finding the **median** :-

f 15, 22, 18, 19, 23, 18

g 8, 12, 14, 30, 6, 34, 24, 16, 21, 17

h 113, 109, 110, 108, 106, 109, 105, 112

i 0·6, 0·7, 0·1, 1·0, 1·6, 0·9, 0·2, 0·3

j $4\frac{1}{2}$, $4\frac{1}{2}$, $5\frac{1}{2}$, $6\frac{1}{2}$, $6\frac{1}{2}$, $7\frac{1}{2}$.

4. Calculate the **mean** for each set of data :-

a 2, 4, 6, 8

b 9, 19, 12, 17, 13

c £8, £9, £10, £28, £24, £5

d 6 cm, 21 cm, 39 cm, 21 cm, 11 cm, 34 cm

e 5·2, 5·1, 2·7, 6·4, 6·8, 2·9, 8·1, 2·4

f 5·85, 0·76, 3·93, 3·86

g 0·5, 0·6, 0·8, 0·5, 1·0, 0·7, 1·1, 0·4

h $125, $118, $128, $121, $143.

5. Calculate the **range**, **mode**, **median** and **mean** for these numbers :-

a 2, 1, 3, 1, 5, 7, 16

b 4·6, 2·2, 5·3, 5·3, 4·0, 5·3, 2·7

c 107, 105, 93, 115, 105, 99

d 40, 32, 23, 30, 55, 25, 27, 40

e 11, 15, 9, 14, 21, 12, 21, 21

f 12 000, 15 000, 17 000, 16 000.

6. Rita buys 10 packets of toffees. The number of chocolate toffees in each packet is :-

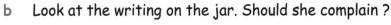

9	7	8	6	9	7	9	10	6	8

a Calculate the :- (i) mode (ii) median (iii) mean.

b How many of the 10 packets have **more** than the mean number of chocolate toffees ?

7. Mel Bought 10 jars of jelly beans containing the following number of beans :-

50, 52, 54, 52, 56, 50, 54, 49, 54, 54.

a Calculate the **mean** number of jelly beans.

b Look at the writing on the jar. Should she complain ?

c Find the **median**.

d What is the **mode** ?

8. 

Marie sat 4 maths tests marked out of 20.
She found her average (**mean**) mark was 17.
She scored 19, 19 and 16 in her first three tests.

What was her mark in the fourth test ?

Compare and Contrast Data

Example :- Look at this set of data :- 5, 7, 2, 9, 10, 2, 3, 4, 57

a Find the **range**.

Range = 57 - 2 = 55

b Find the **mean, median** and **mode**.

Mean = $\frac{5+7+2+9+10+2+3+4+57}{9}$

= 11

Median = 2 2 3 4 |5| 7 9 10 57

= 5

Mode = 2

c Which average is best suited here ?

Median

d Explain why you think the other two averages are less suitable.

Mode ? - only two 2's !

Mean ? - that large 57 distorts the answer and only 1 value above the mean.

Exercise 2

1. *"DW Sports"* announced that the only sizes of trainers that remained in their sale were :-

$2\frac{1}{2}$, 3, $3\frac{1}{2}$, 4, $4\frac{1}{2}$, 6, $6\frac{1}{2}$, 7, $10\frac{1}{2}$, $12\frac{1}{2}$

a What is the mean shoe size ?

b Sally takes a size $3\frac{1}{2}$. How many sizes smaller is this than the mean ?

2. Two 4th year pupils compare their marks for the first 4 science tests of the session.

Test No	1	2	3	4
Ravi	63	77	58	62
Joe	51	80	92	33

a Calculate the **mean** mark for each pupil.

b Who has the lower mean and by how many marks ?

3. Michelle and Daisy are playing darts.

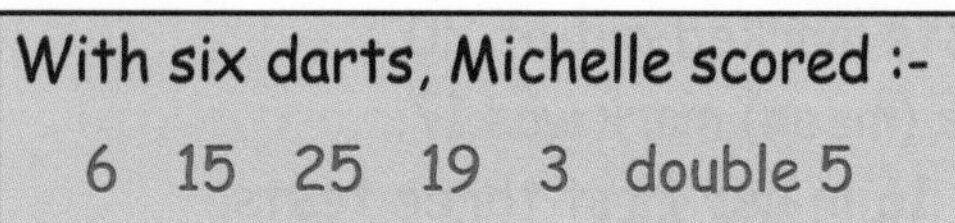
With six darts, Michelle scored :-
6 15 25 19 3 double 5

With her six darts, Daisy scored :-
1 23 17 36 3 double 8

a Calculate the **mean** score for each player.

b Who played better ?

4. The weights of six women are shown :-

45 kg, 55 kg, 68 kg, 45 kg, 52 kg, 54 kg.

a Find the **range** of their weights.

b Calculate the **mode** and **median** weights.

c Choose which is the better average of the two and explain why.

5. Gemma checks her blood glucose level each day and notes the readings.

6·6 6·8 7·0 6·6 6·6 6·9 7·0 6·9 7·0 6·6

a Write down the **mode** and the **mean**.

b Which of these give a clearer indication of how Gemma's glucose levels are ?

6. Shown are the charges quoted by 10 garages for servicing a one year old sports car :-

£60	£80	£90	£100	£110
£60	£120	£55	£220	£125

a Calculate the **median** and the **mean** price.

b Why is it better here to use the median rather than the mean ?

c Why is the mode no use here ?

7. George and his sister went to Disneyland Paris for Easter.

They kept a note as to how long, in minutes, they had to queue to get on the rides.

16 30 25 20 10 110 10 22 40 17

a Calculate the **mean** time waited.

b Find the **median** and **modal** times waited.

c Say which "average" should be chosen to give a fair representation of the data.

8. A Landscape Gardener orders turf from two suppliers, and he recently kept a note of how many days it took for his last 10 orders from each to be delivered.

Green Up	1	12	2	11	15	3	1	10	2	13
Turfers	6	6	8	7	5	6	7	7	5	8

a For each supplier, calculate :-

(i) the **range** (ii) the **mean** number of days.

b As the gardener likes to plan his work in advance he prefers to order from the more **consistent** supplier. Which supplier is that, and why ?

c Give one reason why he might order from his other supplier.

Comparing Data Sets

Statistics Assessment 1

1. Find the **range** of these numbers :- 86, 30, 57, 26, 90, 18, 39, 14, 19.

2. Determine the **mode** for these lengths :-

   9 m, 8 m, 8 m, 10 m, 8 m, 9 m, 8 m, 9 m, 12 m, 12 m, 9 m, 9 m, 12 m.

3. Find the **median** temperature :-

   5°C, –4°C, 2°C, 8°C, –6°C, 6°C, 10°C, –18°C, 5°C, 3°C.

4. Calculate the **mean** weight (grams) :-

   130 g, 50 g, 60 g, 75 g, 105 g, 110 g, 41 g, 69 g.

5. Here are the number of runs scored by a cricketer in his first 6 matches :-

54	62	54	60	54	61

   a Find the **mode** and the **median**.

   b Which one - the mode or the median, gives the better idea of the cricketer's scoring performance ?

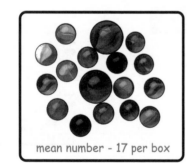

6. mean number - 17 per box

   The contents of ten boxes of marbles are examined.

   The boxes have the following number of marbles :-

   16, 18, 14, 17, 15, 16, 15, 15, 18, 16.

   a Why is the manufacturer's claim wrong ?

   b An eleventh box is examined.

   How many marbles would need to be in that box in order for the manufacturer's claim to **then** be considered to be correct ?

7. Shown is the number of cartons of juice bought by two mums over a few weeks.

Tina	3	4	3	3	3	6	4	3	7
Anne	1	4	4	2	2	3	4	4	3

   a Write down the **modal** amount bought by each mum.

   b Give a reason why it is unfair to say one mum bought more than the other mum by comparing them using the mode. What other "average" is better ?

Graphs, Charts & Tables 2

Drawing Frequency Tables, Bar Graphs and Line Graphs

When setting up Frequency Tables, or drawing statistical graphs like Bar Graphs and Line Graphs, it is important to label them correctly and to show any scale accurately.

Shown below are some hints as to what is expected in each.

Minutes taken to complete a Sudoko Puzzle

Time	*Tally*	*Frequency*
12	||	
13	卌 |	
14		
15		

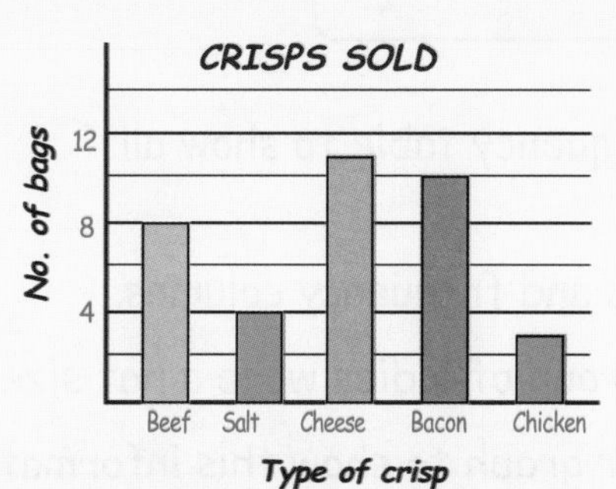

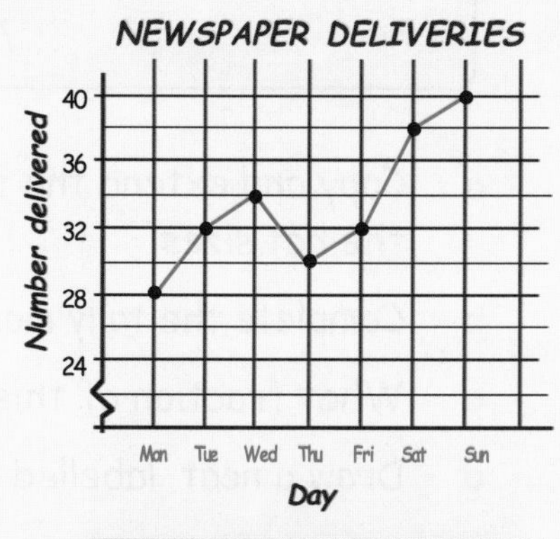

Frequency Table

- Column 1 takes the topic of the question.
- Columns 2 & 3 are always "Tally Marks and Frequency"
- Tally Marks are grouped in 5's.

Bar Graph

- The scale should go up in equal amounts.
- The horizontal and vertical axes should be labelled clearly.
- The graph should be given a title.

Line Graph

- The scale should go up in equal amounts - it does not have to start at 0.
- The horizontal and vertical axes should be labelled clearly.
- The graph should be given a title.

Exercise 1

1. Write down what number each set of tally marks represents :-

   a \|\|\|\| b 卌 卌 c 卌 \|\|\|\| d 卌 卌 卌 \|\|

2. Shown are the times (in minutes) for an S4 class to complete a Sudoko puzzle.

   Copy the frequency table below and complete it.

12	15	13	13	14	16
17	13	14	14	14	17
15	14	12	13	13	15
12	14	16	14	13	12

Time	*Tally*	*Frequency*
12	||	
13	|||	
14		
15		

Remember tally marks are grouped in fives 卌

3. *"Country Hat Shop"* did a survey of ladies' hat sizes in order to help with their monthly ordering.

$7\frac{1}{4}$	$6\frac{1}{2}$	7	$7\frac{1}{4}$	$6\frac{3}{4}$	$6\frac{3}{4}$
$7\frac{1}{2}$	$6\frac{1}{4}$	$6\frac{3}{4}$	7	$7\frac{1}{4}$	$6\frac{1}{2}$
$6\frac{3}{4}$	$7\frac{1}{4}$	7	$6\frac{1}{4}$	$7\frac{1}{4}$	7
7	$6\frac{3}{4}$	$6\frac{1}{2}$	$6\frac{3}{4}$	7	$6\frac{3}{4}$
7	7	7	7	7	$7\frac{3}{4}$

Hat Size	Tally	Frequency
$6\frac{1}{4}$		
$6\frac{1}{2}$		
$6\frac{3}{4}$		
7		
$7\frac{1}{4}$		

a Copy and extend the frequency table to show all the hat sizes.

b Complete the tally marks and frequency columns.

c What fraction of this group of ladies wore a hat size 7 ?

d Draw a neat, labelled bar graph to show this information.

4. This bar chart shows the number of Primary pupils who brought various fruit with them to school one day.

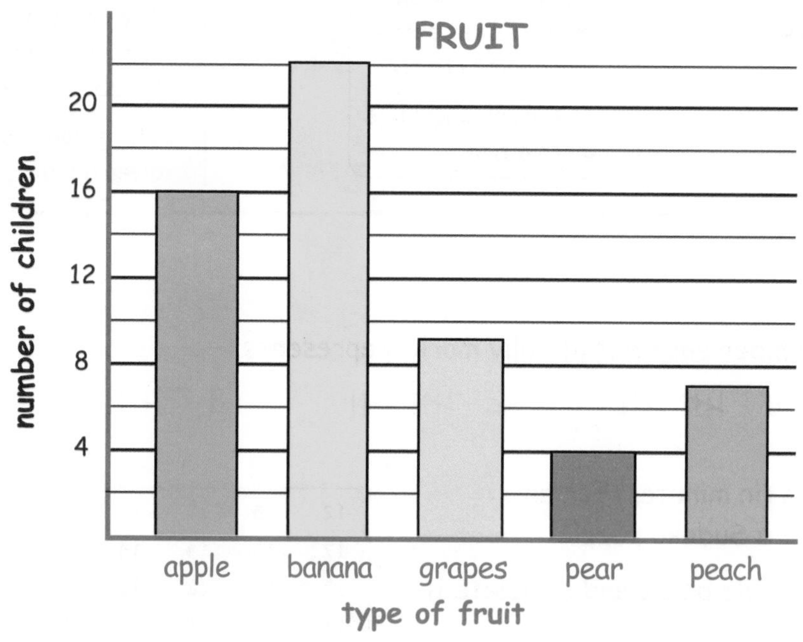

a How many **more** pupils brought a banana rather than a bunch of grapes ?

b Draw a **frequency table** to show how many of each type of fruit was brought to school.

Fruit	Frequency
apple	

5. The owner of a small shop asked 30 customers what kind of tinned soup they liked.

The results are shown in the table :-

pea/ham	tomato	chicken	lentil	oxtail	minestrone
3	9	4	7	1	6

Draw and label a neat **bar graph** to show this information.

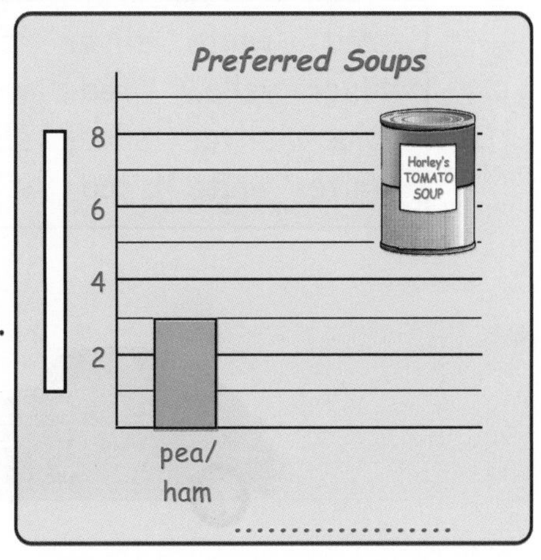

6.

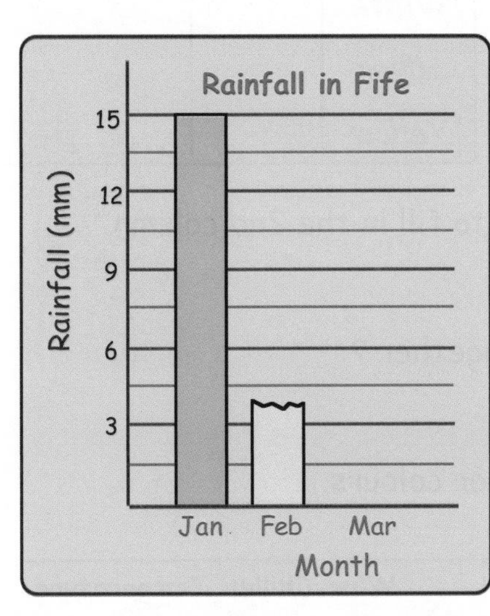

The table below shows the rainfall (in mm) from January to June in a small village in Fife.

Jan	Feb	Mar	Apr	May	June
15	9	12	10·5	3	1·5

Copy and complete the **bar graph** using the information in the table.

7. This table shows the average daily hours of sunshine in Malaga, Spain, from May to November.

May	June	July	Aug	Sept	Oct	Nov
12	14	16	17	10	9	5

Draw a **bar graph** to show the information.

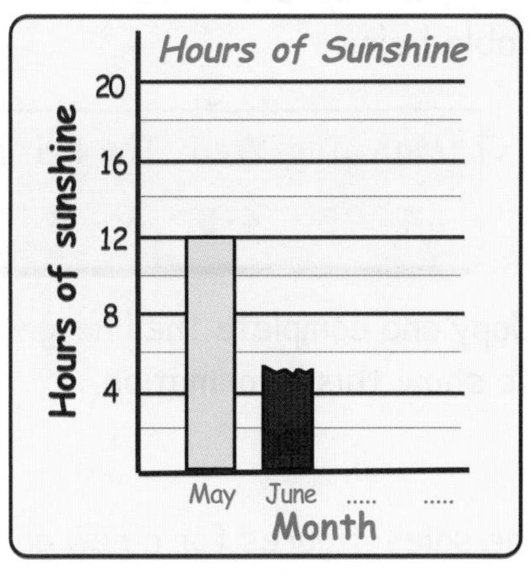

8. *Kerry's Electrical Store* carried out a survey into which TV channel their customers preferred to view. Here are the results of that survey :-

ITV 1	BBC 1	Ch 4	Ch 5	Sky 1	Sky Sports	Sky Movies
45	30	10	25	50	60	5

Decide on a **suitable scale** and draw/label a neat **bar graph** to show these findings.

9. A sample of 20 cars was taken from a car park and the colour of each car was noted.

red	white	silver	blue	silver
silver	yellow	red	white	silver
blue	silver	silver	silver	red
white	white	red	silver	white

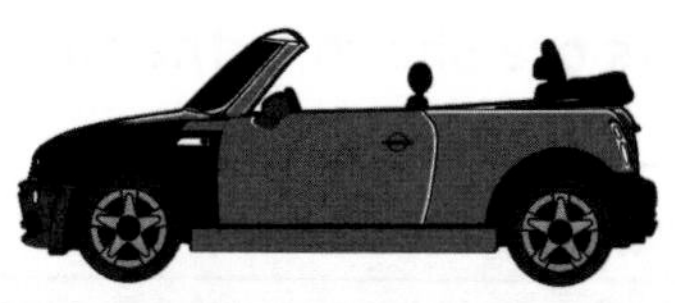

Colour	Tally	Frequency
Red		
Blue		
White		
Silver		
Yellow		

a Copy the frequency table and use tally marks to fill in the 2nd column.

b Fill in the 3rd column in your table.

c How many silver and white cars are there altogether ?

d What fraction of the cars is red ?

e Draw a neat labelled **bar graph** to show the car colours.

10. The temperature of a wine chiller, in °C, is recorded and shown in the table below.

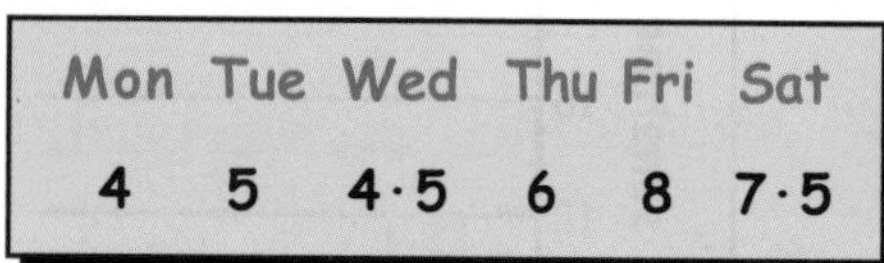

Mon	Tue	Wed	Thu	Fri	Sat
4	5	4·5	6	8	7·5

Copy and complete the **line graph** to show this information.

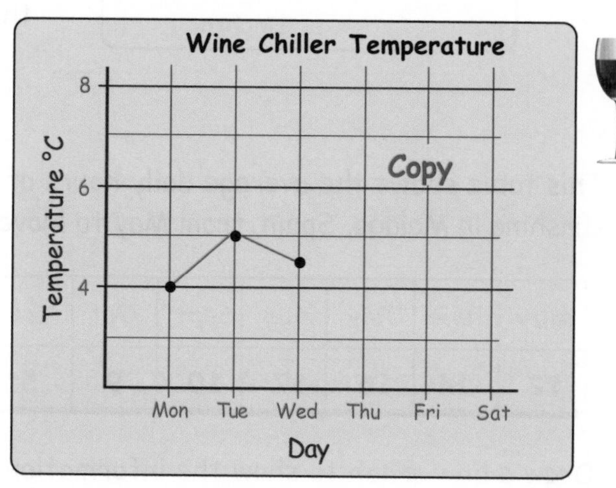

11. The sales' figures for a new game are shown in this table.

Month	*Aug*	*Sep*	*Oct*	*Nov*	*Dec*	*Jan*
Sales (1000's)	10	25	20	30	55	5

a Show the above data in a **line graph** using a scale like the one shown opposite.

b Why were the sales so high in December ?

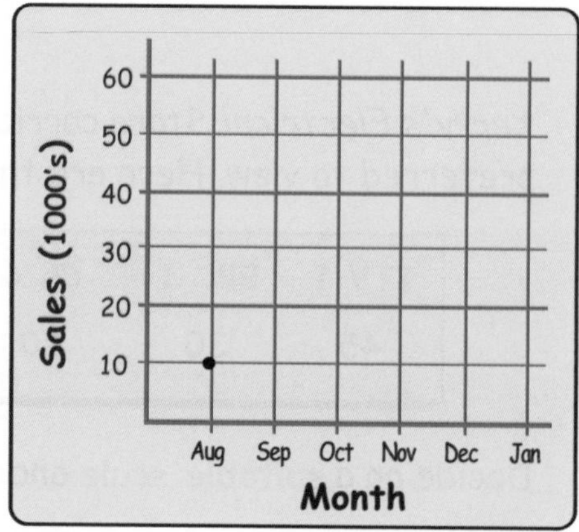

12. 

The temperature (°C) in a pharmacist's medicine cooler is recorded and shown in the table below.

Mon	Tue	Wed	Thu	Fri	Sat
6	7	4	5	8·5	7·5

Draw a **line graph** to show this information.

13. Construct a **line graph** for this data set :-

Height of a tomato plant in cm.

Wk 1	Wk 2	Wk 3	Wk 4	Wk 5	Wk 6
2	3	5	7	10	12

14. The cost of a medium sized pineapple varies at different times of the year.

This table shows the cost in pence of a pineapple from June (2013) to June (2014).

June	Aug	Oct	Dec	Feb	Apr	Jun
40	50	70	90	85	60	45

Draw a **line graph** showing this set of prices.

15. Construct a line graph for the following data which shows the number of ice creams sold from Antonio's ice cream van from February till November 2014.

Month	Feb	Mar	Apr	May	June	Jul	Aug	Sep	Oct	Nov
Sales	100	200	600	1000	1200	1000	900	500	100	50

Make your vertical scale go up in 100's.

16. This table shows six months of car sales from two different car dealers, Arnold Clive and Ron Chorley.

Plot both sets of data on a **comparative line graph**.

	Jul	Aug	Sep	Oct	Nov	Dec
Clive's	100	250	300	250	400	200
Chorley's	300	200	350	450	100	150

Constructing a Pie Chart

TYPE OF HOUSING

bungalow
semi detached villa
detached villa
flat

Pie Chart

- Decide how many sectors the chart has to be split into.
- Decide what each sector represents.
- Colour or shade each sector.
- Label each sector.
- Give the chart a title.

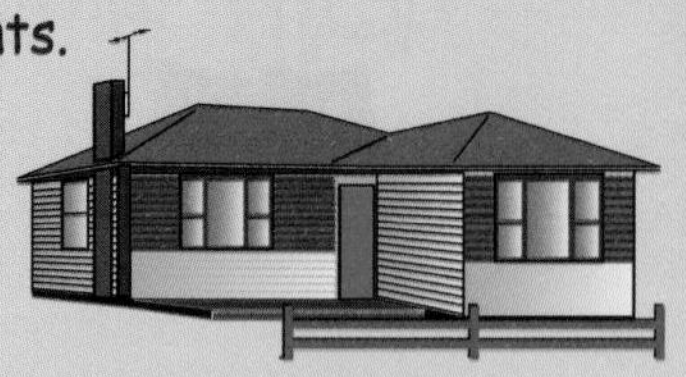

Exercise 2

1. The pie chart shown has been split into 10 sectors.

   a How many sectors will be represented by 50% ?

   b How many sectors will be represented by 10% ?

   c The percentage of cars sold in a garage forecourt were as follows :-

   - 40% Family Saloons
   - 30% Sports
   - 20% 4 x 4's
   - 10% MPV's

Copy (or trace) the blank **pie chart** and complete it, showing the above information.

2. To make her home-made Macaroni Bake, Jaki uses only four ingredients as follows :-

   - 50% macaroni pasta
   - 20% tomato soup
   - 20% diced ham
   - 10% cheese

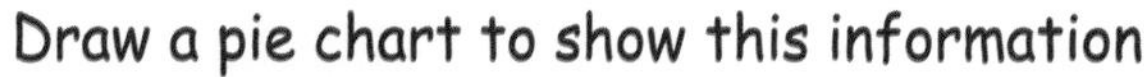

Draw a pie chart to show this information.

3. 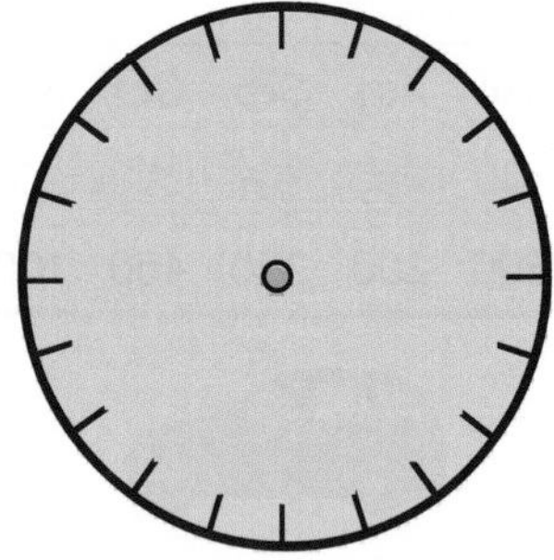

   This pie chart has been split into 20 sectors.

   a How many sectors will be represented by 50% ?

   b How many sectors will be represented by 10% ?

   c How many sectors will be represented by 35% ?

4. COPY

On a Caribbean cruise, it was discovered that :-

- 35% of those on the ship were aged 20-65 years old
- 40% were senior citizens
- 20% were under 20 years old

a If the remainder on board were crew members what percentage was that ?

b Copy (or trace) the blank pie chart and complete it showing the above information.

5. Over the course of a month, appointments at a dental surgery were studied. It was found that :-

- 45% of patients were in for a check-up
- 35% were there to see the hygienist
- 15% were there to get a brace fitted
- the rest required an implant.

a What percentage required an implant ?

b Copy (or trace) the blank pie chart and complete it showing the above information.

6. The information given below shows the most popular answers to the question :-

"If you were given money to renovate one room in your house, which room would you choose" ?

- 45% said "kitchen"
- 25% said "bathroom"
- of the others, half said "bedroom" and half said "living room".

Draw a pie chart to illustrate this, using a "pie" like this one.

7.

There were 60 000 people at the Cup Final.

- 30 000 were supporting Arbroath
- 15 000 were East Stirling supporters
- 12 000 were neutral supporters
- the remainder were football officials and stewards.

Copy (or trace) the blank pie chart and complete it to show the above information.

Drawing a Pie Chart using a Protractor

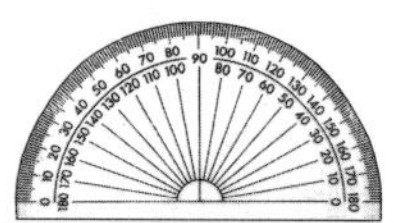

The table of data shows a number of different movie types picked by third year pupils.

Type of Movie	Number
Horror	36
Action	24
Thriller	20
Love Story	10

When drawing a pie chart, it is sometimes easier to add columns to the table for calculations.

Type of Movie	Number	Fraction	Angle
Horror	36	$\frac{36}{90}$	$\frac{36}{90} \times 360 = 144°$
Action	24	$\frac{24}{90}$	$\frac{24}{90} \times 360 = 96°$
Thriller	20	$\frac{20}{90}$	$\frac{20}{90} \times 360 = 80°$
Love Story	10	$\frac{10}{90}$	$\frac{10}{90} \times 360 = 40°$
TOTAL	90	1	360°

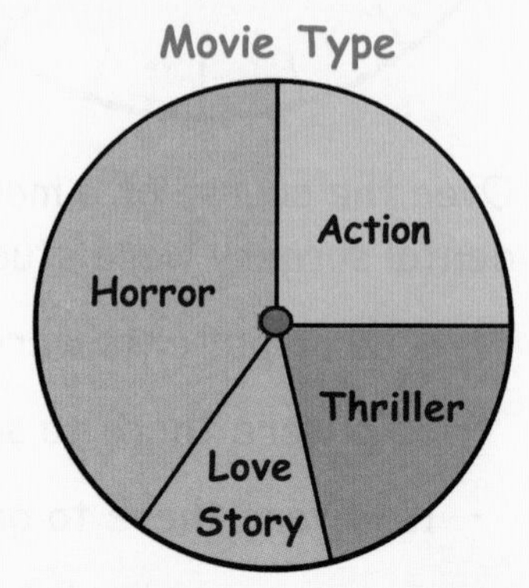

Step 1 :- add up the Numbers column to obtain a total (in this case 90).

Step 2 :- express each "Number" as a fraction of this total, (e.g. $\frac{36}{90}$).

Step 3 :- find that fraction of 360° each time (e.g. $\frac{36}{90} \times 360 = 144°$).

Step 4 :- finally, draw the pie chart using the angles in the table and a protractor.

Exercise 3

1. a Copy and complete the table showing a group of 180 people's favourite vegetable.

   b Construct a pie chart using a pair of compasses, a ruler and a protractor and the table information.

Vegetable	Number	Fraction	Angle
Lettuce	90	$\frac{90}{180}$	$\frac{90}{180} \times 360 = 180°$
Carrot	60	$\frac{60}{180}$	$\frac{60}{180} \times 360 = ...°$
Turnip	20	$\frac{—}{180}$	$\frac{—}{180} \times 360 = ...°$
Cabbage	10	$\frac{—}{180}$	$\frac{—}{180} \times 360 = ...°$
TOTAL	180	1	360°

2. a Copy and complete this table which shows a number of pupils choosing their favourite school holiday.

   b Construct an accurate pie chart showing this information.

Holiday	Number	Fraction	Angle
Summer	3	$\frac{3}{45}$	$\frac{3}{45} \times 360 = 24°$
Christmas	21	$\frac{21}{45}$	$\frac{21}{45} \times 360 = ...°$
Easter	17	$\frac{—}{45}$	$\frac{—}{45} \times 360 = ...°$
October	4	$\frac{—}{45}$	$\frac{—}{45} \times 360 = ...°$
TOTAL	45	1	360°

3. a Copy and complete the table showing a group of teachers' favourite lunchtime drink.

Favourite Drink	Number	Fraction	Angle
Tea	7	$\frac{7}{30}$	$\frac{7}{30}$ × 360 = ...°
Juice	4		× 360 = ...°
Water	6		× 360 = ...°
Coffee	13		× 360 = ...°
TOTAL	30		360°

b Construct an accurate pie chart showing this information.

4. For each table below, copy it (adding new columns to show your working) and construct an accurate pie chart to show the information :-

a

Favourite TV Soap	Number
Corma Street	32
Westenders	24
Nummerdale	3
Next Door	13
TOTAL	....

b

Girls Ages	Number
4 - 6	380
7 - 9	260
10 - 12	60
13 - 15	20
TOTAL	....

5. The table shows the results of a survey asking people's favourite Scottish holiday resort.

Arran	Ayr	St Andrews	Largs	St Andrews	Largs	Ayr	Arran
Largs	St Andrews	Ayr	Largs	Ayr	Largs	St Andrews	Largs
Ayr	Largs	Skye	Arran	Ayr	Skye	Largs	Largs
St Andrews	Ayr	Skye	Largs	Largs	Arran	Skye	St Andrews
Ayr	Largs	Largs	Largs	Ayr	Largs	Ayr	Arran

a Copy and complete the table below :-

Resort	*Tally Mark*	*Number*	*Fraction*	*Angle*
Largs				
Arran				
St Andrews				
Ayr				
Skye				

b Using a pair of compasses, a ruler and a protractor, construct an accurate pie chart for this information.

Drawing a Stem-and-Leaf Diagram

A **stem-and-leaf** diagram is yet another way of displaying information.

Example :-

Here is a list of the ages of people who joined Ferguston Bowling Club this summer :-

38	64	46	65	29	56
43	21	43	60	33	29
59	47	52	24	38	45
26	36	65	68	43	50

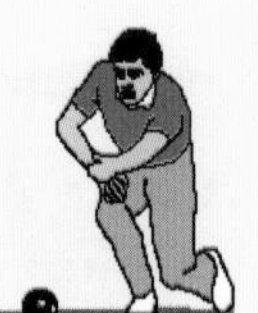

Illustrate this in an **ordered** stem-and-leaf diagram.

You may want to draw up a basic stem-and-leaf diagram, then update it to an ordered one.

UNORDERED

2	6 1 etc
3	8 6 etc
4	3 7
5	9
6	4

Looking at the 1st two columns of the table above

Age in Years

stem	leaves
2	1 4 6 9 9
3	3 6 8 8
4	3 3 3 5 6 7
5	0 2 6 9
6	0 4 5 5 8

Key :-
3 | 8 means **38**

** Note how the ORDERED stem & leaf has a KEY, explaining what the numbers mean.*

Exercise 4

1. From the above table, it can be seen that four people in their 30's joined.

   a How many of those who joined were in their 40's ?

   b What is the age of the youngest person to join ?

   c How many people joined altogether in the summer and what was the range of ages ?

   d What is the **modal** age ?

   e Find the **median** age.

2. The race times, in minutes, for the under-twelve Cumnock Fun Run were recorded in an **unordered** stem and leaf diagram.

   If this unordered diagram was rearranged to form an **ordered** stem-and-leaf diagram the first line would read as :-

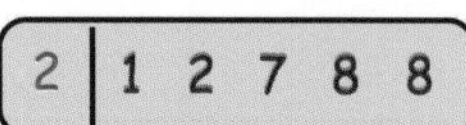

2 | 1 2 7 8 8

Key :-
5 | 2 means **52**

Fun Run Times

2	8 1 8 2 7
3	5 0 2 8 6 3
4	9 5 6 3 7
5	2 0
6	2 0 1

   a Write out the 2nd line **in order**.

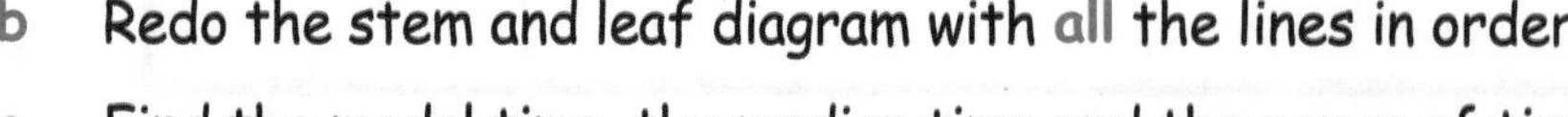

   b Redo the stem and leaf diagram with **all** the lines in order.

   c Find the modal time, the median time and the range of times.

   d How many of the under-twelves took **over** an hour to complete the fun run ?

3. *"PlayGame"* have only 12 computer games left in their sale.

Their prices are shown in a table.

£7	£22	£16	£12
£33	£8	£20	£19
£14	£23	£8	£25

Copy the diagram with the stem and put in the leaves to make it an **ordered** stem and leaf diagram. *(Remember to give it a key).*

stem *leaves*

4.

12	14	24	46	37	11
5	16	29	13	46	49
30	50	33	20	47	17
46	35	47	23	18	8

A teacher recorded the marks (out of 60) for a Science test.

Construct an ordered stem and leaf graph using the information.

5. This table shows how long (in seconds) a group of teenagers were able to hold their breath under water.

   a Construct an ordered stem and leaf diagram.

   b How many managed over 30 seconds ?

   c Find the range, mode and median time.

25	15	48	16	42	35	61
51	18	19	37	57	37	23
30	21	26	61	48	19	23
61	26	43	12	54	60	15

6. This question shows a **back-to-back** stem and leaf diagram, giving the age and gender of people at a retiral party.

   a Explain what you think - 9 9 7 6 **1** 6 7 8 means.

   b How many males at the party are aged :-

   (i) 19 (ii) 38 (iii) 52 ?

   c Find the modal age and median age of the :-

   (i) males (ii) females.

   d How many people were at the party ?

Age of People

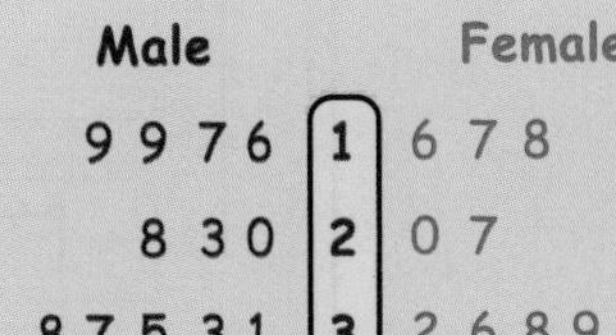

Male		Female
9 9 7 6	**1**	6 7 8
8 3 0	**2**	0 7
8 7 5 3 1	**3**	2 6 8 9
6 2 2 2 2	**4**	0 2 3 5 8
8 3 3	**5**	1 1 7

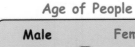

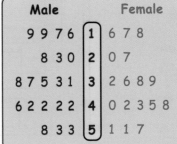

7. The table below gives the ages of a few men and women when they got married.

Men	22	36	45	33	19	22	35	38
Women	20	18	19	23	25	25	30	27

   a Draw an ordered back to back stem and leaf diagram to represent this information.

   b Find the modal and median ages of :- (i) the men (ii) the women.

8. a Draw an ordered back to back stem and leaf diagram showing the details about the heights (*in centimetres*) of the players in two ice hockey teams.

Mohawks	172	156	148	181	160	132	164	157	184	139	157	146
Flyers	145	162	138	182	175	174	167	175	159	150	144	173

   b Write a few sentences comparing the mode and the median of both teams.

Graphs, Charts & Tables 2

Statistics Assessment 2

1. The table shows the results of a survey asking a group of S4 pupils to state what their favourite lunchtime drink was.

Irn Bru	Orange	Cola	Water	Cola	Water	Orange	Irn Bru
Water	Cola	Orange	Water	Orange	Water	Cola	Water
Orange	Water	Lemonade	Irn Bru	Orange	Lemonade	Water	Water
Cola	Orange	Lemonade	Water	Water	Irn Bru	Lemonade	Cola
Orange	Water	Water	Water	Orange	Water	Orange	Irn Bru

a Show all this information in a frequency table.

Drink	Tally	Frequency
irn bru		
water		
....		

b

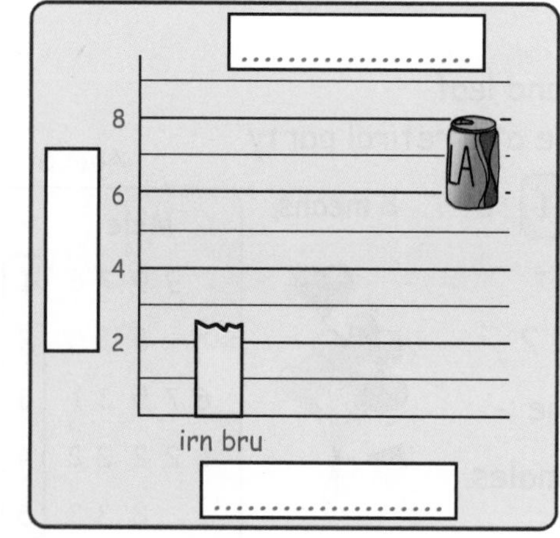

Use the table to help you construct a bar graph to illustrate the data.

2. Use the table below to construct a Comparative Line Graph to show the sales of coffee making machines in 2 stores last week.

	Wed	Thu	Fri	Sat	Sun
Korry's	6	8	4	12	10
Electro	4	6	14	11	12

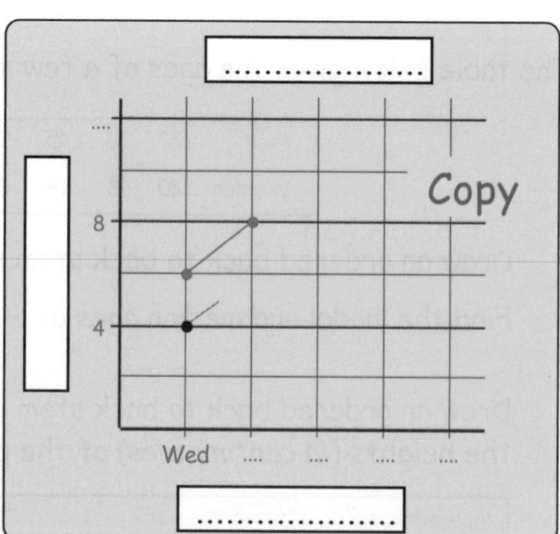

3. A large group of people were asked to name their favourite news channel.

Here are the results :-

- 35% BBC 1
- 30% Sky News
- 20% Channel 5
- the rest chose STV.

Copy (or trace) the blank **pie chart** and complete it showing the above information.

4. The table shows the eye colour of children in a Primary 5 class.

Eye colour	Number	Fraction	Angle
Blue	10	$\frac{10}{30}$	$\frac{10}{30}$ × 360 = ...°
Green	12		× 360 = ...°
Brown	7		× 360 = ...°
Grey	1		× 360 = ...°
TOTAL	**?**		**360°**

a How many children are in the class ?

b Copy and complete the table.

c Construct a neat accurate **pie chart** to show the information.

5. George went online to find the prices of quality inkjet printers.

He found 20 sites which had a printer he could afford and was in stock.

Here are the prices he found :-

£123	£138	£144	£170	£160	£150	£170	£158	£144	£157
£150	£166	£123	£144	£155	£160	£133	£172	£150	£144

a Construct an **ordered stem and leaf diagram**, including a key.

b What is the modal price of the printers ?

c Determine the median price.

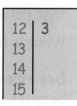

12	3
13	
14	
15	

Scattergraphs

Drawing Scattergraphs

A **Scattergraph** is a statistical graph which makes comparisons of two sets of data.

Example :-

This scattergraph displays the **heights** and **weights** of the players in a Netball team.

- Joy weighs 40 kg.
- Joe is 160 cm tall.
- Jan is 135 cm tall. She weighs 20 kg.

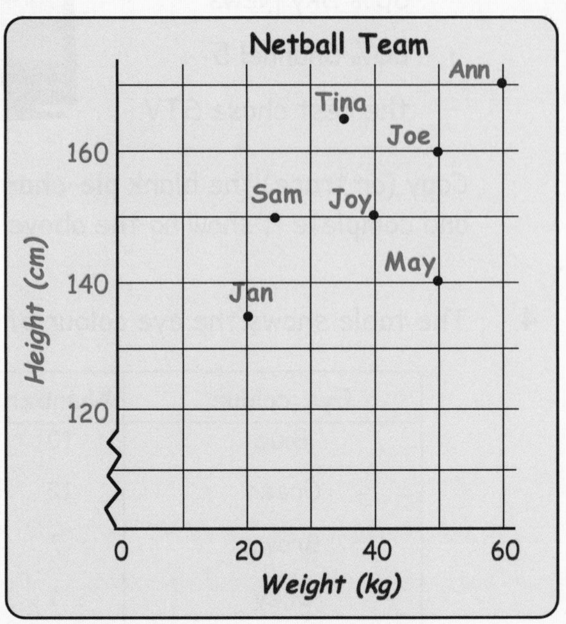

In most scattergraphs you can usually see a relationship (*correlation*) between the two sets of data.

From this graph you could say that the taller you are the heavier you tend to be.

Exercise 1

1. From the scattergraph above, write down the heights and weights of each player.

2. The scattergraph opposite shows the **ages** and **weights** of several children.

   a Who is the :-

   (i) youngest (ii) lightest

   (iii) oldest (iv) heaviest child ?

   b Write down the **age** and **weight** of each child.

   c One child is older than Ali, younger than Pat and is lighter than Shaz.

   What is the child's name ?

   d Describe any **correlation** *(relationship)* between the two sets of data.

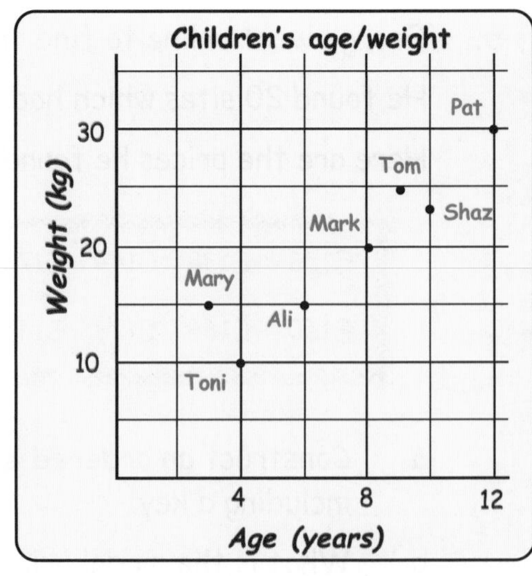

3. This scattergraph shows a correlation between the temperature during the day and the sales of cups of hot soup from Dave's Cafe.

Sales of Cups of Soup

Sales of Hot Soup / *Temperature °C*

a Suggest in words a correlation between the temperature and the sales of cups of hot soup.

b When the temperature was 10°C, how many cups of soup were sold ?

c Use the graph to estimate how many cups of soup will be sold when the temperature is 20°C.

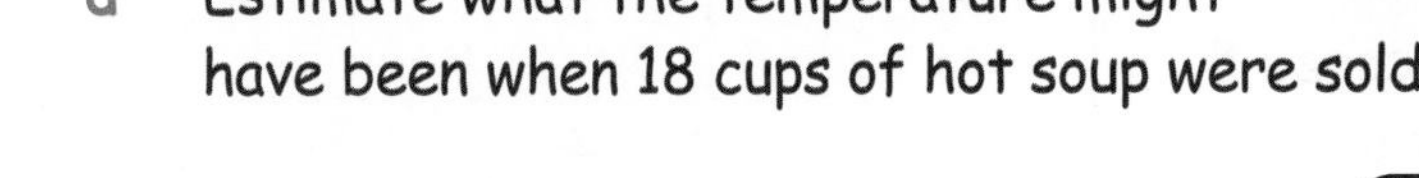

d Estimate what the temperature might have been when 18 cups of hot soup were sold.

4. This scattergraph shows the fares that taxi drivers charge.

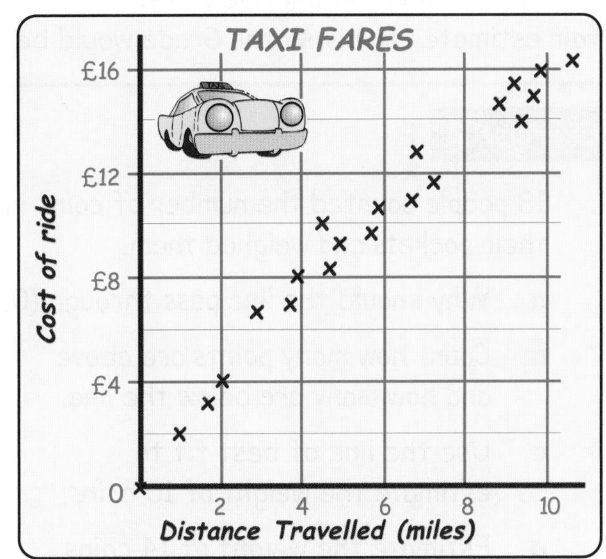

a Is there any correlation between the number of miles travelled and the taxi fare ?

b Why is there a cross at (0, 0) ?

c Use the diagram to find how far you could travel for £6·00.

d Estimate how much an 8 mile journey would cost ?

5. Copy the scattergraph grid from **Question 1**, but plot these pupils on your grid.

Ali is 4 years old and weighs 15 kg.

Jim is 6 years old and weighs 20 kg.

Tia is 7 and weighs 25 kg.

Kol is 10 and weighs 30 kg.

Gio weighs 28 kg and is 9.

Lia weighs 33 kg and is 11.

6. Draw a scattergraph from the data showing heights and shoe sizes of pupils in an S4 class.

	May	Zak	Jack	Tippi	Guy
Height (cm)	120	110	130	145	135
Shoe size	7	6	7	10	8

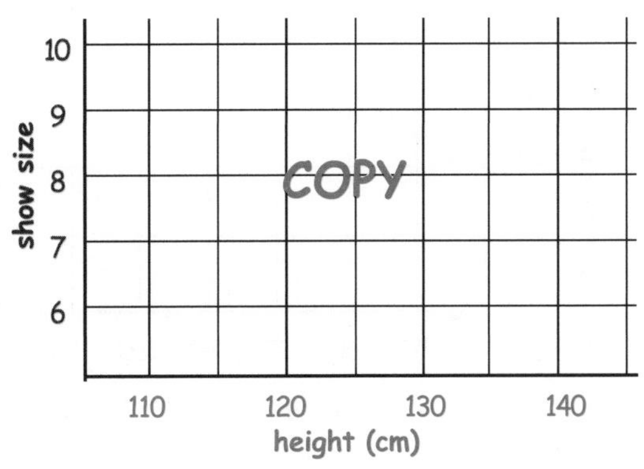

Line of Best Fit

The *correlation* seen here is good enough to allow us to draw a "**best-fitting line**" through the group.

Though the line is only an *estimate*, it should :-

- go through as many points as possible
- split the group so there are roughly as many points above the line as there are below it.

Shown is a good estimate of the **line of best fit**.

We can also use the line to make further **predictions** or **estimates**.

If another boy, Harry, is known to have scored **5** in English, using the line, we can see that a fair estimate for his Maths Grade would be **6**.

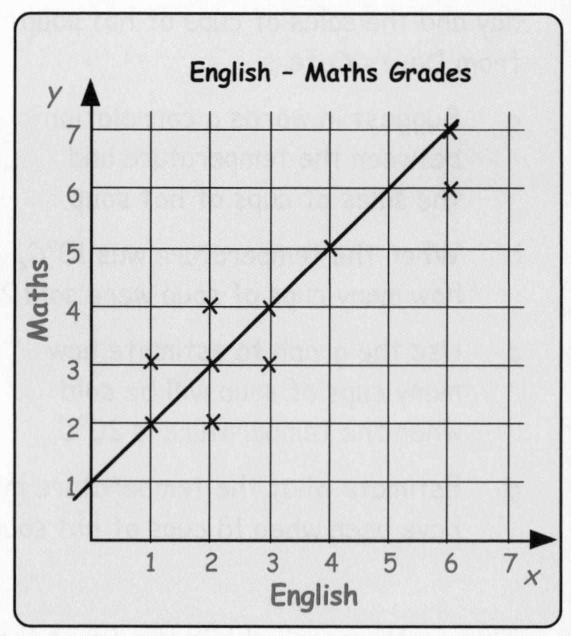

Exercise 2

1. 18 people counted the number of coins in their pockets and weighed them.

   a Why should the line pass through (0, 0) ?

   b Count how many points are above and how many are below the line.

   c Use the line of best fit to estimate the weight of 10 coins.

   d Estimate the weight of 14 coins.

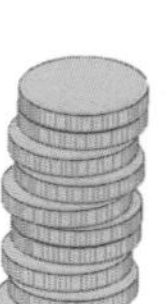

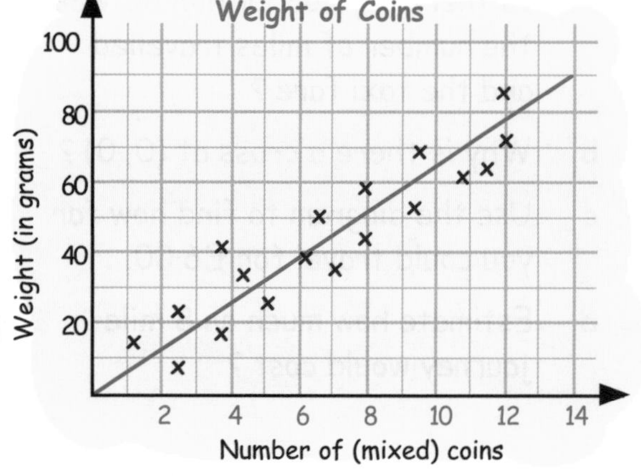

2.

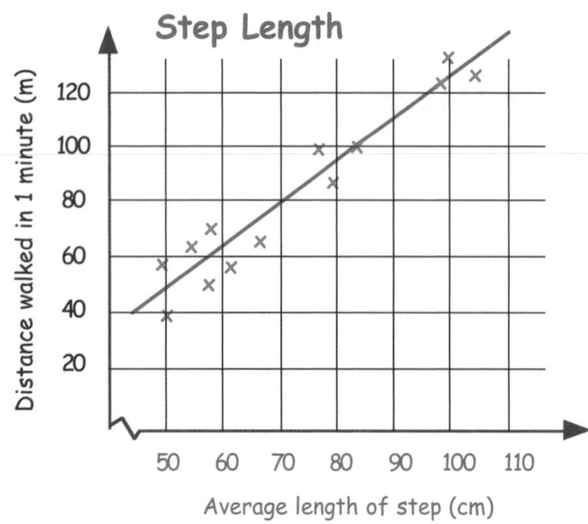

For a group, each person's average step length, and the total distance walked by him/her in a 1 minute period, was recorded.

The scattergraph shows the results along with the line of best fit.

a Joe's average step length is 90 centimetres.

How far should he be able to walk in 1 minute ?

b Debbie walked 80 metres in 1 minute.

Use the line of best fit to estimate Debbie's average step length.

3. This scattergraph shows the number of hours a lady had her central heating on each day, plotted against the average outside daily temperature on each of those days.

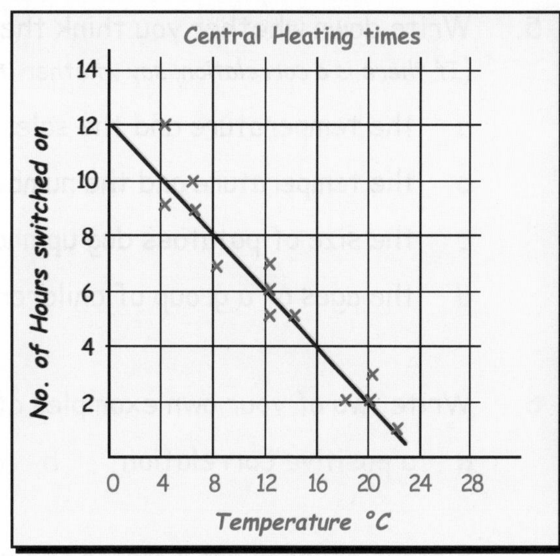

This graph shows a strong negative correlation since all the points lie roughly on a straight line going downwards from left to right.

The line of best fit is also shown.

Use your line to estimate how many hours she would expect to run her central heating for, if the average temperature one day was 16°C.

4. A group of students was asked to say how many hours they studied for a test made up of 50 questions.

The graph shows the number of questions each student got wrong in the test.

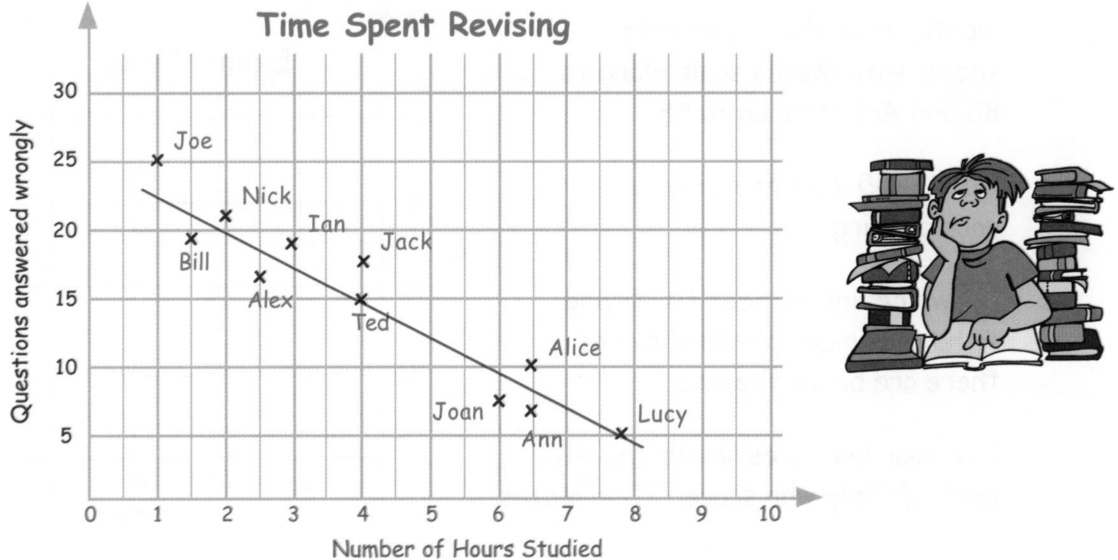

a Describe what kind of correlation there is between the number of hours studied and the number of wrong answers.

b Another student, Nicola, said she had studied for 5 hours for the test.

Estimate how many questions she might be expected to get wrong.

c How many questions might Brian be expected to get wrong if he did not study for the test ?

d

Nancy got all her answers correct.

Use your line of best fit to estimate how many hours she studied for the test.

5. Write down whether you think there will be a correlation between the following :-
(*If there is a correlation, say whether it is positive or negative*).

a the temperature and the sales of ice-cream in June.

b the temperature and the number of people on a beach each day.

c the size of potatoes dug up and the number needed to fill a 5 kg bag.

d the ages of a group of children and the number of coins in their pockets.

6. Write two of your own examples of pairs of measurements where there would be :-

a a positive correlation b a negative correlation c no correlation.

7. Fifteen children sat a Maths and an Art exam. Their marks are listed below.

Maths	60	64	68	76	84	88	74	66	80	88	80	64	80	86	58
Art	58	61	54	44	36	34	44	52	42	30	30	56	40	34	62

a Neatly draw the set of axis shown, with Maths scale along to 88 and Art scale up to 68.

b Plot the 15 sets of marks on your drawing.

c Draw the line of best fit, trying to have as many points above as there are below the line.

d Use your line to estimate the ART mark of Tony who scored 70 in Maths.

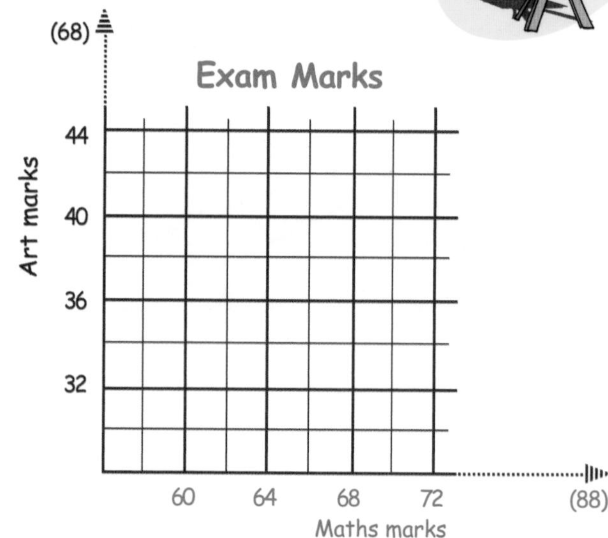

8. The weights and heights of a group of children are recorded in the table below.

Height (cm)	130	140	150	120	155	120	115	140	150	155	125	115	140	145	130	110
Weight (kg)	40	43	48	38	49	40	38	45	46	48	40	36	48	46	42	36

a Draw a scattergraph using the set of axis shown opposite and plot the 16 points of data on your graph.

b Draw a line of best fit.

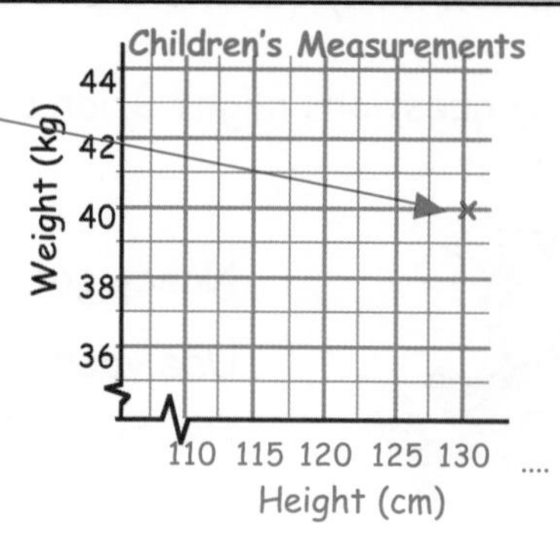

8. c Use your line to estimate how heavy Zoe might be if she is 135 centimetres tall.

d Bobby weighs 47 kilograms.

Use your line of best fit to estimate Bobby's height.

9. Fourteen amateur gardeners were comparing the total weight of tomatoes picked from their tomato plants.

Name	Ted	Ian	Bill	Ed	Joe	Sid	Dan	Len	Bob	Jim	Tom	Lee	Ron	Gus
No. of plants	8	16	19	10	16	20	11	8	15	10	20	6	16	18
Weight (kg)	35	90	90	60	65	105	45	45	70	50	100	30	80	95

a Draw a neat scattergraph and show all 14 sets of data on it.

b Draw the line of best fit.

c Brian had 14 plants.

Use your line to estimate the total weight of Brian's plants.

d John's tomatoes weigh 85 kilograms.

Estimate how many plants John had.

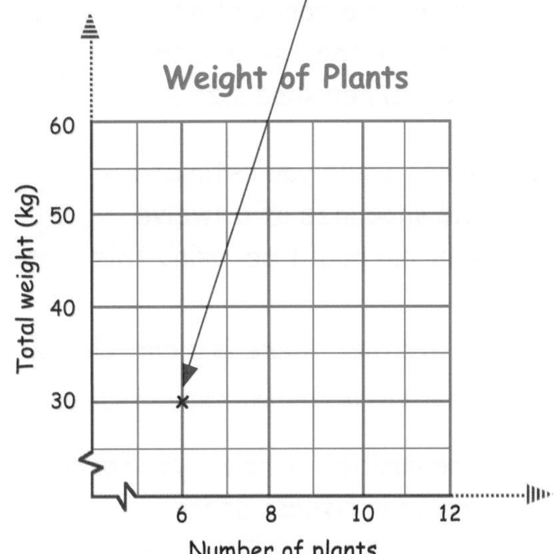

10. Dan was very much overweight.

His doctor put him on a strict diet in January and Dan kept a note at the end of each month of how much weight he had lost (in total).

Month	1	3	5	7	9	11	13	15	17	19	21	23
Total loss (kg)	3·5	4	4	5	5·5	5·5	7	8	6·5	8	9	9·5

a Draw up a set of axes as shown and plot the 12 pairs of pieces of data from the table above.

b Draw a line of best fit on your scattergraph.

c Estimate what his total weight loss might be after :-

(i) 4 months (ii) 8 months

(iii) a year (iv) 2 years.

d Dan actually gained weight at one point.

During which month ?

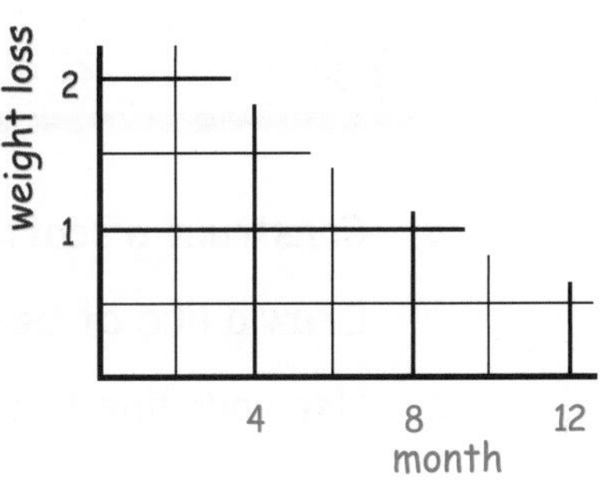

Scattergraphs

Statistics Assessment 3

1. The scattergraph shows the ages and shoe sizes of several children.

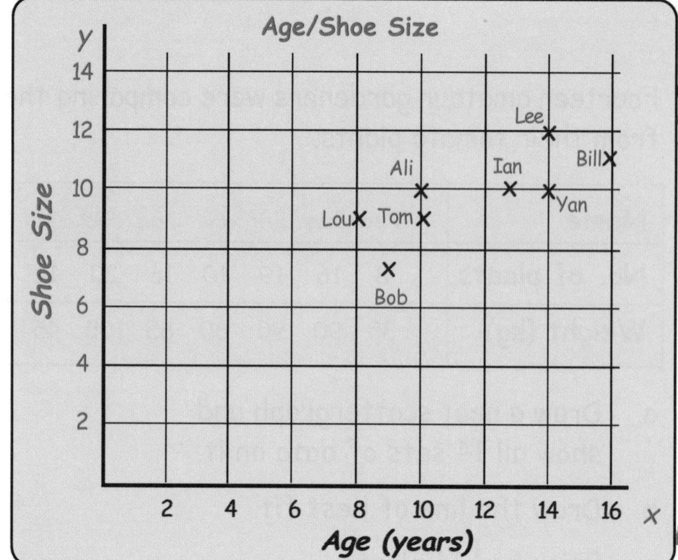

   a Who :-

      (i) is the youngest

      (ii) is the oldest

      (iii) takes the largest shoe ?

   b Is there a correlation between the age of a child and his/her shoe size ?

   c What would you estimate the shoe size of a twelve year old might be, using this graph.

2. State whether there is a correlation between each of the following pairs :-
   (*If there is a correlation, state whether it is positive or negative*).

   a The number of hours you spend exercising and your fitness score.

   b The height and the age of a child.

   c The shoe size of a child and the colour of his/her hair.

   d The sale of woollen scarves and the temperature outside.

3. Eight pupils sit a French exam and an English exam.

   Their results are recorded in the table below.

French	10	35	60	24	56	17	42	49
English	23	57	88	40	85	33	62	?

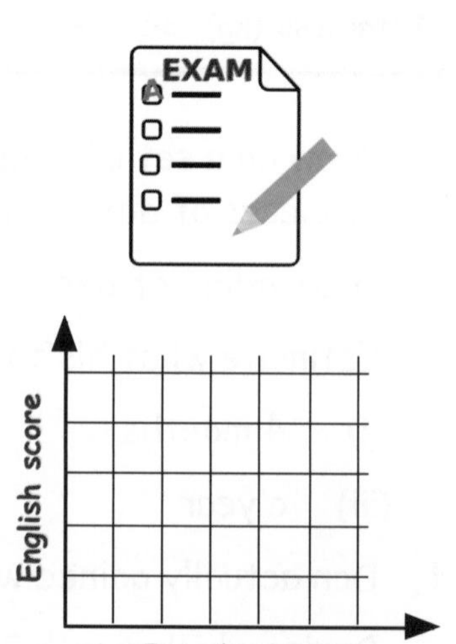

   a Construct a scattergraph from this table.

   b Draw a line of best fit on your scattergraph.

   c Use your line to estimate the missing English mark.

Statistical Chance

Probability in Real Life

Remember :- The PROBABILITY of something happening simply means the FRACTION of times it would happen "in the long run".

Probability is a fraction or decimal and can only take values from 0 to 1.

Examples :- The probability of staying dry when I dive into a pool is 0.

The probability the next baby born in a hospital will be a girl is $\frac{1}{2}$, (0·5).

The probability the sun will rise tomorrow is 1.

Exercise 1

1. This 12 sided dice has the numbers from 1 to 12 marked on it.
   - a What is the probability that when rolled, it stops showing 10 ?

   We say the chances of it showing a 10 is 1 in ......
   - b Does this mean that if we roll the dice 12 times it will stop at 10 exactly 1 time ?
   - c Explain your answer.
   - d How many times might you "roughly" expect a 10 to show if you rolled it :-

     (i) 120 times (ii) 1200 times (iii) 12 000 000 times ?

2. The weatherman says "the chance of it raining in April on any day is 1 in 5".
   - a On how many days in April might you realistically expect rain ?
   - b If it rained on 8 days would you be justified in calling the so called weather expert "rubbish" ?
   - c If not, explain why not.

3. At a charity event, 200 raffle tickets are sold.
   - a If you buy a ticket, what are the chances of it being a winning ticket ?
   - b You buy two strips of 5 tickets. What are your chances now ?
   - c If there are 15 prizes, what are the chances now of winning one of them ?

4. A bag holds 37 red beads, 65 blue beads, 22 green beads and 4 yellow beads.

   To win a game, you must put your hand in and draw out a blue bead.

   Do you have a better than 50-50 chance at winning or not ?

For class discussion :-

5. A roulette wheel has 36 numbers, 1 to 36 + a zero (*37 numbers*)

Since there are 36 numbers, you would think that if you bet on a single number you would get odds of 36 to 1. You don't. You get 35 to 1.

If you put a "chip" across two numbers as shown, you would think the odds would be 36 ÷ 2 = 18 to 1. It's not. You are offered 17 to 1.

If you put a "chip" across 4 numbers as shown, you would think the odds would be 36 ÷ 4 = 9 to 1. It's not. You are offered 8 to 1.

You can use your chip to cover 1, 2, 3, 4, 6, 12 or 18 numbers.

a Try to find where you might place your chip in each of these cases.

b Decide what "odds" you might be offered in each case.

c Discuss whether the casino will win or lose in the short/long term.

6. When you buy a new TV or iPhone, or any electrical goods, the salesman often asks if you would like to buy a 3 year insurance cover on the item. This means that if your TV breaks down, they will cover the repair or replacement cost.

a Find out about the "basic" cover you already have from any manufacturer.

b Joe and Sally buy a new Fridge-Freezer for £595.

They are offered a 3 years' cover plan for £85 per year.

Statistics show that 1 in 10 Freezers break down within 3 years.

Should they take out the extra cover ? Discuss.

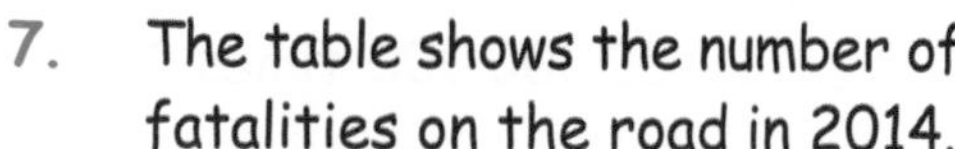

7. The table shows the number of fatalities on the road in 2014.

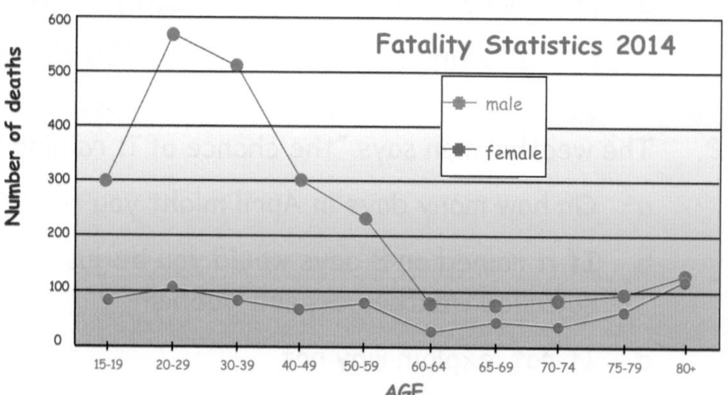

a Discuss the general trend with regard to age and gender.

b Some people think that "very old" people cause or are involved in lots of accidents. Why then is the figure "low" ?

c How do you think these statistics affect how insurance companies determine what the insurance premiums should be for different age groups and sexes ?

d Should there be special rates for women ? Discuss.

e When you become of age to drive, find out what your premium might be. Do you think the actual value of the car you drive will affect your premium ?

8. When you get older, you will probably take out life, car, and house insurance.

Find out what statistical facts might determine how much you might be expected to pay for each of these types of insurance.

For example, will being a smoker or heavy drinker affect your life insurance premium ?

Statistical Chance

Statistics Assessment 4

1. This wheel of fortune has only two sectors.
   You win on blue or you lose on yellow.

   The organisers offer odds of 7 to 1 if you win.

   In the long run, are you likely to come out winning or losing money if you bet on the wheel ?

2. 

   The bookies are offering odds on it snowing on Christmas Day of 10 to 1.

   Over the last 50 years, it has snowed on Christmas Day 6 times.

   Would the odds favour you if you bet on snow next Christmas day ?

3. At a tombola stall, 500 raffle tickets are sold at 20p each.

   a If you buy ten tickets, what are your chances of having a winning ticket ?

   b There are 30 prizes at the tombola stall. Have you a greater than or less than evens chance of winning one of the prizes ?

4. If you go for a day out at the racecourse, the bookie will offer you "odds" when you bet on a horse.

   Note :- (*You need to be at least 18 to gamble in the UK*).

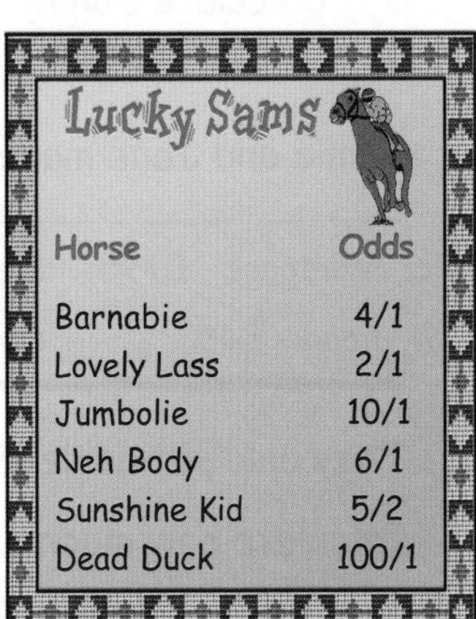

Lucky Sams

Horse	Odds
Barnabie	4/1
Lovely Lass	2/1
Jumbolie	10/1
Neh Body	6/1
Sunshine Kid	5/2
Dead Duck	100/1

   Example :- If you bet £10 on "Neh Body" and it won, the bookie would pay you 6 × your bet, plus your original bet = £60 + £10 = £70.

   a The "favourite" is the horse that pays out least. Which horse is the favourite in this race ?

   b If you bet £25 on the favourite, how much would you get back from the bookie if it came first ?

   c The "outsider" is the horse least likely to win, and it pays out the best odds. Which horse is the outsider here, and how much would I win if I bet £2·00 on it and it came in first ?

   d Why do you think the bookies offer such high odds on the outsider ?

   e What do the odds of 5/2 on Sunshine Kid mean ?

   f If you bet £20 on Sunshine Kid and it won, how much would you get back ?

Unit Assessment
Finance/Statistics

Jamie Stewart works as a teacher and earns £37 800 per year.
His partner, Jane McGavin, works as a gardener and is paid an hourly rate of £8·50.

1. a Calculate Jamie's monthly pay. (1)

   The following deductions are shown on Jamie's monthly pay slip for May :-

   Tax deducted - £702·50, NI deducted - £365·25.

   b Calculate Jamie's net take home pay for May. (2)

2. Jane's timesheet showed that she worked a basic 148 hours in May, as well as 24 hours overtime at time and a half.

   a Calculate Jane's basic pay for May. (2)

   b Calculate her overtime pay and her total pay for the month. (2)

   Jane's deductions for May came to £480·75.

   c Calculate Jane's net take home pay for May. (2)

   d Calculate Jamie and Jane's combined income for May. (1)

3. Jamie and Jane made a list of their monthly expenditure.

Mortgage - £795	Electricity - £185	Council Tax - £220	Mobiles - £69·50
Food - £450	Car Payment - £175	Petrol/Insurance - £295	Clothes - £100

   They also put aside £200 per month towards their holiday fund.

   Calculate how much of their income they have left at the end of May. (3)

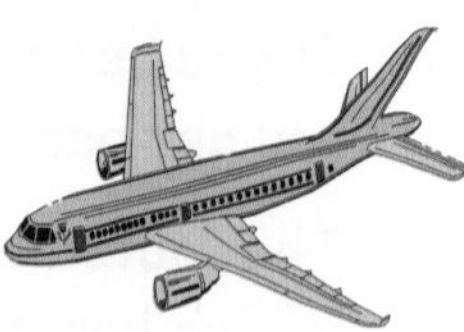

4. They decide to book a week's holiday to Majorca in July.

   They consider two airlines :-

   - Easyfly charges £185 each, plus £15 per person for luggage, (each way).
   - Ryansoar's costs are £232·50 each, but all luggage is free.

     Ryansoar also offers them a 10% reduction as an incentive to fly with them.

   Which airline offers the better deal for Jamie and Jane ? (6)

5. They want to take at least 600 euros with them for spending money.

The Post Office offers a rate of £1 = €1·30.

What is the least amount in £s (to the nearest £1) they need to change, in order that they have the 600 euros they wish to take with them ? (2)

6. As Christmas approaches, Jamie and Jane find they need to borrow £500 to help buy Christmas presents for their parents.

If they take a bank loan out over a year, the annual interest rate is 12·5%

If they pay it back over 6 months, the interest rate is only 10·2%.

a Calculate how much the monthly repayment would be for paying the loan back over 1 year. (3)

b What would each payment be if they only took the loan out for 6 months. (3)

c How much more expensive is it if they take the loan out over 1 year ? (2)

7. 

Over the festive period, they both use taxis a lot to travel around town.

They take a note of the mileage travelled by taxi and the fare charged.

Distance (miles)	5	8	10	3	7	9	12	4	15
Cost of journey (£s)	10·00	£15·00	£19·50	£6·50	£14·50	£17·00	£25·50	£7·50	£28·50

a Draw up a scattergraph on squared paper showing the two axes and plot the 9 sets of data. (2)

b Draw the line of best fit on your graph. (1)

c Use it to estimate the cost of a taxi journey of 11 miles. (1)

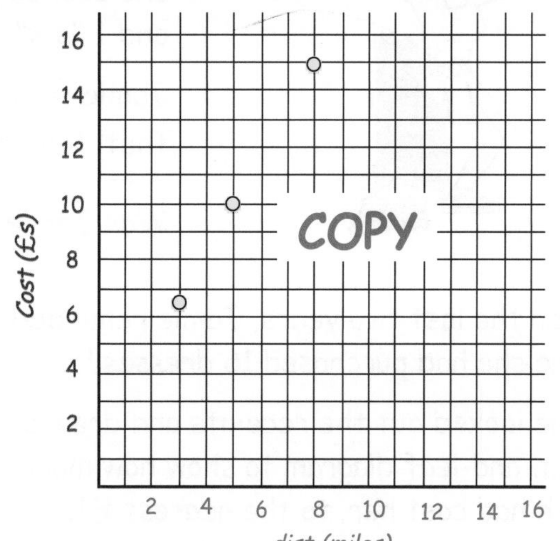

8. Jamie decides it's time to paint the doors and windows on the outside of their house.

They take a walk round their estate one night, noting the various door colours.

red	black	brown	black	blue	brown	blue	red
blue	green	red	red	brown	red	blue	brown
brown	red	brown	blue	red	black	blue	green
red	brown	blue	red	red	brown	red	green

a Show the information in a frequency table. (3)

b Show the information on an appropriate graph. (3)

9. Jamie went for a game of golf with his friend, Andy, to the local nine hole course.

They kept a note of their scores for each hole.

hole	1	2	3	4	5	6	7	8	
Jamie	6	10	7	9	5	2	6	11	7
Andy	7	5	6	8	4	4	7	7	6

a Calculate the mean score and the range of scores for each golfer. (5)

b Make two statements about the golfing skills of the two friends. (2)

10.

Jane is a really good golfer.

The last time she played an 18 hole round, she scored 6 "threes", 8 "fours", 3 "fives and 1 "six".

Jamie worked out that from this, the probability that Jane scored a "five" at a hole was $\frac{1}{5}$.

Was Jamie's calculation correct ? *Explain.*

11. Over the last two years, Jamie reminded Jane she had purchased 16 dresses !

Jane looked out the receipts and drew a stem-and-leaf diagram to show how much each had cost her, to the nearest £1.

How many of her dresses cost over £40 ? (1)

Stem	Leaves
1	9
2	1 1 3 7 9 9
3	0 5 5 7
4	5 8 9 9
5	0 5 5

Key 1 | 9 = £19

Added Value
Specimen Paper 1

20 minutes

Marks

1. At his local Chinese restaurant, Joseph ordered Chicken Noodle Soup at £3·50, Sweet and Sour Chicken at £7·70 and a portion of Egg Fried Rice.

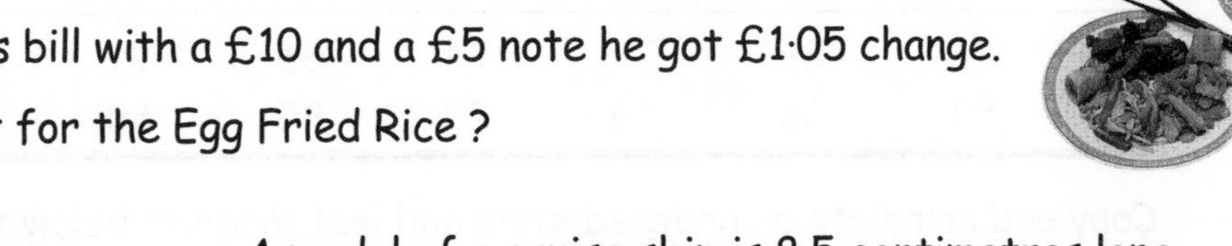

When he paid his bill with a £10 and a £5 note he got £1·05 change.

How much was it for the Egg Fried Rice ? (3)

2. 

A model of a cruise ship is 8·5 centimetres long.

The model was made using a scale of *1 cm = 30 metres*.

What is the length of the real cruise ship ? (3)

3. Eve laid out ten glasses, each with the same amount of water in them.

She poured in the following quantities of diluting orange juice :-

50 ml, 43 ml, 55 ml, 46 ml, 40 ml, 57 ml, 54 ml, 48 ml, 60 ml, 56 ml.

She then threw out the one with least amount of orange for being too watery and also the one with the greatest amount for being too strong.

The eight quantities left were all acceptable.

a From these eight drinks, write down the minimum and the maximum amount of diluting orange juice preferred. (1)

b Write the desired amount of orange juice in tolerance form (.... ± ....) ml. (2)

4. Mr Preston is considering taking out a £10 000 loan with *Jules Bank* to buy a car.

With *Jules Bank*'s 2% per annum interest rate, he would owe £10 200 after 1 year.

The garage he is buying the car from is offering him the same car for £9800 if he takes on their interest rate of 5% per annum.

Which option should Mr Preston take ? *(Give a reason for your answer)* (5)

5. A survey was carried out looking into how long it took seven television companies to answer telephone calls regarding technical faults in their system.

The results, in minutes, are shown below.

13	10	18	8	15	9	11

a Calculate the mean number of minutes taken. (3)

b How many companies took longer than the mean time ? (1)

Added Value
Specimen Paper 2

40 minutes

Marks

1. An insurance salesman keeps a record of how old some of his clients were when they "passed away".

63	72	89	75	74	66	81	88	47
51	53	66	46	79	80	68	43	82

a Copy and complete an ordered stem and leaf diagram below to show this data.

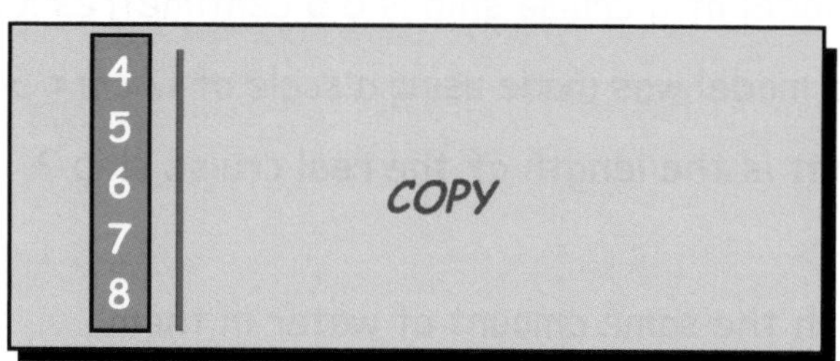

.... (2)

b What was the age of the second oldest person in the group ? (1)

c What was the middle age (median) of the group ? (1)

2. Two plane companies give offers on tours over the lochs of Scotland.

- *"ALLEGRO"* offers a 20 minute tour at a cost of £29.
- *"BONITONS"* offers 25 minutes for £37.

Which company gives better value for money ? (3)

(Explain your choice carefully)

3. a Rick earns £14 an hour as a labourer.

He gets paid time and a half for working Saturdays.

How much did he get for working 6 hours last Saturday ? (2)

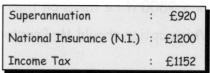

b Rick's wife Alicia gets a gross annual salary of £15 200.

She has to pay the following deductions :-

Superannuation	:	£920
National Insurance (N.I.)	:	£1200
Income Tax	:	£1152

(i) Work out Alesha's total deductions.

(ii) What is her net annual salary ? (2)

4. A full oil storage tank is drained down to allow a repair to be made, because it has a leak.

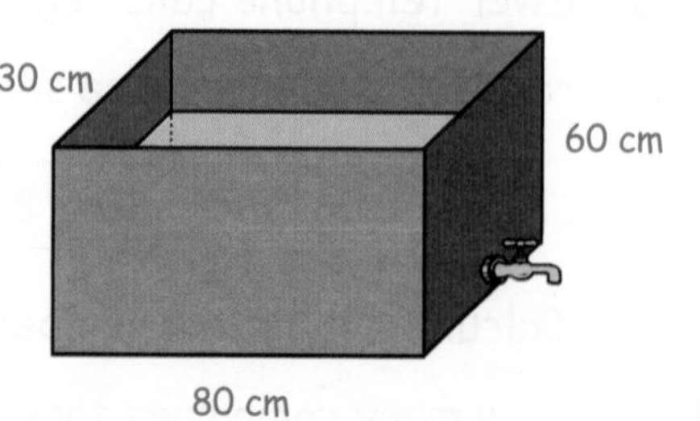

a Calculate the volume of a full tank. (2)

b When the tap is opened, the oil flows out at a rate of 4·5 litres per minute.

How many minutes will it take to empty ? (3)

Marks

5\. a Henry flew from Glasgow at 8 pm on Friday, bound for New Zealand.

Including stops, the 11 000 mile journey took 25 hours.

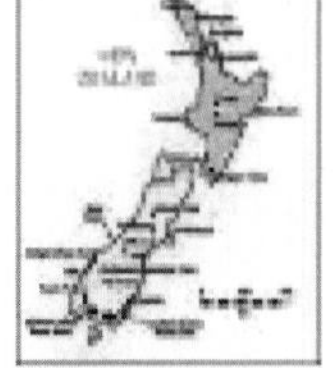

(i) On what day and at what time (our time) did his plane land in New Zealand ? (2)

(ii) Calculate the average speed of the plane, in miles per hour. (3)

b When he returned to the UK he changed 235 New Zealand dollars back into British money at the rate of :-

£1 = 1·89 NZ Dollars.

How much did he get, to the nearest whole pence ? (3)

6\. This pie chart, shows the sale of pies in a butcher's shop one Friday

Butcher's Pie Sales

a What fraction represents :-

(i) Steak (ii) Curry ?

1000 pies were sold altogether that day.

b How many of the pies sold were :-

(i) Mince (ii) Chicken ? (4)

7\. A football pitch measures 40 metres from a corner flag to the centre line.

The distance from the centre spot to the corner flag is 50 metres, as shown.

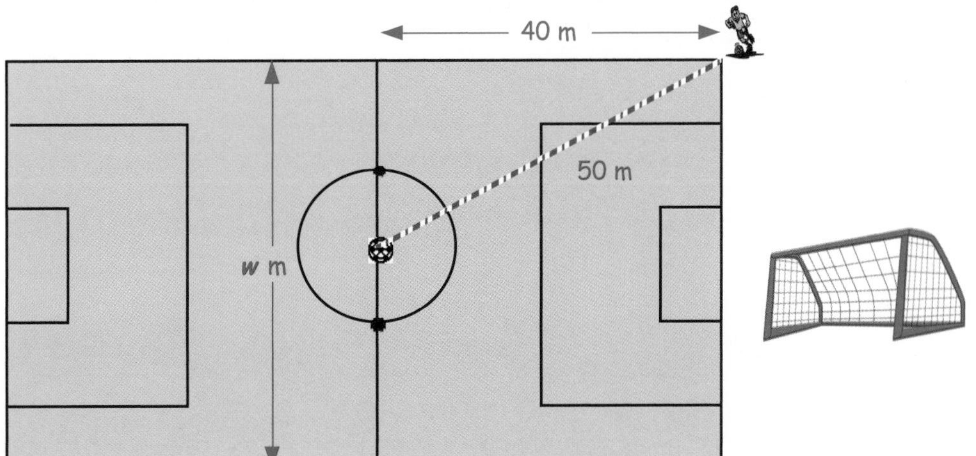

Calculate the width across the pitch. (w metres) (4)

End of National 4 Lifeskills Course

answers to National 4 Lifeskills

Answers to Chapter 0 (page 1)

1. a 12 000 b 36 000
2. 4700 + 1900 = 6600
3. a 10 200 b 16 700
4. a twenty thousand eight hundred and six
   b three million, two hundred and seven thousand and eighty
5. a 3210 b 32 258 c 10 164 d 7538
6. a 15 702 b 108 630 c 1433 d 11 292
7. a 447 g b 4500 ml
8. a 258 b 3·92 c 0·74
9. a 5 017 000 b 3308 c 96 300 d 1600
10. a 30 b 12·1 d 5·10 d 200·0
11. a 22·57 b 85·93 c 48·42 d 15·63
    e 62·39 f 22·24 g 3·95 h 105·28
12. a 60·301 b 0·236 c 34 d 0·068
13. a 4 b 38 c 2 d 24
14. -16°C
15. a -6 b 6 c -4 d -30
16. $^{1}/_{9}$
17. 36%
18. 10%
19. a $^{6}/_{10}$ b $^{14}/_{22}$
20. a $^{3}/_{4}$ b $^{2}/_{3}$
21. a £1·60 b 150 m
22. a £8 b 40p c £3·25
23. 80%
24. Total = £43·25. £45. Change = £1·75 - YES
25. A = 12p per square, B = 11p per square - B √
26. a 3.50 pm b 12.10 am
27. a 2 min 5 sec b 325 mins
28. a 8 min 20 sec b 3 min 25 sec
29. Owens by 3·7 secs
30. 7 hours 15 mins
31. a 70 km/hr b 24 km c 3 hours
32. a 5·2 cm, 52 mm, 5 cm 2 mm
    b 9·7 cm, 97 mm, 9 cm 7 mm
33. a 536 cm b 1004 cm
34. a 2345 g b 5050 g
35. a 3200 ml b 4750 ml
36. In a rect, all angles are 90° - not so in parm
    Rect has 2 lines of symmetry - parm has none
    Rect-diagonals are same length - not in a parm
37. 8
38. A = triangular prism B = square pyramid
    C = cylinder D = cone

Chapter 1 - Whole Numbers

Chapter 1 Exercise 1 - page 4

1. a 2 b 6 c 8 d 20
   e 47 f 81 g 23 h 2
   i 33 j 97
2. a 12 sec b 32 sec c 16 sec d 79 sec
   e 84 sec f 47 sec g 7 sec h 53 sec
3. a 14 b 9 c 30 d 64
   e 39 f 16 g 30 h 64

Chapter 1 Exercise 2 - page 4

1. a 50 b 30 c 20 d 50
   e 70 f 80 g 90 h 60
   i 10 j 110 k 310 l 420
   m 650 n 700 o 5010
2. a 60 cm b 70 cm c 90 cm d 90 cm
   e 100 cm f 180 cm g 550 cm h 800 cm
   i 930 cm j 1010 cm
3. a 100 b 600 c 800 d 500
   e 800 f 700 g 500 h 100
   i 6200 j 4700 k 2600 l 9300
   m 8100 n 3600 o 8500
4. a 2000 b 12 000 c 32 000 d 20 000
   e 34000 f 72 000 g 1000 h 66 000
   i 79 000 j 92 000 k 57 000 l 235 000
   m 624 000 n 362 000 o 799 000

Chapter 1 Exercise 3 - page 5

1. a 900 b 1000 c 4200 d 6000
   e 16 000 f 60 000 g 20 h 20
   i 10 j 800 k 200 l 200
2. 1798
3. a 896 b 1368 c 18 178 d 10 479

Chapter 1 Exercise 4 - page 6

1. a 160 b 90 c 350 d 680
   e 840 f 1260 g 3440 h 6200
   i 9100 j 8010 k 23 090 l 68 040
2. a 1200 b 4500 c 8700 d 5000
   e 20 900 f 43 700 g 78 000 h 90 100
3. a 4000 b 26 000 c 58 000 d 79 000
   e 90 000 f 435 000 g 760 000 h 700 000

Chapter 1 Exercise 5 - page 6

1. a 4 b 9 c 22 d 38
   e 91 f 160 g 720 h 463
   i 500 j 4700 k 8770 l 1395
2. a 7 b 9 c 19 d 53
   e 80 f 210 g 420 h 861
3. a 5 b 18 c 24 d 60
   e 225 f 390 g 510 h 800

Chapter 1 Exercise 6 - page 7

1. a 840 b 570 c 1150 d 1920
   e 3600 f 6200 g 13 000
2. a 3600 b 12 300 c 8500 d 15 400
   e 13 200 f 27 000 g 15 600 h 7000
   i 963 000 j 125 000

Chapter 1 Exercise 7 - page 7

1. a 13 b 9 c 45 d 40
   e 330 f 680 g 920
2. a 91 b 73 c 41 d 65
   e 88 f 31 g 910

Chapter 2 - Decimals

Chapter 2 Exercise 1 - page 9

1. a 0·4 b 0·7 c 1·3
   d 2·5 e 3·3 f 4·6
2. a 0·7 b 1·4 c 2·3
3. a 0·83 b 0·44 c 0·52
   d 1·28 e 2·65 f 0·09
4. a b c

Chapter 2 Exercise 2 - page 10

1. a 7·2 cm b 15·7 cm c 9·9 cm
   d 20·3 cm e 2·4 kg f 3·6 litres
2. a 4·6 oz b 16·7 oz c 37·6 g d 10·0 g
3. a 1·27 cm b 5·96 cm c 4·55 cm
   d 10·28 mm e 0·38 kg f 2·83 pounds
4. a 0·26 m b 3·62 m c 1·37 °C
   d 5·35 °C e 3·04 kg f 0·68 pounds

Chapter 2 Exercise 3 - page 12

1. a 1·36 b 3·72 c 4·62 d 2·76
   e 11·31 f 0·49 g 7·99
2. a 1·44 b 6·05 c 2·85 d 0·78
   e 15·39 f 9·01 g 12·59 h 0·03
3. a 1·29 b 2·97 c 5·33
   d 6·19 e 9·92 f 8·04
   g 4·98 h 6·05 i 10·87
   j 0·28 k 12·11 l 0·09
4. a 4·29 b 4·35 c 3·42
   d 19·24 e 5·73 f 0·75
   g 2·97 h 5·37 i 4·99
5. a 0·43 b 0·58 c 0·44 d 0·86
   e 0·77 f 0·55 g 0·10
6. a £3·85 b 2·08 kg c £7·55
   d $^{5}/_{7}$ = 0·71, $^{2}/_{3}$ = 0·67 (s), $^{7}/_{9}$ = 0·78 (b)

Chapter 2 Exercise 4 - page 14

1. a 22·69 b 46·95 c 62·96
   d 29·64 e 85·94 f 85·01
   g 12·14 h 26·65 i 37·37
   j 12·69 k 24·99 l 30·22
2. a 8·52 b 41·45 c 15·41
   d 28·83 e 29·47 f 12·72
3. a 9·57 b 3·03 c 10·99
   d 8·75 e 33·52 f 79·08
4. a £2·49 b (i) 12·04 kg (ii) 1·54 kg

Chapter 2 Exercise 5 - page 16

1. a 22·4 b 22·56 c 48·56
   d 29·67 e 91·98 f 8·73
   g 95·76 h 194·88 i 67·05
   j 98·7 k 75·42 l 90
2. a 163·7 g b £17·43 c £62·80 d 10·26 L
   e 22 L f 19·38 kg g 444·3 g

Chapter 2 Exercise 6 - page 17

1. a 7·43 b 5·67 c 6·89
d 5·55 e 7·68 f 5·62
g 6·72 h 3·53 i 0·42
j 8·43 k 2·54 l 1·74
2. a £15·54 b 7·27 cm c 15·71
d 1·56 kg e 0·69 L f 45·74 s
g (i) 2·89 kg (ii) 14·45 kg

Chapter 2 Exercise 7 - page 19

1. a 54·6 b 31·9 c 8·5
d 147·2 e 87 f 9
g 213·4 h 67·6 i 827
2. a 76·1 b 18·2 c 6·9 d 63·2
e 161·8 f 475 g 0·3 h 10·8
3. a 932 b 357 c 126·4 d 87·3
e 1218 f 104·9 g 0·1 h 750
4. a 1·9 g b 19 g
5. a 11·5 L b 115 L
6. a 1225 b 467 c 13180
d 4·26 e 3 f 50·5

Chapter 2 Exercise 8 - page 20

1. a 0·58 b 1·72 c 0·265
d 0·076 e 5·9 f 0·006
g 1·83 h 3·372 i 0·6
j 0·421 k 3·57 l 24·21
m 0·856 n 0·7321 o 0·098
p 0·45 q 5·3 r 0·048
s 0·774 t 2·39 u 0·026
2. move all figures 3 places right
3. a 0·2471 b 1·649 c 0·0235
d 0·3652 e 0·069 f 6·75
g 0·65 h 3·275 i 0·0258
4. a 54 p b 4 p c 0·00614 kg
d 8·7 cm e 150 g
5. a 1·2 cm b 4·2 cm c 0·58 cm
d 0·3 cm e 0·07 cm
6. a 4·22 m b 8·05 m c 0·99 m
d 0·467 m f 0·058 m
7. a 43·25 km b 0·437 km
c 0·069 km d 0·0326 km
e 0·0051 km

Chapter 3 - Percentages

Chapter 3 Exercise 1 - page 23

1. a 17/100, 0·17 b 26/100, 0·26
c 48/100, 0·48 d 12/100, 0·12
e 75/100, 0·75 f 6/100, 0·06
g 2/100, 0·02 h 8/100, 0·08
i 10·5/100, 0·105 j 1·2/100, 0·012
2. a 9/20 b 3/10 c 7/20 d 3/5
e 1/2 f 1/4 g 3/4 h 1/10
i 1/20 j 3/25 k 9/25 l 18/25
m 1/25 n 4/5 o 13/20 p 7/25
q 9/10
3. a 18% b 25% c 12% d 40%
e 30% f 55% g 50% h 5%
i 35% j 28% k 12·5% l 62·5%
m 70% n 3%
4. a 70% b 70% c 70% d 30%
e 96% f 90% g 87·5% h 50%
5. Fr - 20%, Ar - 90%, Ge 30%, Mu - 52%
Art - Music - Geography - French

Chapter 3 Exercise 2 - page 24

1. a £6·00 b £7·20 c £2·20 d £144
e £110 f £7·20 g £3888 h £5·85
i 10p j £1·10 k £3·04 l 11p
m 55p n 48p o £8·75 p £5
2. a (i) 117 (ii) 63 b 76 L
c su - 156 g, st - 312 g, pr - 104 g,
fi - 45·5 g, fa - 32·5 g
d 54 kg e £154 f 16 hours

Chapter 3 Exercise 3 - page 26

1. £440 2. £400
3. 73·5 poundals 4. 4900 ft
5. 3·75 metres 6. 53 kg
7. 28°C 8. 896°C
9. 27·6 mph 10. 53 miles
11. £40800 12. £25750
13. 43 days
14. a £651 b £504
c (i) £1720 (ii) £86 (iii) £1806

Chapter 3 Exercise 4 - page 29

1. £48 2. £55·25
3. £414 4. 16250 ft
5. 638 units 6. 147 mph
7. 102 mm 8. 14·4°C
9. 72·8 kg 10. 129 left
11. 8·7 cm 12. £52·50
13. £229·46

Chapter 4 - Fractions

Chapter 4 Exercise 1 - page 32

1. a 1/2 b 3/4 c 1/3 d 1/6
e 2/5 f 1/4 g 1/2 h 5/6
i 2/3 j 5/8
2. a 6 boxes b 3 boxes c 4 boxes
d 9 boxes e 10 boxes f 7 boxes
3. a 1/3 b 1/3 = 2/6
4. a 2/4 b 2/6 c 9/12 = 3/4
5. a 6/8 b 12/16 c 6/8 9/12 12/15 15/20 etc
6. a 2/4 etc b 4/6 etc c 6/10 etc
d 10/12 etc e 2/6 etc f 14/20 etc
7. a (i) 1/6 (ii) 3/5 (iii) 7/10 (iv) 5/11 (v) 11/15 (vi) 9/14
b (i) 1/4 (ii) 3/5 (iii) 1/7 (iv) 7/9 (v) 10/13 (vi) 2/9
c (i) 1/3 (ii) 3/5 (iii) 13/20 (iv) 7/10 (v) 7/11 (vi) 30/41
8. a 3/4 b 1/3 c 1/2 d 2/3
e 3/4 f 2/3 g 4/5 h 1/4
i 4/5 j 7/10 k 1/3 l 3/4
m 10/11 n 3/7 o 3/4 p 1/7
q 3/7 r 3/5 s 5/6 t 4/9

Chapter 4 Exercise 2 - page 34

1. a 8 b 6 c 9
d 10 e 9 f 3
g 5 h 7 i 3
j 5 k 15 l 3
2. a 92 b 95 c 115
d 262 e 323 f 546
g 500 h 123 i 310
3. a 14 b 12
c 4 d 16 e 10
f 9 g 15 h 6
i 9 j 70 k 21
l 15 m 18 n 90
4. a 108 b 105
c 100 d 510 e 980
f 57 g 200 h 159
i 574 j 165 k 740
5. a (i) 630 (ii) 420
b (i) £95 (ii) £57
c (i) 72 (ii) 12

Chapter 4 Exercise 3 - page 36

1. Discussion
2.

100%	50%	$33\frac{1}{3}$ %	25%	20%	10%	5%	1%
1	$\frac{1}{2}$	$\frac{1}{3}$	$\frac{1}{4}$	$\frac{1}{5}$	$\frac{1}{10}$	$\frac{1}{20}$	$\frac{1}{100}$

3. a £10 b £31 c £700
4. a £3 b £50 c £7 d £90
5. a £5 b £9 c £700
6. a £85 b £11 c £12
d £11 e £3 f £22
g £12 h £45 i £130
j £1300 k £60 l £4
7. 70 ladies
8. a £111 b £333
9. a £18 b £36

Chapter 4 Exercise 4 - page 37

1. a 3/4 b 2/5 c 3/5 d 4/5
e 2/3 f 3/10 g 7/10 h 9/10
2. Table copied
3. a £12 b £32 c £12 d £14
4. a (i) £15 (ii) £45 b (i) £5 (ii) £10
c (i) £18 (ii) £72 d (i) £8 (ii) £16
e (i) £7 (ii) £49 f (i) £14 (ii) £42
g (i) £36 (ii) £72 h (i) £50 (ii) £450
i (i) £16 (ii) £8
5. a £21
b £6 c £15 d £32
e £33 f £42 g £33
h £24 i £66 j £104
6. a £84 b £28

Chapter 5 - Time/Distance/Speed

Chapter 5 Exercise 1 - page 40

1. a 0130 b 0445 c 0600
d 1930 e 1415 f 1500
g 0615 h 0820 i 0210
j 0750 k 1200 l 0045
m 1245 n 2115 o 0325
p 2020 q 2355 r 0955
s 2220 t 1134 u 2047
2. a 1.40 am b 11.10 am c 9.25 am
d 2.30 pm e 5.40 pm f 11.15 pm
g 2.45 am h 7.15 pm i 1.10 pm
j 7.03 pm k noon l 6.30 am
m 5.25 am n 3.20 pm o 11.55 pm
p 7.35 pm q 12.20 am r 7.58 am
s 11.47 am t 8.30 pm u 9.55 pm

Chapter 5 Exercise 2 - page 41

1. a 4 hrs b 5 hrs 30 mins
c 7 hrs 30 mins d 3 hrs 45 mins
e 2 hrs 35 mins f 2 hrs 45 mins
g 3 hrs 5 mins h 1 hr 25 mins
i 2 hrs 50 mins j 2 hrs 50 mins
2. 2 hrs 55 mins
3. a (i) 1 hr 5 mins (ii) 1 hr 40 mins
(iii) 6 hr 50 min
b (i) 1.40 pm (ii) 3.20 pm

Chapter 5 Exercise 3 - page 42

1. a 10 km b 12 km c 36 km d 210 km
2. a 92 m b 540 m c 1280 m d 39 m
3. a 20 m b 9 m c 125 m
d 135 km e 2600 m
4. a 1 m b 7 m c 15 m
d 45 km e 14 km
5. a 710 m b 45 m c 15 m

Chapter 5 Exercise 4 - page 43

1. a 4 mph b 7 km/hr c 30 mph d 2100 km/hr
2. a 30 km/hr b 80 mph c 20 m/sec d 6·5 km/hr e 5000 mph f 40 000 km/hr
3. a 80 mph b 310 mph c 83 mph d 11 mph e 69 mph
4. a 42·5mph b 34 mph c 22 mph d 6 mph e 1 metre/hr
5. a 8 km/hr b 28 mph c 26 km/hr d 60 km/hr e 420 mph
6. 70 km/hr
7. a 1 hr 30 min b 200 mph
8. 3 mph

Chapter 5 Exercise 5 - page 45

1. a 1 hr 30 min b 2 hrs 30 min c 3 hrs 15 min d 5 hrs 45 min e 4 hrs 30 min f 6 hrs 15 min g 7 hrs 30 min h 8 hrs 30 min i 2 hrs 15 min j 1 hr 15 min k 4 hrs 45 min l 0 hrs 45 min
2. a 2·5 hrs b 1·25 hrs c 3·75 hrs d 2·25 hrs e 5·5 hrs f 6·5 hrs g 4·75 hrs h 8·75 hrs
3. a 1 hr b 4 hrs c 30 sec d 7 hrs e 4 hrs f 2 hrs g 2 hrs h 1·5 hrs
4. a 11 am b 4 pm c 11.15 am
5. a 1 hr 30 min b 2 hrs 30 min c 1 min 40 secs d 3 hrs 30 min
6. a 60 miles, 2 hrs b 70 miles, 1 hr c 90 miles, 1 hr 30 mins
7. a 1 hr 15 mins b 12.30 pm
8. a 5 hr 30 mins b 1.00 am Sunday
9. 4 seconds

Chapter 5 Exercise 6 - page 47

1. a 3 hrs b 25 km/hr c 100 miles d 70 mph e 4 hr 30 min f 20 metres
2. 80 mph
3. 2 hr 30 min
4. 40 km
5. 185 miles/hr
6. 1 hr 15 mins
7. 18600 miles
8. a 4 mph b 7·5 minutes
9. 2500 miles
10. 3 minutes
11. a Wilma 68 mph - ok b Freddie 72 mph - not ok c Nina 69 mph - ok

Chapter 6 - Area and Perimeter

Chapter 6 Exercise 1 - page 50

1. 15 cm^2
2. a 4 cm^2 b 7 cm^2 c 10 cm^2 d 12 cm^2 e 13 cm^2 f 12 cm^2 g 11 cm^2 h 10 cm^2 i 14 cm^2 j 8 cm^2 k 12 cm^2
3. a 8 cm^2 b 16 cm^2 c 17·5 cm^2 d 24 cm^2 e 12 cm^2
4. a 8 cm^2 b 8 cm^2 c 14 cm^2 d 20 cm^2 e 26 cm^2
5. a 25 cm^2 b 25 cm^2 c 28 cm^2 d 32 cm^2 e 50 cm^2

Chapter 6 Exercise 2 - page 53

1. a/b 12 cm^2 c 12 cm^2
2. 40 cm^2
3. a 54 cm^2 b 35 cm^2 c 30 cm^2 d 165 cm^2 e 49 cm^2 f 300 cm^2
4. a 12 m^2 b 15 m^2 c 26 m^2 d 84 m^2 e 120 m^2

5/ a 320 m^2 b 270 m^2 c 500 m^2

Chapter 6 Exercise 3 - page 55

1. a 24 cm b 41 cm c 58 cm d 28 m e 26·2 mm f 66 cm
2. a 78 cm b 44 m c 20·8 mm
3. 4·6 m

Chapter 6 Exercise 4 - page 56

1. a 4·0 cm, 40 mm, 4 cm 0 mm
   b 5·3 cm, 53 mm, 5 cm 3 mm
   c 6·7 cm, 67 mm, 6 cm 7 mm
   d 7·9 cm, 79 mm, 7 cm 9 mm
   e 2·0 cm, 20 mm, 2 cm 0 mm
   f 8·6 cm, 86 mm, 8 cm 6 mm
2. a 7·1 c, 4·1 cm, 5·5 cm => P = 16·7 cm
   b 4·1 cm, 4·5 cm, 6·9 cm, 3·8 cm => P = 19·3 cm
   c 4·5 cm 4·5 cm, 6·6 cm, 6·6 cm => P = 22·2 cm
   d 5 sides each 3·6 cm => P = 18·0 cm

Chapter 6 Exercise 5 - page 57

1. a 70° b 160° c 90° d 65° e 115° f 95° g 100° h 54 ° i 120°
2. a 60° b 30° c 110° d 140° e 50° f 160°
3. a 27°(±1°) b 112°(±1°) c 41°(±1°) d 115°(±1°) e 108°(±1°) f 140°(±1°) g 12°(±1°) h 175°(±1°)

Chapter 7 - Integers

Chapter 7 Exercise 1 - page 60

1. a 4°C b -4°C c -8°C d -9°C e 6°C f -16°C g -10°C h -30°C
2. a a minus or negative amount = -£50
   b (i) £63·50 in your bank account
   (ii) overdrawn by £40
   (iii) overdrawn by £211·30
3. a -£5 b +£55 c -£80 d -£60
4. a £85 b -£10·60 c -£120
5. a (i) +120 m (ii) +60 m (iii) -60 m (iv) +220 m (v) -140 m (vi) -160 m (vii) +180 m (viii) -100 m
   b (i) 120 m (ii) 320 m
6. 35 BC can be recorded as the year -35

Chapter 7 Exercise 2 - page 62

1. See drawing of thermometer
2. a 9°C b 6°C c 7°C d -4°C e -4°C f -3°C g -14°C h -6°C
3. a 8°C up from b 13°C down from c 15°C down from d 17°C up from e 17°C down from f 35°C up from
4. a -25°C b 250°C
5. a -15°C b -29°C c -57°C

Chapter 7 Exercise 3 - page 63

1. a 13 b 7 c -1 d -3 e 1 f -8 g 1 h -4 i -5 j 2 k 0 l 4 m -10 n -10 o -50 p -270
2. a 3 b -1 c -3 d -4 e -12 f -8 g -47 h -3 i -7 j -14 k -23 l -137 m -20 n -60 o -300 p -193
3. a -1 b -3 c -6 d 2 e -6 f -11 g -12 h -20 i 0 j -131 k -33 l -36 m 5 n -80 o -100 p -34

Chapter 8 - Ratio & Proportion

Chapter 8 Exercise 1 - page 65

1. a 5 : 2 b 2 : 5
2. a 3 : 1 b 1 : 3
3. a 7 : 12 b 12 : 7
4. a 43 : 87 b 87 : 43
5. a 211 : 177 b 177 : 99 c 200 : 211 d 411 : 276
6. a 4 : 5 b 3 : 2 c 3 : 5 d 7 : 3 e 1 : 3 f 1 : 5 g 3 : 4 h 3 : 6
7. various
8. a L = 275 mm, B = 194 mm
   b (i) 275 : 194 (ii) 194 : 275 (iii) 275 : 938 (iv) 938 : 53350
9. a 143 : 37 b 143 : 180
10. a 45 : 57 b 140 : 57 c 45 : 38 d 45 : 57 : 38

Chapter 8 Exercise 2 - page 67

1. 5 : 4
2. 6 : 7
3. a 2 : 3 b 3 : 10 c 1 : 4 d 1 : 14 e 3 : 1 f 2 : 1 g 5 : 4 h 24 : 5 i 4 : 1 j 3 : 7 k 5 : 8 l 9 : 8 m 6 : 5 n 11 : 5 o 8 : 1 p 1 : 8 q 1 : 1000 r 150 : 1 s 1 : 2 t 10 : 1 u 1 : 500 v 1 : 2 000 000
4. a 4 : 3 b 5 : 4
5. a 1000 : 5 b 200 : 1
6. 10 : 120 b 1 : 12
7. a 4 : 1 b 1 : 15 c 5 : 6 d 2 : 3 e 2 : 17 f 1 : 6 g 9 : 2 h 4 : 3 i 6 : 1
8. a 5 : 3 b 20 : 13 c 4 : 3
9. a 5 : 4 b 5 : 6 c 6 : 5 : 4
10. a 13 : 11 b 10 : 7

Chapter 8 Exercise 3 - page 69

1. a 12 b 18 c 16
2. a 32 b 45
3. a 35 b 8 c 27
4. a 21 b 49 c 55 d 154
5. a 36 b (i) 10 (ii) 55 c 54
6. a £80 b £77 c £140
7. 560 000 words
8. a very dark b Light c Mid d Dark e Very Light
9. a 60 b no - only got 132 tins

Chapter 8 Exercise 4 - page 71

1. 20 miles per gallon
2. 60 km/gallon
3. a 12 metres/sec b 2 metres/min c 2·7 kg per day d 8 litres per day e 150 litres per day
4. a 1400 clips per sec
   b (i) 150 000 pins/min (ii) 2500 pins/sec
   c 132 d 1·2 e (i) 125000 (ii) 35
5. David - £7·50/hr, Shona - £8/hr (Shona)
6. Ewan - 4·6/min, Josh - 4·8/min (Josh)
7. a 1·2 b 2·45 c 515
8. Ali - 1·19, Dave - 1·17, Sal - 1·18 (Ali)
9. Investigtion

Chapter 8 Exercise 5 - page 73

1. £27
2. £192·50
3. €9·90
4. a 770 m b 5000 c 7 min d 6 sec

5. a 600 b 4200 c 7200 d 72000
6. a 15 m b £10·40 c 40 mins d 144
7. 16 000 ml
8. 30 times
9. 1155 pages
10. £435
11. 16 litres

Chapter 9 - Converting Measure

Chapter 9 Exercise 1 - page 76

1. a 40 mm b 120 mm c 85 mm
 d 2 mm e 0·6 mm
2. a 30 cm b 7 cm c 3·7 cm
 d 4·2 cm e 0·2 cm
3. a 900 cm b 2000 cm c 640 cm
 d 75 cm e 41·5 cm
4. a 4 m b 1·5 m c 0·5 m
 d 10 m e 0·08 m
5. a 5000 m b 20 000 m c 4500 m
 d 250 m e 125 m
6. a 3 km b 6·4 km c 0·5 km
 d 0·02 km e 0·001 km
7. a 8 km b 15 km c Sarah by 7 km
8. a Zak b 11 mm
9. a 45·26 m b 35 080 mm, 34·7 m, 3460 cm
10. a 184 cm, 1·9 m, 2000 mm, 0·003
 b 10 000 cm, 0·112 km, 1 000 000 mm, 1100 m
11. They are all the same
12. 10·32 km

Chapter 9 Exercise 2 - page 78

1. a 800 cl b 4000 cl c 20 cl d 3 cl
2. a 7 L b 23 L c 8·9 L d 0·01 L
3. a 60 ml b 200 ml c 9 ml d 0·1 ml
4. a 70 cl b 3 cl c 500 cl d 1 cl
5. a 5000 ml b 33000 ml c 100 ml d 10 ml
6. a 4 L b 50 L c 0·35 L d 0·01 L
7. a 40 L b 12 700 L c 0·05 L d 0·8 L
8. a 80 000 cm^3 b 80 litres
9. 1 litre

Chapter 9 Exercise 3 - page 79

1. a 6000 g b 28000 g c 1200 g d 500 g
2. a 7 g b 19 g c 0·6 g d 0·07 g
3. a 8000 kg b 40000 kg c 9500 kg d 240 kg
4. a 8 kg b 0·5 kg c 57 kg d 0·01 kg
5. 2·24 tonnes = 2240 kg
6. 2·76 tonnes = 2760 kg
7. 425 bags
8. Sally - 14·88 kg, Sue - 15·05 kg (Sue by 0·17 kg)
9. a 1600 g b 1·6 kg
10. a 3465 kg b 4 trips

Chapter 10 - Volume

Chapter 10 Exercise 1 - page 82

1. a 5 cm^3 b 9 cm^3 c 10 cm^3
 d 16 cm^3 e 24 cm^3
2. a 6 b 2 c 12 cm^3
3. a 12 b 3 c 36 cm^3
4. a 24 cm^3 b 24 cm^3 c 40 cm^3
 d 54 cm^3 e 75 cm^3
5. a 36 cm^3 b 36 cm^3 c 120 cm^3 d 90 cm^3
6. a 40 cm^3 b 30 cm^3 c 56 cm^3
 d 30 cm^3 e 35 cm^3 f 20 cm^3
 g 40 cm^3 h 60 cm^3 i 70 cm^3
 j 35 cm^3 k 19 cm^3

Chapter 10 Exercise 2 - page 85

1. 480 cm^3
2. 3600 cm^3
3. 120 cm^3
4. 4000 cm^3
5. a 8100 cm^3 b 135 cm^3
 c 10 000 cm^3 d 1536 cm^3
 e 945 cm^3 f 2304 cm^3
 g 11 700 cm^3 h 250 cm^3
 i 1664 cm^3 j 1350 cm^3
 k 180 000 cm^3
6. 1·5 cm
7. a 6 cm b 5 cm c 7 cm

Chapter 10 Exercise 2 - page 87

1. a 3000 cm^3 b 3000 ml
2. 6 x 15 x 10 = 900 cm^3 = 900 ml = 0·9 litre
3. a 2000 cm^3 b 2000 ml c 2 litres
4. a 4 L b 7 L c 13 L
 d 1·5 L e 2·3 L f 10·25 L
 g 0·6 L h 0·4 L i 0·25 L

Chapter 11 - Graphs & Charts

Chapter 11 Exercise 1 - page 89

1. a 250 b 75 c 50
2. a 1 b 6 c 7
 d 33 e few in captivity - endangered
3. a (i) 100 000 (ii) 80 000
 b (i) 120 000 (ii) 50 000 c 80 000
 d (i) Potato (ii) Carrots e 30 000
 f (i) 380 000 (ii) 380 000
 g women - more men don't like vegetables.
4. a (i) 150 (ii) 240 b 3 c Jun - 300
 d Jul - 30 e June and July
5. a (i) 600 (ii) 700 b 7700
 c (i) Aug - Sept (ii) Dec - Jan
 d Dec - Xmas time e rising
6. a most - Labrador, least - Terrier
 b (i) $^4/_{10}$ (ii) $^3/_{10}$ (iii) $^2/_{10}$ (iv) $^1/_{10}$
 c Labrador - Sheepdog - Dalmation - Terrier
 d (i) 50 (ii) 200
7. a Persian & Exotic b (i) $^2/_{20}$ (ii) $^4/_{20}$
 c Persian - Siamese - Abyssinian - Exotic
 d (i) 270 (ii) 150
8. a Friday b Monday
 c (i) $^1/_4$ (ii) $^1/_6$ (iii) $^1/_{12}$ (iv) $^3/_8$
 d (i) 30 (ii) 10 (iii) 15 (iv) 45

Chapter 11 Exercise 2 - page 92

1. a 10 b 5
 c Gerry in July and Bella in September
 d Don in June e Holiday season ?
 f Ken - once in June g 30
2. a as temeprature rises so do sales of ice cream
 b 40 c 20 d about 25°C

Chapter 11 Exercise 3 - page 93

1. a 21, 22, 24, 24, 28, 29
 b 11 c 37 d 12
2. a £1·10, £1·90, £2·00, £2·10, £2·20, £2·30
 £2·50, £2·70, £2·80, £3·10, £3·10, £3·30
 £3·40, £3·90, £4·00, £5·50, £5·70, £5·80
 £5·90
 b £2 level c £3·10 d 5 e 19
3. a 23 b 3·8, 4·7, 4·7, 4·7, 4·8, 4·8, 4·9, 5·0
 c 4 d 0·3, 0·4, 0·8, 0·9, 1·2 e 65·8 kg
4. a 3 b 2 c no - 13 men, 14 women

Chapter 11 Exercise 4 - page 94

1. a (i) Jaws 9 (ii) Horror 3
 b Studio 1-5 pm, Studio 2-5 pm, Studio 3- 7 pm
2. a (i) £250 (ii) £390 (iii) £400 b £480
3. a (i) £4 (ii) £3·50 (iii) £2·50 (iv) £2·00
 b 50p each = £1
4. a (i) ABS (ii) STB (iii) STB b higher rate
5. a £6·00 b £12·50 c £7·50
6. £8·50 + £12·50 + £10·50 = £31·50

Chapter 12 - Probability

Chapter 12 Exercise 1 - page 98

1. a evens b less c more d less
 e certain f less g certain h more
 i imposs j certain k even

Chapter 12 Exercise 2 - page 99

1. a $^3/_7$ b $^2/_7$
2. a 8 b $^1/_8$ c $^1/_8$
 d $^1/_2$ e $^5/_8$
3. a 13 b 1 c $^1/_{13}$
 d $^3/_{13}$ e $^5/_{13}$ f 0
4. a $^3/_{10}$ b $^2/_5$ c $^3/_{10}$
5. a $^1/_2$ b $^1/_2$ c $^1/_{16}$
 d $^1/_4$ e $^9/_{16}$
6. a 0·7 b B - P(red) = 0·75 => B is better
7. P(Mr White searches) = 0·375
 P(Mr Hay searches) = 0·36 - Mr Hay less likely
8. P(A) = 0·625, P(B) = 0·7, P(C) = 0·67 - (B - best)
9. 0·4

Chapter 13 - Gradients

Chapter 13 Exercise 1 - page 106

1. a $^1/_{15}$ Uphill = $^1/_5$, Ross = $^1/_{20}$
 b (i) Uphill (ii) Ross
2. $^{50}/_{350}$ = $^1/_7$
3. a $^2/_{25}$ b $^7/_{80}$
 c (i) Ambrose = 0·08, (ii) Ross = 0·0875 (iii) Ross
4. a $^5/_{100}$ = 0·05 b $^8/_{200}$ = 0·04
 c $^{10}/_{160}$ = 0·0625 d $^{19}/_{190}$ = 0·10
 (iii) Stuart Rd - Davie Ave - Love St -Bolton Way
5. 2·5
6. a 3 b 3·1 c Longer
7. grad = $^{22}/_5$ = 4·4
8. grad = $^{495}/_{1650}$ = 0·3
9. grad = $^{18}/_{120}$ = 0·15
10. A = 0·3, B = 0·35, C = 0·25, D = 0·4
 D is the steepest and C is the shallowest
11. grad = $^{25·5}/_{42·5}$ = 0·6
12. grad = $^{600}/_{800}$ = 0·75

Chapter 14 - Perimeters

Chapter 14 Exercise 1 - page 111

1. 52 cm
2. a 44 cm b 200 mm c 52·6 m
3. 30 cm
4. a 18 cm b 34·2 cm c 105 cm
 d 68 cm e 30 m f 240 mm
5. 65 mm

. a 17 cm b 12·6 m c 62 mm
. 12 cm
. a 14 cm b 220 mm c 5·3 m
. a 19 m b £14·25
0. £3780

hapter 14 Exercise 2 - page 113

. See sketch
. a radius b diam c radius d diam
. a RU b OR, OS and OU
. d 12 cm = 2 x radius length
. a 16 cm b 7 cm c 23·5 cm d 10·2 cm

hapter 14 Practical Exercise - page 114

. a/b/c - Answer should be about 3·14 each time
. Practical 3. 12·56 cm

hapter 14 Exercise 3 - page 115

. 15·7 cm
. 50·24 cm
3. 18·84 cm
. a 12·56 cm b 62·8 cm
 c 9·42 cm d 100·48 cm
 e 11·932 cm f 26·376 cm
 g 43·96 cm h 1·884 cm
5. 37·68 cm
6. a 5·2 cm b 16·328 cm
7. 11·304 cm
8. a 12·56 cm b 87·92 cm
 c 20·096 cm d 301·44 cm
 e 28·26 cm f 40·192 mm
 g 150·72 mm
9. 37·68 cm
10. 157 cm
11. 94·2 cm
12. 138·16 cm
13. 39·25 cm
14. 32·97 m
15. 125·6 cm

Chapter 14 Exercise 4 - page 118

1. a L = 9 cm, P = 48 cm b L = 10 cm, P = 96 cm
 c L = 10 cm, P = 80 cm
2. a missing sides are 6 cm & 10 cm, P = 54 cm
 b missing sides are 12 cm & 18 cm, P = 76 cm
 c missing sides - 8 cm , 5 cm & 5 cm, P = 60 cm
3. a see drawing b 10 cm c 38 cm
4. a 94 cm b 69 cm

Chapter 15 - Area 1

Chapter 15 Exercise 1 - page 120

1. a 24 cm^2 b 30 cm^2 c 65 cm^2
2. a 13·5 m^2 b 11·5 m^2 c 130 mm^2 d 730 m^2

Chapter 15 Exercise 2 - page 121

1. a drawing b drawing c 24 cm^2 d 12 cm^2
2. a 12 cm^2 b 18 cm^2 c 21 cm^2 d 36 cm^2
 e 28 cm^2 f 40 cm^2 g 52·5 cm^2
3. a sketch b 35 cm^2
4. a 48 cm^2 b 75 cm^2 c 160 cm^2
 d 160 cm^2 e 200 cm^2 f 575 cm^2
 g 1850 cm^2 f 6200 cm^2 g 3850 cm^2
5. a 200 mm^2 b 825 mm^2 c 60 m^2
 d 247 cm^2 e 875 mm^2 f 28·5 m^2
6. a Front = 165 m^2, Back = 180·5 m^2 (Back)
 b 15·5 m^2 c £863·75
7. a 480 cm^2 b 1998 g or 1·998 kg

Chapter 15 Exercise 3 - page 124

1. a drawing b drawing c 28 cm^2 d 14 cm^2
2. a drawing b drawing c 12 cm^2 d 6 cm^2
3. a 10 cm^2 b 15 cm^2 c 36 cm^2 d 60 cm^2
 e 72 cm^2 f 175 cm^2 g 575 cm^2 h 187 cm^2
4. A = 980 cm^2, B = 987 cm^2 (B has larger area)
5. Area = 12 x 225 cm^2 = 2700 cm^2
6. Area = 120 m^2 x 2 = 240 m^2
 Cost = (240 ÷ 15) = 16 x £45·75 = £732

Chapter 15 Exercise 4 - page 126

1. a 300 cm^2 b 90 cm^2 c 390 cm^2
2. a 900 cm^2 b 80 cm^2 c 980 cm^2
3. a 424 cm^2 b 396 cm^2 c 428 cm^2 d 270 cm^2
 e 196 cm^2 f 196 cm^2 g 330 cm^2
4. 70 cm^2
5. a 195 cm^2 b 370 cm^2 c 100 cm^2

Chapter 16 - Scale Drawings 1

Chapter 16 Exercise 1 - page 129

Check all drawings

Chapter 16 Exercise 2 - page 131

1. a 18 m b 33 m
2. a 440 cm b 160 cm c 4·4 m by 1·6 m
3. a 250 cm (2·5 m) b 100 cm (1 m)
4. a 180 m by 135 m b P = 630 m
5. 96 cm
6. 4·5 m
7. a 2·7 m b 4·5 m
8. a 5 cm by 3 cm b 2·5 m by 1·5 m
9. 4·2 m
10. 2·4 m
11. 17·5 m
12. a 2·8 cm => 140 miles (all ± 0·2 cm)
 b (i) 2 cm => 100 miles
 (ii) 4 cm => 200 miles
 (iii) 4·5 cm => 225 miles
 (iv) 4·3 cm => 215 miles
 (v) 11·5 cm => 575 miles
 c (i) 2·5 cm - 5·5 cm - 7·7 cm
 (ii) 125 miles - 275 miles - 385 miles
 (iii) 785 miles

Chapter 17 - Area 2

Chapter 17 Exercise 1 - page 135

1. a/b/c - practical d 7 cm by 4 cm
 e 28 cm^2 e 28 cm^2
2. 16 cm^2
3. 40 cm^2
4. a 48 cm^2 b 105 cm^2 c 187 cm^2
 d 72 cm^2 e 64 m^2 f 3600 m^2
5. a 10 cm b 9 cm c 90 cm^2 d 1080 cm^2

Chapter 17 Exercise 2 - page 137

1. a/b - see drawing c 24 cm^2 d 12 cm^2
2. a/b - see drawing c 63 cm^2 d 31·5 cm^2
3. a 18 cm^2 b 120 cm^2 c 88 cm^2
 d 63 cm^2 e 50 cm^2 f 45 cm^2
4. a drawing b 24 cm^2 c 12 cm^2
5. a drawing b 72 cm^2 c 36 cm^2
6. a 27 cm^2 b 30 cm^2 c 110 cm^2
 d 34 cm^2 e 1600 mm^2 f 68 cm^2
7. Left = 30 cm^2, Right = 27·5 cm^2, (Rhombus)

Chapter 17 Exercise 3 - page 140

1. a 9 b 4 c 100 d 81
 e 25 f 144 g 625 h 289
 i 1600 j 14400 k 1·44 l 12·25
 m 10201 n 90·25 o 0·25

Chapter 17 Exercise 4 - page 141

1. a 50·24 cm^2 b 254·34 cm^2
2. 153·86 cm^2
3. a 28·26 cm^2 b 530·66 cm^2 c 1962·5 cm^2
 d 63·585 cm^2 e 346·185 cm^2 f 1·1304 cm^2
4. 706·5 cm^2
5. 254·34 cm^2
6. a 452·16 m^2 b 1·5386 m^2
7. 706·5 cm^2
8. a 10 cm b 628 cm^2
9. a 16·6106 m^2 b 7 tins
10. a 55·3896 m^2 b 7 x £4·80 = £33·60

Chapter 18 - Volumes

Chapter 18 Exercise 1 - page 144

1. 216 cm^3
2. 120 cm^3
3. 600 cm^3
4. a 343 cm^3 b 480 cm^3 c 480 cm^3
5. a 105 m^3 b 108 m^3 c 9 m^3 d 260 m^3
6. 4 cm
7. a 4 cm b 3 cm c 10 cm

Chapter 18 Exercise 2 - page 146

1. a 480 cm^3 b 480 ml
2. a 2400 cm^3 b 2400 ml
3. a 4 L b 8 L c 15 L
 d 1·5 L e 2,3 L f 0·75 L
4. a 48000 cm^3 b 48000 ml c 48 L
5. a yes (10 x 10 x 10 = 1000 ml = 1 litre)
 b 10 x 5 x 20 = 1000 (yes)
 c 20 x 25 x 2 = 1000 (Yes) - too shallow
 d investigation

Chapter 18 Exercise 3 - page 147

1. a 210 cm^3 b 100 cm^3 c 217 cm^3 d 45 cm^3
2. a 54 cm^2 b 270 cm^3
3. a 35 cm^2 b 140 cm^3
4. a 48 cm^2 b 960 cm^3
5. a 48 000 cm^3 b 70 000 cm^3
 c 3200 cm^3 d 1500 cm^3
 e 24 cm^3 f 200 000 cm^3
6. a 1·2 m^2 b 3·6 m^3

Chapter 18 Exercise 4 - page 150

1. a 300 cm^3 b 250 cm^3 c 770 cm^3
 d 185 cm^3 e 114 cm^3 f 270 cm^3
2. a 1099 cm^3 b 452·16 cm^3
 c 602·88 cm^3 d 602·88 cm^3

3. a 7 cm, 2461·76 cm^3 b 5 cm, 1570 cm^3
c 12·5 cm, 3925 cm^3 d 6 cm, 565·2 cm^3
4. a 283 cm^3 b 5699 cm^3
c 5652 cm^3 d 1884 cm^3
e 314 mm^3 f 1356 cm^3

Chapter 19 - Pythagoras

Chapter 19 Exercise 1 - page 153

1. a 2 b 5 c 6 d 7
2. a 9 b 1 c 10 d 8
3. a 0 b 11 c 12 d 13
e 16 f 14 g 20 h 30
i 50 j 1·6
4. a 3·61 b 4·69 c 5·92 d 8·31
e 9·43 f 10·49 g 14·14 h 17·32
i 23·45 j 27·39
5. 5·48 cm

Chapter 19 Exercise 2 - page 154

1. a 9, 16, 25 b 25 c yes
2. a 25, 144, 169 b 169 c yes
3. a 81, 144, 225 b 225 c yes
4. a 64, 225, 289 b 289 c yes
5. a 100, 576, 676 b 676 c yes
6. a 225, 400, 625 b 625 c yes

Chapter 19 Exercise 3 - page 156

1. 10 cm
2. 13 cm
3. a 20 cm b 17 cm c 25 cm
4. 10·30 cm
5. 12·65 cm
6. 15·26 cm
7. 21·1 cm
8. 16·7 cm

Chapter 19 Exercise 4 - page 158

1. 13·60 m
2. 3·61 m
3. 108·17 m
4. 131·24 m
5. 20·62 m
6. 14·87 ft
7. 43·08 cm
8. 97·08 m
9. 3·64 m
10. 25 cm
11. 6·40 m + 7·81 m = 14·21 m
12. 174·93 cm

Chapter 19 Exercise 5 - page 160

1. 20 cm
2. a 8·9 cm b 17·9 cm c 5·7 cm
d 21·2 cm b 20·7 mm c 2 m
3. 4·6 m
4. 20 m
5. 20·7 m
6. 55·9 cm
7. a 20 cm b 34·6 cm
8. 3·3 m

Chapter 19 Exercise 6 - page 162

1. a 8·94 cm b 14·14 cm c 10·63 m
d 16 mm b 13·96 cm c 3·18 m
2. the 3rd side must be bigger than the 10
3. 16·1 cm - the 19·1 should not be bigger than 18
4. 8·35 m
5. 18·36 cm
6. 9·51 m

Chapter 20 - Timetables

Chapter 20 Exercise 1 - page 165

1. a 0230 b 0535 c 0900 d 2030
e 1545 f 1600 g 0825 h 2025
i 0150 j 0625 k 1200 l 0010
m 1210 n 2315 0 0425
2. a 2.50 am b 10.10 am c 7.25 am d 3.30 pm
e 4.50 pm f 11.45 pm g 1.35 am h 8.20 pm
i 2.05 pm j 9.07 pm k noon l 4.30 am
m 5.25 pm n 4.20 pm o 10.59 pm
3. a 3 hr b 4 hrs 30 min
c 6 hrs 45 min d 2 hrs 40 min
e 1 hr 30 min f 2 hrs 40 min
g 1 hr 35 min h 1 hr 50 min
i 4 hrs
4. 10 hr 20 mins

Chapter 20 Exercise 2 - page 166

1. a 2 hr 20 min and 2 hr 25 mins
b 1240 and 0005
c Pitlochrie (15) and Newtonmore (24)
d Pitlochrie and Perth
e Falkirk -> J O'Groats takes 7 hr 30 min
J O'Groats -> Falkirk takes 7 hr 40 mins (✓)
f day as nighttime takes 7 hr and 40 mins
2. 4 hr 40 mins
3. a 6 hr 45 min b 10.10 pm Wed
4. a BBC2 - University Challenge
b Sara Beeny's show on Channel 4 at 8.30 pm
c 5 mins d 10 mins e 1 hr
f Some Irish People tell jokes - BBC2 - 9.45 pm
g 5 minutes h 2 hr 55 mins
i 30 min min + 45 min + 25 min + 10 min = 110 min
You have enough space - less than 120 mins
5. a 4.20 am Tuesday b 11.20 pm (Mon) night
6. 1750 on Saturday night
7. 8.15 am (0815)
8. 1 hour 15 minutes
9. 6 hours 25 mins

Chapter 21 - Formulae

Chapter 21 Exercise 1 - page 170

1. 100
2. a 48 b (i) 3 (ii) 5
3. 84 (more if you use true scoring)
4. a profit = £135 b £73
5. 2700
6. 4 hours 30 mins
7. 7 cm
8. a £40 b £65 c £100
9. a £42·99 b postage cost
10. 4 hrs 20 mins
11. a 25 b 1

Chapter 21 Exercise 2 - page 172

1. a 14 b 290 c 112 d 900
e 39 f 62 g 70 h 10
i 40 j 16 k 59 l 900
2. 50
3. 35
4. a 16°C b 25°C c 34°C d 61°C
5. a 24°C b 23°C c 14°C d 0°C
6. 44·8
7. a £140 b £175
8. 7
9. 3
10. 40
11. £425
12. £70
13. 125 cm^3

Chapter 22 - Scale Drawings 2

Chapter 22 Exercise 1 - page 176

1. rectangle measuring 5 cm by 3 cm
2. rectangle measuring 6 cm by 4 cm
3. rectangle measuring 7 cm by 3·5 cm
4. rectangle measuring 10 cm by 7·5 cm
5. rectangle measuring 8 cm by 6 cm
6. a 9 m and 9 m b

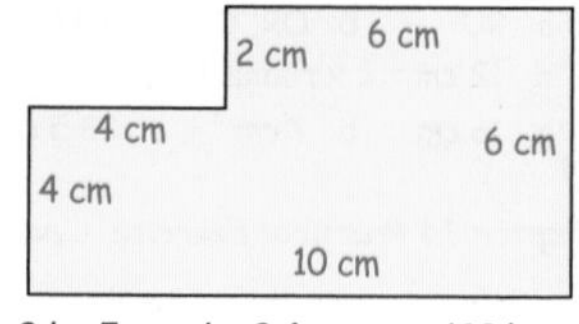

7. a Triangle, 8 by 5 cm b 9·4 cm c 188 km
8. a scale drawing b 6·3 cm => 126 cm

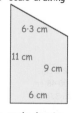

6·3 cm
11 cm
9 cm
6 cm

9. a scale drawing b 5·4 cm => 2·7 m

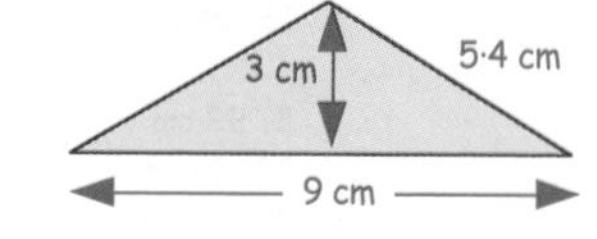

Chapter 22 Exercise 2 - page 178

1.

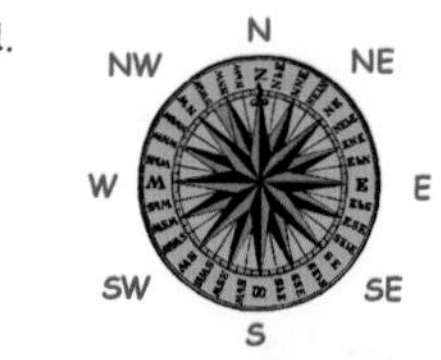

2. a 90° b 180° c 270° d 90°
e 45° f 135 g 135° h 135°
3. a South b SW c SW
4. a (i) Evil Isle (ii) Far out Point
(iii) Reservoir (iv) Brockville
b (i) N (ii) NE (ii) W (iv) SW
c North West

Chapter 22 Exercise 3- page 179

1. 120°
2. a 070° b 160° c 105°
3. a 180° b 090° c 135° d 045°
4. a 270° b 225° c 315°
5. 305°
6. a 240° b 280° c 330°
7. A = 040° B = 095° C = 140° D = 200°
E = 250° F = 295° G = 340°
8. See drawing
9. See scale drawing ND = 8 cm long
10. a scale drawing HT = 6 cm, TM = 8 cm
b 9·1 cm => 45·5 km
11. a scale drawing EP = 9·5 cm, EH = 5·5 cm
b 12·1 cm c 121 km
12. a scale drawing BR = 8 cm, BB = 6·5 cm
b 11·9 cm c 23·8 km
13. a scale drawing DP = 9 cm, PS = 6 cm
b 12·4 cm c 62 km
14. a scale drawing GA = 7 cm, GB = 8 cm
b 10·6 cm b 530 miles

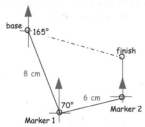

5. a b 7·9 cm => 1580 metres

base 165°
finish
8 cm
6 cm
70°
Marker 1
Marker 2

Chapter 23 - Problem Solving

Chapter 23 Exercise 1 - page 184

1. 25 strips ÷ 3 = 8·333 = 9 rolls = £114·75
2. a 11 m ÷ 2·5 m = 4 strips with a bit left over
   800 cm ÷ 60 =13·3 = 14 strips ÷ 4 = 3·5 = 4 rolls
   Cost = 4 x £12·75 = £51
   b 11 m ÷ 2·4 m = 4·6 = 4 strips & a bit left over
   700 cm ÷ 60 = 11·6 = 12 strips ÷ 4 = 3 rolls
   Cost = 3 x £12·75 = £38·25
3. a 10 x 8 = 80 tiles b £180
4. 12 x 8 = 96 tiles needed => 12 x £24·50 = £294
5. 10 x 8 = 80 - 6 = 72 tiles => need 4 boxes
   cost = 4 x £56 = £224
6. area = (3 + 2·5 + 3 + 2·5) x 2 = 22 - 0·5 = 21·5 m²
   No. of tins = 4 => cost = 4 x £6·95 = £27·80
7. Area = 6 x 6 + 1/2 of 8 x 6 = 60 m²
   Cost = 60 x £108 = £6480
8. a (600 + 300 + 600 + 300) ÷ 60 = 30 strips
   4 strips per roll => 8 rolls
   b cost = 8 x £8·95 = £71·60
9. a 40 m ÷ 4 = 10 strips x 60 m = 600 metres
   No of rolls = 600 ÷ 24 = 25 rolls
   b Cost = 25 x £1250 + 6 x 15 x 24 + 15 x 40
   = £31 250 + £2160 + £600 = £34 010
   c Cost of carpet = £31 250 + 5% = £32 812·50
   Cost = £32812·50 + 48 x 25 + 600 = £34612·50
   d slightly dearer but carpet has no joins
10. Investigation

Chapter 23 Exercise 2 - page 187

1. a 8 x 8 x 4 = 256 b 4 x 8 x 5 = 160
2. No of boxes = 5 x 6 x 3 = 90
   No. of trips = 300 ÷ 90 = 3·3 => 4 trips needed
3. a 200 ÷ 2 = 100 b 2·4 m
4. a 3 x 3 x 10 = 90 b 11 x 7 x 5 = 385
5. 5 x 4 x 6 = 120
6. 5 x 30 x 30 = 4500
7. a 20 x 10 x 7 = 1400
   b Best = (300 ÷ 75) x (400 ÷ 80) x (800 ÷ 65) = 240
8. boxes in 1 crate = 4 x 2 x 2 = 16
   crates per container = 8 x 10 x 8 = 640
   no of teddies = 16 x 640 = 10240
9. a 4 x 3 x 6 = 72 cans b 5 x 2 x 6 = 60 cans
   c No of cans = (10 x 10 x 3) x 72 = 21 600
   No of trips = 1 000 000 ÷ 21600 = 46·3 = 47 trips
10. a drawing b 28 c 29

   d Cost = 5 (P) x £5·95 + 5 (B) x £18·50 = £122·25

Chapter 24 - Tolerance

Chapter 24 Exercise 1 - page 191

1. a 76 mm b 84 mm
2. a (29 - 31) mm b (23 - 27) mm
   c (12 - 18) kg d (16 - 24) kg
   e (45 - 55) ml f (43 - 47) ft
   g (99 - 101) g h (140 - 160) mg
   i (175 - 225) cm j (2·4 - 2·6) km
   k (8·0 - 8·4) m l (22·4 - 23·0) m
   m (44·6 - 44·8) miles n (19·5 - 20·5) kg
   o (59·8 - 60·2) mm p (94·5 - 95·5)°C
   q (8·9 - 9·5) litres r (17 - 20) km
3. a (2·24 - 2·26) mm b (4·72 - 4·78) cm
   c (9·10 - 9·20) g d (0·70 - 0·82) kg
   e (3·16 - 3·26) miles f (30·54 - 30·60) ml
   g (1·96 - 2·00) litres h 2·220 - 2·224) ml
   i (4·050 - 4·058) g
4. a (16 - 22) mm
   b (iii), (iv), (vii), (viii)
5. a (7·7 - 8·1) cm b No
6. a 8·93 secs b 9·03 secs
7. a 7·25 ounces b 8·75 ounces
8. a (238 - 262) grams b No
9. a (i) and (iii) b (i), (ii) and (iii)

Chapter 24 Exercise 2 - page 193

1. (28 ± 2) ft
2. (12 ± 3)°C
3. a (16 ± 1) cm b (45 ± 5) cm
   c (5·5 ± 0·5) cm d (120 ± 10) cm
   e (9·5 ± 0·5) kg f (38 ± 3) mm
   g (4·6 ± 0·2) m h (14·3 ± 0·2) km
   i (0·9 ± 0·2) cm j (30·5 ± 0·3) m
   k (12·9 ± 0·5) g l (500 ± 300) miles
4. a (8·13 ± 0·01) g b (4·05 ± 0·02) cm
   c (0·76 ± 0·02) m d (13·74 ± 0·03) km
   e (7·30 ± 0·02) ft f (0·05 ± 0·04) km
   g (4·00 ± 0·05) g h (0·062 ± 0·002) miles
5. a (70·5 ± 0·3) decibels
   b (i) Q (ii) ok (iii) ok (iv) L
6. (7 ± 4) ft
7. Writing speed = (27 ± 4) words per minute
8. (225 ± 10) grams
9. a £(11·00 ± 0·30) b No
10. (30·9 ± 0·4) secs
11. a (237 ± 7) ml b No
12. a (20·4 ± 4·4) b No

Chapter 25 - Income

Chapter 25 Exercise 1 - page 198

1. £330
2. a £252 b £302·40 c £50·40
3. a Bob - £298·50 Bill - £437·80
   Ted - £557·20 Sue - £348·25
   Fred - £398·00
   b £159·20 c £2039·75
4. £1732·50

Chapter 25 Exercise 2 - page 199

1. £9·80
2. Ari - £14·55, Tina - £9·70,
   Clara - £8·10, Edith - £19·65
3. a £23·75 b £950
4. £1594·08
5. a 162 hrs b £11·00

Chapter 25 Exercise 3 - page 200

1. a £17880 b £20907 c £3027
2. £2678
3. a £14344·20 b £11854·80
   c £24131·40 d £57712·20
4. Jean - £22326, Gina - £22893 => (Gina-£567)
5. Viv - £22893·60, Trish - £24481·60
   (Trish gets paid £1588 more)
6. a £2299 b £1382
7. a £245·25 b £423·50
8. Cathy - £526·50, Ada - £225
9. a £854·35 b £1708·70
10. a £5720 b £1320
11. a £520 b £13 c decrease - £1440·04

Chapter 25 Exercise 4 - page 202

1. a £20564 b £19176
2. a £47726 b £21922
3. a £12852 b £32076 c £42432 d £17625
4. Jeff - £31621, Alec - £31152 => (Jeff - £467)

Chapter 25 Exercise 5 - page 203

1. a £678 b £262·50 c £4200
2. £1428
3. a £560 b £10800 c £8500
4. a £990 b £1840
5. Jackson - £3480, Kenny - £3850, (Kenny - £370)
6 To encourage them to sell more goods.

Chapter 25 Exercise 6 - page 204

1. a £22 b £132
2. £189·60
3. a £233·60 b £306·72
4. £147 b £134·10
5. Electrician - £142·40 Secretary - £100·00
   Brickie - £86·00 Joiner - £108·80
   Plumber - £155·20 Driver - £78·40
6. a £19·80 b £79·20
7. £212·40
8. £292·05
9. a £20·10 b £100·50
10. a £280·80 b £210·60 c £70·20
11. £1855
12. £144
13. a £266 b £491·50
14. £950
15. Overtime Rate = £13·80 Basic Pay = £368
    Overtime pay = £110·40 Total Pay = £478·40
16. Overtime Rate = £12·90 Basic Pay = £309·60
    Overtime pay = £154·80 Total Pay = £464·40
17. Overtime Rate = £23·10 Basic Pay = £585·20
    Overtime pay = £161·70 Total Pay = £746·90
18. Basic Pay = £528 Sunday = £105·60
    Tuesday = £59·40 Total Pay = £693

Chapter 25 Exercise 7 - page 208

1. a £1315 b £1199 c £13677 d £957·30
   e £31171 f £349 g £15720 h £401·15
   i £429·05 j £669·85
2. £2087·35
3. a £18540 b £1545
4. £406·75
5. a £165·75 b £303·76
   c £693·68 d £1174·92
6. a I = £869·15 D = £267·35 N = £601·80
   b I = £997·25 D = £263·93 N = £733·32
   c I = £1365·55 D = £462·04 N = £903·51
   d I = £2178 D = £620·71 N = £1557·29
   e I = £2874·45 D = £792·10 N = £2082·35

Chapter 26 - Foreign Exchange

Chapter 26 Exercise 1 - page 212

1. €625
2. €350
3. $1836
4. 3822 AUD (or A$3822 or just $3822))

5. a €312·50 b €10·00 c $520·20 d 1365 AUD
6. a 2370 HKD b 92500 Yen
c 67500 Rupees d 9250 Kroner
7. 13800 Kroner
8. a $382·50 b €312·50
c 375 francs d 5250 pesos
9. Dearer since £250 = NZ$487·50 - He paid $500
10. a £950 = €1187·50 - dearer in Scotland
b £1800 = $2754 - same price
c £10200 = 918000 rupees - cheaper in Britain

Chapter 26 Exercise 2 - page 214

1. £40
2. £75
3. £150
4. £130
5. a £8 b £15 c £1000
d £2 e £1050 f £2000
6. a €625 b £20
7. a £60 b £20 c £1300 d £45
8. £50
9. £1·40
10. €425 = £340, $459 = £300 - (Kendra in USA)
11. £230
12. a 42 litres b £54·60

Chapter 27 - Banking

Chapter 27 Exercise 1 - page 217

1. It is safer - It gains you interest
2. £240
3. £1050
4. a £260 b £230 c £399 d £280·85
5. a £540 b £756
6. Brian - £192·40, Julie - £192·00 (Brian √)
7. a £240 b £6240
8. a £119 b £3519
9. a £4200 b £824 c £2255 d £18357
10. a 2·9% b £203
11. a £16·10 b £352 c £130·50 d £768

Chapter 27 Exercise 2 - page 219

1. a Scotia Bank b Ms Anne E Strange
c End of August 2018 d April 2014
2. a 16 digit card no. = 2311323458980041
Name is Mrs Ruth Woolie
Sort Code - 200347 Account No. 00176502
b 16 digit card no. = 1817400389880032
Name is Mr Alex Dunbeath
Sort Code - 314502 Account No. 00453198
3. a to distinguish it from other bank branches
b A unique number attached to your account
c If others knew it, they could cash money from your account if they found your card
d Yes and no - It's safer but the tendency is to spend more since it doesn't feel like money
4. Discussion
5. Investigation

Chapter 27 Exercise 3 - page 220

1. £4·80 (+ the original £160)
2. £14·40 (+ the original £480)
3. a 2% b (i) £15·60 (ii) £36 (iii) £6·91
4. a £82 b £902 c £2193·50
5. Vira has the lowest APR - less interest
6. Investigation/discussion

Chapter 27 Exercise 4 - page 221

1. a 11·6% b £46·40 => £446·40 c £37·20
2. a £59·80 => £709·80 b £59·15 per month
3. a £151·20 => £1951·20 b £162·60 per month
4. a Total due = £13740 b £229 /month
5. a 6·5% of £2500 = £162·50
b £81·25 => £2581·25
c £430·21 per month
6. a 12 months costs £3285 ÷ 12 = £273·75/month
6 months costs £3129 ÷ 6 = £521·50/month
b various - 6 months loan incurrs less interest but monthly payments are higher
7. a £73·60
b £873·60 ÷ 12 = £72·80 - yes - within budget
8. a £2847 b Absolutely not
c Might not be able to secure a loan from the bank or an HP agreement with the shop.

Chapter 28 - Comparing Prices

Chapter 28 Exercise 1 - page 224

1. Small - 100 g = £2·50, Large - 100 g = £2·40
Large is better deal by 10p/100 g
2. Small - 100 ml = £1·10, Large - 100 ml = £1·00
Large is better deal by 10p/100 ml
3. Small - 100 g = £1·04, Large - 100 g = £1·05
Small is better deal by 1p/100 g
4. Small - 50 g = £0·50, Large - 50 g = £0·40
Large is better deal by 10p/150 g
5. 4 nights - £80/night, 5 nights - £82/night
4 nights is better by £2 per night
6. 5 nights - £91/night, 7 nights - £90/night
7 nights is better by £1 per night
7. Small - 50 ml = £0·50, Large - 50 ml = £0·40
Large is better deal by 10p/50ml
8. Sm - 20p/100g, Med - 18p/100g Lar - 15p/100g
a Large is better value b Small is worse value
9. Box of 3 = £1·80/ball, Box of 6 = £1·70/ball
Box of 10 = £1·75 per ball
Cheapest per ball is the Box of 6
10. Erskine - £1·31/L, Braehead - £1·26 - Braehead
11. a 60 m^2 b 96 m^2 c Jake = £15·40/m^2
Hannah = £14/m^2 => Hannah got better deal

Chapter 28 Exercise 2 - page 226

1. a Joiner Man = £30 x 4 + £39 = £159
JoineryServices = £25 x 4 + £60 = £160
Joiner Man cheaper this time by £1
b Joiner Man = £30 x 8 + £39 = £279
JoineryServices = £25 x 10 + £60 = £310
Joiner Man cheaper this time by £31
2. a PL Plumbing = £35 x 4 + £25 = £165
The Water Co. = £30 x 5 + £20 = £170
PL Plumbing is cheaper by £5
b PL Plumbing = £35 x 3 + £25 = £130
The Water Co. = £30 x 3 + £20 = £110
The Water Co. is cheaper by £20
3. Tele Media = £40 x 2 + £80 = £160
Phone Wire = £48 x 2 + £70 = £166
Tele Media is cheaper by £6
4. a Chas = £35 x 2 + £75 = £145
b Dave = £30 x 3 + £50 = £140
Dave is cheaper by £5
5. Electrofix = £45 x 4 + £40 + £70 = £290
SparkService = £55 x 4 + £50 = £270
SparkService would have been cheaper by £20
6. a £50 b £30 c (i) £155 (ii) £350
7. a £40 b £20 c (i) £140 (ii) £210
8. a Euan = £40 x 3 + £30 = £150
Terry = £35 x 3 + £60 = £165
Terry is dearer by £15
b 7 hours or more

Chapter 28 Exercise 3 - page 228

1. a Xchange - Less Rupees needed to buy £s
b Xchange - £45, RupRate - £40 - £5 less
2. X-Rate = 245500 Baht, X-Money = 251500 Baht
Xpound = 244900 Baht. => Can get 6600 more
3. a Dumfries Bank b £4
4. You only need to take a 1 year contract
5. a CarLoan - Cheapest rate of interest
b £1650 b £450

Chapter 29 - Budgeting

Chapter 29 Exercise 1 - page 230

1. a No - Only £570 saved b 1 more week
2. Two more weeks => 11 x £12 = £132
3. Anne - £196 ÷ £25 = 7·84 = 8 weeks
Tom - £275 ÷ £40 = 6·875 = 7 weeks => (Tom √)
4. a 13 b 1 more week
5. a £40 + 5 x £5 = £65
b Either budget £65/wk or spend £4 on lunch

Chapter 29 Exercise 2 - page 231

1. a £4·90 b £4·94
2. Cut down on what they spend or ask for a raise
3. Just over £3 (£3·33) - needs to save £3·34/wk
4. a £30 b £70
5. Various - Promise to do chores, Wash her car etc
6. a £50 b Give up the football if possible
7. £105
8. Various choices - Possibly not the football club
9. a 15 x £1·10 = £16·50
b Cinema - £33·75 c £126·45
10. Saves 30 x 99p + 13 x £2·25 = £63·45
If he had saved his £40, would have £103·45
When he spent his £40, he did not have enough
11. Alfie has £30 from car wash and £75 from his paper round => £105, so he can go on trip.

Chapter 29 Exercise 3 - page 233

1. a £320 b £134·80 c £454 d £272
2.

Monthly Budget Planner Sheet for Eve Jones			
INCOME		EXPENDITURE	
Wages	£750·00	Council Tax	£55·00
Child Benefit	£134·80	Electricity	£45·00
Child Tax Credit	£454·00	Car Loan	£108·00
Working Tax Credit	£272·00	Credit Card	£100·00
		Clothing & Shoes	£80·00
		Gas	£80·00
		Food	£320·00
		Rent	£350·00
		Fuel	£70·00
		Car Insurance	£51·00
		TV Licence	£15·00
		Mobile Phone Top-up	£60·00
Over/Under Spend (Income - Expenditure)		£	

3. £1610·80 - £1334·00 = £276·80
4. Council Tax, Rent, Car Loan, Car Insurance, (possibly Gas & Electricity if paid standing order).
5. £276·80 - £220·00 = £56·80
6. Her net income would go up by £250 - £150 = £100 per month - It would help
7. various - discuss

Chapter 29 Exercise 4 - page 234

Needs are food, water, shelter, heat and first aid.
1. a All but the chocolate spread and crisps
b as comfort foods - as a treat for the kids
2. a £13·80 b £2·76
3. a Winter coat (time of year?), possibly pizza
b make-up (possibly pizza)
4. a various - discuss b wants
5. £29·10
6. possibly washing powder and plasters.
7. £18·00 +£13·80 + £25·30 + £29·10 = £86·20. No
8. If she had no means of transport, or was not well or ... etc

Chapter 30 - Comparing Data Sets

Chapter 30 Exercise 1 - page 236

1. a 7 b 39 c 45 d 229
   e 15 f 73 g 6·7 h 3·34
2. a 2 b 5 c 8
   d 4 e 27 f 4·3
3. a 3 b 5 c 44 d 2·7
   e 133 f 18·5 g 16·5
   h 109 i 0·65 j 6
4. a 5 b 14 c £14 d 22 cm
   e 4·95 f 3·6 g 0·7 h $127
5. a R = 15 MO = 1 med = 3 mean = 5
   b R = 3·1 MO = 5·3 med = 4·6 mean = 4·2
   c R = 22 MO = 105 med = 105 mean = 104
   d R = 32 MO = 40 med = 31 mean = 34
   e R = 12 MO = 21 med = 14·5 mean = 15·5
   f R = 5000 MO = - med = 15500 mean = 15000
6. a (i) 9 (ii) 8 (iii) 7·9 b 6
7. a 52·5 b yes c 53 d 54
8. 14

Chapter 30 Exercise 2 - page 238

1. a 6 b $2^1/_2$
2. a Ravi - 65, Joe - 64 b Joe by 1 mark
3. a Michelle - 13, Daisy - 16 -> Daisy
4. a 23 kg b mode = 45 kg, med = 53 kg
   c med is better 45 is not a measure of centre it is in fact the lowest score
5. a mode = 6·6, mean = 6·8
   b probably here the 6·6 - there are 4 of them
6. a med = £95, mean = £102
   b the mean is skewed by the £220 quote
   c The mode is £60 - the lowest quote
7. a 30 b med = 21, mode = 10
   c the median as the 110 skews the results
8. a (i) Green up - 14, Turfers - 3
   (ii) Green Up - 7, Turfers - 6·5
   b Turfers - the variation in delivery date is less
   c The average no of days to delivery is less

Chapter 31 - Graphs, Charts and Tables 2

Chapter 31 Exercise 1 - page 241

1. a 4 b 10 c 9 d 17
2. frequencies are :- 4, 6, 7, 3, 2, 2
3. a $6^1/_4$ - (2), $6^1/_2$ - (3), $6^3/_4$ - (7), 7 - (11), $7^1/_4$ - (5), $7^1/_2$ - (1), $7^3/_4$ - (1)
   c $^{11}/_{30}$ d see bar graph
4. a 13
   b apple (16), ban (22), gra (9), pear (4), pea (7)
5. see bar graph
6. see bar graph
7. see bar graph
8. see bar graph
9. a/b R - 4, B - 2, W - 5, S - 8, Y - 1
   c 13 d $^1/_5$ e see bar graph
10. see line graph
11. a see line graph b Chrismas presents
12. see line graph
13. see line graph
14. see line graph
15. see line graph
16. see comparative line graph

Chapter 30 Exercise 2 - page 246

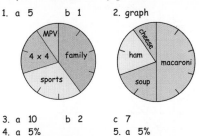

1. a 5 b 1
2. graph
3. a 10 b 2 c 7
4. a 5%
5. a 5%

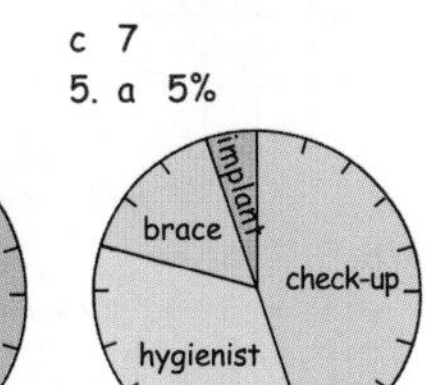

6.
7.

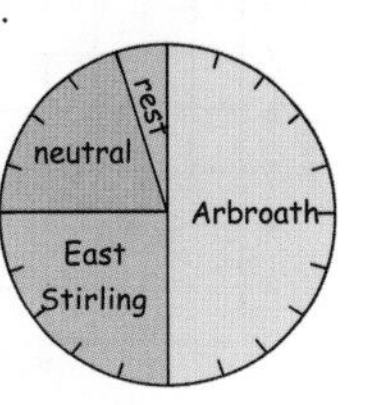

Chapter 30 Exercise 3 - page 248

1. a 180°, 120°, 40°, 20° b graph

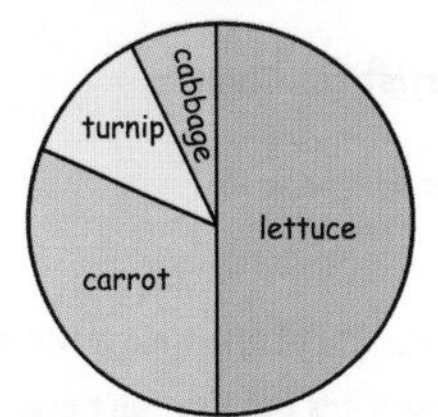

2. a 24°, 168°, 136°, 32° b graph

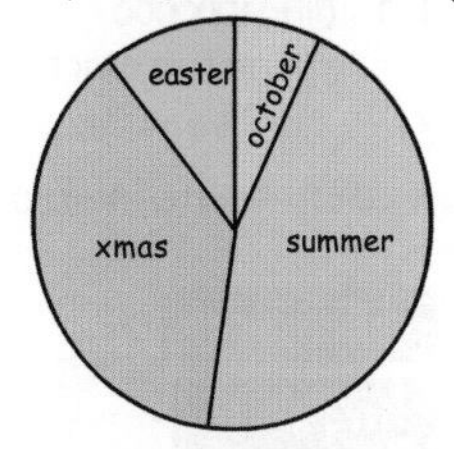

3. a 84°, 48°, 72°, 156° b graph

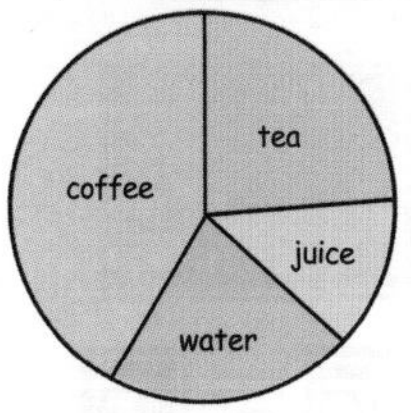

4. a 160°, 120°, 15°, 65° graph b 190°, 130°, 30°, 10° graph

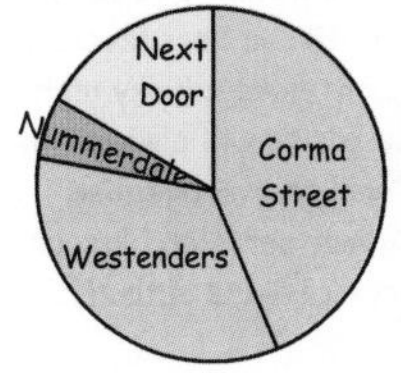

5. Largs - 135°, Arran - 45°, St Andrews - 54° Ayr - 90°, Skye - 36° b graph

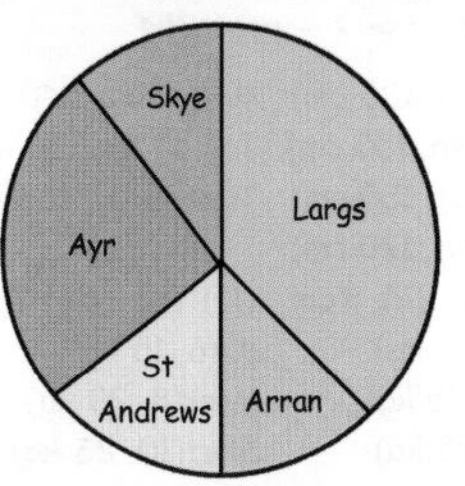

Chapter 30 Exercise 4 - page 250

1. a 6 b 21 c 24 , range = 47
   d 43 e 44
2. a 30, 32, 33, 35, 36, 38 b 2 | 1 = 21 mins

2	1 2 7 8 8
3	0 2 3 5 6 8
4	3 5 6 7 9
5	0 2
6	0 1 2

   c mode = 28, median = 38, range = 41 d 2
3. Stem-and-leaf diagram with 1 | 7 = £17

0	7 8 8
1	2 4 6 9
2	0 2 3 5
3	3

4. Stem-and-leaf diagram with 4 | 6 = 46

0	5 8
1	1 2 3 4 6 7 8
2	0 3 4 9
3	0 3 5 7
4	6 6 6 7 7 9
5	0

5. a Stem-and-leaf with 2 | 1 = 21 seconds

1	2 5 5 6 8 9 9
2	1 3 3 5 6 6
3	0 5 7 7
4	2 3 8 8
5	1 4 7
6	0 1 1 1

   b 14 c R = 49, mode = 61, med = 32·5
6. a men aged 16, 17, 19, 19 & women aged 16, 17, 18
   b (i) 2 (ii) 1 (iii) 0
   c (i) men => mode = 42, med = 36
   women => mode = 51, med = 39 d 37
7. a diagram Key = 1 | 8 and 8 | 1 mean 18

Male		Female
9	1	8 9
2 2	2	0 3 5 5 7
8 6 5 3	3	0
5	4	

   b (i) men => mode = 22, med = 34
   women => mode = 25, med = 24
8. a diagram Key = 13 | 8 and 8 | 13 mean 138

Mohawks		Flyers
9 2	13	8
8 6	14	4 5
7 7 6	15	0 9
4 0	16	2 7
2	17	3 4 5 5
4 1	18	2

   b Mowhaks - mode = 175 cm, med = 157 cm
   Flyers - mode = 157 cm, med = 164·5 cm
   Though the mode is same, median of Flyers is higher and probably average is greater

Chapter 32 - Scattergraphs

Chapter 32 Exercise 1 - page 254

1. a Jan(20 kg, 135 cm) May(50 kg, 140 cm) Sam(25 kg, 150 cm) Joy(40 kg, 150 cm) Joe(50 kg, 160 cm) Tina(35 kg, 165 cm) Ann(60 kg, 170 cm)
2. a (i) Mary (ii) Toni (iii) Pat (iv) Pat
   b Toni(4, 10 kg) Ali(6, 15 kg) Mary(3, 15 kg) Mark(8, 20 kg) Tom(9, 25 kg) Shaz(10, 23 kg) Pat(12, 30 kg)
   c Mark d As child get older it gets heavier
3. a As it gets warmer, less people buy soup.
   b 20 c 10 d (10-12)°C
4. a the longer the journey, the higher the fare
   b No journey means no cost
   c about 3 miles d about £13
5. See diagram
6.

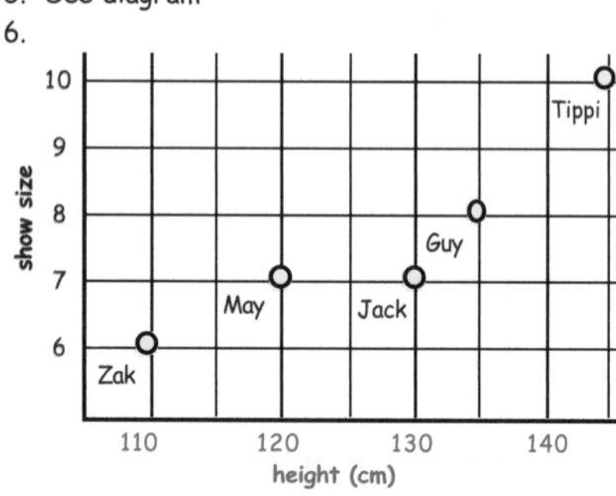

Chapter 32 Exercise 2 - page 256

1. a no coins weigh nothing
   b 8 above and 9 below
   c 65 grams d 90 grams
2. a 110 metres b 70 cm
3. 4 hours
4. a The more you study, the less you get wrong
   b 12 c 25 d 9·5 - 10 hours
5. a strong positive b strong positive
   c strong negative d none
6. various
7. a b c d 50

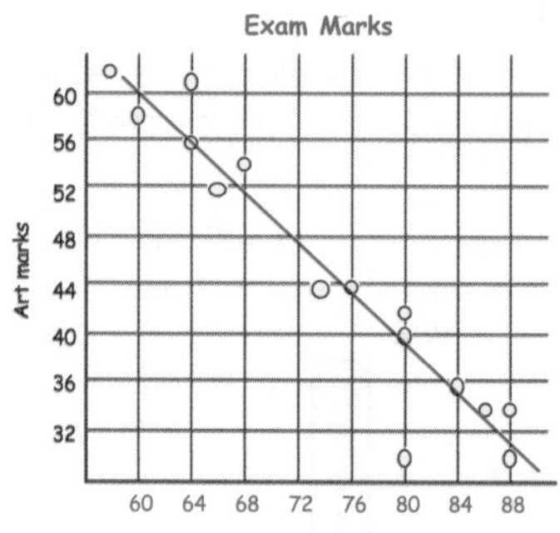

8. a/b c 43 kg d 147-148 cm

Measurements

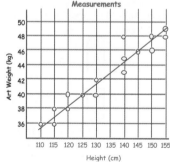

Art Weight (kg)

Height (cm)

9. a/b c 70 kg d 17 plants

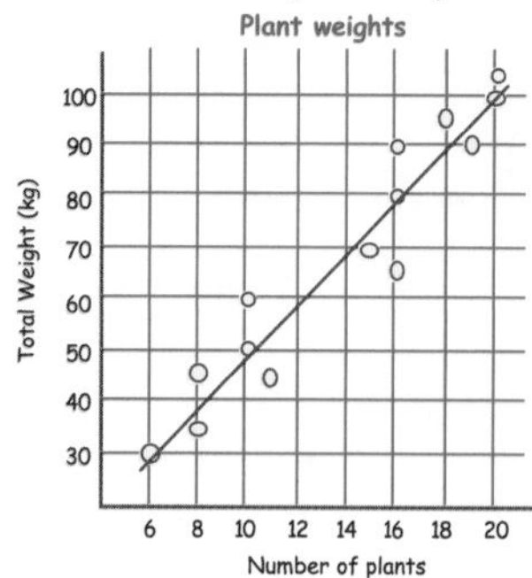

10. a/b

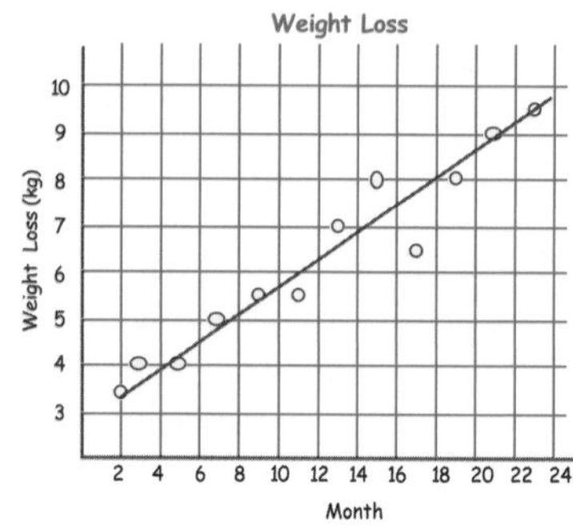

   c (i) 3·8 kg (ii) 5 kg
   (iii) 6·2 kg (iv) (9·5 - 10) kg
   d month 17

Chapter 33 - Statistical Chance

Chapter 33 Exercise 1 - page 261

1. a $^1/_{12}$ b no
   c in the long run, $^1/_{12}$ of the time it will show each of the numbers but you can't predict exactly what will happen on each roll
   d (i) 10 (ii) 100 (iii) 1000000
2. a 6 b no c not an exact science
3. a $^1/_{200}$ b $^1/_{20}$ c $^{15}/_{20} = ^3/_4$
4. P(blue) = $^{65}/_{128}$ = 0·51 --> better than 50-50
5. a various

   3 numbers

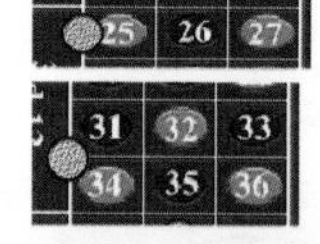

   6 numbers

   12 numbers

   or

   18 numbers

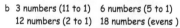

   or

   b 3 numbers (11 to 1) 6 numbers (5 to 1)
   12 numbers (2 to 1) 18 numbers (evens)
   c though someone might have a lucky night, in the long run the casino will always win and the "punters" will on average lose.
6. a Usually you have 1 year parts and labour so the 3 year insurance cover is actually only two years extra.
   b Costs £255 in total for last 2 years cover Only 1 in 10 chance of breakdown probably not worthwhile as after 3 years you probably won't be able to buy any more cover and you've already spent £255.
7. a Young drivers are more at risk and the risk drops as you get older, though over 65, the risk begins to rise.
   Females have less accidents.
   b there are fewer of them on the road and they tend to drive more carefully (slowly ?)
   c Young people's insurance premiums will be higher and older people, especially those who have had fewer accidents will get cheaper insurance.
   d In theory, yes, and that happened with some insurance companies - however, they were no longer allowed to do this due to equality issues.
   e various but generally, it does not matter the value of your car but depends more on the fact that more young people cause accidents and this affects payments to other car users
   Find out about 3rd part or full comprehensive insurance
8. a discussion
   b will cost you more and in some cases insurance companies wo'nt insure people who are heavy smokers or drinkers